WITHIN THE CIRCLE

WITHIN THE CIRCLE

An Anthology of African American Literary Criticism

from the Harlem Renaissance to the Present

Edited by Angelyn Mitchell

DUKE UNIVERSITY PRESS • *Durham and London 1994*

© 1994 Duke University Press
All rights reserved
Printed in the United States of America on acid-free paper ∞
Typeset in Berkeley Medium by Keystone Typesetting, Inc.
Library of Congress Cataloging-in-Publication Data
Within the circle : an anthology of African American literary
criticism from the Harlem Renaissance to the present /
edited by Angelyn Mitchell.
Includes bibliographical references and index.
ISBN 0-8223-1536-X (alk. paper). –ISBN 0-8223-1544-0 (pbk. alk. paper)
1. American literature—Afro-American authors—History and
criticism—Theory, etc. 2. American literature—Afro-American
authors—History and criticism. 3. Afro-Americans in literature.
4. Criticism—United States. I. Mitchell, Angelyn, 1960–
PS153.N5W58 1994
810.9'896073—dc20 94-12711 CIP
Third printing, 1999

To my mother, Evelyn Wiggins Mitchell,
and to the loving memories of
my father, James Judson Mitchell (1923–1987)
my grandmother, Fannie P. Wiggins (1904–1981)
and my grandfather, Rev. Alonza M. Wiggins (1893–1993)

Contents

I did not, when a slave, understand the deep meaning of those rude and apparently incoherent songs. I was myself within the circle; so that I neither saw nor heard as those without might see.—Frederick Douglass, 1845

Fiction is of great value to any people as a preserver of manners and customs—religious, political and social. It is a record of growth and development from generation to generation. No one will do this for us; we must ourselves develop the men and women who will faithfully portray the inmost thoughts and feelings of the Negro with all the fire and romance which lie dormant in our history. —Pauline E. Hopkins, 1900

A people may become great through many means, but there is only one measure by which its greatness is recognized and acknowledged. The final measure of the greatness of all peoples is the amount and standard of the literature and art they have produced. The world does not know that a people is great until that people produces great literature and art. No people that has produced great literature and art has ever been looked upon by the world as distinctly inferior.—James Weldon Johnson, 1921

It is one thing for a race to produce artistic material; it is quite another thing for it to produce the ability to interpret and criticize this material.—W. E. B. DuBois, 1925

Acknowledgments

In the fall of 1989 while a doctoral student at Howard University, I enrolled in a graduate seminar—African American Literary Criticism—directed by Sandra G. Shannon. Little did I know that the subject matter of this seminar would intermittently haunt me over the next five years. At that time no such collection as is offered here existed. While studying the richly diverse history of African American literary criticism from a variety of disparate, sometimes obscure, sources, I realized how necessary and useful such a collection would be to students and scholars of African American and American literature.

As this project has truly been a communal effort, I have incurred many debts. I thank the following members of the Department of English at Howard University who read and gave useful comments on earlier drafts of the introduction: R. Victoria Arana, Theodore R. Hudson, Sandra G. Shannon, and Eleanor W. Traylor. The tracking of copyright permissions allowed me the opportunity to meet new friends and to call upon old friends. I thank Dudley Randall, founder of Broadside Press; E. Ethelburt Miller, Howard University; Ernest Mason, North Carolina Central University, Durham, N.C.; Wilson Flemister, Atlanta University; Cynthia Lewis, Howard University Press; Haki Madhubuti, Third World Press; Anthony Bogucki, Copyright Division, Library of Congress; and all of the permissions editors at the various presses and journals who efficiently answered my requests. I must also say a word of appreciation to the estates of the deceased critics for their cooperation in continuing the work of those departed. I thank Cathy N. Davidson and Michael Moon, both of Duke University, for their gracious encouragement, kind words, and inspiriting interest in my work; I also thank Cathy Davidson for her useful suggestions, which greatly enriched the introduction. Additionally, I thank several of my colleagues at the University of North Carolina, Wilmington (with which I was affiliated 1992–93) for their kind words of encouragement: Keith Newlin, JoAnn Seiple, and Richard Veit. Many thanks to Carol Kolmerten, my colleague at Hood College, for her useful suggestions regarding funding. My students at both the University of North Carolina, Wilmington and Hood College deserve a word of gratitude as they have politely listened to numerous anecdotes pertaining to this book and eagerly awaited its publication. For her useful comments on the introduction and the bibliography, as well as for being (once more) "a friend to my mind," I thank Deborah H. Barnes, of Gettysburg College and a fellow Howard alum. I also thank Duane Cooper, of the University of Maryland—College Park, for his invaluable assistance in compiling the index. I am especially grateful to my editor, Ken Wissoker, who provided me with the best of wise advice and enthusiastic support, and to Duke University Press for its commitment to cultural studies of this sort. I also wish to thank the Danforth Foundation, St. Louis, Mo., for its support while I was a Danforth-Compton fellow at Howard University. I am equally grateful to the National Endowment for the Humanities for a summer stipend which allowed me time to revise.

No words can adequately express my appreciation to my family for their love and encouragement as well as for listening to hours of my ravings (and rantings) about this book. This one is for all of you, especially my uncle, G. Franklin Wiggins; my brother, Steven V. Mitchell; and my sister-friend, Lola Davis. I especially thank my inspiring and courageous mother, Evelyn W. Mitchell, because all that I am that is good I owe to her. Lastly, I must thank Mac for his companionship and his patience.

Introduction

Voices Within the Circle:

A Historical Overview of African American

Literary Criticism

Within the Circle is intended for students and scholars of twentieth-century African American literary criticism and for those interested in modern literary theory and culture. This volume extends from Alain Locke's "The New Negro" (1925) to Sherley Anne Williams's "Some Implications of Womanist Theory" (1990); no period in the history of African American literature and culture is richer or more varied. Ranging from Locke's account of the significance of folk culture in African American arts to Sherley Anne Williams's suggestions for healing the wounds between Black male writers and Black feminist critics who seem to be adversaries, we have here an unfolding documentary of the myriad changes in twentieth-century African American literary thought and culture. By the same token, no period is more difficult to represent adequately in such an anthology. By necessity, important figures must be omitted and others may be represented by selections which highlight only one phase of their work. In the hope of minimizing this problem, I have observed the following editorial criteria:

1. Each selection is significant in itself and has in one way or another influenced subsequent African American criticism. Often, as in the essays on African American feminist criticism, the influence has extended beyond African American culture to American culture in general, as well as to Caribbean and European cultures.
2. Each selection is long enough to present the critic's ideas in a systematic way. Short, isolated, or excerpted selections have been avoided in the belief that they may distort rather than clarify. Likewise, because this anthology is intended for students of African American culture as well as African American literary criticism, essays by African American critics

which concentrate on works of Anglo-American or European prominence have been avoided, except as those selections illuminate African American culture.

3. Finally, each section illustrates a major tradition of African American literary criticism. For this reason, priority has been given to critics who initiated movements or who gave such movements definitive formulation. Of the latter, two essays have been included by Zora Neale Hurston and Barbara Christian, and longer essays by others have been included because of their innovative contributions to contemporary African American literary criticism and culture.

This anthology makes these works accessible so that students and scholars may better understand the diversity and complexity of African American literature and culture.

The Harlem Renaissance

The history of African American literary criticism is in large measure characterized by its sociohistorical character and its response to the political realities facing masses of African Americans. Perhaps due to the overwhelming political and social changes occurring after World War I, the writers of the Harlem Renaissance established the basic postulates of this sociohistorical approach. This period was the inaugurating era of African American literary criticism, and directly or indirectly, all later African American literary criticism is indebted to it. The literary aspect of the Harlem Renaissance started around 1919, coterminously with the Great Migration, reached its peak in the years between 1925 and 1929, and tapered off in the late 1930s. The subject matter of the Harlem Renaissance writers ranges from alienation and irony in Toomer's *Cane* to bourgeois values in Fauset's *Plum Bun,* from female sexuality in Larsen's *Quicksand* and *Passing* to urban life in McKay's *Home to Harlem.* As an artistic, cultural, and social journey of self-discovery, the Harlem Renaissance was a crucial time for all African Americans.

Perhaps American life during the years 1910–1935 may be compared to the turbulent decade of the 1960s in terms of the rapidly changing social and political climates of both periods. Despite the legal protection afforded by the fourteenth and fifteenth amendments, African Americans continued to suffer from racial, economic, and political disenfranchisement. Although the National Association for the Advancement of Colored People (NAACP) was formed in 1910 as a bulwark against racism, racism gained momentum. After proudly serving their country in World War I, numerous African American veterans were the victims of racial assaults. Between 1917–1919, scores of innocent African Americans were brutally lynched. During the "Red Summer" of 1919, race riots devastated at least twenty cities in the North and South; racial conflicts eventually gave rise to a revival of the Ku Klux Klan in 1921. Due to the harsh racial and economic climate of the South, many African Americans migrated to the North in search of a better life; in fact, the Black population in the state of New York more than tripled in a few years. As New York became a central location for African Americans, it also became the center of African American culture and society. While not all of the key figures of the Harlem Renaissance were from Harlem nor did they all live in Harlem, Harlem as place became synonymous with the spirit of change developing in African American life. Consequently, the Harlem Renaissance represents a period of burgeoning creativity and self-reflection in African American art and literature.

As the "new Negro" defined the self through creative expressions, the "new Negro" also examined and interrogated with increasing vigor those creative representations, particularly in race magazines such as *Opportunity*, *Crisis*, and *Messenger*. As the shift in leadership changed soon after the turn of the century from the accommodationist policy of Booker T. Washington to the radical protests of W. E. B. DuBois, African Americans became racially conscious and self-assertive, affirmed their humanity, and demanded respect. Langston Hughes's "The Negro Artist and the Racial Mountain" is a classic statement of this determination:

> We younger Negro artists who create now intend to express our individual dark-skinned selves without fear or shame. If white people are pleased we are glad. If they are not, it doesn't matter. We know we are beautiful. And ugly too. The tom-tom cries and the tom-tom laughs. If colored people are pleased we are glad. If they are not, their displeasure doesn't matter either. We build our temples for tomorrow, strong as we know how, and we stand on top of the mountain, free within ourselves.

A precursor to similar sentiments expressed by members of the 1930s Negritude movement in France, Hughes's statement is among the most defiant of the Harlem Renaissance. By contrast, W. E. B. DuBois expresses a similar "criteria of Negro art," and although it lacks the mass and radical appeal of Hughes's declaration, DuBois makes clear the necessary relationship between art and propaganda—Black art must be propagandistic. Less prescriptive than DuBois, Jessie Fauset, in "The Gift of Laughter," examines the politics of laughter—"our emotional salvation"—in African American drama and life. On the other hand, George Schuyler does not share the same affirmation of Blackness as did Hughes, DuBois, or Fauset. Eschewing discussions of racial or cultural difference in "The Negro-Art Hokum," Schuyler states that "the Aframerican is merely a lampblacked Anglo-Saxon." Obviously, African American critical thought was not then and is not now monolithic. There has been and continues to be a remarkable range of opinion on what constitutes the African American subject. Schuyler's position of 1926 reminds us of recent conservative Black cultural critics such as Shelby Steele and the resurgence of Black conservatism in the 1980s.

Much of the criticism during the Harlem Renaissance centered on seeking recognition for African American artists, on revising negative estimations of them, and on documenting their achievements. Braithwaite's "The Negro in American Literature" and Locke's "The New Negro" are excellent examples of African American criticism devoted to this end. Locke, who often compared the African American's cultural reawakening to the national movements of folk expression that were taking place in Ireland, Czechoslovakia, Yugoslavia, India, China, Egypt, Russia, Palestine, and Mexico, edited a landmark anthology entitled *The New Negro* (1925). Designed specifically to register the interior lives of African Americans and to document them culturally and socially, *The New Negro* reflected the idealism and optimism of most American progressive reformers, black and white. For Locke, DuBois, Braithwaite, James Weldon Johnson, Charles S. Johnson, and other Harlem Renaissance leaders and participants, the creative expressions of African Americans were viewed as a means toward racial equality and as adequate proof of ability to participate in American life and to contribute to American culture.

Perhaps due in part to the influence of an emerging Black middle class, the desire for full participation in American life often led Harlem Renaissance critics to adopt the critical standards of Euro-American culture. The result is that they often viewed African American literature from an evolutionary perspective with the underlying notion that African American literary genius is evolving toward a state of completion and perfection whose ultimate point of reference is "the great tradition" of Western European literary culture. One extension of this assimilationist approach is art-for-art criticism, a critical posture which stems from the assumption that cultural and artistic values are aesthetically good in themselves if they approximate a universally defined sense of the beautiful. The main thrust of this critical position is the assumption that the creation of beauty—art—is irrespective of the social or racial identity of the individual artist. At the core of this idea is a certain universal conception of humanity whose reference point is usually the Euro-American man. William S. Braithwaite can thus write in "The Negro in American Literature" that James Weldon Johnson's poetry is based upon

> a broader contemplation of life, life that is not wholly confined within any racial experience, but through the racial he made articulate that universality of the emotions felt by all mankind. His verse possesses a vigor which definitely breaks away from the brooding minor undercurrents of feelings which have previously characterized the verse of Negro poets.

Concluding, Braithwaite notes, "Here a new literary generation begins; poetry that is racial in substance, but with the universal note, with the conscious background of the full heritage of English poetry." The search here for the ancestry, equivalents, affinities, and precedents of stylistic trends in African American literature in the Euro-American literary tradition is a further trait of the art-for-art trend among Harlem Renaissance critics.

In contrast is a type of criticism during the Harlem Renaissance which recognizes the specific racial, sociocultural character, and historical determination of African American literature and culture and which takes the form of a preoccupation with cultural anthropology. The major task of this cultural criticism is to establish the presence and continuities of varying traditionals—folklore, group customs, beliefs, values, styles—in African American cultural expressions. In addition to Locke, Brown, and Hughes, Zora Neale Hurston belongs to this category. Her essay, "Characteristics of Negro Expression," is among the first by an African American creative writer and critic to offer exploration of this area.

Finally, while most of the critical essays by Harlem Renaissance critics either focused on the general development of African American literature and culture or emphasized the achievements of individual artists, the essay by Sterling Brown, "Our Literary Audience," underscores the institutional grounding of African American literature: that is, its embeddedness in the African American literary public sphere. Brown's approach to African American literature and culture in this essay is unique in a number of ways. It goes beyond the purely descriptive presentation of facts offered by many Harlem Renaissance critics, and it allows for a more thorough exploration of the social and political reading of African American literature. Thus Brown's reader-response approach, which encourages an examination of the psychology behind the African American reading public, has enjoyed widespread

popularity among the generations of African American literary critics, particularly those of the Black Arts Movement, that followed him.

Humanistic/Ethical Criticism and the Protest Tradition

The Great Depression effectively ended the Harlem Renaissance and brought
incredible hardship for the African American masses who were always
among the first not to be hired and the first to be fired. Breadlines, starving
sharecroppers, and dispossessed families were only a fraction of the resulting
disasters. Such sights were viewed by many as part of a larger picture of
capitalism's exploitation of the masses and thus became the rallying point for
African American, nationalist street orators and Marxist activists. With both
the nationalist and Marxist came the ideological shift from the individual
lifting himself above society, i.e., the Harlem Renaissance's "Talented Tenth,"
to the idea of the individual adjusting himself to and becoming a part of
society and the masses. It was this humanistic/ethical and integrationist
emphasis that was to have its day in the 1940s and 1950s as African American
ministers, politicians, and sociologists moved into positions of leadership.
Pushed by the pragmatism of the Depression, creative writers also became
critics as they set the stage for an African American school of protest fiction
and humanistic/ethical criticism.

One of the major writer-critics of this period was Richard Wright. In his
"Blueprint for Negro Writing" written in 1937 while he was a member of the
South Side Writers' Group, Wright states emphatically that

> in order to do justice to his subject matter, in order to depict Negro life
> in all of its manifold and intricate relationships, a deep, informed, and
> complex consciousness is necessary; a consciousness which draws its
> strength upon the fluid lore of a great people, and moulds this lore with
> the concepts that move and direct the forces of history today. Every
> short story, novel, poem, and play should carry within its lines, implied
> or explicit, a sense of the oppression of the Negro people, the danger of
> war, of fascism, of the threatened destruction of culture and civilization;
> and, too, the faith and necessity to build a new world.

Wright's own 1940 novel, *Native Son,* was, accordingly, clearly and deliberately propagandistic. Wright craftfully argues for a humane, socialist society
in which such crimes as the murders that his protagonist, Bigger Thomas,
committed could not conceivably take place. Wright does everything within
his artistic power to convince his reader that Bigger's violent actions, values,

attitudes, and fate are all determined by his place in America. His immediate environment is depicted as being bleak and empty, while the elegant white world around the corner is shown to be cruelly indifferent to his needs. Bigger becomes, in psychological terms, psychotic.

Perhaps no African American novel has received as much critical response from African American literary critics as has Wright's *Native Son*. The novel clearly marked a new departure for African American literary thought. The general tendency on the part of the humanistic/ethical critics was to revise the image of Wright's depiction of the African American and to suggest a more human and more humane African American with a redemptive mission. Perhaps the two most best known representatives of this critical approach are the writer-critics Ralph Ellison and James Baldwin.

Ellison saw Bigger as the product of the so-called scientific perceptions of the sociologist; Baldwin saw Bigger as the product of white liberal thought. For both, Bigger Thomas was the white man's attempt to understand the African American from a vantage point outside of him—the result is a superficial and dehumanized picture, an abstraction. Speaking of the deceptive power of words and its adverse moral consequences, Ellison points out in his essay, "Twentieth-Century Fiction and the Black Mask of Humanity," that "it is unfortunate for the Negro that the most powerful formulations of modern American fictional words have been so slanted against him that when he approaches for a glimpse of himself he discovers an image drained of humanity." "Thus," he continues, "when the white American, holding up most twentieth-century fiction, says, 'This is American reality,' the Negro tends to answer (not at all concerned that Americans tend generally to fight against any but the most flattering imaginative depictions of their lives), 'Perhaps, but you're left this out, and this, and this. And most of all, what you'd have the world accept as *me* isn't even human.'" In short, Wright could only see sociological statistics in Bigger, not the humanity within.

Writing from a very similar standpoint in "Everybody's Protest Novel," James Baldwin seeks to demonstrate that, like Harriet Beecher Stowe in *Uncle Tom's Cabin*, Wright is activated by what he calls a "theological terror, the terror of damnation." Baldwin goes on to say that

Bigger is Uncle Tom's descendant, flesh of his flesh, so exactly opposite a portrait that, when the books are placed together, it seems that the contemporary Negro novelist and the dead New England woman are locked together in a deadly, timeless battle; the one uttering merciless exhortations, the other shouting curses. . . . Bigger's tragedy is not that he is cold or black or hungry, not even that he is American, black; but that he has accepted a theology that denies him life, that he admits the possibility of his being sub-human and feels constrained, therefore, to battle for his humanity according to those brutal criteria bequeathed him at his birth. But our humanity is our burden, our life; we need not battle for it; we need only to do what is infinitely more difficult—that is, accept it. The failure of the protest novel lies in its rejection of life, the human being, the denial of his beauty, dread, power, in its insistence that it is his categorization alone which is real and which cannot be transcended.

The essays by Baldwin and Ellison represent humanistic/ethical criticism at its best among African Americans. That Baldwin and Ellison are both creative writers and critics is characteristic of African American literary criticism and requires brief comment.

It seems without a doubt that the African American writer's incursion into the arena of literary discourse and criticism is a function of two interrelated motivations: one is an attempt to lay bare the peculiar social and philosophical outlook that informs his or her own work; the other is an attempt to use this outlook as a basis for evaluating work by his or her fellow writers. It is perhaps with the latter that students of African American literary criticism should be most concerned. As has been observed in Baldwin and Ellison's work and as will be seen shortly with critics associated with the Black Arts Movement, a common characteristic of the critical pronouncements of most African American writer-critics is the propensity, often unconscious, to evaluate the works of other writers and even the attempt to correct their world and social views through revision according to the writer-critics' own personal world views. As we know, both Ellison and Baldwin created characters radically different from Wright's Bigger Thomas. Ultimately, however, it must be noted that underneath the conflicting positions and world views of African American writer-critics there is a struggle, of confrontation and ideological divergence which cannot be fully explained at the level of a purely structural or aesthetic understanding of African American literature and its criticism. Rather, these differences of opinion attest to the absence of an ideological and, therefore, political consensus among African American writers.

This absence of ideological and political consensus is not, of course, limited to or unique among the writers. It constituted an even greater problem for the professional critic. This bifurcation became obvious when African

American critics debated in *Phylon,* an African American journal founded by DuBois in 1940 which focused on issues of race and culture, and elsewhere, the question of the impact of integration on African American writers. Margaret Walker's retrospective essay, "New Poets," provides a historical overview of the material conditions and aesthetic imperatives under which African American poets of the 1930s and 1940s labored. As integration became more and more a part of American life, literature concerned exclusively with African American life became less popular. Many were happy for the change; others were not so happy. In "American Negro Literature," J. Saunders Redding reveals that he was pleased, as does Arthur P. Davis in "Integration and Race Literature." While both Redding and Davis were aware of and sensitive to the emerging problems facing the African American writer as a result of integration, they were, nevertheless, happy to see that, as Davis observes, African American writers "do naturally and without self-consciousness what the Joyces and Dostoevskys of the world have always done—write intimately and objectively of our own people in universal human terms." Citing writers such as Willard Motley, Frank Yerby, and Margaret Walker, Redding concludes that African American literature had finally found popularity with white audiences. Alternatively, in "What White Publishers Won't Print," Zora Neale Hurston reveals her unhappiness not with the impact of integration on African American writers as such, but with its impact and influence on white publishers who only wanted to see certain images of African Americans. "For various reasons," she wrote, "the average, struggling, non-morbid Negro is the best-kept secret in America." Significantly, Hurston's dissatisfaction with the "literary establishment" was to become one of the major concerns of the critics associated with the Black Arts Movement.

The Black Arts Movement

At the beginning of the 1960s, a large number of African Americans were optimistic about the possibilities of racial and social progress in America. The sit-in demonstrations and freedom rides of 1960 and 1961 led to the formation of the Student Nonviolent Coordinating Committee (SNCC), and the growing civil rights marches encouraged hope for the realization of a more inclusive society. Emotions and hopes of equality climaxed at the 1963 March on Washington, when Dr. Martin Luther King, Jr., described his dream of a united America where all citizens would coexist peacefully. Just as the Civil Rights movement encouraged an aesthetic of integration, the social and political issues of the 1960s generated a new literary politics—a Black Aesthetic, an aesthetic of separatism or, as some called it, the Black Arts Movement (1964–1971). Calling for a destruction of Eurocentric cultural sensibilities, the proponents of the Black Arts Movement sought to establish a Black aesthetic.

America's failure to live up to the promises implied in the civil rights legislation of the early 1960s created widespread frustration and unrest. As had happened in previous decades since Reconstruction, riots erupted in Harlem and other urban areas during the summer of 1964. They were to continue in Watts, Newark, Philadelphia, Detroit, and over fifty other cities for the next two years. In addition to the riots, there were a series of murders which shocked the entire nation. Civil rights activist Medgar Evers was slain in Mississippi one month before the March on Washington in 1963, and in September of the same year, four young African American girls were killed in the bombing by racists of a Birmingham church. Additionally, President John F. Kennedy was assassinated in November of 1963, and the assassinations of Malcolm X, of Dr. Martin Luther King, Jr., and of Senator Robert Kennedy followed in 1965 and 1968.

As a result of these and other tragedies, young African American leaders increasingly challenged the established spokesmen of their communities. Nonviolence and integration were replaced by such watchwords as "racial separatism," "self-help," and the already familiar "Black power." African Americans were urged to take control of the political and economic institutions in their communities and to emphasize their distinctive contributions to American life and the world at large. It was to this end that LeRoi Jones (Amiri Baraka) and others founded the Black Arts Repertory/Theater School in 1964, an event considered as the beginning of the Black Arts Movement.

Due to the political nature of the time, one may wonder what characteristics, if any, distinguish the Black Arts Movement from the Black Power Movement. In the opening lines of his seminal essay "The Black Arts Movement," Larry Neal explains:

> Black art is the aesthetic and spiritual sister of the Black Power concept. As such, it envisions an art that speaks directly to the needs and aspirations of Black America. In order to perform this task, the Black Arts Movement proposes a radical reordering of the western cultural aesthetic. It proposes a separate symbolism, mythology, critique, and iconology. The Black Arts and the Black Power concept both relate broadly to the Afro-American's desire for self-determination and nationhood. Both concepts are nationalistic. One is concerned with the relationship between art and politics; the other with the art of politics.

Broadly speaking, critics associated with the Black Aesthetic movement, a decidedly masculinist movement as gender issues were subsumed by racial matters, advocated that literature become an instrument of separatism and a means of disengaging African Americans from Western culture. For example, Sarah Webster Fabio, one of the movement's few female critics, poetically writes in "Tripping with Black Writing" of the ways in which African American writers throughout the literary tradition have rhetorically disengaged themselves as a strategy of survival and a tool of resistance. For Addison Gayle, Jr., this disengagement meant the "de-Americanization" of Black people.

This de-Americanization of African Americans constituted only one phase of the movement's development. Its members soon came to the conclusion that protest literature and other modes of discourse directed to an unsympathetic American society that refused to recognize Black aesthetic values and standards of beauty were all futile. In his "Cultural Strangulation: Black Literature and the White Aesthetic," Addison Gayle, Jr., echoes Nietzche's call for "a new table of laws." Gayle proclaims, "In similar iconoclastic fashion the proponents of a Black Aesthetic, the idol smashers of America, call for a set of rules by which Black literature and art is to be judged and evaluated. For the historic practice of bowing to other men's gods and definitions has produced a crisis of the highest magnitude, and brought us, culturally, to the limits of racial armageddon. The trends must be reversed." African American critics, consequently, began to encourage African American writers to invest their works not with traditional literary forms such as sonnets and odes but with the distinctive styles, rhythms, and colors of their own race and community.

The following list of aesthetic categories from Don L. Lee's (Haki Madhubuti) "Toward a Definition: Black Poetry of the Sixties (After LeRoi Jones)" is a good example of the Black Aesthetic critic's effort to construct an idiom, symbolism, imagery, mythology, and iconology that reflect the uniqueness of the African American experience:

1. polyrhythmic, uneven, short, and explosive lines;
2. intensity; depth, yet simplicity; spirituality, yet flexibility;
3. irony; humor; signifying;
4. sarcasm—a new comedy;
5. direction; positive movement; teaching; nation building;
6. subject matter—concrete; reflects a collective and personal lifestyle; and
7. music: the unique use of vowels and consonants with the developed rap demands that the poetry be read, and read out loud.

Implicit in these categories is the notion that the "proper" forms of art and literature advocated by the white literary establishment must be suspended and that black art must be created according to the realities of the African American masses. Folk heroes such as Stagolee, Brer' Rabbit, the Signifying Monkey, Malcolm X, Marcus Garvey, and others were all frequently employed in the construction of a black iconology. Black critics, says Hoyt W. Fuller in "Towards a Black Aesthetic," have the responsibility of "approaching the works of black writers assuming these qualities to be present, and with the knowledge that white readers—and white critics—cannot be expected to recognize and to empathize with the subtleties and significance of black style and technique. They have the responsibility of rebutting the white critics and of putting things in the proper perspectives." Another way of putting things in "the proper perspectives" is, according to George E. Kent's "Ethnic Impact in American Literature," through a revisionist pedagogy that decentralizes Anglo-Saxon experiences.

When the activity of Black Aesthetic criticism is viewed in this broad perspective, one can see beyond the limits imposed by traditional criticism's nominal task of judging the merits and analyzing the styles of art objects. The Black Aesthetic critic views himself as an educator, as one must help other African Americans discover and define themselves. Intrinsically related is the more specific image of himself as an aesthetic educator, as one involved in the process of devloping self-awareness of the African American experience in its sensory, imaginative, and social dimensions. He is, in essence, an instructor in artistic perception. He tells his readers what characteristics to look for, places the work in the total context in which African Americans are immersed, and establishes the work's significance for the entirety of African American life. True Black art, according to Fuller, Gayle, Neal, and others, always radically returns African Americans to their roots. The writer that produces anything short of this vision is viewed by the Black Aesthetic critics as being, in the words of LeRoi Jones (Baraka), "just another dead American."

Structuralism, Post-structuralism, and the African American Critic

The emerging conservatism of the Nixon administration (1969–1974) with regard to the struggle for equal opportunity and the noticeable decline in the number of urban riots and "Black power" advocates ushered in a new era for African Americans. In striking contrast to the militant radicals of the 1960s, there were the mainstream academicians and entrepreneurs—young African

American men and women whose primary aspirations in life consisted of integrating within mainstream American society and working toward financial success. Consequently, it was an ideal time for African American critics to pause from purely racial and political issues and to concentrate on literary theory.

One of the first literary methods to influence African American as well as American literary theory was structuralism, a theory founded, in part, on a model of language proposed by Ferdinand de Saussure. According to de Saussure, "no ideas are established in advance, and nothing is distinct before the introduction of linguistic structure" (*Course in General Linguistics*, trans. Wade Baskin, 1916; reprint, London, 1974, 110). Words do not serve as markers that convey notions of a world whose structure and order are received into the mind through perception and afterward objectively described through, and represented by, language. Rather, language itself structures the world. In other words, the world that we know is determined by the language we use.

A good starting point for understanding the influence of structuralism upon African American critics is a book published in 1979 under the auspices of the Modern Language Association—*Afro-American Literature: The Reconstruction of Instruction*, edited by Dexter Fisher and Robert B. Stepto. Both editors proceeded from the assumption that African American literary study was a field in intellectual, scholarly, and pedagogical disarray. Their major target was the sociohistorical approach of the Harlem Renaissance and Black Aesthetic critics. One way to revise and to revitalize African American literary study, they thought, would be to insist on a more "literary" approach to texts. This would mean viewing a novel, for instance, as a function of language and other literary texts rather than as a result of cultural and historical forces. This emphasis on a strictly literary approach and on intertextuality would have the effect of rejuvenating the study of African American literature and of bringing to it, objectively, methodological rigor and theoretical clarity.

One of the contributors to *Afro-American Literature: The Reconstruction of Instruction* who has since done extensive work in the field of African American literary theory is Henry Louis Gates, Jr., author of *The Signifying Monkey: A Theory of African-American Literary Criticism* (1988). Gates states in his "Preface to Blackness: Text and Pretext" that "[t]he correspondence of content between a writer and his world is less significant to literary criticism than is a correspondence of organization or structure, for a relation of content may be a mere reflection of prescriptive, scriptural canon." Calling for a linguistic or a structuralist theoretical application of literary criticism to

African American literature, Gates moves away from the precepts of the Black Arts Movement by positing the ahistoric view that "a literary text is a linguistic event; its explication must be an activity of close textual analysis."

An important work by Robert Stepto, *From Behind the Veil* (1979), extends this emphasis on the linguistic or "literary" approach to African American literature by attempting an "anatomy" of the African American narrative. Stepto sees the narrative tradition as moving largely by the impulse of an intertextual pattern of antiphony or call and response. In his view, certain important nineteenth-century African American narratives by black male writers make a formal "call" which is met by an equally formal "response" in some important twentieth-century African American narratives. By establishing the prominence of this pattern, Stepto seeks to posit a theory of intertextuality in African American narrative. To support his position, Stepto makes extensive allusions to several structuralist literary theoreticians.

Houston A. Baker, Jr., author of *The Journey Back: Issues in Black Literature and Criticism* (1980), *Blues, Ideology, and Afro-American Literature: A Vernacular Theory* (1984), as well as numerous other studies, attempts to mediate the concepts of the Black Arts Movement with the concepts of structuralism. Baker's work is rich, complex, and hence, it defies simple summary. While the essay in this volume by Baker speaks for itself, the following overview of Baker's critical stance from Vincent Leitch's *American Literary Criticism from the Thirties to the Eighties* (New York, 1988) is most instructive for readers approaching Baker for the first time. He writes:

> Baker dedicated himself to an "anthropology of art"—a scientific interdisciplinary method of studying (1) the status of art objects and performances within given cultures, (2) the relationships of specific aesthetic "works" to other entities and systems in a designated culture, and (3) the general nature and function of artistic production and reception therein. Consequently, Baker located works of black literature within *black* American culture. What he sought was a means of depoliticizing, deidealizing, and depersonalizing the powerful premises propounded by the Black Aestheticians. Relying on structuralist thought, he envisioned culture as a linguistic discourse based on systematic rules, principles, and conventions, all of which regularize the social production of art. (346; emphasis in original)

Baker's turn to anthropological structuralism was, Leitch concludes, "designed to move black criticism from polemics to analysis. Because such a project depended on the intimate familiarity of the analyst with the semantic universe of black American culture, white critics unfamiliar with black discourse were at a serious disadvantage and risked ethnocentric distortion" (346).

Although Leitch stresses here the structuralist dimension of Baker's thinking, it is, perhaps more accurately, the "deconstructive" dimension of his thought (that is, the move toward the dismantling of hierarchies established by the dominant discourse) that has exerted the greatest influence on modern African American culture. Of particular interest is the African American critic's effort to revise both the American and African American literary canons. Toni Morrison's "Unspeakable Things Unspoken: The Afro-American Presence in American Literature" speaks forcefully and eloquently on this issue and is reminiscent of George Kent's critical thought. As Morrison makes clear, the American literary canon is composed of the works of white, male American authors generally included in basic American literary college courses and textbooks, and are also those works ordinarily discussed in standard volumes of literary history, bibliography, or criticism. Since the canon involves exclusion and suggestions of "lesser values," expanding the canon has become, since the advent of deconstruction, a major objective of literary practitioners of women's studies, African American studies, and other ethnic studies in the United States.

The fear, nevertheless, remains among African American critics that, when it comes to the African American canon, it is precisely theory itself that poses the greatest danger. One of the most interesting and articulate of these critics is W. Lawrence Hogue who, in the introductory chapter of his book *Discourse and the Other: The Production of the Afro-American Text* (1986), argues that "most Afro-American critical practices . . . do not engage their own productive process. . . . These critical practices ignore the various literary and ideological forces that actually cause certain Afro-American texts to be published, promoted, and certified and others to be subordinated and/or excluded. They ignore the historically and ideologically established way of viewing literary texts and how this established way affects the production of Afro-American literary texts."

In the final two selections of this section, Barbara Christian and Michael Awkward carry on a different sort of debate over theory. Christian, a feminist critic, refuses to appropriate Awkward's theoretical tools—his "appropriative gestures"—in analyzing African American literature. Christian insists on the application of practical criticism—close textual reading—because "critics are no longer concerned with literature, but with other critics' texts, for the critic yearning for attention has displaced the writer and has conceived of himself as the center." Awkward, on the other hand, contends that theoretical criticism offers entrances into the text that may otherwise be closed. Post-structuralist theories, for example, have elicited useful feminist, new historicist, and Marxist readings of African American texts. The primary question that they both raise is what should be the function of Western theoretical paradigms in African American literary criticism. Additionally, should theory be prescriptive or descriptive? These questions continue to elicit raging debate as African American theorists not only in literary studies but also in various branches of the humanities and social sciences have offered various theoretical paradigms, including Afrocentricism, which is reminiscent of the Black Arts Movement's controversial objectives and goals.

Gender, Theory, and African American Feminist Criticism

Feminism seems to gain momentum and then seems to subside at various times throughout Western history. In the decades following the suffrage movement of the early twentieth century, once women had obtained the right to vote, feminist issues gave way to the more immediately urgent problems posed by the Depression and the second world war. Yet it was around this time that the women's movement gained another life. In 1948, just three years after World War II ended and after women obtained the vote in France, a groundbreaking work of feminist theory appeared: Simone de Beauvoir's *The Second Sex*. One of de Beauvoir's major points in this work is that women have always been treated as "the other," "the second sex," something less than men. Women, she asserts, grow up in a patriarchal and repressive society and encounter barriers to the assertion of their individuality and freedom.

In the radicalized atmosphere of the 1960s, many women emerged from the traditional bounds of femininity, but it was not until the 1970s that the feminist movement in America gained momentum, profoundly affecting the lives of women of all ages and social classes. "Consciousness-raising" groups were formed to help women understand what oppressed them and how to liberate themselves, women's studies programs were organized at colleges and universities, other women's groups on all sides of the political spectrum sprang up, and a large number of works on feminist theory began to appear. A forerunner, Alice Walker reconceptualizes African American womanhood in her womanist prose, "In Search of Our Mothers' Gardens." She imaginatively charts the ancestral voyages of precursory Black women artists and charges contemporary Black women with the task of repossessing and re-cuperating those ancestral voices.

Perhaps as a result of the Black Arts Movement during which gender issues were largely ignored, some feminists began to accuse the feminist movement of being too white, too middle-class, and too exclusive in its political orientation. African American as well as Native American, Chicana, and Asian American women in the academy also began to articulate their reservations about the politics of the movement. As Deborah E. McDowell explains in "New Direction for Black Criticism,"

> these early theorists and practitioners of feminist literary criticism were largely white females who, wittingly or not, perpetuated against the Black woman writer the same exclusive practices they so vehemently decried in white male scholars. Seeing the experiences of white women, particularly white middle-class women, as normative, white female scholars proceeded blindly to exclude the work of Black women writers from literary anthologies and critical studies.

McDowell also criticizes influential Black male critics such as Robert Stepto for excluding Black women writers from the African American literary canon. In addition to these exclusions, the success that contemporary Black women writers, such as Alice Walker, Toni Morrison, and Terry McMillan, have enjoyed has given rise to a great deal of misogynistic masculinist crit-icism by such critics as Ishmael Reed, Stanley Crouch, and Charles Johnson.

African American feminist critics also observe that the oppression of Black literary women comes not simply with the obvious patriarchal or racist structures; it can also come, as Barbara Smith's "Toward a Black Feminist Criticism" points out, with the psychological and social formations of gen-dered subjects. Her essay is, accordingly, concerned with the construction and deconstruction of the political, social, psychological, and historical for-mations and processes of gendered texts. This dual effort toward construc-tion and deconstruction, theory and sociopolitical criticism, a telling index of the problems faced by African American feminist critics, is quite charac-teristic of the essays by Mary Helen Washington and Valerie Smith as well. Washington, a feminist literary historian and anthologizer, heeds Walker's charge to recuperate African American literary foremothers. On the other hand, Smith interrogates the relationship between gender and African Amer-ican feminist thought. Also concerned with formations and processes of texts, Hortense Spillers reconfigures the culturally gendered text of the Black female as mother within the context of American society. Retrospectively,

Barbara Christian's "But What Do We Think We're Doing" surveys the history of Black feminist criticism and the various responses from Black feminist critics, and Christian concludes by offering new directions for Black feminist thought. Finally, Sherley Anne Williams offers possible solutions for bridging the sometimes acrimonious divisions between Black feminist critics and Black male writers by reminding us all that literature "is about community and dialogue; theories or ways of reading ought actively to promote the enlargement of both."

Conclusion

The history of African American literary criticism from the Harlem Renaissance to contemporary feminist theory clearly demonstrates that theory and sociopolitical criticism have seldom failed to interact in some manner, whether constructive, controversial, or volatile. As we have also seen, theory has never predominated over the sociopolitical analysis of African American texts as much as it currently seeks to do. Should sociopolitical criticism, with its focus on literary history, be of more importance to African American literature than literary theory? Should Afrocentric ideology govern the theoretical and critical examination of African American literature? Whether we believe that race or gender is a social construct, a biological determinant, or a political reality, what do we make of recent bifurcating debates on racialized or genderized "essentialism"? Too often American literature is presented as a separate entity from African American literature (and vice versa). What implications may be discerned from analyzing these integral relationships? These are only a few of the many necessary questions that students and scholars of African American literature and literary criticism must face. It is hoped that the thirty-seven essays included in this anthology will provide the foundation needed to interrogate the many issues and concerns surrounding the study of African American literary criticism.

I

The Harlem Renaissance

Alain Locke

The New Negro

(1925)

In the last decade something beyond the watch and guard of statistics has happened in the life of the American Negro and the three norns who have traditionally presided over the Negro problem have a changeling in their laps. The Sociologist, the Philanthropist, the Race-leader are not unaware of the New Negro, but they are at a loss to account for him. He simply cannot be swathed in their formulae. For the younger generation is vibrant with a new psychology; the new spirit is awake in the masses, and under the very eyes of the professional observers is transforming what has been a perennial problem into the progressive phases of contemporary Negro life.

Could such a metamorphosis have taken place as suddenly as it had appeared to? The answer is no; not because the New Negro is not here, but because the Old Negro had long become more of a myth than a man. The Old Negro, we must remember, was a creature of moral debate and historical controversy. His has been a stock figure perpetuated as an historical fiction partly in innocent sentimentalism, partly in deliberate reactionism. The Negro himself has contributed his share to this through a sort of protective social mimicry forced upon him by the adverse circumstances of dependence. So for generations in the mind of America, the Negro has been more of a formula than a human being—a something to be argued about, condemned or defended, to be "kept down," or "in his place," or "helped up," to be worried with or worried over, harassed or patronized, a social bogey or a social burden. The thinking Negro even has been induced to share this same general attitude, to focus his attention on controversial issues, to see himself in the distorted perspective of a social problem. His shadow, so to speak, has

This essay first appeared in Alain Locke, ed., *The New Negro: An Anthology* (1925; reprint, New York, 1968).

been more real to him than his personality. Through having had to appeal from the unjust stereotypes of his oppressors and traducers to those of his liberators, friends and benefactors he has had to subscribe to the traditional positions from which his case has been viewed. Little true social or self-understanding has or could come from such a situation.

But while the minds of most of us, black and white, have thus burrowed in the trenches of the Civil War and Reconstruction, the actual march of development has simply flanked these positions, necessitating a sudden re-orientation of view. We have not been watching in the right direction; set North and South on a sectional axis, we have not noticed the East till the sun has us blinking.

Recall how suddenly the Negro spirituals revealed themselves; suppressed for generations under the stereotypes of Wesleyan hymn harmony, secretive, half-ashamed, until the courage of being natural brought them out—and behold, there was folk-music. Similarly the mind of the Negro seems suddenly to have slipped from under the tyranny of social intimidation and to be shaking off the psychology of imitation and implied inferiority. By shedding the old chrysalis of the Negro problem we are achieving something like a spiritual emancipation. Until recently, lacking self-understanding, we have been almost as much of a problem to ourselves as we still are to others. But the decade that found us with a problem has left us with only a task. The multitude perhaps feels as yet only a strange relief and a new vague urge, but the thinking few know that in the reaction the vital inner grip of prejudice has been broken.

With this renewed self-respect and self-dependence, the life of the Negro community is bound to enter a new dynamic phase, the buoyancy from within compensating for whatever pressure there may be of conditions from without. The migrant masses, shifting from countryside to city, hurdle several generations of experience at a leap, but more important, the same thing happens spiritually in the life-attitudes and self-expression of the Young Negro, in his poetry, his art, his education and his new outlook, with the additional advantage, of course, of the poise and greater certainty of knowing what it is all about. From this comes the promise and warrant of a new leadership. As one of them has discerningly put it:

> We have tomorrow
> Bright before us
> Like a flame.

Yesterday, a night-gone thing
A sun-down name.

And dawn today
Broad arch above the road we came.
We march!

This is what, even more than any "most creditable record of fifty years of freedom," requires that the Negro of today be seen through other than the dusty spectacles of past controversy. The day of "aunties," "uncles" and "mammies" is equally gone. Uncle Tom and Sambo have passed on, and even the "Colonel" and "George" play barnstorm roles from which they escape with relief when the public spotlight is off. The popular melodrama has about played itself out, and it is time to scrap the fictions, garret the bogeys and settle down to a realistic facing of facts.

First we must observe some of the changes which since the traditional lines of opinion were drawn have rendered these quite obsolete. A main change has been, of course, that shifting of the Negro population which has made the Negro problem no longer exclusively or even predominantly Southern. Why should our minds remain sectionalized, when the problem itself no longer is? Then the trend of migration has not only been toward the North and the Central Midwest, but city-ward and to the great centers of industry—the problems of adjustment are new, practical, local and not peculiarly racial. Rather they are an integral part of the large industrial and social problems of our present-day democracy. And finally, with the Negro rapidly in process of class differentiation, if it ever was warrantable to regard and treat the Negro *en masse* it is becoming with every day less possible, more unjust and more ridiculous.

In the very process of being transplanted, the Negro is becoming transformed.

The tide of Negro migration, northward and city-ward, is not to be fully explained as a blind flood started by the demands of war industry coupled with the shutting off of foreign migration, or by the pressure of poor crops coupled with increased social terrorism in certain sections of the South and Southwest. Neither labor demand, the boll-weevil nor the Ku Klux Klan is a basic factor, however contributory any or all of them may have been. The wash and rush of this human tide on the beach line of the northern city centers is to be explained primarily in terms of a new vision of opportunity, of social and economic freedom, of a spirit to seize, even in the face of an extortionate and heavy toll, a chance for the improvement of conditions. With each successive wave of it, the movement of the Negro becomes more and more a mass movement toward the larger and the more democratic chance—in the Negro's case a deliberate flight not only from countryside to city, but from medieval America to modern.

Take Harlem as an instance of this. Here in Manhattan is not merely the largest Negro community in the world, but the first concentration in history of so many diverse elements of Negro life. It has attracted the African, the West Indian, the Negro American; has brought together the Negro of the North and the Negro of the South; the man from the city and the man from the town and village; the peasant, the student, the business man, the professional man, artist, poet, musician, adventurer and worker, preacher and criminal, exploiter and social outcast. Each group has come with its own separate motives and for its own special ends, but their greatest experience has been the finding of one another. Proscription and prejudice have thrown these dissimilar elements into a common area of contact and interaction. Within this area, race sympathy and unity have determined a further fusing of sentiment and experience. So what began in terms of segregation becomes more and more, as its elements mix and react, the laboratory of a great race-welding. Hitherto, it must be admitted that American Negroes have been a race more in name than in fact, or to be exact, more in sentiment than in experience. The chief bond between them has been that of a common condition rather than a common consciousness; a problem in common rather than a life in common. In Harlem, Negro life is seizing upon its first chances for group expression and self-determination. It is—or promises at least to be—a race capital. That is why our comparison is taken with those nascent centers of folk-expression and self-determination which are playing a creative part in the world today. Without pretense to their political significance, Harlem has the same role to play for the New Negro as Dublin has had for the New Ireland or Prague for the New Czechoslovakia.

Harlem, I grant you, isn't typical—but it is significant, it is prophetic. No sane observer, however sympathetic to the new trend, would contend that the great masses are articulate as yet, but they stir, they move, they are more than physically restless. The challenge of the new intellectuals among them is clear enough—the "race radicals" and realists who have broken with the old epoch of philanthropic guidance, sentimental appeal and protest. But are we after all only reading into the stirrings of a sleeping giant the dreams of an agitator? The answer is in the migrating peasant. It is the "man farthest down" who is most active in getting up. One of the most characteristic symptoms of this is the professional man himself migrating to recapture his constituency after a vain effort to maintain in some Southern corner what for years back seemed an established living and clientele. The clergyman following his errant flock, the physician or lawyer trailing his clients, supply the true clues. In a real sense it is the rank and file who are leading, and the leaders who are following. A transformed and transforming psychology permeates the masses.

When the racial leaders of twenty years ago spoke of developing race-pride and stimulating race-consciousness, and of the desirability of race solidarity, they could not in any accurate degree have anticipated the abrupt feeling that has surged up and now pervades the awakened centers. Some of the recognized Negro leaders and a powerful section of white opinion identified with "race work" of the older order have indeed attempted to discount this feeling as a "passing phase," an attack of "race nerves" so to speak, an "aftermath of the war," and the like. It has not abated, however, if we are to gauge by the present tone and temper of the Negro press, or by the shift in popular support from the officially recognized and orthodox spokesmen to those of the independent, popular, and often radical type who are unmistakable symptoms of a new order. It is a social disservice to blunt the fact that the Negro of the Northern centers has reached a stage where tutelage, even of the most interested and well-intentioned sort, must give place to new relationships, where positive self-direction must be reckoned with in ever increasing measure. The American mind must reckon with a fundamentally changed Negro.

The Negro too, for his part, has idols of the tribe to smash. If on the one hand the white man has erred in making the Negro appear to be that which would excuse or extenuate his treatment of him, the Negro, in turn, has too often unnecessarily excused himself because of the way he has been treated. The intelligent Negro of today is resolved not to make discrimination an extenuation for his shortcomings in performance, individual or collective; he is trying to hold himself at par, neither inflated by sentimental allowances nor depreciated by current social discounts. For this he must know himself and be known for precisely what he is, and for that reason he welcomes the new scientific rather than the old sentimental interest. Sentimental interest in the Negro has ebbed. We used to lament this as the falling off of our friends; now we rejoice and pray to be delivered both from self-pity and condescension. The mind of each racial group has had a bitter weaning, apathy or hatred on one side matching disillusionment or resentment on the other; but they face each other today with the possibility at least of entirely new mutual attitudes.

It does not follow that if the Negro were better known, he would be better liked or better treated. But mutual understanding is basic for any subsequent cooperation and adjustment. The effort toward this will at least have the effect of remedying in large part what has been the most unsatisfactory feature of our present stage of race relationships in America, namely the fact that the more intelligent and representative elements of the two race groups have at so many points got quite out of vital touch with one another.

The fiction is that the life of the races is separate, and increasingly so. The fact is that they have touched too closely at the unfavorable and too lightly at the favorable levels.

While interracial councils have sprung up in the South, drawing on forward elements of both races, in the Northern cities manual laborers may brush elbows in their everyday work, but the community and business leaders have experienced no such interplay or far too little of it. These segments must achieve contact or the race situation in America becomes desperate. Fortunately this is happening. There is a growing realization that in social effort the cooperative basis must supplant long-distance philanthropy, and that the only safeguard for mass relations in the future must be provided in the carefully maintained contacts of the enlightened minorities of both race groups. In the intellectual realm a renewed and keen curiosity is replacing the recent apathy; the Negro is being carefully studied, not just talked about and discussed. In art and letters, instead of being wholly caricatured, he is being seriously portrayed and painted.

To all of this the New Negro is keenly responsive as an augury of a new democracy in American culture. He is contributing his share to the new social understanding. But the desire to be understood would never in itself have been sufficient to have opened so completely the protectively closed portals of the thinking Negro's mind. There is still too much possibility of being snubbed or patronized for that. It was rather the necessity for fuller, truer self-expression, the realization of the unwisdom of allowing social discrimination to segregate him mentally, and a counter-attitude to cramp and fetter his own living—and so the "spite-wall" that the intellectuals built over the "color-line" has happily been taken down. Much of this reopening of intellectual contacts has centered in New York and has been richly fruitful not merely in the enlarging of personal experience, but in the definite enrichment of American art and letters and in the clarifying of our common vision of the social tasks ahead.

The particular significance in the re-establishment of contact between the more advanced and representative classes is that it promises to offset some of the unfavorable reactions of the past, or at least to resurface race contacts somewhat for the future. Subtly the conditions that are molding a New Negro are molding a new American attitude.

However, this new phase of things is delicate; it will call for less charity but more justice; less help, but infinitely closer understanding. This is indeed a critical stage of race relationships because of the likelihood, if the new temper is not understood, of engendering sharp group antagonism and a second crop of more calculated prejudice. In some quarters, it has already done so. Having weaned the Negro, public opinion cannot continue to paternalize. The Negro today is inevitably moving forward under the control largely of his own objectives. What are these objectives? Those of his outer life are happily already well and finally formulated, for they are none other than the ideals of American institutions and democracy. Those of his inner life are yet in process of formation, for the new psychology at present is more of a consensus of feeling than of opinion, of attitude rather than of program. Still some points seem to have crystallized.

Up to the present one may adequately describe the Negro's "inner objectives" as an attempt to repair a damaged group psychology and reshape a warped social perspective. Their realization has required a new mentality for the American Negro. And as it matures we begin to see its effects; at first, negative, iconoclastic, and then positive and constructive. In this new group psychology we note the lapse of sentimental appeal, then the development of a more positive self-respect and self-reliance; the repudiation of social dependence, and then the gradual recovery from hypersensitiveness and "touchy" nerves, the repudiation of the double standard of judgment with its special philanthropic allowances and then the sturdier desire for objective and scientific appraisal; and finally the rise from social disillusionment to race pride, from the sense of social debt to the responsibilities of social contribution, and offsetting the necessary working and commonsense acceptance of restricted conditions, the belief in ultimate esteem and recognition. Therefore the Negro today wishes to be known for what he is, even in his faults and shortcomings, and scorns a craven and precarious survival at the price of seeming to be what he is not. He resents being spoken of as a social ward or minor, even by his own, and to being regarded a chronic patient for the sociological clinic, the sick man of American Democracy. For the same reasons, he himself is through with those social nostrums and panaceas, the so-called "solutions" of his "problem," with which he and the country have been so liberally dosed in the past. Religion, freedom, education, money—in turn, he has ardently hoped for and peculiarly trusted these things; he still believes in them, but not in blind trust that they alone will solve his life-problem.

Each generation, however, will have its creed, and that of the present is the belief in the efficacy of collective effort, in race cooperation. This deep feeling of race is at present the mainspring of Negro life. It seems to be the outcome of the reaction to proscription and prejudice; an attempt, fairly successful on the whole, to convert a defensive into an offensive position, a handicap into an incentive. It is radical in tone, but not in purpose and only the most stupid forms of opposition, misunderstanding or persecution could make it otherwise. Of course, the thinking Negro has shifted a little toward the left with the world-trend, and there is an increasing group who affiliate with radical and liberal movements. But fundamentally for the present the Negro is radical on race matters, conservative on others, in other words, a "forced radical," a social protestant rather than a genuine radical. Yet under further pressure and injustice iconoclastic thought and motives will inevitably increase. Harlem's quixotic radicalisms call for their ounce of democracy today lest tomorrow they be beyond cure.

The Negro mind reaches out as yet to nothing but American wants, American ideas. But this forced attempt to build his Americanism on race values is a unique social experiment, and its ultimate success is impossible except through the fullest sharing of American culture and institutions. There should be no delusion about this. American nerves in sections unstrung with race hysteria are often fed the opiate that the trend of Negro advance is wholly separatist, and that the effect of its operation will be to encyst the Negro as a benign foreign body in the body politic. This cannot be—even if it were desirable. The racialism of the Negro is no limitation or reservation with respect to American life; it is only a constructive effort to build the obstructions in the stream of his progress into an efficient dam of social energy and power. Democracy itself is obstructed and stagnated to the extent that any of its channels are closed. Indeed they cannot be selectively closed. So the choice is not between one way for the Negro and another way for the rest, but between American institutions frustrated on the one hand and American ideals progressively fulfilled and realized on the other.

There is, of course, a warrantably comfortable feeling in being on the right side of the country's professed ideals. We realize that we cannot be undone without America's undoing. It is within the gamut of this attitude that the thinking Negro faces America, but with variations of mood that are if anything more significant than the attitude itself. Sometimes we have it taken with the defiant ironic challenge of McKay:

Mine is the future grinding down to-day
Like a great landslip moving to the sea,
Bearing its freight of debris far away
Where the green hungry waters restlessly
Heave mammoth pyramids, and break and roar
Their eerie challenge to the crumbling shore.

Sometimes, perhaps more frequently as yet, it is taken in the fervent and almost filial appeal and counsel of Weldon Johnson's:

O Southland, dear Southland!
Then why do you still cling
To an idle age and a musty page,
To a dead and useless thing?

But between defiance and appeal, midway almost between cynicism and hope, the prevailing mind stands in the mood of the same author's *To America*, an attitude of sober query and stoical challenge:

How would you have us, as we are?
Or sinking 'neath the load we bear,
Our eyes fixed forward on a star,
Or gazing empty at despair?

Rising or falling? Men or things?
With dragging pace or footsteps fleet?
Strong, willing sinews in your wings,
Or tightening chains about your feet?

More and more, however, an intelligent realization of the great discrepancy between the American social creed and the American social practice forces upon the Negro the taking of the moral advantage that is his. Only the steadying and sobering effect of a truly characteristic gentleness of spirit prevents the rapid rise of a definite cynicism and counter-hate and a defiant superiority feeling. Human as this reaction would be, the majority still deprecate its advent, and would gladly see it forestalled by the speedy amelioration of its causes. We wish our race pride to be a healthier, more positive achievement than a feeling based upon a realization of the shortcomings of others. But all paths toward the attainment of a sound social attitude have been difficult; only a relatively few enlightened minds have been able as the phrase puts it "to rise above" prejudice. The ordinary man has had until recently only a hard choice between the alternatives of supine and humiliating submission and stimulating but hurtful counter-prejudice. Fortunately from some inner, desperate resourcefulness has recently sprung up the simple expedient of fighting prejudice by mental passive resistance, in other words by trying to ignore it. For the few, this manna may perhaps be effective, but the masses cannot thrive upon it.

Fortunately there are constructive channels opening out into which the balked social feelings of the American Negro can flow freely.

Without them there would be much more pressure and danger than there is. These compensating interests are racial but in a new and enlarged way. One is the consciousness of acting as the advance-guard of the African peoples in their contact with Twentieth Century civilization; the other, the sense of a mission of rehabilitating the race in world esteem from that loss of prestige for which the fate and conditions of slavery have so largely been responsible. Harlem, as we shall see, is the center of both these movements; she is the home of the Negro's "Zionism." The pulse of the Negro world has begun to beat in Harlem. A Negro newspaper carrying news material in English, French and Spanish, gathered from all quarters of America, the West Indies and Africa has maintained itself in Harlem for over five years. Two important magazines, both edited from New York, maintain their news and circulation consistently on a cosmopolitan scale. Under American auspices and backing, three pan-African congresses have been held abroad for the discussion of common interests, colonial questions and the future cooperative development of Africa. In terms of the race question as a world problem, the Negro mind has leapt, so to speak, upon the parapets of prejudice and extended its cramped horizons. In so doing it has linked up with the growing group consciousness of the dark-peoples and is gradually learning their common interests. As one of our writers has recently put it: "It is imperative that we understand the white world in its relations to the non-white world." As with the Jew, persecution is making the Negro international.

As a world phenomenon this wider race consciousness is a different thing from the much asserted rising tide of color. Its inevitable causes are not of our making. The consequences are not necessarily damaging to the best interests of civilization. Whether it actually brings into being new Armadas of conflict or argosies of cultural exchange and enlightenment can only be decided by the attitude of the dominant races in an era of critical change. With the American Negro, his new internationalism is primarily an effort to recapture contact with the scattered peoples of African derivation. Garveyism may be a transient, if spectacular, phenomenon, but the possible role of the American Negro in the future development of Africa is one of the most constructive and universally helpful missions that any modern people can lay claim to.

Constructive participation in such causes cannot help giving the Negro valuable group incentives, as well as increased prestige at home and abroad. Our greatest rehabilitation may possibly come through such channels, but for the present, more immediate hope rests in the revaluation by white and black alike of the Negro in terms of his artistic endowments and cultural contributions, past and prospective. It must be increasingly recognized that the Negro has already made very substantial contributions, not only in his folk-art, music especially, which has always found appreciation, but in larger, though humbler and less acknowledged ways. For generations the Negro has been the peasant matrix of that section of America which has most under-valued him, and here he has contributed not only materially in labor and in social patience, but spiritually as well. The South has unconsciously ab-sorbed the gift of his folk-temperament. In less than half a generation it will be easier to recognize this, but the fact remains that a leaven of humor, sentiment, imagination and tropic nonchalance has gone into the making of the South from a humble, unacknowledged source. A second crop of the Negro's gifts promises still more largely. He now becomes a conscious con-tributor and lays aside the status of a beneficiary and ward for that of a collaborator and participant in American civilization. The great social gain in this is the releasing of our talented group from the arid fields of controversy and debate to the productive fields of creative expression. The especially cultural recognition they win should in turn prove the key to that revalua-tion of the Negro which must precede or accompany any considerable fur-ther betterment of race relationships. But whatever the general effect, the present generation will have added the motives of self-expression and spir-itual development to the old and still unfinished task of making material headway and progress. No one who understandingly faces the situation with its substantial accomplishment or views the new scene with its still more abundant promise can be entirely without hope. And certainly, if in our lifetime the Negro should not be able to celebrate his full initiation into American democracy, he can at least, on the warrant of these things, cele-brate the attainment of a significant and satisfying new phase of group de-velopment, and with it a spiritual Coming of Age.

William Stanley Braithwaite

The Negro in American Literature

(1925)

True to his origin on this continent, the Negro was projected into literature by an overmastering and exploiting hand. In the generations that
he has been so voluminously written and talked about he has been accorded
as little artistic justice as social justice. Antebellum literature imposed the
distortions of moralistic controversy and made the Negro a wax-figure of the
market place: postbellum literature retaliated with the condescending reactions of sentiment and caricature, and made the Negro a *genre* stereotype.
Sustained, serious or deep study of Negro life and character has thus been
entirely below the horizons of our national art. Only gradually through the
dull purgatory of the Age of Discussion, has Negro life eventually issued
forth to an Age of Expression.

Perhaps I ought to qualify this last statement that the Negro was *in* American literature generations before he was part of it as a creator. From his very
beginning in this country the Negro has been, without the formal recognition of literature and art, creative. During more than two centuries of an
enslaved peasantry, the race has been giving evidence, in song and story lore,
of an artistic temperament and psychology precious for itself as well as for its
potential use and promise in the sophisticated forms of cultural expression.
Expressing itself with poignancy and a symbolic imagery unsurpassed, indeed, often unmatched, by any folk-group, the race in servitude was at the
same time the finest national expression of emotion and imagination and the
most precious mass of raw material for literature America was producing.
Quoting these stanzas of James Weldon Johnson's *O Black and Unknown*

This essay first appeared in Alain Locke, ed., *The New Negro: An Anthology* (1925; reprint, New
York, 1968).

Bards, I want you to catch the real point of its assertion of the Negro's way into domain of art:

> O black and unknown bards of long ago,
>   How came your lips to touch the sacred fire?
> How, in your darkness, did you come to know
>   The power and beauty of the minstrel's lyre?
> Who first from midst his bonds lifted his eyes?
>   Who first from out the still watch, lone and long,
> Feeling the ancient faith of prophets rise
>   Within his dark-kept soul, burst into song?
>
> There is a wide, wide wonder in it all,
>   That from degraded rest and servile toil
> The fiery spirit of the seer should call
>   These simple children of the sun and soil.
> O black slave singers, gone, forgot, unfamed,
>   You—you, alone, of all the long, long line
> Of those who've sung untaught, unknown, unnamed,
>   Have stretched out upward, seeking the divine.

How misdirected was the American imagination, how blinded by the dust of controversy and the pall of social hatred and oppression, not to have found it irresistibly urgent to make literary use of the imagination and emotion it possessed in such abundance.

Controversy and moral appeal gave us *Uncle Tom's Cabin,*—the first conspicuous example of the Negro as a subject for literary treatment. Published in 1852, it dominated in mood and attitude the American literature of a whole generation; until the body of Reconstruction literature with its quite different attitude came into vogue. Here was sentimentalized sympathy for a downtrodden race, but one in which was projected a character, in Uncle Tom himself, which has been unequalled in its hold upon the popular imagination to this day. But the moral gain and historical effect of Uncle Tom have been an artistic loss and setback. The treatment of Negro life and character, overlaid with these forceful stereotypes, could not develop into artistically satisfactory portraiture.

Just as in the antislavery period, it had been impaled upon the dilemmas of controversy, Negro life with the Reconstruction became involved in the paradoxes of social prejudice. Between the Civil War and the end of the century the subject of the Negro in literature is one that will some day inspire the literary historian with a magnificent theme. It will be magnificent not because there is any sharp emergence of character or incidents, but because of the immense paradox of racial life which came up thunderingly against the principles and doctrines of democracy, and put them to the severest test that they had known. But in literature, it was a period when Negro life was a shuttlecock between the two extremes of humor and pathos. The Negro was free, and was not free. The writers who dealt with him for the most part refused to see more than skin-deep,—the grin, the grimaces and the picturesque externalities. Occasionally there was some penetration into the heart and flesh of Negro characters, but to see more than the humble happy peasant would have been to flout the fixed ideas and conventions of an entire generation. For more than artistic reasons, indeed against them, these writers refused to see the tragedy of the Negro and capitalized his comedy. The social conscience had as much need for this comic mask as the Negro. However, if any of the writers of the period had possessed gifts of genius of the first caliber, they would have penetrated this deceptive exterior of Negro life, sounded the depths of tragedy in it, and produced a masterpiece.

American literature still feels the hold of this tradition and its indulgent sentimentalities. Irwin Russell was the first to discover the happy, carefree, humorous Negro. He became a fad. It must be sharply called to attention that the tradition of the antebellum Negro is a postbellum product, stranger in truth than in fiction. Contemporary realism in American fiction has not only recorded his passing, but has thrown serious doubts upon his ever having been a very genuine and representative view of Negro life and character. At best this school of Reconstruction fiction represents the romanticized highlights of a regime that as a whole was a dark, tragic canvas. At most, it presents a Negro true to type for less than two generations. Thomas Nelson Page, kindly perhaps, but with a distant view and a purely local imagination did little more than paint the conditions and attitudes of the period contemporary with his own manhood, the restitution of the overlordship of the defeated slave owners in the Eighties. George W. Cable did little more than idealize the aristocratic tradition of the Old South with the Negro as a literary foil. The effects, though not the motives of their work, have been sinister. The "Uncle" and the "Mammy" traditions, unobjectionable as they are in the setting of their day and generation, and in the atmosphere of sentimental humor, can never stand as the great fiction of their theme and subject: the great period novel of the South has yet to be written. Moreover, these type pictures have degenerated into reactionary social fetishes, and from that descended into libelous artistic caricature of the Negro, which has hampered art quite as much as it has embarrassed the Negro.

Of all of the American writers of this period, Joel Chandler Harris has made the most permanent contribution in dealing with the Negro. There is in his work both a deepening of interest and technique. Here at least we have something approaching true portraiture. But much as we admire this lovable personality, we are forced to say that in the Uncle Remus stories the race was its own artist, lacking only in its illiteracy the power to record its speech. In the perspective of time and fair judgment the credit will be divided, and Joel Chandler Harris regarded as a sort of providentially provided amanuensis for preserving the folk tales and legends of a race. The three writers I have mentioned do not by any means exhaust the list of writers who put the Negro into literature during the last half of the nineteenth century. Mr. Howells added a shadowy note to his social record of American life with *An Imperative Duty* and prophesied the Fiction of the Color Line. But his moral scruples—the persistent artistic vice in all his novels—prevented him from consummating a just union between his heroine with a touch of Negro blood and his hero. It is useless to consider any others, because there were none who succeeded in creating either a great story or a great character out of Negro life. Two writers of importance I am reserving for discussion in the group of Negro writers I shall consider presently. One ought perhaps to say in justice to the writers I have mentioned that their nonsuccess was more largely due to the limitations of their social view than of their technical resources. As white Americans of their day, it was incompatible with their conception of the inequalities between the races to glorify the Negro into the serious and leading position of hero or heroine in fiction. Only one man that I recall, had the moral and artistic courage to do this, and he was Stephen Crane in a short story called *The Monster.* But Stephen Crane was a genius, and therefore could not besmirch the integrity of an artist.

With Thomas Dixon, of *The Leopard's Spots,* we reach a distinct stage in the treatment of the Negro in fiction. The portraiture here descends from caricature to libel. A little later with the vogue of the "darkey-story," and its devotees from Kemble and McAllister to Octavus Roy Cohen, sentimental comedy in the portrayal of the Negro similarly degenerated to blatant but diverting farce. Before the rise of a new attitude, these represented the bottom reaction, both in artistic and social attitude. Reconstruction fiction was passing out in a flood of propagandist melodrama and ridicule. One hesitates to lift this material up to the plane of literature even for the purposes of comparison. But the gradual climb of the new literature of the Negro must be traced and measured from these two nadir points. Following *The Leopard's Spots*, it was only occasionally during the next twenty years that the Negro was sincerely treated in fiction by white authors. There were two or three tentative efforts to dramatize him. Sheldon's *The Nigger,* was the one notable early effort. And in fiction Paul Kester's *His Own Country* is, from a purely literary point of view, its outstanding performance. This type of novel failed, however, to awaken any general interest. This failure was due to the illogical treatment of the human situations presented. However indifferent and negative it may seem, there is the latent desire in most readers to have honesty of purpose and a full vision in the artist: and especially in fiction, a situation handled with gloves can never be effectively handled.

The first hint that the American artist was looking at this subject with full vision was in Torrence's *Granny Maumee*. It was drama, conceived and executed for performance on the stage, and therefore had a restricted appeal. But even here the artist was concerned with the primitive instincts of the Race, and, though faithful and honest in his portrayal, the note was still low in the scale of racial life. It was only a short time, however, before a distinctly new development took place in the treatment of Negro life by white authors. This new class of work honestly strove to endow the Negro life with purely aesthetic vision and values, but with one or two exceptions, still stuck to the peasant level of race experience, and gave, unwittingly, greater currency to the popular notion of the Negro as an inferior, superstitious, half-ignorant and servile class of folk. Where they did in a few isolated instances recognize an ambitious impulse, it was generally defeated in the course of the story.

Perhaps this is inevitable with an alien approach, however well-intentioned. The folklore attitude discovers only the lowly and the naive: the sociological attitude.finds the problem first and the human beings after, if at all. But American art in a reawakened seriousness, and using the technique of the new realism, is gradually penetrating Negro life to the core. George Madden Martin, with her pretentious foreword to a group of short stories, *The Children in the Mist*—and this is an extraordinary volume in many ways— quite seriously tried, as a Southern woman, to elevate the Negro to a higher plane of fictional treatment and interest. In succession, followed Mary White Ovington's *The Shadow,* in which Miss Ovington daringly created the kinship of brother and sister between a black boy and white girl, had it brought to disaster by prejudice, out of which the white girl rose to a sacrifice no white girl in a novel had hitherto accepted and endured; then Shands's *White and Black,* as honest a piece of fiction with the Negro as a subject as was ever produced by a Southern pen—and in this story, also, the hero, Robinson, making an equally glorious sacrifice for truth and justice as Miss Ovington's heroine; Clement Wood's *Nigger,* with defects of treatment, but admirable in purpose, wasted though, I think, in the effort to prove its thesis on wholly illogical material; and lastly, T. S. Stribling's *Birthright,* more significant than any of these other books, in fact, the most significant novel on the Negro written by a white American, and this in spite of its totally false conception of the character of Peter Siner.

Mr. Stribling's book broke ground for a white author in giving us a Negro hero and heroine. There is an obvious attempt to see objectively. But the formula of the Nineties,—atavistic race-heredity, still survives and protrudes through the flesh and blood of the characters. Using Peter as a symbol of the man tragically linked by blood to one world and by training and thought to another, Stribling portrays a tragic struggle against the pull of lowly origins and sordid environment. We do not deny this element of tragedy in Negro life,—and Mr. Stribling, it must also be remembered, presents, too, a severe indictment in his painting of the Southern conditions which brought about the disintegration of his hero's dreams and ideals. But the preoccupation, almost obsession of otherwise strong and artistic work like O'Neill's *Emperor Jones, All God's Chillun Got Wings,* and Culbertson's *Goat Alley* with this same theme and doubtful formula of hereditary cultural reversion suggests that, in spite of all good intentions, the true presental of the real tragedy of Negro life is a task still left for Negro writers to perform. This is especially true for those phases of culturally representative race life that as yet have scarcely at all found treatment by white American authors. In corroborating this, let me quote a passage from a recent number of the *Independent,* on the Negro novelist which reads:

During the past few years stories about Negroes have been extremely popular. A magazine without a Negro story is hardly living up to its opportunities. But almost every one of these stories is written in a tone of condescension. The artists have caught the contagion from the writers, and the illustrations are ninety-nine times out of a hundred purely slapstick stuff. Stories and pictures make a Roman holiday for the millions who are convinced that the most important fact about the Negro is that his skin is black. Many of these writers live in the South or are from the South. Presumably they are well acquainted with the Negro, but it is a remarkable fact that they almost never tell us anything vital about him, about the real human being in the black man's skin. Their most frequent method is to laugh at the colored man and woman, to catalogue their idiosyncrasies, their departure from the norm, that is, from the ways of the whites. There seems to be no suspicion in the minds of the writers that there may be a fascinating thought life in the minds of the Negroes, whether of the cultivated or of the most ignorant type. Always the Negro is interpreted in the terms of the white man. Whiteman psychology is applied and it is no wonder that the result often shows the Negro in a ludicrous light.

I shall have to run back over the years to where I began to survey the achievement of Negro authorship. The Negro as a creator in American literature is of comparatively recent importance. All that was accomplished between Phyllis [sic] Wheatley and Paul Laurence Dunbar, considered by critical standards, is negligible, and of historical interest only. Historically it is a great tribute to the race to have produced in Phyllis Wheatley not only the slave poetess in eighteenth century Colonial America, but to know she was as good, if not a better, poetess than Ann [sic] Bradstreet whom literary historians give the honor of being the first person of her sex to win fame as a poet in America.

Negro authorship may, for clearer statement, be classified into three main activities: Poetry, Fiction, and the Essay, with an occasional excursion into other branches. In the drama, until very recently, practically nothing worth while has been achieved, with the exception of Angelina Grimké's *Rachel,* notable for its somber craftsmanship. Biography has given us a notable life story, told by himself, of Booker T. Washington. Frederick Douglass's story of his life is eloquent as a human document, but not in the graces of narration and psychologic portraiture, which has definitely put this form of literature in the domain of the fine arts. Indeed, we may well believe that the efforts of controversy, of the huge amount of discursive and polemical articles dealing chiefly with the race problem, that have been necessary in breaking and clearing the impeded pathway of racial progress, have absorbed and in a way dissipated the literary energy of many able Negro writers.

Let us survey briefly the advance of the Negro in poetry. Behind Dunbar, there is nothing that can stand the critical test. We shall always have a sentimental and historical interest in those forlorn and pathetic figures who cried in the wilderness of their ignorance and oppression. With Dunbar we have our first authentic lyric utterance, an utterance more authentic, I should say, for its faithful rendition of Negro life and character than for any rare or subtle artistry of expression. When Mr. Howells, in his famous introduction to the

Lyrics of Lowly Life, remarked that Dunbar was the first black man to express the life of his people lyrically, he summed up Dunbar's achievement and transported him to a place beside the peasant poet of Scotland, not for his art, but precisely because he made a people articulate in verse.

The two chief qualities in Dunbar's work are, however, pathos and humor, and in these he expresses that dilemma of soul that characterized the race between the Civil War and the end of the nineteenth century. The poetry of Dunbar is true to the life of the Negro and expresses characteristically what he felt and knew to be the temper and condition of his people. But its moods reflect chiefly those of the era of Reconstruction and just a little beyond,—the limited experience of a transitional period, the rather helpless and subservient era of testing freedom and reaching out through the difficulties of life to the emotional compensations of laughter and tears. It is the poetry of the happy peasant and the plaintive minstrel. Occasionally, as in the sonnet to *Robert Gould Shaw* and the *Ode to Ethiopia* there broke through Dunbar, as through the crevices of his spirit, a burning and brooding aspiration, an awakening and virile consciousness of race. But for the most part, his dreams were anchored to the minor whimsies; his deepest poetic inspiration was sentiment. He expressed a folk temperament, but not a race soul. Dunbar was the end of a regime, and not the beginning of a tradition, as so many careless critics, both white and colored, seem to think.

After Dunbar many versifiers appeared,—all largely dominated by his successful dialect work. I cannot parade them here for tag or comment, except to say that few have equalled Dunbar in this vein of expression, and none have deepened it as an expression of Negro life. Dunbar himself had clear notions of its limitations;—to a friend in a letter from London, March 15, 1897, he says: "I see now very clearly that Mr. Howells has done me irrevocable harm in the dictum he laid down regarding my dialect verse." Not until James W. Johnson published his *Fiftieth Anniversary Ode* on the emancipation in 1913, did a poet of the race disengage himself from the background of mediocrity into which the imitation of Dunbar snared Negro poetry. Mr. Johnson's work is based upon a broader contemplation of life, life that is not wholly confined within any racial experience, but through the racial he made articulate that universality of the emotions felt by all mankind. His verse possesses a vigor which definitely breaks away from the brooding minor undercurrents of feeling which have previously characterized the verse of Negro poets. Mr. Johnson brought, indeed, the first intellectual substance to the content of our poetry, and a craftsmanship which, less spontaneous than that of Dunbar's, was more balanced and precise.

Here a new literary generation begins; poetry that is racial in substance, but with the universal note, with the conscious background of the full heritage of English poetry. With each new figure somehow the gamut broadens and the technical control improves. The brilliant succession and maturing powers of Fenton Johnson, Leslie Pinckney Hill, Everett Hawkins, Lucien Watkins, Charles Bertram Johnson, Joseph Cotter, Georgia Douglas Johnson, Roscoe Jameson and Anne Spencer bring us at last to Claude McKay and the poets of the younger generation and a poetry of the masterful accent and high distinction. Too significantly for mere coincidence, it was the stirring year of 1917 that heard the first real masterful accent in Negro poetry. In the September *Crisis* of that year, Roscoe Jameson's *Negro Soldiers* appeared:

> These truly are the Brave,
> These men who cast aside
> Old memories to walk the blood-stained pave
> Of Sacrifice, joining the solemn tide
> That moves away, to suffer and to die
> For Freedom—when their own is yet denied!
> O Pride! A Prejudice! When they pass by
> Hail them, the Brave, for you now crucified.

The very next month, under the pen name of Eli Edwards, Claude McKay printed in *The Seven Arts,*

> *The Harlem Dancer*
> Applauding youths laughed with young prostitutes
>   And watched her perfect, half-clothed body sway;
> Her voice was like the sound of blended flutes
>   Blown by black players upon a picnic day.
> She sang and danced on gracefully and calm,
>   The light gauze hanging loose about her form;
> To me she seemed a proudly-swaying palm
>   Grown lovelier for passing through a storm.
>
> Upon her swarthy neck black, shiny curls
>   Profusely fell; and, tossing coins in praise
> The wine-flushed, bold-eyed boys, and even the girls
>   Devoured her with their eager, passionate gaze;
> But, looking at her falsely-smiling face
>   I knew her self was not in that strange place.

With Georgia Johnson, Anne Spencer and Angelina Grimké, the Negro woman poet significantly appears. Mrs. Johnson especially has voiced in true poetic spirit the lyric cry of Negro womanhood. In spite of lapses into the sentimental and the platitudinous, she has an authentic gift. Anne Spencer, more sophisticated, more cryptic but also more universal, reveals quite another aspect of poetic genius. Indeed, it is interesting to notice how today Negro poets waver between the racial and the universal notes.

Claude McKay, the poet who leads his generation, is a genius meshed in this dilemma. His work is caught between the currents of the poetry of protest and the poetry of expression; he is in turn the violent and strident propagandist, using his poetic gifts to clothe arrogant and defiant thoughts, and then the pure lyric dreamer, contemplating life and nature with a wistful sympathetic passion. When the mood of *Spring in New Hampshire* or the sonnet *The Harlem Dancer* possesses him, he is full of that spirit and power of beauty that flowers above any and all men's harming. How different in spite of the admirable spirit of courage and defiance, are his poems of which the sonnet *If We Must Die* is a typical example. Negro poetic expression hovers for the moment, pardonably perhaps, over the race problem, but its highest allegiance is to Poetry—it must soar.

Let me refer briefly to a type of literature in which there have been many pens, but a single mind. Dr. DuBois is the most variously gifted writer which the race has produced. Poet, novelist, sociologist, historian and essayist, he has produced books in all these fields with the exception, I believe, of a formal book of poems, and has given to each the distinction of his clear and exact thinking, and of his sensitive imagination and passionate vision. *The Souls of Black Folk* was the book of an era; it was a painful book, a book of tortured dreams woven into the fabric of the sociologist's document. This book has more profoundly influenced the spiritual temper of the race than any other written in its generation. It is only through the intense, passionate idealism of such substance as makes *The Souls of Black Folk* such a quivering rhapsody of wrongs endured and hopes to be fulfilled that the poets of the race with compelling artistry can lift the Negro into the only full and complete nationalism he knows—that of the American democracy. No other book has more clearly revealed to the nation at large the true idealism and high aspiration of the American Negro.

In this book, as well as in many of Dr. DuBois's essays, it is often my personal feeling that I am witnessing the birth of a poet, phoenix-like, out of a scholar. Between *The Souls of Black Folk* and *Darkwater,* published four years ago, Dr. DuBois has written a number of books, none more notable, in my opinion, than his novel *The Quest of the Silver Fleece,* in which he made Cotton the great protagonist of fate in the lives of the Southern people, both white and black. I only know of one other such attempt and accomplishment in American fiction—that of Frank Norris—and I am somehow of the opinion that when the great epic novel of the South is written this book will prove to have been its forerunner. Indeed, the Negro novel is one of the great potentialities of American literature. Must it be written by a Negro? To recur to the article from which I have already quoted:

> The white writer seems to stand baffled before the enigma and so he expends all his energies on dialect and in general on the Negro's minstrel characteristics. . . . We shall have to look to the Negro himself to go all the way. It is quite likely that no white man can do it. It is reasonable to suppose that his white psychology will always be in his way. I am not thinking at all about a Negro novelist who shall arouse the world to the horror of the deliberate killings by white mobs, to the wrongs that condemn a free people to political serfdom. I am not thinking at all of the propaganda novel, although there is enough horror and enough drama in the bald statistics of each one of the annual Moton letters to keep the whole army of writers busy. But the Negro novelist, if he ever comes, must reveal to us much more than what a Negro thinks about when he is being tied to a stake and the torch is being applied to his living flesh; much more than what he feels when he is being crowded off the sidewalk by a drunken rowdy who may be his intellectual inferior by a thousand leagues. Such a writer, to succeed in a big sense, would have to forget that there are white readers; he would have to lose self-consciousness and forget that his work would be placed before a white jury. He would have to be careless as to what the white critic might think of it; he would need the self-assurance to be his own critic. He would have to forget for the time being, at least, that any white man ever attempted to dissect the soul of a Negro.

What I here quote is both an inquiry and a challenge! Well informed as the writer is, he does not seem to detect the forces which are surely gathering to produce what he longs for.

The development of fiction among Negro authors has been, I might almost say, one of the repressed activities of our literary life. A fair start was made the last decade of the nineteenth century when Chestnutt [sic] and Dunbar were turning out both short stories and novels. In Dunbar's case, had he lived, I think his literary growth would have been in the evolution of the Race novel as indicated in *The Uncalled* and the *Sport of the Gods*. The former was, I think, the most ambitious literary effort of Dunbar; the latter was his most significant; significant because, thrown against the background of New York City, it displayed the life of the race as a unit, swayed by currents of existence, of which it was and was not a part. The story was touched with that shadow of destiny which gave to it a purpose more important than the mere racial machinery of its plot. But Dunbar in his fiction dealt only successfully with the same world that gave him the inspiration for his dialect poems; though his ambition was to "write a novel that will deal with the educated class of my own people." Later he writes of *The Fanatics:* "You do not know how my hopes were planted in that book, but it has utterly disappointed me." His contemporary, Charles W. Chestnutt [*sic*], was concerned more primarily with the fiction of the Color Line and the contacts and conflicts of its two worlds. He was in a way more successful. In the five volumes to his credit, he has revealed himself as a fiction writer of a very high order. But after all Mr. Chestnutt is a storyteller of genius transformed by racial earnestness into the novelist of talent. His natural gift would have found freer vent in a flow of short stories like Bret Harte's, to judge from the facility and power of his two volumes of short stories, *The Wife of His Youth and Other Stories* and *The Conjure Woman*. But Mr. Chestnutt's serious effort was in the field of the novel, where he made a brave and partially successful effort to correct the distortions of Reconstruction fiction and offset the school of Page and Cable. Two of these novels, *The Marrow of Tradition* and *The House Behind the Cedars,* must be reckoned among the representative period novels of their time. But the situation was not ripe for the great Negro novelist. The American public preferred spurious values to the genuine; the coinage of the Confederacy was at literary par. Where Dunbar, the sentimentalist, was welcome, Chestnutt, the realist, was barred. In 1905 Mr. Chestnutt wrote *The Colonel's Dream,* and thereafter silence fell upon him.

From this date until the past year, with the exception of *The Quest of the Silver Fleece,* which was published in 1911, there has been no fiction of importance by Negro authors. But then suddenly there comes a series of books, which seems to promise at least a new phase of race fiction, and possibly the era of the major novelists. Mr. Walter White's novel *The Fire in the Flint* is a swift moving straightforward story of the contemporary conflicts of black manhood in the South. Coming from the experienced observation of the author, himself an investigator of many lynchings and riots, it is a social document story of firsthand significance and importance; too vital to be labelled and dismissed as propaganda, yet for the same reason too unvarnished and realistic a story to be great art. Nearer to the requirements of art comes Miss Jessie Fauset's novel *There is Confusion*. Its distinction is to have created an entirely new milieu in the treatment of the race in fiction. She has taken a class within the race of established social standing, tradition and culture, and given in the rather complex family story of *The Marshalls* a social document of unique and refreshing value. In such a story, race fiction, detaching itself from the limitations of propaganda on the one hand and genre fiction on the other, emerges from the color line and is incorporated into the body of general and universal art.

Finally in Jean Toomer, the author of *Cane*, we come upon the very first artist of the race, who with all an artist's passion and sympathy for life, its hurts, its sympathies, its desires, its joys, its defeats and strange yearnings, can write about the Negro without the surrender or compromise of the artist's vision. So objective is it, that we feel that it is a mere accident that birth or association has thrown him into contact with the life he has written about. He would write just as well, just as poignantly, just as transmutingly, about the peasants of Russia, or the peasants of Ireland, had experience brought him in touch with their existence. *Cane* is a book of gold and bronze, of dusk and flame, of ecstasy and pain, and Jean Toomer is a bright morning star of a new day of the race in literature.

Jessie Fauset

The Gift of Laughter

(1925)

The black man bringing gifts, and particularly the gift of laughter, to the
American stage is easily the most anomalous, the most inscrutable figure of the century. All about him and within himself stalks the conviction
that like the Irish, the Russian and the Magyar he has some peculiar offering
which shall contain the very essence of the drama. Yet the medium through
which this unique and intensely dramatic gift might be offered has been so
befogged and misted by popular preconception that the great gift, though
divined, is as yet not clearly seen.

Popular preconception in this instance refers to the pressure of white
opinion by which the American Negro is surrounded and by which his true
character is almost submerged. For years the Caucasian in America has
persisted in dragging to the limelight merely one aspect of Negro characteristics, by which the whole race has been glimpsed, through which it has been
judged. The colored man who finally succeeds in impressing any considerable number of whites with the truth that he does not conform to these
measurements is regarded as the striking exception proving an unshakable
rule. The medium then through which the black actor has been presented to
the world has been that of the "funny man" of America. Ever since those far-
off times directly after the Civil War when white men and colored men too,
blacking their faces, presented the antics of plantation hands under the
caption of "Georgia Minstrels" and the like, the edict has gone forth that the
black man on the stage must be an end-man.

In passing one pauses to wonder if this picture of the black American as a
living comic supplement has not been painted in order to camouflage the

This essay first appeared in Alaine Locke, ed., *The New Negro: An Anthology* (1925; reprint, New
York, 1968).

real feeling and knowledge of his white compatriot. Certainly the plight of the slaves under even the mildest of masters could never have been one to awaken laughter. And no genuinely thinking person, no really astute observer, looking at the Negro in modern American life, could find his condition even now a first aid to laughter. That condition may be variously deemed hopeless, remarkable, admirable, inspiring, depressing; it can never be dubbed merely amusing.

It was the colored actor who gave the first impetus away from this buffoonery. The task was not an easy one. For years the Negro was no great frequenter of the theater. And no matter how keenly he felt the insincerity in the presentation of his kind, no matter how ridiculous and palpable a caricature such a presentation might be, the Negro auditor with the helplessness of the minority was powerless to demand something better and truer. Artist and audience alike were in the grip of the minstrel formula. It was at this point in the eighteen-nineties that Ernest Hogan, pioneer comedian of the better type, changed the tradition of the merely funny, rather silly "end-man" into a character with a definite plot in a rather loosely constructed but none the less well outlined story. The method was still humorous, but less broadly, less exclusively. A little of the hard luck of the Negro began to creep in. If he was a buffoon, he was a buffoon wearing his rue. A slight, very slight quality of the Harlequin began to attach to him. He was the clown making light of his troubles but he was a wounded, a sore-beset clown.

This figure became the prototype of the plays later presented by those two great characters, Williams and Walker. The ingredients of the comedies in which these two starred usually consisted of one dishonest, overbearing, flashily dressed character (Walker) and one kindly, rather simple, hard-luck personage (Williams). The interest of the piece hinged on the juxtaposition of these two men. Of course these plays, too, were served with a sauce of humor because the public, true to its carefully taught and rigidly held tradition, could not dream of a situation in which colored people were anything but merely funny. But the hardships and woes suffered by Williams, ridiculous as they were, introduced with the element of folk comedy some element of reality.

Side by side with Williams and Walker, who might be called the apostles of the "legitimate" on the stage for Negroes, came the merriment and laughter and high spirits of that incomparable pair, Cole and Johnson. But they were essentially the geniuses of musical comedy. At that time their singers and dancers outsang and outdanced the neophytes of contemporary white musical comedies even as their followers to this day outsing and outdance in their occasional appearances on Broadway their modern neighbors. Just what might have been the ultimate trend of the ambition of this partnership, the untimely death of Mr. Cole rendered uncertain; but speaking offhand I should say that the relation of their musical comedy idea to the fixed plot and defined dramatic concept of the Williams and Walker plays molded the form of the Negro musical show which still persists and thrives on the contemporary stage. It was they who capitalized the infectious charm of so much rich dark beauty, the verve and abandon of Negro dancers, the glorious fullness of Negro voices. And they produced those effects in the *Red Shawl* in a manner still unexcelled, except in the matter of setting, by any latter-day companies.

But Williams and Walker, no matter how dimly, were seeking a method whereby the colored man might enter the "legitimate." They were to do nothing but pave the way. Even this task was difficult but they performed it well.

Those who knew Bert Williams say that his earliest leanings were toward the stage, but that he recognized at an equally early age that his color would probably keep him from ever making the "legitimate." Consequently, deliberately, as one who desiring to become a great painter but lacking the means for travel and study might take up commercial art, he turned his attention to minstrelsy. Natively he possessed the art of mimicry; intuitively he realized that his first path to the stage must lie along the old recognized lines of "funny man." He was, as few of us recall, a Jamaican by birth; the ways of the American Negro were utterly alien to him and did not come spontaneously; he set himself therefore to obtaining a knowledge of them. For choice he selected, perhaps by way of contrast, the melancholy out-of-luck Negro, shiftless, doleful, "easy"; the kind that tempts the world to lay its hand none too lightly upon him. The pursuit took him years, but at length he was able to portray for us not only that "typical Negro" which the white world thinks is universal but also the special types of given districts and localities with their own peculiar foibles of walk and speech and jargon. He went to London and studied before Pietro, greatest pantomimist of his day, until finally he, too, became a recognized master in the field of comic art.

But does anyone who realizes that the foibles of the American Negro were painstakingly acquired by this artist, doubt that Williams might just as well have portrayed the Irishman, the Jew, the Englishman abroad, the Scotchman or any other of the vividly etched types which for one reason or another lend themselves so readily to caricature? Can anyone presume to say that a man who travelled *north, east, south* and *west* and even abroad in order to acquire accent and jargon, aspect and characteristic of a people to which he was bound by ties of blood but from whom he was natively separated by training and tradition, would not have been able to portray with equal effectiveness what, for lack of a better term, we must call universal roles?

There is an unwritten law in America that though white may imitate black, black, even when superlatively capable, must never imitate white. In other words, grease-paint may be used to darken but never to lighten.

Williams' color imposed its limitations upon him even in his chosen field. His expansion was always upward but never outward. He might portray black people along the gamut from roustabout to unctuous bishop. But he must never stray beyond those limits. How keenly he felt this few of us knew until after his death. But it was well known to his intimates and professional associates. W. C. Fields, himself an expert in the art of amusing, called him "the funniest man I ever saw and the saddest man I ever knew."

He was sad with the sadness of hopeless frustration. The gift of laughter in his case had its source in a wounded heart and in bleeding sensibilities.

That laughter for which we are so justly famed has had in late years its overtones of pain. Now for some time past it has been used by colored men who have gained a precarious footing on the stage to conceal the very real dolor raging in their breasts. To be by force of circumstances the most dramatic figure in a country; to be possessed of the wells of feeling, of the most spontaneous instinct for effective action and to be shunted no less always into the role of the ridiculous and funny,—that is enough to create the quality of bitterness for which we are ever so often rebuked. Yet that same laughter influenced by these same untoward obstacles has within the last four years known a deflection into another channel, still productive of mirth, but even more than that of a sort of cosmic gladness, the joy which arises spontaneously in the spectator as a result of the sight of its no less spontaneous bubbling in others. What hurt most in the spectacle of the Bert Williams' funny man and his forerunners was the fact that the laughter which he created must be objective. But the new "funny man" among black comedians is essentially funny himself. He is joy and mischief and rich, homely native humor personified. He radiates good feeling and happiness; it is with him now a state of being purely subjective. The spectator is infected with his high spirits and his excessive good will; a stream of well-being is projected across the footlights into the consciousness of the beholder.

This phenomenon has been especially visible in the rendition of the colored musical "shows," *Shuffle Along, Runnin' Wild, Liza,* which livened up Broadway recently for a too brief season. Those of us who were lucky enough to compare with the usual banality of musical comedy, the verve and pep, the liveliness and gayety of those productions will not soon forget them. The medley of shades, the rich colorings, the abundance of fun and spirits on the part of the players all combined to produce an atmosphere which was actually palpable, so full was it of the ecstasy and joy of living. The singing was inimitable; the work of the chorus apparently spontaneous and unstudied. Emotionally they garnished their threadbare plots and comedy tricks with the genius of a new comic art.

The performers in all three of these productions gave out an impression of sheer happiness in living such as I have never before seen on any stage except in a riotous farce which I once saw in Vienna and where the same effect of superabundant vitality was induced. It is this quality of vivid and untheatrical portrayal of sheer emotion which seems likely to be the Negro's chief contribution to the stage. A comedy made up of such ingredients as the music of Sissle and Blake, the quaint, irresistible humor of Miller and Lyles, the quintessence of jazzdom in the Charleston, the superlativeness of Miss Mills' happy abandon could know no equal. It would be the line by which all other comedy would have to be measured. Behind the banalities and claptrap and crudities of these shows, this supervitality and joyousness glow from time to time in a given step or gesture or in the teasing assurance of such a line as: "If you've never been vamped by a brown-skin, you've never been vamped at all."

And as Carl van Vechten recently in his brilliant article, *Prescription for the Negro Theater,* so pointedly advises and prophesies, once this spirit breaks through the silly "childish adjuncts of the minstrel tradition" and drops the unworthy formula of unoriginal imitation of the stock revues, there will be released on the American stage a spirit of comedy such as has been rarely known.

The remarkable thing about this gift of ours is that it has its rise, I am convinced, in the very woes which beset us. Just as a person driven by great sorrow may finally go into an orgy of laughter, just so an oppressed and too hard driven people breaks over into compensating laughter and merriment. It is our emotional salvation. There would be no point in mentioning this rather obvious fact were it not that it argues also the possession on our part of a histrionic endowment for the portrayal of tragedy. Not without reason has tradition made comedy and tragedy sisters and twins, the capacity for one argues the capacity for the other. It is not surprising then that the period that sees the Negro actor on the verge of great comedy has seen him breaking through to the portrayal of serious and legitimate drama. No one who has seen Gilpin and Robeson in the portrayal of *The Emperor Jones* and of *All God's Chillun* can fail to realize that tragedy, too, is a vastly fitting role for the Negro actor. And so with the culminating of his dramatic genius, the Negro actor must come finally through the very versatility of his art to the universal role and the main tradition of drama, as an artist first and only secondarily as a Negro.

Nor when within the next few years, this question comes up, as I suspect it must come up with increasing insistence, will the more obvious barriers seem as obvious as they now appear. For in this American group of the descendants of Mother Africa, the question of color raises no insuperable barrier, seeing that with chameleon adaptability we are able to offer white colored men and women for *Hamlet, The Doll's House* and the *Second Mrs. Tanqueray;* brown men for *Othello;* yellow girls for *Madam Butterfly;* black men for *The Emperor Jones.* And underneath and permeating all this bewildering array of shades and tints is the unshakable precision of an instinctive and spontaneous emotional art.

   All this beyond any doubt will be the reward of the "gift of laughter" which many black actors on the American stage have proffered. Through laughter we have conquered even the lot of the jester and the clown. The parable of the one talent still holds good and because we have used the little which in those early painful days was our only approach we find ourselves slowly but surely moving toward that most glittering of all goals, the freedom of the American stage. I hope that Hogan realizes this and Cole and Walker, too, and that lastly Bert Williams the inimitable, will clap us on with those tragic black-gloved hands of his now that the gift of his laughter is no longer tainted with the salt of chagrin and tears.

George S. Schuyler

The Negro-Art Hokum

(1926)

Negro art "made in America" is as nonexistent as the widely advertised profundity of Cal Coolidge, the "seven years of progress" of Mayor Hylan, or the reported sophistication of New Yorkers. Negro art there has been, is, and will be among the numerous black nations of Africa; but to suggest the possibility of any such development among the ten million colored people in this republic is self-evident foolishness. Eager apostles from Greenwich Village, Harlem, and environs proclaimed a great renaissance of Negro art just around the corner waiting to be ushered on the scene by those whose hobby is taking races, nations, peoples, and movements under their wing. New art forms expressing the "peculiar" psychology of the Negro were about to flood the market. In short, the art of Homo Africanus was about to electrify the waiting world. Skeptics patiently waited. They still wait.

True, from dark-skinned sources have come those slave songs based on Protestant hymns and Biblical texts known as the spirituals, work songs and secular songs of sorrow and tough luck known as the blues, that outgrowth of ragtime known as jazz (in the development of which whites have assisted), and the Charleston, an eccentric dance invented by the gamins around the public marketplace in Charleston, S.C. No one can or does deny this. But these are contributions of a caste in a certain section of the country. They are foreign to Northern Negroes, West Indian Negroes, and African Negroes. They are no more expressive or characteristic of the Negro race than the music and dancing of the Appalachian highlanders or the Dalmation peasantry are expressive or characteristic of the Caucasian race. If one wishes to speak of the musical contributions of the peasantry of the South, very well. Any group under similar circumstances would have produced

This essay first appeared in *The Nation*, 122 (1926).

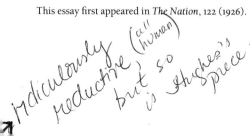

something similar. It is merely a coincidence that this peasant class happens to be of a darker hue than the other inhabitants of the land. One recalls the remarkable likeness of the minor strains of the Russian mujiks to those of the Southern Negro.

As for the literature, painting, and sculpture of Aframericans—such as there is—it is identical in kind with the literature, painting, and sculpture of white Americans: that is, it shows more or less evidence of European influence. In the field of drama little of any merit has been written by and about Negroes that could not have been written by whites. The dean of the Aframerican literati is W. E. B. DuBois, a product of Harvard and German universities; the foremost Aframerican sculptor is Meta Warwick Fuller, a graduate of leading American art schools and former student of Rodin; while the most noted Aframerican painter, Henry Ossawa Tanner, is dean of American painters in Paris and has been decorated by the French Government. Now the work of these artists is no more "expressive of the Negro soul"— as the gushers put it—than are the scribblings of Octavus Cohen or Hugh Wiley.

This, of course, is easily understood if one stops to realize that the Aframerican is merely a lampblacked Anglo-Saxon. If the European immigrant after two or three generations of exposure to our schools, politics, advertising, moral crusades, and restaurants becomes indistinguishable from the mass of Americans of the older stock (despite the influence of the foreign-language press), how much truer must it be of the sons of Ham who have been subjected to what the uplifters call Americanism for the last three hundred years. Aside from his color, which ranges from very dark brown to pink, your American Negro is just plain American. Negroes and whites from the same localities in this country talk, think, and act about the same. Because a few writers with a paucity of themes have seized upon imbecilities of the Negro rustics and clowns and palmed them off as authentic and characteristic Aframerican behavior, the common notion that the black American is so "different" from his white neighbor has gained wide currency. The mere mention of the word "Negro" conjures up in the average white American's mind a composite stereotype of Bert Williams, Aunt Jemima, Uncle Tom, Jack Johnson, Florian Slappey, and the various monstrosities scrawled by the cartoonists. Your average Aframerican no more resembles this stereotype than the average American resembles a composite of Andy Gump, Jim Jeffries, and a cartoon by Rube Goldberg.

Again, the Africamerican is subject to the same economic and social forces that mold the actions and thoughts of the white Americans. He is not living in a different world as some whites and a few Negroes would have us believe. When the jangling of his Connecticut alarm clock gets him out of his Grand Rapids bed to a breakfast similar to that eaten by his white brother across the street; when he toils at the same or similar work in mills, mines, factories, and commerce alongside the descendants of Spartacus, Robin Hood, and Eric the Red; when he wears similar clothing and speaks the same language with the same degree of perfection; when he reads the same Bible and belongs to the Baptist, Methodist, Episcopal, or Catholic church; when his fraternal affiliations also include the Elks, Masons, and Knights of Pythias; when he gets the same or similar schooling, lives in the same kind of houses, owns the same makes of cars (or rides in them), and nightly sees the same Hollywood version of life on the screen; when he smokes the same brands of tobacco, and avidly peruses the same puerile periodicals; in short, when he responds to the same political, social, moral, and economic stimuli in precisely the same manner as his white neighbor, it is sheer nonsense to talk about "racial differences" as between the American black man and the American white man. Glance over a Negro newspaper (it is printed in good Americanese) and you will find the usual quota of crime news, scandal, personals, and uplift to be found in the average white newspaper—which, by the way, is more widely read by the Negroes than is the Negro press. In order to satisfy the cravings of an inferiority complex engendered by the colorphobia of the mob, the readers of the Negro newspapers are given a slight dash of racialistic seasoning. In the homes of the black and white Americans of the same cultural and economic level one finds similar furniture, literature, and conversation. How, then, can the black American be expected to produce art and literature dissimilar to that of the white American?

Consider Coleridge-Taylor, Edward Wilmot Blyden, and Claude McKay, the Englishmen; Pushkin, the Russian; Bridgewater, the Pole; Antar, the Arabian; Latino, the Spaniard; Dumas, *père* and *fils,* the Frenchmen; and Paul Laurence Dunbar, Charles W. Chestnutt [*sic*], and James Weldon Johnson, the Americans. All Negroes; yet their work shows the impress of nationality rather than race. They all reveal the psychology and culture of their environment—their color is incidental. Why should Negro artists of America vary from the national artistic norm when Negro artists in other countries have not done so? If we can foresee what kind of white citizens will inhabit this neck of the woods in the next generation by studying the sort of education and environment the children are exposed to now, it should not be difficult to reason that the adults of today are what they are because of the education and environment they were exposed to a generation ago. And that education and environment were about the same for blacks and whites. One contemplates the popularity of the Negro-art hokum and murmurs, "How come?"

This nonsense is probably the last stand of the old myth palmed off by Negrophobists for all these many years, and recently rehashed by the sainted Harding, that there are "fundamental, eternal, and inescapable differences" between white and black Americans. That there are Negroes who will lend this myth a helping hand need occasion no surprise. It has been broadcast all over the world by the vociferous scions of slaveholders, "scientists" like Madison Grant and Lothrop Stoddard, and the patriots who flood the treasury of the Ku Klux Klan; and is believed, even today, by the majority of free, white citizens. On this baseless premise, so flattering to the white mob, that the blackamoor is inferior and fundamentally different, is erected the postulate that he must needs be peculiar; and when he attempts to portray life through the medium of art, it must of necessity be a peculiar art. While such reasoning may seem conclusive to the majority of Americans, it must be rejected with a loud guffaw by intelligent people.

Langston Hughes

The Negro Artist and the Racial Mountain

(1926)

(Cullen)

One of the most promising of the young Negro poets said to me once, "I want to be a poet—not a Negro poet," meaning, I believe, "I want to write like a white poet"; meaning, subconsciously, "I would like to be a white poet"; meaning behind that, "I would like to be white." And I was sorry the young man said that, for no great poet has ever been afraid of being himself. And I doubted then that, with his desire to run away spiritually from his race, this boy would ever be a great poet. But this is the mountain standing in the way of any true Negro art in America—this urge within the race toward whiteness, the desire to pour racial individuality into the mold of American standardization, and to be as little Negro and as much American as possible.

But let us look at the immediate background of this young poet. His family is of what I suppose one would call the Negro middle class: people who are by no means rich, yet never uncomfortable nor hungry—smug, contented, respectable folk, members of the Baptist church. The father goes to work every morning. He is a chief steward at a large white club. The mother sometimes does fancy sewing or supervises parties for the rich families of the town. The children go to a mixed school. In the home they read white papers and magazines. And the mother often says, "Don't be like niggers" when the children are bad. A frequent phrase from the father is, "Look how well a white man does things." And so the word white comes to be unconsciously a symbol of all the virtues. It holds for the children beauty, morality and money. The whisper of "I want to be white" runs silently through their minds. This young poet's home is, I believe, a fairly typical home of the colored middle class. One sees immediately how difficult it would be for an artist born in such a home to interest himself in interpreting the beauty of his

This essay first appeared in *The Nation*, 122 (1926).

own people. He is never taught to see that beauty. He is taught rather not to see it, or if he does, to be ashamed of it when it is not according to Caucasian patterns.

For racial culture the home of a self-styled "high-class" Negro has nothing better to offer. Instead there will perhaps be more aping of things white than in a less cultured or less wealthy home. The father is perhaps a doctor, lawyer, landowner, or politician. The mother may be a social worker, or a teacher, or she may do nothing and have a maid. Father is often dark but he has usually married the lightest woman he could find. The family attends a fashionable church where few really colored faces are to be found. And they themselves draw a color line. In the North they go to white theaters and white movies. And in the South they have at least two cars and a house "like white folks." Nordic manners, Nordic faces, Nordic hair, Nordic art (if any), and an Episcopal heaven. A very high mountain indeed for the would-be racial artist to climb in order to discover himself and his people.

But then there are the low-down folks, the so-called common element, and they are the majority—may the Lord be praised! The people who have their nip of gin on Saturday nights and are not too important to themselves or the community, or too well fed, or too learned to watch the lazy world go round. They live on Seventh Street in Washington or State Street in Chicago and they do not particularly care whether they are like white folks or anybody else. Their joy runs, bang! into ecstasy. Their religion soars to a shout. Work maybe a little today, rest a little tomorrow. Play awhile. Sing awhile. O, let's dance! These common people are not afraid of spirituals, as for a long time their more intellectual brethren were, and jazz is their child. They furnish a wealth of colorful, distinctive material for any artist because they still hold their own individuality in the face of American standardizations. And per-haps these common people will give to the world its truly great Negro artist, the one who is not afraid to be himself. Whereas the better-class Negro would tell the artist what to do, the people at least let him alone when he does appear. And they are not ashamed of him—if they know he exists at all. And they accept what beauty is their own without question.

Certainly there is, for the American Negro artist who can escape the re-strictions the more advanced among his own group would put upon him, a great field of unused material ready for his art. Without going outside his race, and even among the better classes with their "white" culture and con-scious American manners, but still Negro enough to be different, there is sufficient matter to furnish a black artist with a lifetime of creative work. And when he chooses to touch on the relations between Negroes and whites in *reductive / essentialist in his theories? Racial individuality?* (handwritten annotations)

this country, with their innumerable overtones and undertones, surely, and especially for literature and the drama, there is an inexhaustible supply of themes at hand. To these the Negro artist can give his racial individuality, his heritage of rhythm and warmth, and his incongruous humor that so often, as in the Blues, becomes ironic laughter mixed with tears. But let us look again at the mountain.

A prominent Negro clubwoman in Philadelphia paid eleven dollars to hear Raquel Meller sing Andalusian popular songs. But she told me a few weeks before she would not think of going to hear "that woman," Clara Smith, a great black artist, sing Negro folksongs. And many an upper-class Negro church, even now, would not dream of employing a spiritual in its services. The drab melodies in white folks' hymnbooks are much to be preferred. "We want to worship the Lord correctly and quietly. We don't believe in 'shouting.' Let's be dull like the Nordics," they say, in effect.

The road for the serious black artist, then, who would produce a racial art is most certainly rocky and the mountain is high. Until recently he received almost no encouragement for his work from either white or colored people. The fine novels of Chesnutt go out of print with neither race noticing their passing. The quaint charm and humor of Dunbar's dialect verse brought to him, in his day, largely the same kind of encouragement one would give a sideshow freak (A colored man writing poetry! How odd!) or a clown (How amusing!).

The present vogue in things Negro, although it may do as much harm as good for the budding colored artist, has at least done this: it has brought him forcibly to the attention of his own people among whom for so long, unless the other race had noticed him beforehand, he was a prophet with little honor. I understand that Charles Gilpin acted for years in Negro theaters without any special acclaim from his own, but when Broadway gave him eight curtain calls, Negroes, too, began to beat a tin pan in his honor. I know a young colored writer, a manual worker by day, who had been writing well for the colored magazines for some years, but it was not until he recently broke into the white publications and his first book was accepted by a prominent New York publisher that the "best" Negroes in his city took the trouble to discover that he lived there. Then almost immediately they decided to give a grand dinner for him. But the society ladies were careful to whisper to his mother that perhaps she'd better not come. They were not sure she would have an evening gown.

The Negro artist works against an undertow of sharp criticism and misunderstanding from his own group and unintentional bribes from the whites.

"O, be respectable, write about nice people, show how good we are," say the Negroes. "Be stereotyped, don't go too far, don't shatter our illusions about you, don't amuse us too seriously. We will pay you," say the whites. Both would have told Jean Toomer not to write *Cane*. The colored people did not praise it. The white people did not buy it. Most of the colored people who did read *Cane* hate it. They are afraid of it. Although the critics gave it good reviews the public remained indifferent. Yet (excepting the work of DuBois) *Cane* contains the finest prose written by a Negro in America. And like the singing of Robeson it is truly racial.

But in spite of the Nordicized Negro intelligentsia and the desires of some white editors we have an honest American Negro literature already with us. Now I await the rise of the Negro theater. Our folk music, having achieved world-wide fame, offers itself to the genius of the great individual American Negro composer who is to come. And within the next decade I expect to see the work of a growing school of colored artists who paint and model the beauty of dark faces and create with new technique the expressions of their own soul-world. And the Negro dancers who will dance like flame and the singers who will continue to carry our songs to all who listen—they will be with us in even greater numbers tomorrow.

Most of my own poems are racial in theme and treatment, derived from the life I know. In many of them I try to grasp and hold some of the meanings and rhythms of jazz. I am sincere as I know how to be in these poems and yet after every reading I answer questions like these from my own people: "Do you think Negroes should always write about Negroes? I wish you wouldn't read some of your poems to white folks. How do you find anything interesting in a place like a cabaret? Why do you write about black peoople? You aren't black. What makes you do so many jazz poems?"

But jazz to me is one of the inherent expressions of Negro life in America: the eternal tom-tom beating in the Negro soul—the tom-tom of revolt against weariness in a white world, a world of subway trains and work, work, work; the tom-tom of joy and laughter, and pain swallowed in a smile. Yet the Philadelphia clubwoman is ashamed to say that her race created it and she does not like me to write about it. The old subconscious "white is best" runs through her mind. Years of study under white teachers, a lifetime of white books, pictures, and papers, and white manners, morals, and Puritan standards made her dislike the spirituals. And now she turns up her nose at jazz and all its manifestations—likewise almost everything else distinctly racial. She doesn't care for the Winold Reiss portraits of Negroes because they are "too Negro." She does not want a true picture of herself from anybody. She wants the artist to flatter her, to make the white world believe that all Negroes are as smug and as near white in soul as she wants to be. But, to my mind, it is the duty of the younger Negro artist, if he accepts any duties at all from outsiders, to change through the force of his art that old whispering, "I want to be white," hidden in the aspirations of his people, to "Why should I want to be white? I am a Negro—and beautiful!"

So I am ashamed for the black poet who says, "I want to be a poet, not a Negro poet," as though his own racial world were not as interesting as any other world. I am ashamed, too, for the colored artist who runs from the painting of Negro faces to the painting of sunsets after the manner of the academicians because he fears the strange un-whiteness of his own features. An artist must be free to choose what he does, certainly, but he must also never be afraid to do what he might choose.

Let the blare of Negro jazz bands and the bellowing voice of Bessie Smith singing Blues penetrate the closed ears of the colored near-intellectuals until they listen and perhaps understand. Let Paul Robeson singing "Water Boy," and Rudolph Fisher writing about the streets of Harlem, and Jean Toomer holding the heart of Georgia in his hands, and Aaron Douglas drawing strange black fantasies cause the smug Negro middle class to turn from their white, respectable, ordinary books and papers to catch a glimmer of their own beauty. We younger Negro artists who create now intend to express our individual dark-skinned selves without fear or shame. If white people are pleased we are glad. If they are not, it doesn't matter. We know we are beautiful. And ugly too. The tom-tom cries and the tom-tom laughs. If colored people are pleased we are glad. If they are not, their displeasure doesn't matter either. We build our temples for tomorrow, strong as we know how, and we stand on top of the mountain, free within ourselves.

W. E. B. DuBois

Criteria of Negro Art

(1926)

I do not doubt but there are some in this audience who are a little disturbed at the subject of this meeting, and particularly at the subject I have chosen. Such people are thinking something like this: "How is it that an organization like this, a group of radicals trying to bring new things into the world, a fighting organization which has come up out of the blood and dust of battle, struggling for the right of black men to be ordinary human beings—how is it that an organization of this kind can turn aside to talk about Art? After all, what have we who are slaves and black to do with Art?"

Or perhaps there are others who feel a certain relief and are saying, "After all it is rather satisfactory after all this talk about rights and fighting to sit and dream of something which leaves a nice taste in the mouth."

Let me tell you that neither of these groups is right. The thing we are talking about tonight is part of the great fight we are carrying on and it represents a forward and an upward look—a pushing onward. You and I have been breasting hills; we have been climbing upward; there has been progress and we can see it day by day looking back along blood-filled paths. But as you go through the valleys and over the foothills, so long as you are climbing, the direction,—north, south, east or west,—is of less importance. But when gradually the vista widens and you begin to see the world at your feet and the far horizon, then it is time to know more precisely whither you are going and what you really want.

What do we want? What is the thing we are after? As it was phrased last night it had a certain truth: We want to be Americans, full-fledged Americans, with all the rights of other American citizens. But is that all? Do we want simply to be Americans? Once in a while through all of us there flashes

This essay first appeared in *Crisis*, 32 (October 1926).

some clairvoyance, some clear idea, of what America really is. We who are dark can see America in a way that white Americans can not. And seeing our country thus, are we satisfied with its present goals and ideals?

In the high school where I studied we learned most of Scott's "Lady of the Lake" by heart. In after life once it was my privilege to see the lake. It was Sunday. It was quiet. You could glimpse the deer wandering in unbroken forests; you could hear the soft ripple of romance on the waters. Around me fell the cadence of that poetry of my youth. I fell asleep full of the enchantment of the Scottish border. A new day broke and with it came a sudden rush of excursionists. They were mostly Americans and they were loud and strident. They poured upon the little pleasure boat,—men with their hats a little on one side and drooping cigars in the wet corners of their mouths; women who shared their conversation with the world. They all tried to get everywhere first. They pushed other people out of the way. They made all sorts of incoherent noises and gestures so that the quiet home folk and the visitors from other lands silently and half-wonderingly gave way before them. They struck a note not evil but wrong. They carried, perhaps, a sense of strength and accomplishment, but their hearts had no conception of the beauty which pervaded this holy place.

If you tonight suddenly should become full-fledged Americans; if your color faded, or the color line here in Chicago was miraculously forgotten; suppose, too, you became at the same time rich and powerful;—what is it that you would want? What would you immediately seek? Would you buy the most powerful of motor cars and outrace Cook County? Would you buy the most elaborate estate on the North Shore? Would you be a Rotarian or a Lion or a What-not of the very last degree? Would you wear the most striking clothes, give the richest dinners and buy the longest press notices?

Even as you visualize such ideals you know in your hearts that these are not the things you really want. You realize this sooner than the average white American because, pushed aside as we have been in America, there has come to us not only a certain distaste for the tawdry and flamboyant but a vision of what the world could be if it were really a beautiful world; if we had the true spirit; if we had the Seeing Eye, the Cunning Hand, the Feeling Heart; if we had, to be sure, not perfect happiness, but plenty of good hard work, the inevitable suffering that always comes with life; sacrifice and waiting, all that—but, nevertheless, lived in a world where men know, where men create, where they realize themselves and where they enjoy life. It is that sort of a world we want to create for ourselves and for all America.

After all, who shall describe Beauty? What is it? I remember tonight four beautiful things: The Cathedral at Cologne, a forest in stone, set in light and changing shadow, echoing with sunlight and solemn song; a village of the Veys in West Africa, a little thing of mauve and purple, quiet, lying content and shining in the sun; a black and velvet room where on a throne rests, in old and yellowing marble, the broken curves of the Venus of Milo; a single phrase of music in the Southern South—utter melody, haunting and appealing, suddenly arising out of night and eternity, beneath the moon.

Such is Beauty. Its variety is infinite, its possibility is endless. In normal life all may have it and have it yet again. The world is full of it; and yet today the mass of human beings are choked away from it, and their lives distorted and made ugly. This is not only wrong, it is silly. Who shall right this well-nigh universal failing? Who shall let this world be beautiful? Who shall restore to men the glory of sunsets and the peace of quiet sleep?

We black folk may help for we have within us as a race new stirrings; stirrings of the beginning of a new appreciation of joy, of a new desire to create, of a new will to be; as though in this morning of group life we had awakened from some sleep that at once dimly mourns the past and dreams a splendid future; and there has come the conviction that the Youth that is here today, the Negro Youth, is a different kind of Youth, because in some new way it bears this mighty prophecy on its breast, with a new realization of itself, with new determination for all mankind.

What has this Beauty to do with the world? What has Beauty to do with Truth and Goodness—with the facts of the world and the right actions of men? "Nothing," the artists rush to answer. They may be right. I am but an humble disciple of art and cannot presume to say. I am one who tells the truth and exposes evil and seeks with Beauty and for Beauty to set the world right. That somehow, somewhere eternal and perfect Beauty sits above Truth and Right I can conceive, but here and now and in the world in which I work they are for me unseparated and inseparable.

This is brought to us peculiarly when as artists we face our own past as a people. There has come to us—and it has come especially through the man we are going to honor tonight*—a realization of that past, of which for long years we have been ashamed, for which we have apologized. We thought nothing could come out of that past which we wanted to remember; which we wanted to hand down to our children. Suddenly, this same past is taking on form, color and reality, and in a half shamefaced way we are beginning to be proud of it. We are remembering that the romance of the world did not die

*Carter Godwin Woodson, 12th Spingarn Medallist.

and lie forgotten in the Middle Age; that if you want romance to deal with you must have it here and now and in your own hands.

I once knew a man and woman. They had two children, a daughter who was white and a daughter who was brown; the daughter who was white married a white man; and when her wedding was preparing the daughter who was brown prepared to go and celebrate. But the mother said, "No!" and the brown daughter went into her room and turned on the gas and died. Do you want Greek tragedy swifter than that?

Or again, here is a little Southern town and you are in the public square. On one side of the square is the office of a colored lawyer and on all the others sides are men who do not like colored lawyers. A white woman goes into the black man's office and points to the white-filled square and says, "I want five hundred dollars now and if I do not get it I am going to scream."

Have you heard the story of the conquest of German East Africa? Listen to the untold tale: There were 40,000 black men and 4,000 white men who talked German. There were 20,000 black men and 12,000 white men who talked English. There were 10,000 black men and 400 white men who talked French. In Africa then where the Mountains of the Moon raised their white and snowcapped heads into the mouth of the tropic sun, where Nile and Congo rise and the Great Lakes swim, these men fought; they struggled on mountain, hill and valley, in river, lake and swamp, until in masses they sickened, crawled and died; until the 4,000 white Germans had become mostly bleached bones; until nearly all the 12,000 white Englishmen had returned to South Africa, and the 400 Frenchmen to Belgium and Heaven; all except a mere handful of the white men died; but thousands of black men from East, West and South Africa, from Nigeria and the Valley of the Nile, and from the West Indies still struggled, fought and died. For four years they fought and won and lost German East Africa; and all you hear about it is that England and Belgium conquered German Africa for the allies!

Such is the true and stirring stuff of which Romance is born and from this stuff come the stirrings of men who are beginning to remember that this kind of material is theirs; and this vital life of their own kind is beckoning them on.

The question comes next as to the interpretation of these new stirrings, of this new spirit: Of what is the colored artist capable? We have had on the part of both colored and white people singular unanimity of judgment in the past. Colored people have said: "This work must be inferior because it comes from colored people." White people have said: "It is inferior because it is done by colored people." But today there is coming to both the realization that the work of the black man is <u>not always inferior</u>. Interesting stories come to us. A

professor in the University of Chicago read to a class that had studied literature a passage of poetry and asked them to guess the author. They guessed a
goodly company from Shelley and Robert Browning down to Tennyson and
Masefield. The author was Countée Cullen. Or again the English critic John
Drinkwater went down to a Southern seminary, one of the sort which "fin-
ishes" young white women of the South. The students sat with their wooden
faces while he tried to get some response out of them. Finally he said, "Name
me some of your Southern poets." They hesitated. He said finally, "I'll start
out with your best: Paul Laurence Dunbar!"

With the growing recognition of Negro artists in spite of the severe handicaps, one comforting thing is occurring to both white and black. They are
whispering, "Here is a way out. Here is the real solution of the color problem.
The recognition accorded Cullen, Hughes, Fauset, White and others shows
there is no real color line. Keep quiet! Don't complain! Work! All will be
well!"

I will not say that already this chorus amounts to a conspiracy. Perhaps I
am naturally too suspicious. But I will say that there are today a surprising number of white people who are getting great satisfaction out of these
younger Negro writers because they think it is going to stop agitation of the
Negro question. They say, "What is the use of your fighting and complaining;
do the great thing and the reward is there." And many colored people are all
too eager to follow this advice; especially those who are weary of the eternal
struggle along the color line, who are afraid to fight and to whom the money
of philanthropists and the alluring publicity are subtle and deadly bribes.
They say, "What is the use of fighting? Why not show simply what we
deserve and let the reward come to us?"

And it is right here that the National Association for the Advancement of
Colored People comes upon the field, comes with its great call to a new
battle, a new fight and new things to fight before the old things are wholly
won; and to say that the Beauty of Truth and Freedom which shall some day
be our heritage and the heritage of all civilized men is not in our hands yet
and that we ourselves must not fail to realize.

There is in New York tonight a black woman molding clay by herself in a
little bare room, because there is not a single school of sculpture in New York
where she is welcome. Surely there are doors she might burst through, but
when God makes a sculptor He does not always make the pushing sort of
person who beats his way through doors thrust in his face. This girl is
working her hands off to get out of this country so that she can get some sort
of training.

∧
STILL HAVE POOR
OPPORTUNITIES
TO EXPLORE
ARTISTRY

There was Richard Brown. If he had been white he would have been alive today instead of dead of neglect. Many helped him when he asked but he was not the kind of boy that always asks. He was simply one who made colors sing.

There is a colored woman in Chicago who is a great musician. She thought she would like to study at Fontainebleau this summer where Walter Damrosch and a score of leaders of Art have an American school of music. But the application blank of this school says: "I am a white American and I apply for admission to the school." *STILL HAVE PREJUDICE*

We can go on the stage; we can be just as funny as white Americans wish us to be; we can play all the sordid parts that America likes to assign to Negroes; but for any thing else there is still small place for us. *MARGINALIZED*

And so I might go on. But let me sum up with this: Suppose the only Negro who survived some centuries hence was the Negro painted by white Americans in the novels and essays they have written. What would people in a hundred years say of black Americans? Now turn it around. Suppose you were to write a story and put in it the kind of people you know and like and imagine. You might get it published and you might not. And the "might not" is still far bigger than the "might." The white publishers catering to white folk would say, "It is not interesting"—to white folk, naturally not. They want Uncle Toms, Topsies, good "darkies" and clowns. I have in my office a story with all the earmarks of truth. A young man says that he started out to write and had his stories accepted. Then he began to write about the things he knew best about, that is, about his own people. He submitted a story to a magazine which said, "We are sorry, but we cannot take it." "I sat down and revised my story, changing the color of the characters and the locale and sent it under an assumed name with a change of address and it was accepted by the same magazine that had refused it, the editor promising to take anything else I might send in providing it was good enough."

We have, to be sure, a few recognized and successful Negro artists; but they are not all those fit to survive or even a good minority. They are but the remnants of that ability and genius among us whom the accidents of education and opportunity have raised on the tidal waves of chance. We black folk are not altogether peculiar in this. After all, in the world at large, it is only the accident, the remnant, that gets the chance to make the most of itself; but if this is true of the white world it is infinitely more true of the colored world. It is not simply the great clear tenor of Roland Hayes that opened the ears of America. We have had many voices of all kinds as fine as his and America was and is as deaf as she was for years to him. Then a foreign land heard

Hayes and put its imprint on him and immediately America with all its imitative snobbery woke up. We approved Hayes because London, Paris and Berlin approved him and not simply because he was a great singer.

Thus it is the bounden duty of black America to begin this great work of the creation of Beauty, of the preservation of Beauty, of the realization of Beauty, and we must use in this work all the methods that men have used before. And what have been the tools of the artist in times gone by? First of all, he has used the Truth—not for the sake of truth, not as a scientist seeking truth, but as one upon whom Truth eternally thrusts itself as the highest handmaid of imagination, as the one great vehicle of universal understanding. Again artists have used Goodness—goodness in all its aspects of justice, honor and right—not for sake of an ethical sanction but as the one true method of gaining sympathy and human interest.

The apostle of Beauty thus becomes the apostle of Truth and Right not by choice but by inner and outer compulsion. Free he is but his freedom is ever bounded by Truth and Justice; and slavery only dogs him when he is denied the right to tell the Truth or recognize an ideal of Justice.

Thus all Art is propaganda and ever must be, despite the wailing of the purists. I stand in utter shamelessness and say that whatever art I have for writing has been used always for propaganda for gaining the right of black folk to love and enjoy. I do not care a damn for any art that is not used for propaganda. But I do care when propaganda is confined to one side while the other is stripped and silent.

In New York we have two plays: "White Cargo" and "Congo." In "White Cargo" there is a fallen woman. She is black. In "Congo" the fallen woman is white. In "White Cargo" the black woman goes down further and further and in "Congo" the white woman begins with degradation but in the end is one of the angels of the Lord. You know the current magazine story: A young white man goes down to Central America and the most beautiful colored woman there falls in love with him. She crawls across the whole isthmus to get to him. The white man says nobly, "No." He goes back to his white sweetheart in New York.

In such cases, it is not the positive propaganda of people who believe white blood divine, infallible and holy to which I object. It is the denial of a similar right of propaganda to those who believe black blood human, lovable and inspired with new ideals for the world. White artists themselves suffer from this narrowing of their field. They cry for freedom in dealing with Negroes because they have so little freedom in dealing with whites. DuBose Heywood writes "Porgy" and writes beautifully of the black Charleston underworld. But why does he do this? Because he cannot do a similar thing for the white people of Charleston, or they would drum him out of town. The only chance he had to tell the truth of pitiful human degradation was to tell it of colored people. I should not be surprised if Octavius Roy Cohen had approached the *Saturday Evening Post* and asked permission to write about a different kind of colored folk than the monstrosities he has created; but if he has, the *Post* has implied, "No. You are getting paid to write about the kind of colored people you are writing about."

In other words, the white public today demands from its artists, literary and pictorial, racial prejudgment which deliberately distorts Truth and Justice, as far as colored races are concerned, and it will pay for no other.

On the other hand, the young and slowly growing black public still wants its prophets almost equally unfree. We are bound by all sorts of customs that have come down as secondhand soul clothes of white patrons. We are ashamed of sex and we lower our eyes when people will talk of it. Our religion holds us in superstition. Our worst side has been so shamelessly emphasized that we are denying we have or ever had a worst side. In all sorts of ways we are hemmed in and our new young artists have got to fight their way to freedom.

The ultimate judge has got to be you and you have got to build yourselves up into that wide judgment, that catholicity of temper which is going to enable the artist to have his widest chance for freedom. We can afford the Truth. White folk today cannot. As it is now we are handing everything over to a white jury. If a colored man wants to publish a book, he has got to get a white publisher and a white newspaper to say it is great; and then you and I say so. We must come to the place where the work of art when it appears is reviewed and acclaimed by our own free and unfettered judgment. And we are going to have a real and valuable and eternal judgment only as we make ourselves free of mind, proud of body and just of soul to all men.

And then do you know what will be said? It is already saying. Just as soon as true Art emerges; just as soon as the black artist appears, someone touches the race on the shoulder and says, "He did that because he was an American, not because he was a Negro; he was born here; he was trained here; he is not a Negro—what is a Negro anyhow? He is just human; it is the kind of thing you ought to expect."

I do not doubt that the ultimate art coming from black folk is going to be just as beautiful, and beautiful largely in the same ways, as the art that comes from white folk, or yellow, or red; but the point today is that until the art of the black folk compels recognition they will not be rated as human. And when through art they compell [sic] recognition then let the world discover if it will that their art is as new as it is old and as old as new.

I had a classmate once who did three beautiful things and died. One of them was a story of a folk who found fire and then went wandering in the gloom of night seeking again the stars they had once known and lost; suddenly out of blackness they looked up and there loomed the heavens; and what was it that they said? They raised a mighty cry: "It is the stars, it is the ancient stars, it is the young and everlasting stars!"

Sterling A. Brown

Our Literary Audience

(1930)

We have heard in recent years a great deal about the Negro artist. We have heard excoriations from the one side, and flattery from the other. In some instances we have heard valuable honest criticism. One vital determinant of the Negro artist's achievement or mediocrity has not been so much discussed. I refer to the Negro artist's audience, within his own group. About this audience a great deal might be said.

I submit for consideration this statement, probably no startling discovery: that those who might be, who should be a fit audience for the Negro artist are, taken by and large, fundamentally out of sympathy with his aims and his genuine development.

I am holding no brief for any writer, or any coterie of writers, or any racial credo. I have as yet, no logs to roll, and no brickbats to heave. I have however a deep concern with the development of a literature worthy of our past, and of our destiny; without which literature certainly, we can never come to much. I have a deep concern with the development of an audience worthy of such a literature.

"Without great audiences we cannot have great poets." Whitman's trenchant commentary needs stressing today, universally. But particularly do we as a racial group need it? There is a great harm that we can do our incipient literature. With a few noteworthy exceptions, we are doing that harm, most effectually. It is hardly because of malice; it has its natural causes; but it is nonetheless destructive.

We are not a reading folk (present company of course forever excepted). There are reasons, of course, but even with those considered, it remains true that we do not read nearly so much as we should. I imagine our magazine

This essay first appeared in *Opportunity*, February 1930.

editors and our authors if they chose, could bear this out. A young friend, on a book-selling project, filling in questionnaires on the reason why people did not buy books, wrote down often, with a touch of malice—"Too much bridge." Her questionnaires are scientific with a vengeance.

When we do condescend to read books about Negroes, we seem to read in order to confute. These are sample ejaculations: *"But we're not all like that." "Why does he show such a level of society? We have better Negroes than that to write about." "What effect will this have on the opinions of white people."* (Alas, for the ofay, forever ensconced in the lumber yard!) . . . *"More dialect. Negroes don't use dialect anymore."* Or if that sin is too patent against the Holy Ghost of Truth—*"Negroes of my class don't use dialect anyway."* (Which *mought* be so, and then again, which *moughtn't.*)

Our criticism is vitiated therefore in many ways. Certain fallacies I have detected within at least the last six years are these:

> We look upon Negro books regardless of the author's intention, as representative of all Negroes, i.e. as sociological documents.
>
> We insist that Negro books must be idealistic, optimistic tracts for race advertisement.
>
> We are afraid of truth telling, of satire.
>
> We criticize from the point of view of bourgeois America, of racial apologists.

In this division there are, of course, overlappings. Moreover all of these fallacies might be attributed to a single cause, such as an apologistic chip on the shoulder attitude, imposed by circumstance; an arising snobbishness; a delayed Victorianism; or a following of the wrong lead. Whatever may be the primary impulse, the fact remains that if these standards of criticism are perpetuated, and our authors are forced to heed them, we thereby dwarf their stature as interpreters.

One of the most chronic complaints concerns this matter of Representativeness. An author, to these sufferers, never intends to show a man who happens to be a Negro, but rather to make a blanket charge against the race. The syllogism follows: Mr. A. shows a Negro who steals; he means by this that all Negroes steal; all Negroes do not steal; Q.E.D. Mr. A. is a liar, and his book is another libel on the race.

For instance, *Emperor Jones* is considered as sociology rather than drama; as a study of the superstition, and bestiality, and charlatanry of the group, rather than as a brilliant study of a hard-boiled pragmatist, far more "American" and "African," and a better man in courage, and resourcefulness than those ranged in opposition to him. To the charge that I have misunderstood the symbolism of Brutus Jones' visions, let me submit that superstition is a human heritage, not peculiar to the Negro, and that the beat of the tom-tom, as heard even in a metropolitan theatre, can be a terrifying experience to many regardless of race, if we are to believe testimonies. But no, O'Neill is "showing us the Negro race," not a shrewd Pullman Porter, who had for a space, a run of luck. By the same token, is Smithers a picture of the white race? If so, O'Neill is definitely propagandizing against the Caucasian. O'Neill must be an East Indian.

All God's Chillun Got Wings is a tract, say critics of this stamp, against intermarriage; a proof of the inferiority of the Negro (why he even uses the word Nigger!!! when he could have said Nubian or Ethiopian!); a libel stating that Negro law students all wish to marry white prostitutes. (The word prostitute by the way, is cast around rather loosely, with a careless respect for the Dictionary, as will be seen later.) This for as humane an observation of the wreck that prejudice can bring to two poor children, who whatever their frailties, certainly deserve no such disaster!

This is not intended for any defense of O'Neill, who stands in no need of any weak defense I might urge. It is to show to what absurdity we may sink in our determination to consider anything said of Negroes as a wholesale indictment or exaltation of all Negroes. We are as bad as Schuyler says many of "our white folks" are; we can't admit that there are individuals in the group, or at least we can't believe that men of genius whether white or colored can see those individuals.

Of course, one knows the reason for much of this. Books galore have been written, still are written with a definite inclusive thesis, purposing generally to discredit us. We have seen so much of the razor toting, gin guzzling, chicken stealing Negro; or the pompous walking dictionary spouting malapropisms; we have heard so much of "learned" tomes, establishing our characteristics, "appropriativeness," short memory for joys and griefs, imitativeness, and general inferiority. We are certainly fed up.

This has been so much our experience that by now it seems we should be able to distinguish between individual and race portraiture, i.e., between literature on the one hand and pseudoscience and propaganda on the other. These last we have with us always. From Dixon's melodramas down to Roark Bradford's funny stories, from Thomas Nelson Page's "Ole Virginny retainers" to Bowyer Campbell's *Black Sadie* the list is long and notorious. One doesn't wish to underestimate this prejudice. It is ubiquitous and dangerous. When it raises its head it is up to us to strike, and strike hard. But when it doesn't exist, there is no need of tilting at windmills.

In some cases the author's design to deal with the entire race is explicit, as in Vachel Lindsay's *The Congo,* subtitled "A Study of the Negro Race"; in other cases, implicit. But an effort at understanding the work should enable us to detect whether his aim is to show one of ours, or all of us (in the latter case, whatever his freedom from bias, doomed to failure). We have had such practice that we should be rather able at this detection.

We have had so much practice that we are thin-skinned. Anybody would be. And it is natural that when pictures of us were almost entirely concerned with making us out to be either brutes or docile housedogs, i.e., infrahuman, we should have replied by making ourselves out superhuman. It is natural that we should insist that the pendulum be swung back to its other extreme. Life and letters follow the law of the pendulum. Yet, for the lover of the truth, neither extreme is desirable. And now, if we are coming of age, the truth should be our major concern.

This is not a disagreement with the apologistic belief in propaganda. Propaganda must be counter checked by propaganda. But let it be found where it should be found, in books explicitly propagandistic, in our newspapers, which perhaps must balance white playing up of crime with our own playing up of achievement; in the teaching of our youth that there is a great deal in our racial heritage of which we may be justly proud. Even so, it must be artistic, based on truth, not on exaggeration.

Propaganda, however legitimate, can speak no louder than the truth. Such a cause as ours needs no dressing up. The honest, unvarnished truth, presented as it is, is plea enough for us, in the unbiased courts of mankind. But such courts do not exist? Then what avails thumping the tub? Will that call them into being? Let the truth speak. There has never been a better persuader.

Since we need truthful delineation, let us not add every artist whose picture of us may not be flattering to our long list of traducers. We stand in no need today of such a defense mechanism. If a white audience today needs assurance that we are not all thievish or cowardly or vicious, it is composed of half wits, and can never be convinced anyway. Certainly we can never expect to justify ourselves by heated denials of charges which perhaps have not even been suggested in the work we are denouncing.

To take a comparison at random. Ellen Glasgow has two recent novels on the Virginia gentry. In one she shows an aging aristocrat, a self-appointed lady killer, egocentric, slightly ridiculous. In another she shows three lovely ladies who stooped to "folly." It would be a rash commentator who would say that Ellen Glasgow, unflinching observer though she is, means these pictures to be understood as ensemble pictures of all white Virginians. But the same kind of logic that some of us use on our books would go farther; it would make these books discussions of *all* white Americans.

Such reasoning would be certainly more ingenious than intelligent.

The best rejoinder to the fuming criticism "But all Negroes aren't like that" should be "Well, what of it. Who said so?" or better, "Why bring that up?" . . . But if alas we must go out of our group for authority, let this be said, "All Frenchwomen aren't like Emma Bovary but *Madame Bovary* is a great book; all Russians aren't like Vronsky, but *Anna Karenina* is a great book; all Norwegians aren't like Oswald but *Ghosts* is a great play." Books about us may not be true of all of us; but that has nothing to do with their worth.

As a corollary to the charge that certain books "aiming at representativeness" have missed their mark, comes the demand that our books must show our "best." Those who criticize thus, want literature to be "idealistic"; to show them what we should be like, or more probably, what we should like to be. There's a great difference. It is sadly significant also, that by "best" Negroes, these idealists mean generally the upper reaches of society; i.e. those with money.

Porgy, because it deals with Catfish Row is a poor book for this audience; *Green Thursday,* dealing with cornfield rustics, is a poor book; the *Walls of Jericho* where it deals with a piano mover, is a poor book. In proportion as a book deals with our "better" class it is a better book.

According to this scale of values, a book about a Negro and a mule would be, because of the mule, a better book than one about a muleless Negro; about a Negro and a horse and buggy a better book than about the mule owner; about a Negro and a Ford, better than about the buggy rider; and a book about a Negro and a Rolls Royce better than one about a Negro and a Ford. All that it seems our writers need to do, to guarantee a perfect book and deathless reputation is to write about a Negro and an aeroplane. Unfortunately, this economic hierarchy does not hold in literature. It would rule out most of the Noble prize winners.

Now Porgy in his goat cart, Kildee at his ploughing, Shine in a Harlem poolroom may not be as valuable members of the body economic and politic as "more financial" brethren. (Of course, the point is debatable.) But that books about them are less interesting, less truthful, and less meritorious as works of art, is an unwarranted assumption.

Some of us look upon this prevailing treatment of the lowly Negro as a

concerted attack upon us. But an even cursory examination of modern literature would reveal that the major authors everywhere have dealt and are
dealing with the lowly. A random ten, coming to mind, are Masefield, Hardy,
Galsworthy in England; Synge and Joyce in Ireland; Hamsun in Norway;
O'Neill, Willa Cather, Sherwood Anderson, Ernest Hemingway in America.
Not to go back to Burns, Crabbe, Wordsworth. The dominance of the lowly
as subject matter is a natural concomitant to the progress of democracy.

This does not mean that our books must deal with the plantation or lowly
Negro. Each artist to his taste. Assuredly let a writer deal with that to which
he can best give convincing embodiment and significant interpretation. To
insist otherwise is to hamper the artist, and to add to the stereotyping which
has unfortunately, been too apparent in books about us. To demand on the
other hand that our books exclude treatment of any character other than the
"successful" Negro is a death warrant to literature.

Linked with this is the distaste for dialect. This was manifested in our
much earlier thrice told denial of the spirituals. James Weldon Johnson aptly
calls this "Second Generation Respectability."

Mr. Johnson is likewise responsible for a very acute criticism of dialect,
from a literary point of view, rather than from that of "respectability." Now
much of what he said was deserved. From Lowell's *Bigelow Papers* through
the local colorists, dialect, for all of its rather eminent practitioners, has been
a bit too consciously "*quaint,*" too *condescending.* Even in Maristan Chap-
man's studies in Tennessee mountainers there is a hint of "outlandishness"
being shown for its novelty, not for its universality.

Negro dialect, however, as recorded by the most talented of our observers
today, such as Julia Peterkin, Howard Odum, and Langston Hughes, has
shown itself capable of much more than the "limited two stops, pathos and
humor." Of course, Akers and Octavus Roy Cohen still clown, and show us
Negroes who never were, on land or sea, and unreconstructed Southrons
show us the pathetic old mammy weeping over vanished antebellum glories.
But when we attack these, we do not attack the medium of expression. The
fault is not with the material. If Daniel Webster Davis can see in the Negro
"peasant" only a comic feeder on hog meat and greens, the fault is in Davis'
vision, not in his subject.

Lines like these transcend humor and pathos:
"I told dem people if you was to come home cold an' stiff in a box, I
could look at you same as a stranger an' not a water wouldn' drean out
my eye."

Or this:
"Death, ain't yuh got no shame?"
Or this:
"Life for me ain't been no crystal stair."
Or:
"She walked down the track, an' she never looked back.
I'm goin' whah John Henry fell dead."

Julia Peterkin, Heyward, the many other honest artists have shown us what is to be seen, if we have eyes and can use them.

There is nothing "degraded" about dialect. Dialectical peculiarities are universal. There is something about Negro dialect, in the idiom, the turn of the phrase, the music of the vowels and consonants that is worth treasuring.

Are we to descend to the level of the lady who wanted Swing Low, Sweet Chariot metamorphosed into "Descend, welcome vehicle, approaching for the purpose of conveying me to my residence?"

Those who are used only to the evasions and reticences of Victorian books, or of Hollywood(!) (i.e. the products of Hollywood, not the city as it actually is) are or pretend to be shocked by the frankness of modern books on the Negro. That the "low" rather than the "lowly" may often be shown; that there is pornography I do not doubt. But that every book showing frankly aspects of life is thereby salacious, I do stoutly deny. More than this, the notions that white authors show only the worst in Negro life and the best in theirs; that Negro authors show the worst to sell out to whites, are silly, and reveal woeful ignorance about modern literature.

Mamba and Hagar are libellous portraits say some; *Scarlet Sister Mary* is a showing up of a "prostitute" say others. "Our womanhood is defamed." Nay, rather, our intelligence is defamed, by urging such nonsense. For these who must have glittering falsifications of life, the movie houses exist in great plenty.

The moving picture, with its enforced happy ending, may account for our distaste for tragedy; with its idylls of the leisure class, may account for our distaste for Negro portraiture in the theatre. Maybe a shrinking optimism causes this. Whatever the reason, we do not want to see Negro plays. Our youngsters, with some Little Theatre Movements the honorable exceptions, want to be English dukes and duchesses, and wear tuxedoes and evening gowns. Our "best" society leaders want to be mannequins.

Especially taboo is tragedy. Into these tragedies, such as *In Abraham's*

Bosom we read all kinds of fantastic lessons. "Intended to show that the Negro never wins out, but always loses." "Intended to impress upon us the futility of effort on our part." Some dramatic "critics" say in substance that the only value of plays like *Porgy,* or *In Abraham's Bosom* is that they give our actors parts. "Worthwhile," "elevating" shows do not get a chance. They are pleading, one has reason to suspect, for musical comedy which may have scenes in cabarets, and wouldn't be confined to Catfish Row. With beautiful girls in gorgeous "costumes," rather than Negroes in more but tattered clothing.

"These plays are depressing," say some. Alas, the most depressing thing is such criticism. Should one insist that *In Abraham's Bosom* is invigorating, inspiring; showing a man's heroic struggle against great odds, showing the finest virtue a man can show in the face of harsh realities,—enduring courage; should one insist upon that, he would belong to a very small minority, condemned as treasonous. We seem to forget that for the Negro to be conceived as a tragic figure is a great advance in American Literature. The aristocratic concept of the lowly as clowns is not so far back. That the tragedy of this "clown" meets sympathetic reception is a step forward in race relations.

I sincerely hope that I have not been crashing in open doors. I realize that there are many readers who do not fit into the audience I have attempted to depict. But these exceptions seem to me to fortify the rule. There are wise leaders who are attempting to combat supersensitive criticism. The remarks I have seen so much danger in are not generally written. But they are prevalent and powerful.

One hopes that they come more from a misunderstanding of what literature should be, than from a more harmful source. But from many indications it seems that one very dangerous state of mind produces them. It may be named—lack of mental bravery. It may be considered as a cowardly denial of our own.

It seems to acute observers that many of us, who have leisure for reading are ashamed of being Negroes. This shame make us harsher to the shortcomings of some perhaps not so fortunate economically. There seems to be among us a more fundamental lack of sympathy with the Negro farthest down, than there is in other groups with the same Negro.

To recapitulate. It is admitted that some books about us are definite propaganda; that in the books about us, the great diversity of our life has not been shown (which should not be surprising when we consider how recent is this movement toward realistic portraiture), that dramas about the Negro character are even yet few and far between. It is insisted that these books should be judged as works of literature; i.e., by their fidelity to the truth of their particular characters, not as representative pictures of all Negroes; that they should not be judged at all by the level of society shown, not at all as good or bad according to the "morality" of the characters; should not be judged as propaganda when there is no evidence, explicit or implicit, that propaganda was intended. Furthermore those who go to literature as an entertaining building up of dream worlds, purely for idle amusement, should not pass judgment at all on books which aim at fidelity to truth.

One doesn't wish to be pontifical about this matter of truth. "What is truth, asked Pontius Pilate, and would not stay for an answer." The answer would have been difficult. But it surely is not presumptuous for a Negro, in Twentieth Century America, to say that showing the world in idealistic rose colors is not fidelity to truth. We have got to look at our times and at ourselves searchingly and honestly; surely there is nothing of the farfetched in that injunction.

But we are reluctant about heeding this injunction. We resent what doesn't flatter us. One young man, Allison Davis, who spoke courageously and capably his honest observation about our life has been the target of second rate attacks ever since. George Schuyler's letter bag seems to fill up whenever he states that even the slightest something may be rotten on Beale Street or Seventh Avenue. Because of their candor, Langston Hughes and Jean Toomer, humane, fine grained artists both of them, have been received in a manner that should shame us. This is natural, perhaps, but unfortunate. Says J. S. Collis in a book about Bernard Shaw, "The Irish cannot bear criticism; for like all races who have been oppressed they are still *without mental bravery.* They are afraid to see themselves exposed to what they imagine to be adverse criticism. . . . But the future of Ireland largely depends upon *how much she is prepared to listen to criticism* and how far she is capable of preserving peace between able men." These last words are worthy of our deepest attention.

We are cowed. We have become typically bourgeois. Natural though such an evolution is, if we are *all* content with evasion of life, with personal complacency, we as a group are doomed. If we pass by on the other side, despising our brothers, we have no right to call ourselves men.

Crime, squalor, ugliness there are in abundance in our Catfish Rows, in our Memphis dives, in our Southwest Washington. But rushing away from them surely isn't the way to change them. And if we refuse to pay them any attention, through unwillingness to be depressed, we shall eventually, be dragged down to their level. We, or our children. And that is true "depression."

But there is more to lowliness than "lowness." If we have eyes to see, and willingness to see, we might be able to find in Mamba, an astute heroism, in Hagar a heartbreaking courage, in Porgy, a nobility, and in E. C. L. Adams' Scrip and Tad, a shrewd, philosophical irony. And all of these qualities we need, just now, to see in our group.

Because perhaps we are not so far from these characters, being identified racially with them, at least, we are revolted by Porgy's crapshooting, by Hagar's drinking, by Scarlet Sister Mary's scarletness. We want to get as far away as the end of the world. We do not see that Porgy's crapshooting is of the same fabric, fundamentally, psychologically, as a society lady's bridge playing. And upon honest investigation it conceivably might be found that it is not moral lapses that offend, so much as the showing of them, and most of all, the fact that the characters belong to a low stratum of society. Economically low, that is. No stratum has monopoly on other "lowness."

If one is concerned only with the matter of morality he could possibly remember that there is no literature which is not proud of books that treat of characters no better "morally" than Crown's Bess and Scarlet Sister Mary. But what mature audience would judge a book by the morality of its protagonist? Is *Rollo* a greater book than *Tom Jones* or even than *Tom Sawyer*?

Negro artists have enough to contend with in getting a hearing, in isolation, in the peculiar problems that beset all artists, in the mastery of form and in the understanding of life. It would be no less disastrous to demand of them that they shall evade truth, that they shall present us a Pollyanna philosophy of life, that, to suit our prejudices, they shall lie. It would mean that as self-respecting artists they could no longer exist.

The question might be asked, why should they exist? Such a question deserves no reply. It merely serves to bring us, alas, to the point at which I started.

Without great audiences we cannot have great literature.

Zora Neale Hurston

Characteristics of Negro Expression

(1934)

Drama

The Negro's universal mimicry is not so much a thing in itself as an evidence of something that permeates his entire self. And that thing is drama.

His very words are action words. His interpretation of the English language is in terms of pictures. One act described in terms of another. Hence the rich metaphor and simile.

The metaphor is of course very primitive. It is easier to illustrate than it is to explain because action came before speech. Let us make a parallel. Language is like money. In primitive communities actual goods, however bulky, are bartered for what one wants. This finally evolves into coin, the coin being not real wealth but a symbol of wealth. Still later even coin is abandoned for legal tender, and still later for checks in certain usages.

Every phase of Negro life is highly dramatized. No matter how joyful or how sad the case there is sufficient poise for drama. Everything is acted out. Unconsciously for the most part of course. There is an impromptu ceremony always ready for every hour of life. No little moment passes unadorned.

Now the people with highly developed languages have words for detached ideas. That is legal tender. "That-which-we-squat-on" has become "chair." "Groan-causer" has evolved into "spear," and so on. Some individuals even conceive of the equivalent of check words, like "ideation" and "pleonastic." Perhaps we might say that *Paradise Lost* and *Sartor Resartus* are written in check words.

The primitive man exchanges descriptive words. His terms are all close-

This essay first appeared in Nancy Cunard, ed. *Negro: An Anthology* (London, 1934; reprint, New York, 1984).

fitting. Frequently the Negro, even with detached words in his vocabulary—not evolved in him but transplanted on his tongue by contact—must add action to it to make it do. So we have "chop-axe," "sitting-chair," "cook-pot" and the like because the speaker has in his mind the picture of the object in use. Action. Everything illustrated. So we can say the white man thinks in a written language and the Negro thinks in hieroglyphics.

A bit of Negro drama familiar to all is the frequent meeting of two opponents who threaten to do atrocious murder one upon the other.

Who has not observed a robust young Negro chap posing upon a street corner, possessed of nothing but his clothing, his strength and his youth? Does he bear himself like a pauper? No, Louis XIV could be no more insolent in his assurance. His eyes say plainly "Female, halt!" His posture exults "Ah, female, I am the eternal male, the giver of life. Behold in my hot flesh all the delights of this world. Salute me, I am strength." All this with a languid posture, there is no mistaking his meaning.

A Negro girl strolls past the corner lounger. Her whole body panging and posing. A slight shoulder movement that calls attention to her bust, that is all of a dare. A hippy undulation below the waist that is a sheaf of promises tied with conscious power. She is acting out "I'm a darned sweet woman and you know it."

These little plays by strolling players are acted out daily in a dozen streets in a thousand cities, and no one ever mistakes the meaning.

Will to Adorn

The will to adorn is the second most notable characteristic in Negro expression. Perhaps his idea of ornament does not attempt to meet conventional standards, but it satisfies the soul of its creator.

In this respect the American Negro has done wonders to the English language. It has often been stated by etymologists that the Negro has introduced no African words to the language. This is true, but it is equally true that he has made over a great part of the tongue to his liking and has had his revision accepted by the ruling class. No one listening to a Southern white man talk could deny this. Not only has he softened and toned down strongly consonanted words like "aren't" to "aint" and the like, he has made new force words out of old feeble elements. Examples of this are "ham-shanked," "battle-hammed," "double-teen," "bodaciously," "muffle-jawed."

But the Negro's greatest contribution to the language is: (1) the use of metaphor and simile; (2) the use of the double descriptive; (3) the use of verbal nouns.

I. Metaphor and Simile
One at a time, like lawyers going to heaven.
You sho is propaganda.
Sobbing hearted.
I'll beat you till: (*a*) rope like okra, (*b*) slack like lime, (*c*) smell like onions.
Fatal for naked.
Kyting along.
That's a lynch.
That's a rope.
Cloakers—deceivers.
Regular as pig-tracks.
Mule blood—black molasses.
Syndicating—gossiping.
Flambeaux—cheap café (lighted by flambeaux).
To put yo'self on de ladder.

2. The Double Descriptive
High-tall.
Little-tee-ninchy (tiny).
Low-down.
Top-superior.
Sham-polish.
Lady-people.
Kill-dead.
Hot-boiling.
Chop-axe.
Sitting-chairs.
De watch wall.
Speedy-hurry.
More great and more better.

3. Verbal Nouns
She features somebody I know.
Funeralize.
Sense me into it.
Puts the shamery on him.

'Taint everybody you kin confidence.
I wouldn't friend with her.
Jooking—playing piano or guitar as it is done in Jook-houses
(houses of ill-fame).
Uglying away.
I wouldn't scorn my name all up on you.
Bookooing (beaucoup) around—showing off.

Nouns from Verbs
Won't stand a broke.
She won't take a listen.
He won't stand straightening.
That is such a complement.
That's a lynch.

The stark, trimmed phrases of the Occident seem too bare for the voluptuous child of the sun, hence the adornment. It arises out of the same impulse as the wearing of jewelry and the making of sculpture—the urge to adorn.

On the walls of the homes of the average Negro one always finds a glut of gaudy calendars, wall pockets and advertising lithographs. The sophisticated white man or Negro would tolerate none of these, even if they bore a likeness to the Mona Lisa. No commercial art for decoration. Nor the calendar nor the advertisement spoils the picture for this lowly man. He sees the beauty in spite of the declaration of the Portland Cement Works or the butcher's announcement. I saw in Mobile a room in which there was an overstuffed mohair living-room suite, an imitation mahogany bed and chifforobe, a console victrola. The walls were gaily papered with Sunday supplements of the *Mobile Register.* There were seven calendars and three wall pockets. One of them was decorated with a lace doily. The mantel-shelf was covered with a scarf of deep homemade lace, looped up with a huge bow of pink crepe paper. Over the door was a huge lithograph showing the Treaty of Versailles being signed with a Waterman fountain pen.

It was grotesque, yes. But it indicated the desire for beauty. And decorating a decoration, as in the case of the doily on the gaudy wall pocket, did not seem out of place to the hostess. The feeling back of such an act is that there can never be enough of beauty, let alone too much. Perhaps she is right. We each have our standards of art, and thus are we all interested parties and so unfit to pass judgment upon the art concepts of others.

Whatever the Negro does of his own volition he embellishes. His religious service is for the greater part excellent prose poetry. Both prayers and sermons are tooled and polished until they are true works of art. The supplication is forgotten in the frenzy of creation. The prayer of the white man is considered humorous in its bleakness. The beauty of the Old Testament does not exceed that of a Negro prayer.

Angularity

After adornment the next most striking manifestation of the Negro is Angularity. Everything that he touches becomes angular. In all African sculpture and doctrine of any sort we find the same thing.

Anyone watching Negro dancers will be struck by the same phenomenon. Every posture is another angle. Pleasing, yes. But an effect achieved by the very means which an European strives to avoid.

The pictures on the walls are hung at deep angles. Furniture is always set at an angle. I have instances of a piece of furniture in the *middle* of a wall being set with one end nearer the wall than the other to avoid the simple straight line.

Asymmetry

Asymmetry is a definite feature of Negro art. I have no samples of true Negro painting unless we count the African shields, but the sculpture and carvings are full of this beauty and lack of symmetry.

It is present in the literature, both prose and verse. I offer an example of this quality in verse from Langston Hughes:

> I ain't gonna mistreat ma good gal any more,
> I'm just gonna kill her next time she makes me sore.
>
> I treats her kind but she don't do me right,
> She fights and quarrels most ever' night.
>
> I can't have no woman's got such low-down ways
> Cause de blue gum woman aint de style now'days.
>
> I brought her from the South and she's goin on back,
> Else I'll use her head for a carpet track.

It is the lack of symmetry which makes Negro dancing so difficult for white dancers to learn. The abrupt and unexpected changes. The frequent change of key and time are evidences of this quality in music. (Note the St. Louis Blues.)

The dancing of the justly famous Bo-Jangles and Snake Hips are excellent examples.

The presence of rhythm and lack of symmetry are paradoxical, but there they are. Both are present to a marked degree. There is always rhythm, but it is the rhythm of segments. Each unit has a rhythm of its own, but when the whole is assembled it is lacking in symmetry. But easily workable to a Negro who is accustomed to the break in going from one part to another, so that he adjusts himself to the new tempo.

Dancing

Negro dancing is dynamic suggestion. No matter how violent it may appear to the beholder, every posture gives the impression that the dancer will do much more. For example, the performer flexes one knee sharply, assumes a ferocious face mask, thrusts the upper part of the body forward with clenched fists, elbows taut as in hard running or grasping a thrusting blade. That is all. But the spectator himself adds the picture of ferocious assault, hears the drums and finds himself keeping time with the music and tensing himself for the struggle. It is compelling insinuation. That is the very reason the spectator is held so rapt. He is participating in the performance himself— carrying out the suggestions of the performer.

The difference in the two arts is: the white dancer attempts to express fully; the Negro is restrained, but succeeds in gripping the beholder by forcing him to finish the action the performer suggests. Since no art ever can express all the variations conceivable, the Negro must be considered the greater artist, his dancing is realistic suggestion, and that is about all a great artist can do.

Negro Folklore

Negro folklore is not a thing of the past. It is still in the making. Its great variety shows the adaptability of the black man: nothing is too old or too new, domestic or foreign, high or low, for his use. God and the Devil are paired, and are treated no more reverently than Rockefeller and Ford. Both of these men are prominent in folklore, Ford being particularly strong, and they talk and act like good-natured stevedores or mill-hands. Ole Massa is some-times a smart man and often a fool. The automobile is ranged alongside of the oxcart. The angels and the apostles walk and talk like section hands. And through it all walks Jack, the greatest culture hero of the South; Jack beats them all—even the Devil, who is often smarter than God.

Culture Heroes

The Devil is next after Jack as a culture hero. He can outsmart everyone but Jack. God is absolutely no match for him. He is good-natured and full of humor. The sort of person one may count on to help out in any difficulty.

Peter the Apostle is the third in importance. One need not look far for the explanation. The Negro is not a Christian really. The primitive gods are not deities of too subtle inner reflection; they are hardworking bodies who serve their devotees just as laboriously as the suppliant serves them. Gods of physical violence, stopping at nothing to serve their followers. Now of all the apostles Peter is the most active. When the other ten fell back trembling in the garden, Peter wielded the blade on the posse. Peter first and foremost in all action. The gods of no peoples have been philosophic until the people themselves have approached that state.

The rabbit, the bear, the lion, the buzzard, the fox are culture heroes from the animal world. The rabbit is far in the lead of all the others and is blood brother to Jack. In short, the trickster-hero of West Africa has been transplanted to America.

John Henry is a culture hero in song, but no more so than Stacker Lee, Smokey Joe or Bad Lazarus. There are many, many Negroes who have never heard of any of the song heroes, but none who do not know John (Jack) and the rabbit.

Examples of Folklore and the Modern Culture Hero

WHY DE PORPOISE'S TAIL IS ON CROSSWISE

Now, I want to tell you 'bout de porpoise. God had done made de world and everything. He set de moon and de stars in de sky. He got de fishes of de sea, and de fowls of de air completed.

He made de sun and hung it up. Then He made a nice gold track for it to run on. Then He said, "Now, Sun, I got everything made but Time. That's up to you. I want you to start out and go round de world on dis track just as fast as you kin make it. And de time it takes you to go and come, I'm going to call day and night." De Sun went zoonin' on cross de elements. Now, de porpoise was hanging round there and heard God what he tole de Sun, so he decided he'd take dat trip round de world hisself. He looked up and saw de Sun kytin' along, so he lit out too, him and dat Sun!

So de porpoise beat de Sun round de world by one hour and three minutes. So God said, "Aw naw, this aint gointer do! I didn't mean for nothin' to be faster than de Sun!" So God run dat porpoise for three days before he run him down and caught him, and took his tail off and put it on crossways to slow him up. Still he's de fastest thing in de water. And dat's why de porpoise got his tail on crossways.

ROCKEFELLER AND FORD

Once John D. Rockefeller and Henry Ford was woofing at each other. Rockefeller told Henry Ford he could build a solid gold road round the world. Henry Ford told him if he would he would look at it and see if he liked it, and if he did he would buy it and put one of his tin lizzies on it.

Originality

It has been said so often that the Negro is lacking in originality that it has almost become a gospel. Outward signs seem to bear this out. But if one looks closely its falsity is immediately evident.

It is obvious that to get back to original sources is much too difficult for any group to claim very much as a certainty. What we really mean by originality is the modification of ideas. The most ardent admirer of the great Shakespeare cannot claim first source even for him. It is his treatment of the borrowed material.

So if we look at it squarely, the Negro is a very original being. While he lives and moves in the midst of a white civilization, everything that he touches is reinterpreted for his own use. He has modified the language, mode of food preparation, practice of medicine, and most certainly the religion of his new country, just as he adapted to suit himself the Sheik haircut made famous by Rudolph Valentino.

Everyone is familiar with the Negro's modification of the whites' musical instruments, so that his interpretation has been adopted by the white man himself and then reinterpreted. In so many words, Paul Whiteman is giving an imitation of a Negro orchestra making use of white-invented musical instruments in a Negro way. Thus has arisen a new art in the civilized world, and thus has our so-called civilization come. The exchange and re-exchange of ideas between groups.

Imitation

The Negro, the world over, is famous as a mimic. But this in no way damages his standing as an original. Mimicry is an art in itself. If it is not, then all art must fall by the same blow that strikes it down. When sculpture, painting, acting, dancing, literature neither reflect nor suggest anything in nature or human experience we turn away with a dull wonder in our hearts at why the thing was done. Moreover, the contention that the Negro imitates from a feeling of inferiority is incorrect. He mimics for the love of it. The group of Negroes who slavishly imitate is small. The average Negro glories in his ways. The highly educated Negro the same. The self-despisement lies in a middle class who scorns to do or be anything Negro. "That's just like a Nigger" is the most terrible rebuke one can lay upon this kind. He wears drab clothing, sits through a boresome church service, pretends to have no interest in the community, holds beauty contests, and otherwise apes all the mediocrities of the white brother. The truly cultured Negro scorns him, and the Negro "farthest down" is too busy "spreading his junk" in his own way to see or care. He likes his own things best. Even the group who are not Negroes but belong to the "sixth race," buy such records as "Shake dat thing" and "Tight lak dat." They really enjoy hearing a good bible-beater preach, but wild horses could drag no such admission from them. Their ready-made expression is: "We done got away from all that now." Some refuse to countenance Negro music on the grounds that it is niggerism, and for that reason should be done away with. Roland Hayes was thoroughly denounced for singing spirituals until he was accepted by white audiences. Langston Hughes is not considered a poet by this group because he writes of the man in the ditch, who is more numerous and real among us than any other.

But, this group aside, let us say that the art of mimicry is better developed in the Negro than in other racial groups. He does it as the mockingbird does it, for the love of it, and not because he wishes to be like the one imitated. I saw a group of small Negro boys imitating a cat defecating and the subsequent toilet of the cat. It was very realistic, and they enjoyed it as much as if they had been imitating a coronation ceremony. The dances are full of imitations of various animals. The buzzard lope, walking the dog, the pig's hind legs, holding the mule, elephant squat, pigeon's wing, falling off the log, seabord (imitation of an engine starting), and the like.

Absence of the Concept of Privacy

It is said that Negroes keep nothing secret, that they have no reserve. This ought not to seem strange when one considers that we are an outdoor people accustomed to communal life. Add this to all-permeating drama and you have the explanation.

There is no privacy in an African village. Loves, fights, possessions are, to misquote Woodrow Wilson, "Open disagreements openly arrived at." The community is given the benefit of a good fight as well as a good wedding. An audience is a ncessary part of any drama. We merely go with nature rather than against it.

Discord is more natural than accord. If we accept the doctrine of the survival of the fittest there are more fighting honors than there are honors for other achievements. Humanity places premiums on all things necessary to its well-being, and a valiant and good fighter is valuable in any community. So why hide the light under a bushel? Moreover, intimidation is a recognized part of warfare the world over, and threats certainly must be listed under that head. So that a great threatener must certainly be considered an aid to the fighting machine. So then if a man or woman is a facile hurler of threats why should he or she not show their wares to the community? Hence the holding of all quarrels and fights in the open. One relieves one's pent-up anger and at the same time earns laurels in intimidation. Besides, one does the community a service. There is nothing so exhilarating as watching well-matched opponents go into action. The entire world likes action, for that matter. Hence prize-fighters become millionaires.

Likewise lovemaking is a biological necessity the world over and an art among Negroes. So that a man or woman who is proficient sees no reason why the fact should not be moot. He swaggers. She struts hippily about. Songs are built on the power to charm beneath the bedclothes. Here again we have individuals striving to excel in what the community considers an art. Then if all of his world is seeking a great lover, why should he not speak right out loud?

It is all in a viewpoint. Lovemaking and fighting in all their branches are high arts, other things are arts among other groups where they brag about their proficiency just as brazenly as we do about these things that others consider matters for conversation behind closed doors. At any rate, the white man is despised by Negroes as a very poor fighter individually, and a very poor lover. One Negro, speaking of white men, said, "White folks is alright when dey gits in de bank and on de law bench, but dey sho' kin lie about wimmen folks."

I pressed him to explain. "Well you see, white mens makes out they marries wimmen to look at they eyes, and they know they gits em for just what us gits em for. 'Nother thing, white mens say they goes clear round de world and wins all de wimmen folks way from they men folks. Dat's a lie too. They don't win nothin, they buys em. Now de way I figgers it, if a woman don't want me enough to be wid me, 'thout I got to pay her, she kin rock right on, but these here white men don't know what to do wid a woman when they gits her—dat's how come they gives they wimmen so much. They got to. Us wimmen works jus as hard as us does an come home an sleep wid us every night. They own wouldn't do it and its de mens fault. Dese white men done fooled theyself bout dese wimmen.

"Now me, I keeps me some wimmens all de time. Dat's whut dey wuz put here for—us mens to use. Dat's right now, Miss. Y'all wuz put here so us mens could have some pleasure. Course I don't run round like heap uh men folks. But if my ole lady go way from me and stay more'n two weeks, I got to git me somebody, aint I?"

The Jook

Jook is the word for a Negro pleasure house. It may mean a bawdy house. It may mean the house set apart on public works where the men and women dance, drink and gamble. Often it is a combination of all these.

In past generations the music was furnished by "boxes," another word for guitars. One guitar was enough for a dance; to have two was considered excellent. Where two were playing one man played the lead and the other seconded him. The first player was "picking" and the second was "framming," that is, playing chords while the lead carried the melody by dexterous finger work. Sometimes a third player was added, and he played a tom-tom effect on the low strings. Believe it or not, this is excellent dance music.

Pianos soon came to take the place of the boxes, and now player-pianos and victrolas are in all of the Jooks.

Musically speaking, the Jook is the most important place in America. For in its smelly, shoddy confines has been born the secular music known as blues, and on blues has been founded jazz. The singing and playing in the true Negro style is called "jooking."

The songs grow by incremental repetition as they travel from mouth to mouth and from Jook to Jook for years before they reach outside ears. Hence the great variety of subject-matter in each song.

The Negro dances circulated over the world were also conceived inside the Jooks. They too make the round of Jooks and public works before going into the outside world.

In this respect it is interesting to mention the Black Bottom. I have read several false accounts of its origin and name. One writer claimed that it got its name from the black sticky mud on the bottom of the Mississippi river. Other equally absurd statements gummed the press. Now the dance really originated in the Jook section of Nashville, Tennessee, around Fourth Avenue. This is a tough neighborhood known as Black Bottom—hence the name.

The Charleston is perhaps forty years old, and was danced up and down the Atlantic seaboard from North Carolina to Key West, Florida.

The Negro social dance is slow and sensuous. The idea in the Jook is to gain sensation, and not so much exercise. So that just enough foot movement is added to keep the dancers on the floor. A tremendous sex stimulation is gained from this. But who is trying to avoid it? The man, the woman, the time and the place have met. Rather, little intimate names are indulged in to heap fire on fire.

These too have spread to all the world.

The Negro theatre, as built up by the Negro, is based on Jook situations, with women, gambling, fighting, drinking. Shows like "Dixie to Broadway" are only Negro in cast, and could just as well have come from pre-Soviet Russia.

Another interesting thing—Negro shows before being tampered with did not specialize in octoroon chorus girls. The girl who could hoist a Jook song from her belly and lam it against the front door of the theatre was the lead, even if she were as black as the hinges of hell. The question was "Can she jook?" She must also have a good belly wobble, and her hips must, to quote a popular work song, "Shake like jelly all over and be so broad, Lawd, Lawd, and be so broad." So that the bleached chorus is the result of a white demand and not the Negro's.

The woman in the Jook may be nappy headed and black, but if she is a good lover she gets there just the same. A favorite Jook song of the past has this to say:

> *Singer:*   It aint good looks dat takes you through dis world.
> *Audience:* What is it, good mama?

Singer: Elgin[1] movements in your hips
              Twenty years guarantee.

And it always brought down the house too.

    Oh de white gal rides in a Cadillac,
    De yaller[2] gal rides de same,
    Black gal rides in a rusty Ford
    But she gits dere just de same.

The sort of woman her men idealize is the type that is put forth in the theatre. The art-creating Negro prefers a not too thin woman who can shake like jelly all over as she dances and sings, and that is the type he put forth on the stage. She has been banished by the white producer and the Negro who takes his cue from the white.

Of course a black woman is never the wife of the upper class Negro in the North. This state of affairs does not obtain in the South, however. I have noted numerous cases where the wife was considerably darker than the husband. People of some substance, too.

This scornful attitude towards black women receives mouth sanction by the mud-sills.

Even on the works and in the Jooks the black man sings disparagingly of black women. They say that she is evil. That she sleeps with her fists doubled up and ready for action. All over they are making a little drama of waking up a yaller wife and a black one.

A man is lying beside his yaller wife and wakes her up. She says to him, "Darling, do you know what I was dreaming when you woke me up?" He says, "No honey, what was you dreaming?" She says, "I dreamt I had done cooked you a big, fine dinner and we was setting down to eat out de same plate and I was setting on yo' lap jus huggin you and kissin you and you was so sweet."

Wake up a black woman, and before you kin git any sense into her she be done up and lammed you over the head four or five times. When you git her quiet she'll say, "Nigger, know whut I was dreamin when you woke me up?"

You say, "No honey, what was you dreamin?" She says, "I dreamt you shook yo' rusty fist under my nose and I split yo' head open wid a axe."

But in spite of disparaging fictitious drama, in real life the black girl is

[1]Elegant(?).
[2]Yaller (yellow), light mulatto.

drawing on his account at the commissary. Down in the Cypress Swamp as he swings his axe he chants:

> Dat ole black gal, she keep on grumblin,
> New pair shoes, new pair shoes,
> I'm goint to buy her shoes and stockings
> Slippers too, slippers too.

Then adds aside: "Blacker de berry, sweeter de juice."

To be sure the black gal is still in power, men are still cutting and shooting their way to her pillow. To the queen of the Jook!

Speaking of the influence of the Jook, I noted that Mae West in "Sex" had much more flavor of the turpentine quarters than she did of the white bawd. I know that the piece she played on the piano is a very old Jook composition. "Honey let yo' drawers hang low" had been played and sung in every Jook in the South for at least thirty-five years. It has always puzzled me why she thought it likely to be played in a Canadian bawdy house.

Speaking of the use of Negro material by white performers, it is astonishing that so many are trying it, and I have never seen one yet entirely realistic. They often have all the elements of the song, dance, or expression, but they are misplaced or distorted by the accent falling on the wrong element. Every one seems to think that the Negro is easily imitated when nothing is further from the truth. Without exception I wonder why the blackface comedians *are* blackface; it is a puzzle—good comedians, but darn poor niggers. Gershwin and the other "Negro" rhapsodists come under this same axe. Just about as Negro as caviar or Ann Pennington's athletic Black Bottom. When the Negroes who knew the Black Bottom in its cradle saw the Broadway version they asked each other, "Is you learnt dat *new* Black Bottom yet?" Proof that it was not *their* dance.

And God only knows what the world has suffered from the white damsels who try to sing Blues.

The Negroes themselves have sinned also in this respect. In spite of the goings up and down on the earth, from the original Fisk Jubilee Singers down to the present, there has been no genuine presentation of Negro songs to white audiences. The spirituals that have been sung around the world are Negroid to be sure, but so full of musicians' tricks that Negro congregations are highly entertained when they hear their old songs so changed. They never use the new style songs, and these are never heard unless perchance some daughter or son has been off to college and returns with one of the old songs with its face lifted, so to speak.

I am of the opinion that this trick style of delivery was originated by the Fisk Singers; Tuskeegee and Hampton followed suit and have helped spread this misconception of Negro spirituals. This Glee Club style has gone on so long and become so fixed among concert singers that it is considered quite authentic. But I say again, that not one concert singer in the world is singing the songs as the Negro song-makers sing them.

If anyone wishes to prove the truth of this let him step into some unfashionable Negro church and hear for himself.

To those who want to institute the Negro theatre, let me say it is already established. It is lacking in wealth, so it is not seen in the high places. A creature with a white head and Negro feet struts the Metropolitan boards. The real Negro theatre is in the Jooks and the cabarets. Self-conscious individuals may turn away the eye and say, "Let us search elsewhere for our dramatic art." Let 'em search. They certainly won't find it. Butter Beans and Susie, Bo-Jangles and Snake Hips are the only performers of the real Negro school it has ever been my pleasure to behold in New York.

Dialect

If we are to believe the majority of writers of Negro dialect and the burnt-cork artists, Negro speech is a weird thing, full of "ams" and "Ises." Fortunately we don't have to believe them. We may go directly to the Negro and let him speak for himself.

I know that I run the risk of being damned as an infidel for declaring that nowhere can be found the Negro who asks "am it?" nor yet his brother who announces "Ise uh gwinter." He exists only for a certain type of writers and performers.

Very few Negroes, educated or not, use a clear clipped "I." It verges more or less upon "Ah." I think the lip form is responsible for this to a great extent. By experiment the reader will find that a sharp "I" is very much easier with a thin taut lip than with a full soft lip. Like tightening violin strings.

If one listens closely one will note too that a word is slurred in one position in the sentence but clearly pronounced in another. This is particularly true of the pronouns. A pronoun as a subject is likely to be clearly enunciated, but slurred as an object. For example: "You better not let me ketch yuh."

There is a tendency in some localities to add the "h" to "it" and pronounce it "hit." Probably a vestige of old English. In some localities "if" is "ef."

In storytelling "so" is universally the connective. It is used even as an introductory word, at the very beginning of a story. In religious expression "and" is used. The trend in stories is to state conclusions; in religion, to enumerate.

I am mentioning only the most general rules in dialect because there are so many quirks that belong only to certain localities that nothing less than a volume would be adequate.

Humanistic/Ethical Criticism
and the Protest Tradition

Richard Wright

Blueprint for Negro Writing

(1937)

The Role of Negro Writing: Two Definitions

Generally speaking, Negro writing in the past has been confined to humble novels, poems, and plays, prim and decorous ambassadors who went a-begging to white America. They entered the Court of American Public Opinion dressed in the knee-pants of servility, curtsying to show that the Negro was not inferior, that he was human, and that he had a life comparable to that of other people. For the most part these artistic ambassadors were received as though they were French poodles who do clever tricks.

White America never offered these Negro writers any serious criticism. The mere fact that a Negro could write was astonishing. Nor was there any deep concern on the part of white America with the role Negro writing should play in American culture; and the role it did play grew out of accident rather than intent or design. Either it crept in through the kitchen in the form of jokes; or it was the fruits of that foul soil which was the result of a liaison between inferiority-complexed Negro "geniuses" and burnt-out white Bohemians with money.

On the other hand, these often technically brilliant performances by Negro writers were looked upon by the majority of literate Negroes as something to be proud of. At best, Negro writing has been something external to the lives of educated Negroes themselves. That the productions of their writers should have been something of a guide in their daily living is a matter which seems never to have been raised seriously.

Under these conditions Negro writing assumed two general aspects: (1) It became a sort of conspicuous ornamentation, the hallmark of "achievement."

This essay first appeared in *New Challenge*, 11 (1937).

(2) It became the voice of the educated Negro pleading with white America for justice.

Rarely was the best of this writing addressed to the Negro himself, his needs, his sufferings, his aspirations. Through misdirection, Negro writers have been far better to others than they have been to themselves. And the mere recognition of this places the whole question of Negro writing in a new light and raises a doubt as to the validity of its present direction.

The Minority Outlook

Somewhere in his writings Lenin makes the observation that oppressed minorities often reflect the techniques of the bourgeoisie more brilliantly than some sections of the bourgeoisie themselves. The psychological importance of this becomes meaningful when it is recalled that oppressed minorities, and especially the petty bourgeois sections of oppressed minorities, strive to assimilate the virtues of the bourgeoisie in the assumption that by doing so they can lift themselves into a higher social sphere. But not only among the oppressed petty bourgeoisie does this occur. The workers of a minority people, chafing under exploitation, forge organizational forms of struggle to better their lot. Lacking the handicaps of false ambition and property, they have access to a wide social vision and a deep social consciousness. They display a greater freedom and initiative in pushing their claims upon civilization than even do the petty bourgeoisie. Their organizations show greater strength, adaptability, and efficiency than any other group or class in society.

That Negro workers, propelled by the harsh conditions of their lives, have demonstrated this consciousness and mobility for economic and political action there can be no doubt. But has this consciousness been reflected in the work of Negro writers to the same degree as it has in the Negro workers' struggle to free Herndon and the Scottsboro Boys, in the drive toward unionism, in the fight against lynching? Have they as creative writers taken advantage of their unique minority position?

The answer decidedly is no. Negro writers have lagged sadly, and as time passes the gap widens between them and their people.

How can this hiatus be bridged? How can the enervating effects of this longstanding split be eliminated?

In presenting questions of this sort an attitude of self-consciousness and self-criticism is far more likely to be a fruitful point of departure than a mere recounting of past achievements. An emphasis upon tendency and experiment, a view of society as something becoming rather than as something fixed and admired is the one which points the way for Negro writers to stand shoulder to shoulder with Negro workers in mood and outlook.

A Whole Culture

There is, however, a culture of the Negro which is his and has been addressed to him; a culture which has, for good or ill, helped to clarify his consciousness and create emotional attitudes which are conducive to action. This culture has stemmed mainly from two sources: (1) the Negro church; and (2) the folklore of the Negro people.

It was through the portals of the church that the American Negro first entered the shrine of western culture. Living under slave conditions of life, bereft of his African heritage, the Negroes' struggle for religion on the plantations between 1820–60 assumed the form of a struggle for human rights. It remained a relatively revolutionary struggle until religion began to serve as an antidote for suffering and denial. But even today there are millions of American Negroes whose only sense of a whole universe, whose only relation to society and man, and whose only guide to personal dignity comes through the archaic morphology of Christian salvation.

It was, however, in a folklore molded out of rigorous and inhuman conditions of life that the Negro achieved his most indigenous and complete expression. Blues, spirituals, and folk tales recounted from mouth to mouth; the whispered words of a black mother to her black daughter on the ways of men, to confidential wisdom of a black father to his black son; the swapping of sex experiences on street corners from boy to boy in the deepest vernacular; work songs sung under blazing suns—all these formed the channels through which the racial wisdom flowed.

One would have thought that Negro writers in the last century of striving at expression would have continued and deepened this folk tradition, would have tried to create a more intimate and yet a more profoundly social system of artistic communication between them and their people. But the illusion that they could escape through individual achievement the harsh lot of their race swung Negro writers away from any such path. Two separate cultures sprang up: one for the Negro masses, unwritten and unrecognized; and the other for the sons and daughters of a rising Negro bourgeoisie, parasitic and mannered.

Today the question is: Shall Negro writing be for the Negro masses, molding the lives and consciousness of those masses toward new goals, or shall it continue begging the question of the Negroes' humanity?

The Problem of Nationalism in Negro Writing

In stressing the difference between the role Negro writing failed to play in the lives of the Negro people, and the role it should play in the future if it is to serve its historic function; in pointing out the fact that Negro writing has been addressed in the main to a small white audience rather than to a Negro one, it should be stated that no attempt is being made here to propagate a specious and blatant nationalism. Yet the nationalist character of the Negro people is unmistakable. Psychologically this nationalism is reflected in the whole of Negro culture, and especially in folklore.

In the absence of fixed and nourishing forms of culture, the Negro has a folklore which embodies the memories and hopes of his struggle for freedom. Not yet caught in paint or stone, and as yet but feebly depicted in the poem and novel, the Negroes' most powerful images of hope and despair still remains in the fluid state of daily speech. How many John Henrys have lived and died on the lips of these black people? How many mythical heroes in embryo have been allowed to perish for lack of husbanding by alert intelligence?

Negro folklore contains, in a measure that puts to shame more deliberate forms of Negro expression, the collective sense of Negro life in America. Let those who shy at the nationalist implications of Negro life look at this body of folklore, living and powerful, which rose out of a unified sense of a common life and a common fate. Here are those vital beginnings of a recognition of value in life as it is *lived*, a recognition that marks the emergence of a new culture in the shell of the old. And at the moment this process starts, at the moment when a people begin to realize a *meaning* in their suffering, the civilization that engenders that suffering is doomed.

The nationalist aspects of Negro life are as sharply manifest in the social institutions of Negro people as in folklore. There is a Negro church, a Negro press, a Negro social world, a Negro sporting world, a Negro business world, a Negro school system, Negro professions; in short, a Negro way of life in America. The Negro people did not ask for this, and deep down, though they express themselves through their institutions and adhere to this special way of life, they do not want it now. This special existence was forced upon them from without by lynch rope, bayonet and mob rule. They accepted these negative conditions with the inevitability of a tree which must live or perish in whatever soil it finds itself.

The few crumbs of American civilization which the Negro has got from the tables of capitalism have been through these segregated channels. Many

Negro institutions are cowardly and incompetent; but they are all that the Negro has. And, in the main, any move, whether for progress or reaction, must come through these institutions for the simple reason that all other channels are closed. Negro writers who seek to mold or influence the consciousness of the Negro people must address their messages to them through the ideologies and attitudes fostered in this warping way of life.

The Basis and Meaning of Nationalism in Negro Writing

The social institutions of the Negro are imprisoned in the Jim Crow political system of the South, and this Jim Crow political system is in turn built upon a plantation-feudal economy. Hence, it can be seen that the emotional expression of group-feeling which puzzles so many whites and leads them to deplore what they call "black chauvinism" is not a morbidly inherent trait of the Negro, but rather the reflex expression of a life whose roots are imbedded deeply in Southern soil.

Negro writers must accept the nationalist implications of their lives, not in order to encourage them, but in order to change and transcend them. They must accept the concept of nationalism because, in order to transcend it, they must *possess* and *understand* it. And a nationalist spirit in Negro writing means a nationalism carrying the highest possible pitch of social consciousness. It means a nationalism that knows its origins, its limitations; that is aware of the dangers of its position; that knows its ultimate aims are unrealizable within the framework of capitalist America; a nationalism whose reason for being lies in the simple fact of self-possession and in the consciousness of the interdependence of people in modern society.

For purposes of creative expression it means that the Negro writer must realize within the area of his own personal experience those impulses which, when prefigured in terms of broad social movements, constitute the stuff of nationalism.

For Negro writers even more so than for Negro politicians, nationalism is a bewildering and vexing question, the full ramifications of which cannot be dealt with here. But among Negro workers and the Negro middle class the spirit of nationalism is rife in a hundred devious forms; and a simple literary realism which seeks to depict the lives of these people devoid of wider social connotations, devoid of the revolutionary significance of these nationalist tendencies, must of necessity do a rank injustice to the Negro people and alienate their possible allies in the struggle for freedom.

Social Consciousness and Responsibility

The Negro writer who seeks to function within his race as a purposeful agent has a serious responsibility. In order to do justice to his subject matter, in order to depict Negro life in all of its manifold and intricate relationships, a deep, informed, and complex consciousness is necessary; a consciousness which draws for its strength upon the fluid lore of a great people, and molds this lore with the concepts that move and direct the forces of history today.

With the gradual decline of the moral authority of the Negro church, and with the increasing irresolution which is paralyzing Negro middle class leadership, a new role is devolving upon the Negro writer. He is being called upon to do no less than create values by which his race is to struggle, live and die.

By his ability to fuse and make articulate the experiences of men, because his writing possesses the potential cunning to steal into the inmost recesses of the human heart, because he can create the myths and symbols that inspire a faith in life, he may expect either to be consigned to oblivion, or to be recognized for the valued agent he is.

This raises the question of the personality of the writer. It means that in the lives of Negro writers must be found those materials and experiences which will create a meaningful picture of the world today. Many young writers have grown to believe that a Marxist analysis of society presents such a picture. It creates a picture which, when placed before the eyes of the writer, should unify his personality, organize his emotions, buttress him with a tense and obdurate will to change the world.

And, in turn, this changed world will dialectically change the writer. Hence, it is through a Marxist conception of reality and society that the maximum degree of freedom in thought and feeling can be gained for the Negro writer. Further, this dramatic Marxist vision, when consciously grasped, endows the writer with a sense of dignity which no other vision can give. Ultimately, it restores to the writer his lost heritage, that is, his role as a creator of the world in which he lives, and as a creator of himself.

Yet, for the Negro writer, Marxism is but the starting point. No theory of life can take the place of life. After Marxism has laid bare the skeleton of society, there remains the task of the writer to plant flesh upon those bones out of his will to live. He may, with disgust and revulsion, say *no* and depict the horrors of capitalism encroaching upon the human being. Or he may, with hope and passion, say *yes* and depict the faint stirrings of a new and emerging life. But in whatever social voice he chooses to speak, whether positive or negative, there should always be heard or *over*-heard his faith, his necessity, his judgement.

His vision need not be simple or rendered in primer-like terms; for the life of the Negro people is not simple. The presentation of their lives should be simple, yes; but all the complexity, the strangeness, the magic wonder of life that plays like a bright sheen over the most sordid existence, should be there. To borrow a phrase from the Russians, it should have a *complex simplicity*. Eliot, Stein, Joyce, Proust, Hemingway, and Anderson; Gorky, Barbusse, Nexo, and Jack London no less than the folklore of the Negro himself should form the heritage of the Negro writer. Every iota of gain in human thought and sensibility should be ready grist for his mill, no matter how farfetched they may seem in their immediate implications.

The Problem of Perspective

What vision must Negro writers have before their eyes in order to feel the impelling necessity for an about-face? What angle of vision can show them all the forces of modern society in process, all the lines of economic development converging toward a distant point of hope? Must they believe in some "ism"?

They may feel that only dupes believe in "isms"; they feel with some measure of justification that another commitment means only another disillusionment. But anyone destitute of a theory about the meaning, structure and direction of modern society is a lost victim in a world he cannot understand or control.

But even if Negro writers found themselves through some "ism," how would that influence their writing? Are they being called upon to "preach"? To be "salesmen"? To "prostitute" their writing? Must they "sully" themselves? Must they write "propaganda"?

No; it is a question of awareness, of consciousness; it is, above all, a question of perspective.

Perspective is that part of a poem, novel, or play which a writer never puts directly upon paper. It is that fixed point in intellectual space where a writer stands to view the struggles, hopes, and sufferings of his people. There are times when he may stand too close and the result is a blurred vision. Or he may stand too far away and the result is a neglect of important things.

Of all the problems faced by writers who as a whole have never allied themselves with world movements, perspective is the most difficult of achievement. At its best, perspective is a preconscious assumption, something which a writer takes for granted, something which he wins through his living.

A Spanish writer recently spoke of living in the heights of one's time. Surely, perspective means just *that*.

It means that a Negro writer must learn to view the life of a Negro living in New York's Harlem or Chicago's South Side with the consciousness that one-sixth of the earth surface belongs to the working class. It means that a Negro writer must create in his readers' minds a relationship between a Negro woman hoeing cotton in the South and the men who loll in swivel chairs in Wall Street and take the fruits of her toil.

Perspective for Negro writers will come when they have looked and brooded so hard and long upon the harsh lot of their race and compared it with the hopes and struggles of minority peoples everywhere that the cold facts have begun to tell them something.

The Problem of Theme

This does not mean that a Negro writer's sole concern must be with rendering the social scene; but if his conception of the life of his people is broad and deep enough, if the sense of the *whole* life he is seeking is vivid and strong in him, then his writing will embrace all those social, political, and economic forms under which the life of his people is manifest.

In speaking of theme one must necessarily be general and abstract; the temperament of each writer molds and colors the world he sees. Negro life may be approached from a thousand angles, with no limit to technical and stylistic freedom.

Negro writers spring from a family, a clan, a class, and a nation; and the social units in which they are bound have a story, a record. Sense of theme will emerge in Negro writing when Negro writers try to fix this story about some pole of meaning, remembering as they do so that in the creative process meaning proceeds *equally* as much from the contemplation of the subject matter as from the hopes and apprehensions that rage in the heart of the writer.

Reduced to its simplest and most general terms, theme for Negro writers will rise from understanding the meaning of their being transplanted from a "savage" to a "civilized" culture in all of its social, political, economic, and emotional implications. It means that Negro writers must have in their consciousness the foreshortened picture of the *whole*, nourishing culture from which they were torn in Africa, and of the long, complex (and for the most part, unconscious) struggle to regain in some form and under alien conditions of life a *whole* culture again.

It is not only this picture they must have, but also a knowledge of the social and emotional milieu that gives it tone and solidity of detail. Theme for Negro writers will emerge when they have begun to feel the meaning of the history of their race as though they in one life time had lived it themselves throughout all the long centuries.

Autonomy of Craft

For the Negro writer to depict this new reality requires a greater discipline and consciousness than was necessary for the so-called Harlem school of expression. Not only is the subject matter dealt with far more meaningful and complex, but the new role of the writer is qualitatively different. The Negro writers' new position demands a sharper definition of the status of his craft, and a sharper emphasis upon its functional autonomy.

Negro writers should seek through the medium of their craft to play as meaningful a role in the affairs of men as do other professionals. But if their writing is demanded to perform the social office of other professions, then the autonomy of craft is lost and writing detrimentally fused with other interests. The limitations of the craft constitute some of its greatest virtues. If the sensory vehicle of imaginative writing is required to carry too great a load of didactic material, the artistic sense is submerged.

The relationship between reality and the artistic image is not always direct and simple. The imaginative conception of a historical period will not be a carbon copy of reality. Image and emotion possess a logic of their own. A vulgarized simplicity constitutes the greatest danger in tracing the reciprocal interplay between the writer and his environment.

Writing has its professional autonomy; it should complement other professions, but it should not supplant them or be swamped by them.

The Necessity for Collective Work

It goes without saying that these things cannot be gained by Negro writers if their present mode of isolated writing and living continues. This isolation exists *among* Negro writers as well as *between* Negro and white writers. The Negro writers' lack of thorough integration with the American scene, their lack of a clear realization among themselves of their possible role, have bred generation after generation of embittered and defeated literati.

Barred for decades from the theater and publishing houses, Negro writers have been *made* to feel a sense of difference. So deep has this white-hot iron of exclusion been burnt into their hearts that thousands have all but lost the desire to become identified with American civilization. The Negro writers' acceptance of this enforced isolation and their attempt to justify it is but a defense-reflex of the whole special way of life which has been rammed down their throats.

This problem, by its very nature, is one which must be approached contemporaneously from *two* points of view. The ideological unity of Negro writers and the alliance of that unity with all the progressive ideas of our day is the primary prerequisite for collective work. On the shoulders of white writers and Negro writers alike rest the responsibility of ending this mistrust and isolation.

By placing cultural health above narrow sectional prejudices, liberal writers of all races can help to break the stony soil of aggrandizement out of which the stunted plants of Negro nationalism grow. And, simultaneously, Negro writers can help to weed out these choking growths of reactionary nationalism and replace them with hardier and sturdier types.

These tasks are imperative in light of the fact that we live in a time when the majority of the most basic assumptions of life can no longer be taken for granted. Tradition is no longer a guide. The world has grown huge and cold. Surely this is the moment to ask questions, to theorize, to speculate, to wonder out of what materials can a human world be built.

Each step along this unknown path should be taken with thought, care, self-consciousness, and deliberation. When Negro writers think they have arrived at something which smacks of truth, humanity, they should want to test it with others, feel it with a degree of passion and strength that will enable them to communicate it to millions who are groping like themselves.

Writers faced with such tasks can have no possible time for malice or jealousy. The conditions for the growth of each writer depend too much upon the good work of other writers. Every first-rate novel, poem, or play lifts the level of consciousness higher.

J. Saunders Redding

American Negro Literature

(1949)

There is this about literature by American Negroes—it has uncommon resilience. Three times within this century it has been done nearly to death: once by indifference, once by opposition, and once by the unbounded enthusiasm of its well-meaning friends.

By 1906, Charles W. Chesnutt, the best writer of prose fiction the race had produced, was silent; Paul Laurence Dunbar, the most popular poet, was dead. After these two, at least in the general opinion, there were no other Negro writers. Booker Washington had published *Up from Slavery*, but Washington was no writer—he was the orator and the organizer of the march to a questionable new Canaan. The poetic prose of DuBois, throbbing in *The Souls of Black Folk*, had not yet found its audience. Polemicists like Monroe Trotter, Kelly, Miller and George Forbes were faint whispers in a lonesome wood. Indifference had stopped the ears of all but the most enlightened who, as often as not, were derisively labeled "nigger lovers."

But this indifference had threatened even before the turn of the century. Dunbar felt it, and the purest stream of his lyricism was made bitter and all but choked by it. Yearning for the recognition of his talent as it expressed itself in the pure English medium, he had to content himself with a kindly, but condescending praise of his dialect pieces. Time and again he voiced the sense of frustration brought on by the neglect of what he undoubtedly considered his best work. Writing dialect, he told James Weldon Johnson, was "the only way he could get them to listen to him." His literary friend and sponsor, William D. Howells, at that time probably the most influential critic in America, passing over Dunbar's verse in pure English with only a glance, urged him to write "of his own race in its own accents of our English."

This essay first appeared in *The American Scholar*, 18 (1949).

During Dunbar's lifetime, his pieces in pure English appeared more or less on sufferance. The very format of the 1901 edition of *Lyrics of the Hearthside,* the book in which most of his nondialect poetry was published, suggests this. No fancy binding on this book, no handsome paper, no charming, illustrative photographs. *Lyrics of the Hearthside* was the least publicized of all his books of poetry, and four lines from his "The Poet" may tell why.

> He sang of love when earth was young,
> And love itself was in his lays,
> But, ah, the world it turned to praise
> A jingle in a broken tongue.

Enough has been said about the false concepts, the stereotypes which were effective—and to some extent are still effective—in white America's thinking about the Negro for the point not to be labored here. History first, and then years of insidious labor to perpetuate what history had wrought, created these stereotypes. According to them, the Negro was a buffoon, a harmless child of nature, a dangerous despoiler (the concepts were contradictory), an irresponsible beast of devilish cunning—soulless, ambitionless and depraved. The Negro, in short, was a higher species of some creature that was not quite man.

What this has done to writing by American Negroes could easily be imagined, even without the documentation, which is abundant. No important critic of writing by American Negroes has failed to note the influence of the concept upon it. Sterling Brown, one of the more searching scholars in the field, gives it scathing comment in "The Negro Author and His Publisher." James Weldon Johnson touches upon it in his preface to the 1931 edition of his anthology, but he does so even more cogently in "The Negro Author's Dilemma." The introduction to Countee Cullen's *Caroling Dusk* is a wry lament over it. In *The New Negro,* Alain Locke expresses the well-founded opinion that the Negro "has been a stock figure perpetuated as an historical fiction partly in innocent sentimentalism, partly in deliberate reactionism."

There can be no question as to the power of the traditional concepts. The Negro writer reacted to them in one of two ways. Either he bowed down to them, writing such stories as would do them no violence; or he went to the opposite extreme and wrote for the purpose of invalidating, or at least denying, the tradition. Dunbar did the former. Excepting only a few, his short stories depict Negro characters as whimsical, simple, folksy, not-too-bright souls, all of whose social problems are little ones, and all of whose emotional cares can be solved by the intellectual or spiritual equivalent of a stick of red peppermint candy. It is of course significant that three of his four novels are not about Negroes at all; and the irony of depicting himself as a white youth in his spiritual autobiography, *The Uncalled*, needs no comment.

Charles Chesnutt's experience is also to the point. When his stories began appearing in the *Atlantic Monthly* in 1887, it was not generally known that their author was a Negro. Stories like "The Gray Wolf's Ha'nt" and "The Goophered Grapevine" were so detached and objective that the author's race could not have been detected from a reading of them. The editor of the *Atlantic Monthly*, Walter H. Page, fearing that public acknowledgment of it would do the author's work harm, was reluctant to admit that Chesnutt was a Negro, and the fact of his race was kept a closely guarded secret for a decade.

It was this same fear that led to the rejection of Chesnutt's first novel, *The House behind the Cedars*, for "a literary work by an American of acknowledged color was a doubtful experiment . . . entirely apart from its intrinsic merit." The reception of Chesnutt's later books—those that came after 1900—was to prove that literary works by an "American of color" were more than doubtful experiments. *The Colonel's Dream* and *The Marrow of Tradition* did not pay the cost of the paper and the printing. They were honest probings at the heart of a devilish problem; they were, quite frankly, propaganda. But the thing that made the audience of the day indifferent to them was their attempt to override the concepts that were the props of the dialect tradition. Had Chesnutt not had a reputation as a writer of short stories (which are, anyway, his best work), it is likely that his novels would not have been published at all.

The poetry of Dunbar and the prose of Chesnutt proved that even with the arbitrary limitations imposed upon them by historical convention, Negro writers could rise to heights of artistic expression. They could even circumvent the convention, albeit self-consciously, and create credible white characters in a credible white milieu.

II

After about 1902, indifference began to crystallize into opposition to the culture-conscious, race-conscious Negro seeking honest answers to honest questions. It was opposition to the Negro's democratic ambitions which were just then beginning to burgeon. It was opposition to the Negro who was weary of his role of clown, scapegoat, doormat. And it was, of course, opposition to the Negro writer who was honest and sincere and anxious beyond the bounds of superimposed racial polity.

There is danger here of oversimplifying a long and complex story. Even with the advantage of hindsight, it is hard to tell what is cause and what effect. But let us have a look at some of the more revealing circumstances. In 1902 came Thomas Dixon's *The Leopard's Spots,* and three years later *The Clansman.* They were both tremendously popular. In 1906 there were race riots in Georgia and Texas, in 1908 in Illinois. . . . By this later year, too, practically all of the Southern states had disfranchised the Negro and made color caste legal. . . . The Negro's talent for monkeyshines had been exploited on the stage, and coon songs (some by James Weldon Johnson and his brother!) had attained wide popularity. Meantime, in 1904, Thomas Nelson Page had published the bible of reactionism, *The Negro, the Southerner's Problem.* And, probably most cogent fact of all, Booker Washington had reached the position of undisputed leader of American Negroes by advocating a racial policy strictly in line with the traditional concept.

There had been a time when the old concept of the Negro had served to ease his burden. He had been laughed at, tolerated, and genially despaired of as hopeless in a modern, dynamic society. White Americans had become used to a myth—had, indeed, convinced themselves that myth was reality. All the instruments of social betterment—schools, churches, lodges— adopted by colored people were the subjects of ribald jokes and derisive laughter. Even the fact that the speeches which Booker Washington was making up and down the country could have been made only by a really intelligent and educated man did not strike them as a contradiction of the concept. And anyway, there was this about Washington: he was at least half-white, and white blood in that proportion excused and accounted for many a thing, including being intelligent, lunching with President Theodore Roosevelt, and getting an honorary degree from Harvard.

Today any objective judgment of Booker Washington's basic notion must be that it was an extension of the old tradition framed in new terms. He preached a message of compromise, of humility, of patience. Under the impact of social change the concept was modified to include the stereotype of the Negro as satisfied peasant, a docile servitor under the stern but kindly eye of the white boss; a creature who had a place, knew it, and would keep it unless he got *bad* notions from somewhere. The merely laughable coon had become also the cheap laborer who could be righteously exploited for his own good and to the greater glory of God. By this addition to the concept, the Negro-white status quo—the condition of inferior-superior caste—could be maintained in the face of profound changes in the general society.

What this meant to the Negro artist and writer was that he must, if he wished an audience, adhere to the old forms and the acceptable patterns. It meant that he must work within the limitations of the concept, or ignore his racial kinship altogether and leave unsounded the profoundest depths of the peculiar experiences which were his by reason of his race. But fewer and fewer Negro writers were content with the limitations. The number of dialect pieces (the term includes the whole tradition) written after 1907 is very small indeed. Among Negro writers the tradition had lost its force and its validity. White writers like Julia Peterkin and Gilmore Millen, and, in a different way, Carl Van Vechten and DuBose Heyward, were to lend it a spurious strength down through the 1920's.

Negro writers of unmistakable talent chose the second course, and some of them won high critical praise for their work in nonracial themes. Their leader was William Stanley Braithwaite. Save only a few essays written at the behest of his friend, W. E. B. DuBois, nothing that came from his pen had anything about it to mark it as Negro. His leading essays in the Boston *Transcript,* his anthologies of magazine verse, and his own poetry, might just as well have been written by someone with no background in the provocative experience of being colored in America.

Though the other Negro poets of this genre (which was not entirely a genre) developed a kind of dilettantist virtuosity, none carried it to Braithwaite's amazing lengths of self-conscious contrivance. They were simpler and more conventional in their apostasy. Alice Dunbar, the widow of Paul, wrote sonnets of uncommon skill and beauty. Georgia Johnson and Anne Spenser were at home in the formal lyric, and James Weldon Johnson in "The White Witch" and "My City" set a very high standard for his fellow contributors to the *Century Magazine.*

But given the whole web of circumstance—empirical, historic, racial, psychological—these poets must have realized that they could not go on in this fashion. With a full tide of race-consciousness bearing in upon them individually and as a group, they could not go on forever denying their racehood. To try to do this at all was symptomatic of neurotic strain. They could not go on, and they did not. The hardiest of them turned to expression of another kind the moment the pressure was off.

The pressure was not off for another decade and a half. As a matter of fact, it mounted steadily. For all of Booker Washington's popularity and ideological appeal among whites, who had set him up as *the* leader of the Negro race, and for all of his power, there was rebellion against him in the forward ranks of Negroes. Rebellion against Washington meant dissatisfaction with the social and economic goals which he had persuaded white Americans were the proper goals for the Negro race. The whites had not counted on this disaffection, and their reaction to it was willful, blind opposition.

What had happened was that Booker Washington, with the help of the historic situation and the old concept, had so thoroughly captured the minds of most of those white people who were kindly disposed to Negroes that not another Negro had a chance to be heard. Negro schools needing help could get it from rich and powerful whites only through Booker Washington. Negro social thought wanting a sounding board could have it only with the sanction of the Principal of Tuskegee. Negro politicians were helpless without his endorsement. Negro seekers after jobs of any consequence in either public or private capacities begged recommendations from Booker Washington.

This despotic power—and there is scarcely another term for it—was stultifying to many intelligent Negroes, especially in the North. White editors, who would have published anything under the signature of Booker Washington, consistently rejected all but the most innocuous work of other Negroes. Publishers were not interested in the ideas of Negroes unless those ideas conformed to Washington's, or in creative work by and about Negroes unless they fell into the old pattern.

So intelligent, articulate Negroes grew insurgent, and the leader of this insurgence was W. E. B. DuBois. Nor was his the only voice raised in protest. Charles Chesnutt spoke out, and so did John Hope and Kelly Miller. In 1900 the *Chicago Defender* had been founded, and in 1901 Monroe Trotter's *Boston Guardian*. Courageous as these polemical organs were, they had not yet grown into full effectiveness. Neither had DuBois, but he was growing fast. By 1903 the Atlanta University Studies of the Negro were coming out regularly under his editorship. In that year he published *The Souls of Black Folk*, which contained the essay "Of Mr. Booker T. Washington and Others," sharply critical of the Tuskegee leader. DuBois was in on the founding of the National Association for the Advancement of Colored People, and in 1910 he became editor of the new monthly, the *Crisis*.

From the very first the *Crisis* was much more than the official organ of the NAACP. It was a platform for the expression of all sorts of ideas that ran counter to the notion of Negro inferiority. Excepting such liberal and nonpopular journals as the *Atlantic Monthly* and *World's Work* and the two or three Negro newspapers that had not been bought or throttled by the "Tuskegee Machine," the *Crisis* was the only voice the Negro had. The opposition to that voice was organized around the person and the philosophy of Booker Washington, and there were times when this opposition all but drowned out the voice.

Nevertheless protestation and revolt were becoming bit by bit more powerful reagents in the social chemistry that produced the New Negro. Year by year more Negroes were transformed—and a lot of them needed transforming. Once James Weldon Johnson himself had written "coon songs" and been content to carol with sweet humility "Lift Every Voice and Sing." When Johnson wrote it in 1900, it had the approval of Booker Washington and became the "Negro National Anthem." Then followed Johnson's period of apostasy and such jejune pieces as "The Glory of the Day Was in Her Face," among others. But in 1912, when he was already forty-one, he wrote the novel *The Autobiography of an Ex-Colored Man,* and in 1917 he cried out bitterly that Negroes must cease speaking "servile words" and must "stand erect and without fear."

III

Other factors than simple protest contributed to the generation of the New Negro. In the first place, the notions regarding the Old Negro were based on pure myth. The changes occurring at the onset of war in Europe sloughed off some of the emotional and intellectual accretions, and the Negro stood partially revealed for what he was—a fellow whose opportunities had been narrowed by historical fallacies, "a creature of moral debate," but a man pretty much as other men. The war, which made him an intersectional migrant, proved that he, too, sought more economic opportunities, the protection of laws evenhandedly administered, the enlargement of democracy. He, too, was a seeker for the realities in the American dream.

But when in 1917 the Negro was called upon to protect that dream with his blood, he revealed himself more fully. He asked questions and demanded answers. Whose democracy? he wanted to know; and why, and wherefore? There followed the promises, which were certainly sincerely meant in the stress of the times. Then came the fighting and dying—and, finally, came a thing called Peace. But in 1919 and after, there were the race riots in the nation's capital, in Chicago, in Chester, Pennsylvania, and in East St. Louis.

By this time the New Negro movement was already stirring massively along many fronts. In the 1920's Negroes cracked through the prejudices that had largely confined them to supernumerary roles on Broadway. *Shuffle Along* was praised as "a sparkling, all-Negro musical of unusual zest and talent." Charles Gilpin's portrayal of the Emperor Jones was the dramatic triumph of 1921. The Garvey Movement, fast getting out of bounds, swept the country like a wildfire. James Weldon Johnson published an anthology of

Negro verse. The monumental historical studies of the Negro were begun by Carter Woodson. *The Gift of Black Folk, Color, Fire In the Flint, Weary Blues, God's Trombones, Walls of Jericho,* and *Home to Harlem* had all been published, read, discussed, praised or damned by 1928.

Fortunately some of the talents that produced these works were genuine. Had this not been so, the New Negro movement in art and literature would surely have come to nothing. The best of Johnson, Hughes, Cullen, McKay, Fisher and DuBois would have lived without the movement, but the movement without them would have gone the way of mah-jongg. Their work considerably furthered the interest of white writers and critics in Negro material and Negro art expression. Whatever else Eugene O'Neill, Paul Rosenfeld and DuBose Heyward did, they gave validity to the new concept of the Negro as material for serious artistic treatment.

Writing by Negroes beginning with this period and continuing into the early thirties had two distinct aspects. The first of these was extremely arty, self-conscious and experimental. Jean Toomer's *Cane* and the "racial-rhythm" and jazz-rhythm poetry of Hughes represent it most notably, while the magazines *Harlem* and *Fire,* which published a quantity of nonsense by writers unheard of since, were its special organs. But the times were themselves arty and experimental. That Negro writers could afford to be touched by these influences was a good sign. It was healthy for them to be blown upon by the winds of literary freedom—even of license—that blew upon e. e. cummings, Dos Passos and Hemingway. If their self-conscious experimentation proved nothing lasting, it at least worked no harm.

One searches in vain for a phrase to characterize the exact impulses behind the second aspect, which is the one best remembered. It was chock-full of many contradictory things. It showed itself naive and sophisticated, hysterical and placid, frivolous and sober, free and enslaved. It is simple enough to attribute this contrariety to the effects of the war; but the atavistic release of certain aberrant tendencies in writing by Negroes in this period cannot be matched in all the rest of contemporary writing. The period produced the poignant beauty of Johnson's *God's Trombones* and the depressing futility of Thurman's *The Blacker the Berry.* Within a span of five years McKay wrote the wholesome *Banjo* and the pointlessly filthy *Banana Bottom.* The Hughes who wrote "I've Known Rivers" and "Mother to Son" could also find creative satisfaction in the bizarre "The Cat and the Saxophone."

The mass mind of white America fastened upon the exotic and the atavistic elements and fashioned them into a fad, the commercialized products of which were manufactured in Harlem. That that Harlem itself was largely synthetic did not seem to matter. It was "nigger heaven." There, the advertised belief was, Dullness was dethroned: Gaiety was king! The rebels from Sauk Center and Winesburg, Main Street and Park Avenue, sought carnival in Harlem. "Life," the burden of the dithyrambics ran, "had surge and sweep there, and blood-pounding savagery."

Commercialism was the bane of the Negro renaissance of the twenties. Jazz music became no longer the uninhibited expression of unlearned music-makers, but a highly sophisticated pattern of musical sounds. The "Charleston" and the "Black Bottom" went down to Broadway and Park Avenue. Losing much of its folk value, the blues became the "torch song" eloquently sung by Ruth Etting and Helen Morgan. Negro material passed into the less sincere hands of white artists, and Negro writers themselves, from a high pitch of creation, fell relatively and pathetically silent.

IV

When Richard Wright's *Uncle Tom's Children* was published in 1938, only the least aware did not realize that a powerful new pen was employing itself in stern and terrible material; when *Native Son* appeared in 1940, even the least aware realized it. The first book is a clinical study of human minds under the stress of violence; the second is a clinical study of the social being under the cumulative effects of organized repression. The two books complement each other. The theme of both is prejudice, conceptual prejudgment—the effects of this upon the human personality. For Wright deals only incidentally—and for dramatic purposes, and because of the authenticity of empiricism—with *Negro* and *white.* "Bigger Thomas was not black all the time," Wright wrote in "How Bigger Was Born." "He was white, too, and there were literally millions of him, *everywhere.* . . . Certain modern experiences were creating types of personalities whose existence ignored racial and national lines. . . ."

Some critics have said that the wide appeal of Wright's work (it has been translated into a dozen languages) is due to the sensationalism in it, but one can have serious doubts that the sensationalism comes off well in translation. What does come off well is the concept of the primary evil of prejudice. This all peoples would understand, and a delineation of its effects, particular though it be, interests them in the same way and for the same reason that love interests them. *Black Boy,* which does not prove the point, does not deny it either. Even here it may be argued that Wright delineates and skewers home the point that "to live habitually as a superior among inferiors . . . is a temptation and a hubris, inevitably deteriorating."

So Wright is a new kind of writer in the ranks of Negroes. He has extricated himself from the dilemma of writing exclusively for a Negro audience and limiting himself to a glorified and race-proud picture of Negro life, and of writing exclusively for a white audience and being trapped in the old stereotypes and fixed opinions that are bulwarks against honest creation. Negro writers traditionally have been impaled upon one or the other horn of this dilemma, sometimes in spite of their efforts to avoid it. Langston Hughes was sincere when he declared, back in the twenties, that Negro writers cared nothing for the pleasure or displeasure of either a white or a colored audience—he was sincere, but mistaken.

A writer writes for an audience. Until recently Negro writers have not believed that the white audience and the colored audience were essentially alike, because, in fact, they have not been essentially alike. They have been kept apart by a wide sociocultural gulf, by differences of concept, by cultivated fears, ignorance, race- and caste-consciousness. Now that gulf is closing, and Negro writers are finding it easier to appeal to the two audiences without being either false to the one or subservient to the other. Thus Margaret Walker, writing for the two audiences now becoming one, can carry away an important poetry prize with her book *For My People*. No longer fearing the ancient interdiction, Chester Himes in *If He Hollers Let Him Go* and *Lonely Crusade* writes of the sexual attraction a white woman feels for a Negro man. In *Knock On Any Door* Willard Motley can concern himself almost entirely with white characters. On the purely romantic and escapist side, Frank Yerby's *The Foxes of Harrow* sells over a million copies, and *The Vixens* and *The Golden Hawk* over a half-million each. Anthologists no longer think it risky to collect, edit and issue the works of Negro writers.

Facing up to the tremendous challenge of appealing to two audiences, Negro writers are extricating themselves from what has sometimes seemed a terrifying dilemma. Working honestly in the material they know best, they are creating for themselves a new freedom. Though what is happening seems very like a miracle, it has been a long, long time preparing. Writing by American Negroes has never before been in such a splendid state of health, nor had so bright and shining a future before it.

Zora Neale Hurston

What White Publishers Won't Print

(1950)

I have been amazed by the Anglo-Saxon's lack of curiosity about the internal lives and emotions of the Negroes, and for that matter, any non-Anglo-Saxon peoples within our borders, above the class of unskilled labor.

This lack of interest is much more important than it seems at first glance. It is even more important at this time than it was in the past. The internal affairs of the nation have bearings on the international stress and strain, and this gap in the national literature now has tremendous weight in world affairs. National coherence and solidarity is implicit in a thorough understanding of the various groups within a nation, and this lack of knowledge about the internal emotions and behavior of the minorities cannot fail to bar out understanding. Man, like all the other animals fears and is repelled by that which he does not understand, and mere difference is apt to connote something malign.

The fact that there is no demand for incisive and full-dress stories around Negroes above the servant class is indicative of something of vast importance to this nation. This blank is NOT filled by the fiction built around upper-class Negroes exploiting the race problem. Rather, it tends to point it up. A college-bred Negro still is not a person like other folks, but an interesting problem, more or less. It calls to mind a story of slavery time. In this story, a master with more intellectual curiosity than usual, set out to see how much he could teach a particularly bright slave of his. When he had gotten him up to higher mathematics and to be a fluent reader of Latin, he called in a neighbor to show off his brilliant slave, and to argue that Negroes had brains just like the slave-owners had, and given the same opportunities, would turn out the same.

This essay first appeared in *Negro Digest*, 8 (April 1950).

The visiting master of slaves looked and listened, tried to trap the literate slave in Algebra and Latin, and failing to do so in both, turned to his neighbor and said:

"Yes, he certainly knows his higher mathematics, and he can read Latin better than many white men I know, but I cannot bring myself to believe that he understands a thing that he is doing. It is all an aping of our culture. All on the outside. You are crazy if you think that it has changed him inside in the least. Turn him loose, and he will revert at once to the jungle. He is still a savage, and no amount of translating Virgil and Ovid is going to change him. In fact, all you have done is to turn a useful savage into a dangerous beast."

That was in slavery time, yes, and we have come a long, long way since then, but the troubling thing is that there are still too many who refuse to believe in the ingestion and digestion of western culture as yet. Hence the lack of literature about the higher emotions and love life of upperclass Negroes and the minorities in general.

Publishers and producers are cool to the idea. Now, do not leap to the conclusion that editors and producers constitute a special class of unbelievers. That is far from true. Publishing houses and theatrical promoters are in business to make money. They will sponsor anything that they believe will sell. They shy away from romantic stories about Negroes and Jews because they feel that they know the public indifference to such works, unless the story or play involves racial tension. It can then be offered as a study in Sociology, with the romantic side subdued. They know the skepticism in general about the complicated emotions in the minorities. The average American just cannot conceive of it, and would be apt to reject the notion, and publishers and producers take the stand that they are not in business to educate, but to make money. Sympathetic as they might be, they cannot afford to be crusaders.

In proof of this, you can note various publishers and producers edging forward a little, and ready to go even further when the trial balloons show that the public is ready for it. This public lack of interest is the nut of the matter.

The question naturally arises as to the why of this indifference, not to say skepticism, to the internal life of educated minorities.

The answer lies in what we may call THE AMERICAN MUSEUM OF UNNATURAL HISTORY. This is an intangible built on folk belief. It is assumed that all non-Anglo-Saxons are uncomplicated stereotypes. Everybody knows all about them. They are lay figures mounted in the museum where all may take them in at a glance. They are made of bent wires without insides at all. So how could anybody write a book about the nonexistent?

The American Indian is a contraption of copper wires in an eternal war-bonnet, with no equipment for laughter, expressionless face and that says "How" when spoken to. His only activity is treachery leading to massacres. Who is so dumb as not to know all about Indians, even if they have never seen one, nor talked with anyone who ever knew one?

The American Negro exhibit is a group of two. Both of these mechanical toys are built so that their feet eternally shuffle, and their eyes pop and roll. Shuffling feet and those popping, rolling eyes denote the Negro, and no characterization is genuine without this monotony. One is seated on a stump picking away on his banjo and singing and laughing. The other is a most amoral character before a sharecropper's shack mumbling about injustice. Doing this makes him out to be a Negro "intellectual." It is as simple as all that.

The whole museum is dedicated to the convenient "typical." In there is the "typical" Oriental, Jew, Yankee, Westerner, Southerner, Latin, and even out-of-favor Nordics like the German. The Englishman "I say old chappie," and the gesticulating Frenchman. The least observant American can know them all at a glance. However, the public willingly accepts the untypical in Nordics, but feels cheated if the untypical is portrayed in others. The author of *Scarlet Sister Mary* complained to me that her neighbors objected to her book on the grounds that she had the characters thinking, "and everybody know that Nigras don't think."

But for the national welfare, it is urgent to realize that the minorities do think, and think about something other than the race problem. That they are very human and internally, according to natural endowment, are just like everybody else. So long as this is not conceived, there must remain that feeling of unsurmountable difference, and difference to the average man means something bad. If people were made right, they would be just like him.

The trouble with the purely problem arguments is that they leave too much unknown. Argue all you will or may about injustice, but as long as the majority cannot conceive of a Negro or a Jew feeling and reacting inside just as they do, the majority will keep right on believing that people who do not look like them cannot possibly feel as they do, and conform to the established pattern. It is well known that there must be a body of waived matter, let us say, things accepted and taken for granted by all in a community before there can be that commonality of feeling. The usual phrase is having things in common. Until this is thoroughly established in respect to Negroes in America, as well as of other minorities, it will remain impossible for the majority to conceive of a Negro experiencing a deep and abiding love and not just the passion of sex. That a great mass of Negroes can be stirred by the pageants of Spring and Fall; the extravaganza of summer, and the majesty of winter. That they can and do experience discovery of the numerous subtle faces as a foundation for a great and selfless love, and the diverse nuances that go to destroy that love as with others. As it is now, this capacity, this evidence of high and complicated emotions, is ruled out. Hence the lack of interest in a romance uncomplicated by the race struggle has so little appeal.

This insistence on defeat in a story where upperclass Negroes are portrayed, perhaps says something from the subconscious of the majority. Involved in western culture, the hero or the heroine, or both, must appear frustrated and go down to defeat, somehow. Our literature reeks with it. Is it the same as saying, "You can translate Virgil, and fumble with the differential calculus, but can you really comprehend it? Can you cope with our subtleties?"

That brings us to the folklore of "reversion to type." This curious doctrine has such wide acceptance that it is tragic. One has only to examine the huge literature on it to be convinced. No matter how high we may *seem* to climb, put us under strain and we revert to type, that is, to the bush. Under a superficial layer of western culture, the jungle drums throb in our veins.

This ridiculous notion makes it possible for that majority who accept it to conceive of even a man like the suave and scholarly Dr. Charles S. Johnson to hide a black cat's bone on his person, and indulge in a midnight voodoo ceremony, complete with leopard skin and drums if threatened with the loss of the presidency of Fisk University, or the love of his wife. "Under the skin . . . better to deal with them in business, etc., but otherwise keep them at a safe distance and under control. I tell you, Carl Van Vechten, think as you like, but they are just not like us."

The extent and extravagance of this notion reaches the ultimate in nonsense in the widespread belief that the Chinese have bizarre genitals, because of that eye-fold that makes their eyes seem to slant. In spite of the fact that no biology has ever mentioned any such difference in reproductive organs makes no matter. Millions of people believe it. "Did you know that a Chinese has. . . ." Consequently, their quiet contemplative manner is interpreted as a sign of slyness and a treacherous inclination.

But the opening wedge for better understanding has been thrust into the crack. Though many Negroes denounced Carl Van Vechten's *Nigger Heaven* because of the title, and without ever reading it, the book, written in the deepest sincerity, revealed Negroes of wealth and culture to the white public.

It created curiosity even when it aroused skepticism. It made folks want to know. Worth Tuttle Hedden's *The Other Room* has definitely widened the opening. Neither of these well-written works take a romance of upperclass Negro life as the central theme, but the atmosphere and the background is there. These works should be followed up by some incisive and intimate stories from the inside.

The realistic story around a Negro insurance official, dentist, general practitioner, undertaker and the like would be most revealing. Thinly disguised fiction around the well known Negro names is not the answer, either. The "exceptional" as well as the Ol' Man Rivers has been exploited all out of context already. Everybody is already resigned to the "exceptional" Negro, and willing to be entertained by the "quaint." To grasp the penetration of western civilization in a minority, it is necessary to know how the average behaves and lives. Books that deal with people like in Sinclair Lewis' *Main Street* is the necessary métier. For various reasons, the average, struggling, nonmorbid Negro is the best-kept secret in America. His revelation to the public is the thing needed to do away with that feeling of difference which inspires fear, and which ever expresses itself in dislike.

It is inevitable that this knowledge will destroy many illusions and romantic traditions which America probably likes to have around. But then, we have no record of anybody sinking into a lingering death on finding out that there was no Santa Claus. The old world will take it in its stride. The realization that Negroes are no better nor no worse, and at times just as boring as everybody else, will hardly kill off the population of the nation.

Outside of racial attitudes, there is still another reason why this literature should exist. Literature and other arts are supposed to hold up the mirror to nature. With only the fractional "exceptional" and the "quaint" portrayed, a true picture of Negro life in America cannot be. A great principle of national art has been violated.

These are the things that publishers and producers, as the accredited representatives of the American people, have not as yet taken into consideration sufficiently. Let there be light!

Margaret Walker

New Poets

(1950)

During the past twenty years of literary history in America, Negroes have enjoyed unusual prominence as poets. At least ten books of poetry by new poets have received serious critical comment in leading literary magazines and columns. If we can believe the additional comments in anthologies of American poetry and books of literary criticism, Negroes writing poetry have gone a long way toward achieving full literary status as American writers; and they have thus attained a measure of integration into contemporary schools of literary thought.

A backward look into American life during these two decades should provide a reason for this literary development and resurgence. It must also accountably tell the background of such poetry, and at the same time provide a basis for predicting the future of poetry written by Negroes in America. Let us, therefore, consider, first, the socioeconomic and political factors which have influenced the poetry of the past twenty years.

During the Twenties we spoke of the New Negro and the Negro Renaissance. At that time such figures as James Weldon Johnson, Langston Hughes, Countee Cullen, Claude McKay, and Jean Toomer emerged as the spokesmen of the New Negro. Rich white patrons or "angels" who could and did underwrite the poetry of Negroes by helping to support Negroes who were interested in writing poetry did so as a fad to amuse themselves and their guests at some of the fabulous parties of the Twenties. They considered the intelligent, sensitive, and creative Negro as the talented tenth, exotic, bizarre, and unusual member of his race; and they indulgently regarded the poetry of the Negro as the prattle of a gifted child. Negro people as a mass showed little appreciation for poetry and offered very little audience for the Negro writ-

This essay first appeared in Phylon, 10 (1950).

ing poetry. Whatever Negro people thought about the poetry written about Negro life did not seem to matter. In the final analysis the audience and the significant critics were white. Negroes as a whole knew too little about their own life to analyze correctly and judge astutely their own literary progress as poets. Isolated from the literary life of whites and confused by the segregated pattern of economic and political life, it was only natural that the point of view of these writers was limited. They lacked social perspective and suffered from a kind of literary myopia. They seemed constantly to beg the question of the Negro's humanity, perhaps as an answer to the white patron's attitude that Negroes are only children anyway. *God's Trombones* by James Weldon Johnson, *The Weary Blues* by Langston Hughes, *Color* and *Copper Sun* by Countee Cullen, and *Harlem Shadows* by Claude McKay were published during the Twenties. Each was received as justification that the Negro race could produce geniuses and that it was nothing short of remarkable that "God should make a poet black and bid him sing." Titles of books as well as eloquent short lyrics such as "O Black and Unknown Bards," and "I, too, sing America . . . I am the darker brother" all reflected an intense desire to justify the Negro as a human being. These books sold well among whites but none of them ranked in a "best-seller" class. People did not buy poetry, certainly not poetry by Negroes. It was a day of individual literary patronage when a rich "angel" adopted a struggling poor artist and made an exotic plaything out of any "really brilliant Negro."

The halcyon days of individual patronage of the arts were ended with the stockmarket crash at the end of the Twenties. The gay hayride of the flaming and gilded Twenties had come to a jolting stop and the depression of the Thirties began to make its first inroads into American life. Hoover persisted so long in predicting that prosperity was just around the corner that it became a standing joke. Men appeared on street corners selling apples, and there was talk of an American dole such as England had already experienced. Early in 1932 before the repeal of prohibition and the ending of the speakeasies that had been an institution of the Twenties, it was a common sight to see streets of large cities littered with sprawling drunkards. The parks were full of unemployed men, shabby and helpless, wearing beaten and hopeless faces. Grant Park in Chicago was a notable example. Evictions were common and Communism was on the march. What chance did the luxury of art have at such a time?

Roosevelt's New Deal not only averted a bloody social revolution in 1932 and 1933 by bracing the tottering economic structure of the country, but it also ushered into existence the boon to art and letters in the form of the

Works Progress Administration. The WPA meant two things of far-reaching significance to Negroes who were writers. It meant, first, (as it meant to whites) money on which to exist and provision for the meager security necessary in order to create art. It meant, second, that Negroes who were creative writers, and poets especially, were no longer entirely isolated from other writers. In cities above the Mason-Dixon line where the Writers Projects drew no color line a new school of black and white writers mushroomed overnight into being.

The cry of these writers was the cry of social protest: protest against the social ills of the day which were unemployment, slums, crime and juvenile delinquency, prejudice, poverty, and disease. The New Deal struggled to alleviate these social ills while the writers led the vanguard of literary protest and agitation for a better world. The decade of the nineteen-thirties therefore became known as the socially-conscious Thirties. Negroes joined the ranks of these socially-conscious writers and Negroes who were writing poetry in particular were poets of social protest. At least three new poets appeared during the Thirties with books of poetry of obvious social significance.

Southern Road by Sterling Brown appeared in 1932. It was chiefly concerned with the plight of Negroes in the South. Ballads in this volume such as the "Slim Greer Series" are some of the finest in the annals of American poetry regardless of the color of the author. One of Mr. Brown's later poems, "Old Lem," which first appeared in magazines and anthologies in the Thirties, is an outstanding example of social protest and clearly reflects the mood of the period.

> I talked to old Lem
> And old Lem said:
>   "They weigh the cotton
>   They store the corn
>   We only good enough
>   To work the rows;
>   They run the commissary
>   They keep the books
>   We gotta be grateful
>   For being cheated;
>   Whippersnapper clerks
>   Call us out of our name
>   We got to say mister
>   To spindling boys

They make our figgers
Turn somersets
We buck in the middle
Say, 'Thankyuh, sah.'
They don't come by ones
They don't come by twos
But they come by tens.

Black Man's Verse and *I Am the American Negro* by Frank Marshall Davis appeared in 1935 and 1937 respectively. These two volumes of poetry, although technically rough and uneven, were scathing books of social protest. An example of such social protest may be seen in the following excerpt from one of Mr. Davis' poems, "Portrait of the Cotton South":

Well, you remakers of America
You apostles of Social Change
Here is pregnant soil
Here are grass roots of a nation.
But the crop they grow is Hate and Poverty.
By themselves they will make no change
Black men lack the guts
Po' whites have not the brains
And the big land owners want Things as They Are.

Black Labor Chant by David Wadsworth Cannon, who died before his volume of verse was published in 1939, celebrated the Negro's joining ranks with the upsurging Labor movement, particularly the cio, and continued in general in the vein of social protest.

Although the outbreak of the Second World War changed the note of social significance, bringing as it did prosperity at home in the United States, and ushering into the world the Atomic Age, the strong note of anxiety it bred was not felt at first in the literature of the period. For at least a decade longer the poetry of American Negroes continued to reflect the mood of the Thirties. A half dozen books of poetry published during the Forties reflect either a note of social protest or a growing concern with the terrible reality of war.

Heart-Shape in the Dust by Robert Hayden appeared in 1940 followed by *For My People* by Margaret Walker in 1942. *Rendezvous With America* by Melvin Tolson was published in 1944; *A Street in Bronzeville* by Gwendolyn Brooks in 1945; and *Powerful Long Ladder* by Owen Dodson appeared in 1946.

The first three poets each reflected in varying degrees the note of social protest in their respective volumes of poetry. The last two poets showed a growing concern with the grim reality of war.

Contrast the tone of the poems of the Twenties with examples of the poetry of the early Forties reflecting as they did the social consciousness of the Thirties. From Robert Hayden's early work, *Heart-Shape in the Dust,* an excerpt from the poem, "Speech," follows:

> Hear me, white brothers,
> Black brothers, hear me:
> I have seen the hand
> Holding the blowtorch
> To the dark, anguish-twisted body;
> I have seen the hand
> Giving the high-sign
> To fire on the white pickets;
> And it was the same hand,
> Brothers, listen to me,
> It was the same hand.

From Margaret Walker's poem, "For My People":

> For my people standing staring trying to fashion a better way from confusion, from hypocrisy and misunderstanding, trying to fashion a world that will hold all the people, all the faces, all the Adams and Eves and their countless generations;
>
> Let a new earth rise. Let another world be born. Let a bloody peace be written in the sky. Let a second generation full of courage issue forth; let a people loving freedom come to growth. Let a beauty full of healing and a strength of final clenching be the pulsing in our spirits and our blood. Let the martial songs be written, let the dirges disappear. Let a race of men now rise and take control.

From Melvin Tolson's poem, "Dark Symphony":

> Out of abysses of Illiteracy
> Through labyrinths of Lies,
> Across wastelands of Disease . . .
> We advance!
> Out of dead-ends of Poverty,
> Through wildernesses of Superstition,

> Across barricades of Jim Crowism
> We advance!
> With the Peoples of the World . . .
> We advance!

In each of these three illustrations of poetry published during the early Forties may be detected the note of social protest, a growing perspective beyond the point of view of race, and a militant attitude not evidenced in the poets of the Twenties.

Gwendolyn Brooks and Owen Dodson published in 1945 and 1946 and their works show a growing concern with the problem of war. They show more than any of the aforementioned poets a growing global perspective which has become a keynote of current poetry. In her volume, *A Street in Bronzeville,* Miss Brooks writes about "Gay Chaps at the Bar":

> We knew how to order . . .
> But nothing ever taught us to be islands
>
> .   .   .   .
>
> No stout
> Lesson showed how to chat with death. We brought
> No brass fortissimo, among our talents,
> To holler down the lions in this air.

In Owen Dodson's poems, "Black Mother Praying," and "Conversation on V," the question of race is presented within the framework of war. The following excerpt is taken from "Conversation on V:"

> V stands for Victory.
> Now what is this here Victory?
> It what we get when we fight for it.
> Ought to be Freedom, God do know that.

Common Peoples Manifesto by Marcus Christian was published in 1948. It has probably not received as widespread critical notice as it deserves, but in several reviews mention has been made of its "considerable merit." It, too, reflects the social note of protest that was typical of the poetry of the Thirties.

The period of greatest intensification of the social note in poetry written by Negroes extends roughly from 1935 to 1945. Summing up the period, generally speaking, we can see that the New Negro came of age during the Thirties. He grew away from the status of the exotic, the accidentally unusual

Negro, the talented tenth of what the white audience chose to consider an otherwise mentally infantile minority group whole masses were illiterate, disfranchised, exploited, and oppressed. Negroes became members of a new school of writers who were no longer isolated because of color, who were integrated around the beliefs that created the New Deal. They were the poets of social protest who began to catch a glimmer of a global perspective, who as spokesmen for their race did not beg the question of their humanity, and who cried out to other peoples over the earth to recognize race prejudice as a weapon that is as dangerous as the atomic bomb in the threat to annihilation of culture and peace in the western world.

Any literary development of the Negro in the Thirties was directly due to his social development. During the Thirties the Negro people made great social strides. The New Deal opened many avenues of opportunity and development to the masses of Negro people. The economic standards of the Negro race rose higher than ever in the history of his life in this Country. As a result of free art for all the people, a cultural renaissance in all the arts swept the United States. This created a new intelligentsia with a genuine appreciation for the creative arts and a recognition for all cultural values. Labor was stimulated by the unionization together of black and white labor and this in turn strengthened the political voice of the people. Consequently the literary audience widened and the Negro people themselves grew in intellectual awareness.

Three books published during the Forties, however, show a marked departure from the note of social protest. These books are *From the Shaken Tower* by Bruce McWright, published in Great Britain in 1944; *The Lion and the Archer* by Robert Hayden and Myron O'Higgins, published as a brochure in 1948; and Gwendolyn Brooks' Pulitzer Prize-winning volume, *Annie Allen,* which was published in 1949. Each one of these books is less preoccupied with the theme of race as such. Race is rather used as a point of departure toward a global point of view than as the central theme of one obsessed by race. This global perspective is an important new note in poetry. The tendency is toward internationalism rather than toward nationalism and racism. Because modern inventions have shortened the time involved in transportation and communications to such an amazing degree our world has shrunk to a small community of nations and mankind is forced to recognize the kinship of all peoples. Thus we have a basis for new conceptions that of necessity lead us in new directions.

These new poets of the late Forties also remind us that there are other factors in the writing of poetry that are equally as important as perspective.

They focus our attention on craftsmanship with their return to an emphasis on form. The new poetry has universal appeal coupled with another definite mark of neoclassicism, the return to form. They show an emphasis placed on technique rather than subject matter, and a moving toward intellectual themes of psychological and philosophical implications which border on obscurantism. These poems are never primitive, simple, and commonplace.

What technical advances have these poets of our new classical age shown over the poets of the Twenties and the Thirties?

Looking back to the Twenties one quickly recognizes that the poets of the Negro Renaissance varied technically from the strictly classical and conventional poetry to the utterly unconventional. Countee Cullen was an outstanding example of the true classicist who had been schooled thoroughly in versification and all the types and forms of poetry. His classical education was clearly reflected in his poetry. On the other hand, Langston Hughes introduced the pattern of the "blues" into poetry. He made no pretense of being the poets' poet, of writing intellectual poetry, or conforming to any particular school of aesthetics. The pattern of the "blues" was, nevertheless, the first new Negro idiom introduced into American poetry since the time of Paul Laurence Dunbar and his Negro dialect that was typical of the antebellum plantation life. The poetry of Negroes that was published during the Thirties was primarily free verse. Technically there were no innovations.

Currently, the new poets, however, are so concerned with form that they are often interested in form to the exclusion of everything else and thus are in danger of sacrificing sense for sound, or meaning for music. As a result of this tendency much of recent poetry by white writers in America has been labelled obscurantist. Can this charge be safely levelled at recent poetry by Negroes?

Such a charge has already been levelled at *Annie Allen* when the book was mentioned in a recent issue of *Phylon*. It was then stated that the poem, "the birth in a narrow room," has too many elliptical or truncated lines. This seems a minor technical matter of not too great importance since it does not actually destroy the meaning of the poem. The lines under question follow:

> Weeps out of western country something new.
> Blurred and stupendous. Wanted and unplanned.
> Winks. Twines, and weakly winks
> Upon the milk-glass fruit bowl, iron pot,
> The bashful china child tipping forever
> Yellow apron and spilling pretty cherries.

Does this make sense? Obviously when one reads the entire poem in terms of the title, the poem does make sense, and that should be all that really matters.

The fact that Miss Brooks displays an excellent knowledge of form, whether in the versatile handling of types of forms of poetry included in *Annie Allen* or in the metrical variations in the volume, can be readily seen as proof of this new emphasis upon conventional form. She skillfully handles a number of stanzaic forms including couplets, quatrains, the Italian Terza Rima, and even in the Anniad, the difficult rime-royal or the seven line stanza named for Chaucer. Here is a perfect example:

> Think of thaumaturgic lass
> Looking in her looking-glass
> At the unembroidered brown;
> Printing bastard roses there;
> Then emotionally aware
> Of the black and boisterous hair
> Taming all that anger down.

In addition to these conventional forms she includes several poems written in free verse as well as occasional lines of blank verse. In regard to types she includes short lyrics, ballads, and sonnets written with veteran aplomb. As a whole, *Annie Allen* is a fine delineation of the character of a young Negro woman from childhood through adolescence to complete maturity, but with slight racial exceptions it could apply to any female of a certain class and society. The entire volume is tinged with an highly sophisticated humor and is not only technically sure but also vindicates the promise of *A Street in Bronzeville*. Coming after the long hue and cry of white writers that Negroes as poets lack form and intellectual acumen, Miss Brooks' careful craftsmanship and sensitive understanding reflected in *Annie Allen* are not only personal triumphs but a racial vindication.

There may be more reason to level the charge of obscurantism at the poetry of Myron O'Higgins in *The Lion and the Archer*, written in collaboration with Robert Hayden. Although the vocabulary is no more intellectual than that of Miss Brooks, and there are several magnificent poems in this brochure—new in note, and vital—there seems more obscurity and ambiguity in the use of poetic symbols and imagery, as for example:

> But that day in between
> comes back with two lean cats

who run in checkered terror
through a poolroom door
and bolting from a scream
a keen knife marks with sudden red
the gaming green
. . . a purple billiard ball
explodes the color scheme.

Robert Hayden shows a decided growth and advance in this volume over his first, *Heart-Shape in the Dust,* which was uneven and lacked the grasp of a true Negro idiom which he seemed to be seeking at that time. His sense of choric movement and his understanding and perspective of peoples have increased to a telling degree and he writes now with due maturity and power:

Now as skin-and-bones Europe hurts all over from the swastika's
hexentanz: oh think of Anton, Anton brittle, Anton crystalline;
think what the winter moon, the leper beauty of a Gothic tale, must see:
the ice-azure likeness of a young man reading, carved most craftily.

In Bruce McWright there is authentic reporting of World War II but even the title of his book, *From the Shaken Tower,* reflects the questions of our present-day age. War has further denounced the ivory towers because war is the grim reality that ends the romantic dreams and airy castle building. The poets of the Thirties said that ivory towers were not fit habitations for poets anyway; they should be social prophets, preachers, teachers, and leaders. Now, with the threat of annihilation hanging over the civilized world of western culture, whether by atomic or hydrogen bomb, with the tremendous wave of social revolution sweeping through the world, men have felt themselves spiritually bankrupt. There is therefore a wave of religious revival, especially in America, whether through fear and hysteria, or from a genuine desire for inner self-analysis, reflection and introspective knowledge that may lead, thereby, to a spiritual panacea which we seek for the ills of the world. Whether to Catholicism, Existentialism, or Communism, modern man is turning to some definite belief around which to integrate his life and give it true wholeness and meaning. Consequently there has already been noted among white writers a decided religious revival. Whereas Marxism was the intellectual fad of the Thirties, religion has become the intellectual fad at present in America where the political and economic structures have definitely reverted to an extremely conservative position. The religious pathway of T. S. Eliot, prophet of the spiritual wasteland, technical pioneer, and most influential name among poets during the Thirties, has been followed by W. H. Auden. Robert Lowell, a Pulitzer Prize poet of a few years ago, is a Catholic convert. Thus far no Negro recently writing poetry has reflected this religious revival, but we may well expect this tendency.

Negroes not only have grown up as poets technically with volumes of poetry showing a growing concern with craftsmanship, social perspective, and intellectual maturity, but they have also begun to reap the rewards in the form of laurels due them for their labors. They have received a greater measure of consideration from literary critics and judges of literary competitions than ever before in the history of writing by Negroes in America. Not only have Negroes succeeded in winning many philanthropic grants such as Rosenwalds and Guggenheims which have provided the wherewithal to pursue creative projects and develop burgeoning talents, but also many other honors and awards have been granted to poets of the Negro race. These have included grants from the Academy of Arts and Letters and the Yale Award for a promising younger poet. Now in 1950 has come the signal achievement with the awarding of the Pulitzer Prize for Poetry to Gwendolyn Brooks for her volume, *Annie Allen*. This is the first time in the history of this Prize that a Negro has won this national honor. With this announcement comes not only the recognition of the fact that poetry by Negroes has come of age but also that the Negro has finally achieved full status in the literary world as an American poet.

What, then, is the future of the Negro writing poetry in America? It would seem from these remarks that the outlook is bright and hopeful. It is a fact that some of the most significant poetry written in America during the past two decades has been written by Negroes. Now, what is the promise? Is there hope that it will be fulfilled? Is the Negro as a poet doomed to annihilation because he is part of a doomed Western world, or is that Western culture really doomed? Is our society already a fascist society? If it is, what hope has our literature? If these are only bogeymen, then whither are we turning? Is our path toward religious revival, neoclassicism, internationalism as a result of global perspectives and world government, or what?

From such young poets as M. Carl Holman must come the answer. Deeply concerned with the psychological, yet aware of our physical world, he shares a growing understanding of our spiritual problems with some of the most mature craftsmen practicing the art of poetry. He bears watching as a poet who is technically aware and intellectually worthy of his salt.

If we are truly in a transitional stage of social evolution, a state of flux, of cataclysmic socioeconomic and political upheaval that will ultimately and inevitably shape our literary life, this will soon be clear. Now, the shape of our emerging society is dimly shadowed by many imponderables. The future of the Negro writing poetry in America is bright only if the future of the world is bright, and if he with the rest of his world can survive the deadly conflicts that threaten him and his total freedom, the awful anticipation of which now hangs over his head like the sword of Damocles.

Ralph Ellison

Twentieth-Century Fiction

and the Black Mask of Humanity

(1953)

W hen this essay was published in 1953, it was prefaced with the following note:
"*When I started rewriting this essay it occurred to me that its value might be somewhat increased if it remained very much as I wrote it during 1946. For in that form it is what a young member of a minority felt about much of our writing. Thus I've left in much of the bias and short-sightedness, for it says perhaps as much about me as a member of a minority as it does about literature. I hope you still find the essay useful, and I'd like to see an editorial note stating that this is an unpublished piece written not long after the Second World War.*"

Perhaps the most insidious and least understood form of segregation is that of the word. And by this I mean the word in all its complex formulations, from the proverb to the novel and stage play, the word with all its subtle power to suggest and foreshadow overt action while magically disguising the moral consequences of that action and providing it with symbolic and psychological justification. For if the word has the potency to revive and make us free, it has also the power to blind, imprison and destroy.

The essence of the word is its ambivalence, and in fiction it is never so effective and revealing as when both potentials are operating simultaneously, as when it mirrors both good and bad, as when it blows both hot and cold in the same breath. Thus it is unfortunate for the Negro that the most powerful formulations of modern American fictional words have been so slanted against him that when he approaches for a glimpse of himself he discovers an image drained of humanity.

This essay first appeared in *Confluence*, December 1953.

Obviously the experiences of Negroes—slavery, the grueling and continuing fight for full citizenship since Emancipation, the stigma of color, the enforced alienation which constantly knifes into our natural identification with our country—have not been that of white Americans. And though as passionate believers in democracy Negroes identify themselves with the broader American ideals, their sense of reality springs, in part, from an American experience which most white men not only have not had, but one with which they are reluctant to identify themselves even when presented in forms of the imagination. Thus when the white American, holding up most twentieth-century fiction, says, "This is American reality," the Negro tends to answer (not at all concerned that Americans tend generally to fight against any but the most flattering imaginative depictions of their lives), "Perhaps, but you've left out this, and this, and this. And most of all, what you'd have the world accept as *me* isn't even human."

Nor does he refer only to second-rate works but to those of our most representative authors. Either like Hemingway and Steinbeck (in whose joint works I recall not more than five American Negroes) they tend to ignore them, or like the early Faulkner, who distorted Negro humanity to fit his personal versions of Southern myth, they seldom conceive Negro characters possessing the full, complex ambiguity of the human. Too often what is presented as the American Negro (a most complex example of Western man) emerges an oversimplified clown, a beast or an angel. Seldom is he drawn as that sensitively focused process of opposites, of good and evil, of instinct and intellect, of passion and spirituality, which great literary art has projected as the image of man. Naturally, the attitude of Negroes toward this writing is one of great reservation. Which, indeed, bears out Richard Wright's remark that there is in progress between black and white Americans a struggle over the nature of reality.

Historically this is but a part of that larger conflict between older, dominant groups of white Americans, especially the Anglo-Saxons, on the one hand, and the newer white and nonwhite groups on the other, over the major group's attempt to impose its ideals upon the rest, insisting that its exclusive image be accepted as *the* image of the American. This conflict should not, however, be misunderstood. For despite the impact of the American idea upon the world, the "American" himself has not (fortunately for the United States, its minorities, and perhaps for the world) been finally defined. So that far from being socially undesirable this struggle between Americans as to what the American is to be is part of that democratic process through which the nation works to achieve itself. Out of this conflict the ideal American character—a type truly great enough to possess the greatness of the land, a delicately poised unity of divergencies—is slowly being born.

But we are concerned here with fiction, not history. How is it then that our naturalistic prose—one of the most vital bodies of twentieth-century fiction, perhaps the brightest instrument for recording sociological fact, physical action, the nuance of speech, yet achieved—becomes suddenly dull when confronting the Negro?

Obviously there is more in this than the mere verbal counterpart of lynching or segregation. Indeed, it represents a projection of processes lying at the very root of American culture and certainly at the central core of its twentieth-century literary forms, a matter having less to do with the mere "reflection" of white racial theories than with processes molding the attitudes, the habits of mind, the cultural atmosphere and the artistic and intellectual traditions that condition men dedicated to democracy to practice, accept and, most crucial of all, often blind themselves to the essentially undemocratic treatment of their fellow citizens.

It should be noted here that the moment criticism approaches Negro-white relationships it is plunged into problems of psychology and symbolic ritual. Psychology, because the distance between Americans, Negroes and whites, is not so much spatial as psychological; while they might dress and often look alike, seldom on deeper levels do they think alike. Ritual, because the Negroes of fiction are so consistently false to human life that we must question just what they truly represent, both in the literary work and in the inner world of the white American.*

Despite their billings as images of reality, these Negroes of fiction are counterfeits. They are projected aspects of an internal symbolic process

---

*Perhaps the ideal approach to the work of literature would be one allowing for insight into the deepest psychological motives of the writer at the same time that it examined all external sociological factors operating within a given milieu. For while objectively a social reality, the work of art is, in its genesis, a projection of a deeply personal process, and any approach that ignores the personal at the expense of the social is necessarily incomplete. Thus when we approach contemporary writing from the perspective of segregation, as is commonly done by sociology-minded thinkers, we automatically limit ourselves to one external aspect of a complex whole, which leaves us little to say concerning its personal, internal elements. On the other hand, American writing has been one of the most important twentieth-century literatures, and though negative as a social force it is technically brilliant and emotionally powerful. Hence were we to examine it for its embodiment of these positive values, there would be other more admiring things to be said.

through which, like a primitive tribesman dancing himself into the group frenzy necessary for battle, the white American prepares himself emotionally to perform a social role. These fictive Negroes are not, as sometimes interpreted, simple racial clichés introduced into society by a ruling class to control political and economic realities. For although they are manipulated to that end, such an externally one-sided interpretation relieves the individual of personal responsibility for the health of democracy. Not only does it forget that a democracy is a collectivity of *individuals,* but it never suspects that the tenacity of the stereotype springs exactly from the fact that its function is no less personal than political. Color prejudice springs not from the stereotype alone, but from an internal psychological state; not from misinformation alone, but from an inner need to believe. It thrives not only on the obscene witch-doctoring of men like Jimmy Byrnes and Malan, but upon an inner craving for symbolic magic. The prejudiced individual creates his own stereotypes, very often unconsciously, by reading into situations involving Negroes those stock meanings which justify his emotional and economic needs.

Hence whatever else the Negro stereotype might be as a social instrumentality, it is also a key figure in a magic rite by which the white American seeks to resolve the dilemma arising between his democratic beliefs and certain antidemocratic practices, between his acceptance of the sacred democratic belief that all men are created equal and his treatment of every tenth man as though he were not.

Thus on the moral level I propose that we view the whole of American life as a drama acted out upon the body of a Negro giant, who, lying trussed up like Gulliver, forms the stage and the scene upon which and within which the action unfolds. If we examine the beginning of the Colonies, the application of this view is not, in its economic connotations at least, too farfetched or too difficult to see. For then the Negro's body was exploited as amorally as the soil and climate. It was later, when white men drew up a plan for a democratic way of life, that the Negro began slowly to exert an influence upon America's moral consciousness. Gradually he was recognized as the human factor placed outside the democratic master plan, a human "natural" resource who, so that white men could become more human, was elected to undergo a process of institutionalized dehumanization.

Until the Korean War this moral role had become obscured within the staggering growth of contemporary science and industry, but during the nineteenth century it flared nakedly in the American consciousness, only to be repressed after the Reconstruction. During periods of national crises, when the United States rounds a sudden curve on the pitch-black road of history, this moral awareness surges in the white American's conscience like a raging river revealed at his feet by a lightning flash. Only then is the veil of anti-Negro myths, symbols, stereotypes and taboos drawn somewhat aside. And when we look closely at our literature it is to be seen operating even when the Negro seems most patently the little man who isn't there.

I see no value either in presenting a catalogue of Negro characters appearing in twentieth-century fiction or in charting the racial attitudes of white writers. We are interested not in quantities but in qualities. And since it is impossible here to discuss the entire body of this writing, the next best thing is to select a framework in which the relationships with which we are concerned may be clearly seen. For brevity let us take three representative writers: Mark Twain, Hemingway and Faulkner. Twain for historical perspective and as an example of how a great nineteenth-century writer handled the Negro; Hemingway as the prime example of the artist who ignored the dramatic and symbolic possibilities presented by this theme; and Faulkner as an example of a writer who has confronted Negroes with such mixed motives that he has presented them in terms of both the "good nigger" and the "bad nigger" stereotypes, and who yet has explored perhaps more successfully than anyone else, either white or black, certain forms of Negro humanity.

For perspective let us begin with Mark Twain's great classic, *Huckleberry Finn*. Recall that Huckleberry has run away from his father, Miss Watson and the Widow Douglas (indeed the whole community, in relation to which he is a young outcast) and has with him as companion on the raft upon which they are sailing down the Mississippi the Widow Watson's runaway Negro slave, Jim. Recall, too, that Jim, during the critical moment of the novel, is stolen by two scoundrels and sold to another master, presenting Huck with the problem of freeing Jim once more. Two ways are open: he can rely upon his own ingenuity and "steal" Jim into freedom or he might write the Widow Watson and request reward money to have Jim returned to her. But here is a danger in this course, remember, since the angry widow might sell the slave down the river into a harsher slavery. It is this course which Huck starts to take, but as he composes the letter he wavers.

"It was a close place." [he tells us] "I took it [the letter] up, and held it in my hand. I was trembling, because I'd got to decide forever, 'twixt two things, and I knowed it. I studied a minute, sort of holding my breath, and then says to myself:

"'Alright, then, I'll *go* to hell"—and tore it up, . . . It was awful thoughts and awful words, but they was said . . . And I let them stay said, and never thought no more about reforming. I shoved the whole thing out of my head and said I would take up wickedness again, which was in my line, being brung up to it, and the other warn't. And for a starter I would . . . steal Jim out of slavery again. . . ."

And a little later, in defending his decision to Tom Sawyer, Huck comments, "I know you'll say it's dirty, low-down business but *I'm* low-down. And I'm going to steal him . . ."

We have arrived at a key point of the novel and, by an ironic reversal, of American fiction, a pivotal moment announcing a change of direction in the plot, a reversal as well as a recognition scene (like that in which Oedipus discovers his true identity) wherein a new definition of necessity is being formulated. Huck Finn has struggled with the problem poised by the clash between property rights and human rights, between what the community considered to be the proper attitude toward an escaped slave and his knowledge of Jim's humanity, gained through their adventures as fugitives together. He has made his decision on the side of humanity. In this passage Twain has stated the basic moral issue centering around Negroes and the white American's democratic ethics. It dramatizes as well the highest point of tension generated by the clash between the direct, human relationships of the frontier and the abstract, inhuman, market-dominated relationships fostered by the rising middle class—which in Twain's day was already compromising dangerously with the most inhuman aspects of the defeated slave system. And just as politically these forces reached their sharpest tension in the outbreak of the Civil War, in *Huckleberry Finn* (both the boy and the novel) their human implications come to sharpest focus around the figure of the Negro.

Huckleberry Finn knew, as did Mark Twain, that Jim was not only a slave but a human being, a man who in some ways was to be envied, and who expressed his essential humanity in his desire for freedom, his will to possess his own labor, in his loyalty and capacity for friendship and in his love for his wife and child. Yet Twain, though guilty of the sentimentality common to humorists, does not idealize the slave. Jim is drawn in all his ignorance and superstition, with his good traits and his bad. He, like all men, is ambiguous, limited in circumstance but not in possibility. And it will be noted that when Huck makes his decision he identifies himself with Jim and accepts the judgment of his super-ego—that internalized representative of the community—that his action is evil. Like Prometheus, who for mankind stole fire from the gods, he embraces the evil implicit in his act in order to affirm his belief in humanity. Jim, therefore, is not simply a slave, he is a symbol of humanity, and in freeing Jim, Huck makes a bid to free himself of the conventionalized evil taken for civilization by the town.

This conception of the Negro as a symbol of Man—the reversal of what he represents in most contemporary thought—was organic to nineteenth-century literature. It occurs not only in Twain but in Emerson, Thoreau, Whitman and Melville (whose symbol of evil, incidentally, was white), all of whom were men publicly involved in various forms of deeply personal rebellion. And while the Negro and the color black were associated with the concept of evil and ugliness far back in the Christian era, the Negro's emergence as a symbol of value came, I believe, with Rationalism and the rise of the romantic individual of the eighteenth century. This, perhaps, because the romantic was in revolt against the old moral authority, and if he suffered a sense of guilt, his passion for personal freedom was such that he was willing to accept evil (a tragic attitude) even to identifying himself with the "noble slave"—who symbolized the darker, unknown potential side of his personality, that underground side, turgid with possibility, which might, if given a chance, toss a fistful of mud into the sky and create a "shining star."

Even that prototype of the bourgeois, Robinson Crusoe, stopped to speculate as to his slave's humanity. And the rising American industrialists of the late nineteenth century were to rediscover what their European counterparts had learned a century before: that the good man Friday was as sound an investment for Crusoe morally as he was economically, for not only did Friday allow Crusoe to achieve himself by working for him, but by functioning as a living scapegoat to contain Crusoe's guilt over breaking with the institutions and authority of the past, he made it possible to exploit even his guilt economically. The man was one of the first missionaries.

Mark Twain was alive to this irony and refused such an easy (and dangerous) way out. Huck Finn's acceptance of the evil implicit in his "emancipation" of Jim represents Twain's acceptance of his personal responsibility in the condition of society. This was the tragic face behind his comic mask.

But by the twentieth century this attitude of tragic responsibility had disappeared from our literature along with that broad conception of democracy which vitalized the work of our greatest writers. After Twain's compelling image of black and white fraternity the Negro generally disappears from fiction as a rounded human being. And if already in Twain's time a novel which was optimistic concerning a democracy which would include all men could not escape being banned from public libraries, by our day his great drama of interracial fraternity had become, for most Americans at least, an amusing boy's story and nothing more. But, while a boy, Huck Finn has become by the somersault motion of what William Empson terms "pastoral," an embodiment of the heroic, and an exponent of humanism. Indeed, the historical and artistic justification for his adolescence lies in the fact that Twain was depicting a transitional period of American life; its artistic justification is that adolescence is the time of the "great confusion" during which both individuals and nations flounder between accepting and rejecting the responsibilities of adulthood. Accordingly, Huck's relationship to Jim, the river, and all they symbolize, is that of a humanist; in his relation to the community he is an individualist. He embodies the two major conflicting drives operating in nineteenth-century America. And if humanism is man's basic attitude toward a social order which he accepts, and individualism his basic attitude toward one he rejects, one might say that Twain, by allowing these two attitudes to argue dialectically in his work of art, was as highly moral an artist as he was a believer in democracy, and vice versa.

History, however, was to bring an ironic reversal to the direction which Huckleberry Finn chose, and by our day the divided ethic of the community had won out. In contrast with Twain's humanism, individualism was thought to be the only tenable attitude for the artist.

Thus we come to Ernest Hemingway, one of the two writers whose art is based most solidly upon Mark Twain's language, and one who perhaps has done most to extend Twain's technical influence upon our fiction. It was Hemingway who pointed out that all modern American writing springs from *Huckleberry Finn.* (One might add here that equally as much of it derives from Hemingway himself.) But by the twenties the element of rejection implicit in Twain had become so dominant an attitude of the American writer that Hemingway goes on to warn us to "stop where the Nigger Jim is stolen from the boys. That is the real end. The rest is just cheating."

So thoroughly had the Negro, both as man and as a symbol of man, been pushed into the underground of the American conscience that Hemingway missed completely the structural, symbolic and moral necessity for that part of the plot in which the boys rescue Jim. Yet it is precisely this part which gives the novel its significance. Without it, except as a boy's tale, the novel is meaningless. Yet Hemingway, a great artist in his own right, speaks as a victim of that culture of which he is himself so critical, for by his time that growing rift in the ethical fabric pointed out by Twain had become completely sundered—snagged upon the irrepressible moral reality of the Negro. Instead of the single democratic ethic for every man, there now existed two: one, the idealized ethic of the Constitution and the Declaration of Independence, reserved for white men; and the other, the pragmatic ethic designed for Negroes and other minorities, which took the form of discrimination. Twain had dramatized the conflict leading to this division in its earlier historical form, but what was new here was that such a moral division, always a threat to the sensitive man, was ignored by the artist in the most general terms, as when Hemingway rails against the rhetoric of the First World War.

Hemingway's blindness to the moral values of *Huckleberry Finn* despite his sensitivity to its technical aspects duplicated the one-sided vision of the twenties. Where Twain, seeking for what Melville called "the common continent of man," drew upon the rich folklore of the frontier (not omitting the Negro's) in order to "Americanize" his idiom, thus broadening his stylistic appeal, Hemingway was alert only to Twain's technical discoveries—the flexible colloquial language, the sharp naturalism, the thematic potentialities of adolescence. Thus what for Twain was a means to a moral end became for Hemingway an end in itself. And just as the trend toward technique for the sake of technique and production for the sake of the market lead to the neglect of the human need out of which they spring, so do they lead in literature to a marvelous technical virtuosity won at the expense of a gross insensitivity to fraternal values.

It is not accidental that the disappearance of the human Negro from our fiction coincides with the disappearance of deep-probing doubt and a sense of evil. Not that doubt in some form was not always present, as the works of the lost generation, the muckrakers and the proletarian writers make very clear. But it is a shallow doubt, which seldom turns inward upon the writer's own values; almost always it focuses outward, upon some scapegoat with which he is seldom able to identify himself as Huck Finn identified himself with the scoundrels who stole Jim and with Jim himself. This particular naturalism explored everything except the nature of man.

And when the artist would no longer conjure with the major moral problem in American life, he was defeated as a manipulator of profound social passions. In the United States, as in Europe, the triumph of industrialism had repelled the artist with the blatant hypocrisy between its ideals and its acts. But while in Europe the writer became the most profound critic of these matters, in our country he either turned away or was at best halfhearted in his opposition—perhaps because any profound probing of human values, both within himself and within society, would have brought him face to face with the rigidly tabooed subject of the Negro. And now the tradition of avoiding the moral struggle had led not only to the artistic segregation of the Negro but to the segregation of real fraternal, i.e., democratic, values.

The hard-boiled school represented by Hemingway, for instance, is usually spoken of as a product of World War I disillusionment, yet it was as much the product of a tradition which arose even before the Civil War—that tradition of intellectual evasion for which Thoreau criticized Emerson in regard to the Fugitive Slave Law, and which had been growing swiftly since the failure of the ideals in whose name the Civil War was fought. The failure to resolve the problem symbolized by the Negro has contributed indirectly to the dispossession of the artist in several ways. By excluding our largest minority from the democratic process, the United States weakened all national symbols and rendered sweeping public rituals which would dramatize the American dream impossible; it robbed the artist of a body of unassailable public beliefs upon which he could base his art; it deprived him of a personal faith in the ideals upon which society supposedly rested; and it provided him with no tragic mood indigenous to his society upon which he could erect a tragic art. The result was that he responded with an attitude of rejection, which he expressed as artistic individualism. But too often both his rejection and individualism were narrow; seldom was he able to transcend the limitations of pragmatic reality, and the quality of moral imagination—the fountainhead of great art—was atrophied within him.

Malraux has observed that contemporary American writing is the only important literature not created by intellectuals, and that the creators possess "neither the relative historical culture, nor the love of ideas (a prerogative of professors in the United States)" of comparable Europeans. And is there not a connection between the non-intellectual aspects of this writing (though many of the writers are far more intellectual than they admit or than Malraux would suspect) and its creators' rejection of broad social responsibility, between its nonconcern with ideas and its failure to project characters who grasp the broad sweep of American life, or who even attempt to state its fundamental problems? And has not this affected the types of heroes of this fiction, is it not a partial explanation of why it has created no characters possessing broad insight into their situations or the emotional, psychological and intellectual complexity which would allow them to possess and articulate a truly democratic world view?

It is instructive that Hemingway, born into a civilization characterized by violence, should seize upon the ritualized violence of the culturally distant

Spanish bullfight as a laboratory for developing his style. For it was, for Americans, an amoral violence (though not for the Spaniards) which he was seeking. Otherwise he might have studied that ritual of violence closer to home, that ritual in which the sacrifice is that of a human scapegoat, the lynching bee. Certainly this rite is not confined to the rope as agency, nor to the South as scene, nor even to the Negro as victim.

But let us not confuse the conscious goals of twentieth-century fiction with those of the nineteenth century, let us take it on its own terms. Artists such as Hemingway were seeking a technical perfection rather than moral insight. (Or should we say that theirs was a morality of technique?) They desired a style stripped of unessentials, one that would appeal without resorting to what was considered worn-out rhetoric, or best of all without any rhetoric whatsoever. It was felt that through the default of the powers that ruled society the artist had as his major task the "pictorial presentation of the evolution of a personal problem." Instead of recreating and extending the national myth as he did this, the writer now restricted himself to elaborating his personal myth. And although naturalist in his general style, he was not interested, like Balzac, in depicting a society, or even, like Mark Twain, in portraying the moral situation of a nation. Rather he was engaged in working out a personal problem through the evocative, emotion-charged images and ritual-therapy available through the manipulation of art forms. And while art was still an instrument of freedom, it was now mainly the instrument of a questionable personal freedom for the artist, which too often served to enforce the "unfreedom" of the reader.

This because it is not within the province of the artist to determine whether his work is social or not. Art by its nature is social. And while the artist can determine within a certain narrow scope the type of social effect he wishes his art to create, here his will is definitely limited. Once introduced into society, the work of art begins to pulsate with those meanings, emotions, ideas brought to it by its audience and over which the artist has but limited control. The irony of the "lost generation" writers is that while disavowing a social role it was the fate of their works to perform a social function which reenforced those very social values which they most violently opposed. How could this be? Because in its genesis the work of art, like the stereotype, is personal; psychologically it represents the socialization of some profoundly personal problem involving guilt (often symbolic murder—parricide, fratricide—incest, homosexuality, all problems at the base of personality) from which by expressing them along with other elements (images, memories, emotions, ideas) he seeks transcendence. To be effective as personal fulfillment, if it is to be more than dream, the work of art must simultaneously evoke images of reality and give them formal organization. And it must, since the individual's emotions are formed in society, shape them into socially meaningful patterns (even Surrealism and Dadaism depended upon their initiates). Nor, as we can see by comparing literature with reportage, is this all. The work of literature differs basically from reportage not merely in its presentation of a pattern of events, nor in its concern with emotion (for a report might well be an account of highly emotional events), but in the deep personal necessity which cries full-throated in the work of art and which seeks transcendence in the form of ritual.

Malcolm Cowley, on the basis of the rites which he believes to be the secret dynamic of Hemingway's work, has identified him with Poe, Hawthorne and Melville, "the haunted and nocturnal writers," he calls them, "the men who dealt with images that were symbols of an inner world." In Hemingway's work, he writes, "we can recognize rites of animal sacrifice . . . of sexual union . . . of conversion . . . and of symbolic death and rebirth." I do not believe, however, that the presence of these rites in writers like Hemingway is as important as the fact that here, beneath the deadpan prose, the cadences of understatement, the anti-intellectualism, the concern with every "fundamental" of man except that which distinguishes him from the animal—that here is the twentieth-century form of that magical rite which during periods of great art has been to a large extent public and explicit. Here is the literary form by which the personal guilt of the pulverized individual of our rugged era is expatiated: not through his identification with the guilty acts of an Oedipus, a Macbeth or a Medea, by suffering their agony and loading his sins upon their "strong and passionate shoulders," but by being gored with a bull, hooked with a fish, impaled with a grasshopper on a fishhook; not by identifying himself with human heroes, but with those who are indeed defeated.

On the social level this writing performs a function similar to that of the stereotype: it conditions the reader to accept the less worthy values of society, and it serves to justify and absolve our sins of social irresponsibility. With unconscious irony it advises stoic acceptance of those conditions of life which it so accurately describes and which it pretends to reject. And when I read the early Hemingway I seem to be in the presence of Huckleberry Finn who, instead of identifying himself with humanity and attempting to steal Jim free, chose to write the letter which sent him back into slavery. So that now he is a Huck full of regret and nostalgia, suffering a sense of guilt that fills even his noondays with nightmares, and against which, like a terrified child avoiding the cracks in the sidewalk, he seeks protection through the compulsive minor rituals of his prose.

The major difference between nineteenth- and twentieth-century writers is not in the latter's lack of personal rituals—a property of all fiction worthy of being termed literature—but in the social effect aroused within their respective readers. Melville's ritual (and his rhetoric) was based upon materials that were more easily available, say, than Hemingway's. They represented a blending of his personal myth with universal myths as traditional as any used by Shakespeare or the Bible, while until *For Whom the Bell Tolls* Hemingway's was weighted on the personal side. The difference in terms of perspective of belief is that Melville's belief could still find a public object. Whatever else his works were "about" they also managed to be about democracy. But by our day the democratic dream had become too shaky a structure to support the furious pressures of the artist's doubt. And as always when the belief which nurtures a great social myth declines, large sections of society become prey to superstition. For man without myth is Othello with Desdemona gone: chaos descends, faith vanishes and superstitions prowl in the mind.

Hard-boiled writing is said to appeal through its presentation of sheer fact, rather than through rhetoric. The writer puts nothing down but what he pragmatically "knows." But actually one "fact" itself—which in literature must be presented simultaneously as image and as event—became a rhetorical unit. And the symbolic ritual which has set off the "fact"—that is, the fact unorganized by vital social myths (which might incorporate the findings of science and still contain elements of mystery)—is the rite of superstition. The superstitious individual responds to the capricious event, the fact that seems to explode in his face through blind fatality. For it is the creative function of myth to protect the individual from the irrational, and since it is here in the realm of the irrational that, impervious to science, the stereotype grows, we see that the Negro stereotype is really an image of the unorganized, irrational forces of American life, forces through which, by projecting them in forms of images of an easily dominated minority, the white individual seeks to be at home in the vast unknown world of America. Perhaps the object of the stereotype is not so much to crush the Negro as to console the white man.

Certainly there is justification for this view when we consider the work of William Faulkner. In Faulkner most of the relationships which we have pointed out between the Negro and contemporary writing come to focus: the social and the personal, the moral and the technical, the nineteenth-century emphasis upon morality and the modern accent upon the personal myth. And on the strictly literary level he is prolific and complex enough to speak for those Southern writers who are aggressively anti-Negro and for those younger writers who appear most sincerely interested in depicting the Negro as a rounded human being. What is more, he is the greatest artist the South has produced. While too complex to be given more than a glance in these notes, even a glance is more revealing of what lies back of the distortion of the Negro in modern writing than any attempt at a group survey might be.

Faulkner's attitude is mixed. Taking his cue from the Southern mentality in which the Negro is often dissociated into a malignant stereotype (the bad nigger) on the one hand and a benign stereotype (the good nigger) on the other, most often Faulkner presents characters embodying both. The dual function of this dissociation seems to be that of avoiding moral pain and thus to justify the South's racial code. But since such a social order harms whites no less than blacks, the sensitive Southerner, the artist, is apt to feel its effects acutely—and within the deepest levels of his personality. For not only is the social division forced upon the Negro by the ritualized ethic of discrimination, but upon the white man by the strictly enforced set of anti-Negro taboos. The conflict is always with him. Indeed, so rigidly has the recognition of Negro humanity been tabooed that the white Southerner is apt to associate any form of personal rebellion with the Negro. So that for the Southern artist the Negro becomes a symbol of his personal rebellion, his guilt and his repression of it. The Negro is thus a compelling object of fascination, and this we see very clearly in Faulkner.

Sometimes in Faulkner the Negro is simply a villain, but by an unconsciously ironic transvaluation his villainy consists, as with Loosh in *The Unvanquished*, of desiring his freedom. Or again the Negro appears benign, as with Ringo, of the same novel, who uses his talent not to seek personal freedom but to remain the loyal and resourceful retainer. Not that I criticize loyalty in itself, but that loyalty given where one's humanity is unrecognized seems a bit obscene. And yet in Faulkner's story, "The Bear," he brings us as close to the moral implication of the Negro as Twain or Melville. In the famous "difficult" fourth section, which Malcolm Cowley advises us to skip very much as Hemingway would have us skip the end of *Huckleberry Finn*, we find an argument in progress in which one voice (that of a Southern abolitionist) seeks to define Negro humanity against the other's enumeration of those stereotypes which many Southerners believe to be the Negro's basic traits. Significantly the mentor of the young hero of this story, a man of great moral stature, is socially a Negro.

Indeed, through his many novels and short stories, Faulkner fights out the moral problem which was repressed after the nineteenth century, and it was shocking for some to discover that for all his concern with the South, Faulkner was actually seeking out the nature of man. Thus we must turn to him for that continuity of moral purpose which made for the greatness of our classics. As for the Negro minority, he has been more willing perhaps than any other artist to start with the stereotype, accept it as true, and then seek out the human truth which it hides. Perhaps his is the example for our writers to follow, for in his work technique has been put once more to the task of creating value.

Which leaves these final things to be said. First, that this is meant as no plea for white writers to define Negro humanity, but to recognize the broader aspects of their own. Secondly, Negro writers and those of the other minorities have their own task of contributing to the total image of the American by depicting the experience of their own groups. Certainly theirs is the task of defining Negro humanity, as this can no more be accomplished by others than freedom, which must be won again and again each day, can be conferred upon another. A people must define itself, and minorities have the responsibility of having their ideals and images recognized as part of the composite image which is that of the still forming American people.

The other thing to be said is that while it is unlikely that American writing will ever retrace the way to the nineteenth century, it might be worthwhile to point out that for all its technical experimentation it is nevertheless an ethical instrument, and as such it might well exercise some choice in the kind of ethic it prefers to support. The artist is no freer than the society in which he lives, and in the United States the writers who stereotype or ignore the Negro and other minorities in the final analysis stereotype and distort their own humanity. Mark Twain knew that in *his* America humanity masked its face with blackness.

James Baldwin

Everybody's Protest Novel

(1955)

In *Uncle Tom's Cabin,* that cornerstone of American social protest fiction, St. Clare, the kindly master, remarks to his coldly disapproving Yankee cousin, Miss Ophelia, that, so far as he is able to tell, the blacks have been turned over to the devil for the benefit of the whites in this world—however, he adds thoughtfully, it may turn out in the next. Miss Ophelia's reaction is, at least, vehemently right-minded: "This is perfectly horrible!" she exclaims. "You ought to be ashamed of yourselves!"

Miss Ophelia, as we may suppose, was speaking for the author; her exclamation is the moral, neatly framed, and incontestable like those improving mottoes sometimes found hanging on the walls of furnished rooms. And, like these mottoes, before which one invariably flinches, recognizing an insupportable, almost an indecent glibness, she and St. Clare are terribly in earnest. Neither of them questions the medieval morality from which their dialogue springs: black, white, the devil, the next world—posing its alternatives between heaven and the flames—were realities for them as, of course, they were for their creator. They spurned and were terrified of the darkness, striving mightily for the light; and considered from this aspect, Miss Ophelia's exclamation, like Mrs. Stowe's novel, achieves a bright, almost a lurid significance, like the light from a fire which consumes a witch. This is the more striking as one considers the novels of Negro oppression written in our own, more enlightened day, all of which say only: "This is perfectly horrible! You ought to be ashamed of yourselves!" (Let us ignore, for the moment, those novels of oppression written by Negroes, which add only a raging, near-paranoiac postscript to this statement and actually reinforce, as I hope to make clear later, the principles which activate the oppression they decry.)

This essay first appeared in James Baldwin, *Notes of a Native Son* (Boston, 1955).

Uncle Tom's Cabin is a very bad novel, having, in its self-righteous, virtuous sentimentality, much in common with *Little Women*. Sentimentality, the ostentatious parading of excessive and spurious emotion, is the mark of dishonesty, the inability to feel; the wet eyes of the sentimentalist betray his aversion to experience, his fear of life, his arid heart; and it is always, therefore, the signal of secret and violent inhumanity, the mask of cruelty. *Uncle Tom's Cabin*—like its multitudinous, hard-boiled descendants—is a catalogue of violence. This is explained by the nature of Mrs. Stowe's subject matter, her laudable determination to flinch from nothing in presenting the complete picture; an explanation which falters only if we pause to ask whether or not her picture is indeed complete; and what constriction or failure of perception forced her to so depend on the description of brutality—unmotivated, senseless—and to leave unanswered and unnoticed the only important question: what it was, after all, that moved her people to such deeds.

But this, let us say, was beyond Mrs. Stowe's powers; she was not so much a novelist as an impassioned pamphleteer; her book was not intended to do anything more than prove that slavery was wrong; was, in fact, perfectly horrible. This makes material for a pamphlet but it is hardly enough for a novel; and the only question left to ask is why we are bound still within the same constriction. How is it that we are so loath to make a further journey than that made by Mrs. Stowe, to discover and reveal something a little closer to the truth?

But that battered word, truth, having made its appearance here, confronts one immediately with a series of riddles and has, moreover, since so many gospels are preached, the unfortunate tendency to make one belligerent. Let us say, then, that truth, as used here, is meant to imply a devotion to the human being, his freedom and fulfillment; freedom which cannot be legislated, fulfillment which cannot be charted. This is the prime concern, the frame of reference; it is not to be confused with a devotion to Humanity which is too easily equated with a devotion to a Cause; and Causes, as we know, are notoriously bloodthirsty. We have, as it seems to me, in this most mechanical and interlocking of civilizations, attempted to lop this creature down to the status of a time-saving invention. He is not, after all, merely a member of a Society or a Group or a deplorable conundrum to be explained by Science. He is—and how old-fashioned the words sound!—something more than that, something resolutely indefinable, unpredictable. In overlooking, denying, evading his complexity—which is nothing more than the disquieting complexity of ourselves—we are diminished and we perish; only within this web of ambiguity, paradox, this hunger, danger, darkness, can we find at once ourselves and the power that will free us from ourselves. It is this power of revelation which is the business of the novelist, this journey toward a more vast reality which must take precedence over all other claims. What is today parroted as his Responsibility—which seems to mean that he must make formal declaration that he is involved in, and affected by, the lives of other people and to say something improving about this somewhat self-evident fact—is, when he believes it, his corruption and our loss; moreover, it is rooted in, interlocked with and intensifies this same mechanization. Both *Gentleman's Agreement* and *The Postman Always Rings Twice* exemplify this terror of the human being, the determination to cut him down to size. And in *Uncle Tom's Cabin* we may find foreshadowing of both: the formula created by the necessity to find a lie more palatable than the truth has been handed down and memorized and persists yet with a terrible power.

It is interesting to consider one more aspect of Mrs. Stowe's novel, the method she used to solve the problem of writing about a black man at all. Apart from her lively procession of field hands, house niggers, Chloe, Topsy, etc.—who are the stock, lovable figures presenting no problem—she has only three other Negroes in the book. These are the important ones and two of them may be dismissed immediately, since we have only the author's word that they are Negro and they are, in all other respects, as white as she can make them. The two are George and Eliza, a married couple with a wholly adorable child—whose quaintness, incidentally, and whose charm, rather put one in mind of a darky bootblack doing a buck and wing to the clatter of condescending coins. Eliza is a beautiful, pious hybrid, light enough to pass—the heroine of *Quality* might, indeed, be her reincarnation—differing from the genteel mistress who has overseered her education only in the respect that she is a servant. George is darker, but makes up for it by being a mechanical genius, and is, moreover, sufficiently un-Negroid to pass through town, a fugitive from his master, disguised as a Spanish gentleman, attracting no attention whatever beyond admiration. They are a race apart from Topsy. It transpires by the end of the novel, through one of those energetic, last-minute convolutions of the plot, that Eliza has some connection with French gentility. The figure from whom the novel takes its name, Uncle Tom, who is a figure of controversy yet, is jet-black, wooly-haired, illiterate; and he is phenomenally forbearing. He has to be; he is black; only through this forbearance can he survive or triumph. (*Cf.* Faulkner's preface to *The Sound and the Fury:* These others were not Compsons. They were black:—They endured.) His triumph is metaphysical, unearthly; since he is black, born without the light, it is only through humility, the incessant

(margin note, handwritten:) PAINTS BLACK CHARACTERS AS DEVOID OF BLACK QUALITIES,

mortification of the flesh, that he can enter into communion with God or man. The virtuous rage of Mrs. Stowe is motivated by nothing so temporal as a concern for the relationship of men to one another—or, even, as she would have claimed, by a concern for their relationship to God—but merely by a panic of being hurled into the flames, of being caught in traffic with the devil. She embraced this merciless doctrine with all her heart, bargaining shamelessly before the throne of grace: God and salvation becoming her personal property, purchased with the coin of her virtue. Here, black equates with evil and white with grace; if, being mindful of the necessity of good works, she could not cast out the blacks—a wretched, huddled mass, apparently, claiming, like an obsession, her inner eye—she could not embrace them either without purifying them of sin. She must cover their intimidating nakedness, robe them in white, the garments of salvation; only thus could she herself be delivered from ever-present sin, only thus could she bury, as St. Paul demanded, "the carnal man, the man of the flesh." Tom, therefore, her only black man, has been robbed of his humanity and divested of his sex. It is the price for that darkness with which he has been branded.

Uncle Tom's Cabin, then, is activated by what might be called a theological terror, the terror of damnation; and the spirit that breathes in this book, hot, self-righteous, fearful, is not different from that spirit of medieval times which sought to exorcize evil by burning witches; and is not different from that terror which activates a lynch mob. One need not, indeed, search for examples so historic or so gaudy; this is a warfare waged daily in the heart, a warfare so vast, so relentless and so powerful that the interracial handshake or the interracial marriage can be as crucifying as the public hanging or the secret rape. This panic motivates our cruelty, this fear of the dark makes it impossible that our lives shall be other than superficial; this, interlocked with and feeding our glittering, mechanical, inescapable civilization which has put to death our freedom.

This, notwithstanding that the avowed aim of the American protest novel is to bring greater freedom to the oppressed. They are forgiven, on the strength of these good intentions, whatever violence they do to language, whatever excessive demands they make of credibility. It is, indeed, considered the sign of a frivolity so intense as to approach decadence to suggest that these books are both badly written and wildly improbable. One is told to put first things first, the good of society coming before niceties of style or characterization. Even if this were incontestable—for what exactly is the "good" of society?—it argues an insuperable confusion, since literature and sociology are not one and the same; it is impossible to discuss them as if they were. Our

passion for categorization, life neatly fitted into pegs, has led to an unfore-
seen, paradoxical distress; confusion, a breakdown of meaning. Those categories which were meant to define and control the world for us have boomer-
anged us into chaos; in which limbo we whirl, clutching the straws of our
definitions. The "protest" novel, so far from being disturbing, is an accepted
and comforting aspect of the American scene, ramifying that framework we
believe to be so necessary. Whatever unsettling questions are raised are
evanescent, titillating; remote, for this has nothing to do with us, it is safely
ensconced in the social arena, where, indeed, it has nothing to do with
anyone, so that finally we receive a very definite thrill of virtue from the fact
that we are reading such a book at all. This report from the pit reassures us of
its reality and its darkness and of our own salvation; and "As long as such
books are being published," an American liberal once said to me, "everything
will be all right."

But unless one's ideal of society is a race of neatly analyzed, hardworking
ciphers, one can hardly claim for the protest novels the lofty purpose they
claim for themselves or share the present optimism concerning them. They
emerge for what they are: a mirror of our confusion, dishonesty, panic,
trapped and immobilized in the sunlit prison of the American dream. They
are fantasies, connecting nowhere with reality, sentimental; in exactly the
same sense that such movies as *The Best Years of Our Lives* or the works of Mr.
James M. Cain are fantasies. Beneath the dazzling pyrotechnics of these
current operas one may still discern, as the controlling force, the intense
theological preoccupations of Mrs. Stowe, the sick vacuities of *The Rover
Boys*. Finally, the aim of the protest novel becomes something very closely
resembling the zeal of those alabaster missionaries to Africa to cover the
nakedness of the natives, to hurry them into the pallid arms of Jesus and
thence into slavery. The aim has now become to reduce all Americans to the
compulsive, bloodless dimensions of a guy named Joe.

It is the peculiar triumph of society—and its loss—that it is able to convince those people to whom it has given inferior status of the reality of this
decree; it has the force and the weapons to translate its dictum into fact, so
that the allegedly inferior are actually made so, insofar as the societal realities
are concerned. This is a more hidden phenomenon now than it was in the
days of serfdom, but it is no less implacable. Now, as then, we find ourselves
bound, first without, then within, by the nature of our categorization. And
escape is not effected through a bitter railing against this trap; it is as though
this very striving were the only motion needed to spring the trap upon us.
We take our shape, it is true, within and against that cage of reality be-

queathed us at our birth; and yet it is precisely through our dependence on this reality that we are most endlessly betrayed. Society is held together by our need; we bind it together with legend, myth, coercion, fearing that without it we will be hurled into that void, within which, like the earth before the Word was spoken, the foundations of society are hidden. From this void—ourselves—it is the function of society to protect us; but it is only this void, our unknown selves, demanding, forever, a new act of creation, which can save us—"from the evil that is in the world." With the same motion, at the same time, it is this toward which we endlessly struggle and from which, endlessly, we struggle to escape.

It must be remembered that the oppressed and the oppressor are bound together within the same society; they accept the same criteria, they share the same beliefs, they both alike depend on the same reality. Within this cage it is romantic, more, meaningless, to speak of a "new" society as the desire of the oppressed, for that shivering dependence on the props of reality which he shares with the *Herrenvolk* makes a truly "new" society impossible to conceive. What is meant by a new society is one in which inequalities will disappear, in which vengeance will be exacted; either there will be no oppressed at all, or the oppressed and the oppressor will change places. But, finally, as it seems to me, what the rejected desire is, is an elevation of status, acceptance within the present community. Thus, the African, exile, pagan, hurried off the auction block and into the fields, fell on his knees before that God in Whom he must now believe; who had made him, but not in His image. This tableau, this impossibility, is the heritage of the Negro in America: *Wash me,* cried the slave to his Maker, *and I shall be whiter, whiter than snow!* For black is the color of evil; only the robes of the saved are white. It is this cry, implacable on the air and in the skull, that he must live with. Beneath the widely published catalogue of brutality—bringing to mind, somehow, an image, a memory of church-bells burdening the air—is this reality which, in the same nightmare notion, he both flees and rushes to embrace. In America, now, this country devoted to the death of the paradox—which may, therefore, be put to death by one—his lot is as ambiguous as a tableau by Kafka. To flee or not, to move or not, it is all the same; his doom is written on his forehead, it is carried in his heart. In *Native Son,* Bigger Thomas stands on a Chicago street corner watching airplanes flown by white men racing against the sun and "Goddamn" he says, the bitterness bubbling up like blood, remembering a million indignities, the terrible, rat-infested house, the humiliation of home-relief, the intense, aimless, ugly bickering, hating it; hatred smoulders through these pages like sulphur fire. All of Bigger's life is controlled, defined by his hatred and his fear. And later, his fear drives him to murder and his hatred to rape; he dies, having come, through this violence, we are told, for the first time, to a kind of life, having for the first time redeemed his manhood. Below the surface of this novel there lies, as it seems to me, a continuation, a complement of that monstrous legend it was written to destroy. Bigger is Uncle Tom's descendant, flesh of his flesh, so exactly opposite a portrait that, when the books are placed together, it seems that the contemporary Negro novelist and the dead New England woman are locked together in a deadly, timeless battle; the one uttering merciless exhortations, the other shouting curses. And, indeed, within this web of lust and fury, black and white can only thrust and counterthrust, long for each other's slow, exquisite death; death by torture, acid, knives and burning; the thrust, the counterthrust, the longing making the heavier that cloud which blinds and suffocates them both, so that they go down into the pit together. Thus has the cage betrayed us all, this moment, our life, turned to nothing through our terrible attempts to insure it. For Bigger's tragedy is not that he is cold or black or hungry, not even that he is American, black; but that he has accepted a theology that denies him life, that he admits the possibility of his being subhuman and feels constrained, therefore, to battle for his humanity according to those brutal criteria bequeathed him at his birth. But our humanity is our burden, our life; we need not battle for it; we need only to do what is infinitely more difficult—that is, accept it. The failure of the protest novel lies in its rejection of life, the human being, the denial of his beauty, dread, power, in its insistence that it is his categorization alone which is real and which cannot be transcended.

Arthur P. Davis

Integration and Race Literature

(1956)

Integration is the most vital issue in America today. The word is on every tongue, and it has acquired all kinds of meanings and connotations. The idea—not the fact obviously—but the idea of integration threatens to split the nation into two hostile camps. As the Negro is the center of this violent controversy, his reaction to it is of supreme importance. In this paper I wish to examine one segment of that reaction—that of the Negro creative artist. How has the integration issue affected him? It is my belief that the concept of integration has already produced a major trend or change in our literature, and that as integration becomes a reality, it will transform Negro writing even more drastically. The rest of this article will be an attempt to illustrate and uphold this thesis.

But before we explore these changes, let us examine the peculiar period in which the Negro writer finds himself because of the integration movement. In the phrase of Matthew Arnold, he is actually living "between two worlds"—one not yet dead, the other not fully born. It is obvious to even the most rabid critic that racial conditions in America are far better than they have ever been before. Barriers are falling in all areas. The armed forces are integrated. Most Southern universities have Negro students, and the Supreme Court has sounded the legal death knell of segregation in public schools. The State Department and the better Northern schools are vying with each other to enlist the services of outstanding race scholars. In practically all states Negroes can now vote without risking their lives; and though the Till Case may seem to deny it, lynching is a dead practice. In short, despite the last desperate and futile efforts of frightened and panicky Southerners, the country has committed itself spiritually to integration. As yet, it is

This essay first appeared in *Phylon*, 17.2 (1956).

still largely a spiritual commitment, but it has changed radically the racial climate of America.

This change of climate, however, has inadvertently dealt the Negro writer a crushing blow. Up to the present decade, our literature has been predominantly a protest literature. Ironical though it may be, we have capitalized on oppression (I mean, of course, in a literary sense). Although we may deplore and condemn the cause, there is great creative motivation in a movement which brings all members of a group together and cements them in a common bond. And that is just what segregation did for the Negro, especially during the Twenties and Thirties when full segregation was not only practiced in the South but tacitly condoned by the whole nation. As long as there was this common enemy, we had a common purpose and a strong urge to transform into artistic terms our deep-rooted feelings of bitterness and scorn. When the enemy capitulated, he shattered our most fruitful literary tradition. The possibility of imminent integration has tended to destroy the protest element in Negro writing.

And one must always keep in mind the paradox involved. We do not have actual integration anywhere. We have surface integration and token integration in many areas, but the everyday pattern of life for the overwhelming majority of Negroes is unchanged, and probably will be for the next two or three decades. But we do have—and this is of the utmost importance—we do have the spiritual climate which will eventually bring about complete integration. The Negro artist recognizes and acknowledges that climate; he accepts it on good faith; and he is resolved to work with it at all costs. In the meantime, he will have to live between worlds, and that for any artist is a disturbing experience. For the present-day Negro artist—especially the writer in his middle years—it becomes almost a tragic experience because it means giving up a tradition in which he has done his apprentice and journeyman work, giving it up when he is prepared to make use of that tradition as a master craftsman.

Another disturbing factor which must be considered here is that this change of climate came about rather suddenly. Perhaps it would be more exact to say that the full awareness came suddenly because there were signs of its approach all during the Forties, and Negro writers from time to time showed that they recognized these signs. But the full awareness did not come until the present decade, and it came with some degree of abruptness. For example, all through World War II, all through the Forties, the Negro writer was still grinding out protest and Problem novels, most of them influenced by *Native Son*. The list of these works is impressive: *Blood on the Forge* (1941),

White Face (1943), *If He Hollers* (1943), *The Street* (1946), *Taffy* (1951), and there were others—practically all of them naturalistic novels with the same message of protest against America's treatment of its black minority. The poets wrote in a similar vein. *For My People* (1942), *Freedom's Plow* (1943), *A Street in Bronzeville* (1945), and *Powerful Long Ladder* (1946) all had strong protest elements, all dealt in part with the Negro's fight against segregation and discrimination at home and in the armed forces. Noting the dates of these works, one realizes that, roughly speaking, up to 1950 the protest tradition was in full bloom, and that most of our best writers were still using it. And then with startling swiftness came this awareness of a radical change in the nation's climate; and with it the realization that the old protest themes had to be abandoned. The new climate tended to date the Problem works of the Forties as definitely as time had dated the New Negro "lynching-passing" literature of the Twenties and Thirties. In other words, protest writing has become the first casualty of the new racial climate.

Faced with the loss of his oldest and most cherished tradition, the Negro writer has been forced to seek fresh ways to use his material. First of all, he has attempted to find new themes within the racial framework. Retaining the Negro character and background, he has shifted his emphasis from the protest aspect to Negro living and placed it on the problems and conflicts within the group itself. For example, Chester Himes, pursuing this course in his latest novel, *Third Generation,* explores school life in the Deep South. His main conflict in this work is not concerned with interracial protest but with discord within a Negro family caused by color differences. The whole racial tone of this novel is quite different from that of *If He Hollers,* which, as stated above, is a typical protest work. One came out in 1943, the other in 1953. The two books are a good index to the changes which took place in the decade separating them.

In like manner, Owen Dodson and Gwendolyn Brooks in their novels, *Boy at the Window* and *Maud Martha,* respectively, show this tendency to find new themes within the racial framework. Both of these publications are "little novels," written in the current style, giving intimate and subtle vignettes of middle class living. Their main stress is on life within the group, not on conflict with outside forces. Taking a different approach, William Demby, in *Beetlecreek,* completely reversed the protest pattern by showing the black man's inhumanity to his white brother. In *The Outsider,* Richard Wright has taken an even more subtle approach. He uses a Negro main character, but by adroitly and persistently minimizing that character's racial importance, he succeeds in divorcing him from any association with the traditional protest alignment. And Langston Hughes in his latest work, *Sweet Flypaper of Life,* though using all Negro characters, does not even remotely touch on the matter of interracial protest. All of these authors, it seems to me, show their awareness of the new climate by either playing down or avoiding entirely the traditional protest approach.

Another group of writers have elected to show their awareness by avoiding the Negro character. Among them are William Gardner Smith (*Anger at Innocence*), Ann Petry (*Country Place*), Richard Wright (*Savage Holiday*), and Willard Motley (*Knock on Any Door*). None of these works has Negro main characters. With the exception of *Knock on Any Door,* each is a "second" novel, following a work written in the Forties which has Negro characters and background, and which is written in the protest vein. In each case the first work was highly popular, and yet each of these novelists elected to avoid the theme which gave him his initial success. The effect of the changed climate, it seems to me, is obvious here.

I realize that Frank Yerby with his ten or more best sellers in a row should be listed in this group. Yerby, however, has never used a Negro background or Negro principal characters for his novels. His decision not to make use of the Negro protest tradition came so early in his career, we cannot use it as a case in point at this time. But it is interesting to note that Yerby's first published work, a short story, was written in the protest tradition.

So far I have spoken only of the novelists, but the Negro poets have also sensed the change of climate in America and have reacted to it. Incidentally, several of our outstanding protest poets of the Thirties and Forties have simply dropped out of the picture as poets. I cannot say, of course, that the new climate alone has silenced them, but I do feel that it has been a contributing cause. It is hard for a mature writer to slough off the tradition in which he has worked during all of his formative years. Acquiring a new approach in any field of art is a very serious and trying experience. One must also remember that the protest tradition was no mere surface fad with the Negro writer. It was part of his self-respect, part of his philosophy of life, part of his inner being. It was almost a religious experience with those of us who came up through the dark days of the Twenties and Thirties. When a tradition so deeply ingrained is abandoned, it tends to leave a spiritual numbness—a kind of void not easily filled with new interests or motivations. Several of our ablest poets—and novelists too, for that matter—have not tried to fill that void.

But a few of our poets have met the challenge of the new climate, among them Langston Hughes, M. B. Tolson, Robert Hayden, and several others. A comparison of their early and later works will show in each case a tendency either to avoid protest themes entirely or to approach them much more subtly and obliquely. Compare, for example, Tolson's *Rendezvous with America* (1944) with a *Libretto for the Republic of Liberia* (1953). The thumping rhythms of the protest verse in the former work have given way in the latter to a new technique, one that is influenced largely by Hart Crane. With this work, Tolson has turned his back on the tradition in which he came to maturity, and he has evidently done so successfully. Concerning the work, Allen Tate feels that: "For the first time . . . a Negro poet has assimilated completely the full poetic language of his time and, by implication, the language of the Anglo-American poetic tradition." A younger poet like Gwendolyn Brooks, in her poetic career, as brief as it is, also illustrates this change in attitude. There is far more racial protest in *A Street in Bronzeville* than in her latest Pulitzer-Prize-winning volume, *Annie Allen*. Moreover, the few pieces in the latter book which concern the Problem are different in approach and in technique from those in the first work. This tendency to avoid too much emphasis on Problem poetry is also seen, curiously enough, in a very recent anthology, *Lincoln University Poets,* edited by Waring Cuney, Langston Hughes, and Bruce Wright. Several of the Lincoln poets were writing during the New Negro period when the protest tradition was at its height, but these editors, two of them New Negro poets themselves, took great pains to keep the protest pieces down to the barest minimum; and those which they included are relatively mild.

Summing up then, I think we can safely say that the leaven of integration is very much at work. It has forced the Negro creative artist to play down his most cherished tradition; it has sent him in search of new themes; it has made him abandon, at least on occasion, the Negro character and background; and it has possibly helped to silence a few of the older writers now living.

The course of Negro American literature has been highlighted by a series of social and political crises over the Negro's position in America. The Abolition Movement, the Civil War, Reconstruction, World War I, and the Riot-Lynching Period of the Twenties all radically influenced Negro writing. Each crisis in turn produced a new tradition in our literature; and as each crisis has passed, the Negro writer has dropped the special tradition which the occasion demanded and moved towards the mainstream of American literature. The Integration Controversy is another crisis and from it we hope that the Negro will move permanently into full participation in American life—social, economic, political and literary.

But what about the literature of this interim between two worlds—between a world of dying segregation and one of a developing integration? It is my belief that this period will produce for a while a series of "goodwill books"—novels and short stories for the most part in which the emphasis will be on what the Negro journalists now call "positive reporting." In an all-out effort to make integration become a reality, the Negro writer will tend to play down the remaining harshness in Negro American living and to emphasize the progress towards equality. This new type of work will try to do in fiction what Roi Ottley has done in *No Green Pastures*. May I say in passing that I do not imply any praise of this work. It simply illustrates for me a trend which I feel will become more and more popular during this interim period. May I also add that this type of goodwill publication will lend itself to all kinds of abuse at the hands of mercenary charlatans; it will create other stereotypes more unbelievable than those we already have, but it will be immensely popular.

During this interim there will also come into fashion another type of racial publication—racial fiction that, without using the Problem, will do for the internal life of Negroes what *Marty* has done for New York Italian-American family and group life and what a host of works in recent years have done for Irish-American life. With the pressure of segregation lightened, the Negro artist will find it easy to draw such pictures of his people. He will discover, what we all know in our objective moments, that there are many facets of Negro living—humorous, pathetic, and tragic—which are not directly touched by the outside world. Hughes' *Sweet Flypaper of Life* is, I believe, a forerunner of many more works of this type.

And when we finally reach that stage in which we can look at segregation in the same way that historians now regard the Inquisition or the Hitler Era in Germany or any other evil period of the past, we shall then do naturally and without self-consciousness what the Joyces and Dostoevskys of the world have always done—write intimately and objectively of our own people in universal human terms.

The Black Arts Movement

LeRoi Jones (Amiri Baraka)

The Myth of a "Negro Literature"

(1966)

The mediocrity of what has been called "Negro Literature" is one of the most loosely held secrets of American culture. From Phyllis Wheatley to Charles Chesnutt, to the present generation of American Negro writers, the only recognizable accretion of tradition readily attributable to the black producer of a formal literature in this country, with a few notable exceptions, has been of an almost agonizing mediocrity. In most other fields of "high art" in America, with the same few notable exceptions, the Negro contribution has been, when one existed at all, one of impressive mediocrity. Only in music, and most notably in blues, jazz, and spirituals, i.e., "Negro Music," has there been a significantly profound contribution by American Negroes.

There are a great many reasons for the spectacular vapidity of the American Negro's accomplishment in other formal, serious art forms—social, economic, political, etc.—but one of the most persistent and aggravating reasons for the absence of achievement among serious Negro artists, except in Negro music, is that in most cases the Negroes who found themselves in a position to pursue some art, especially the art of literature, have been members of the Negro middle class, a group that has always gone out of its way to cultivate any mediocrity, as long as that mediocrity was guaranteed to prove to America, and recently to the world at large, that they were not really who they were, i.e., Negroes. Negro music alone, because it drew its strengths and beauties out of the depth of the black man's soul, and because to a large extent its traditions could be carried on by the lowest classes of Negroes, has been able to survive the constant and willful dilutions of the black middle class. Blues and jazz have been the only consistent exhibitors of "Negritude" in formal American culture simply because the bearers of its tradition main-

This essay first appeared in LeRoi Jones, *Home: Social Essays* (New York, 1966).

tained their essential identities as Negroes; in no other art (and I will persist
in calling Negro music, Art) has this been possible. Phyllis Wheatley and her
pleasant imitations of 18th century English poetry are far and, finally, ludicrous departures from the huge black voices that splintered southern nights
with their *hollers, chants, arwhoolies,* and *ballits.* The embarrassing and inverted paternalism of Charles Chesnutt and his "refined Afro-American"
heroes are far cries from the richness and profundity of the blues. And it is
impossible to mention the achievements of the Negro in any area of artistic
endeavor with as much significance as in spirituals, blues and jazz. There has
never been an equivalent to Duke Ellington or Louis Armstrong in Negro
writing, and even the best of contemporary literature written by Negroes
cannot yet be compared to the fantastic beauty of the music of Charlie
Parker.

American Negro music from its inception moved logically and powerfully
out of a fusion between African musical tradition and the American experience. It was, and continues to be, a natural, yet highly stylized and personal
version of the Negro's life in America. It is, indeed, a chronicler of the Negro's
movement, from African slave to American slave, from Freedman to Citizen.
And the literature of the blues is a much more profound contribution to
Western culture than any other literary contribution made by American
Negroes. Moreover, it is only recently that formal literature written by American Negroes has begun to approach the literary standards of its model, i.e.,
the literature of the white middle class. And only Jean Toomer, Richard
Wright, Ralph Ellison, and James Baldwin have managed to bring off examples of writing, in this genre, that could succeed in passing themselves off as
"serious" writing, in the sense that, say, the work of Somerset Maugham is
"serious" writing. That is, serious, if one has never read Herman Melville or
James Joyce. And it is part of the tragic naivete of the middle class (brow)
writer, that he has not.

Literature, for the Negro writer, was always an example of "culture." Not
in the sense of the more impressive philosophical characteristics of a particular social group, but in the narrow sense of "cultivation" or "sophistication"
by an individual within that group. The Negro artist, because of his middle-
class background, carried the artificial social burden as the "best and most
intelligent" of Negroes and usually entered into the "serious" arts to exhibit
his familiarity with the social graces, i.e., as a method or means of displaying
his participation in the "serious" aspects of American culture. To be a writer
was to be "cultivated," in the stunted bourgeois sense of the word. It was also
to be a "quality" black man. It had nothing to do with the investigation of the

human soul. It was, and is, a social preoccupation rather than an aesthetic one. A rather daring way of status seeking. The cultivated Negro leaving those ineffectual philanthropies, Negro colleges, looked at literature merely as another way of gaining prestige in the white world for the Negro middle class. And the literary and artistic models were always those that could be socially acceptable to the white middle class, which automatically limited them to the most spiritually debilitated imitations of literature available. Negro music, to the middle class, black and white, was never socially acceptable. It was shunned by blacks ambitious of "waking up white," as low and degrading. It was shunned by their white models simply because it was produced by blacks. As one of my professors at Howard University protested one day, "It's amazing how much bad taste the blues display." Suffice it to say, it is in part exactly this "bad taste" that has continued to keep Negro music as vital as it is. The abandonment of one's local (i.e., place or group) emotional attachments in favor of the abstract emotional response of what is called "the general public" (which is notoriously white and middle class) has always been the great diluter of any Negro culture. "You're acting like a nigger," was the standard disparagement. I remember being chastised severely for daring to eat a piece of watermelon on the Howard campus. "Do you realize you're sitting near the highway?" is what the man said, "This is the capstone of Negro education." And it is too, in the sense that it teaches the Negro how to make out in the white society, using the agonizing overcompensation of pretending he's also white. James Baldwin's play, *The Amen Corner,* when it appeared at the Howard Players theatre, "set the speech department back ten years," an English professor groaned to me. The play depicted the lives of poor Negroes running a storefront church. Any reference to the Negro-ness of the American Negro has always been frowned upon by the black middle class in their frenzied dash toward the precipice of the American mainstream.

High art, first of all, must reflect the experiences of the human being, the emotional predicament of the man, as he exists, in the defined world of his being. It must be produced from the legitimate emotional resources of the soul in the world. It can *never* be produced by evading these resources or pretending that they do not exist. It can never be produced by appropriating the withered emotional responses of some strictly social idea of humanity. High art, and by this I mean any art that would attempt to describe or characterize some portion of the profound meaningfulness of human life with any finality or truth, cannot be based on the superficialities of human existence. It must issue from *real* categories of human activity, *truthful* accounts of human life, and not fancied accounts of the attainment of cultural privilege by some willingly preposterous apologists for one social "order" or another. Most of the formal literature produced by Negroes in America has never fulfilled these conditions. And aside from Negro music, it is only in the "popular traditions" of the so-called lower class Negro that these conditions are fulfilled as a basis for human life. And it is because of this "separation" between Negro life (as an emotional experience) and Negro art, that, say, Jack Johnson or Ray Robinson is a larger cultural hero than any Negro writer. It is because of this separation, even evasion, of the emotional experience of Negro life, that Jack Johnson is a more modern political symbol than most Negro writers. Johnson's life, as proposed, certainly, by his career, reflects much more accurately the symbolic yearnings for singular values among the great masses of Negroes than any black novelist has yet managed to convey. Where is the Negro-ness of a literature written in imitation of the meanest of social intelligences to be found in American culture, i.e., the white middle class? How can it even begin to express the emotional predicament of black Western man? Such a literature, even if its "characters" *are* black, takes on the emotional barrenness of its model, and the blackness of the characters is like the blackness of Al Jolson, an unconvincing device. It is like using black checkers instead of white. They are still checkers.

The development of the Negro's music was, as I said, direct and instinctive. It was the one vector out of African culture impossible to eradicate completely. The appearance of blues as a native *American* music signified in many ways the appearance of American Negroes where once there were African Negroes. The emotional fabric of the music was colored by the emergence of an American Negro culture. It signified that culture's strength and vitality. In the evolution of form in Negro music it is possible to see not only the evolution of the Negro as a cultural and social element of American culture, but also the evolution of that culture itself. The "Coon Shout" proposed one version of the American Negro—and of America; Ornette Coleman proposes another. But the point is that both these versions are accurate and informed with a legitimacy of emotional concern nowhere available in what is called "Negro Literature," and certainly not in the middlebrow literature of the white American.

The artifacts of African art and sculpture were consciously eradicated by slavery. Any African art that based its validity on the production of an artifact, i.e., some *material* manifestation such as a wooden statue or a woven cloth, had little chance of survival. It was only the more "abstract" aspects of African culture that could continue to exist in slave America. Africanisms

(margin note: SEPERATION REAL LIFE v. ART.)

still persist in the music, religion, and popular cultural traditions of American Negroes. However, it is not an African art American Negroes are responsible for, but an American one. The traditions of Africa must be utilized within the culture of the American Negro where they *actually* exist, and not because of a defensive rationalization about the *worth* of one's ancestors or an attempt to capitalize on the recent eminence of the "new" African nations. Africanisms do exist in Negro culture, but they have been so translated and transmuted by the American experience that they have become integral parts of that experience.

The American Negro has a definable and legitimate historical tradition, no matter how painful, in America, but it is the only place such a tradition exists, simply because America is the only place the American Negro exists. He is, as William Carlos Williams said, "A pure product of America." The paradox of the Negro experience in America is that it is a separate experience, but inseparable from the complete fabric of American life. The history of Western culture begins for the Negro with the importation of the slaves. It is almost as if all Western history before that must be strictly a learned concept. It is only the American experience that can be a persistent cultural catalyst for the Negro. In a sense, history for the Negro, before America, must remain an emotional abstraction. The cultural memory of Africa informs the Negro's life in America, but it is impossible to separate it from its American transformation. Thus, the Negro writer if he wanted to tap his legitimate cultural tradition should have done it by utilizing the entire spectrum of the American experience from the point of view of the emotional history of the black man in this country: as its victim and its chronicler. The soul of such a man, as it exists outside the boundaries of commercial diversion or artificial social pretense. But without a deep commitment to cultural relevance and intellectual purity this was impossible. The Negro as a writer, was always a social object, whether glorifying the concept of white superiority, as a great many early Negro writers did, or in crying out against it, as exemplified by the stock "protest" literature of the thirties. He never moved into the position where he could propose his own symbols, erect his own personal myths, as any great literature must. Negro writing was always "after the fact," i.e., based on known social concepts within the structure of bourgeois idealistic projections of "their America," and an emotional climate that never really existed.

The most successful fiction of most Negro writing is in its emotional content. The Negro protest novelist postures, and invents a protest quite amenable with the tradition of bourgeois American life. He never reaches the central core of the America which *can* cause such protest. The intellectual traditions of the white middle class prevent such exposure of reality, and the black imitators reflect this. The Negro writer on Negro life in America postures, and invents a Negro life, and an America to contain it. And even most of those who tried to rebel against that *invented* America were trapped because they had lost all touch with the reality of their experience within the *real* America, either because of the hidden emotional allegiance to the white middle class, or because they did not realize where the reality of their experience lay. When the serious Negro writer disdained the "middlebrow" model, as is the case with a few contemporary black American writers, he usually rushed headlong into the groves of the Academy, perhaps the most insidious and clever dispenser of middlebrow standards of excellence under the guise of "recognizable tradition." That such recognizable tradition is necessary goes without saying, but even from the great philosophies of Europe a contemporary usage must be established. No poetry has come out of England of major importance for forty years, yet there are would-be Negro poets who reject the gaudy excellence of 20th century American poetry in favor of disembowelled Academic models of second-rate English poetry, with the notion that somehow it is the only way poetry should be written. It would be better if such a poet listened to Bessie Smith sing *Gimme A Pigfoot*, or listened to the tragic verse of a Billie Holiday, than be content to imperfectly imitate the bad poetry of the ruined minds of Europe. And again, it is this striving for *respectability* that has it so. For an American, black or white, to say that some hideous imitation of Alexander Pope means more to him, emotionally, than the blues of Ray Charles or Lightnin' Hopkins, it would be required for him to have completely disappeared into the American Academy's vision of a Europeanized and colonial American culture, or to be lying. In the end, the same emotional sterility results. It is somehow much more tragic for the black man.

A Negro literature, to be a legitimate product of the Negro experience in America, must get at that experience in exactly the terms America has proposed for it, in its most ruthless identity. Negro reaction to America is as deep a part of America as the root causes of that reaction, and it is impossible to accurately describe that reaction in terms of the American middle class; because for them, the Negro has never really existed, never been glimpsed in anything even approaching the complete reality of his humanity. The Negro writer has to go from where he actually is, completely outside of that conscious white myopia. That the Negro does exist is the point, and as an element of American culture he is completely misunderstood by Americans.

The middlebrow, commercial Negro writer assures the white American that, in fact, he doesn't exist, and that if he does, he does so within the perfectly predictable fingerpainting of white bourgeois sentiment and understanding. Nothing could be further from the truth. The Creoles of New Orleans resisted "Negro" music for a time as raw and raucous, because they thought they had found a place within the white society which would preclude their being Negroes. But they were unsuccessful in their attempts to "disappear" because the whites themselves reminded them that they were still, for all their assimilation, "just coons." And this seems to me an extremely important idea, since it is precisely this bitter insistence that has kept what can be called "Negro Culture" a brilliant amalgam of diverse influences. There was always a border beyond which the Negro could not go, whether musically or socially. There was always a possible limitation to any dilution or excess of cultural or spiritual reference. The Negro could not ever become white and that was his strength; at some point, always, he could not participate in the dominant tenor of the white man's culture, yet he came to understand that culture as well as the white man. It was at this juncture that he had to make use of other resources, whether African, subcultural, or hermetic. And it was this boundary, this no-man's-land, that provided the logic and beauty of his music. And this is the only way for the Negro artist to provide his version of America—from that no-man's-land outside the mainstream. A no-man's-land, a black country, completely invisible to white America, but so essentially part of it as to stain its whole being an ominous gray. Were there really a Negro literature, now it could flower. At this point when the whole of Western society might go up in flames, the Negro remains an integral part of that society, but continually outside it, a figure like Melville's Bartleby. He is an American, capable of identifying emotionally with the fantastic cultural ingredients of this society, but he is also, forever, outside that culture, an invisible strength within it, an observer. If there is ever a Negro literature, it must disengage itself from the weak, heinous elements of the culture that spawned it, and use its very existence as evidence of a more profound America. But as long as the Negro writer contents himself with the imitation of the useless ugly inelegance of the stunted middle-class mind, academic or popular, and refuses to look around him and "tell it like it is"—preferring the false prestige of the black bourgeosie or the deceitful "acceptance" of *buy and sell* America, something never included in the legitimate cultural tradition of "his people"—he will be a failure, and what is worse, not even a significant failure. Just another dead American.

George E. Kent

Ethnic Impact in American Literature:

Reflections on a Course

(1967)

What I wish to describe is the idea of the literary section of an inter-disciplinary course, its patterns and critical approaches. First, I shall briefly outline the complete course and practical aim; then devote the rest of the essay to the literary aspects.

In the summer of 1966, under NDEA sponsorship, Wesleyan University in Middletown, Connecticut, offered an interdisciplinary course designed to give high school English teachers in newly integrated urban schools an intensive introduction to the tensions, pressures, and values of Negro culture and personality and some exposure to the historical and value patterns of other minorities who had found a place in the "mainstream." The sections of the course were entitled: "The Ethnic Writer in Urban American Culture" and "A Psychological Analysis of the Sociological Literature of the American Negro." Dr. Ronald Forgus, Chairman of the Psychology Department, Lake Forest College, Lake Forest, Illinois, taught the Psychological Analysis, and challenged the teachers to evaluate their role as teachers and counselors of Negro students. Mrs. Alberta Lindsey of Rust College, Holly Springs, Mississippi, served as staff consultant, with the task of helping the teachers of the course to maintain touch with the living density of Negro life and history and mediating relevant issues between teachers and students. There were also numerous special consultants for workshop sessions, and a bibliography that enabled some novels and autobiographies to be studied from both a psychological and a literary point of view. The response from the students in a follow-up study indicates that a considerable impact was made upon their subsequent practices and planning.

However, the primary focus of this paper is upon the literary subject

This essay first appeared in *College Language Association Journal*, 11 (1967).

matter and certain critical reflections that, for the most part, informed the course, but in a few instances were in gestation as the course developed.

To include literary works of other minorities and to give something of the backgrounds of the minorities were of the first importance. What was shed immediately is the popular view: that the entry of the Irish, the Jew and others into American culture was a simple matter of hard work and ingenuity. Instead, the reader encounters intense pathos, the ingredients of the tragicomic and the tragic—and the fortuitous. One sees blood upon the floor—both of the body and of the spirit and the lip-sucking bewilderment at the shattering of identity and the threat of stillbirth, and one remembers all those blank and baffled peasant faces that survive now mainly as museum footnotes. Through Oscar Handlin's *The Uprooted* and other sources, I tried to give a careful picture of the pain and poignancy of the immigrant experience.

Taking the peak period of immigration during the Nineteenth and early Twentieth Centuries, I tried to illustrate the institutional supports that survived the abandoned homeland and nurtured personality, organization, and the desperate thrust for adjustment. For example, the political experience of the Irishman developed under the extreme pressure over several centuries in his homeland, the supports behind the family, the rallying point of the Catholic church in social and political affairs, the existence of a relatively simple American economy abounding in jobs for unskilled labor, and the American Civil War, in which the Irishman, according to Shannon in his history *The American Irish* was able to transform the stereotype of the brawling, drunken Irishman into that of the manly, aggressive, fighting patriot, were aspects of the cultural supports that aided his integration and assimilation. Given the foregoing supports, the Irish were able to create Irish power. In the case of the Eastern Jews, obviously, the tight religious and social culture brought from the homeland, the self-government in the Tshtetl, the commercial experience—70 percent being skilled workers, and the level of literacy, were powerful means of sustaining personality and achieving transcendence. Thus another advantage of treating other minorities and their backgrounds is the emergence of the self-evident fact, so frequently ignored: that although the problems and adjustments of all minorities to American culture are related, there is also the stark evidence of uniqueness.

The first ethnic group presented was entitled, "The Anglo-Saxon as a Conscious Minority." What do I mean by "Anglo-Saxons?" I use the term loosely to include those of English descent who dominated this country and the so-called assimilables—many who scrambled upon boats rather subsequent to the *Mayflower* but upon arrival immediately felt what sociologists used to call "a consciousness of kind." I used the expression also to indicate the moral climate the immigrants were integrating into, for the climate is an important ingredient conveniently overlooked in the term *mainstream*. Many major statements of American literature reflect the climate, through characters of a rather intense self-consciousness frequently producing the greatest intensities, revulsions and loneliness: Ishmael contemplating the sea; Emerson shouting feverishly about the glories of the private citadel; Walt Whitman loving too compulsively and vociferously for the comfort of the beloved; Huck Finn begging peace from the river; and Thoreau, at Walden Pond, pointing out that loneliness is not really loneliness.

What I actually chose was Henry Adams, *The Autobiography of Henry Adams* and the complete William Faulkner's "The Bear." The works were first approached in the purer literary fashion and then used to analyze the self-proclaimed and self-congratulated role of the American Anglo-Saxon as the bearer of Western culture, in its pristine forms. The values analyzed were as follows:

1. the drive to mastery over nature, and the intrepid manipulation of nature
2. the drive of massive and intricate social organization
3. the possession of a problem solving optimism
4. the possession of a status endowing religion, Christianity
5. versions of rationality and commonsense as effective tools in dealing with reality
6. the compulsive drive for intense individualism and self-consciousness

Culturally, it seems to me, it is precisely the roles of *The Autobiography of Henry Adams* and Faulkner's "The Bear" to register an artistic sense of the shakiness of the values at the very center. Thus, Henry Adams, living at a time when the back edge of the values cut toward the possessor, agonized over the breakdown of puritanical and Eighteenth Century values, and suggested a consequent loss, at the center, of moral force—a world collapsing under the weight of the American Civil War, rampant commercialism, international intrigue and complexity, and the general shattering of spiritual unity. The impact of the *Autobiography* upon T. S. Eliot and other writers of the 1920s is well known.

Faulkner is concerned with a similar loss of order and value. Isaac, of "The Old People" and "The Bear," is concerned about the corrupting effects of the drive to mastery over nature, the cancerous degeneration of the social organization, the intrinsic meaning of Christianity, the development of intense self-consciousness, versions of rationality and commonsense, the destructiveness of rampaging commercialism, and a general degeneration of human value. The foregoing, of course, among other concerns. Nor is Isaac the only one of Faulkner's boys to fret and fuss and worry over such things—indeed the art of each work in which his boys appear shows them to be, themselves, victims of an intense, neutralizing, and thus crippling self-consciousness. What all this adds up to is an awareness of the loss of the order based upon the Southern aristocratic deal, and of the things that had festered at its roots even while it was sending pridefully skyward the glossy shoots of its culture.

Some such set of moral complexities as above confronted immigrants who greeted the Statue of Liberty during the peak immigration periods. Some such picture was observed by Negroes with what Faulkner frequently called "dark inscrutable eyes."

If we look at such a work as James T. Farrell's *Studs Lonigan* trilogy, we get an artistic projection of the working out of values at a particular moment of self-consciousness, the very moment when a group can look hind and fore and ask what is it all coming to. The moment before the loss of distinctive identity. At such a time, a rare richness pours from the artist into the American literary stream; the values by which the group has survived and seems to have prevailed and the values of the "mainstream" and the national and international forces are placed under intense artistic scrutiny, thereby forming a highly tensioned symbiosis. Leslie Fiedler, speaking with particular reference to the Jewish Community in his essay "The Breakthrough: The American Jewish Novelist and the Fictional Image of the Jew,"[1] states that the appearance of a major writer to communicate a group's dilemma is evidence that the inward life of the group is well enough defined to sustain him, and "to provide him with something substantial against which to define himself in protest."[2] What one hears in the art speech, I think, is that the very success of "having arrived" has intensified the encounter with Nothingness—that age-old enemy of Mankind, who so long ago slithered into the Garden of Eden. "Man, I'm still here," he now says in elegant tones, standing upon the porch of the suburban or ex-urban homes, staring out of the neon lights of his eyes, and reaching forth his cool, enfolding arms. And thus neither the values of the dominant culture nor those of the minority culture find an expressway to utopia. If we understand such ambiguities, we take a step toward understanding the ambiguities and growls of many Negro writers.

Well. I suggest that in the *Studs Lonigan* trilogy one sees and hears a series of ceremonies and rituals and institutions and values that had helped to sustain the Irish immigrant, but no longer energized his confrontation with reality. The current sputters into futile sparks. Pugnacity loses itself in merely brutal and degrading displays; home is merely a place of resounding pronouncements; the father parrots the romanticized values of an olden time and is simply bewildered because the sure-fire principles create no flaming inspiration for his sons; the mother simpers about the children; the parochial school acts out rituals that communicate brutality and stupidity only; and the church spouts a bigoted conception of Americanism, womanhood, manhood, nationality, racism, etc. In the context, the individual Studs Lonigan flounders, alienated, but not quite able to know why: corrupted and perverted is his sense of beauty, manhood, and purpose. Shortly after Farrell's portrait appeared, the Irish moved into the "mainstream."

For the Eastern Jewish patterns, several writers and works are penetrating. Irving Howe's introductory essay to *A Treasury of Yiddish Literature* analyzes the literary tradition. Leslie Fiedler, in several essays; Michael Gold in *Jews Without Money;* Henry Roth in *Call It Sleep;* and Bernard Malamud, in general, were extremely helpful. I would add to them random readings in *Commentary,* Jewish history, and the *Old Testament.* The class was assigned Bernard Malamud's *The Assistant,* a novel that ambiguously places the values deriving from the central works of Jewish culture alongside the values of the optimistic "mainstream" American culture. The truth that emerges is in the tension of those values—rather than in either set alone. Morris Bober, the repository of Jewish values, represents the law of the Torah and the pain of values won in the cauldron of Russia and preserved in the Tshtetl, the little settlements to which most Eastern Jews had been confined; the acceptance of suffering as a way of life; the aspiration to justice and honesty—virtues expressed tragically and tragicomically, all in the face of an optimistic American culture in which the good life was supposed to drop upon the ambitious, the imaginative, the resourceful, the beautiful, and the brave. On the one hand, Morris Bober powerfully symbolizes the value of suffering: "What do you suffer for?" Frank (the Italian) asks. "I suffer for you," Morris said calmly.[3] Frank Alpine, who becomes a Jew, illustrates the need in one's being for the ordering law of suffering. Asked again by Frank what he means, Morris replies: "I mean you suffer for me."[4] But on the other hand, Morris has a daughter, Helen, confronting directly the strains and tensions of American culture, a person who is beginning to reflect the intense American individuality and self-consciousness—and yet must love the old man and his values that simply make life confusing to her. Upon Morris's death, she confesses that he was a somewhat ridiculous and likeable man, but not admirable. "He made himself a victim. He could, with a little more courage, have been more than he was." Such is the situation as Helen Bober and her like stand poised to enter the "mainstream."

When we speak of Negro cultural values, we encounter certain liberals and some Negroes who are wont to say that what we are talking about is habits deriving from slavery and the ghettos—and let's get rid of them real fast, wholesale. Their attitude accepts unconditionally those unrelieved sociological images of the maimed and the diseased and the perverted. The images are powerful because, like frozen food in the supermarkets, they package easily, market easily, and are arranged easily on the shelves of the compartments of our minds; but they seem to me to be insufficiently related to the density and complexity of reality. It is not necessary, either, to assume a complete dichotomy between Negro experience and the values of Western culture or to become shiny-eyed over some sort of mystique. Cultural values are won in the hard crucible of experience, the dirt and the grime, as well as the sky and the far horizon. Perhaps what Negroes are up against is the age-old problem of the necessity for, not a casting out of hard won values, but rather a transvaluation of values. (Patience, for example, does make a good slave, but also, creatively and aggressively exercised, the builder, the inventor, and the revolutionist.) Here are some of the key values that seem frequently to be reflected by Negro folk literature and by outstanding Negro writers:

1. The insistence upon a tough-minded grip upon reality
2. A willingness to confront the self searchingly and even with laughter
3. Patience and endurance
4. Humor as a tool for transcendence
5. A sort of deadend courage, and not so deadend
6. An acceptance of the role of suffering in retaining one's humanity and in retaining some perspective on the humanity of the oppressor
7. A high development of dissimulation and camouflage
8. A sense of something more than this world and of its rhythms
9. A deep sense of the inexorable limitations of life and all that we associate with the tragic and tragicomic vision
10. Ceremonies of poise in a nonrational universe (The hipsters and the cool-cats play an endless satire upon Western assumptions of rationality.)

"Who wills to be a Negro?" cries Ralph Ellison, the outstanding writer, in *Shadow and Act*. "I do!"[5]

And he is not alone.

Obviously, there is not time to illustrate in detail. I suggest very careful attention to Ralph Ellison's *Shadow and Act,* which despite some excesses in emphasizing the positive, is a brilliant theory of culture. The varieties of folk expression—slave narratives, spirituals, the blues, work-songs, etc., tend to embody some such set of values. They can be heard if one listens not merely to the contents of the works but also to what the *form* is saying. The better Negro writers frequently express several of the values. Charles W. Chestnutt's [sic] Josh Green in *The Marrow of Tradition* and Bud Johnson in his *The Colonel's Dream,* the latter character a victim of the convict lease system, are types of rock-bottom courage. Some of the best poems of Langston Hughes reflect the poise amidst the nonrationality of the Western system. Such conscious artists as Richard Wright, James Baldwin and Ralph Ellison tend to occupy the whole spread of values. Richard Wright's sharp negative approach to some Negro values, I found very useful, since all values have negative aspects and sometimes cut back at the possessor. In several short stories in *Uncle Tom's Children,* Wright tended to see effectiveness in the Negro culture, although the values are usually in tension with the mores of the broader culture and within the Negro character, himself. In *Native Son* most Negro values are seen negatively against the background of urban onslaught. In *Black Boy,* the viewpoint is negative, as Wright notoriously said:

> Whenever I thought of the essential bleakness of black life in America, I knew that Negroes had never been allowed to catch the full spirit of Western civilization, that they lived somehow in it but not of it. And when I brooded upon the cultural barrenness of black life, I wondered if clean, positive tenderness, love, honor, and the capacity to remember were native with man.[6]

Wright is particularly offended with the tendency to camouflage and dissimulation, the training away from curiosity, the otherworldliness, the repression, engendered in the culture. Certainly, one great value of Wright is that he very early saw the destructiveness of the modern city upon a people ill-supported by the institutions and devices, which most immigrant groups could count upon. He is particularly useful in his portrayal of the Negro cultural values under tension from their clash with American middle-class structure.

Although I am sympathetic to Ellison's argument that his own inspiration comes from sources broader, more varied, and richer than Wright, and that black writers should not be considered as simply developing in a kind of black apostolic succession, I freely used him and Baldwin to illustrate a different and more positive approach to black cultural values. As early as 1945 in the *Antioch Review,* Ellison in "Richard Wright's Blues" tried to come to terms with Wright's viewpoint:

> Wright knows perfectly well that Negro life is a by-product of Western civilization, and that in it, if only one possesses the humanity and humility to see, are to be discovered all those impulses, tendencies, life and cultural forms to be found elsewhere in Western society.[7]

In an early short story, "That I Had the Wings," Ellison portrayed a young boy arising to a sense of self-consciousness and aspiration, who is rebuked for his aspirations by an aunt, who invokes the suppressive element of Negro culture. (That's for white folks.) In "Flying Home," a reverse situation occurs: a character who literally must crash his plane and land in the care of the folk values before he can gain the strength to confront Western culture. Incidentally, the airplane is a great Western symbol for both Wright and Ellison. In *Invisible Man,* we have a veritable textbook concerning the power of Negro cultural values, and a considerable satire focused upon the negative aspects: particularly the drive to dissimulation and camouflage. It may be said that the invisible narrator tends to gain power and identity as he negotiates a correct relationship with his own culture and learns the limitations of Western values—as well as their challenge.

Despite the title of the course, The Ethnic Writer in Urban American Culture, I tried to make clear that the tensions of which America is now conscious did not spring to birth with the 1954 Supreme Court Decision on school desegregation. So, in relationship to the protest tradition, we read such works as *David Walker's Appeal,* a pre–Civil War book with a Malcolm X scream and venom; *Narrative of the Life of Frederick Douglass,* for some artistic sense of the meaning of slavery; *Up From Slavery by Booker T. Washington,* with the perspective broadened by Douglass's *Narrative* and DuBois's *The Souls of Black Folks* (for it is mandatory that the perspective be broadened). We read James Weldon Johnson's *The Autobiography of an Ex-Colored Man,* representative poets since 1900, and selections of prose where novels were out of print. Of the so-called Harlem Renaissance novelists, only Claude McKay's *Home to Harlem* is in print and thus available for general assignment, although individual members of the class read such other novels of the period as were available in the Wesleyan University Library. For the folk tradition, Langston Hughes and Arna Bontemps, *The Book of Negro Folklore* was essential. As to very contemporary writing, Wright, Ellison, and Baldwin, and Herbert Hill's anthology, *Soon One Morning,* were important sources.

For background, a history of the Negro is mandatory, since the American educational system fosters historical ignorance regarding Negroes and leaves most people unprepared for the simplest intelligent discussion of issues. John Hope Franklin's *From Slavery to Freedom* is, on all grounds, preferable. There were many reference works on literary and sociological background, and my preference, in sociology was for some old-timers who do *not* make a fetish of a kind of statistical orientation that seems to flatten out both reality and humanity and to turn tendencies into absolute with jet speed: Charles S. Johnson, *Shadow of the Plantation,* Hortense Powdermaker, *After Freedom;* Allison Davis, *Deep South;* and Horace Cayton, *Black Metropolis.* On slavery, Kenneth Stampp's *The Peculiar Institution* is extremely useful—as is Stanley Elkin's *Slavery,* although I think that his theory of a widespread existence of real-life Samboes founders in the face of a single simple question: How could his Samboes, of induced imbecility, have created the body of folk materials that we have, with its insights on the human condition and the Creator?

Although the attempt was made to place the literature in a variety of contexts, the stress was upon a rigorous literary criticism. The question that the class was supposed to answer for each work was whether the author seemed to have penetrated conventional assumptions about reality suffi-ciently to render the privateness and complexity of the Negro experience. Autobiography was useful in indicating objectively the complexity of Negro life, for often autobiography pointed to a complexity which the artist had not imaged fully in novels and other literary forms. The following autobiog-raphies have very complex situations that have unexploited possibilities: James Weldon Johnson, *Along This Way;* Claude McKay, *A Long Ways From Home,* Zora Neale Hurston's *Dust Tracks on a Road;* Richard Wright, *Black Boy* and "I Tried to be a Communist"; Pauli Murray, *Proud Shoes;* Katherine Dunham, *A Touch of Innocence;* and Horace Cayton, *Long Old Road.* A par-ticular value of the critical approach is that it tends to put such popular, misleading labels as "assimilationism" and "cultural dualism" into proper perspective, and lead to a deeper discovery of the literature.

Such were the inner patterns of the course, in its attempt to render the imaginative sense of minority groups' experiences as they mounted high points of self-consciousness. The pain of this consciousness is unalleviated by the fact that the group leaves its impress upon the dominant culture, and even as it loses the one-to-one contact between its values and "reality." Later, it assumes outwardly the contours of the Anglo-Saxon, and a new generation arises who remembers only faintly the travails of Joseph and the tribe, and who as descendant can enter the tragic experience of the fathers only in the most external ceremonies. Certainly, a good deal of tragic meaning is lost which would deepen our lives.

The Negro minority stands out in stark uniqueness. Sociologically, we may well ponder the blunt words of Charles E. Silberman in *Crisis in Black and White:* "The European Ethnic groups . . . could move into the main-stream of American life without forcing before hand any drastic rearrangements of attitudes and institutions. For the Negro to do so, however, will require the most radical changes in the whole structure of American society."[8] Literarily, we may well ponder two symbols of terrifying power near the end of Chapter 10 in Ralph Ellison's *Invisible Man:* the iron bridge of technology which threatens to become autonomous to the destruction of all humanistic values and the nightmare of castration experienced by the invisible narrator:

> But now they [all opponents to identity] came forward with a knife, holding me; and I felt the bright red pain and they took the two bloody blobs and cast them over the bridge, and out of my anguish I saw them curve up and catch beneath the apex of the curving arch of the bridge, to hang there, dripping down through the sunlight into the dark red water. And while the others laughed, before my pain-sharpened eyes the whole world was slowly turning red.
> "Now you're free of illusions," Jack said . . .[9]

Without illusions, the invisible narrator feels painful and empty, but points out that it is not only "my generations wasting upon the water—"

> "But your sun . . ."
> "Yes?"
> "And your moon . . ."
> "He's crazy!"
> "Your world . . ."
> "I knew he was a mystic idealist!" Tobitt said.
> "Still," I said, "there's your universe, and that drip-drop upon the water you hear is all the history you've made, all you're going to make."[10]

As slave of technology, the scene implies in part, the American idealistic struggles and proclamations become an exercise in narcissism and abstract universalism. One may hear this castration rage from the frustrated ghettos crescendoing out of today's television news.

And finally, the adaptability of the course. The interdisciplinary approach is very useful, although not indispensable. The materials combine easily with history or sociology or psychology. The full value of the course, I think, is best delivered if the instructors agree, from the outset, upon the kinds of faculties and truth which each discipline emphasizes: the more scientific emphasizing the rational, categorizing, and data-collecting faculties; the literary emphasizing imaginative sweep and the attempt to recapture the contradictory density and complexity of the stream of life. The Negro father or family in sociology, for example, is not interchangeable with the Negro father or family in literature, and the course is immediately reduced if the distinction is not clear. Obviously, the course can be offered in the conventional one instructor pattern. Some version of the course, whichever approach is used, would fill an alarming gap in the high school curriculum where Negro and white students tend to confront the Negro experience as simply a blank or a problem.

Part of the adapting is in terms of people. For the white student, the sheer speed of change in public surface tends to make unrecognizable, quaint or esoteric tendencies and patterns that had their grip upon white lives well up into the Twentieth Century. Religious fundamentalism and extreme poverty are examples, and may be placed in proper context by reference to various American writers of great power. The teacher should also be wary of any occasional tendency to substitute a stereotyped, push-button liberalism for literary understanding. For a black student, in integrated schools, the lethargy of social change may influence his reception of a particular work. The situations presented in the hard-hitting naturalistic style of many outstanding Negro writers may still be very close by, uncomfortably so—or conversely, the situations may seem very different from the particular high school student's middle-class environment. The answer is still the placement of the writing in the appropriate context, an effort required for teaching literature, anyway. One useful context is that of the folk values, but there are also plenty of general American contexts to be drawn upon.

The exciting aspect of the course is that it utilizes a very urgent motivation of both black and white students: To get some deeper than conventional sense of America and their identity. The vanguard of students, in general, are seeking through a variety of confrontations: the campus and various public issues claim their passionate involvement. A growing number of black students are demanding the right to a positive identity that takes no upward slant toward middle-class values. The polite search is over. The vanguard have sought their identity in the backroads of Mississippi, and often under the clubs of jailers who attempted to imprint their identity in blood. They have sought it in the souls of gnarled and starving sharecroppers and headragged mothers. What they seem to be seeking is a means, not merely to fit into the Western world, but to negotiate manly terms with it. The actions of the vanguards have probably done little to shake up our lethargic curriculums. Maybe the question that we ought to face is whether through some courses that emphasize relevance, without abating a jot of universality, intellectual rigor, and critical analysis, academia can speak more intimately to some of the intellectual hunger of our students and time.

Notes

1   Joseph J. Waldmeir, ed., *Recent American Fiction* (Boston, 1963), 95.
2   Ibid.
3   Bernard Malamud, *The Assistant* (New York, 1957), 99.
4   Ibid., 100.
5   Ralph Ellison, *Shadow and Act* (New York, 1964), 132.
6   Richard Wright, *Black Boy* (New York, 1945), 33.
7   Ralph Ellison, *Shadow and Act*, 93.
8   Charles E. Silberman, *Crisis in Black and White* (New York, 1964), 43.
9   Ralph Ellison, *Invisible Man* (New York, 1952), 493.
10   Ibid.

Larry Neal

The Black Arts Movement

(1968)

1.

The Black Arts Movement is radically opposed to any concept of the artist that alienates him from his community. Black Art is the aesthetic and spiritual sister of the Black Power concept. As such, it envisions an art that speaks directly to the needs and aspirations of Black America. In order to perform this task, the Black Arts Movement proposes a radical reordering of the western cultural aesthetic. It proposes a separate symbolism, mythology, critique, and iconology. The Black Arts and the Black Power concept both relate broadly to the Afro-American's desire for self-determination and nationhood. Both concepts are nationalistic. One is concerned with the relationship between art and politics; the other with the art of politics.

Recently, these two movements have begun to merge: the political values inherent in the Black Power concept are now finding concrete expression in the aesthetics of Afro-American dramatists, poets, choreographers, musicians, and novelists. A main tenet of Black Power is the necessity for Black people to define the world in their own terms. The Black artist has made the same point in the context of aesthetics. The two movements postulate that there are in fact and in spirit two Americas—one black, one white. The Black artist takes this to mean that his primary duty is to speak to the spiritual and cultural needs of Black people. Therefore, the main thrust of this new breed of contemporary writers is to confront the contradictions arising out of the Black man's experience in the racist West. Currently, these writers are reevaluating western aesthetics, the traditional role of the writer, and the social

This essay first appeared in *The Drama Review*, 12.4 (1968).

function of art. Implicit in this reevaluation is the need to develop a "Black aesthetic." It is the opinion of many Black writers, I among them, that the Western aesthetic has run its course: it is impossible to construct anything meaningful within its decaying structure. We advocate a cultural revolution in art and ideas. The cultural values inherent in western history must either be radicalized or destroyed, and we will probably find that even radicalization is impossible. In fact, what is needed is a whole new system of ideas. Poet Don L. Lee expresses it:

> . . . We must destroy Faulkner, dick, jane, and other perpetuators of evil. It's time for DuBois, Nat Turner, and Kwame Nkrumah. As Frantz Fanon points out: destroy the culture and you destroy the people. This must not happen. Black artists are culture stabilizers; bringing back old values, and introducing new ones. Black Art will talk to the people and with the will of the people stop impending "protective custody."

The Black Arts Movement eschews "protest" literature. It speaks directly to Black people. Implicit in the concept of "protest" literature, as Brother Knight has made clear, is an appeal to white morality:

> Now any Black man who masters the technique of his particular art form, who adheres to the white aesthetic, and who directs his work toward a white audience is, in one sense, protesting. And implicit in the act of protest is the belief that a change will be forthcoming once the masters are aware of the protestor's "grievance" (the very word connotes begging, supplications to the gods). Only when that belief has faded and protestings end, will Black art begin.

Brother Knight also has some interesting statements about the development of a "Black aesthetic":

> Unless the Black artist establishes a "Black aesthetic" he will have no future at all. To accept the white aesthetic is to accept and validate a society that will not allow him to live. The Black artist must create new forms and new values, sing new songs (or purify old ones); and along with other Black authorities, he must create a new history, new symbols, myths and legends (and purify old ones by fire). And the Black artist, in creating his own aesthetic, must be accountable for it only to the Black people. Further, he must hasten his own dissolution as an individual (in the Western sense)—painful though the process may be, having been breast-fed the poison of "individual experience."

When we speak of a "Black aesthetic" several things are meant. First, we assume that there is already in existence the basis for such an aesthetic. Essentially, it consists of an African-American cultural tradition. But this aesthetic is finally, by implication, broader than that tradition. It encompasses most of the useable elements of Third World culture. The motive behind the Black aesthetic is the destruction of the white thing, the destruction of white ideas, and white ways of looking at the world. The new aesthetic is mostly predicated on an Ethics which asks the question: whose vision of the world is finally more meaningful, ours or the white oppressors'? What is truth? Or more precisely, whose truth shall we express, that of the oppressed or of the oppressors? These are basic questions. Black intellectuals of previous decades failed to ask them. Further, national and international affairs demand that we appraise the world in terms of our own interests. It is clear that the question of human survival is at the core of contemporary experience. The Black artist must address himself to this reality in the strongest terms possible. In a context of world upheaval, ethics and aesthetics must interact positively and be consistent with the demands for a more spiritual world. Consequently, the Black Arts Movement is an ethical movement. Ethical, that is, from the viewpoint of the oppressed. And much of the oppression confronting the Third World and Black America is directly traceable to the Euro-American cultural sensibility. This sensibility, anti-human in nature, has, until recently, dominated the psyches of most Black artists and intellectuals; it must be destroyed before the Black creative artist can have a meaningful role in the transformation of society.

It is this natural reaction to an alien sensibility that informs the cultural attitudes of the Black Arts and the Black Power movement. It is a profound ethical sense that makes a Black artist question a society in which art is one thing and the actions of men another. The Black Arts Movement believes that your ethics and your aesthetics are one. That the contradictions between ethics and aesthetics in western society is symptomatic of a dying culture.

The term "Black Arts" is of ancient origin, but it was first used in a positive sense by LeRoi Jones:

> We are unfair
> And unfair
> We are black magicians
> Black arts we make
> in black labs of the heart

The fair are fair
and deathly white

The day will not save them
And we own the night

There is also a section of the poem "Black Dada Nihilismus" that carries the same motif. But a fuller amplification of the nature of the new aesthetics appears in the poem "Black Art":

Poems are bullshit unless they are
teeth or trees or lemons piled
on a step. Or black ladies dying
of men leaving nickel hearts
beating them down. Fuck poems
and they are useful, would they shoot
come at you, love what you are,
breathe like wrestlers, or shudder
strangely after peeing. We want live
words of the hip world, live flesh &
coursing blood. Hearts and Brains
Souls splintering fire. We want poems
like fists beating niggers out of Jocks
or dagger poems in the slimy bellies
of the owner-jews . . .

Poetry is a concrete function, an action. No more abstractions. Poems are physical entities: fists, daggers, airplane poems, and poems that shoot guns. Poems are transformed from physical objects into personal forces:

. . . Put it on him poem. Strip him naked
to the world. Another bad poem cracking
steel knuckles in a jewlady's mouth
Poem scream poison gas on breasts in green berets . . .

Then the poem affirms the integral relationship between Black Art and Black people:

. . . Let Black people understand
that they are the lovers and the sons
of lovers and warriors and sons

> of warriors Are poems & poets &
> all the loveliness here in the world

It ends with the following lines, a central assertion in both the Black Arts Movement and the philosophy of Black Power:

> We want a black poem. And a
> Black World.
> Let the world be a Black Poem
> And let All Black People Speak This Poem
> Silently
> Or LOUD

The poem comes to stand for the collective conscious and unconscious of Black America—the real impulse in back of the Black Power movement, which is the will toward self-determination and nationhood, a radical reordering of the nature and function of both art and the artist.

2.

In the spring of 1964, LeRoi Jones, Charles Patterson, William Patterson, Clarence Reed, Johnny Moore, and a number of other Black artists opened the Black Arts Repertoire Theatre School. They produced a number of plays including Jones' *Experimental Death Unit # One, Black Mass, Jello,* and *Dutchman.* They also initiated a series of poetry readings and concerts. These activities represented the most advanced tendencies in the movement and were of excellent artistic quality. The Black Arts School came under immediate attack by the New York power structure. The Establishment, fearing Black creativity, did exactly what it was expected to do—it attacked the theatre and all of its values. In the meantime, the school was granted funds by OEO through HARYOU-ACT. Lacking a cultural program itself, HARYOU turned to the only organization which addressed itself to the needs of the community. In keeping with its "revolutionary" cultural ideas, the Black Arts Theatre took its programs into the streets of Harlem. For three months, the theatre presented plays, concerts, and poetry readings to the people of the community. Plays that shattered the illusions of the American body politic, and awakened Black people to the meaning of their lives.

Then the hawks from the OEO moved in and chopped off the funds. Again, this should have been expected. The Black Acts Theatre stood in radical opposition to the feeble attitudes about culture of the "War On Poverty" bureaucrats. And later, because of internal problems, the theatre was forced to close. But the Black Arts group proved that the community could be served by a valid and dynamic art. It also proved that there was a definite need for a cultural revolution in the Black community.

With the closing of the Black Arts Theatre, the implications of what Brother Jones and his colleagues were trying to do took on even more significance. Black Art groups sprang up on the West Coast and the idea spread to Detroit, Philadelphia, Jersey City, New Orleans, and Washington, D.C. Black Arts movements began on the campuses of San Francisco State College, Fisk University, Lincoln University, Hunter College in the Bronx, Columbia University, and Oberlin College. In Watts, after the rebellion, Maulana Karenga welded the Black Arts Movement into a cohesive cultural ideology which owed much to the work of LeRoi Jones. Karenga sees culture as the most important element in the struggle for self-determination:

> Culture is the basis of all ideas, images and actions. To move is to move culturally, i.e. by a set of values given to you by your culture.
>
> Without a culture Negroes are only a set of reactions to white people.

The seven criteria for culture are:
1. Mythology
2. History
3. Social Organization
4. Political Organization
5. Economic Organization
6. Creative Motif
7. Ethos

In drama, LeRoi Jones represents the most advanced aspects of the movement. He is its prime mover and chief designer. In a poetic essay entitled "The Revolutionary Theatre," he outlines the iconology of the movement:

> The Revolutionary Theatre should force change: it should be change. (All their faces turned into the lights and you work on them black nigger magic, and cleanse them at having seen the ugliness. And if the beautiful see themselves, they will love themselves.) We are preaching virtue again, but by that to mean NOW, toward what seems the most constructive use of the word.

The theatre that Jones proposes is inextricably linked to the Afro-American political dynamic. And such a link is perfectly consistent with

Black America's contemporary demands. For theatre is potentially the most social of all of the arts. It is an integral part of the socializing process. It exists in direct relationship to the audience it claims to serve. The decadence and inanity of the contemporary American theatre is an accurate reflection of the state of American society. Albee's *Who's Afraid of Virginia Woolf?* is very American: sick white lives in a homosexual hell hole. The theatre of white America is escapist, refusing to confront concrete reality. Into this cultural emptiness come the musicals, an up-tempo version of the same stale lives. And the use of Negroes in such plays as *Hello Dolly* and *Hallelujah Baby* does not alert their nature; it compounds the problem. These plays are simply hipper versions of the minstrel show. They present Negroes acting out the hang-ups of middle-class white America. Consequently, the American theatre is a palliative prescribed to bourgeois patients who refuse to see the world as it is. Or, more crucially, as the world sees them. It is no accident, therefore, that the most "important" plays come from Europe—Brecht, Weiss, and Ghelderode. And even these have begun to run dry.

The Black Arts theatre, the theatre of LeRoi Jones, is a radical alternative to the sterility of the American theatre. It is primarily a theatre of the Spirit, confronting the Black man in his interaction with his brothers and with the white thing.

> Our theatre will show victims so that their brothers in the audience will be better able to understand that they are brothers of victims, and that they themselves are blood brothers. And what we show must cause the blood to rush, so that prerevolutionary temperaments will be bathed in this blood, and it will cause their deepest souls to move, and they will find themselves tensed and clenched, even ready to die, at what the soul has been taught. We will scream and cry, murder, run through the streets in agony, if it means some soul will be moved, moved to actual life understanding of what the world is, and what it ought to be. We are preaching virtue and feeling, and a natural sense of the self in the world. All men live in the world, and the world ought to be a place for them to live.

[margin note: ART BLACK SHOULD WAKE UP AUDIENCES]

The victims in the world of Jones' early plays are Clay, murdered by the white bitch-goddess in *Dutchman,* and Walker Vessels, the revolutionary in *The Slave.* Both of these plays present Black men in transition. Clay, the middle-class Negro trying to get himself a little action from Lula, digs himself and his own truth only to get murdered after telling her like it really is:

Just let me bleed you, you loud whore, and one poem vanished. A whole people neurotics, struggling to keep from being sane. And the only thing that would cure the neurosis would be your murder. Simple as that. I mean if I murdered you, then other white people would understand me. You understand? No, I guess not. If Bessie Smith had killed some white people she wouldn't needed that music. She could have talked very straight and plain about the world. Just straight two and two are four. Money. Power. Luxury. Like that. All of them. Crazy niggers turning their back on sanity. When all it needs is that simple act. Just murder. Would make us all sane.

But Lula understands, and she kills Clay first. In a perverse way it is Clay's nascent knowledge of himself that threatens the existence of Lula's idea of the world. Symbolically, and in fact, the relationship between Clay (Black America) and Lula (white America) is rooted in the historical castration of black manhood. And in the twisted psyche of white America, the Black man is both an object of love and hate. Analogous attitudes exist in most Black Americans, but for decidedly different reasons. Clay is doomed when he allows himself to participate in Lula's "fantasy" in the first place. It is the fantasy to which Frantz Fanon alludes in *The Wretched Of The Earth* and *Black Skins, White Mask:* the native's belief that he can acquire the oppressor's power by acquiring his symbols, one of which is the white woman. When Clay finally digs himself it is too late.

Walker Vessels, in *The Slave,* is Clay reincarnated as the revolutionary confronting problems inherited from his contact with white culture. He returns to the home of his ex-wife, a white woman, and her husband, a literary critic. The play is essentially about Walker's attempt to destroy his white past. For it is the past, with all of its painful memories, that is really the enemy of the revolutionary. It is impossible to move until history is either recreated or comprehended. Unlike Todd, in Ralph Ellison's *Invisible Man,* Walker cannot fall outside history. Instead, Walker demands a confrontation with history, a final shattering of bullshit illusions. His only salvation lies in confronting the physical and psychological forces that have made him and his people powerless. Therefore, he comes to understand that the world must be restructured along spiritual imperatives. But in the interim it is basically a question of *who* has power:

Easley. You're so wrong about everything. So terribly, sickeningly wrong. What can you change? What do you hope to change? Do you think

Negroes are better people than whites . . . that they can govern a society *better* than whites? That they'll be more judicious or more tolerant? Do you think they'll make fewer mistakes? I mean really, if the Western white man has proved one thing . . . it's the futility of modern society. So the have-not peoples become the haves. Even so, will that change the essential functions of the world? Will there be more love or beauty in the world . . . more knowledge . . . because of it?

Walker. Probably. Probably there will be more . . . if more people have a chance to understand what it is. But that's not even the point. It comes down to baser human endeavor than any social-political thinking. What does it matter if there's more love or beauty? Who the fuck cares? Is that what the Western ofay thought while he was ruling . . . that his rule somehow brought more love and beauty into the world? Oh, he might have thought that concomitantly, while sipping a gin rickey and scratching his ass . . . but that was not ever the point. Not even on the Crusades. The point is that you had your chance, darling, now these other folks have theirs. *Quietly.* Now they have theirs.

Easley: God, what an ugly idea.

This confrontation between the black radical and the white liberal is symbolic of larger confrontations occurring between the Third World and Western society. It is a confrontation between the colonizer and the colonized, the slavemaster and the slave. Implicit in Easley's remarks is the belief that the white man is culturally and politically superior to the Black Man. Even though Western society has been traditionally violent in its relation with the Third World, it sanctimoniously deplores violence or self assertion on the part of the enslaved. And the Western mind, with clever rationalizations, equates the violence of the oppressed with the violence of the oppressor. So that when the native preaches self-determination, the Western white man cleverly misconstrues it to mean hate of *all* white men. When the Black political radical warns his people not to trust white politicians of the left and the right, but instead to organize separately on the basis of power, the white man cries: "racism in reverse." Or he will say, as many of them do today: "We deplore both white and black racism." As if the two could be equated.

There is a minor element in *The Slave* which assumes great importance in a later play entitled *Jello*. Here I refer to the emblem of Walker's army: a red-mouthed grinning field slave. The revolutionary army has taken one of the most hated symbols of the Afro-American past and radically altered its meaning. This is the supreme act of freedom, available only to those who

have liberated themselves psychically. Jones amplifies this inversion of emblem and symbol in *Jello* by making Rochester (Ratfester) of the old Jack
Benny (Penny) program into a revolutionary nationalist. Ratfester, ordinarily
the supreme embodiment of the Uncle Tom Clown, surprises Jack Penny by
turning on the other side of the nature of the Black man. He skillfully, and
with an evasive black humor, robs Penny of all of his money. But Ratfester's
actions are "moral." That is to say, Ratfester is getting his back pay; payment
of a long overdue debt to the Black man. Ratfester's sensibilities are different
from Walker's. He is *blues people* smiling and shuffling while trying to figure
out how to destroy the white thing. And like the blues man, he is the master
of the understatement. Or in the Afro-American folk tradition, he is the
Signifying Monkey, Shine, and Stagolee all rolled into one. There are no
stereotypes any more. History has killed Uncle Tom. Because even Uncle
Tom has a breaking point beyond which he will not be pushed. Cut deeply
enough into the most docile Negro, and you will find a conscious murderer.
Behind the lyrics of the blues and the shuffling porter looms visions of white
throats being cut and cities burning.

Jones' particular power as a playwright does not rest solely on his revolutionary vision, but is instead derived from his deep lyricism and spiritual
outlook. In many ways, he is fundamentally more a poet than a playwright.
And it is his lyricism that gives body to his plays. Two important plays in this
regard are *Black Mass* and *Slave Ship. Black Mass* is based on the Muslim
myth of Yacub. According to this myth, Yacub, a Black scientist, developed
the means of grafting different colors of the Original Black Nation until a
White Devil was created. In *Black Mass,* Yacub's experiments produce a
raving White Beast who is condemned to the coldest regions of the North.
The other magicians implore Yacub to cease his experiments. But he insists
on claiming the primacy of scientific knowledge over spiritual knowledge.
The sensibility of the White Devil is alien, informed by lust and sensuality.
The Beast is the consummate embodiment of evil, the beginning of the
historical subjugation of the spiritual world.

Black Mass takes place in some prehistorical time. In fact, the concept of
time, we learn, is the creation of an alien sensibility, that of the Beast. This is a
deeply weighted play, a colloquy on the nature of man, and the relationship
between legitimate spiritual knowledge and scientific knowledge. It is LeRoi
Jones' most important play mainly because it is informed by a mythology
that is wholly the creation of the Afro-American sensibility.

Further, Yacub's creation is not merely a scientific exercise. More fundamentally, it is the aesthetic impulse gone astray. The Beast is created merely

for the sake of creation. Some artists assert a similar claim about the nature of art. They argue that art need not have a function. It is against this decadent attitude toward art—ramified throughout most of Western society—that the play militates. Yacub's real crime, therefore, is the introduction of a meaningless evil into a harmonious universe. The evil of the Beast is pervasive, corrupting everything and everyone it touches. What was beautiful is twisted into an ugly screaming thing. The play ends with destruction of the holy place of the Black Magicians. Now the Beast and his descendants roam the earth. An offstage voice chants a call for the Jihad to begin. It is then that myth merges into legitimate history, and we, the audience, come to understand that all history is merely someone's version of mythology.

Slave Ship presents a more immediate confrontation with history. In a series of expressionistic tableaux it depicts the horrors and the madness of the Middle Passage. It then moves through the period of slavery, early attempts at revolt, tendencies toward Uncle Tom-like reconciliation and betrayal, and the final act of liberation. There is no definite plot (LeRoi calls it a pageant), just a continuous rush of sound, groans, screams, and souls wailing for freedom and relief from suffering. This work has special affinities with the New Music of Sun Ra, John Coltrane, Albert Ayler, and Ornette Coleman. Events are blurred, rising and falling in a stream of sound. Almost cinematically, the images flicker and fade against a heavy backdrop of rhythm. The language is spare, stripped to the essential. It is a play which almost totally eliminates the need for a text. It functions on the basis of movement and energy—the dramatic equivalent of the New Music.

3.

LeRoi Jones is the best known and the most advanced playwright of the movement, but he is not alone. There are other excellent playwrights who express the general mood of the Black Arts ideology. Among them are Ron Milner, Ed Bullins, Ben Caldwell, Jimmy Stewart, Joe White, Charles Patterson, Charles Fuller, Aisha Hughes, Carol Freeman, and Jimmy Garrett.

Ron Milner's *Who's Got His Own* is of particular importance. It strips bare the clashing attitudes of a contemporary Afro-American family. Milner's concern is with legitimate manhood and morality. The family in *Who's Got His Own* is in search of its conscience, or more precisely its own definition of life. On the day of his father's death, Tim and his family are forced to examine the inner fabric of their lives; the lies, self-deceits, and sense of powerlessness in a white world. The basic conflict, however, is internal. It is rooted in the historical search for black manhood. Tim's mother is representative of a generation of Christian Black women who have implicitly understood the brooding violence lurking in their men. And with this understanding, they have interposed themselves between their men and the object of that violence—the white man. Thus unable to direct his violence against the oppressor, the Black man becomes more frustrated and the sense of powerlessness deepens. Lacking the strength to be a man in the white world, he turns against his family. So the oppressed, as Fanon explains, constantly dreams violence against his oppressor, while killing his brother on fast weekends.

Tim's sister represents the Negro woman's attempt to acquire what Eldridge Cleaver calls "ultrafemininity." That is, the attributes of her white upper-class counterpart. Involved here is a rejection of the body-oriented life of the working class Black man, symbolized by the mother's traditional religion. The sister has an affair with a white upper-class liberal, ending in abortion. There are hints of lesbianism, i.e. a further rejection of the body. The sister's life is a pivotal factor in the play. Much of the stripping away of falsehood initiated by Tim is directed at her life, which they have carefully kept hidden from the mother.

Tim is the product of the new Afro-American sensibility, informed by the psychological revolution now operative within Black America. He is a combination ghetto soul brother and militant intellectual, very hip and slightly flawed himself. He would change the world, but without comprehending the particular history that produced his "tyrannical" father. And he cannot be the man his father was—not until he truly understands his father. He must understand why his father allowed himself to be insulted daily by the "honky" types on the job; why he took a demeaning job in the "shit-house"; and why he spent on his family the violence that he should have directed against the white man. In short, Tim must confront the history of his family. And that is exactly what happens. Each character tells his story, exposing his falsehood to the other until a balance is reached.

Who's Got His Own is not the work of an alienated mind. Milner's main thrust is directed toward unifying the family around basic moral principles, toward bridging the "generation gap." Other Black playwrights, Jimmy Garrett for example, see the gap as unbridgeable.

Garrett's *We Own the Night* takes place during an armed insurrection. As the play opens we see the central characters defending a section of the city against attacks by white police. Johnny, the protagonist, is wounded. Some of his Brothers intermittently fire at attacking forces, while others look for medical help. A doctor arrives, forced at gun point. The wounded boy's mother also comes. She is a female Uncle Tom who berates the Brothers and their cause. She tries to get Johnny to leave. She is hysterical. The whole idea of Black people fighting white people is totally outside of her orientation. Johnny begins a vicious attack on his mother, accusing her of emasculating his father—a recurring theme in the sociology of the Black community. In Afro-American literature of previous decades the strong Black mother was the object of awe and respect. But in the new literature her status is ambivalent and laced with tension. Historically, Afro-American women have had to be the economic mainstays of the family. The oppressor allowed them to have jobs while at the same time limiting the economic mobility of the Black man. Very often, therefore, the woman's aspirations and values are closely tied to those of the white power structure and not to those of her man. Since he cannot provide for his family the way white men do, she despises his weakness, tearing into him at every opportunity until, very often, there is nothing left but a shell.

The only way out of this dilemma is through revolution. It either must be an actual blood revolution, or one that psychically redirects the energy of the oppressed. Milner is fundamentally concerned with the latter and Garrett with the former. Communication between Johnny and his mother breaks down. The revolutionary imperative demands that men step outside the legal framework. It is a question of erecting *another* morality. The old constructs do not hold up, because adhering to them means consigning oneself to the oppressive reality. Johnny's mother is involved in the old constructs. Manliness is equated with white morality. And even though she claims to love her family (her men), the overall design of her ideas are against black manhood. In Garrett's play the mother's morality manifests itself in a deep-seated hatred of Black men; while in Milner's work the mother understands, but holds her men back.

The mothers that Garrett and Milner see represent the Old Spirituality—the Faith of the Fathers of which DuBois spoke. Johnny and Tim represent the New Spirituality. They appear to be a type produced by the upheavals of the colonial world of which Black America is a part. Johnny's assertion that he is a criminal is remarkably similar to the rebel's comments in Aimé Césaire's play, *Les Armes Miraculeuses* (*The Miraculous Weapons*). In that play the rebel, speaking to his mother, proclaims: "My name—an offense; my Christian name—humiliation; my status—a rebel; my age—the stone age." To which the mother replies: "My race—the human race. My religion—brotherhood." The Old Spirituality is generalized. It seeks to recognize Universal Humanity. The New Spirituality is specific. It begins by seeing the world from the concise point-of-view of the colonialized. Where the Old Spirituality would live with oppression while ascribing to the oppressors an innate goodness, the New Spirituality demands a radical shift in point-of-view. The colonialized native, the oppressed must, of necessity, subscribe to a *separate* morality. One that will liberate him and his people.

The assault against the Old Spirituality can sometimes be humorous. In Ben Caldwell's play, *The Militant Preacher,* a burglar is seen slipping into the home of a wealthy minister. The preacher comes in and the burglar ducks behind a large chair. The preacher, acting out the role of the supplicant minister begins to moan, praying to De Lawd for understanding.

In the context of today's politics, the minister is an Uncle Tom, mouthing platitudes against self-defense. The preacher drones in a self-pitying monologue about the folly of protecting oneself against brutal policeman. Then the burglar begins to speak. The preacher is startled, taking the burglar's voice for the voice of God. The burglar begins to play on the preacher's old time religion. He *becomes* the voice of God insulting and goading the preacher on until the preacher's attitudes about protective violence change. The next day the preacher emerges militant, gun in hand, sounding like Reverend Cleage in Detroit. He now preaches a new gospel—the gospel of the gun, an eye for an eye. The gospel is preached in the rhythmic cadences of the old Black church. But the content is radical. Just as Jones inverted the symbols in *Jello,* Caldwell twists the rhythms of the Uncle Tom preacher into the language of the new militancy.

These plays are directed at problems within Black America. They begin with the premise that there is a well defined Afro-American audience. An audience that must see itself and the world in terms of its own interests. These plays, along with many others, constitute the basis for a viable movement in the theatre—a movement which takes as its task a profound re-evaluation of the Black man's presence in America. The Black Arts Movement represents the flowering of a cultural nationalism that has been suppressed since the 1920s. I mean the "Harlem Renaissance"—which was essentially a failure. It did not address itself to the mythology and the lifestyles of the Black community. It failed to take roots, to link itself concretely to the struggles of that community, to become its voice and spirit. Implicit in the Black Arts Movement is the idea that Black people, however dispersed, constitute a *nation* within the belly of white America. This is not a new idea. Garvey said it and the Honorable Elijah Muhammad says it now. And it is on this idea that the concept of Black Power is predicated.

Afro-American life and history is full of creative possibilities, and the movement is just beginning to perceive them. Just beginning to understand that the most meaningful statements about the nature of Western society must come from the Third World of which Black America is a part. The thematic material is broad, ranging from folk heroes like Shine and Stagolee to historical figures like Marcus Garvey and Malcolm X. And then there is the struggle for Black survival, the coming confrontation between white America and Black America. If art is the harbinger of future possibilities, what does the future of Black America portend?

Hoyt W. Fuller

Towards A Black Aesthetic

(1968)

The black revolt is as palpable in letters as it is in the streets, and if it has not yet made its impact upon the Literary Establishment, then the nature of the revolt itself is the reason. For the break between the revolutionary black writers and the "literary mainstream" is, perhaps of necessity, cleaner and more decisive than the noisier and more dramatic break between the black militants and traditional political and institutional structures. Just as black intellectuals have rejected the NAACP, on the one hand, and the two major political parties on the other, and gone off in search of new and more effective means and methods of seizing power, so revolutionary black writers have turned their backs on the old "certainties" and struck out in new, if uncharted, directions. They have begun the journey toward a black aesthetic.

The road to that place—if it exists at all—cannot, by definition, lead through the literary mainstreams. Which is to say that few critics will look upon the new movement with sympathy, even if a number of publishers might be daring enough to publish the works which its adherents produce. The movement will be reviled as "racism-in-reverse," and its writers labeled "racists," opprobrious terms which are flung lightly at black people now that the piper is being paid for all the long years of rejection and abuse which black people have experienced at the hands of white people—with few voices raised in objection.

Is this too harsh and sweeping a generalization? White people might think so; black people will not; which is a way of stating the problem and the prospect before us. Black people are being called "violent" these days, as if violence is a new invention out of the ghetto. But violence against the black minority is in-built in the established American society. There is no need for

This essay first appeared in *The Critic*, 26.5 (1968).

the white majority to take to the streets to clobber the blacks, although there certainly is *enough* of that; brutalization is inherent in all the customs and practices which bestow privileges on the whites and relegate the blacks to the status of pariahs.

These are old and well-worn truths which hardly need repeating. What is new is the reaction to them. Rapidly now, black people are turning onto that uncertain road, and they are doing so with the approval of all kinds of fellow-travellers who ordinarily are considered "safe" for the other side. In the fall 1967 issue of the *Journal of the National Medical Association* (all-black), for example, Dr. Charles A. De Leon of Cleveland, Ohio, explained why the new turn is necessary: "If young Negroes are to avoid the unnecessary burden of self-hatred (via identification with the aggressor) they will have to develop a keen faculty for identifying, fractionating out, and rejecting the absurdities of the conscious as well as the unconscious white racism in American society from what is worthwhile in it."

Conscious and unconscious white racism is everywhere, infecting all the vital areas of national life. But the revolutionary black writer, like the new breed of militant activist, has decided that white racism will no longer exercise its insidious control over his work. If the tag of "racist" is one the white critic will hang on him in dismissing him, then he is more than willing to bear that. He is not going to separate literature from life. ✳

But just how widespread is white racism—conscious and unconscious—in the realm of letters? In a review of Gwendolyn Brooks's *Selected Poems* in the old *New York Herald Tribune Book Week* back in October 1963, poet Louis Simpson began by writing that the Chicago poet's book of poems "contains some lively pictures of Negro life," an ambiguous enough opener which did not necessarily suggest a literary putdown. But Mr. Simpson's next sentence dispelled all ambiguity. "I am not sure it is possible for a Negro to write well without making us aware he is a Negro," he wrote. "On the other hand, if being a Negro is the only subject, the writing is not important."

All the history of American race relations is contained in that appraisal, despite its disingenuousness. It is civilized, urbane, gentle and elegant; and it is arrogant, condescending, presumptuous and racist. To most white readers, no doubt, Mr. Simpson's words, if not his assessment, seemed eminently sensible; but it is all but impossible to imagine a black reader not reacting to the words with unalloyed fury.

Both black and white readers are likely to go to the core of Mr. Simpson's statement, which is: "if being a Negro is the only subject, the writing is not important." The white reader will, in all probability, find that clear and acceptable enough; indeed, he is used to hearing it. "Certainly," the argument might proceed, "to be important, writing must have *universal values, universal implications;* it cannot deal exclusively with Negro problems." The plain but unstated assumption being, of course, that there are no "universal values" and no "universal implications" in Negro life.

Mr. Simpson is a greatly respected American poet, a winner of the Pulitzer Prize for poetry, as is Miss Brooks, and it will be considered the depth of irresponsibility to accuse him of the viciousness of racism. He is probably the gentlest and most compassionate of men. Miss Brooks, who met Mr. Simpson at the University of California not many months after the review was published, reported that the gentleman was most kind and courteous to her. There is no reason to doubt it. The essential point here is not the presence of overt hostility; it is the absence of clarity of vision. The glass through which black life is viewed by white Americans is, inescapably (it is a matter of extent), befogged by the hot breath of history. True "objectivity" where race is concerned is as rare as a necklace of Hope diamonds.

In October 1967, a young man named Jonathan Kozol published a book called *Death at an Early Age,* which is an account of his experiences as a teacher in a predominantly Negro elementary school in Boston. Mr. Kozol broke with convention in his approach to teaching and incurred the displeasure of a great many people, including the vigilant policeman father of one of his few white pupils. The issue around which the young teacher's opponents seemed to rally was his use of a Langston Hughes poem in his classroom. Now the late Langston Hughes was a favorite target of some of the more aggressive right-wing pressure groups during his lifetime, but it remained for an official of the Boston School Committee to come to the heart of the argument against the poet. Explaining the opposition to the poem used by Mr. Kozol, the school official said that "no poem by any Negro author can be considered permissible if it involves suffering."

There is a direct connecting line between the school official's rejection of Negro poetry which deals with suffering and Mr. Simpson's facile dismissal of writing about Negroes "only." Negro life, which is characterized by suffering imposed by the maintenance of white privilege in America, must be denied validity and banished beyond the pale. The facts of Negro life accuse white people. In order to look at Negro life unflinchingly, the white viewer either must relegate it to the realm of the subhuman, thereby justifying an attitude of indifference, or else the white viewer must confront the imputation of guilt against him. And no man who considers himself humane wishes to admit complicity in crimes against the human spirit.

There is a myth abroad in American literary criticism that Negro writing has been favored by a "double standard" which judges it less stringently. The opposite is true. No one will seriously dispute that, on occasions, critics have been generous to Negro writers, for a variety of reasons; but there is no evidence that generosity has been the rule. Indeed, why should it be assumed that literary critics are more sympathetic to blacks than are other white people? During any year, hundreds of mediocre volumes of prose and poetry by white writers are published, little noted, and forgotten. At the same time, the few creative works by black writers are seized and dissected and, if not deemed of the "highest" literary quality, condemned as still more examples of the failure of black writers to scale the rare heights of literature. And the condemnation is especially strong for those black works which have not screened their themes of suffering, redemption and triumph behind frail facades of obscurity and conscious "universality."

Central to the problem of the irreconcilable conflict between the black writer and the white critic is the failure of recognition of a fundamental and obvious truth of American life—that the two races are residents of two separate and naturally antagonistic worlds. No manner of well-meaning rhetoric about "one country" and "one people," and even about the two races' long joint-occupancy of this troubled land, can obliterate the high, thick dividing walls which hate and history have erected—and maintain—between them. The breaking down of those barriers might be a goal, worthy or unworthy (depending on viewpoint), but the reality remains. The world of the black outsider, however much it approximates and parallels and imitates the world of the white insider, by its very nature is inheritor and generator of values and viewpoints which threaten the insiders. The outsiders' world, feeding on its own sources, fecundates and vibrates, stamping its progeny with its very special ethos, its insuperably logical bias.

The black writer, like the black artist generally, has wasted much time and talent denying a propensity every rule of human dignity demands that he possess, seeking an identity that can only do violence to his sense of self. Black Americans are, for all practical purposes, colonized in their native land, and it can be argued that those who would submit to subjection without struggle deserve to be enslaved. It is one thing to accept the guiding principles on which the American republic ostensibly was founded; it is quite another thing to accept the prevailing practices which violate those principles.

The rebellion in the streets is the black ghetto's response to the vast distance between the nation's principles and its practices. But that rebellion has roots which are deeper than most white people know; it is many-veined, and its blood has been sent pulsating to the very heart of black life. Across this country, young black men and women have been infected with a fever of affirmation. They are saying, "We are black and beautiful," and the ghetto is reacting with a liberating shock of realization which transcends mere chauvinism. They are rediscovering their heritage and their history, seeing it with newly focused eyes, struck with the wonder of that strength which has enabled them to endure and, in spirit, to defeat the power of prolonged and calculated oppression. After centuries of being told, in a million different ways, that they were not beautiful, and that whiteness of skin, straightness of hair, and aquilineness of features constituted the only measures of beauty, black people have revolted. The trend has not yet reached the point of avalanche, but the future can be clearly seen in the growing number of black people who are snapping off the shackles of imitation and are wearing their skin, their hair, and their features "natural" and with pride. In a poem called "Nittygritty," which is dedicated to poet LeRoi Jones, Joseph Bevans Bush put the new credo this way:

> . . . We all gonna come from behind those
> Wigs and start to stop using those
> Standards of beauty which can never
> Be a frame for our reference; wash
> That excess grease out of our hair,
> Come out of that bleach bag and get
> Into something meaningful to us as
> Nonwhite people—Black people . . .

If the poem lacks the resonances of William Shakespeare, that is intentional. The "great bard of Avon" has only limited relevance to the revolutionary spirit raging in the ghetto. Which is not to say that the black revolutionaries reject the "universal" statements inherent in Shakespeare's works; what they do reject, however, is the literary assumption that the style and language and the concerns of Shakespeare establish the appropriate limits and "frame of reference" for black poetry and people. This is above and beyond the doctrine of revolution to which so many of the brighter black intellectuals are committed, that philosophy articulated by the late Frantz Fanon which holds that, in the time of revolutionary struggle, the traditional Western liberal ideals are not merely irrelevant but they must be assiduously

REINVENTING FORM . — BLACK AESTHETIC .

opposed. The young writers of the black ghetto have set out in search of a black aesthetic, a system of isolating and evaluating the artistic works of black people which reflect the special character and imperatives of black experience.

That was the meaning and intent of poet-playwright LeRoi Jones' aborted Black Arts Theater in Harlem in 1965, and it is the generative idea behind such later groups and institutions as Spirit House in Newark, the Black House in San Francisco, the New School of Afro-American Thought in Washington, D.C., the Institute for Black Studies in Los Angeles, Forum '66 in Detroit, and the Organization of Black American Culture in Chicago. It is a serious quest, and the black writers themselves are well aware of the possibility that what they seek is, after all, beyond codifying. They are fully aware of the dual nature of their heritage, and of the subtleties and complexities; but they are even more aware of the terrible reality of their outsideness, of their political and economic powerlessness, and of the desperate racial need for unity. And they have been convinced, over and over again, by the irrefutable facts of history and by the cold intransigence of the privileged white majority that the road to solidarity and strength leads inevitably through reclamation and indoctrination of black art and culture.

In Chicago, the Organization of Black American Culture has moved boldly toward a definition of a black aesthetic. In the writers' workshop sponsored by the group, the writers are deliberately striving to invest their work with the distinctive styles and rhythms and colors of the ghetto, with those peculiar qualities which, for example, characterize the music of a John Coltrane or a Charlie Parker or a Ray Charles. Aiming toward the publication of an anthology which will manifest this aesthetic, they have established criteria by which they measure their own work and eliminate from consideration those poems, short stories, plays, essays and sketches which do not adequately reflect the black experience. What the sponsors of the workshop most hope for in this delicate and dangerous experiment is the emergence of new black critics who will be able to articulate and expound the new aesthetic and eventually set in motion the long overdue assault against the restrictive assumptions of the white critics.

It is not that the writers of OBAC have nothing to start with. That there exists already a mystique of blackness even some white critics will agree. In the November 1967 issue of *Esquire* magazine, for instance, George Frazier, a white writer who is not in the least sympathetic with the likes of LeRoi Jones, nevertheless did a commendable job of identifying elements of the black mystique. Discussing "the Negro's immense style, a style so seductive that it's little wonder that black men are, as Shakespeare put it in *The Two Gentlemen of Verona*, 'pearls in beauteous ladies' eyes,'" Mr. Frazier singled out the following examples:

"The formal daytime attire (black sack coats and striped trousers) the Modern Jazz Quartet wore when appearing in concert; the lazy amble with which Jimmy Brown used to return to the huddle; the delight the late 'Big Daddy' Lipscomb took in making sideline tackles in full view of the crowd and the way, after crushing a ball carrier to the ground, he would chivalrously assist him to his feet; the constant cool of 'Satchel' Paige; the chic of Bobby Short; the incomparable grace of John Bubbles—things like that are style and they have nothing whatsoever to do with ability (although the ability, God wot, is there, too). It is not that there are no white men with style, for there is Fred Astaire, for one, and Cary Grant, for another, but that there are so very, very few of them. Even in the dock, the black man has an air about him—Adam Clayton Powell, so blithe, so self-possessed, so casual, as contrasted with Tom Dodd, sanctimonious, whining, an absolute disgrace. What it is that made Miles Davis and Cassius Clay, Sugar Ray Robinson and Archie Moore and Ralph Ellison and Sammy Davis, Jr. seem so special was their style. . . .

"And then, of course, there is our speech.

"For what nuances, what plays of light and shade, what little sharpnesses our speech has are almost all of them, out of the black world—the talk of Negro musicians and whores and hoodlums and whatnot. 'Cool' and all the other words in common currency came out of the mouths of Negroes.

" 'We love you madly,' said Duke Ellington, and now the phrase is almost a cliché. But it is a quality of the Negro's style—that he is forever creative, forever more stylish. There was a night when, as I stood with Duke Ellington outside the Hickory House, I looked up at the sky and said, 'I hope it's a good day tomorrow. I want to wake up early.'

" 'Any day I wake up,' said Ellington, 'is a good day.'

"And that was style."

Well, yes. . . .

Black critics have the responsibility of approaching the works of black writers assuming these qualities to be present, and with the knowledge that white readers—and white critics—cannot be expected to recognize and to empathize with the subtleties and significance of black style and technique. They have the responsibility of rebutting the white critics and of putting things in the proper perspective. Within the past few years, for example, Chicago's white critics have given the backs of their hands to worthy works by black playwrights, part of their criticism directly attributable to their ignorance of the intricacies of black style and black life. Oscar Brown, Jr.'s rockingly soulful *Kicks and Company* was panned for many of the wrong reasons; and Douglas Turner Ward's two plays, *Day of Absence* and *Happy Ending,* were tolerated as labored and a bit tasteless. Both Brown and Ward had dealt satirically with race relations, and there were not many black people in the audiences who found themselves in agreement with the critics. It is the way things are—but not the way things will continue to be if the OBAC writers and those similarly concerned elsewhere in America have anything to say about it.

Addison Gayle, Jr.

Cultural Strangulation: Black Literature

and the White Aesthetic

(1971)

"This assumption that of all the hues of God, whiteness is inherently and obviously better than brownness or tan leads to curious acts. . . ."—W. E. B. DuBois

The expected opposition to the concept of a "Black Aesthetic" was not long in coming. In separate reviews of *Black Fire,* an anthology edited by LeRoi Jones and Larry Neal, critics from the Saturday Review and the New York Review of Books presented the expected rebuttal. Agreeing with Ralph Ellison that sociology and art are incompatible mates, these critics, nevertheless, invoked the cliches of the social ideology of the "we shall overcome" years in their attempt to steer Blacks from "the path of literary fantasy and folly."

Their major thesis is simple: There is no Black aesthetic because there is no white aesthetic. The Kerner Commission Report to the contrary, America is not two societies but one. Therefore, Americans of all races, colors and creeds share a common cultural heredity. This is to say that there is one predominant culture—the American culture—with tributary national and ethnic streams flowing into the larger river. Literature, the most important by-product of this cultural monolith, knows no parochial boundaries. To speak of a Black literature, a Black aesthetic, or a Black state, is to engage in racial chauvinism, separatist bias, and Black fantasy.

The question of a white aesthetic, however, is academic. One has neither to talk about it nor define it. Most Americans, black and white, accept the existence of a "White Aesthetic" as naturally as they accept April 15th as the deadline for paying their income tax—with far less animosity towards the former than the latter. The white aesthetic, despite the academic critics, has

This essay first appeared in Addison Gayle, ed., *The Black Aesthetic* (New York, 1971).

always been with us: for long before Diotima pointed out the way to heavenly beauty to Socrates, the poets of biblical times were discussing beauty in terms of light and dark—the essential characteristics of a white and black aesthetic—and establishing the dichotomy of superior versus inferior which would assume body and form in the eighteenth century. Therefore, more serious than a definition, is the problem of tracing the white aesthetic from its early origins and afterwards, outlining the various changes in the basic formula from culture to culture and from nation to nation. Such an undertaking would be more germane to a book than an essay; nevertheless, one may take a certain starting point and, using selective nations and cultures, make the critical point, while calling attention to the necessity of a more comprehensive study encompassing all of the nations and cultures of the world.

Let us propose Greece as the logical starting point, bearing in mind Will Durant's observation that "all of Western Civilization is but a footnote to Plato," and take Plato as the first writer to attempt a systematic aesthetic. Two documents by Plato, *The Symposium* and *The Republic,* reveal the twin components of Plato's aesthetic system.

In *The Symposium,* Plato divides the universe into spheres. In one sphere, the lower, one finds the forms of beauty; in the other, the higher, beauty, as Diotima tells Socrates, is absolute and supreme. In *The Republic,* Plato defines the poet as an imitator (a third-rate imitator—a point which modern critics have long since forgotten) who reflects the heavenly beauty in the earthly mirror. In other words, the poet recreates beauty as it exists in heaven; thus the poet, as Neo-Platonists from Aquinas to Coleridge have told us, is the custodian of beauty on earth.

However, Plato defines beauty only in ambiguous, mystical terms; leaving the problem of a more circumscribed, secular definition to philosophers, poets, and critics. During most of the history of the Western world, these aestheticians have been white; therefore, it is not surprising that, symbolically and literally, they have defined beauty in terms of whiteness. (An early contradiction to this tendency is the Marquis de Sade who inverted the symbols, making black beautiful, but demonic, and white pure, but sterile—the Marquis is considered by modern criticism to have been mentally deranged.)

The distinction between whiteness as beautiful (good) and blackness as ugly (evil) appears early in the literature of the middle ages—in the Morality Plays of England. Heavily influenced by both Platonism and Christianity, these plays set forth the distinctions which exist today. To be white was to be pure, good, universal, and beautiful; to be black was to be impure, evil, parochial, and ugly.

The characters and the plots of these plays followed this basic format. The villain is always evil, in most cases the devil; the protagonist, or hero, is always good, in most cases, angels or disciples. The plot then is simple; good (light) triumphs over the forces of evil (dark). As English literature became more sophisticated, the symbols were made to cover wider areas of the human and literary experience. To love was divine; to hate, evil. The fancied mistress of Petrarch was the purest of the pure; Grendel's mother, a creature from the "lower regions and marshes," is, like her son, a monster; the "bad" characters in Chaucer's *Canterbury Tales* tell dark stories; and the Satan of *Paradise Lost* must be vanquished by Gabriel, the angel of purity.

These ancients, as Swift might have called them, established their dichotomies as a result of the influences of Neo-Platonism and Christianity. Later, the symbols became internationalized. Robert Burton, in *The Anatomy of Melancholy*, writes of "dark despair" in the seventeenth century, and James Boswell describes melancholia, that state of mind common to intellectuals of the 17th and 18th centuries, as a dark, dreaded affliction which robbed men of their creative energies. This condition—dark despair or melancholia—was later popularized in what is referred to in English literature as its "dark period"—the period of the Grave Yard School of poets and the Gothic novels.

The symbols thus far were largely applied to conditions, although characters who symbolized evil influences were also dark. In the early stages of English literature, these characters were mythological and fictitious and not representative of people of specific racial or ethnic groups. In the eighteenth century English novel, however, the symbolism becomes ethnic and racial.

There were forerunners. As early as 1621, Shakespeare has Iago refer to Othello as that "old Black ewe," attaching the mystical sexual characteristic to blackness which would become the motive for centuries of oppressive acts by white Americans. In *The Tempest*, Shakespeare's last play, Caliban, though not ostensibly black, is nevertheless a distant cousin of the colonial Friday in Daniel Defoe's *Robinson Crusoe*.

Robinson Crusoe was published at a historically significant time. In the year 1719, the English had all but completed their colonization of Africa. The slave trade in America was on its way to becoming a booming industry; in Africa, Black people were enslaved mentally as well as physically by such strange bedfellows as criminals, businessmen, and Christians. In the social and political spheres, a rationale was needed, and help came from the artist— in this case, the novelist—in the form of *Robinson Crusoe*. In the novel, Defoe brings together both Christian and Platonic symbolism, sharpening the dichotomy between light and dark on the one hand, while on the other establishing a criterion for the inferiority of Black people as opposed to the superiority of white.

One need only compare Crusoe with Friday to validate both of these statements. Crusoe is majestic, wise, white and a colonialist; Friday is savage, ignorant, black and a colonial. Therefore, Crusoe, the colonialist, has a double task. On the one hand he must transform the island (Africa—unproductive, barren, dead) into a little England (prosperous, life-giving, fertile), and he must recreate Friday in his own image, thus bringing him as close to being an Englishman as possible. At the end of the novel, Crusoe has accomplished both undertakings; the island is a replica of "mother England"; and Friday has been transformed into a white man, now capable of immigrating to the land of the gods.

From such mystical artifacts has the literature and criticism of the Western world sprung; and based upon such narrow prejudices as those of Defoe, the art of Black people throughout the world has been described as parochial and inferior. Friday was parochial and inferior until, having denounced his own culture, he assimilated another. Once this was done, symbolically, Friday underwent a change. To deal with him after the conversion was to deal with him in terms of a character who had been civilized and therefore had moved beyond racial parochialism.

However, Defoe was merely a hack novelist, not a thinker. It was left to shrewder minds than his to apply the rules of the white aesthetic to the practical areas of the Black literary and social worlds, and no shrewder minds were at work on this problem than those of writers and critics in America. In America, the rationale for both slavery and the inferiority of Black art and culture was supplied boldly, without the trappings of eighteenth century symbolism.

In 1867, in a book entitled *Nojoque: A Question for a Continent,* Hinton Helper provided the vehicle for the cultural and social symbols of inferiority under which Blacks have labored in this country. Helper intended, as he states frankly in his preface, "to write the negro out of America." In the headings of the two major chapters of the book, the whole symbolic apparatus of the white aesthetic handed down from Plato to America is graphically revealed: the heading of one chapter reads: "Black: A Thing of Ugliness, Disease"; another heading reads: "White: A Thing of Life, Health, and Beauty."

Under the first heading, Helper argues that the color black "has always been associated with sinister things such as mourning, the devil, the darkness of night." Under the second, "White has always been associated with the light of day, divine transfiguration, the beneficent moon and stars . . . the fair complexion of romantic ladies, the costumes of Romans and angels, and the white of the American flag so beautifully combined with blue and red without ever a touch of the black that has been for the flag of pirates."

Such is the American critical ethic based upon centuries of distortion of the Platonic ideal. By not adequately defining beauty, and implying at least that this was the job of the poet, Plato laid the foundation for the white aesthetic as defined by Daniel Defoe and Hinton Helper. However, the uses of that aesthetic to stifle and strangle the cultures of other nations is not to be attributed to Plato but, instead, to his hereditary brothers far from the Aegean. For Plato knew his poets. They were not, he surmised, a very trusting lot and, therefore, by adopting an ambiguous position on symbols, he limited their power in the realm of aesthetics. For Plato, there were two kinds of symbols: natural and proscriptive. Natural symbols corresponded to absolute beauty as created by God; proscriptive symbols, on the other hand, were symbols of beauty as proscribed by man, which is to say that certain symbols are said to mean such and such by man himself.

The irony of the trap in which the Black artist has found himself throughout history is apparent. Those symbols which govern his life and art are proscriptive ones, set down by minds as diseased as Hinton Helper's. In other words, beauty has been in the eyes of an earthly beholder who has stipulated that beauty conforms to such and such a definition. To return to Friday, Defoe stipulated that civilized man was what Friday had to become, proscribed certain characteristics to the term "civilized," and presto, Friday, in order not to be regarded as a "savage under Western eyes," was forced to conform to this ideal. How well have the same stipulative definitions worked in the artistic sphere! Masterpieces are made at will by each new critic who argues that the subject of his doctoral dissertation is immortal. At one period of history, John Donne, according to the critic Samuel Johnson, is a second rate poet; at another period, according to the critic T. S. Eliot, he is one of the finest poets in the language. Dickens, argues Professor Ada Nisbet, is one of England's most representative novelists, while for F. R. Leavis, Dickens' work does not warrant him a place in *The Great Tradition*.

When Black literature is the subject, the verbiage reaches the height of the ridiculous. The good "Negro Novel," we are told by Robert Bone and Herbert Hill, is that novel in which the subject matter moves beyond the limitations of narrow parochialism. Form is the most important criterion of the work of art when Black literature is evaluated, whereas form, almost nonexistent in

Dostoyevsky's *Crime and Punishment,* and totally chaotic in Kafka's *The Trial,* must take second place to the supremacy of thought and message.

Richard Wright, says Theodore Gross, is not a major American novelist; while Ralph Ellison, on the strength of one novel, is. LeRoi Jones is not a major poet, Ed Bullins not a major playwright, Baldwin incapable of handling the novel form—all because white critics have said so.

Behind the symbol is the object or vehicle, and behind the vehicle is the definition. It is the definition with which we are concerned, for the extent of the cultural strangulation of Black literature by white critics has been the extent to which they have been allowed to define the terms in which the Black artist will deal with his own experience. The career of Paul Laurence Dunbar is the most striking example. Having internalized the definitions handed him by the American society, Dunbar would rather not have written about the Black experience at all, and three of his novels and most of his poetry support this argument. However, when forced to do so by his white liberal mentors, among them was the powerful critic, William Dean Howells, Dunbar deals with Blacks in terms of buffoonery, idiocy and comedy.

Like so many Black writers, past and present, Dunbar was trapped by the definitions of other men, never capable of realizing until near the end of his life, that those definitions were not god-given, but man-given; and so circumscribed by tradition and culture that they were irrelevant to an evaluation of either his life or his art.

In a literary conflict involving Christianity, Zarathustra, Friedrich Nietzsche's iconoclast, calls for "a new table of the laws." In similar iconoclastic fashion, the proponents of a Black Aesthetic, the idol smashers of America, call for a set of rules by which Black literature and art is to be judged and evaluated. For the historic practice of bowing to other men's gods and definitions has produced a crisis of the highest magnitude, and brought us, culturally, to the limits of racial armageddon. The trend must be reversed.

The acceptance of the phrase "Black is Beautiful" is the first step in the destruction of the old table of the laws and the construction of new ones, for the phrase flies in the face of the whole ethos of the white aesthetic. This step must be followed by serious scholarship and hard work; and Black critics must dig beneath the phrase and unearth the treasure of beauty lying deep in the untoured regions of the Black experience—regions where others, due to historical conditioning and cultural deprivation, cannot go.

Don L. Lee (Haki Madhubuti)

Toward a Definition: Black Poetry of the Sixties

(After LeRoi Jones)

(1971)

We are going to talk about black art forms and movements. Those black artists that are active and hip would gladly agree, I'm sure, that black music is our most advanced form of black art. The reasons for this are innumerable, but basically that, regardless of outward conditions during slavery, post-slavery, etc., black music was able to endure and grow as (1) a communicative language, (2) a sustaining spiritual force, (3) an entertaining outlet, (4) a creative extension of our African selves, (5) one of the few mediums of expression that was open and virtually free of interferences.

Very few people understand the music of John Coltrane; his early critics and some of his fellow musicians called him crazy. Clifford Brown and Charlie Parker were giants in their time, but they stayed broke (penniless). Thelonius Monk transformed and enlarged the sounds of the piano, but he is still not taught in our institutions of higher learning. What this gets down to is that to understand the aesthetic of black art or that which is uniquely black, we must start with the art form that was least distorted and was not molded into that which is referred to as a pure product of European-American culture.

In reading LeRoi Jones's critique in *Black Music,* we come to understand that there are two distinct levels on which the aesthetic works: gut-emotion level, which must predominate, and a technical level, which must not be *too* obvious but must seem (and in fact be) natural and real. Jones goes on to say: "The white musicians' commitment to jazz, the *ultimate concern,* proposed that the subcultural attitudes that reduced the music as a profound expression of human feelings, could be *learned* and need not be passed on as a secret blood rite. And Negro is essentially the expression of an attitude, or a

This essay first appeared in Addison Gayle, ed., *The Black Aesthetic* (New York, 1971).

collection of attitudes, about the world, and only secondarily an attitude about the way music is made."

As a collection of attitudes about the world, the aesthetic moves toward a semblance of a definition if we can understand the sensibility of the persons we are trying to reach. Especially since we are to deal with black poetry of the sixties, we must understand that which went down before the decade of the sixties. Also, poetry as most of us understand it, *is* rather an exclusive art form written and preferred by the intellectually astute. That is to say, the poetry on the written page very seldom found its way into the home or neighborhood of the common black man, i.e., poetry in my home was almost as strange as money.

The one subject that wasn't taught, but was consciously learned in our early educational experiences was that writing of any kind was something that black people *just didn't do.* Today it's popular to refer back to the Harlem Renaissance of the twenties as a successful "Negro" literary movement in black letters. That statement is only partially true; actually, the arts or black arts as we now know them were alive and active only at a very superficial, elitest level, being mainly patronized by the uptown whites, e.g., Carl Van Vechten, Max Eastman, DuBose Heyward, etc. Whereas, black people in Harlem hardly knew that anything of a literary movement was in process, let alone took part in it. Langston Hughes clarifies this in his autobiography, *The Big Sea.* He states: "The ordinary Negroes hadn't heard of the Negro Renaissance." Which is to imply that because of its restrictions, the black literary movement of the twenties forecast its own death. Out of the many writers who took part, only a few are still widely read today: Langston Hughes, Sterling A. Brown, Arna Bontemps, and Claude McKay.

Sensibility: awareness, consciousness, fineness of feeling. Actually, what it gets down to is, that which shaped our sensibilities shaped us. What was it? Why are some of us Negroes, some blacks, and some don't know what we are? Most of us have been shaped by the same consciousness: a white nationalist consciousness called Americanism that's really a refined, or unrefined, depending on your viewpoint, weak version of the European sensibility. Whereas, black people in this country are products of a dual culture: the duality is that of being formally educated as a "European-American" and informally schooled as a black man, i.e., public schools or private schools in the A.M. and street schools and home schools in the P.M.

The black sensibility is not new. The only thing new about blackness today is the magnitude in which it has been generated and the amount of people it has reached. You see, there has always been a visible portion of the "Negro people" that were black, but then they were dismissed as being *crazy*.

Aesthetic: "The branch of philosophy dealing with the beautiful, chiefly with respect to theories of its essential character, tests by which it may be judged, and its relation to the human mind; also, the branch of psychology treating of the sensations and emotions evoked by the fine arts and belles-lettres." (Webster's)

A Black Aesthetic would, in effect, encompass much of the definition above, but in the context of Western culture is and becomes a serious and profound variation on a loose theme. Harold Cruse, in his *Crisis of the Negro Intellectual,* gives a view of the prevailing school of criticism: "The impact of the Negro presence on American art forms has been tremendous, and also historically conditioned; but this fact the American psyche is loath to admit in its established critical school of thought. As Americans, white people in America are also Westerners, and American white values are shaped by Western cultural values. Americans possess no critical standards for the cultural arts that have not been derived from the European experience. On the other hand, the basic ingredients for native (non-European) American originality in art forms derive from American Negroes, who came to America from a non-Western background. We need only point to American music to prove the point. Thus in American art a peculiar kind of cultural duality exists, which is an ideological reflection of the basic attitudes of blacks and whites toward each other."

Black poetry of the sixties is not too different from black poetry of the forties and fifties; there has always existed in the verse a certain amount of blackness. But in the sixties the black arts emerged as never before: e.g., music, theater (black drama), art (painting, sculpture), film, prose (novel, essay), and poetry. The new and powerful voices of the sixties came to light mainly because of the temper of the times; it accented the human-rights struggle of black people in the world. Also, television played a very important role in projecting blackness in the early sixties—mainly in a gross misunderstanding, over-representing it as something new and queer. The men of the moment were: John Coltrane, LeRoi Jones, Cecil Taylor, James Baldwin, Charles White, Marion Brown, Ornette Coleman, Don Cherry, John A. Williams, Lerone Dennett, Mari Evans, William Melvin Kelley, John O. Killens, Grachun Manour III, Thelonius Monk, Sunny Murray, Ed Bullins, Ronald Milner, Calvin C. Hernton, Larry Neal, Dudley Randall, James Brown, A. B. B. Spellman, Lew Alcindor, Hoyt Fuller, Conrad Kent

Rivers, Archie Shepp, Sun Ra, Pharaoh Sanders, Gwendolyn Brooks, Malcolm X, Frantz Fanon, Martin Luther King, and we can go on for days.

Black art of the sixties, on the national scene, started with the advent of LeRoi Jones (Ameer Baraka) and the black theater. We in the Midwest felt the pressures from both the west and the east coasts. In the vanguard in terms of publishing black writing was *Negro Digest* under the extraordinary editorship of Hoyt Fuller, and a new quarterly came into existence in the mid-sixties, *The Journal of Black Poetry,* edited by quietly patient Joe Goncalves. Other publications that regularly published black poets were: *Soul Book, Black Dialogue, Liberator,* and *Black Expression.* New presses to emerge in the sixties that concentrated on poetry books were led by Broadside Press of Detroit, Michigan, under the editorship of Dudley Randall (a nationally known poet himself), Jihad Press of Newark, Free Black Press of Chicago, Black Dialogue Press of New York by way of California, the Journal of Black Poetry Press of California, and the Third World Press of Chicago. Broadside Press has been by far the most successful and productive.

The Poetry: The language of the new writers seems to move in one direction; that is to say that the poets of the sixties are actually defining and legitimizing their own communicative medium. We will see that the language as a whole is not formal or proper Anglo-Saxon English. It carries its own syntax, which is not conventional, and by Western standards could be referred to as noncommunicative, obscene, profane, or vulgar. In short, it's the language of the street, charged so as to heighten the sensitivity level of the reader. We find that this concentration on language is not unique to black poets of the sixties. James Weldon Johnson, in his *American Negro Poetry,* talks about two poets of another generation that were experimenters and innovators in language: "Langston Hughes and Sterling A. Brown do use a dialect; but it is not the dialect of the comic minstrel tradition; it is the common, racy, living, authentic speech of the Negro in certain phases of real life." So we find that language is constant only as man is.

The decade of the sixties, especially that of the mid-sixties, brought to us a new consciousness, a perception that has come to be known as a *black consciousness.* Embodied in most of the poetry of the sixties, we find at least a semblance of this sensibility. Along with the new awareness, we get a form that on the surface speaks of newness (actually, most of the forms and styles used by the newer poets may be as confusing as some of the new black music forms). In effect, the form that is used may be a starting point for determining and categorizing the Black Aesthetic. Some of the common occurrences, we find in the black poets of the sixties are:

1. polyrhythmic, uneven, short, and explosive lines
2. intensity; depth, yet simplicity; spirituality, yet flexibility
3. irony; humor; signifying
4. sarcasm—a new comedy
5. direction; positive movement; teaching, nation-building
6. subject matter—concrete; reflects a collective and personal life-style.
7. music: the unique use of vowels and consonants with the developed rap demands that the poetry be real, and read out loud.

All that's mentioned above, and more, can be seen much more clearly in some of the poetry. First, exclusion is automatic in a critique of this kind; I've purposely restricted myself to the poets who have published widely and in most cases have published several books. These writers look upon themselves as black men or black women first, then as poets. Thus, understanding their responsibility to themselves and to their community is a priority in no uncertain terms. Ron Wellburn said of the new poets: "No poets in America serve in such a priestly capacity as do black poets. Priests, musicians, deacons, chanters, poets—all bear the song and its power as their unfailing weapon."

Mari Evans moves beyond the self-reliant assertion of the natural fact in her poem *I Am a Black Woman*—not just a woman. Mari in this poem creates an identity, a personality, a role that is not newly black, but generically and historically black: "Look on me and be renewed." One may contrast her with Stephanie in her book *Moving Deep*, in which Stephanie characterizes herself as woman, a lover—simply; or with West Indian poets who prior to 1939 made a point of being "universal," which was to be not specifically black. Indeed, Mari is universal here in exploring the natural arena of the role of the woman in human society. Her historical identity is created through allusions to Nat Turner and "Anzio"—all caught in a historical timelessness. She was/is always there. The naturalness and the biological origins of herself are poignant, yet stoically strong:

> I saw my mate leap screaming to the sea and I
> with these hands
> cupped the lifebreath from my issue in the canebrake.

A kind of mystical yet hard strength reminiscent of Jean Toomer's women in *Cane*. The woman herein recreated is not fragmented, hysterical, doesn't have sexual problems with her mate, doesn't feel caught up in a "liberated womanhood" complex/bag—which is to say she is not out to define herself (that is, from the position of weakness, as "the others" do) and thus will not be looked upon as an aberration of the twentieth-century white woman.

Margaret Danner is a poet of African descent. Africa is throughout her poetry. If a true test for a black poem is whether you can tell the author's color, we find that Sister Danner's poem *And Through the Caribbean Sea* is an interesting example, because she does not mention the word black in the poem. But there is no doubt as to who she is. The colors are not literally black, but still black:

> We, like shades that were first conjured up
> by an African witch-doctor's ire,
> (indigo for the drum and the smoke of night,
>
> tangerine for the dancing smudged fire)
> have been forced to exist in a huge kaleidoscope world.
> We've been shifting with time and sifting through
> space,
>
> at each whimsical turn of the hands that have thrown
> the Kaleidoscope, until any pattern or place
> or shade is our own. . . .

The bright arrangement of red and tangerine is very black, whether here, in the West Indies, or in Africa. Also, the poem is very subtle. She begins her poem with an inclusive "we," which means she acknowledges that she herself is a part of the kaleidoscopic arrangement; and then with subtle simile immediately establishes the link, tells who "we" are, which is the same as saying where we came from. All her references are African—indigo, drum, dancing, tangerine, African mask! Those references or allusions that are not African are meant to indicate a loss of identity: Louis Quinze Frame, Rococo, etc.

Eugene Perkins and Ebon emerged in the late sixties as two of the stronger men poets. Perkins becomes a poet because he's a man of his time and place: America, Chicago, Now. In *Black Patches,* from his book *Black Is Beautiful,* the colors are copper and ebony. Black Chicago is recreated into an analytical photograph. A white social worker might make references to Woodlawn and Robert Taylor Holmes, but would hardly see them for what they are:

> The Congo Villages stand unclaimed under the
> shadows of grotesque tenements
> and the towering concrete
> of welfare prisons. . . .

Critics would call his references metaphors, but politically they are profound and well-stated truisms. It is Fanon and Nkrumah; it's Lumumba, DuBois, and Stokely, all squeezed and purified in four simple lines. He knows the beauty of the lifestyle, but also its weaknesses:

> A carnival strip in an ebony jungle
> Still clinging to a tradition
>   of self styled hustlers
>   Jewish economy
>   and street corner preachers

A distinct few white people even allude to the "black patches" of this continent, but because they think they're liberal (and are in reality stupid), they can't creatively criticize as Perkins does. With this in mind, we realize how much of a poet Brother Perkins is when he cops the lid off white boy's facade:

> hide marijuana cigarettes
> between the pages of "Black Boy"
> and "The Rise and Fall of the Third Reich"

Ebon also lends his interpretation to that which he considers black. Anyone who has ever heard Ebon read can still hear and see the deep voice bounding out like a black barker at a secret blood rite, as in *Legacy: In Memory of Trane,* from his book *Revolution:*

> Juba-Lover
> bringing tales of
> Coaldust gods
> wrapped in sound.
> striving to journey home.
> beyond the light
> into darkness . . .
> into Truth
> his voice a glistening Nommo
> speechless now, hushed by
> milky smiles
> and snow June hate.
> leaving songs of praise
> a path to dance beyond . . .
> a journey quest to selfhood . . .
> a love supremely unafraid . . .

> black bright, and binding
> ear to sight unseen.

The first stanza of this strong poem is jubilant with flowing lines and images of Africa, precious, but hidden. The use of Nommo becomes its own meaning: the word, the power of the word, communication. He mixes his metaphors and if one is familiar with the music of John Coltrane, one will understand his reversal of images and double use of allusion: "a love supremely unafraid." And again his mixing of metaphor: "black bright, and binding ear to sight unseen." Whereas Coltrane becomes an image of links and heritage, and not a weird extension of a Western musician.

Toward the end of the sixties, we were introduced to poets such as Nikki Giovanni, S. E. Anderson, Jayne Cortez, June Meyer, Audre Lorde, Sterling Plumpp, Mae Jackson, Julia Fields, Marvin X, Alicia L. Johnson, Jon Eckels, Charles K. Moreland, Jr., Rockie D. Taylor, Xavier Nicholas, Askia Muhammed Touré, Doc Long, Ted Joans, and Larry Neal, with the stronger voices of Etheridge Knight, Sonia Sanchez, Carolyn Rodgers, Norman Jordan, Keorapetse Kgositsile, and Johari Amini (Jewel C. Latimore) that continued to deafen us.

Sonia Sanchez has moments of personal loneliness that are not akin to some philosophical abstraction, but come because of the absence of someone, her man, which is real. She is also intense and able to do many things at the same time, as in *Short Poem,* from her first published book, *Homecoming:*

> My old man
> tells me i'm
> so full of sweet
> pussy he can
> smell me coming.
> maybe
>   i
>   shd
>   bottle
>   it   and
>   sell it
>   when he goes.

It screams the fertile sense of being a woman desired; irony suggests an attitude toward a sex life that's natural (it can't be sold): revealing-self blues—obscenity that's funny and easy to relate to if you are black.

On the other hand, there is the formality and traditional verse form of Etheridge Knight. Gwendolyn Brooks said of Brother Knight: "[his] poetry is a major announcement. And there is blackness, inclusive, possessed and given: freed and terrible and beautiful."

Blackness:

> Hard Rock was "known not to take no shit
> From nobody," and he had the scars to prove it:
> Split purple lips, lumped ears, welts above
> His yellow eyes, and one long scar that cut
> Across his temple and plowed through a thick
> Canopy of kinky hair.

Freed:

> He sees through stone
> he has the secret
> eyes this old black one
> who under prison skies
> sits pressed by the sun
> against the western wall
> his pipe between purple gums.

Terrible and Beautiful:

> Now you take ol Rufus. He beat drums,
> was free and funky under the arms,
> fucked white girls, jumped off a bridge
> (and thought nothing of the sacrilege),
> he copped out—and he was over twenty-one.

We get a great deal in the poetry of Etheridge Knight; it's folkish as an African folk tale. It is simple/deep, as though the man has actually lived his words. He uses traditional lines, and we can see that obvious care is taken to bring forth the most meaning. He has the ability to say much in a few words. Each poem becomes a complete story that is not over- or understated.

Because of space limitations, I can't deal with other poets of merit. But I would like to mention that poets such as Lucille Clifton, Barbara D. Mahone, Zack Gilbert, Arthur Pfister, Jr., Ahmed Legraham Alhamisi, Stanley Crouch, Jay Wright, Kirk Hall, Edward S. Spriggs, Ron Wellburn, Lance Jeffers, Carol Freeman, D. L. Graham, and Bob Hamilton will be, along with the others mentioned earlier, poets to watch in the seventies. The seventies will be the decade of nation building for black people. The poets, with their special brand of insight and courage, will be in the forefront. Also, we'll see a deeper appreciation of Africa and that which is African. African literature as well as African-American literature will be placed in the positive context both deserve; bringing forth African poets like Léopold Senghor, David Diop, John Pepper Clark, Christopher Okigbo, Wole Soyinka, Léon Damas, and Aimé Césaire—all of whom are already established poets in their respective homelands, but relatively unknown in the United States.

Finally, the Black Aesthetic cannot be defined in any definite way. To accurately and fully define a Black Aesthetic would atuomatically limit it. What we've tried to do is relate specific points of reference. After all, that which is called the white (Western) aesthetic is continuously reconsidered every time a new writer, painter, or what they call a musician comes on the scene. We now know that there are nuances and ideas that are purely African. In the same vein, we can see things and ideas that are purely black, or African-American. We've talked about the music and we've seen it in the poetry, but that which we consider uniquely black can also be viewed in the way we prepare and eat food, the way we dance, our mode of dress, our loose walk, and in the way we talk and relate to each other.

What most of the young writers are doing is taking the lead in defining that which is of value to them, and doing this gives legitimacy to the community from which it stems. Therefore, these writers undertake a rather pragmatic and realistic look at the real world. Most of them grew up on Malcolm X and Frantz Fanon, and they nonromantically understand that we are an African people, but are also aware of the precariousness of the great African-past cult. As Fanon states, "I admit that all the proofs of a wonderful Songhai civilization will not change the fact that today the Songhais are underfed and illiterate, thrown between sky and water with empty heads and empty eyes." And what the younger writers of the sixties (most under thirty-five) are saying is that in order for the heads and eyes to be filled, we have to develop that which is necessary to fill them. Nation-building is the call; understanding how others have survived in this country, we as writers must contribute to the positive direction that is needed. Creativity and individuality are the two nouns most often used to describe an artist of any kind. Black poets ascribe to both, but understand that both must not interfere with us, black people, as a whole. Black poets of the sixties have moved to create images that reflect a positive movement for black people and people of the world. The poets understand their own growth and education from a new perspective. They comprehend that if all you are exposed to is Charlie Chan, you'll have Charlie Chan mentality. John Legett, in *The New York Times Book Review,* talking about the WASP vision, said: "I practice the Wasp novel. I can hardly do otherwise. I write of a Wasp world for the good and simple reason that I know it best." Just as there are the French writer, the Jewish writer, the Russian writer, the African writer, we have the black, or African-American, writer. Black poets have discovered their uniqueness, their beauty, their tales, their history, and have diligently moved to enlighten their people and the world's people in an art form that's called poetry, but to them is another extension of black music.

Sarah Webster Fabio

Tripping with Black Writing

(1971)

The move toward liberation from slave to serf to self, for Black folk, has meant a long, arduous trip. The history of this development, which we might call "The Black Experience," has been chronicled in the annals of Black Literature. Always the movement has had to be bilateral—that is, both external and internal; language has played an important part in communicating the experience from within and without. And while Blacks have had to define and validate Black reality, they, concurrently, have had to protest and protect themselves from exploitation and dehumanization. They had to not only devise ways of speaking in tongues so that "the man" could not always understand everything, but also had to speak out of both sides of their mouths—hurrahing Black; badmouthing White.

Original hoodoo, badmouthing the man, forerunners of the "Stomp Me, O Lord" slave accounts and protests Black-perspective accounts of what was really going down with the wind, start with Lucy Terry, digging the scene of an Indian Massacre, 1746:

> And had not her petticoats stopt her
> The awful creatures had not cotched her
> And tommyhawked her on the head
> And left her on the ground for dead.

Or Jupiter Hammon on *An Evening Thought, Salvation by Christ, with Penitential Cries,* turning hearts and souls away from an unbearable reality to spiritualism:

This essay first appeared in Addison Gayle, ed., *The Black Aesthetic* (New York, 1971).

Lord turn our dark benighted Souls;
Give us a true Motion,
And let the Hearts of all the World,
Make Christ their Salvation.

Early turnings; trying to turn these bedeviled mothers around, shame them in their human trafficking; these wrenchings of conscience from those short on conscience but long on bread and black gold—earliest forms of Black power. Image-making from early days from pure spirit and communion with nature. Nation-building from the ground. Loss of king-of-the-jungle images, lion-and-panther form. Beaten to the ground; gagged and shackled, but singing free:

Keep a-inching along
like a poor inch worm
JESUS IS COMING BY AND BY.

Or George Moses Horton transcending that hell-bound scene in *On Liberty and Slavery*, rapping on "the man," calling on the ancestors' spirit world:

Say unto foul oppression, Cease:
Ye tyrants rage no more,
And let the joyful trump of peace,
Now bid the vassal soar.
Soar on the pinions of that dove
Which long has cooed for thee,
And breathed her notes from Afric's grove,
The Sound of liberty. . . .

And with *The Life of Olanudah Equiano or Gustavus Vassa, The African, Written by Himself*, the beginning of the Black gift to American Mainstream Literature, a new genre—the slave narrative. "For-real" world literature. Gustavus Vassa running it down how he was run across the world, making giant steps, building civilization. Born in Benin, slaved in Virginia and Pennsylvania, farmed-out on a Caribbean plantation, working out as an abolitionist in England—as a self-made man. Bootstrap pulling; defying laws of gravity and gravitation. Gaming for self, and bootstrap-yanking for brother boots.

Getting that soul together in times of dehumanization and desecration of the souls of Black men. *Life and Times*, Frederick Douglass, a put-down as early as 1845; altogether in 1881. Whipping it to the original outhouse ruler of the "Harry Sam" vintage, Abe Lincoln; running down such a heavy game that runaway slave turns presidential adviser and Consul General to Haiti. Shades of Papa Doc! Wearing two faces. Seer. Invoking spirits, calling for an exorcism of the spirit and body of racism manifested by *Dred Scott* decision and the act of nullifying the Fourteenth Amendment in 1883. Instances of bad Supreme Court decisions which made him cry out:

> But when a deed is done for slavery, caste, and oppression; and a blow is struck at human progress, whether so intended or not, the heart of humanity sickens in sorrow and writhes in pain. It makes us feel as if some one were stamping upon the graves of our mothers, or desecrating our sacred temples. Only base men and oppressors can rejoice in a triumph of injustice over the weak and defenseless, for weakness ought itself to protect from assaults of pride, prejudice, and power. . . .
>
> No man can put a chain about the ankle of his fellow-man, without at last finding the other end of it about his own neck.
>
> The lesson of all the ages upon this point is, that a wrong done to one man is a wrong done to all men. It may not be felt at the moment, and the evil may be long delayed, but so sure as there is a moral government of the universe, so sure will the harvest of evil come.

Stomp us, O Lord! Getting into the power of speaking in tongues. W. E. B. DuBois. *The Souls of Black Folk.* Those of the double consciousness, born with veils over their eyes . . . From *Darkwater,* "A Litany at Atlanta, Done at Atlanta, in the Day of Death, 1906":

> . . . Wherefore do we pray? Is not the God of the fathers dead? Have not seers seen in Heaven's halls Thine hearsed and lifeless form stark amidst the black and rolling smoke of sin, where all along bow bitter forms of endless dead? . . . Thou art still the God of our black fathers, and in Thy soul's soul sit some soft darkenings of the evening, some shadowings of the velvet night.

Stomp us, O Lord! James Weldon Johnson raising *God's Trombones,* giving a new folk "Creation," rhapsodizing about Africa's prodigal son's return home. Setting the beat of marching feet on the road to victory in "Lift Every Voice and Sing":

> . . . Stony the road we trod,
> Bitter the chastening rod,
> Felt in the days when hope unborn had died;

Yet with a steady beat,
Have not our weary feet
Come to the place for which our fathers sighed?

Speaking in tongues. Uncle Julius, in "The Goophered Grapevine," describes one of Sycorax's daughters, Aun' Peggy, who has goophered, cunju'd, bewitched the scuppernon' vineyard:

She sa'ntered 'roun' mongs' de vimes, en tuk a leaf fum dis one, en a grape-hull fum dat one, en a grape-seed fum annuder one; en den a little twig fum here, en a little pinch er dirt fum dere,—en put it all in a big black bottle, wid a snake's toof en a speckle' hen's gall en some ha'rs fum a black cat's tail, en den fill' de bottle wid scuppernon' wine.

Speaking in tongues and running his games. Charles Chesnutt. And Paul Laurence Dunbar running it down how "We wear the Mask/That grins and lies." An African orientation . . .

Alain Locke—that necessary critic for *The New Negro;* a special critic for a special time. Harlem Renaissance. Fathering Negritude. Giving the possibility of showing forth a triumph of spirit and mind. A decolonized mind shining through colonial language. Locke sees Caliban's early move:

. . . Then eventually came the time when the hectic rhetoric and dogged moralism had to fall back in sheer exhaustion on the original basis of cultural supply. Through Dunbar,—part of whose poetry, nevertheless, reflects the last stand of this rhetorical advance, Negro poetry came penitently back to the folk-tradition, and humbled itself to dialect for fresh spiritual food and raiment.

William Stanley Braithwaite, who gave America the possibility of an American poetry, speaks of Dunbar as closing one age in Black poetry and beginning another. Check out the Sesqui-Centennial Edition of *Braithwaite's Anthology of Magazine Verse for 1926, Yearbook of American Poetry.* Black poetry—a main tributary of mainstream American poetry. A Black man willing to bring an indigenous, nonderivative poetry into being. He got lost in the shuffle after 1929. But he'd done his thing. Sterling Brown, one of the most capable writers using Black form chronicling the literary movement in *Negro Caravan.* Sterling Brown in his *Negro Poetry and Drama* said this:

"Dialect, or the speech of the people, is capable of expressing whatever the people are. And the folk Negro is a great deal more than a buffoon or a plaintive minstrel. Poets more intent upon learning the ways of the folk, their speech, and their character, that is to say better poets, could have smashed the mold. But first they would have had to believe in what they were doing. And this was difficult in a period of conciliation and middle class striving for recognition and respectability."

Early there was a self-consciousness and a mold which a deriding white America put on Black folk speech. This meant that many feigned representing folk speech, according to Brown, by:

"A few pat phrases, a few stock situations and characteristics, some misspelling: these were the chief things necessary. The wit and beauty possible to folk speech, the folk-shrewdness, the humanity, the stoicism of these people they seldom say."

The Harlem Renaissance period closed the credibility gap between the Black man, his articulation of his experience, and his selfhood. Zora Neal [sic] Hurston, anthropologist, throwing light on language. Open the way for today's freedom-wigged freaks. Stone-cold, bad-blood revolutionaries. Escapees from prisons of Anglo rhetoric. Frontiersmen in the lumbering netherlands of Black language. Medicine men schooled in witchcraft, black magic, the voodoo of words. Immortalized, subterranean, out-of-this-world travelers. Dutchmen. LeRois. LeRoi Joneses. Quick-change sleight-of-hand magicians. Dons. Don Lees. Changing. "Change your enemy change your change change change your enemy change change . . . change your mind nigger." Killens. Killens' chilluns. On their jobs. Taking care of business. "Deniggerizing the world." Voodoo cowboys. Loop Garoo Kids. Riding loose— cool ones—into the whirlwind of change; who, as they gallop into town, have a "posse of spells phone in sick." Ishmaels. Ishmael Reeds. Yeah. Yellow Back Radio Done Show Good Broke-Down. Up against the wall, Prospero.

Calibans all. Exploding Prospero's premises with extraordinary, for-real, supernatural departures. Trips. More benevolent despotism, spelled Tyranny. Any way you look at it. And his gift of language—his "prison in which Caliban's achievements will be realized and restricted"—is a boomerang. New-breed Blacks, those desperadoes who "Take the Money and Run," leave "the man" behind bound and bankrupt; marooned on a barren island of derivative Anglo-Saxon, European-like culture. Walled in by the "law and order" of his own restrictive rhetoric. And those newly free? They are on their jobs making jujus, working their mojos, peeping Chuck's hold cards.

Understanding the real meaning of his excessive articulation of so much nonsense. Seers and sages. Reporters such as Eldridge Cleaver sending back messages about the "technologically gifted moon men": "I heard what he said; he said 'oink.'" LeRoi Jones-created criminals intent on robbing the family of its jewels in *Home on the Range*. Mystified, momentarily, with the father's talk, "Crillilly bagfest. Gobble Gobble. Gobble." But understand their task is to give these robots the gift of soul, of language of the real world. Once more, Mr. Tooful: "I was born in Kansas City in 1920. My father was the vice-president of a fertilizer company. Before that we were phantoms. . . ." Which explains all that shit. Packaged under the brand name of "Standard English," mainstream American literature. Or Sister Carolyn Rodgers taking a look at the spineless, flat imitation in "Portrait of a White Nigger!" who "talks like/a biscuit that will/not rise . . . got a jelly mind/and shimmy thighs"; whose purpose in life is reduced to an endless search trying "to find the MAGIC that/will/PRESTO"/Black/off/ . . ."

No mere children of nature these. They are indeed, Sycorax-the-Sorceress' offspring. With magic potions to tame the beasts of nature. With so many thumping, twangling instruments giving the beat. Informing William Melvin Kelley and his likes that he moves to the rhythms of *A Different Drummer.* Dere's Us'ns and dere's *Dem.* Magic knowledge. Source of power found rooted in the residue of a wellspring of aged and ageless African native culture—soul. Spooky Stuff. Sins of the father's revisited! Great balls of fire!!! Brother, brush off your Br'er Rabbit's foot. Shine up your John-The-Conqueror root. Whip up your own brand gris-gris. It's Voodoo time again.

LeRoi Jones, dramatizing the dilemma. Don Lee, chronicling the changes. Ishmael Reed, S-p-e-l-l-i-n-g it out. Nikki Giovanni, recording "Records": "a negro needs to kill/something/trying to record/that this country must be/ destroyed/if we are to live/must be destroyed if we are to live/must be destroyed if we are to live." Jimmy Garret, bucking the whitewashed system. White power—the same which done got his mama—challenged to a duel. By a deathly game of dozens, in the one-act *And We Own the Night*. Cracker-walled prisons of rhetoric crumbled before the double-whammied eyes of crumb-snatching blues logic, Semple-fied by Langston Hughes, passed on as sacrament to Stanley Crouch and Dante. Stone walls of martial law and bad conditions failing to imprison the spirit of Blacks. Etheridge Knight, breaking through in *Cell Song,* answering the call to "take/your words and scrape/ the sky, shake rain/on the desert, sprinkle/salt on the tail/of a girl . . ." And

Sonia Sanchez preparing for *Homecoming:* "Leaving behind me/all those hide and/seek faces . . . I have learned it/ain't like they say/in the newspapers." Soul talk for soul folk. *Boss Soul,* by Sarah Fabio: " . . . gut bucket, gospel spiritual, jazz/touching cords of Feeling any live person/has to tune into or turn on to that/special deepdown/inside you thing."

New Day. Dawn. Light of Broken Night. Night breaks. Night trippers. Check out the Bad, Bold scene of the Mojo workers. Dig the star-crossed bones uncovered by Ishmael Reed in *15 Nigromancers From Now.* If you dare. Any day or night—or séance in between—get on down to what's really there. Clean-picked bones. The skulls of ones who talked too much. Get to that. Another necessary trip: *Amistad,* with Charles Harris and John Williams piloting.

Black writers, finding themselves up a tree with "the man's" rhetoric and aesthetic, which hangs them up, lynching their black visions, cut it loose. All the way—swinging free. Flying home. Wings flapping, raucously, in the breeze. So many unnatural demands from the establishment, the tradition, beamed into a subject people from a hostile, alien culture, shined off as irrelevant, self-defeating. Needing to respond as integral beings not having to compromise integrity. Bringing black perspective, black aesthetic, black rhetoric, black language to add authenticity to the felt reality. Knowing America has no rhetoric matching its racist reality; no reality matching its "universal" and "democratic" idealistic state of existence. Knowing the simple-minded, fascist, pseudo-Europeanized mandate of "universality" to be a funky issue in any aesthetic consideration. A hustle to make walleyed, white-eyed America the all-seeing Cyclops of our age.

Giving the finger to blind justice. Peeping the loosened blindfold. Peeping her peeping; favoring the apples of her eye—rotten though they may be. Playing the game of dozens with her. Combating her status-quo games. Knowing the truth about this society. One that devaluates the lives of a people for the duration of its existence. One that dehumanizes them for fun and profit. A mere matter of pragmatism and utilitarianism. Knowing that society to be guilty of: emasculating manhood; deflowering womanhood; exploiting spirit and soul; blinding vision; binding motion; dulling sensitivity; gagging speech.

Black Writing—repressed, suppressed, ignored, denounced. Black Writers having rained upon them not respect, riches, rewards, but disrespect, discouragement, nonrecognition, deculturation, assimilation, isolation, starvation, expatriation, derangement, criminal indictment. LeRoi Jones's case but a recent and flagrant example of a system's way of dealing with creative liberated black minds. The same brutal white backlash that cut the cord of David Walker's life after his writing of his "Appeal" in the early nineteenth century still tears at the flesh of articulate Blacks of the recent past and the present—men such as Malcolm X, Martin Luther King, Eldridge Cleaver, Bobby Seale.

No turning back, though. This is the day of Biggers and ghosts of Biggers. Black writers—most of them poets plus—have always been barometers, even when America kept bell jars on them. Have always been/still are/will be. Always traveling with ears to the ground; attuned to the drumbeats of the age. Check out the Harlem Renaissance poets, such as Langston Hughes, Claude McKay, Sterling Brown. Check out the post depression poets of the thirties, including Richard Wright. Check out Margaret Walker's words to her people in the early forties. Check out the poets in *Beyond the Blues*, a time when Black poetry was so far underground it had to travel to England for publication. Check out Black poets publishing with Broadside Press, Third World Press, Success Press. Check out Black periodicals—*Journal of Black Poetry, Black Dialogue, Negro Digest, Liberator.*

Take the A-Train to Black liberation. Black writing of the seventies will be the Sweet Chariots of our time: swinging low/swinging high/swinging free. Communicant. Continuum. Change. Consummation.

IV

Structuralism, Post-Structuralism,
and the African American Critic

Henry Louis Gates, Jr.

Preface to Blackness: Text and Pretext

(1978)

For Soule is forme, and doth the bodie make.—Edmund Spenser, 1596

Music is a world within itself, with a language we all understand.—Stevie Wonder, 1976

The idea of a determining formal relation between literature and social institutions does not in itself explain the sense of urgency that has, at least since the publication in 1760 of *A Narrative of the Uncommon Sufferings and Surprising Deliverance of Briton Hammon, a Negro Man,*[1] characterized nearly the whole of Afro-American writing. This idea has often encouraged a posture that belabors the social and documentary status of black art, and indeed the earliest discrete examples of written discourse by slave and ex-slave came under a scrutiny not primarily literary. Formal writing, beginning with the four autobiographical slave narratives published in English between 1760 and 1798, was taken to be collective as well as functional. Because narratives documented the potential for "culture," that is, for manners and morals, the command of written English virtually separated the African from the Afro-American, the slave from the ex-slave, titled property from fledgling human being. Well-meaning abolitionists cited these texts as proof of the common humanity of bondsman and lord; yet these same texts also demonstrated the contrary for proponents of the antebellum world view—that the African imagination was merely derivative. The command of a written language, then, could be no mean thing in the life of the slave: Learning to read, the slave narratives repeat again and again, was a decisive political act; learning to write, as measured by an eighteenth-century scale of culture and

This essay first appeared in Dexter Fisher and Robert Stepto, eds., *Afro-American Literature: The Reconstruction of Instruction* (New York, 1978).

society, was an irreversible step away from the cotton field toward a freedom even larger than physical manumission. What the use of language entailed for personal social mobility and what it implied about the public Negro mind made for the onerous burden of literacy, a burden having very little to do with the use of language as such, a burden so pervasive that the nineteenth-century quest for literacy and the twentieth-century quest for form became the central, indeed controlling, metaphors (if not mythical matrices) in Afro-American narrative. Once the private dream fused with a public, and therefore political, imperative, the Negro arts were committed; the pervasive sense of fundamental urgency and unity in the black arts became a millenial, if not precisely apocalyptic, force.

I do not mean to suggest that these ideas were peculiar to eighteenth-century American criticism. For example, we learn from Herder's Prize Essay of 1773 on the *Causes of the Decline of Taste in Different Nations* that in Germany "the appreciation of various folk and Gothic literatures and the comparative study of ancient, eastern, and modern foreign literatures (the criticism of literature by age and race) were strongly established, and these interests profoundly affected theories about the nature of literature as the expression of, or the power that shaped, human cultures or human nature in general." William K. Wimsatt also remarks that Friedrick Schlegel "only accented an already pervasive view when he called poetry the most specifically human energy, the central document of any culture."[2] It should not surprise us, then, that *Poems on Various Subjects, Religious and Moral, by Phillis Wheatley, Negro Servant to Mr. Wheatley of Boston,* the first book of poems published by an African in English,[3] became, almost immediately after its publication in London in 1773, the international antislavery movement's most salient argument for the African's innate mental equality. That the book went to five printings before 1800 testified far more to its acceptance as a "legitimate" product of "the African muse," writes Henri Grégoire[4] in 1808, than to the merit of its sometimes vapid elegiac verse. The no fewer than eighteen "certificates of authenticity" that preface the book, including one by John Hancock and another by the Governor of Massachusetts, Thomas Hutchinson, meant to "leave no doubt, that she is its author."[5] Literally scores of public figures—from Voltaire to George Washington, from Benjamin Rush to Benjamin Franklin—reviewed Wheatley's book, yet virtually no one discussed the book as poetry. It was an unequal contest: The documentary status of black art assumed priority over mere literary judgment; criticism rehearsed content to justify one notion of origins or another.

Of these discussions, it was Thomas Jefferson's that proved most seminal to the shaping of the Afro-American critical activity. Asserted primarily to debunk the exaggerated claims of the abolitionists, Thomas Jefferson's remarks on Phillis Wheatley's poetry, as well as on Ignatius Sancho's *Letters*,[6] exerted a prescriptive influence over the criticism of the writing of blacks for the next 150 years. "Never yet," Jefferson prefaces his discussion of Wheatley, "could I find a Black that had uttered a thought above the level of plain narration; never seen even an elementary trait of painting or sculpture." As a specimen of the human mind, Jefferson continued, Wheatley's poems as poetry did not merit discussion. "Religion," he writes, "indeed has produced a Phillis Whately [sic] but it could not produce a poet." "The compositions published under her name," Jefferson concludes, "are below the dignity of criticism. The heroes of the *Dunciad* are to her, as Hercules to the author of the poem." As to Sancho's *Letters*, Jefferson says:

> his imagination is wild and extravagant, escapes incessantly from every restraint of reason and taste, and, in the course of its vagaries, leaves a tract of thought as incoherent and eccentric, as is the course of a meteor through the sky. His subjects should have led him to a process of sober reasoning: yet we find him always substituting sentiment for demonstration.[7]

Jefferson's stature demanded response: from black writers, refutations of his doubts about their very capacity to imagine great art and hence to take a few giant steps up the Great Chain of Being; from would-be critics, encyclopaedic and often hyperbolic replies to Jefferson's disparaging generalizations. The critical responses included Thomas Clarkson's Prize Essay, written in Latin at Cambridge in 1785 and published as *An Essay on the Slavery and Commerce of the Human Species, Particularly the African* (1788), and the following, rather remarkable, volumes: Gilbert Imlay's *A Topographical Description of the Western Territory of North America* (1793); the Marquis de Bois-Robert's two-volume *The Negro Equalled by Few Europeans* (1791); Thomas Branagan's *Preliminary Essay* on the *Oppression of the Exiled Sons of Africa* (1804); The Abbé Grégoire's *An Enquiry concerning the Intellectual and Moral Faculties, and Literature of Negroes . . .* (1808); Samuel Stanhope Smith's *An Essay on the Causes of the Variety of the Human Complexion and Figure in the Human Species* (1810); Lydia Child's *An Appeal in Favor of That Class of Americans Called Africans* (1833); B. B. Thatcher's *Memoir of Phillis Wheatley, a Native American and a Slave* (1834); Abigail Mott's *Biographical*

Sketches and Interesting Anecdotes of Persons of Color (1838); R. B. Lewis' *Light and Truth* (1844); Theodore Hally's *A Vindication of the Capacity of the Negro Race* (1851); R. T. Greener's urbane long essay in *The National Quarterly Review* (1880); Joseph Wilson's rather ambitious *Emancipation: Its Course and Progress from 1481 B.C. to A.D. 1875* (1882); William Simmon's *Men of Mark* (1887); Benjamin Brawley's *The Negro in Literature and Art* (1918) and Joel A. Rodgers' two-volume *The World's Great Men of Color* (1946).

Even more telling, for our purposes here, is that the almost quaint authenticating signatures and statements that prefaced Wheatley's book became, certainly through the period of Dunbar and Chesnutt and even until the middle of the Harlem Renaissance, fixed attestations of the "specimen" author's physical blackness. This sort of authenticating color description was so common to these prefaces that many late nineteenth- and early twentieth-century black reviewers, particularly in the *African Methodist Episcopal Church Review,* the *Southern Workman,* the *Voice of the Negro, Alexander's Magazine,* and *The Colored American,* adopted it as a political as well as rhetorical strategy to counter the intense and bitter allegations of African inferiority popularized by journalistic accounts and "colorations" of social Darwinism. Through an examination of a few of these prefaces, I propose to sketch an ironic circular thread of interpretation that commences in the eighteenth century but does not reach its fullest philosophical form until the decade between 1965 and 1975: the movement from blackness as a physical concept to blackness as a metaphysical concept. Indeed, this movement became the very text and pretext of the "Blackness" of the recent Black Arts movement, a solidly traced hermeneutical circle into which all of us find ourselves drawn.

II

Even before Jefferson allowed himself the outrageous remark that "the improvement of the blacks in body and mind, in the first instance of their mixture with the whites, has been observed by every one, and proves that their inferiority is not the effect merely of their condition of life,"[8] advocates of the unity of the human species had forged a union of literary tradition, individual talent, and innate racial capacity. Phillis Wheatley's "authenticators," for instance, announced that:

> We whose Names are under-written, do assure the world, that the POEMS specified in the following Page, were (as we verily believe)

written by *Phillis,* a young Negro Girl, who was but a few years since, brought an uncultured Barbarian from Africa, and has ever since been and now is, under the Disadvantage of serving as a Slave of a Family in this Town. She has been examined by some of the best Judges, and is thought qualified to write them.[9]

Further, Wheatley herself asks indulgence of the critic, considering the occasion of her verse. "As her Attempts in Poetry are now sent into the World, it is hoped the critic will not severely censure their Defects; and we presume they have too much Merit to be cast aside with contempt, as worthless and trifling effusions." "With all their Imperfections," she concludes, "the poems are now humbly submitted to the Perusal of the Public."[10] Other than the tone of the author's preface, there was little here that was "humbly submitted" to Wheatley's public. Her volume garnered immense interest as to the nature of the African imagination. So compelling did evidence of the African's artistic abilities prove to be to Enlightenment speculation on the idea of progress and the scala naturae that just nine years after Wheatley's *Poems* appeared, over one thousand British lords and ladies subscribed to have published Ignatius Sancho's collected letters. Even more pertinent in our context, Joseph Jekyll, M.P., prefaced the volume with a full biographical account of the colorful Sancho's life, structured curiously about the received relation between "genius" and "species."

People were also fascinated by the "African mind" presented in the collected letters of Ignatius Sancho. Named "from a fancied resemblance to the Squire of Don Quixote,"[11] Sancho had his portrait painted by Gainsborough and engraved by Bartolozzi. He was a correspondent of Garrick and Sterne and, apparently, something of a poet as well: "A commerce with the Muses was supported amid the trivial and momentary interruptions of a shop," Jekyll writes. Indeed, not only were "the Poets studied, and even imitated with some success," but "two pieces were constructed for the stage." In addition to his creative endeavors, Sancho was a critic—perhaps the first African critic of the arts to write in English. His "theory of Music was discussed, published, and dedicated to the Princess Royal, and Painting was so much within the circle of Ignatius Sancho's judgment and criticism," Jekyll observes, "that several artists paid great *deference* to his opinion."

Jekyll's rather involved biography is a pretext to display the artifacts of the sable mind, as was the very publication of the *Letters* themselves. "Her motives for laying them before the publick were," the publisher admits, "the desire of showing that an untutored African may possess abilities equal to an

European." Sancho was an "extraordinary Negro," his biographer relates, although he was a bit better for being a bit bad. "Freedom, riches, and leisure, naturally led to a disposition of African tendencies into indulgences; and that which dissipated the mind of Ignatius completely drained the purse," Jekyll puns. "In his attachment to women, he displayed a profuseness which not unusually characterizes the excess of the passion." "Cards had formerly seduced him," we are told, "but an unsuccessful contest at cribbage with a Jew, who won his cloaths, had determined to abjure the propensity which appears to be innate among his countrymen." Here, *again,* we see drawn the thread between phylogeny and ontogeny: "a French writer relates," Jekyll explains, "that in the kingdoms of Ardrah, Whydah, and Benin, a Negro will stake at play his fortune, his children, and his liberty." Thus driven to distraction, Sancho was "induced to consider the stage" since "his complexion suggested an offer to the manager of attempting Othello and Oroonoko; but a defective and incorrigible articulation rendered it abortive."

Colorful though Jekyll's anecdotes are, they are a mere pretext for the crux of his argument: a disquisition on cranial capacity, regional variation, skin color, and intelligence. The example of Sancho, made particularly human by the citation of his foibles, is meant to put to rest any suspicion as to the native abilities of the Negro:

> Such was the man whose species philosophers and anatomists have endeavored to degrade as a deterioration of the human; and such was the man whom Fuller, with a benevolence and quaintness of phrase peculiarly his own, accounted "God's Image, though cut in Ebony." To the harsh definition of the naturalist, oppressions political and legislative have been added; and such are hourly aggravated towards this unhappy race of men by vulgar prejudice and popular insult. To combat these on commercial principles, has been the labour of [others]—such an effort here, [he concludes ironically] would be an impertinent digression.

That Sancho's attainments are not merely isolated exceptions to the general morass is indicated by the state of civilization on the African "slave-coast." Jekyll continues:

> Of those who have speculatively visited and described the slave-coast, there are not wanting some who extol the mental abilities of the natives. [Some] speak highly of their mechanical powers and indefatigable industry. [Another] does not scruple to affirm, that their ingenuity rivals the Chinese.

What is more, these marks of culture and capacity signify an even more telling body of data, since the logical extensions of mechanical powers and industry are sublime arts and stable polity:

> He who could penetrate the interior of Africa, might not improbably discover negro arts and polity, which could bear little analogy to the ignorance and grossness of slaves in the sugar-islands, expatriated in infamy; and brutalized under the whip and the task-master.

"And he," Jekyll summarizes, "who surveys the extent of intellect to which Ignatius Sancho had attained self-education, will perhaps conclude, that the perfection of the reasoning faculties does not depend on the colour of a common integument."[12]

Jekyll's preface became a touchstone for the literary anthropologists who saw in black art a categorical repository for the African's potential to deserve inclusion in the human community. Echoes of Jekyll's language resound throughout the prefaces to slave testimony. Gustavus Vassa's own claim in 1789 that the African's contacts with "liberal sentiments" and "the Christian religion" have "exalted human nature" is vouched for by more than one hundred Irish subscribers. Charles Ball's editor asserts in 1836 that Ball is "a common negro slave, embued by nature with a tolerable portion of intellectual capacity."[13] Both Garrison's and Phillip's prefaces to *The Narrative of the Life of Frederick Douglass* (1845) and James McCune Smith's introduction to Douglass' *My Bondage and My Freedom* (1855)[14] attest to Douglass' African heritage and former bestial status. McCune Smith proffers the additional claims for literary excellence demanded by the intensity of doubt toward the black African's mental abilities:

> the Negro, for the first time in the world's history brought in full contact with high civilization, must prove his title first to all that is demanded for him; in the teeth of unequal chances, he must prove himself equal to the mass of those who oppress him—therefore, absolutely superior to his apparent fate, and to their relative ability. And it is most cheering to the friends of freedom, to-day, that evidence of this equality is rapidly accumulating, not from the ranks of the half-freed colored people of the free states, but from the very depths of slavery itself; the indestructible equality of man to man is demonstrated by the ease with which black men, scarce one remove from barbarism—if slavery can be honored with such a distinction—vault into the high places of the most advanced and painfully acquired civilization.

What is more germane is a review of Douglass' *Narrative* that emphasizes the relevance of each "product" of the African mind almost as another primary argument in the abolitionists' brief against slavery:

> Considered merely as a narrative, we have never read one more simple, true, coherent, and warm with genuine feeling. It is an excellent piece of writing, and on that score to be prized as a specimen of the powers of the black race, which prejudice persists in disputing. We prize highly all evidence of this kind, and it is becoming more abundant.[15]

These readings of blackness discuss the very properties of property. In fact, what we discover here is a correlation between property and properties and between character and characteristics, which proved so pervasive in the latter half of the nineteenth century that Booker T. Washington's *Up from Slavery,* for example, becomes, after its seventh chapter, the autobiography of an institution, thereby detaching itself somewhat from the slave narrative tradition, where the structural movement was from institution and property to man.

This relation between essence and value, between ethics and aesthetics, became, at least as early as William Dean Howells' 1896 review of Paul Laurence Dunbar's "Majors and Minors,"[16] a correlation between a metaphysical blackness and a physical blackness. Howells emphasizes almost immediately Dunbar's appearance:

> the face of a young negro, with the race's traits strangely accented: the black skin, the wooly hair, the thick, outrolling lips, and the mild, soft eyes of the pure African type. One cannot be very sure, ever, about the age of those people, but I should have thought that this poet was about twenty years old; and I suppose that a generation ago he would have been worth, apart from his literary gift, twelve or fifteen hundred dollars, under the hammer.

Howells makes a subtle shift here from properties to property. Moreover, he outlines the still prevalent notion that treats art as artifact:

> He is, so far as I know, the first man of his color to study his race objectively, to analyze it to himself, and then to represent it in art as he felt it and found it to be; to represent it humorously, yet tenderly, and above all so faithfully that we know the portrait to be undeniably like. A race which has reached this effect in any of its members can no longer be

held wholly uncivilized; and intellectually Mr. Dunbar makes a stronger claim for the negro than the negro yet has done.

Howells then makes the leap so crucial to this discussion, and so crucial to the aesthetics of the Black Arts movement:

If his Minors [the dialect pieces] had been written by a white man, I should have been struck by their very uncommon quality; I should have said that they were wonderful divinations. But since they are expressions of a race-life from within the race, they seem to me infinitely more valuable and significant. I have sometimes fancied that perhaps the negroes *thought* black, and *felt* black: that they were racially so utterly alien and distinct from ourselves that there never could be common intellectual and emotional ground between us, and that whatever eternity might do to reconcile us, the end of time would find us far asunder as ever. But this little book, has given me pause in my speculation. Here in the artistic effect at least, is white thinking and white feeling in a black man, and perhaps the human unity, and not the race unity, is the precious thing, the divine thing, after all. God hath made of one blood all nations of men: perhaps the proof of this saying is to appear in the arts, and our hostilities and prejudices are to vanish in them.

Here in Howells we find suggestions of imperatives for the cultural renaissance that DuBois would outline in the *Crisis* just fifteen years later. Here in Howells we find the premise that would assume a shape in the fiction of a "New Negro." Here we find the sustained apocalyptic notion of the Negro arts, about which Carl Van Vechten and James Weldon Johnson would correspond at length. Here we find the supposition, elaborated on at length by DuBois and even William Stanley Braithwaite, by Langston Hughes and Claude McKay, that, while blacks and whites are in essence different, that difference can be mediated through the media of art. The Black Christ would be a poetaster. And the physical blackness to which would testify critics as unalike as I. A. Richards at Cambridge and Max Eastman at the *Liberator,* referred to in separate prefaces to different volumes by Claude McKay in 1919 and 1922, would resurface in subtler form in Allen Tate and Irving Howe. Tate and Howe, the ideological counterparts of Richards and Eastman, would in 1950 and 1963 reassert a metaphysical blackness to which they were somehow privy, Tate's New Critical "extrinsic" fallacies notwithstanding. Yet if we see this remarkably persistent idea become Don L. Lee's pernicious preface to

Gwendolyn Brooks's *Report from Part One,* we can perhaps take comfort in Black Arts poet Larry Neal's sensitive authenticating preface to Kimberly Benston's subtle readings of the plays of Imamu Baraka. As blind men, we have traced the circle.

III

The confusion of realms, of art with propaganda, plagued the Harlem Renaissance in the 1920s. A critical determination—a mutation of principles set in motion by Matthew Arnold's *Culture and Anarchy,* simplified thirty years later into Booker Washington's "toothbrush and bar of soap," and derived from Victorian notions of "uplifting" spiritual and moral ideals that separated the savage (noble or not) from the realm of culture and the civilized mind—meant that only certain literary treatments of black people could escape community censure. The race against Social Darwinism and the psychological remnants of slavery meant that each piece of creative writing became a political statement. Each particular manifestation served as a polemic: "Another bombshell fired into the heart of bourgeois culture," as *The World Tomorrow* editorialized in 1921. "The black writer," said Richard Wright, "approached the critical community dressed in knee pants of servility, curtseying to show that the Negro was not inferior, that he was human, and that he had a gift comparable to other men."[17] As early as 1921, W. E. B. DuBois wrote of this in the *Crisis:*

> Negro art is today plowing a difficult row. We want everything that is said about us to tell of the best and highest and noblest in us. We insist that our Art and Propaganda be one. We fear that evil in us will be called racial, while in others it is viewed as individual. We fear that our shortcomings are not merely human. . . .[18]

And, as late as 1925, even as sedate an observer as Heywood Broun argued that only through Art would the Negro gain his freedom: "A supremely great negro artist," he told the New York Urban League, "who could catch the imagination of the world, would do more than any other agency to remove the disabilities against which the negro now labors."[19] Further, Broun remarked that this artist-redeemer could come at any time, and he asked his audience to remain silent for ten seconds to imagine that coming! Ambiguity in language, then, and "feelings that are general" (argued for as early as 1861 by Frances E. W. Harper) garnered hostility and suspicion from the critical minority; ambiguity was a threat to "knowing the lines." The results on a growing black literature were disastrous, these perorations themselves dubious. Black literature came to be seen as a cultural artifact (the product of unique historical forces) or as a document and witness to the political and emotional tendencies of the Negro victim of white racism. Literary theory became the application of a social attitude.

By the apex of the Harlem Renaissance, then, certain latent assumptions about the relationships between "art" and "life" had become prescriptive canon. In 1925, DuBois outlined what he called "the social compulsion" of black literature, built as it was, he contended, on "the sorrow and strain inherent in American slavery, on the difficulties that sprang from emancipation, on the feelings of revenge, despair, aspiration, and hatred which arose as the Negro struggled and fought his way upward."[20] Further, he made formal the mechanistic distinction between "method" and "content," the same distinction that allowed James Weldon Johnson to declare with glee that, sixty years after slavery, all that separated the black poet from the white was "mere technique!" Structure, by now, was atomized: "Form" was merely a surface for a reflection of the world, the "world" here being an attitude toward race; form was a repository for the disposal of ideas; message was not only meaning but value; poetic discourse was taken to be literal, or once removed; language lost its capacity to be metaphorical in the eyes of the critic; the poem approached the essay, with referents immediately perceivable; literalness precluded the view of life as "allegorical"; and black critics forgot that writers approached things through words, not the other way around. The functional and didactic aspects of formal discourse assumed primacy in normative analysis. The confusion of realms was complete: The critic became social reformer, and literature became an instrument for the social and ethical betterment of the black man.

So, while certain rather conservative notions of art and culture wove themselves into F. R. Leavis' *Scrutiny* in Cambridge in the 1930s, blacks borrowed whole the Marxist notion of base and superstructure and made of it, if you will, race and superstructure. Here, as in Wright's "Blueprint for Negro Literature," for example, "race" in American society was held to determine the social relations that determine consciousness, which, in turn, determines actual ideas and creative works. "In the beginning was the deed," said Trotsky in an attack on the Formalists; now, the deed was *black*.

This notion of race and superstructure became, during the 1940s and 1950s, in one form or another the mode of criticism of black literature. As would be expected, critics urged the supremacy of one extraliterary idea after another, as Ralph Ellison "challenged" Richard Wright on one front and

James Baldwin on another. But race as the controlling "mechanism" in critical theory reached its zenith of influence and mystification when LeRoi Jones metamorphosed himself into Imamu Baraka, and his daishiki-clad, Swahili-named "harbari gani" disciples "discovered" they were black. With virtually no exceptions, black critics employed "blackness"-as-theme to forward one argument or another for the amelioration of the Afro-American's social dilemma. Yet, the critical activity altered little, whether that "message" was integration or whether it was militant separation. Message was the medium; message reigned supreme; form became a mere convenience or, worse, a contrivance.

The commonplace observation that black literature with very few exceptions has failed to match pace with a sublime black music stems in large measure from this concern with *statement*. Black music, by definition, could never utilize the schism between form and content, because of the nature of music. Black music, alone of the black arts, has developed free of the imperative, the compulsion, to make an explicit political statement. Black musicians, of course, had no choice: Music groups masses of nonrepresentational material into significant form; it is the audible embodiment of form. All this, however, requires a specific mastery of technique, which cannot be separated from "poetic insight." There could be no "knowing the lines" in the creation of black music, especially since the Afro-American listening audience had such a refined and critical aesthetic sense. Thus, Afro-America has a tradition of masters, from Bessie Smith through John Coltrane, unequalled, perhaps, in all of modern music. In literature, however, we have no similar development, no sustained poignancy in writing. In poetry, where the command of language is indispensable if only because poetry thickens language and thus draws attention from its referential aspect, we have seen the growth of what the poet Ted Joans calls the "Hand-Grenade" poets,[21] who concern themselves with futile attempts to make poetry preach, which poetry is not capable of doing so well. And the glorification of this poetry (especially the glorification of Baraka and Don Lee's largely insipid rhetoric), in which we feel the unrelenting vise of the poet's grip upon our shoulders, has become the principal activity of the "New Black" critic. The suppositions on which this theory of criticism rests are best explicated through a close reading of four texts that, conveniently, treat poetry, literary history, and the novel.

Stephen Henderson's *Understanding the New Black Poetry* is the first attempt at a quasi-formalistic analysis of black poetry.[22] It is of the utmost importance to the history of race and superstructure criticism because it attempts to map a black poetic landscape, identifying inductively those unique cultural *artifacts* that critics, "especially white critics," have "widely misunderstood, misinterpreted, and undervalued for a variety of reasons—aesthetic, cultural, and political." Henderson's work is seminal insofar as he is concerned with the uses of language, but in the course of his study he succumbs to the old idea of advancing specific ideological prerequisites.

Henderson readily admits his bias: He equates aesthetics and ethics. "Ultimately," he says, "the 'beautiful' is bound up with the truth of a people's history, as they perceive it themselves." This absolute of truth Henderson defines in his fifth definition of what "Black poetry is chiefly": "Poetry by any identifiably Black person whose ideological stance vis-à-vis the history and aspirations of his people since slavery [is] adjudged by them to be 'correct.'" Hence, an ideal of truth, which exists in fact for the black poet to "find," is a "Black" truth. And "Black" is integral to the poetic equation, since "if there is such a *commodity* as 'blackness' in literature (and I assume that there is), it should somehow be found in concentrated or in residual form in the poetry" (italics added).

Had Henderson elaborated on "residual form" in literary language, measured formally, structurally, or linguistically, he would have revolutionized black literary criticism and brought it into the twentieth century. But his theory of poetry is based on three sometimes jumbled "broad categories" that allow the *black* critic to define "norms" of "blackness." The first of these is an oversimplified conception of "theme": "that which is spoken of, whether the specific subject matter, the emotional response to it, or its intellectual formulation." The second is "structure," by which Henderson intends "chiefly some aspect of the poem such as diction, rhythm, figurative language, which goes into the total makeup." (At times, he notes, "I use the word in an extended sense to include what is usually called genre.") His third critical tool, the scale by which he measures the "commodity" he calls "Blackness," is "saturation." He means by this "several things, chiefly the communication of 'Blackness' and fidelity to the observed or intuited truth of the Black Experience in the United States."

Now, the textual critic has problems with Henderson's schema not only because it represents an artificial segmentation of poetic structure (which can never, in fact, be discussed as if one element existed independently of the rest) but also because that same schema tends to be defined in terms of itself, and hence is tautological. Henderson defines "theme," for example, as "perhaps the simplest and most apparent" of the three. By theme, however, he means a poem's paraphrased level of "meaning." To illustrate this, he contrasts a George Moses Horton quatrain with a couplet from Countée Cullen.

The "ambiguity" of the former lines, he concludes, defined for us insofar as "it might evoke a sympathetic tear from the eye of a white [Jewish] New York professor meditating upon his people's enslavement in ancient Egypt, does make it a less precise kind of ['Black'] statement than Cullen's, because in the latter the irony cannot be appreciated without understanding the actual historical debasement of the African psyche in America." Thus, the principal corollary to the theorem of "black themes" is that the closer a "theme" approaches cultural exclusivity, the closer it comes to a higher "fidelity." Moreover, he allows himself to say, had Shakespeare's Sonnet 130 "been written by an African at Elizabeth's court, would not the thematic meaning change?" That leap of logic is difficult to comprehend, for a poem is above all atemporal and must cohere at a symbolic level, if it coheres at all. In some fairness to Stephen Henderson, much of the poetry from which he is extracting his theory *is used* in the language game of *giving information*. Stephen Henderson's problem is, in short, the "poetry" prompting his theory; he has only followed that poetry's lead and in that way left himself open to Wittgenstein's remonstration: "Do not forget that a poem, even though it is composed in the language of information, is not used in the language of giving information."

The most promising of Henderson's categories is "structure," and yet it is perhaps the most disappointing. By "structure," he means that "Black poetry is most distinctively Black" whenever "it derives its form from two basic sources, Black speech and Black music." At first glance, this idea seems exciting, since it implies a unique, almost intangible use of language peculiar to Afro-Americans. On this one could build, nay one *must* build, that elusive "Black Aesthetic" the race and superstructure critics have sought in vain. But Henderson's understanding of speech as referent is not linguistic; he means a *literal* referent to nonpoetic discourse and makes, unfortunately, no allowances for the manner in which poetic discourse differs from prosaic discourse or "instances" of speech. He provides us with an elaborate and complicated taxonomy of referents to speech and to music, yet unaccountably ignores the fact that the "meaning" of a word in a poem is derived from its context within that poem, as well as from its context in our actual, historical consciousness. But a taxonomy is a tool to knowledge, not knowledge itself. The use of language is not a stockpile of referents or forms, but an activity.

Henderson remarks with some astonishment that "Black speech in this country" is remarkable in that "certain words and constructions seem to carry an inordinate charge of emotional and psychological weight." These, he calls "mascon" words, borrowing the acronym from NASA, where it is employed to describe a "massive concentration" of matter beneath the lunar surface. What he is describing, of course, is not unique to black poetic discourse; it is common to all poetic uses of language in all literatures and is what helps to create ambiguity, paradox, and irony. This, of course, has been stated adamantly by the "practical critics" since the 1920s—those same "New" critics Henderson disparages. These usages, however, do make black poetic language unique and argue strongly for a compilation of a "black" dictionary of discrete examples of specific signification, where "Black English" departs from "general usage." They are not, I am afraid, found only in the language of black folks in this country. Had Henderson identified some criteria by which we could define an oral tradition in terms of the "grammar" it superimposes on nonliterary discourse, then shown how this comes to bear on literary discourse, and further shown such "grammars" to be distinctly black, then his contribution to our understanding of language and literature would have been no mean thing indeed.

His final category, "saturation," is the ultimate tautology: Poetry is "Black" when it communicates "Blackness." The more a text is "saturated," the "Blacker" the text. One imagines a daishiki-clad Dionysus weighing the saturated, mascon lines of Countée Cullen against those of Langston Hughes, as Paul Laurence Dunbar and Jean Toomer are silhouetted by the flames of Nigger Hell. The blacker the berry, the sweeter the juice.

Should it appear that I have belabored my reading of this theory, it is not because it is the weakest of the three theories of black literature. In fact, as I will try to show, Henderson's is by far the most imaginative of the three and has, at least, touched on areas critical to the explication of black literature. His examination of form is the first in a "race and superstructure" study and will most certainly give birth to more systematic and less polemical studies. But the notions implicit and explicit in Henderson's ideas are shared by Houston A. Baker, Jr., and Addison Gayle as well.

In the first essay of *Long Black Song, Essays in Black American Literature and Culture*,[23] Houston Baker proffers the considerable claim that black culture, particularly as "measured" through black folklore and literature, serves in intent and effect as an "index" of repudiation not only of white Western values and white Western culture but of white Western literature as well. "In fact," he writes, "it is to a great extent the culture theorizing of whites that has made for a separate and distinctive black American culture. That is to say, one index of the distinctiveness of black American culture is the extent to which it repudiates the culture theorizing of the white Western world." Repudiation, he continues, "is characteristic of black American folklore; and this is one of the most important factors in setting black American literature

apart from white American literature." Further, "Black folklore and the black
American literary tradition that grew out of it reflect a culture that is distinctive both of white American and of African culture, and therefore neither can
provide valid standards by which black American folklore and literature may
be judged." A text becomes "blacker," it surely follows, to the extent that it
serves as an "index of repudiation." Here we find an ironic response to
Harold Bloom's *Anxiety of Influence* in what we could characterize as an
"Animosity of Influence."

Baker discusses this notion of influence between black and white American culture at length. "Call it black, Afro-American, Negro," he writes, "the
fact remains that there is a fundamental, qualitative difference between it and
white American culture." The bases of this "fundamental, qualitative difference" are, first, that "black American culture was developed orally or musically for many years"; second, that "black American culture was never characterized by a collective ethos"; and, finally, that "one of [black American
culture's] most salient characteristics is an index of repudiation." Oral, col-
lectivistic, and repudiative, he concludes, "each of these aspects helps to
distinguish black American culture from white American culture."

These tenets suggest that there must be an arbitrary relation between a
sign and its referent; indeed, that all meaning is culture-bound. Yet what we
find elaborated here are rather oversimplified, basically political, criteria,
which are difficult to verify, partly because they are not subject to *verbal*
analysis (that is, can this sense of *difference* be measured through the literary
uses of language?), partly because the *thematic* analytical tools employed
seem to be useful primarily for black naturalist novels or for the mere paraphrasing of poetry, partly because the matter of influence is almost certainly
too subtle to be traced in other than close textual readings, and finally
because his three bases of "fundamental, qualitative difference" seem to me
too unqualified. There is so much more to Jean Toomer, Zora Hurston,
Langston Hughes, Sterling Brown, Ralph Ellison, Leon Forrest, Ishmael
Reed, Toni Morrison, and Alice Walker than their "index of repudiation,"
whatever that is. Besides, at least Toomer, Ellison, and Reed have taken care
to discuss the complex matter of literary ancestry, in print and without. It is
one of the ironies of the study of black literature that our critical activity is,
almost by definition, a comparative one, since many of our writers seem to
be influenced by Western masters, writing in English as well as outside it, as
they are by indigenous, Afro-American oral or even written forms. That the
base for our literature is an oral one is certainly true; but, as Millman Parry
and Albert Lord have amply demonstrated,[24] so is the base of the whole of

Western literature, commencing with the Hebrews and the Greeks. Nevertheless, Baker does not suggest any critical tools for explicating the oral tradition in our literature, such as the formulaic studies so common to the subject. Nor does he suggest how folklore is displaced in literature, even though, like Henderson, he does see it at "the base of the black literary tradition." That black culture is characterized by a collective ethos most definitely demands some qualification, since our history, literary and extra-literary, often turns on a tension, a dialectic, between the private perceptions of the individual and the white public perceptions of that same individual.

Nor does Baker's thought-provoking contention of the deprivation of the American frontier stand to prove this thesis:

> When the black American reads Frederick Jackson Turner's *The Frontier in American History,* he feels no regret over the end of the Western frontier. To black America, *frontier* is an alien word; for, in essence, all frontiers established by the white psyche have been closed to the black man. Heretofore, later, few have been willing to look steadily at America's past and acknowledge that the black man was denied his part in the frontier and his share of the nation's wealth.

Yet, at least Ralph Ellison has written extensively on the fact of the frontier (physical and metaphysical) and its centrality to his sensibility. Further, Ishmael Reed uses the frontier again and again as a central trope.

Part of the problem here is not only Baker's exclusive use of thematic analysis to attempt to delineate a literary tradition but also his implicit stance that literature functions primarily as a cultural artifact, as a repository for ideas. "It is impossible to comprehend the process of transcribing cultural values," he says (in his essay "Racial Wisdom and Richard Wright's *Native Son*"), "without an understanding of the changes that have characterized both the culture as a whole and the lives of its individual transcribers." Further, "Black American literature has a human immediacy and a pointed relevance which are obscured by the overingenious methods of the New Criticism, or any other school that attempts to talk of works of art as though they had no creators or of sociohistorical factors as though they did not filter through the lives of individual human beings." Here we find the implicit thesis in *Long Black Song,* the rather Herderian notion of literature as primarily the reflection of ideas and experiences outside of it. It is not, of course, that literature is unrelated to culture, to other disciplines, or even to other arts; it is not that words and usage somehow exist in a vacuum or that the literary work of art occupies an ideal or reified, privileged status, the province of some elite cult of culture. It is just that the literary work of art is a system of signs that may be decoded with various methods, all of which assume the fundamental unity of form and content and all of which demand close reading. Only the rare critic, such as Michael G. Cooke, Nathan A. Scott, or Sherley Williams, has made of thematic analysis the subtle tool that intelligent, sensitive reading requires. Baker seems to be reading black texts in a particular fashion for other than literary purposes. In *Singers of Daybreak: Studies in Black American Literature*,[25] he suggests these purposes. "What lies behind the neglect of black American literature," he asserts, "is not a supportable body of critical criteria that includes a meaningful definition of *utile* and *dulce*, but a refusal to believe that blacks possess the humanity requisite for the production of works of art." Baker finds himself shadowboxing with the ghostly judgments of Jefferson on Phillis Wheatley and Ignatius Sancho; his blows are often telling, but his opponent's feint is deadly.

If Houston Baker's criticism teaches us more about his attitude toward being black in white America than it does about black literature, then Addison Gayle, Jr.'s *The Way of the New World* teaches us even less.[26] Gayle makes no bones about his premises:

> To evaluate the life and culture of black people, it is necessary that one live the black experience in a world where substance is more important than form, where the social takes precedence over the aesthetic, where each act, gesture, and movement is political, and where continual rebellion separates the insane from the sane, the robot from the revolutionary.

Gayle's view of America, and of the critic, means that he can base his "literary judgments" on some measure of ideology; and he does. Regrettably, he accuses James Baldwin of "ignorance of black culture." His praise of John A. Williams seems predicated on an affinity of ideology. He praises John Killens' *And Then We Heard the Thunder* because he "creates no images of racial degradation." For him, the "central flaw" of the protagonist in *Invisible Man* ("an otherwise superb novel") is "attributable more to Ellison's political beliefs than to artistic deficiency." In Addison Gayle, we see race and superstructure criticism at its basest: Not only is his approach to literature deterministic, but his treatment of the critical activity itself demonstrates an alarming disrespect for qualified scholarship.

What is wrong with employing race and superstructure as critical premises? This critical activity sees language and literature as reflections of "Blackness." It postulates "Blackness" as an entity, rather than as metaphor or sign. Thus, the notion of a signified *black* element in literature retains a certain impressiveness insofar as it exists in some mystical kingdom halfway between a fusion of psychology and religion on the one hand and the Platonic Theory of Ideas on the other. Reflections of this "Blackness" are more or less "literary" according to the ideological posture of the critic. Content is primary over form and indeed is either divorced completely from form, in terms of genesis and normative value, or else is merely facilitated by form as a means to an end. In this criticism, rhetorical value judgments are closely related to social values. This method reconstitutes "message," when what is demanded is a deconstruction of a literary system.

The race and superstructure critics would have us believe that the function of the critic is to achieve an intimate knowledge of a literary text by recreating it from the inside: Critical thought must become the thought criticized. Only a black man, therefore, can think (hence, rethink) a "black thought." Consciousness is predetermined by culture and color. These critics, in Todorov's phrase, "recreate" a text either by repeating its own words in their own order or by establishing a relationship between the work and some system of ideas outside it. They leave no room for the idea of literature as a system. Normative judgments stem from how readily a text yields its secrets or is made to confess falsely on the rack of "black reality."

Yet, perceptions of reality are in no sense absolute; reality is a function of our senses. Writers present models of reality, rather than a description of it, though obviously the two may be related variously. In fact, fiction often contributes to cognition by providing models that highlight the nature of things precisely by their failure to coincide with it. Such, certainly, is the case in science fiction. Too, the thematic studies so common to black criticism suffer from a similar fallacy. Themes in poetry, for instance, are rarely reducible to literal statement; literature approaches its richest development when its "presentational symbolism" (as opposed by Suzanne Langer to its "literal discourse") cannot be reduced to the form of a literal proposition. Passages for creative discourse cannot be excerpted and their "meaning" presented independent of context. For Ralph Ellison, invisibility was not a matter of being seen but rather a refusal to run the gamut of one's own humanity.

"Blackness," as these critics understand it, is weak in just the decisive area where practical criticism is strong: in its capacity to give precise accounts of actual consciousness, rather than a scheme or a generalization. And the reason for the corresponding weakness is not difficult to find: It lies in the received formula of race and superstructure, which converts far too readily to the simple repetition of ideology. The critical method, then, is reductionist; literary discourse is described mechanically by classifications that find their ultimate meaning and significance somewhere else.

Ultimately, black literature is a verbal art like other verbal arts. "Blackness" is not a material object or an event but a metaphor; it does not have an "essence" as such but is defined by a network of relations that form a particular aesthetic unity. Even the slave narratives offer the text as a world, as a system of signs. The black writer is the point of consciousness of his language. If he does embody a "Black Aesthetic," then it can be measured not by "content," but by a complex structure of meanings. The correspondence of content between a writer and his world is less significant to literary criticism than is a correspondence of organization or structure, for a relation of content may be a mere reflection of prescriptive, scriptural canon, such as those argued for by Baker, Gayle, and Henderson. A relation of structure, on the other hand, according to Raymond Williams, "can show us the organizing principles by which a particular view of the world, and from that the coherence of the social group which maintains it, really operates in consciousness."[27] If there is a relationship between social and literary "facts," it must be found here.

To paraphrase René Wellek, black literature may well be dark, mysterious, and foreboding, but it is certainly not beyond careful scrutiny and fuller understanding. The tendency toward thematic criticism implies a marked inferiority complex: Afraid that our literature cannot sustain sophisticated verbal analysis, we view it from the surface merely and treat it as if it were a Chinese lantern with an elaborately wrought surface, parchment-thin but full of hot air. Black critics have enjoyed such freedom in their "discipline" that we find ourselves with no discipline at all. The present set of preconceptions has brought readers and writers into a blind alley. Literary images, even black ones, are combinations of words, not of absolute or fixed things. The tendency of black criticism toward an ideological absolutism, with its attendant Inquisition, must come to an end. A literary text is a linguistic event; its explication must be an activity of close textual analysis. Simply because Bigger Thomas kills Mary Dalton and tosses her body into a furnace, *Native Son* is not necessarily a "blacker" novel than *Invisible Man*—Gayle notwithstanding. We urgently need to direct our attention to the nature of black figurative language, to the nature of black narrative forms, to the history and theory of Afro-American literary criticism, to the fundamental unity and form of content, and to the arbitrary relations between the sign and its referent. Finally, we must begin to understand the nature of intertextuality, that is, the nonthematic manner by which texts—poems and novels—respond to other texts. All cats may be black at night, but not to other cats.

Notes

1 Briton Hammon, *A Narrative of the Uncommon Sufferings and Surprising Deliverance of Briton Hammon, a Negro Man* (Boston, 1760).

2 William Wimsatt and Cleanth Brooks, *Literary Criticism: A Short History* (New York, 1969), 366.

3 Phillis Wheatley, *Poems* (Philadelphia, 1773), vii.

4 *De la littérature des nègres, ou recherches sur leurs facultés intellectuelles, leurs qualités morales, et leur littérature* (Paris, 1808), 140.

5 Eugene Parker Chase, *Our Revolutionary Forefathers, The Letters of Francois, Marquis de Barbé-Marbois during His Residence in the United States as Secretary of the French Legation, 1779–1884* (New York, 1929), 84–85.

6 *Letters of the Late Ignatius Sancho, an African* (London, 1783), vi.

7 *Notes on the State of Virginia* (London, 1787), Bk. II, 196.

8 Ibid., 196.

9 Wheatley, vii.

10 Ibid., vi.

11 Sancho, vi.

12 Ibid., xiv–xvi.

13 Charles Ball, *Fifty Years in Chains; Or, The Life of an American Slave* (New York, 1858), 3.

14 Introduction, *My Bondage and My Freedom* (New York, 1855), xvii–xxxi.

15 *New York Tribune*, 10 June 1845, 1, col. 1. Reprint in *Liberator*, 30 May 1845, 97.

16 "Majors and Minors," *North American Review*, 27 June 1896, 630.

17 "Blueprint for Negro Writing," in this volume, 97–106.

18 "Negro Art," *Crisis*, 22 (June 1921), 55–56.

19 *New York Times*, 26 Jan. 1925, 3.

20 "The Social Origins of American Negro Art," *Modern Quarterly*, 3 (Autumn 1925), 53.

21 "Ted Joans: Tri-Continental Poet," *Transition*, 48 (1975), 4–12.

22 *Understanding the New Black Poetry* (New York, 1972). All subsequent quotes are from pp. 3–69.

23 *Long Black Song* (Charlottesville, 1972).

24 Albert Lord, *The Singer of Tales* (Cambridge, 1960).

25 *Singers of Daybreak: Studies in Black American Literature* (Washington, D.C., 1974).

26 *The Way of the New World* (Garden City, N.Y., 1975).

27 "Base and Superstructure in Marxist Cultural Theory," *New Left Review*, 82 (Dec., 1973), 3–16.

Robert B. Stepto

I Rose and Found My Voice: Narration, Authentication,

and Authorial Control in Four Slave Narratives

(1979)

The strident, moral voice of the former slave recounting, exposing, appealing, apostrophizing, and above all *remembering* his ordeal in bondage is the single most impressive feature of a slave narrative. This voice is striking because of what it relates, but even more so because the slave's acquisition of that voice is quite possibly his only permanent achievement once he escapes and casts himself upon a new and larger landscape. In their most elementary form, slave narratives are full of other voices which are frequently just as responsible for articulating a narrative's tale and strategy. These other voices may belong to various "characters" in the "story," but mainly they appear in the appended documents written by slaveholders and abolitionists alike. These documents—and voices—may not always be smoothly integrated with the former slave's tale, but they are nevertheless parts of the narrative. Their primary function is, of course, to authenticate the former slave's account; in doing so, they are at least partially responsible for the narrative's acceptance as historical evidence. However, in literary terms, the documents collectively create something close to a dialogue—of forms as well as voices—which suggests that, in its primal state or first phase, the slave narrative is an *eclectic narrative* form. A "first phase" slave narrative that illustrates these points rather well is Henry Bibb's *Narrative of the Life and Adventures of Henry Bibb, an American Slave* (1849).

When the various forms (letters, prefaces, guarantees, tales) and their accompanying voices become integrated in the slave narrative text, we are presented with another type of basic narrative which I call an *integrated narrative*. This type of narrative represents the second phase of slave narra-

This essay first appeared in Robert B. Stepto, *From Behind the Veil: A Study of Afro-American Narrative* (Chicago, 1979).

tive narration; it usually yields a more sophisticated text, wherein most of the literary and rhetorical functions previously performed by several texts and voices (the appended prefaces, letters, and documents as well as the tale) are now rendered by a loosely unified single text and voice. In this second phase, the authenticating documents "come alive" in the former slave's tale as speech and even action; and the former slave—often while assuming a deferential posture toward his white friends, editors, and guarantors—carries much of the burden of introducing and authenticating his own tale. In short, as my remarks on Solomon Northrup's *Twelve Years a Slave* (1854) will suggest, a "second phase" narrative is a more sophisticated narrative because the former slave's voice is responsible for much more than recounting the tale.

Because an integrated or second-phase narrative is less a collection of texts and more a unified narrative, we may say that, in terms of narration, the integrated narrative is in the process of becoming—irrespective of authorial intent—a generic narrative, by which I mean a narrative of discernible genre such as history, fiction, essay, or autobiography. This process is no simple "gourd vine" activity: an integrated narrative does not become a generic narrative overnight, and indeed, there are no assurances that in becoming a new type of narrative it is transformed automatically into a distinctive generic text. What we discover, then, is a third phase to slave narration wherein two developments may occur: the integrated narrative (phase II) may be dominated either by its tale or by its authenticating strategies. In the first instance, as we see in Frederick Douglass's *Narrative of the Life of Frederick Douglass, an American Slave, Written by Himself* (1845), the narrative and moral energies of the former slave's voice and tale so resolutely dominate the narrative's authenticating machinery (voices, documents, rhetorical strategies) that the narrative becomes, in thrust and purpose, far more metaphorical than rhetorical. When the integrated narrative becomes, in this way, a figurative account of action, landscape, and heroic self-transformation, it is so close generally to history, fiction, and autobiography that I term it a *generic narrative.*

In the second instance, as we see in William Wells Brown's *Narrative of the Life and Escape of William Wells Brown* (1852; appended to his novel, *Clotel, or The President's Daughter*), the authenticating machinery either remains as important as the tale or actually becomes, usually for some purpose residing outside the text, the dominant and motivating feature of the narrative. Since this is also a sophisticated narrative phase, figurative presentations of action, landscape, and self may also occur; however, such developments are rare and always ancillary to the central thrust of the text. When the authenticating

The Three Phases of Narration

PHASE I: Basic Narrative (a): "Eclectic Narrative"—authenticating documents and strategies (sometimes including one by the author of the tale) are *appended* to the tale

↓

PHASE II: Basic Narrative (b): "Integrated Narrative"—authenticating documents and strategies are *integrated* into the tale and formally become voices and/or characters in the tale

|
ㄥ↘

PHASE III:

| (a) "Generic Narrative"—authenticating documents and strategies are totally *subsumed by the tale*; the slave narrative becomes an identifiable generic text, e.g., autobiography | (b) "Authenticating Narrative"—the tale is *subsumed by the authenticating strategy*; the slave narrative becomes an authenticating document for other, usually generic, texts, e.g., novels, histories |

machinery dominates in this fashion, the integrated narrative becomes an *authenticating narrative.*

As these remarks suggest, one reason for investigating the phases of slave narrative narration is to gain a clearer view of how some slave narrative types become generic narratives, and how, in turn, generic narratives—once formed, shaped, and set in motion by certain distinctly Afro-American cultural imperatives—have roots in the slave narratives. All this is, of course, central to our discussion of Washington's *Up from Slavery*, DuBois's *The Souls of Black Folk*, Johnson's *The Autobiography of an Ex-Coloured Man*, Wright's *Black Boy*, and Ellison's *Invisible Man*. Moreover, it bears on our ability to distinguish between narrative modes and forms, and to describe what we see. When a historian or literary critic calls a slave narrative an autobiography, for example, what he or she sees most likely is a first-person narrative that possesses literary features to distinguish it from ordinary documents providing historical and sociological data. But a slave narrative is *not* necessarily an autobiography. We need to observe the finer shades between the more easily discernible categories of narration, and we must discover whether these stops arrange themselves in progressive, contrapuntal, or dialectic fashion—or if they possess any arrangement at all. As the scheme described above and diagrammed above suggests, I believe there are at least four identifiable modes of narration within the slave narratives, and that all four have a direct bearing on the development of subsequent Afro-American narrative forms.

Phase I: Eclectic Narrative

Henry Bibb's *Narrative of the Life and Adventures of Henry Bibb, an American Slave*, begins with several introductory documents offering, collectively, what may be the most elaborate guarantee of authenticity found in the slave narrative canon. What is most revealing—in terms of eclectic narrative form, authenticating strategy, and race rituals along the color line—is the segregation of Bibb's own "Author's Preface" from the white-authored texts of the "Introduction." Bibb's "Author's Preface" is further removed from the preceding introductory texts by the fact that he does not address or acknowledge what has gone before. There is no exchange, no verbal bond, between the two major units of introductory material; this reflects not only the quality of Bibb's relations with his benefactors, but also his relatively modest degree of control over the text and event of the narrative itself.

The "Introduction" is basically a frame created by Bibb's publisher, Lucius Matlack, for the presentation of guarantees composed mostly by abolitionists in Detroit (where, in freedom, Bibb chose to reside). Yet Matlack, as the publisher, also has his own authenticating duties to perform. He assures the reader that while he did indeed "examine" and "prepare" Bibb's manuscript, "The work of preparation . . . was that of orthography and punctuation merely, an arrangement of the chapters, and a table of contents—little more than falls to the lot of publishers generally." When Matlack tackles the issue of the tale's veracity, he mutes his own voice and offers instead those of various "authentic" documents gathered by the abolitionists. These gentlemen, all members of the Detroit Liberty Association, appear most sympathetic to Bibb, especially since he has spoken before their assemblies and lived an exemplary Christian life in their midst. To aid him—and their cause—they have interrogated Bibb (to which he submitted with "praiseworthy spirit") and have solicited letters from slaveholders, jailors, and Bibb's acquaintances, so that the truth of his tale might be established. No fewer than six of these letters plus the conclusion of the Association's report, all substantiating Bibb's story, appear in the "Introduction"; and, as if to "guarantee the guarantee," a note certifying the "friendly recommendation" of the abolitionists and verifying Bibb's "correct deportment" (composed, quite significantly, by a Detroit *judge*) is appended as well.

The elaborate authenticating strategy contained in Matlack's "Introduction" is typical of those found in the first-phase or eclectic narrative. The publisher or editor, far more than the former slave, assembles and manipulates the authenticating machinery, and seems to act on the premise that

POSITIVE CORRELATION B/W DOCUMENTS & CREDIBILITY

there is a direct correlation between the quantity of documents or texts assembled and the readership's acceptance of the narrative as a whole. I would like to suggest that Matlack's "Introduction" also constitutes a literary presentation of race rituals and cultural conditions, and that, as such, it functions as a kind of metaphor in the narrative.

To be sure, Matlack displays typical nineteenth-century American enthusiasm and superficiality when he writes of the literary merits of slave narratives: "Gushing fountains of poetic thought have started from beneath the rod of violence, that will long continue to slake the feverish thirst of humanity outraged, until swelling to a flood it shall rush with wasting violence over the ill-gotten heritage of the oppressor." However, the thrust of his "Introduction" is to guarantee the truth of a tale and, by extension, the *existence* of a man calling himself Henry Bibb. In his own aforementioned remarks regarding the preparation of Bibb's text for publication, Matlack appears to address the issue of the author's—Bibb's—credibility. However, the issue is really the audience's—white America's—credulity: their acceptance not so much of the former slave's escape and newfound freedom, but of his literacy. Many race rituals are enacted here, not the least of which is Matlack's "conversation" with white America across the text and figurative body of a silent former slave. The point we may glean from them all is that, insofar as Bibb must depend on his publisher to be an intermediary between his text and his audience, he relinquishes control of the narrative—which is, after all, the vehicle for the account of how he obtained his voice in freedom.

While we are impressed by the efforts of the Detroit Liberty Association's members to conduct an investigation of Bibb's tale, issue a report, and lend their names to the guarantee, we are still far more overwhelmed by the examples of the cultural disease with which they wrestle than by their desire to find a cure. That disease is, of course, cultural myopia, the badge and sore bestowed upon every nation mindlessly heedful of race ritual instead of morality: Henry Bibb is alive and well in Detroit, but by what miraculous stroke will he, as a man, be able to cast his shadow on this soil? The effort in the narrative's "Introduction" to prove that Bibb exists, and hence has a tale, goes far to explain why a prevailing metaphor in Afro-American letters is, in varying configurations, one of invisibility and translucence. Indirectly, and undoubtedly on a subconscious level, Matlack and the abolitionists confront the issue of Bibb's inability "to cast his shadow." But even in their case we may ask: Are they bolstering a cause, comforting a former slave, or recognizing a man?

The letters from the slaveholders and jailors Bibb knew while in bondage must not be overlooked here, for they help illuminate the history of the disease we are diagnosing. The letter from Silas Gatewood, whose father once owned Bibb, is designed solely to portray Bibb as "a notorious liar . . . and a rogue." Placed within the compendium of documents assembled by the abolitionists, the letter completes, through its nearly hysterical denunciation of Bibb, the "Introduction's" portrait of America at war with itself. The debate over Bibb's character, and, by extension, his right to a personal history bound to that of white Americans, is really nothing less than a literary omen of the Civil War. In this regard, the segregation of Bibb's "Author's Preface" from the introductory compendium of documents is, even more than his silence within the compendium, indicative of how the former slave's voice was kept muted and distant while the nation debated questions of slavery and the Negro's humanity. SILENCED VOICE IN THEIR OWN FIGHT.

Bibb's "Preface" reveals two features to his thinking, each of which helps us see how the former slave approached the task of composing a narrative. In answer to his own rhetorical question as to why he wrote the narrative, he replies, "in no place have I given orally the detail of my narrative; and some of the most interesting events of my life have never reached the public ear." This is not extraordinary except in that it reminds us of the oral techniques and traditions that lay behind most of the written narratives. The former slave's accomplishment of a written narrative should by no means be minimized, but we must also recognize the extent to which the abolitionist lecture circuit, whether in Michigan, Maine, or New York, gave former slaves an opportunity to structure, to embellish, and above all to polish an oral version of their tale—and to do so before the very audiences who would soon purchase hundreds, if not thousands, of copies of the written account. The former slave, not altogether unlike the semi-literate black preacher whose sermons were (and are) masterpieces of oral composition and rhetorical strategy, often had a fairly well developed version of his or her tale either memorized or (more likely) sufficiently *patterned* for effective presentation, even before the question of written composition was entertained. Certainly such was the case for Bibb, and this reminds us not to be too narrow when we call the basic slave narrative an eclectic narrative form. Oral as well as written forms are part of the eclectic whole.

The second revealing feature of Bibb's "Preface" returns us to a point on which his publisher, Matlack, began. Bibb appears extremely aware of the issue of his authorship when he writes:

The reader will remember that I make no pretension to literature; for I can truly say, that I have been educated in the school of adversity, whips,

and chains. Experience and observation have been my principal teachers, with the exception of three weeks schooling which I have had the
good fortune to receive since my escape from the "grave yard of the
mind," or the dark prison of human bondage.

That Bibb had only three weeks of formal schooling is astonishing; however,
I am intrigued even more by the two metaphors for slavery with which he
concludes. While both obviously suggest confinement—one of the mind, the
other of his body—it seems significant that Bibb did not choose between the
two (for reasons of style, if no other). Both images are offered *after* the act of
writing his tale, possibly because Bibb is so terribly aware of both. His body is
now free, his mind limber, his voice resonant; together they and his tale, if
not his narrative, are his own.

On a certain level, we must study Matlack's "Introduction," with all its
documents and guarantees, and Bibb's "Author's Preface" as a medley of
voices, rather than as a loose conglomerate of discrete and even segregated
texts. Together, both in what they do and do not say, these statements reflect
the passions, politics, interpersonal relations, race rituals, and uses of language of a cross-section of America in the 1840s. But on another level, we
must hold fast to what we have discovered regarding how Bibb's removal
from the primary authenticating documents and strategy (that is, from the
"Introduction") weakens his control of the narrative and, in my view, rele-
gates him to a posture of partial literacy. Bibb's tale proves that he has acquired a voice, but his narrative shows that his voice does not yet control the
imaginative forms which his personal history assumes in print.

In the Bibb narrative, the various texts within the "Introduction" guarantee Bibb and his tale; Bibb sustains this strategy of guarantee late in his tale by
quoting letters and proclamations by many of the same figures who provided
documents for the "Introduction." As we will discover in Solomon Northup's
narrative, this use of authenticating documents within the text of the tale
indicates the direction of more sophisticated slave narrative texts. Indeed,
the question of whether the authenticating documents and strategies have
been integrated into the central text (usually the tale) of the slave narrative is
a major criterion by which we may judge author and narrative alike. The
inclusion and manipulation of peripheral documents and voices suggests a
remarkable level of literacy and self-assurance on the part of the former
slave, and the reduction of many texts and strategies into one reflects a
search, irrespective of authorial intent, for a more sophisticated written narrative form. Here, then, is a point of departure from which we may study the

development of pregeneric narratives into generic and other sophisticated narrative types.

Phase II: Integrated Narrative

While I am not prepared to classify Solomon Northup's *Twelve Years a Slave* (1854) as an autobiography, it is certainly a more sophisticated text than Henry Bibb's, principally because its most important authenticating document is integrated into the tale as a voice and character. *Twelve Years a Slave* is, however, an integrated narrative unsure of itself. Ultimately, its authenticating strategy depends as much upon an appended set of authenticating texts as upon integrated documents and voices.

In comparison to the Bibb "Introduction," the Northup introductory materials appear purposely short and undeveloped. Northup's editor and amanuensis, a Mr. David Wilson, offers a one-page "Preface," not a full-blown "Introduction," and Northup's own introductory words are placed in the first chapter of his tale, rather than in a discrete entry written expressly for that purpose. Wilson's "Preface" is, predictably, an authenticating document, formulaically acknowledging whatever "faults of style and of expression" the narrative may contain while assuring the reader that he, the editor and a white man, is convinced of Northup's strict adherence to the truth. Northup's own contributions, like Bibb's, are not so much anthenticating as they are reflective of what a slave may have been forced to consider while committing his tale to print.

Northup's first entry is simply and profoundly his signature—his proof of literacy writ large, with a bold, clear hand. It appears beneath a pen-and-ink frontispiece portrait entitled "Solomon in His Plantation Suit." His subsequent entries quite self-consciously place his narrative amid the antislavery literature of the era, in particular, with Harriet Beecher Stowe's *Uncle Tom's Cabin* (1852) and *Key to Uncle Tom's Cabin* (1853). If one wonders why Northup neither establishes his experience among those of other kidnapped and enslaved blacks nor positions his narrative with other narratives, the answer is provided in part by his dedicatory page. There, after quoting a passage from *Key to Uncle Tom's Cabin* which, in effect, verifies his account of slavery because it is said to "form a striking parallel" to Uncle Tom's, Northup respectfully dedicates his narrative to Miss Stowe, remarking that his tale affords "another *Key to Uncle Tom's Cabin.*"

This is no conventional dedication; it tells us much about the requisite act of authentication. While the Bibb narrative is authenticated by documents provided by the Detroit Liberty Association, the Northup narrative begins the process of authentication by assuming kinship with a popular antislavery novel. Audience, and the former slave's relationship to that audience, are the key issues here: authentication is, apparently, a rhetorical strategy designed not only for verification purposes, but also for the task of initiating and insuring a readership. No matter how efficacious it undoubtedly was for Northup (or his editor) to ride Miss Stowe's coattails and share in her immense notoriety, one cannot help wondering about the profound implications involved in authenticating personal history by binding it to historical fiction. In its way, this strategy says as much about a former slave's inability to confirm his existence and "cast his shadow" as does the more conventional strategy observed in the Bibb narrative. Apparently, a novel may authenticate a personal history, especially when the personal history is that of a former slave.

While not expressing the issue in these terms, Northup seems to have thought about the dilemma of authentication and that of slave narratives competing with fictions of both the pro- and anti-slavery variety. He writes:

Since my return to liberty, I have not failed to perceive the increasing interest throughout the Northern states, in regard to the subject of Slavery. Works of fiction, professing to portray its features in their more pleasing as well as more repugnant aspects, have been circulated to an extent unprecedented, and, as I understand, have created a fruitful topic of comment and discussion.

I can speak of Slavery only so far as it came under my own observation—only so far as I have known and experienced it in my own person. My object is, to give a candid and truthful statement of facts: to repeat the story of my life, without exaggeration, leaving it for others to determine, whether even the pages of fiction present a picture of more cruel wrong or a severer bondage.

Clearly, Northup felt that the authenticity of his tale would not be taken for granted, and that, on a certain peculiar but familiar level enforced by rituals along the color line, his narrative would be viewed as a fiction competing with other fictions. However, in this passage Northup also inaugurates a counterstrategy. His reference to his own observation of slavery may be a just and subtle dig at the "armchair sociologists" of North and South alike, who wrote of the slavery question amid the comforts of their libraries and verandas. But more important, in terms of plot as well as point of view, the remark establishes Northup's authorial posture as a "participant-observer" in the truest and (given his bondage) most regrettable sense of the phrase. In these terms, then, Northup contributes personally to the authentication of *Twelve Years a Slave*: he challenges the authenticity of the popular slavery fictions and their power of authenticating his own personal history by first exploiting the bond between them and his tale and then assuming the posture of an authenticator. One needn't delve far into the annals of American race relations for proof that Northup's rhetorical strategy is but a paradigm for the classic manipulation of the master by the slave.

As the first chapter of *Twelve Years a Slave* unfolds, Northup tells of his family's history and circumstances. His father, Mintus Northup, was a slave in Rhode Island and in Rensselaer County, New York, before gaining his freedom in 1803 upon the death of his master. Mintus quickly amassed property and gained suffrage; he came to expect the freedoms that accompany self-willed mobility and self-initiated employment, and gave his son, Solomon, the extraordinary advantage of being born a free man. As a result, Solomon writes of gaining "an education surpassing that ordinarily bestowed upon children in our condition," and he recollects leisure hours "employed over my books, or playing the violin." Solomon describes employment (such as lumber-rafting on Lake Champlain) that was not only profitable but also, in a way associated with the romance of the frontier, adventurous and even manly. When Solomon Northup married Anne Hampton on Christmas Day of 1829, they did not jump over a broomstick, as was the (reported) lot of most enslaved black Americans; rather, the two were married by a magistrate of the neighborhood, Timothy Eddy, Esq. Furthermore, their first home was neither a hovel nor a hut but the "Fort House," a residence "lately occupied by Captain Lathrop" and used in 1777 by General Burgoyne.

This saga of Solomon's heritage is full of interest, and it has its rhetorical and strategical properties as well. Northup has begun to establish his authorial posture removed from the condition of the black masses in slavery—a move which, as we have indicated, is as integral to the authenticating strategy as to the plot of his tale. In addition to portraying circumstances far more pleasant and fulfilling than those which he suffers in slavery, Northup's family history also yields some indication of his relations with whites in the district, especially the white Northups. Of course, these indications also advance both the plot and the authenticating strategy. One notes, for example, that while Mintus Northup did indeed migrate from the site of his enslavement once he was free, he retained the Northup surname and labored for a relative of his former master. Amid his new prosperity and mobility, Mintus maintained fairly amicable ties with his past; apparently this set the

tone for relations between Northups, black and white. One should be wary
of depicting New York north of Albany as an ideal or integrated area in the
early 1800s, but the black Northups had bonds with whites—perhaps blood
ties. To the end Solomon depends on these bonds for his escape from slavery
and for the implicit verification of his tale.

In the first chapter of *Twelve Years a Slave*, Henry B. Northup, Esq., is
mentioned only briefly as a relative of Mintus Northup's former master; in
the context of Solomon's family history, he is but a looming branch of the
(white) Northup family tree. However, as the tale concludes, Henry Northup
becomes a voice and character in the narrative. He requests various legal
documents essential to nullifying Solomon's sale into bondage; he inquires
into Solomon's whereabouts in Bayou Boeuf, Louisiana; he presents the facts
before lawyers, sheriffs, and Solomon's master, Edwin Epps; he pleads Solomon's case against his abductors before a District of Columbia court of law;
and, most important, after the twelve years of assault on Solomon's sense of
identity, Henry Northup utters, to Solomon's profound thanksgiving, Solomon's given name—not his slave name. In this way Henry Northup enters
the narrative, and whatever linguistic authentication of the tale Solomon
inaugurated by assuming the rather objective posture of the participant-
observer-authenticator is concluded and confirmed, not by appended letter,
but by Henry Northup's presence.

This strategy of authentication functions hand in hand with the narrative's strategy of reform. Like the carpenter, Bass, who jeopardizes his own
safety by personally mailing Solomon's appeals for help to New York, Henry
Northup embodies the spirit of reform in the narrative. In terms of reform
strategy, Henry Northup and Bass—who, as a Canadian, represents a variation on the archetype of deliverance in Canada—are not only saviors but also
models whose example might enlist other whites in the reform cause. Certainly abolitionists near and far could identify with these men, and that
was important. Slave narratives were often most successful when they were
as subtly pro-abolition as they were overtly anti-slavery—a consideration
which could only have exacerbated the former slave's already sizeable problems with telling his tale in such a way that he, and not his editors or
guarantors, controlled it.

But Henry Northup is a different kind of savior from Bass: he is an American descended from slaveowners, and he shares his surname with the kidnapped Solomon. Furthermore, his posture as a family friend is inextricably
bound to his position in the tale as a lawyer. At the end of *Twelve Years a
Slave*, Henry Northup appears in Louisiana as an embodiment of the law, as

well as of Solomon Northup's past (in all its racial complexity) come to reclaim him. In this way, Solomon's *tale* assumes the properties of an integrated narrative—the authenticating texts (here, the words and actions of Henry Northup) are integrated into the former slave's tale. But in what follows after the tale, we see that Solomon's *narrative* ultimately retrogresses to the old strategies of a phase-one eclectic narrative. Whereas the Bibb narrative begins with a discrete set of authenticating texts, the Northup narrative ends with such a set—an "Appendix."

The Northup Appendix contains three types of documents. First comes the New York state law, passed May 14, 1840, employed by Henry Northup and others to reclaim Solomon Northup from bondage in Louisiana. There follows a petition to the Governor of New York from Solomon's wife, Ann Northup, replete with legal language that persists in terming her a "memorialist." The remaining documents are letters, mostly from the black Northups' white neighbors, authenticating Solomon's claim that he is a free Negro. Despite our initial disappointment upon finding such an orthodox authenticating strategy appended to what had heretofore been a refreshingly sophisticated slave narrative (the narrative does not need the Appendix to fulfill its form), the Appendix does have its points of interest. Taken as a whole, it portrays the unfolding of a law; the New York law with which it begins precipitates the texts that follow, notably, in chronological order. On one level, then, Northup's Appendix is, far more than Bibb's Introduction, a story in epistolary form that authenticates not only his tale but also those voices within the tale, such as Henry Northup's. On another level, however, the Appendix becomes a further dimension to the reform strategy subsumed within the narrative. Just as Bass and Henry Northup posture as model reformers, the narrative's Appendix functions as a primer, complete with illustrative documents, on how to use the law to retrieve kidnapped free Negroes. Thus, the Appendix, as much as the tale itself, can be seen (quite correctly) as an elaborate rhetorical strategy against the Fugitive Slave Law of 1850.

In the end, the Northup narrative reverts to primitive authenticating techniques, but that does not diminish the sophistication and achievement of the tale within the narrative. We must now ask: To what end does the immersion of authenticating documents and strategies within the texture of Northup's tale occur? Furthermore, is this goal literary or extraliterary? In answering these questions we come a little closer, I think, to an opinion on whether narratives like Northup's may be autobiographies.

Northup's conscious or unconscious integration and subsequent manipulation of authenticating voices advances his tale's plot and most certainly advances his narrative's validation and reform strategies. However, it does little to develop what Albert Stone has called a literary strategy of self-presentation. The narrative renders an extraordinary experience, but not a remarkable self. The two need not be exclusive, as Frederick Douglass's 1845 *Narrative* illustrates, but in the Northup book they appear to be distinct entities, principally because of the eye or "I" shaping and controlling the narration. Northup's eye and "I" are not so much introspective as they are inquisitive; even while in the pit of slavery in Louisiana, Northup takes time to inform us of various farming methods and of how they differ from practices in the North. Of course, this remarkable objective posture results directly from Northup assuming the role of a participant-observer for authentication purposes. But it all has a terrible price. Northup's tale is neither the history nor a metaphor for the history of his life; and because this is so, his tale cannot be called autobiographical.

Phase IIIa: Generic Narrative

In the first two phases of slave narrative narration we observe the former slave's ultimate lack of control over his own narrative, occasioned primarily by the demands of audience and authentication. This dilemma is not unique to the authors of these narratives; indeed, many modern black writers still do not control their personal history once it assumes literary form. For this reason, Frederick Douglass's *Narrative of the Life of Frederick Douglass, an American Slave, Written by Himself* (1845) seems all the more a remarkable literary achievement. Because it contains several segregated narrative texts—a preface, a prefatory letter, the tale, an appendix—it appears to be, in terms of the narrative phases, a rather primitive slave narrative. But each ancillary text is drawn to the tale by some sort of extraordinary gravitational pull or magnetic attraction. There is, in short, a dynamic energy between the tale and each supporting text that we do not discover in the Bibb or Northup narratives, save perhaps in the relationship between Solomon Northup and his guarantor-become-character, Henry Northup. The Douglass narrative is an integrated narrative of a very special order. The integrating process does, in a small way, pursue the conventional path found in Northup's narrative, creating characters out of authenticating texts (William Lloyd Garrison silently enters Douglass's tale at the very end); however, its new and major thrust is the creation of that aforementioned energy which binds the supporting texts to the tale, while at the same time removing them from participation in the narrative's rhetorical and authenticating strategies. Douglass's tale dominates the narrative because it alone authenticates the narrative.

The introductory texts to the tale are two in number: a "Preface" by William Lloyd Garrison, the famous abolitionist and editor of *The Liberator;* and a "Letter from Wendell Phillips, Esq.," who was equally well known as an abolitionist, crusading lawyer, and judge. In theory, each of these introductory documents should be classic guarantees written almost exclusively for a white reading public, concerned primarily and ritualistically with the white validation of a newfound black voice, and removed from the tale in such ways that the guarantee and tale vie silently and surreptitiously for control of the narrative as a whole. But these entries are not fashioned that way. To be sure, Garrison offers a conventional guarantee when he writes, "Mr. Douglass has very properly chosen to write his own Narrative, in his own style, and according to the best of his ability, rather than to employ some one else. It is, therefore, entirely his own production; and . . . it is, in my judgment, highly creditable to his head and heart." And Phillips, while addressing Douglass, most certainly offers a guarantee to "another" audience as well:

> Every one who has heard you speak has felt, and, I am confident, every one who read your book will feel, persuaded that you give them a fair specimen of the whole truth. No one-sided portrait,—no wholesale complaints,—but strict justice done, whenever individual kindliness has neutralized, for a moment, the deadly system with which it was strangely allied.

But these passages dominate neither the tone nor the substance of their respective texts.

Garrison is far more interested in writing history (specifically, that of the 1841 Nantucket Anti-Slavery Convention, and the launching of Douglass's career as a lecture agent for various antislavery societies) and recording his own place in it. His declaration, "I shall never forget his [Douglass's] first speech at the convention," is followed within a paragraph by, "*I rose,* and declared that PATRICK HENRY, of revolutionary fame, never made a speech more eloquent in the cause of liberty . . . *I reminded* the audience of the peril which surrounded this self-emancipated young man . . . *I appealed* to them, whether they would ever allow him to be carried back into slavery,—law or no law, constitution or no constitution" (italics added). His "Preface" ends, not with a reference to Douglass or his tale, but with an apostrophe very much like one he would use to exhort and arouse an antislavery assembly.

With the following cry Garrison hardly guarantees Douglass's tale, but enters and reenacts his own abolitionist career instead:

> Reader! are you with the man-stealers in sympathy and purpose, or on the side of their down-trodden victims? If with the former, then you are the foe of God and man. If with the latter, what are you prepared to do and dare in their behalf? Be faithful, be vigilant, be untiring in your efforts to break every yoke, and let the oppressed go free. Come what may—cost what may—inscribe on the banner which you unfurl to the breeze, as your religious and political motto—"No COMPROMISE WITH SLAVERY! NO UNION WITH SLAVEHOLDERS!"

In the light of this closure, and (no matter how hard we try to ignore it) the friction that developed between Garrison and Douglass in later years, we might be tempted to see Garrison's "Preface" at war with Douglass's tale for authorial control of the narrative as a whole. Certainly there is a tension, but that tension is stunted by Garrison's enthusiasm for Douglass's tale. Garrison writes:

> This *Narraive* contains many affecting incidents, many *passages* of great eloquence and power; but I think the most thrilling one of them all is the *description* DOUGLASS gives of his feelings, as he stood soliloquizing respecting his fate, and the chances of his one day being a free man. . . . Who can read that *passage,* and be insensible to its pathos and sublimity? [Italics added.]

Here Garrison does, probably subconsciously, an unusual and extraordinary thing—he becomes the first guarantor we have seen in this study who not only directs the reader to the tale, but also acknowledges the tale's singular rhetorical power. Garrison enters the tale by being at the Nantucket convention with Douglass in 1841 (the same year Solomon Northup was kidnapped) and by, in effect, authenticating the impact, rather than the facts, of the tale. He fashions his own apostrophe, but finally he remains a member of Douglass's audience far more than he assumes the posture of a competing or superior voice. In this way Garrison's "Preface" stands outside Douglass's tale but is steadfastly bound to it.

Such is the case for Wendell Phillips's "Letter" as well. As I have indicated, it contains passages which seem addressed to credulous readers in need of a "visible" authority's guarantee, but by and large the "Letter" is directed to Frederick Douglass alone. It opens with "My Dear Friend," and there are many extraliterary reasons for wondering initially if the friend is actually Frederick. Shortly thereafter, however, Phillips declares, "I am glad the time has come when the 'lions write history,'" and it becomes clear that he both addresses Douglass and writes in response to the tale. These features, plus Phillips's specific references to how Douglass acquired his "A B C" and learned "where the 'white sails' of the Chesapeake were bound," serve to integrate Phillips's "Letter" into Douglass's tale.

Above all, we must understand in what terms the "Letter" is a cultural and linguistic event. Like the Garrison document, it presents its author as a member of Douglass's audience; but the act of letterwriting, of correspondence, implies a moral and linguistic parity between a white guarantor and black author which we haven't seen before—and which we do not always see in American literary history *after* 1845. The tone and posture initiated in Garrison's "Preface" are completed and confirmed in Phillips's "Letter"; while these documents are integrated into Douglass's tale, they remain segregated outside the tale in the all-important sense that they yield Douglass sufficient narrative and rhetorical space in which to render personal history in—and as—a literary form.

What marks Douglass's narration and control of his tale is his extraordinary ability to pursue several types of writing with ease and with a degree of simultaneity. The principal types of writing we discover in the tale are: syncretic phrasing, introspective analysis, internalized documentation, and participant observation. Of course, each of these types has its accompanying authorial posture, the result being that even the telling of the tale (as distinct from the content of the tale) yields a portrait of a complex individual marvelously facile with the tones, shapes, and dimensions of his voice.

Douglass's syncretic phrasing is often discussed; the passage most widely quoted is probably, "My feet have been so cracked with the frost, that the pen with which I am writing might be laid in the gashes." The remarkable clarity of this language needs no commentary, but what one admires as well is Douglass's ability to conjoin past and present, and to do so with images that not only stand for different periods in his personal history but also, in their fusion, speak of his evolution from slavery to freedom. The pen, symbolizing the quest for literacy fulfilled, actually measures the wounds of the past, and this measuring process becomes a metaphor in and of itself for the artful composition of travail transcended. While I admire this passage, I find even more intriguing the syncretic phrases that pursue a kind of acrid punning upon the names of Douglass's oppressors. A minor example appears early in the tale, when Douglass deftly sums up an overseer's character by writing, "Mr. Severe was rightly named: he was a cruel man." Here Douglass is content with "glossing" the name; but late in the tale, just before attempting to escape in 1835, he takes another oppressor's name and does not so much gloss it or play with it as *work upon* it—to such an extent that, riddled with irony, it is devoid of its original meaning: "At the close of the year 1834, Mr. Freeland again hired me of my master, for the year 1835. But, by this time, I began to want to live *upon free land* as well as *with Freeland;* and I was no longer content, therefore, to live with him or any other slaveholder." Of course, this is effective writing—far more effective than what is found in the average slave narrative. But my point is that Douglass seems to fashion these passages for both his readership and himself. Each example of his increasing facility and wit with language charts his ever-shortening path to literacy; thus, in their way, Douglass's syncretic phrases reveal his emerging comprehension of freedom and literacy, and are another introspective tool by which he may mark the progress of his personal history.

But the celebrated passages of introspective analysis are even more pithy and direct. In these, Douglass fashions language as finely honed and balanced as an aphorism or Popean couplet, and thereby orders his personal history with neat, distinct, and credible moments of transition. When Mr. Auld forbids Mrs. Auld from teaching Douglass the alphabet, for example, Douglass relates, "From that moment, I understood the pathway from slavery to freedom. . . . Whilst I was saddened by the thought of losing the aid of my kind mistress, I was gladdened by the invaluable instruction which, by the merest accident, I gained from my master." The clarity of Douglass's revelation is as unmistakable as it was remarkable. As rhetoric, the passage is successful because its nearly extravagant beginning is finally rendered quite acceptable by the masterly balance and internal rhyming of "saddened" and "gladdened," which is persuasive because it is pleasant and because it offers the illusion of a reasoned conclusion.

Balance is an important feature to two other equally celebrated passages which open and close Douglass's telling of his relations with Mr. Covey, an odd (because he *worked* in the fields alongside the slaves) but vicious overseer. At the beginning of the episode, in which Douglass finally fights back and draws Covey's blood, he writes: "You have seen how a man was made a slave; you shall see how a slave was made a man." And at the end of the episode, to bring matters linguistically as well as narratively full circle, Douglass declares: "I now resolved that, however long I might remain a slave in form, the day has passed forever when I could be a slave in fact. I did not hesitate to let it be known of me, that the white man who expected to succeed in whipping, must also succeed in killing me."

The sheer poetry of these statements is not lost on us, nor is the reason why the poetry was created in the first place. One might suppose that in another age Douglass's determination and rage would take a more effusive expression, but I cannot imagine that to be the case. In the first place, his linguistic model is obviously scriptural; and in the second, his goal, as Albert Stone has argued, is the presentation of a *"historical* self," not the record of temporary hysteria.

This latter point, to refer back to the Northup narrative, is one of the prime distinctions between Solomon Northup and Frederick Douglass—one which ultimately persuades me that Douglass is about the business of discovering how personal history may be transformed into autobiography, while Northup is not. Both narratives contain episodes in which the author finally stands up to and soundly beats his overseer, but while Douglass performs this task and reflects upon its place in his history, Northup resorts to effusion:

As I stood there, feelings of unutterable agony overwhelmed me. I was conscious that I had subjected myself to unimaginable punishment. The reaction that followed my extreme ebullition of anger produced the most painful sensations of regret. An unfriended, helpless slave—what could I *do,* what could I *say,* to justify, in the remotest manner, the heinous act I had committed . . . I tried to pray . . . but emotion choked my utterance, and I could only bow my head upon my hands and weep.

Passages such as these may finally link certain slave narratives with the popular sentimental literary forms of the nineteenth century, but Douglass's passages of introspective analysis create fresh space for themselves in the American literary canon.

Internal documentation in Douglass's tale is unusual in that, instead of reproducing letters and other documents written by white guarantors within the tale or transforming guarantees into characters, Douglass internalizes documents which, like the syncretic and introspective passages, order his personal history. Again a comparison of Douglass and Northup is useful, because while both authors present documents having only a secondary function in the authenticating process, their goals (and, perhaps one might say, their ambitions) seem quite different.

Northup, for example, documents slave songs in two major passages: first in the text of the tale, and then in a segregated text serving as a musical interlude between the tale and the Appendix. His discussion of the songs within the tale is one dimensional, by which I mean it merely reflects his limited comprehension and appreciation of the songs at a given moment in his life.

Rather than establishing Northup within the slave community, remarks like "those unmeaning songs, composed rather for [their] adaptation to a certain tune or measure, than for the purpose of expressing any distinct idea" or "equally nonsensical, but full of melody" serve only to reinforce his displacement as a participant-observer. One might have assumed that Northup (who was, after all, kidnapped into slavery partly because of his musicianship) found music a bond between him and his enslaved brethren, and in passages such as these would relinquish or soften his objective posture. But apparently the demands of audience and authentication precluded such a shift.

In contrast, Douglass's discussion of slave songs begins with phrases such as "wild songs" and "unmeaning jargon" but concludes, quite typically for him, with a study of how he grew to "hear" the songs and how that hearing affords yet another illumination of his path from slavery to freedom:

> I did not, when a slave, understand the deep meaning of those rude and apparently incoherent songs. I was myself within the circle; so that I neither saw nor heard as those without might see and hear. They told a tale of woe which was then altogether beyond my feeble comprehension. . . . Every tone was a testimony against slavery, and a prayer to God for deliverance from chains. The hearing of those wild notes always depressed my spirit, and filled me with ineffable sadness. I have frequently found myself in tears while hearing them. The mere recurrence to those songs, even now, afflicts me; and while I am writing these lines, an expression of feeling has already found its way down my cheek.

 The tears of the past and present interflow. Douglass not only documents his saga of enslavement but also, with typical recourse to syncretic phrasing and introspective analysis, advances his presentation of self.

Douglass's other internalized documents are employed with comparable efficiency, as we see in the episode where he attempts an escape in 1835. There the document reproduced is the pass or "protection" Douglass wrote for himself and his compatriots in the escape plan:

> This is to certify that I, the undersigned, have given the bearer, my servant, full liberty to go to Baltimore, and spend the Easter holidays. Written with mine own hand, &c., 1835.
>   William Hamilton,
>   Near St. Michael's, in Talbot county, Maryland.

The protection exhibits Douglass's increasingly refined sense of how to manipulate language—he has indeed come a long way from that day when Mr.

Auld halted his A B C lessons. But even more impressive, I believe, is the act of reproducing the document itself. We know from the tale that each slave managed to destroy his pass when the scheme was thwarted; Douglass is reproducing his language from memory, and there is no reason to doubt a single jot of his recollection. He can draw so easily from the wellsprings of memory because the protection is not a mere scrap of memorabilia, but a veritable roadsign on his path to freedom and literacy. In this sense, his protection assumes a place in Afro-American letters as an antedating trope for such documents as "The Voodoo of Hell's Half Acre" in Richard Wright's *Black Boy*, and the tale framed by the prologue and epilogue in Ralph Ellison's *Invisible Man*.

All of the types of narrative discourse discussed thus far reveal features of Douglass's particular posture as a participant-observer narrator, a posture that is as introspective as Solomon Northup's is inquisitive. But the syncretic phrases, introspective studies, and internalized documents only exhibit Douglass as a teller and doer, and part of the great effect of his tale depends upon what he does *not* tell, what he refuses to reenact in print. Late in the tale, at the beginning of the eleventh chapter, Douglass writes:

> I now come to that part of my life during which I planned, and finally succeeded in making, my escape from slavery. But before narrating any of the peculiar circumstances, I deem it proper to make known my intention not to state all the facts connected with the transaction . . . I deeply regret the necessity that impels me to suppress any thing of importance connected with my experience in slavery. It would afford me great pleasure indeed, as well as materially add to the interest of my narrative, were I at liberty to gratify a curiosity, which I know exists. . . . But I must deprive myself of this pleasure, and the curious gratification which such a statement would afford. I would allow myself to suffer under the greatest imputations which evil-minded men might suggest, rather than exculpate myself, and thereby run the hazard of closing the slightest avenue by which a brother slave might clear himself of the chains and fetters of slavery.

John Blassingame has argued, in *The Slave Community* (1972), that one way to test a slave narrative's authenticity is by gauging how much space the narrator gives to relating his escape, as opposed to describing the conditions of his captivity. If the adventure, excitement, and perils of the escape seem to be the *raison, d'être* for the narrative's composition, then the narrative is quite possibly an exceedingly adulterated slave's tale or a bald fiction. The theory does not always work perfectly: Henry "Box" Brown's narrative and that of William and Ellen Craft are predominantly recollections of extraordinary escapes; yet, as far as we can tell, these are authentic tales. But Blassingame's theory nevertheless has great merit, and I have often wondered to what extent it derives from the example of Douglass's tale and from his fulminations against those authors who unwittingly excavate the Underground Railroad and expose it to the morally thin mid-nineteenth-century American air. Douglass's tale is spectacularly free from suspicion because he never divulges a detail of his escape to New York. (That information is given ten years later, in *My Bondage and My Freedom* and other statements.) This marvelously rhetorical omission or silence both sophisticates and authenticates his posture as a participant-observer narrator. When a narrator wrests this kind of preeminent authorial control from the ancillary voices in the narrative, we may say that he controls the presentation of his personal history, and that his tale is becoming autobiographical. In this light, then, Douglass's last few sentences of the tale take on special meaning:

> But, while attending an anti-slavery convention at Nantucket, on the 11th of August, 1841, I felt strongly moved to speak. . . . It was a severe cross, and I took it up reluctantly. The truth was, I felt myself a slave, and the idea of speaking to white people weighed me down. I spoke but a few moments, when I felt a degree of freedom, and said what I desired with considerable ease. From that time until now, I have been engaged in pleading the case of my brethren—with what success, and what devotion, I leave those acquainted with my labors to decide.

With these words, the *narrative,* as Albert Stone has remarked, comes full circle. We are returned not to the beginning of the *tale,* but to Garrison's prefatory remarks on the convention and Douglass's first public address. This return may be pleasing in terms of the sense of symmetry it affords, but it is also a remarkable feat of rhetorical strategy: having traveled with Douglass through his account of his life, we arrive in Nantucket in 1841 to hear him speak. We become, along with Mr. Garrison, his audience. The final effect is that Douglass reinforces his posture as an articulate hero, while supplanting Garrison as the definitive historian of his past.

Even more important, I think, is Douglass's final image of a slave shedding his last fetter and becoming a man by first finding his voice and then, as surely as light follows dawn, speaking "with considerable ease." In one brilliant stroke, the quest for freedom and literacy, implied from the start even by the narrative's title, is resolutely consummated.

The final text of the narrative, the Appendix, differs from the one attached to the Northup narrative. It is not a series of letters and legal documents, but a discourse by Douglass on *his* view of Christianity and Christian practice, as opposed to what he exposed in his tale to be the bankrupt, immoral faith of slaveholders. As rhetorical strategy, the discourse is effective because it lends weight and substance to what passes for a conventional complaint of slave narrators, and because Douglass's exhibition of faith can only enhance his already considerable posture as an articulate hero. But more specifically, the discourse is most efficacious because at its heart lies a vitriolic poem written by a northern Methodist minister that Douglass introduces by writing: "I conclude these remarks by copying the following portrait of the religion of the south, (which is, by communion and fellowship, the religion of the north,) which I soberly affirm is 'true to life,' and without caricature or the slightest exaggeration." The poem is strong and imbued with considerable irony, but what we must appreciate here is the effect of the white North-erner's poem conjoined with Douglass's *authentication* of the poem. The tables are clearly reversed: Douglass has not only controlled his personal history, but also fulfilled the prophecy suggested by his implicit authentica-tion of Garrison's "Preface" by explicitly authenticating what is convention-ally a white Northerner's validating text. Douglass's narrative thus offers what is unquestionably our best portrait in Afro-American letters of the requisite act of assuming authorial control. An author can go no further than Douglass did without himself writing all the texts constituting the narrative.

Phase IIIb: Authenticating Narrative

In an authenticating narrative, represented here by William Wells Brown's *Narrative of the Life and Escape of William Wells Brown* (not to be confused with Brown's 1847 volume, *Narrative of William Wells Brown, a Fugitive Slave, Written by Himself*), the narrator exhibits considerable control of his narra-tive by becoming an editor of disparate texts for authentication purposes, far more than for the goal of recounting personal history. The texts Brown displays include passages from his speeches and other writings, but for the most part they are testimonials from antislavery groups in both America and England, excerpts from reviews of his travel book, *Three Years in Europe* (1852), selections from antislavery verse, and, quite significantly, letters to Brown's benefactors from his last master in slavery, Mr. Enoch Price of St. Louis. Brown's control of his narrative is comparable to Douglass's, but while Douglass gains control by improving upon the narrative failures of authors

like Henry Bibb, Brown's control represents a refinement of the authenticating strategies used by publishers like Bibb's Lucius Matlack, who edited
and deployed authenticating documents very much like those gathered by
Brown. In this way, Brown's narrative is not so much a tale of personal history
as it is a conceit upon the authorial mode of the white guarantor. Control and
authentication are achieved, but at the enormous price of abandoning the
quest to present personal history in and as literary form.

Brown's "Preface," written notably by himself and not by a white guarantor, is peculiar in that it introduces both his narrative and the text authenticated by the narrative, *Clotel; or, The President's Daughter.* By and large, the
tone of the "Preface" is sophisticated and generally that of a self-assured
writer. Unlike Bibb or Northup, Brown does not skirmish with other authenticators for authorial control of the text, nor is he anxious about competition
from other literary quarters of the antislavery ranks. He scans briefly the
history of slavery in North America and reasons, with the British (with
whom he resides after passage of the 1850 Fugitive Slave Law), that they who
controlled the American colonies when slavery was introduced should feel "a
lively interest in its abolition." All this is done without resort to conventional
apologia or the confession of verbal deficiencies; Brown is humble not so
much in his rhetoric as in his goal: "If the incidents set forth in the following
pages should add anything new to the information already given to the
public through similar publications, and should thereby aid in bringing
British influence to bear upon American slavery, the main object for which
this work was written will have been accomplished." That Brown introduces
a personal narrative and a somewhat fictive narrative (*Clotel*) with language
and intentions commonly reserved for works of history and journalism constitutes his first admission of being motivated by extraliterary concerns. His
second admission emerges from his persistent use of the term "memoir." In
contrast to a confession or autobiography, a memoir refers specifically to an
author's recollections of his public life, far more than to his rendering of
personal history as literary form or metaphor. This former kind of portrait is,
of course, exactly what Brown give us in his narrative.

The narrative is, as I have indicated, bereft of authorship. Brown rarely
renders in fresh language those incidents of which he has written elsewhere;
he simply quotes himself. His posture as the editor and not the author of his
tale disallows any true expression of intimacy with his personal past. This
feature is reinforced by certain objectifying and distancing qualities created
by third-person narration. Brown's 1847 narrative begins, "I was born in
Lexington, Ky. The man who stole me as soon as I was born, recorded the

births of all the infants which he claimed to be born his property, in a book which he kept for that purpose. . . ." Thus, it inaugurates the kind of personal voice and hardboiled prose which is Brown's contribution to early Afro-American letters. In contrast, the opening of the 1852 narrative is flat, without pith or strength: "William Wells Brown, the subject of this narrative, was born a slave in Lexington, Kentucky, not far from the residence of the late Hon. Henry Clay." These words do not constitute effective writing, but that is not Brown's goal. The goal is, rather, authentication, and the seemingly superfluous aside about Henry Clay—which in another narrative might very well generate the first ironic thrust against America's moral blindness—appears for the exclusive purpose of validation. In this way Brown commences an authentication strategy which he will pursue throughout the tale.

The tale or memoir is eclectic in its collection of disparate texts; however, very few of the collected texts merit discussion. I will simply list their types to suggest both their variety and their usefulness to Brown:

1. The scrap of verse, usually effusive, always saccharine, culled from anti-slavery poets known and unknown. The verse expresses high sentiment and deep emotion when the text requires it, engages the popular reading public, and suggests erudition and sensitivity.

2. Quotations from Brown's speeches at famous institutions like Exeter Hall and from "addresses" bestowed on him after such speeches. These advance the memoir, embellish Brown's résumé, and authenticate his claim that he was where he said he was.

3. Quotations from Brown's travel book, *Three Years in Europe,* and from the book's reviews. The passages of personal history advance the memoir and validate "The energy of the man," as well as call attention to the book. The reviews call further attention to the book, and authenticate Brown's literacy and good character.

4. Testimonies and testimonials from various abolitionist groups in the United States and England, white and colored. These texts profess the success of Brown's labors as a lecturing agent, "commend him to the hospitality and encouragement of all true friends of humanity," and, upon his departure for England, provide him with what Douglass would have termed a "protection" for his travels. These are, in short, recommending letters attached to Brown's résumé validating his character and the fact that he is a fugitive slave.

5. Two letters from a former master, Enoch Price of St. Louis, dated before and after the Fugitive Slave Law was passed in 1850.

The Enoch Price letters are undoubtedly the most interesting documents in Brown's compendium, and he makes good narrative use of them. While the other assembled documents merely serve the authenticating strategy, Price's letters, in their portrait of a slaveholder ironically invoking the dictates of fair play while vainly attempting to exact a bargain price for Brown from his benefactors, actually tell us something about Brown's circumstances. Despite the lionizing illustrated by the other documents, Brown is still not a free man. He is most aware of this, and for this reason the narrative concludes, not with another encomium, but with the second of Price's letters once again requesting payment—payment for lost property, payment for papers that will set Brown free. All Brown can do under the circumstances is refuse to acknowledge Price's supposed right to payment, and order his present condition by controlling not so much his tale, which is his past, as the authentication of himself, which is his present and possibly his future. As the editor of his résumé—his present circumstance—Brown must acknowledge slavery's looming presence in his life, but he can also attempt to bury it beneath a mountain of antislavery rhetoric and self-authenticating documentation. Through the act of self-authentication Brown may contextualize slavery and thereby control it. In these terms, then, the heroic proportions to Brown's editorial act of including and manipulating Enoch Price's letters become manifest.

Brown's personal narrative most certainly authenticates himself, but how does it also authenticate *Clotel?* The answer takes us back to Brown's "Preface," where he outlines the extraliterary goals of both narratives, and forward to the concluding chapter of *Clotel*, where he writes:

> My narrative has now come to a close. I may be asked, and no doubt shall, Are the various incidents and scenes related founded in truth? I answer, Yes. I have personally participated in many of those scenes. Some of the narratives I have derived from other sources; many from the lips of those who, like myself, have run away from the land of bondage. . . . To Mrs. Child, of New York, I am indebted for part of a short story. American Abolitionist journals are another source from whence some of the characters appearing in my narrative are taken. All these combined have made up my story.

Brown's personal narrative functions, then, as a successful rhetorical device, authenticating his *access* to the incidents, characters, scenes, and tales which collectively make up *Clotel*. In the end, we witness a dynamic interplay between the two narratives, established by the need of each for resolution and authentication within the other. Since *Clotel* is not fully formed as either a fiction or a slave narrative, it requires completion of some sort, and finds this when it is transformed into a fairly effective antislavery device through linkage with its prefatory authenticating text. Since Brown's personal narrative is not fully formed as either an autobiography or a slave narrative, it requires fulfillment as a literary form through intimacy with a larger, more developed but related text. *Clotel* is no more a novel than Brown's preceding personal narrative is autobiography, but together they represent a roughly hewn literary tool which is, despite its defects, a sophisticated departure from the primary phases of slave narration and authentication.

Brown's personal narrative is hardly an aesthetic work, but that is because Brown had other goals in mind. He is willing to forsake the goal of presenting personal history in literary form in order to promote his books and projects like the Manual Labor School for fugitive slaves in Canada, to authenticate *Clotel*, and to authenticate himself while on British soil. He is willing to abandon the goals of true authorship and to assume instead the duties of an editor in order to gain some measure of control over the present, as opposed to illuminating the past. Brown's narrative is present and future oriented: most of his anecdotes from the past are offered as testimony to the energy and character he will bring to bear on future tasks. In short, just as Douglass inaugurates the autobiographical mode in Afro-American letters, Brown establishes what curiously turns out to be the equally common mode of the authenticating narrative. To see the popularity and great effect of the Afro-American authenticating narrative—once it assumes a more sophisticated form—one need look no further than Booker T. Washington's *Up from Slavery*.

Houston A. Baker, Jr.

Generational Shifts and the Recent Criticism

of Afro-American Literature

(1981)

There exist any number of possible ways to describe changes that have occurred in Afro-American literary criticism during the past four decades. If one assumes a philosophical orientation, one can trace a movement from democratic pluralism ("integrationist poetics") through romantic Marxism (the "Black Aesthetic") to a version of Aristotelian metaphysics (the "Reconstruction of Instruction"). From another perspective, one can describe the ascendant class interests that have characterized Afro-America since World War II, forcing scholars, in one instance, to assess Afro-American expressive culture at a mass level and, in another instance, to engage in a kind of critical "professionalism" that seems contrary to mass interests. One can survey, on yet another level, transformations in the recent criticism of Afro-American literature from a perspective in the philosophy of science; from this vantage point, one can explore conceptual, or "paradigm," changes that have marked the critical enterprise in recent years. These various levels of analysis can be combined, I think, in the notion of the "generational shift."

A "generational shift" can be defined as an ideologically motivated movement overseen by young or newly-emergent intellectuals who are dedicated to refuting the work of their intellectual predecessors and to establishing a new framework of intellectual inquiry. The affective component of such shifts is described by Lewis Feuer: "Every birth or revival of an ideology is borne by a new generational wave: in its experience, each such new intellectual generation feels everything is being born anew, that the past is meaningless, or irrelevant, or nonexistent."[1] The new generation's break with the past is normally signaled by its adoption of what the philosopher of science Thomas S. Kuhn (to whose work I shall return later) designates a new

This essay first appeared in *Black American Literature Forum*, 15 (Spring 1981).

"paradigm"; i.e., a new set of guiding assumptions that unifies the intellectual community.[2]

In the recent criticism of Afro-American literature, there have been two distinct generational shifts. Both have involved ideological and aesthetic reorientations, and both have been accompanied by shifts in literary-critical and literary-theoretical paradigms. The first such shift occurred during the mid-1960s. It led to the displacement of what might be described as integrationist poetics and gave birth to a new object or scholarly investigation.

II

The dominant critical perspective on Afro-American literature during the late 1950s and early 1960s might be called the poetics of integrationism. Richard Wright's essay "The Literature of the Negro in the United States," which appears in his 1957 collection entitled *White Man, Listen!*, offers an illustration of integrationist poetics.[3] Wright optimistically predicts that Afro-American literature may soon be indistinguishable from the mainstream of American arts and letters. The basis for his optimism is the Supreme Court's decision in *Brown* vs. *Topeka Board of Education* (1954), in which the Court ruled that the doctrine "separate but equal" was inherently unequal. According to Wright, this ruling ensures a future "equality" in the experiences of black and white Americans, and this equality of *social* experience will translate in the literary domain as a homogeneity of *represented* experience (103–105). When Afro-American writers have achieved such equality and homogeneity, they will stand at one with the majority culture—in a relationship that Wright terms "entity" (72).

But the foregoing stipulations apply only to what Wright calls the "Narcissistic Level"—i.e., the self-consciously literate level—of Afro-American culture (84–85). At the folk, or mass, level the relationship between Afro-American and the majority culture has always been one of "identity" (as in "the black person's quest for identity"), or separateness (72). And though Wright argues that the self-consciously literate products of Afro-America that signify a division between cultures (e.g., "protest" poems and novels) may disappear relatively quickly under the influence of the Brown decision, he is not so optimistic with regard to the "Forms of Things Unknown" (83)— i.e., the expressive products of the black American masses. For blues, jazz, work songs, and verbal forms such as folktales, boasts, toasts, and dozens are functions of the black masses' relationship of "identity" with the mainstream culture. They signal, that is to say, *an absence of equality* and represent a *sensualization* of the masses' ongoing suffering (83). They are, according to Wright, improvisational forms filled "with a content wrung from a bleak and barren environment, an environment that stung, crushed, all but killed" (84). Only when the "Forms of Things Unknown" have disappeared altogether, or when conditions have been realized that enable them to be raised to a level of self-conscious art, will one be able to argue that an egalitarian ideal has been achieved in American life and art. The only course leading to such a positive goal, Wright implies, is momentous social action like that represented by the 1954 Supreme Court decision.

Hence, the black spokesman who champions a poetics of integrationism is constantly in search of social indicators (such as the Brown decision) that signal a democratic pluralism in American life. The implicit goal of this philosophical orientation is a raceless, classless community of men and women living in perfect harmony (105). The integrationist critic, as Wright demonstrates, founds his predictions of a future, homogeneous body of American creative expression on such social *evidence* as the Emancipation Proclamation, Constitutional amendments, Supreme Court decisions, or any one of many other documented claims that suggest that America is moving toward a pluralistic ideal. The tone that such critics adopt is always one of optimism.

Arthur P. Davis offers a striking example of an Afro-American critic who has repeatedly sought to discover evidence to support his arguments that a oneness of all Americans and a harmonious merger of disparate forms of American creative expression are impending American social realities. What seems implicit in Davis's critical formulations is a call for Afro-American writers to speed the emergence of such realities by offering genuine, *artistic* contributions to the kind of classless, raceless literature that he and other integrationist critics assume will carry the future. An injunction of this type can be inferred, for example, from the 1941 "Introduction" to *The Negro Caravan,* the influential anthology of Afro-American expression that Davis coedited with Sterling Brown and Ulysses Lee:

> The editors . . . do not believe that the expression "Negro literature" is an accurate one, and in spite of its convenient brevity, they have avoided using it. "Negro literature" has no application if it means *structural peculiarity,* or a Negro school of writing. The Negro writes in the forms evolved in English and American literature. . . . The editors consider Negro writers to be American writers, and literature by American Negroes to be a segment of American literature. . . . The chief cause for

objection to the term is that "Negro literature" is too easily placed by certain critics, white and Negro, in an alcove apart. The next step is a double standard of judgment, which is dangerous for the future of Negro writers.[4] (my italics)

In the 1950s and 1960s, Davis continued to champion the poetics implicit in such earlier work as *The Negro Caravan*. His essay "Integration and Race Literature," which he presented to the first conference of Afro-American writers sponsored by the American Society of African Culture in 1959, states:

The course of Negro American literature has been highlighted by a series of social and political crises over the Negro's position in America. The Abolition Movement, the Civil War, Reconstruction, World War I, and the riot-lynching period of the twenties all radically influenced Negro writing. Each crisis in turn produced a new tradition in our literature; and as each crisis has passed, the Negro writer has dropped the social tradition which the occasion demanded and moved towards the mainstream of American literature. The integration controversy is another crisis, and from it we hope that the Negro will move permanently into full participation in American life—social, economic, political, and literary.[5]

The stirring drama implied here of black writers finding their way through various "little" traditions to the glory of the "great" mainstream is a function of Davis's solid faith in American pluralistic ideals. He regards history and society from a specific philosophical and ideological standpoint: Afro-Americans and their expressive traditions, like other minority cultures, have always moved unceasingly toward a unity with American majority culture. He thus predicts—like Wright—the eventual disappearance of social conditions that produce literary works of art that are identifiable (in terms of "structural peculiarity") as "Negro" or "Afro-American" literature.

Wright and Davis represent a generation whose philosophy, ideology, and attendant poetics support the vanishing of Afro-American literature qua *Afro-American* literature. I shall examine this proposition at greater length in the next section. At this point, I simply want to suggest that the consequences of this generational position for literary-critical axiology can be inferred from the "Introduction" to *The Negro Caravan*. The editors of that work assert: "They [Afro-American writers] must ask that their books be judged as books, without sentimental allowances. In their own defense they must demand a single standard of criticism" (7). This assertion suggests that black writers should construct their works in ways that make them accept-able in the sight of those who mold a "single standard of criticism" in Amer-ica. These standard bearers were for many years, however, a small, exclusive community of individuals labelled by black spokesmen of the sixties as the "white, literary-critical establishment." And only a poetics buttressed by a philosophical viewpoint that augured the eventual unification of *all* talented creative men and women as judges could have prompted such able spokes-men as Wright, Brown, and Davis to consider that works of Afro-American literature and verbal art be subjected to a "single standard" of American literary-critical judgment.

III

The generational shift that displaced the integrationist poetics just described brought forth a group of intellectuals most clearly distinguished from its predecessors by its different ideological and philosophical posture vis-à-vis American egalitarian ideals. After the arrests, bombings, and assassinations that comprised the white South's reaction to nonviolent, direct-action pro-tests by hundreds of thousands of civil rights workers from the late fifties to the mid-sixties, it was difficult for even the most committed optimist to feel that integration was an impending American social reality.[6] Rather than searching for documentary evidence and the indelible faith necessary to argue for an undemonstrated American egalitarianism, the emerging genera-tion set itself the task of analyzing the nature, aims, ends, and arts of those hundreds of thousands of their own people who were assaulting America's manifest structures of exclusion.

   The Afro-American masses demonstrated through their violent acts ("ur-ban riots") in Harlem, Watts, and other communities throughout the nation that they were intent on black social and political sovereignty in America. Their acts signaled the birth of a new ideology, one that received its proper name in 1966,[7] when Stokely Carmichael designated it "Black Power":

> [Black Power] is a call for black people in this country to unite, to
> recognize their heritage, to build a sense of community. It is a call for
> black people to begin to define their own goals, to lead their own
> organizations and to support those organizations. It is a call to reject the
> racist institutions and values of [American] society.[8]

This definition, drawn from Carmichael and Charles Hamilton's work en-titled *Black Power,* expresses a clear imperative for Afro-Americans to focus their social efforts and political vision on their *own* self-interests. This particularity of Black Power—its sharp emphasis on the immediate concerns of Afro-Americans themselves—was a direct counterthrust by an emergent generation to the call for a general, raceless, classless community of men and women central to an earlier integrationist framework. The community that was of interest to the emergent generation was not a future generation of integrated Americans, but rather a present, vibrant group of men and women who constituted the heart of Afro-America. The Afro-American masses became, in the late sixties and early seventies, both subject and audience for the utterances of black political spokesmen moved by a new ideology.

The poetics accompanying the new ideological orientation were first suggested by Amiri Baraka (LeRoi Jones) in an address entitled "The Myth of a 'Negro Literature,'" which he presented to the American Society of African Culture in 1962:

Where is the Negro-ness of a literature written in imitation of the meanest of social intelligences to be found in American culture, i.e., the white middle class? How can it even begin to express the emotional predicament of black Western man? Such a literature, even if its "characters" *are* black, takes on the emotional barrenness of its model, and the blackness of the characters is like the blackness of Al Jolson, an unconvincing device. It is like using black checkers instead of white. They are still checkers.[9]

At the self-consciously literate level of Afro-American expression, the passage implies, black spokesmen have deserted the genuine emotional referents and the authentic experiential categories of black life in America. The homogeneity between their representations of experience and those of the white mainstream are a cause for disgust rather than an occasion for rejoicing. Finally, the quoted passage implies that the enervating merger of black and white expression at the "Narcissistic" level (to use Wright's phrase) of Afro-American life is a result of the black writer's acceptance of a "single standard of criticism" molded by white America. Baraka, thus, inverts the literary-critical optimism and axiology of an earlier generation, rejecting entirely the notion that "Negro Literature" should not stand apart as a unique body of expression. It is precisely the desertion by black writers of those aspects of Afro-American life that foster the uniqueness and authenticity of black expression that Baraka condemns most severely in his essay.

But where, then, does one discover in Afro-America genuine reflections of the true emotional referents and experiential categories of black life if not in its self-consciously literate works of art? Like the more avowedly political spokesmen of his day, Baraka turned to the world of the masses, and there he discovered the "forms of things unknown" (Wright's designation for black, folk expressive forms):

> Negro music alone, because it drew its strengths and beauties out of the depth of the black man's soul, and because to a large extent its traditions could be carried on by the lowest classes of Negroes, has been able to survive the constant and willful dilutions of the black middle class. Blues and jazz have been the only consistent exhibitors of "Negritude" in formal American culture simply because the bearers of its tradition maintained their essential identities as Negroes; in no other art (and I will persist in calling Negro music Art) has this been possible. (165–66)

In this statement, Baraka seems to parallel the Richard Wright of an earlier generation. But while Wright felt that the disappearance of the "forms of things unknown" would signal a positive stage in the integration of American life and art, Baraka established the Harlem Black Arts Repertory Theatre/School in 1965 as an enterprise devoted to the continuance, development, and strengthening of the "coon shout," blues, jazz, holler, and other expressive forms of the "lowest classes of Negroes."[10] He, and other artists who contributed to the establishment of the school, felt that the perpetuation of such forms would help give birth to a new black nation. Larry Neal, who worked with Baraka during the mid-sixties, delineates both the complementarity of the Black Arts and Black Power movements and the affective component of·a generational shift in his often-quoted essay "The Black Arts Movement":

> Black Art is the aesthetic and spiritual sister of the Black Power concept. As such, it envisions an art that speaks directly to the needs and aspirations of Black America. In order to perform this task, the Black Arts Movement proposes a radical reordering of the western cultural aesthetic. It proposes a separate symbolism, mythology, critique, and iconology.[11]

The Black Arts Movement, therefore, like its ideological counterpart Black Power, was concerned with the articulation of experiences (and the satisfaction of audience demands) that found their essential character among the black urban masses. The guiding assumption of the movement was that if a literary-critical investigator looked to the characteristic musical and verbal forms of the masses, he would discover unique aspects of Afro-American creative expression—aspects of form and performance—that lay closest to the veritable emotional referents and experiential categories of Afro-American culture. The result of such critical investigations, according to Neal and other spokesmen such as Baraka and Addison Gayle, Jr. (to name but three prominent advocates for the Black Arts), would be the discovery of a "Black Aesthetic"—i.e., a distinctive code for the creation and evaluation of black art. From an assumed "structural peculiarity" of Afro-American expressive culture, the emergent generation of intellectuals proceeded to assert a *sui generis* tradition of Afro-American art and a unique "standard of criticism" suitable for its elucidation.

Stephen Henderson's essay entitled "The Forms of Things Unknown," which stands as the introduction to his anthology *Understanding the New Black Poetry*, offers one of the most suggestive illustrations of this discovery process at work.[12] Henderson's formulations mark a high point in the first generational shift in the recent criticism of Afro-American literature because he is a spokesman *par excellence* for what emerged from his generation as a new object of literary-critical and literary-theoretical investigation. Before turning to the specifics of his arguments, however, I want to focus for a moment on the work of Thomas Kuhn to clarify what I mean by a "new object" of investigation.

IV

In his work *The Structure of Scientific Revolutions*, Kuhn sets out to define the nature of a scientific "revolution," or shift in the fundamental ways in which the scientific community perceives and accounts for phenomena. He first postulates that the guiding construct in the practice of normal science is what he defines as the "paradigm"; i.e., a constellation of "beliefs, values, techniques and so on shared by the members of a given community."[13] He further defines a paradigm as the "universally recognized scientific achieve-ments that for a time provide model problems and solutions to a community of practitioners [of normal science]" (viii). A paradigm, thus, sets the param-eters of scholarly investigation, constraining both the boundaries of an in-vestigator's perception and the degree of legitimacy attributed to various problems and methodologies. A forceful example of a scientific revolution and its enabling paradigm shift was the displacement of geocentricism by a Copernican cosmology. Kuhn writes: "The Copernicans who denied its tra-ditional title 'planet' to the sun were not only learning what 'planet' meant or what the sun was. Instead, they were changing the meaning of 'planet' so that it could continue to make useful distinctions in a world where all celestial bodies, not just the sun, were seen differently from the way they had been seen before" (128–29).

The effects of this kind of paradigmatic shift on assumptions and higher-order rules of a scholarly community are additionally clarified when Kuhn says:

> Led by a new paradigm, scientists adopt new instruments and look in new places. Even more important, during revolutions scientists see new and different things when looking with familiar instruments in places they have looked before. It is rather as if the professional community had been suddenly transported to another planet where *familiar objects are seen in a different light and are joined by unfamiliar ones as well* . . . paradigm changes . . . cause scientists to see the world of their research-engagement differently. In so far as their only recourse to that world is through what they see and do, we may want to say that after a revolution scientists are responding to a different world. (my italics, 111)

Kuhn cites as an experimental instance of such change in perception the classic work of George M. Stratton. Stratton fitted his subjects with goggles that contained inverting lenses. Initially, these subjects saw the world upside down and existed in a state of extreme disorientation. Eventually, though, their entire visual field flipped over, and:

> Thereafter, objects are again seen as they had been before the goggles were put on. The assimilation of a previously anomalous visual field . . . reacted upon and changed the field itself. Literally as well as metaphorically . . . [the subject] accustomed to inverting lenses . . . [underwent] *a revolutionary transformation of vision.* (my italics, 112)

In terms of the present discussion of Afro-American literary criticism, I want to suggest that Stephen Henderson and other Afro-American intellectuals of his generation fomented a change in the perceptual field of Afro-American literary study that amounted, finally, to a "revolutionary transformation" of literary-critical and literary-theoretical vision vis-à-vis black expressive culture. Before the mid-sixties scholars were led by an integrationist paradigm that permitted them to perceive as "literature" or "art" only those Afro-American expressive works that approached or conformed to the "single standard of criticism" advocated by the editors of *The Negro Caravan.* In adopting such a "standard," an integrationist poetics bound its perceptual field and constrained its domain of legitimate investigative problems to Afro-

American expressive objects and events that came nearest this standard. Under the old paradigm, therefore, a scholar could not *see* that "Negro music" qua "*Negro* music" or "Negro Poetry" qua "*Negro* poetry" constituted *art*. For "Negro-ness" was viewed by the old paradigm as a condition (a set of properties of "structural peculiarities") that excluded such a phenomenon as "*Negro* poetry" from the artworld.[14] The integrationists held it as a first law that *art* was an American area of achievement in which race and class did not comprise significant variables. To discover, assert, or label the "Negro-ness" or "Blackness" of an expressive work as a fundamental condition of its "artistic-ness" was, thus, for the new generation to "flip over" the integrationist field of vision. And this revised perceptual orientation is precisely what Henderson and his contemporaries achieved. Their efforts made it possible for literary-critical and literary-theoretical investigators to see "familiar objects" in a different light and to include previously "unfamiliar" objects in an expanded (and sharply modified) American artworld. In "The Forms of Things Unknown," Henderson masterfully outlines the hypotheses, boundaries, and legitimate problems of the new paradigmatic framework called the "Black Aesthetic."

V

Henderson's assumption is that in literature there exists "such a commodity as 'blackness'" (3). He further argues that this "commodity" should be most easily located in poetry "since poetry is the most concentrated and the most allusive of the verbal arts" (3). Implicit in these statements is Henderson's claim that an enabling condition for art (and particularly for "poetry") in Afro-American culture is the possession of *blackness* by an expressive object or event. The ontological status—the very condition of being—of *Afro-American* poetic expression is, in fact, a function of this commodity of blackness. The most legitimate paradigmatic question that a literary-critical investigator or a literary theorist can pose, therefore, is: In what place and by what means does the commodity "blackness" achieve form and substance?

The title of Henderson's essay suggests the answer he provides to this question. He states that blackness must be defined, at a *structural* level of expressive objects and events, as an "interior dynamism" that derives its force from the "inner life" of the Afro-American folk (5–6). And he is quite explicit that what he intends by "inner life" is, in fact, the constellation of cultural values and beliefs that characterizes what the philosopher Albert Hofstadter calls a "reference public." Hofstadter writes:

Predication of "good" . . . tends to lose meaningful direction when the public whose valuations are considered in judging the object is not specified. I do not see how we can hope to speak sensibly about the aesthetic goodness of objects unless we think of them in the context of reception and valuation by persons, the so-called "context of consumption." Properties by virtue of which we value objects aesthetically—e.g., beauty, grace, charm, the tragic, the comic, balance, proportion, expressive symbolism, versimilitude, propriety—always require some reference to the apprehending and valuing person. . . . Any public taken as the public referred to in a normative esthetic judgment I shall call the judgment's *reference public*. The reference public is the group whose appreciations or valuations are used as data on which to base the judgment. It is the group to which universality of appeal may or may not appertain.[15]

Henderson says that the existence of black poetry is a function of a black audience's concurrence that a particular verbal performance (whether written or oral) by some person of "known Black African ancestry" is, in fact, poetry (7). The array of values and beliefs—the cultural codes—that allows a black reference public to make such a normative judgment constitutes the inner life of the folk. "Inner life," then—on the assumption that the operative codes of a culture are historically conditioned and are maintained at a level of interacting cultural systems—is translated as "ethnic roots." Questions of the ontology and valuation of a black poem, according to Henderson, "can not be resolved without considering the ethnic roots of Black poetry, which I insist are ultimately understood only by Black people themselves" (7–8). What he seeks to establish, or to support, with this claim, I think, is a kind of cultural holism—an interconnectedness (temporally determined) of a cultural discourse—that can only be successfully apprehended through a set of theoretical concepts and critical categories arrived at by in-depth investigation of the fundamental expressive manifestations of a culture.

In order to achieve such apprehension, the literary investigator (like the cultural anthropologist) must go the best available informants; i.e., to natives of the culture, or to the "reference public." "One must not consider the poem in isolation," writes Henderson, "but in relationship to the reader/audience, and the reader to the wider context of the phenomenon which we call, for the sake of convenience, the Black Experience" (62). His tone approximates even more closely that of cultural anthropology in the following stipulations on literary-critical axiology:

. . . the recognition of Blackness in poetry is a value judgment which on certain levels and in certain instances, notably in matters of meanings that go beyond questions of structure and theme, must rest upon one's immersion in the totality of the Black Experience. It means that the ultimate criteria for critical evaluation must be found in the sources of the creation, that is, in the Black Community itself. (65–66)

The notion that a conditioning cultural holism is a necessary consideration in the investigation of a culture's works of verbal art receives yet another designation that has anthropological parallels when Henderson talks of a "Soul Field." Field theory in anthropology stresses the continuous nature of conceptual structures that make up various areas, or "fields," of a culture, e.g., kinship or color terms and their attendant *connotations* or *sense*. For Henderson, the "Soul Field" of Afro-American culture is "the complex galaxy of personal, social, institutional, historical, religious, and mythical meanings that affect everything we say or do as Black people sharing a common heritage" (41). In this definition, "meanings" is the operative term, and it situates the author's designation of "field" decisively within the realm of semantics. Henderson's "Soul Field" is, thus, similar to J. Trier's *Sinnfeld,* or conceptual field; i.e., the area of a culture's linguistic system that contains the encyclopedia or mappings of various "senses" of lexical items drawn from the same culture's *Wortfeld,* or lexicon.[16]

The theoretical concepts and critical categories for analyzing black poetry that Henderson sets forth in "The Forms of Things Unknown" are coextensive with the case he makes for the holism and continuity of Afro-American culture. His three major categories are theme, structure, and saturation. And in dividing each category into analytic subsets, he never loses sight of the "inner life" of the folk, of that interconnected "field" of uniquely black meanings and values that he postulates as the essential determinants of these subsets. He, thus, seeks to ensure a relationship of identity between his own critical categories and the "real," experiential categories of Afro-American life. For example, he identifies "theme" with what he perceives as the *actual* guiding concern of the collective, evolving consciousness of Afro-American.

He finds that the most significant concern of that consciousness has always been "the idea of liberation" (18) and suggests that the "old word, 'freedom,'" might be substituted for this phrase to denote the overriding theme (i.e., that which is "being spoken of") of Afro-American expressive culture. Hence, a "real" lexical category ("freedom") and its complex conceptual mappings in Afro-American culture are identified as one subset of the critical category "theme." Similarly, the *actual* speech and music of Afro-American culture and their various forms, techniques, devices, nuances, rules, and so on are identified as fundamental structural referents in the continuum of black expressive culture:

> Structurally speaking . . . whenever Black poetry is most distinctively and effectively *Black*, it derives its form from two basic sources, Black speech and Black music. . . . By Black speech I mean the speech of the majority of Black people in this country. . . . This includes the techniques and timbres of the sermon and other forms of oratory, the dozens, the rap, the signifying, and the oral folktale. . . . By Black music I mean essentially the vast fluid body of Black song—spirituals, shouts, jubilees, gospel songs, field cries, blues, pop songs by Blacks, and, in addition, jazz (by whatever name one calls it) and non-jazz by Black composers who *consciously or unconsciously* draw upon the Black musical tradition. (30–31)

Here, Henderson effectively delineates a continuum of Afro-American verbal and musical expressive behavior that begins with everyday speech and popular music and extends to works of "high art."

Finally, "saturation" is a category in harmony with the assumed uniqueness of both the Afro-American *Sinnfeld* and *Wortfeld*. For Henderson insists that "saturation" is a perceptual category that has to do with a distinctive semantics:

> Certain words and constructions [e.g., *rock, jelly, jook*] seem to carry an inordinate charge of emotional and psychological weight [in Afro-American culture], so that whenever they are used they set all kinds of bells ringing, all kinds of synapses snapping, on all kinds of levels. . . . I call such words 'mascon' words. . . . to mean *a massive concentration of Black experiential energy* which powerfully affects the meaning of Black speech, Black song, and Black poetry—if one, indeed, has to make such distinctions. (43)

From an assumed "particularity," wholeness, and continuity of Afro-American culture—characteristics that manifest themselves most clearly among the Afro-American folk or masses—Henderson, thus, moves to the articulation of theoretical concepts and critical categories that provide what he calls "a way of speaking about all kinds of Black poetry despite the kinds of questions that can be raised" (10). He proposes, in short, a theory to account for the continuity—the unity in theme, structure, and semantics—of black speech, music, and poetry (both oral and written). He refuses, from the outset, to follow a traditional literary-critical path; i.e., predicating this continuity on history or chronology alone. Instead, he observes the contemporary scene in Afro-American poetry (i.e., the state of the art of black poetry in the 1960s and early 1970s) and realizes that the oral tradition of the urban masses is the dominant force shaping the work of Afro-American poets. From this modern instantiation of the reciprocity between expressive folk culture and self-conscious, literary expression, he proposes that *all* black "poetic" expression can be understood in terms of such a reciprocal pattern. "Understanding" the "new black poetry" in its relationship to black urban folk culture, therefore, provides direction and definition in the larger enterprise of understanding the artistic codes—or the cultural system that is "art"—in black American culture. A comprehension of the "forms of things unknown" and the cultural anthropologic assumptions that it presupposes lead to the discovery a unique artistic tradition, one embodying peculiar themes, structures, and meanings.

The "Black Aesthetic" signaled for Henderson and his contemporaries the codes that determine the tradition as well as the theoretical standpoint (one marked by appropriate categories) that would enable one to see, to "speak about," this tradition. And like new paradigms, the "Black Aesthetic" had distinctly perceptual and semantic ramifications. It changed the meaning of both "black" and "aesthetic" in the American literary-critical universe of discourse so that these terms could continue to make "useful distinctions" in a world where works of Afro-American expressive art had come to be seen quite differently from the manner in which they were viewed by an old integrationist paradigm.

VI

Earlier, I referred to the philosophical orientation of the Black Aesthetic as romantic Marxism. Having discussed Henderson's work, perhaps I can now clarify this designation. For me, the fact that the aesthetics of the Black Arts movement were idealistically centered in the imagination of the black critical observer makes them "romantic."[17] This critical centrality of the Afro-American mind is illustrated by Henderson's assumption that "Blackness" is not a theoretical reification, but a reality, accessible only to those who can "imagine" in uniquely black ways. From this perspective, the word "understanding" in the title of his anthology is a sign for spiritual journey in which what the *black* imagination seizes upon as *black* must be *black,* whether it existed before or not.

The notion of a "reference public" gives way, therefore, at a lower level of the Black Aesthetic's argument, to a kind of impressionistic chauvinism. For it is, finally, *only* the black imagination that can experience blackness, in poetry, or in life. As a result, the creative and critical framework suggested by Henderson resembles, at times, a closed circle:

> . . . for one who is totally immersed, as it were, or saturated in the Black Experience the slightest formulation of the typical or true-to-life [Black] experience, whether positive or negative, is enough to bring on at least subliminal recognition [of the "formulation" of the experience as "Black"]. . . . I have tried to postulate a concept that would be useful in talking about what Black people feel is their distinctiveness, without being presumptuous enough to attempt a description or definition of it. This quality or condition of Black awareness I call *saturation.* I intend it as a sign, like the mathematical symbol *infinity,* or the term "Soul." It allows us to talk about the thing [a "distinctive" feeling of "Blackness"], even to some extent to use it, though we can't, thank God! ultimately abstract and analyze it: it must be experienced. (63–68)

"Saturation" also gives way, then, at a lower level of the argument to cultural xenophobia. Rather than an indicator for a *sui generis* semantics, it becomes a mysterious trait of consciousness. In "Saturation: Progress Report on a Theory of Black Poetry," an article that appeared two years after his anthology, Henderson comments on the critical reactions that his romantic specifications evoked:

> Some people—critics, white and Black—have difficulty with this last standard [i.e., the critical standard of "intuition" for judging the successful rendering of "Black poetic structure"]. They call it mysterious, mystical, chauvinistic, and even (in a slightly different context) a "curious metaphysical argument" (Saunders Redding). I call it *saturation.* I authenticate it from personal experience. To those critics I say: Remember Keats did the same, proving poetic experience by his pulse and the "holiness of the imagination."[18]

But if Henderson's romanticism led him to chauvinistically posit an "intuitive sense," a "condition" of "Blackness" that can only be grasped by the "saturated" or "immersed" black imagination, it also led him to suggest the kind of higher-order, cultural-anthropological argument that I have extrapolated from his work and discussed in the preceding section. I think the romanticism of Henderson and his contemporaries—like that of romantics gone before who believed they were compelled to "create a system or be enslav'd by another Man's"—lay in their metaphysical rebelliousness, their willingness to postulate a positive and distinctive category of existence ("Blackness") and then to read the universe in terms of that category.[19] The predication of such a category was not only a radical political act designed to effect the liberation struggles of Afro-America, but also a bold critical act designed to break the interpretive monopoly on Afro-American expressive culture that had been held from time immemorial by a white, literary-critical establishment that set a "single standard of criticism":

> If the critic is half worth his salt, then he would attempt to describe what occurs in the poem and to *explain*—to the extent that it is possible—how the "action" takes place, i.e., how the elements of the work interact with one another to produce its effect. And if one of those elements is "Blackness"—as value, as theme, or as structure, especially the latter—then he is remiss in his duty if he does not attempt to deal with it in some logical, orderly manner.[20]

Given Henderson's arguments for the black person's own intuitive sense of experience as the only valid guide to the recognition of "Blackness" as an "element," it seems unlikely that many white critics would prove "worth their salt" vis-à-vis Afro-American literature and criticism. And there is a kind of implicit antinomianism in the following assertion from his essay "The Question of Form and Judgment in Contemporary Black American Poetry: 1962–1977": "Historically, the question of what constitutes a Black poem or how to judge one does not really come to a head until the 1960s and the promulgation of the Black Aesthetic in literature and the other arts. In a special sense . . . 'Black' poetry was invented in the 1960s along with the radicalization of the word 'Black' and the emergence of the Black Power philosophy."[21] Here, the faith that postulated "Blackness" as a distinctive category of existence is seen as the generative source of a new art, politics, and criticism nullifying the interpretive authority of a white, critical orthodoxy.

The rebelliousness that seemed to close the circle of Afro-American criticism to white participants, however, was not only romantic, it was also Marxist. Henderson and his contemporaries attempted to base their arguments for an Afro-American intuitive sense of "Blackness" on the notion that such a sense was a function of the continuity of Afro-American culture. The distinctive cultural circumstances that comprised the material bases of Afro-American culture—i.e., the means and instrumentalities of production, distribution, and consumption that marked the formation and growth of an African culture in America—were always seen by spokesmen for the Black Aesthetic as determinants of a *consciousness* that was distinctively "Black." And the most accurate reflection of the economics of slavery (and their subsequent forms) in the American economy was held to take place at a mass or folk level. Hence, the expressive forms of black folk consciousness were defined by Black Aestheticians as underdetermined by material circumstances that vary within a narrow range. To take up such forms is to find oneself involved with the "authentic" or basic (as in the "material base") categories of Afro-American existence. "Culture determines consciousness" became a watchword for the Black Aesthetic, and by "culture" its spokesmen meant a complex of material and expressive components that could only be discovered at a mass level of Afro-American experience. It was their emphasis on this level—an emphasis motivated by a paradoxical desire to ground an idealistic rebelliousness in a materialist reading of history—that led to a deepened scholarly interest during the sixties and early seventies in both Afro-American folklore and other black expressive forms that had long been (in Henderson's words) "under siege" by "white critical condescension and snobbery, and more recently, outright pathological ignorance and fear."[22] And through their investigation of the "forms of things unknown" in recent years, some white critics were able to reenter the critical circle.[23] They reentered, however, not as superordinate authorities, but as serious scholars working in harmony with some of the fundamental postulates of the Black Aesthetic.

There is also a more clichéd sense in which the Black Aesthetic was Marxist, and it finds its best illustration in the insistence by spokesmen for the new paradigm that expressive culture has a "social function." Black Aestheticians were quick to assert that works of verbal art have direct effects in the solution of social problems and in the shaping of social consciousness. The prescriptive formulations of a spokesman like Ron Karenga demonstrate this aspect of the Black Aesthetic: "All black art, irregardless of any technical requirements, must have three basic characteristics which make it revolutionary. In brief, it must be functional, collective and committing."[24] Like Mao Tse-Tung, whom he is paraphrasing, Karenga and other spokesmen for the Black Arts felt that poems and novels could (and *should*) be designed to move audiences to revolutionary action.

It should be clear at this point that there were blatant weaknesses in the critical framework that actually accompanied the postulates of the Black Aesthetic. Too often in their attempts to locate the parameters of Afro-American culture, spokesmen for the new paradigm settled instead for a romantically-conceived domain of "race." And their claims to have achieved a scholarly consensus on "culture" sometimes revealed themselves as functions of a defensive chauvinism on the part of spokesmen who had gained the limelight. What is encouraging though, in any evaluation of the Afro-American intellectual milieu during the later stages of the Black Arts movement is that Black Aesthetic spokesmen *themselves* first pointed out (and suggested ways beyond) such critical and theoretical weaknesses.

In his essay "The Black Contribution to American Letters: The Writer as Activist—1960 and After," Larry Neal identifies the Black Aesthetic's interest in an African past and in African-American folklore as a species of Herderian nationalism and goes on to say: "Nationalism, wherever it occurs in the modern world, must legitimize itself by evoking the muse of history. This is an especially necessary step where the nation or group feels that its social oppression is inextricably bound up with the destruction of its traditional culture and with the suppression of that culture's achievements in the intellectual sphere."[25] A social group's reaction in such nationalistic instances, according to Neal, is understandably (though also, regrettably) one of total introspection—i.e., drawing in unto itself and labeling the historically oppressive culture as "the enemy" (782). A fear of the destruction of Afro-American culture by an "aggressive and alien" West, for example, prompted Black Aesthetic spokesmen to think only in racial terms and to speak only in "strident" tones as a means of defending their culture against what they perceived as threats from the West. Such a strategy, however, in Neal's view, represents a confusion of politics and art, an undesirable conflation of the "public" domain of social activism and the "private" field of language reserved for artistic creation and literary-theoretical investigation.

Such a response is, in his estimation, finally a form of distorted "Marxist literary theory in which the concept of race is substituted for the Marxist idea of class" (783). The attempt to apply the "ideology of race to artistic creation" (784), he says, is simply a contemporary manifestation of Afro-American literature's (and, by implication, literary criticism's) historical dilemma:

The historical problem of black literature is that it has in a sense been perpetually hamstrung by its need to address itself to the question of racism in America. Unlike black music, it has rarely been allowed to exist on its own terms, but rather [has] been utilized as a means of public relations in the struggle for human rights. Literature can indeed make excellent propaganda, but through propaganda alone the black writer can never perform the highest function of his art: that of revealing to man his most enduring human possibilities and limitations. (784)

In order to perform the "highest function" of artistic creation and criticism the black spokesman must concentrate his attention and efforts on "method"—on "form, structure, and genre"—rather than on "experience" or "content" (783–84). Neal, therefore, who called in the sixties for a literature and a criticism that spoke "directly to the needs and aspirations of black people," ends his later essay by calling for a creativity that projects "the accumulated weight of the world's aesthetic, intellectual, and historical experience" as a function of its mastery of "form." His revised formalist position leads not only to a condemnation of the critical weaknesses of former allies in the Black Aesthetic camp, but also to a valorization of the theoretical formulations of such celebrated "Western" theoreticians as Northrop Frye and Kenneth Burke (783–84).

A new order of literary-critical and literary-theoretical thought—one that sought to situate the higher-order rules of the Black Aesthetic within a contemporary universe of literary-theoretical discourse—was signaled during the mid-seventies not only by Neal's essay, but also by symposia and conferences on the Black Arts that occurred throughout the United States.[26] It was at one such symposium that Henderson presented his essay "The Question of Form and Judgement," which I have previously cited.[27] Like Neal, Henderson is drawn to a more formalist critique in his 1977 essay. For example, he implicitly rejects an intuitive "saturation" in favor of a more empirical approach to literary study: "in criticism, intuition, though vital, is not enough. The canons, the categories, the dynamics must be as clear and reasoned as possible. These must rest on a sound empirical base" (36). This "sound empirical base" is, in the final analysis, a *data base* acquired through the kind of cultural-anthropological investigation that I suggested when discussing "The Forms of Things Unknown." "Black poetry," Henderson continues, "can and should be judged by the same standards that any other poetry is judged by—by those standards which validly arise out of the culture" (33). And the primary and secondary sources that he takes up in his 1977 discussion indicate that he has a very clear notion of "culture" as a category in literary study.

I think it would be incorrect to assert that the mid- and later-seventies witnessed a total revisionism on the part of former advocates for the Black Aesthetic. It seems fair, however, to say that some early spokesmen had by this time begun to point out weaknesses of the structure they had raised on the ideological foundations of Black Power. The defensive inwardness of the Black Aesthetic—its manifest appeal to a racially-conditioned, revolutionary, and intuitive standard of critical judgment—made the new paradigm an ideal instrument of vision for those who wished to usher into the world new and *sui generis* Afro-American objects of investigation. Ultimately, though, such introspection could not answer the kinds of theoretical questions occasioned by the entry of these objects into the world. In a sense, the Afro-American literary-critical investigator had been given—through a bold act of the critical imagination—a unique literary tradition but no distinctive theoretical vocabulary with which to discuss this tradition. He had been given linguistic forms of power and beauty, but the language meted out by Karenga and others of his ilk was, sometimes, little more than a curse. A new paradigm (one coextensive with a contemporary universe whose participants were attempting to formulate adequate, theoretical ways of discussing art) was in order.

VII

Discussing the manner of progression of a new philosophical posture born of a generational shift, Feuer comments:

> . . . from its point of origin with an insurgent generational group, the new emotional standpoint, the new perspective, the new imagery, the new metaphors and idioms spread to the more conventional sections of their own generation, then to their slightly older opponents and their relative elders. Thus, by the time that conservative Americans spoke of themselves as 'pragmatic,' and virtually every American politician defined himself as a 'pragmatist,' the word 'pragmatist' had become a cliché, and its span as a movement was done. A new insurgent generation would perforce have to explore novel emotions, images, and idioms in order to define its own independent character, its own 'revolutionary' aims against the elders.[28]

One might substitute "Black Aesthetic" and "Black Aesthetician" for the implied "pragmatism" and the explicit "pragmatist" of the foregoing remarks. For by the end of the 1970s, the notion of a uniquely Afro-American field of aesthetic experience marked by unique works of verbal and literary art had become a commonplace in American literary criticism. The philosophical tenets that supported early manifestations of this notion, however, had been discredited by the failure of revolutionary black social and political groups to achieve their desired ends. "Black Power," that is to say, as a motivating philosophy for the Black Aesthetic, was deemed an ideological failure by the mid-seventies because it had failed to give birth to a sovereign Afro-American state within the United States. Hence, those who adopted fundamental postulates of the Black Aesthetic as givens in the late seventies did so without a corresponding acceptance of its initial philosophical buttresses.

The "imagery" of a new and resplendent nation of Afro-Americans invested with Black Power, like the "emotional standpoint" which insisted that this hypothetical nation should have a collective and functional literature and criticism, gave way in the late seventies to a new idiom. In defining its independent character, a new group of intellectuals found it *de rigueur* to separate the language of criticism from the vocabulary of political ideology. Their supporting philosophical posture for this separation was a dualism predicated on a distinction between "literary" and "extraliterary" realms of human behavior. Their proclaimed mission was to "reconstruct" the pedagogy and study of Afro-American literature so that it would reflect the most advanced thinking of a contemporary universe of literary-theoretical discourse. This goal was similar in some respects to the revisionist efforts of Neal and Henderson discussed in the preceding section. Like their immediate forerunners, the "reconstructionists" were interested in establishing a sound theoretical framework for the future study of Afro-American literature. In their attempts to achieve this goal, however, some spokesmen for the new generation (whose work I shall discuss shortly) were hampered by a literary-critical "professionalism" that was a function of their emergent class interests.

At the outset of the present essay, I implied that the notion "generational shifts" was sufficient to offer some account of the "ascendant class interests that have characterized Afro-America since World War II." The emergence of a mass, black audience, which was so important for the Black Power and Black Arts movements, was the first instance that I had in mind.[29] But the vertical mobility of Afro-Americans prompted by black political activism during the sixties and early seventies also resulted in the emergence during the 1970s of what has been called a "new black middle class."[30] The opening of the doors, personnel rosters, and coffers of the white academy to minority groups effected by the radical politics of the past two decades provided the conditions of possibility for the appearance of Afro-American critics who have adopted postures, standards, and vocabularies of their white compeers. The disappearance of a mass black audience for both literary-critical and revolutionary-political discourse brought about by the billions of dollars and countless man-hours spent to suppress the American radical left in recent years has been ironically accompanied, therefore, by the emergence of Afro-American spokesmen whose class status (new, black middle-class) and privileges are, in fact, contingent upon their adherence to accepted (i.e., white) standards of their profession. Bernard Anderson's reflections on the situation of black corporate middle-managers who assumed positions in the late sixties and early seventies serve as well to describe the situation of a new group of Afro-American literary critics:

> As pioneers in a career-development process, these [black] managers face challenges and uncertainties unknown to most white managers. Many feel an extra responsibility to maintain high performance levels, and most recognize an environment of competition that will tolerate only slight failure. . . . Some black middle managers feel the need to conform to a value system alien to the experience of most black Americans but essential for success in professional management.[31]

One result of a class-oriented professionalism among Afro-American literary critics has been a sometimes uncritical imposition upon Afro-American culture of literary theories borrowed from prominent white scholars.

When such borrowings have occurred among the generation that displaced the Black Aesthetic, the outcome has sometimes been disastrous for the course of Afro-American literary study. For instead of developing the mode of analysis suggested by the higher-order arguments of a previous generation, the emergent generation has chosen to distinguish Afro-American literature as an autonomous cultural domain and to criticize it in terms "alien" to the implied cultural-anthropological approach of the Black Aesthetic. Rather than attempting to assess the merits of the Black Aesthetic's methodological assumptions, that is to say, the new generation has adopted the "professional" assumptions (and attendant jargon) that mark the world of white academic literary critics. A positive outcome to the emergent generation's endeavors has been a strong and continuing emphasis on the necessity for an adequate theoretical framework for the study of Afro-American literature. The negative results of their efforts have been an unfortunate burdening of the universe of discourse surrounding Afro-American culture with meaningless jargon and the articulation of a variety of lamentably confused utterances on language, literature, and culture. The emergent generation is fundamentally correct, I feel, in its call for serious literary study of Afro-American literature. But it is misguided, I believe, in its wholesale adoption of terminology and implicit assumptions of white, "professional" critics. A view of essays by principal spokesmen for the new theoretical prospect will serve to clarify these judgments. The essays appear in the handbook of the new generation entitled *Afro-American Literature: The Reconstruction of Instruction* (1979).[32]

Edited by Dexter Fisher and Robert B. Stepto, *Afro-American Literature* "grew out of the lectures and course design workshops of the 1977 Modern Language Association/National Endowment for the Humanities Summer Seminar on Afro-American Literature" (p. 1). The volume sets forth basic tenets of a new paradigm. The guiding assumption—i.e., that a literature known as "Afro-American" exists in the world—is stated as follows by Stepto in his "Introduction": "[Afro-American] literature fills bookstore shelves and, increasingly, the stacks of libraries; symposia and seminars on the literature are regularly held; prominent contemporary black writers give scores of readings; and so the question of the literature's existence, at this juncture in literary studies, is not at issue" (1). The second, fundamental assumption—i.e., that literature consists in "written art" (3)—is implied by Stepto later in the same "Introduction" when he is describing the unit of *Afro-American Literature* devoted to "Afro-American folklore *and* Afro-American literature as well as Afro-American folklore *in* Afro-American literature" (3–4). According to the editor, folklore can be transformed into a "written art" that may, in turn, comprise "fiction" (4). Further, he suggests that the "folk" roots of a work like Frederick Douglass's *Narrative of the Life of Frederick Douglass* are to be distinguished from its "literary roots" (5). The condition signaled by "written" seems at first glance, therefore, a necessary one for "literary" and "literature" in Stepto's thinking.

There is, however, some indication in the "Introduction" that the new generation does not wish to confine its definition of the "literary" exclusively to what is "written." At the midpoint of his opening remarks, Stepto asserts that there are "discrete literary texts that are inherently interdisciplinary (e.g., blues) and often multigeneric (dialect voicings in all written art forms)" (3). If "blues" and "dialect voicings" constitute, respectively, a literary text and a genre, then it would appear to follow that *any distinctly Afro-American expressive form* (not merely *written* ones) can be encompassed by the "literary" domain. The boundaries of the new generation's theoretical inquiries, therefore, can apparently be expanded at will to include whatever seems distinctly expressive in Afro-America. Stepto suggests, for example, that "a methodology for an integrated study of *Afro-American folklore* and literature" (my italics, 4) should form part of the scholar-teacher's tools. And he goes on to propose that there are "various ways in which an instructor . . . can present a *collection of art forms* and still respond to the literary qualities of many of those forms in the course of the presentation" (my italics, 3). On one hand, then, the new prospect implies a rejection of modes of inquiry that are sociological in character or that seek to explore ranges of experience lying beyond the transactions of an exclusive sphere of written art: "central . . . to this volume as a whole" is a rejection of "extraliterary values, ideas, and pedagogical constructions that have plagued the teaching of . . . [Afro-American] literature" (2). On the other hand, the new prospect attempts to preserve a concern for the "forms of things unknown" (e.g., blues) by reading them under the aspect of a Procrustean definition of "literary." Similarly, it attempts to maintain certain manifestations of Afro-American ordinary discourse (e.g., dialect voicings) as legitimate areas of study by reading them as literary genre. Finally, the new prospect, as defined by Stepto, implies that the entire realm of the Afro-American arts can be subsumed by the "literary" since any collection of black art forms can be explicated in terms of its "literary qualities." Such qualities, under the terms of the new prospect, take on the character of sacrosanct, cultural universals (a point to which I shall return shortly).

Kuhn points out that a paradigmatic shift in a community's conception of the physical world results in "the whole conceptual web whose strands are space, time, matter, force and so on" being shifted and "laid down again on nature whole" (149). While the earlier Black Aesthetic was concerned to determine how the commodity of "blackness" shaped the Afro-American artistic domain, the emergent theoretical prospect attempts to discover how the qualities of a "literary" domain shape Afro-American life as a whole. There is, thus, a movement from the whole culture to the part signaled by the most recent generational shift in Afro-American literary criticism. For what the new group seeks to specify is a new "literary" conceptual scheme for apprehending Afro-American culture. This project constitutes its main theoretical goal. Two of *Afro-American Literature*'s most important essays—Stepto's "Teaching Afro-American Literature: Survey or Tradition: The Reconstruction of Instruction" and Henry Louis Gates, Jr.'s "Preface to Blackness: Text and Pretext"—are devoted to this goal.

Stepto's basic premise in "Teaching Afro-American Literature" is that the typical (i.e., normative) teacher of Afro-American literature is a harried, irresponsible pedagogue ignorant of the "inner" workings of the Afro-American literary domain. It follows from this proposition that pedagogy surrounding the literature must be reconstructed on a sound basis by someone familiar with the "myriad cultural metaphors," "coded structures," and "poetic rhetoric" of Afro-America (9). Stepto asserts that only a person who has learned *to read* the discrete literary texts of Afro-America in ways that ensure a proximity and "intimacy, with writers and texts outside the normal boundaries of nonliterary structures" (16) can achieve this required familiarity. According to the author, moreover, it is a specific form of "literacy"—of proficient reading—that leads to the reconstruction of instruction.

Understandably, given the author's earlier claims, this literacy is not based on a comprehension or study of "extraliterary" structures. Its epistemological foundation is, instead, the instructor's apprehension and comprehension of what Stepto calls the "Afro-American canonical story or pregeneric myth, the particular historicity of the Afro-American literary tradition, and the Afro-American landscape or *genius loci*" (18). This "pregeneric myth," according to Stepto, is "the quest for freedom *and* literacy" (18), and he further asserts that the myth is an "aesthetic and rhetorical principle" that can serve as the basis for constructing a proper course in Afro-American literature (17). The Afro-American "pregeneric myth" is, therefore, (at one and the same instant) somehow a prelinguistic reality, a quest, and a pedagogical discovery principle.

It is at this point in Stepto's specifications that what I earlier referred to as an "unfortunate burdening" of the universe of discourse surrounding Afro-American culture with jargon becomes apparent. For the author's formulations on a "pregeneric myth" reflect his metaphysical leanings far more clearly than they project a desirable methodological competence. They signal, in fact, what I called at the outset of this essay a "version of Aristotelian metaphysics." Stepto's pregeneric myth has the character of prime matter capable of assuming an unceasing variety of forms. Just as for Aristotle "the elements are the simplest physical things, and within them the distinction of matter and form can only be made by an abstraction of thought,"[33] so for Stepto the pregeneric myth is *informed matter* that serves as the core and essence of that which is "literary" in Afro-America. It is the substance out of which all black expression molds itself: "The quest for freedom and literacy is found in every major text . . ." (18). Further: "If an Afro-American literary tradition exists, it does so not because there is a sizeable chronology of authors and texts but because those authors and texts seek collectively their own literary forms—their own admixture of genre—bound historically and linguistically to a shared pregeneric myth" (19).

A simplifed statement of the conceptual scheme implied by Stepto's notion of cultural evolution would be: The various *structures* of a culture derive from the informed matter of myth. The principal difficulty with this notion is that the author fails to make clear the mode of being of a "myth" that is not only *pregeneric,* but also, it would seem, *prelinguistic.* "Nonliterary structures," Stepto tells us, evolve "almost exclusively from freedom myths devoid of linguistic properties" (18). Such structures, we are further told, "speak rarely to questions of freedom *and* literacy" (18). The question one must pose in light of such assertions is: Are "nonliterary structures" indeed devoid of linguistic properties? If so, then "literacy" and "freedom" can scarcely function as dependent variables in a single, generative myth. For under conditions of mutual inclusiveness (where the variables are, *ab initio,* functions of one another) the structures generated from the myth could not logically be devoid of that which is essential to literacy, i.e., *linguistic properties.* It is important to note, for example, that the "nonliterary" structure known as the *African Methodist Episcopal Church* preserves in its name, and particularly in the linguistic sign "African," a marker of the structure's cultural origin and orientation. And it is difficult to imagine the kind of cognition that would be required to summon to consciousness *cultural structures* devoid of all linguistic properties such as a name, a written history, or a controlling interest in the semantic field of a culture's language. But, perhaps, what Stepto actually meant to suggest by his statement was that "freedom myths" are devoid of linguistic properties. Under this interpretation of his statement, however, one would have to adopt a philosophically idealistic conception of myth that seems contrary to the larger enterprise of the reconstructionists. For Stepto insists that the "reconstruction" of Afro-American literary instruction is contingent upon the discoverability through "literacy" (a process of *linguistic* transaction) of the Afro-American pregeneric myth. And how could such a goal be achieved if myths existed only as *prelinguistic,* philosophical ideals? In sum, Stepto seems to have adopted a critical rhetoric that plays him false. Having assumed some intrinsic merit and inherent clarity in the notion "pregeneric myth," he fails to analytically delineate the mode of existence of such a myth or to clarify the manner in which it is capable of generating two *distinct kinds* of cultural structures.

One sign of the problematical status of this myth in Stepto's formulations is the apparent "agentlessness" of its operations. According to the author, the pregeneric myth is simply "set in motion" (20), and one can observe its "motion through both chronological and linguistic time" (19). Yet, the efficacy of motion suggested here seems to have no historically based community of agents or agencies for its origination or perpetuation. The myth and its operations, therefore, are finally reduced in Stepto's thinking to an aberrant version of Aristotle's "unmoved mover." For Aristotle specifies that the force which moves the "first heaven" has "no contingency; it is not subject even to minimal change (spatial motion in a circle), since that is what it originates."[34] Stepto, however, wants both to posit an "unmoved" substance as his pregeneric myth *and* to claim that this myth *moves* as "literary history." In fact, he designates the shape of its literary-historical movement as a circle—a "magic circle" or *temenos*—representing one kind of ideal harmony, or perfection of motion.

At this point in his description, Stepto (not surprisingly) feels compelled to illustrate his formulations with examples drawn from the Afro-American literary tradition. He first asserts that the phrase "the black belt" is one of Afro-America's metaphors for the *genius loci* (a term borrowed from Geoffrey Hartman signifying "spirit of place") that resides within the interior of the "magic circle" previously mentioned (20). Employing this metaphor, the late-nineteenth-century founder and president of Tuskegee Institute, Booker T. Washington, wrote:

> So far as I can learn the term was first used to designate a part of the country which was distinguished by the colour of the soil. The part of the country possessing this thick, dark soil was, of course, the part of the south where the slaves were most profitable, and consequently they were taken there in the largest numbers. Later, and especially since the war, the term seems to be used wholly in a political sense—that is, to designate the counties where the black people out number the white.[35]

Stepto feels that this description comprises an act of disingenuity on Washington's part. However, when he proceeds to demonstrate that Washington's statement is a "literary offense" (something akin to a sin of shallowness in the reading of metaphor) vis-à-vis the metaphor "the black belt," Stepto does not summon logical, rhetorical, or linguistic criteria. In condemning Washington for describing only geological and political dimensions of the black belt rather than historical and symbolic dimensions, Stepto summons "extraliterary" criteria, insisting that the turn-of-the-century black leader's "offense" was committed in order to insure his success in soliciting philanthropic funds for Tuskegee. The author of *Up From Slavery*, in Stepto's view, merely glossed the metaphor "the black belt" in order to keep his white, potential benefactors happy.

We, thus, find ourselves thrust into the historical dust and heat of turn-of-the-century white philanthropy in America. And what Stepto calls a "geographical metaphor" (i.e., "the black belt") becomes, in his own reading, simply a sign for one American region where such philanthropy had its greatest impact. Contrary to his earlier injunction, therefore, Stepto allows a "nonliterary structure" to become central to his own "reading of art" (20). He assumes, however, that he has achieved his interpretation of Washington solely on the basis of his own "literacy" in regard to the black leader's employment of metaphor. He further assumes that when he contrasts W. E. B. DuBois's employment of "the black belt" with Washington's usage that he is engaged in a purely "literary" act of "reading within tradition" (21). But if the "tradition" that he has in mind requires a comprehension of turn-of-the-century white philanthropy where Washington is concerned, then surely Stepto does his reader a disservice when he fails to reveal that DuBois's "rhetorical journey into the soul of a race" (21) in fact curtailed white philanthropy to Atlanta University, cost DuBois his teaching position at the same university, and led the author of *The Souls of Black Folk* to an even deeper engagement with the metaphor "the black belt."

In his attempt to maintain the exclusively "literary" affiliations of a pregeneric myth and its operations, Stepto introduces historical and sociological structures into his reading only where they will not seem to conflict dramatically with his claim that all necessary keys for literacy in the tradition generated by the pregeneric myth are linguistically situated within the texts of black authors themselves. Such reading is, at best, an exercise in the positing of cultural metaphors followed by attempts to fit such metaphors into a needlessly narrow framework of interpretation. Yet, Stepto asserts "it is reading of this sorth that our instructor's new pedagogy should both emulate and promote" (21).

Rather than offering additional examples of such reading, Stepto turns to a consideration of what one early-twentieth-century critic called the relationship between "tradition and the individual talent."[36] For Stepto, this relationship is described as the tension between "Genius and *genius loci*" and between *temenos* and *genius loci*. And the mediation between these facets of Afro-American culture constitutes what the author calls "modal improvisation." Although his borrowed terminology is almost hopelessly confusing here, what Stepto seems to suggest is that the Afro-American literature instructor must engage in "literate" communion with the inner dynamics of the region of Afro-America comprised by a pregeneric myth and its myriad forms and operations. The instructor's pedagogical "genius" consists in his ability to comprehend the "eternal landscape" (22) that is the pregeneric myth—i.e., the sacred domain of the "literary" in Afro-American culture.

An "eternal landscape" (without beginning or end and agentless in its creation and motions) is but another means of denoting for Stepto what he describes earlier in his essay as the "various dimensions of literacy achieved within the *deeper recesses* of the art form" (my italics, 13). At another point in "Teaching Afro-American Literature," the author speaks of an "*immersion in* the multiple images and landscapes of metaphor" (my italics, 15). This cumulative employment of images of a sacred interiority seems to suggest that Stepto believes there is an inner sanctum of pregeneric, mythic, literary "intimacy" resident in works of Afro-American art. Further, he seems to feel that entrance to this sanctum can be gained only by the initiated. One might posit, therefore, that what is presented by "Teaching Afro-American Literature" is a scheme of mystical literacy that finally comprises what might be called a *theology of literacy*. For the "conceptual web" laid upon Afro-America by Stepto's essay asserts the primacy and sacredness among cultural activities of the literary-critical and literary-theoretical enterprise. The argument of the essay is, in the end, a religious interpretation *manqué,* complete with an unmoved mover, a priestly class of "literate" initiates, and an eternal landscape of cultural metaphor that can be obtained by those who are free of literary "offense." And the "qualities" that derive from such a landscape (since they are coextensive with the generation of cultural structure) operate as "universals."

The articulation of such a literary-critical orthodoxy is scarcely a new departure in the history of literary criticism. In his "General Introduction" to *The English Poets* published in 1880, Matthew Arnold wrote: "More and more mankind will discover that we have to turn to poetry to interpret life for us, to console us, to sustain us. Without poetry, our science will appear incomplete; and most of what now passes for religion and philosophy will be replaced by poetry."[37] As a function of this conceptualization of the "higher uses" of poetry, Arnold confidently proclaimed: "In poetry, which is thought and art in one, it is the glory, the eternal honour, that charlatanism shall have no entrance; that this noble sphere be kept inviolate and inviolable" (3). Stepto's assumption that his "reconstructed" scheme for teaching Afro-American literature may "nuture literacy in the academy" (23) is certainly akin to Arnold's formulations on the exalted mission of poetry. And his zeal in preserving "inviolate" the sacred domain of the literary surely constitutes a modern, Arnoldian instance of a theology of literacy. As a function of this zeal, Stepto condemns with fierce self-righteousness any pedagogical con-

textualization of Afro-American literature that might lead a student to ascribe to, say, a Langston Hughes poem, a use-value, or meaning, in opposition to the kind of linguistic and rhetorical values made available by the
reconstruction of instruction.

The author of "Teaching Afro-American Literature" emerges as a person
incapable of acknowledging that the decision to investigate the material
bases of the society that provided enabling conditions for Hughes's metaphors is a sound literary-theoretical decision. Semantic and pragmatic considerations of metaphor suggest that the information communicated by metaphor is hardly localized in a given image on a given page (or, exclusively
within the confines of a "magical" literary circle). Rather, the communication
process is a function of myriad factors; e.g., a native speaker's ability to
recognize ungrammatical sentences, the vast store of encyclopedic knowledge constituting a speech community's common knowledge of objects and
concepts, relevant information supplied by the verbal context of a specific
metaphoric text, and, finally, the relevant knowledge brought to bear by an
"introjecting" listener or reader.[38] Conceived under these terms, metaphoric
communication may actually be more fittingly comprehended by an investigation of the material bases of society than by an initiate's passage "from
metaphor to metaphor and from image to image of the same metaphor in
order to locate the Afro-American *genius loci*" (21). Hughes is, perhaps, more
comprehensible, for example, within the framework of Afro-American verbal and musical *performance* than within the borrowed framework for the
description of *written* inscriptions of cultural metaphor adduced by Stepto.
Only a full investigation of Afro-American metaphor—an analysis based on
the best theoretical models available—will enable a student to decide.

The zeal that forced Stepto to adopt a narrow, "literary" conception of
metaphor should not be totally condemned. For it is correct (and fair)
to point out that a kind of sacred crusade did seem in order by the mid-
seventies to modify or "reconstruct" the instruction and study of Afro-
American literature that were not then based on sound theoretical foundations. While I do not think the type of mediocre instruction and misguided
criticism that Stepto describes were, in fact, as prevalent as he assumes, I do
feel that there were enough charlatans about in the mid-seventies to justify
renewed vigilance and effort. But though one comes away from "Teaching
Afro-American Literature" with a fine sense of these villains, one does not
depart the essay (or others in *Afro-American Literature*) with a sense that the
reconstructionists are either broadminded or well-informed in their preach-
ments. In fact, I think the instructor who seeks to model his course on

the formulations of Stepto might find himself as nonplused as the critic who attempts to pattern his investigative strategies on the model implicit in Gates's "Preface to Blackness: Text and Pretext."

Just as Stepto's work begins with the assumption that the pedagogy surrounding Afro-American literature rests on a mistake, so Gates's essay commences with the notion that the criticism of Afro-American literature (prior to 1975) rested upon a mistake. This mistake, according to Gates, consisted in the assumption by past critics that a "determining formal relation" exists between "literature" and "social institutions."

> The idea of a determining formal relation between literature and social institutions does not in itself explain the sense of urgency that has, at least since the publication in 1760 of *A Narrative of the Uncommon Sufferings and Surprising Deliverance of Briton Hammon, a Negro Man,* characterized nearly the whole of Afro-American writing. This idea has often encouraged a posture that belabors the social and documentary status of black art, and indeed the earliest discrete examples of written discourse by slave and ex-slave came under a scrutiny not primarily literary. (235, this volume)

For Gates, "social institutions" is an omnibus category equivalent to Stepto's "nonliterary structures." Such institutions include: the philosophical musings of the Enlightenment on the "African Mind," eighteenth-century debates concerning the African's place in the great chain of being, the politics of abolitionism, or (more recently) the economics, politics, and sociology of the Afro-American liberation struggle in the twentieth century. Gates contends that Afro-American literature has repeatedly been interpreted and evaluated according to criteria derived from such "institutions."

As a case in point, he surveys the critical response that marked the publication of Phillis Wheatley's *Poems on Various Subjects, Religious and Moral,* discovering that "almost immediately after its publication in London in 1773," the black Boston poet's collection became "the international antislavery movement's most salient argument for the African's innate mental equality" (236). Gates goes on to point out that "literally scores of public figures" provided prefatory signatures, polemical reviews, or "authenticating" remarks dedicated to proving that Wheatley's verse was (or was not, as the case may be) truly the product of an African imagination. Such responses were useless in the office of criticism, however, because "virtually no one," according to Gates, "discusses . . . [Wheatley's collection] as poetry" (236). Hence: "The documentary status of black art assumed priority over mere literary judgment; criticism rehearsed content to justify one notion of origins or another" (236).

Thomas Jefferson's condemnation (on "extra-literary" grounds) of Wheatley and of the black eighteenth-century epistler Ignatius Sancho set an influential model for the discussion of Afro-American literature that, in Gates's view, "exerted a prescriptive influence over the criticism of the writings of blacks for the next 150 years" (237). Jefferson's recourse to philosophical, political, religious, economic and other cultural systems for descriptive and evaluative terms in which to discuss black writing was, in short, a *mistake* that has been replicated through the decades by both white and Afro-American commentators. William Dean Howells, the writers of the Harlem Renaissance, and, most recently, according to Gates, spokesmen for the Black Aesthetic have repeated the critical offense of Jefferson. They have assumed that there is, in fact, a determining formal relation between literature and other cultural institutions and that various dimensions of these other institutions constitute areas of knowledge relevant to literary criticism. Gates says, "No," in thunder, to such assumptions. For as he reviews the "prefaces" affixed to various Afro-American texts through the decades, he finds no useful criteria for the practice of literary criticism. He discovers only introductory remarks that are "pretexts" for discussing African humanity, or for displaying "artifacts of the sable mind" (239), or for chronicling the prefacer's own "attitude toward being black in white America" (252).

Like Larry Neal,[39] Gates concludes that such "pretexts" and the lamentable critical situation that they imply are functions of the powerful influence of "race" as a variable in all spheres of American intellectual endeavor related to Afro-America. And like Neal, he states that racial considerations have been substituted for "class" as a category in the thinking of those who have attempted to criticize Afro-American literature, resulting in what he calls "race and superstructure" criticism: "blacks borrowed whole the Marxist notion of base and superstructure and made of it, if you will, race and superstructure" (245). Gates also believes that Afro-American creative writers have fallen prey to the mode of thought that marks "race and superstructure" criticism. For these writers have shaped their work on polemical, documentary lines designed to prove the equality of Afro-Americans or to argue a case for their humanity. And in the process, they have neglected the "literary" engagement that results in true art.

What, then, is the path that leads beyond the critical and creative failings of the past? According to Gates, it lies in a semiotic understanding of literature as a "system" of signs that stand in an "arbitrary" relationship to social reality (250–52). Having drawn a semiotic circle around literature, however, he moves rapidly to disclaim the notion that literature as a "system" is radically distinct from other domains of culture:

> It is not, of course, that literature is unrelated to culture, to other disciplines, or even to other arts; it is not that words and usage somehow exist in a vacuum or that the literary work of art occupies an ideal or reified, privileged status, that province of some elite cult of culture. It is just that the literary work of art is a system of signs that may be decoded with various methods, all of which assume the fundamental unity of form and content and all of which demand close reading. (251–52)

The epistemology on which this description rests is stated as follows:

> . . . perceptions of reality are in no sense absolute; reality is a function of our senses. Writers present models of reality, rather than a description of it, though obviously the two may be related variously. In fact, fiction often contributes to cognition by providing models that highlight the nature of things precisely by their failure to coincide with it. Such certainly is the case in science fiction. (253)

The semiotic notion of literature and culture implied by Gates seems to combine empiricism (reality as a "function of our senses") with an ontology of the sign that suggests that signs are somehow "natural" or "inherent" to human beings. For if "reality" is, indeed, a function of our senses, then observation and study of these physiological capacities should yield some comprehension of a subject's "reality." In truth, however, it is not these physiological processes in themselves that interest Gates, but rather the operation of such processes under the conditions of "models" of cognition, which, of course, is a very different thing. For if one begins not with the senses, but with cognition, then one is required to ask: How are "models" of cognition conceived, articulated, and transmitted in human cultures? Certainly, one of the obvious answers here is *not* that human beings are endowed at birth with a "system of signs," but rather that *models of cognition are conceived in, articulated through, and transmitted by language.* And like other systems of culture, language *is* a "social institution." Hence, if cognitive "models" of "fiction" differ from those of other spheres of human behavior, they do not do so because fiction is somehow discontinuous with social institutions. In fact, it is the attempt to understand the coextensiveness of language *as a social institution* and literature *as a system within it* that constitutes what is, perhaps, the defining process of literary-theoretical study in our day.

When, therefore, Gates proposes metaphysical and behavioral models that suggest that a literature, or even a single text (254), exists as a structured "world" ("a system of signs") that can be comprehended without reference to "social institutions," he seems misguided in his claims and only vaguely aware of recent developments in literary study, symbolic anthropology, linguistics, the psychology of perception, and other related areas of intellectual inquiry. He seems, in fact, to have adopted, without qualification, a theory of the literary sign (of the "word" in a literary text) that presupposes a privileged status for the creative writer: "The black writer is the point of consciousness of his language" (254). What this assertion means to Gates is that a writer is more capable than others in society of producing a "complex structure of meanings"—a linguistic structure that (presumably) corresponds more closely than those produced by non-writers—to the organizing principles by which a group's world view operates in consciousness (254).

One might be at a loss to understand how a writer can achieve this end unless he is fully aware of language *as a social institution* and of the relationship that language bears to other institutions that create, shape, maintain, and transmit a society's "organizing principles." Surely, Gates does not mean to suggest that the mind of the writer is an autonomous semantic domain where complex structures are conceived and maintained "non-linguistically." On the other hand, if such structures of meaning are, in fact, "complex" *because* they are linguistically maintained, then so, too, are similar structures that are conceived by nonwriters.

That is to say, Gates renders but small service to the office of theoretical distinction when he states that "a poem is above all atemporal and must cohere at a symbolic level, if it coheres at all" (248), or when he posits that "literature approaches its richest development when its 'presentational symbolism' (as opposed by Suzanne Langer to its 'literal discourse') cannot be reduced to the form of a literal proposition" (253). The reason such sober generalities contribute little to our understanding of literature, of course, is that Gates provides no just notion of the nature of "literal discourse," failing to admit both its social-institutional status and its fundamental existence as a symbolic system. On what basis, then, except a somewhat naive belief in the explanatory power of semiotics can he suggest a radical disjunction between literature and other modes of linguistic behavior in a culture? The critic who attempted to pattern his work on Gates's model would find himself confronted by a theory of language, literature, and culture that suggests that "literary" meanings are conceived in a nonsocial, non-institutional manner by the "point of consciousness" of a language and are maintained and transmitted in an agentless fashion within a closed circle of "intertextuality" (254). It does seem, therefore, that despite his disclaimer, Gates feels that "literature is unrelated to culture." For culture consists in the interplay of various human symbolic systems, an interplay that is essential to the production and comprehension of meaning. Gates's independent literary domain, which produces meanings from some mysteriously nonsocial, noninstitutional medium, bears no relationship to such a process.

One reason Gates fails to articulate an adequate theory of literary semantics in his essay, I think, is that he allots an inordinate amount of space to the castigation of his critical forebears. And his attacks are often restatements of shortcomings that his predecessors had recognized and discussed by the later seventies. Yet Gates provides elaborate detail in, for example, his analysis of the Black Aesthetic.

Among the many charges that he levels against Stephen Henderson, Addison Gayle, Jr., and the present author is the accusation that the spokesmen for a Black Aesthetic assumed they could "achieve an intimate knowledge of a literary text by recreating it from the inside: Critical thought must become the thought criticized" (253). Though Gates employs familiar terminology here,[40] what he seems to object to in the work of Black Aesthetic spokesmen is their treatment of the text as subject. He levels the charge, in short, that these spokesmen postulated a tautological, literary-critical circle, assuming that the thought of an Afro-American literary text was "black thought" and, hence, could be "re-thought" only by a black critic. And while there is some merit in this charge (as Henderson's and Neal's previously mentioned reconsiderations of their initial critical postures make clear), it is scarcely true, as Gates argues, that Black Aestheticians did nothing in their work but reiterate presuppositions about "black thought" and then interpret Afro-American writing in accord with the entailments of such presuppositions. For the insular vision that would have resulted from this strategy would not have enabled Black Aestheticians to discuss and interpret Afro-American verbal behavior in the holistic ways conceived by Henderson, Neal, Gayle, and the present author. Spokesmen for the Black Aesthetic seldom conceived of the "text" as a *closed* enterprise. Instead, they normally thought (at the higher level of their arguments) of the text as an occasion for transactions between writer and reader, between performer and audience. And far from insisting that the written text is, in itself, a repository of inviolable "black thought" to be preserved at all costs, they called for the "destruction of the text"—for an open-endedness of performance and response that created conditions of possibility for the emergence of both new meanings and new strategies of verbal transaction.[41] True, such spokesmen never saw the text as discontinuous with its social origins, but then they also never conceived of these "origins" as somehow divorced from the semantics of the metaphorical instances represented in black "artistic" texts. In short, they never thought of culture under the terms of a semiotic analysis that restricted its formulations to the literary domain alone.

On the other hand, they were certainly never so innocent as Gates would have one believe. Their semantics were never so crude as to permit them to accept the notion that the words of a literary text stand in a one-to-one relationship to the "things" of Afro-American culture. In fact, they were so intent on discovering the full dimensions of the artistic "word" that they attempted to situate its various manifestations within a continuum of verbal behavior in Afro-American culture as a whole. Further, they sought to understand this continuum within the complex webs of interacting cultural systems that ultimately gave meaning to such words.

Rather than a referential semantics, therefore, what was implicit in the higher-order arguments of Black Aesthetic spokesmen (as I have attempted to demonstrate in my earlier discussions) was an anthropological approach to Afro-American art. I think, in fact, that Gates recognizes this and is, finally, unwilling to accept the kind of critical responsibilities signaled by such an enterprise. For though he spends a great deal of energy arguing with Henderson's and my own assumptions on Afro-American culture, he refuses (not without some disingenuity) to acknowledge our *actual readings of Afro-American texts*. The reason for this refusal, I think, is that our readings bring together, in what one hopes are useful ways, our knowledge of various social institutions, or cultural systems (including language), in our attempts to reveal the *sui generis* character of Afro-American artistic texts. Gates's formulations, however, imply an ideal critic whose readings would summon knowledge *only* from the literary system of Afro-America. The semantics endorsed by his ideal critic would *not* be those of a culture. They would constitute, instead, the specially consecrated meanings of an intertextual world of "written art."

The emphasis on "close reading" (252) in Gates's formulations, therefore, might justifiably be designated a call for a "closed" reading of selected Afro-American written texts. In fact, the author implies that the very defining criteria of a culture may be extrapolated from selected written, literary texts rather than vice-versa (250). For example, if any Afro-American literary artist has entertained the notion of "frontier," then Gates feels the notion must have defining force in Afro-American culture (251). Only by ignoring the mass level of Afro-America and holding up the "message" of literary works of art by Ralph Ellison and Ishmael Reed as "normative" utterances in Afro-American culture can Gates support such a claim. His claim is, thus, a function of the privileged status he grants to the writer and the elitist status that he bestows on "literary uses of language" (250).

But if it is true that scholarly investigations of an Afro-American expressive tradition must begin at a mass level—at the level of the "forms of things unknown"—then Gates's claim that the notion of "frontier" has defining force in Afro-America would have to be supported by the testimony of, say, the blues, work songs, or early folktales of Afro-America. And I think that an emphasis on frontier, in the sense intended by Frederick Jackson Turner, is scarcely to be discerned in these cultural manifests.

Gates, however, is interested only in what *writers* (as "points of consciousness") have to say, and he seems to feel no obligation to turn to Afro-American folklore. In fact, when he comments on Henderson's formulations on Afro-American folk language, or vernacular, he reveals not only a lack of interest in folk processes, but also some profound misconceptions about the nature of Afro-American language.

Henderson attempts to establish a verbal and musical continuum of expressive behavior in Afro-American culture as an analytical category. In this process, he encounters certain verbal items that seem to claim (through usage) expansive territory in the Afro-American "sign field." Gates mistakenly assumes that Henderson is setting such items (e.g., "jook," "jelly") apart from a canon of "ordinary" usage as "poetic discourse." This assumption is a function of Gates's critical methodology, which is predicated on a distinction between ordinary and poetic discourse. And the assumption compels him to cast aspersions on the originality of Henderson's work by asserting that "practical critics" since the 1920s (249) have been engaged in actions similar to those of the Black Aesthetic spokesman.

The fault here is that Gates fails to recognize that Henderson is *not* seeking to isolate a lexicon of Afro-American "poetic" usages, nor to demonstrate how such usages "superimpose" a "grammar" (Gates's notion) on "nonliterary discourse" (249). Henderson is concerned, instead, to demonstrate that Afro-American ordinary discourse is, in fact, continuous with Afro-American artistic discourse and that an investigation of the black oral tradition would finally concern itself not simply with a lexicon, but also with a "grammar" adequate to describe the syntax and phonology of *all* Afro-American speech.

Gates is incapable of understanding this notion, however, because he believes that the artistic domain is unrelated to ordinary, "social" modes of behavior. Hence, he is enamored of the written, literary work, suggesting that a mere dictionary of black "poetic" words and their "specific signification" would lead to an understanding of how "Black English" departs from "general usage" (249). This view of language is coextensive with his views of literature and culture. For it concentrates solely on words as "artistic" words and ignores the complexities of the syntax and phonology that give resonance to such words. "A literary text," Gates writes, "is a linguistic event; its explication must be an activity of close textual analysis" (254).

It is not, however, the "text" that constitutes an "event" (if by this Gates means a process of linguistic transaction). It is rather the reading or performance by human beings of a kind of score, or graphemic record, if you will, that constitutes *the event* and, in the process, produces (or reproduces) the meaningful text. And the observer or critic who wishes to "analyze" such a text must have a knowledge of far more than the mere words of the performers. He should, it seems to me, have some theoretically adequate notions of the entire array of cultural forces which shape the performers' or readers' cognition and allow them to actualize the text as an instance of a distinctive cultural semantics. Gates has no such notions to bring to bear. And his later essay in *Afro-American Literature* entitled "Dis and Dat: Dialect and the Descent" reveals some confusion on issues of both language and culture.

Briefly, we are told by Gates that "culture is imprisoned in a linguistic contour that no longer matches . . . the changing landscape of fact" (92). This appears a mild form of Whorfianism[42] until one asks: How do "facts" achieve a nonlinguistic existence? The answer is that *they do not achieve such an existence.* Placed in proper perspective, Gates's statement simply means that different communities of speakers of the same language have differential access to "modern" ideas. But in his efforts to preserve language apart from the other social institutions, Gates ignores agents or speakers until he wishes to add further mystery and distinctiveness to his own conceptions of language. When he finally comes to reflect on speakers, he invokes the notion of "privacy," insisting that lying and remaining silent both offer instances of the employment of a "personal" thesaurus by a speaker (93). Now, this conception stands in contrast to Gates's earlier Whorfianism.[43] And, to my knowledge, it possesses little support in the literature of linguistics or semiotics.

The notions that Gates advocates presuppose uniquely "personal" meanings for lexical items that form part of a culture's "public discourse." But what is unique, or personal, about these items is surely their difference from public discourse; their very identity, that is to say, is a function of public discourse. Further, the ability to use such lexical items to lie, or to misinform, scarcely constitutes an argument for privacy. Umberto Eco, for example, writes:

> A sign is everything which can be taken as significantly substituting for something else. This something else does not necessarily have to exist or to actually be somewhere at the moment in which a sign stands for it. Thus *semiotics is in principle the discipline studying everything which can be used in order to lie.* If something cannot be used to tell a lie, conversely it cannot be used to tell the truth: it cannot in fact be used "to tell" at all.[44]

The *word,* in short, becomes a sign by being able *to tell,* and unless Gates means to propose the idealistic notion that each human mind generates its own system of meaningful, nonpublic signs, it is difficult to understand how he conceives of sign usage in lying as an instance of "private" usage of language. His goal in "Dis and Dat" (an unfortunate choice of lexical items for his title since the phonological feature *d* for *th* is not unique to Black English Vernacular, but rather can be found in other nonstandard language varieties) is to define Afro-American "dialect" as a kind of "private," subconscious code signifying a "hermetic closed world" (94). The problem with this very suggestive notion, however, is that Gates not only seems to misunderstand the issue of privacy in language and philosophy, but also seems to fail to comprehend the nature of Black English Vernacular as a natural language.

He bases his understanding of this language on a nineteenth-century magazine article by a writer named James A. Harrison, who asserted that "the poetic and multiform messages which nature sends him [the Afro-American] through his auditory nerve" are reproduced, in words, by the Afro-American (95). Gates takes Harrison's claims seriously, assuming that there is a fundamental physiological difference between the linguistic behavior of Afro-Americans and other human beings: "One did not believe one's eyes, were one black; one believed [presumably on the basis of the Afro-American's direct auditory contact with nature] . . . one's ears" (109). On the basis of such problematical linguistic and cultural assumptions as the foregoing, Gates proposes that Black English Vernacular was essentially musical, poetical, spoken discourse generated by means other than those employed to generate standard English and maintained by Afro-Americans as a code of symbolic inversion.

There are reasons for studying the process of symbolic, linguistic inversion in Afro-American culture, and, indeed, for studying the relationship between the tonal characteristics of African languages (which is what both Harrison and Gates have in mind when they say "musical") in relationship to Afro-American speech. Such study, however, should not be grounded on the assertions of Wole Soyinka, Derek Walcott, or James A. Harrison (Gates's sources). It should be a matter of careful, holistic cultural analysis that summons as evidence a large, historical body of informed comment and scholarship on Black English Vernacular. A beginning has been made in this direction by Henderson in his previously-mentioned essay "The Question of Form and Judgment," which commences with the assumption that a discussion of Afro-American poetry (whether written in "dialect" or in standard English) must be based on sound historical notions of Black English Vernacular resulting from detailed research.[45]

Neither Gates nor Stepto, who are the principal spokesmen for the new theoretical prospect in *Afro-American Literature,* has undertaken the detailed research in various domains of Afro-American culture that leads to adequate theoretical formulations. Stepto's stipulations on the ontology of a pregeneric myth from which all Afro-American cultural "structures" originate are just as problematical as Gates's notions of a generative, artistic "point of consciousness" whose "literary uses of language" are independent of "social institutions." The narrowness of Stepto's conception of the "literary" forces him to adopt "nonliterary" criteria in his reading of *Up From Slavery.* And the instability of Gates's views of language and culture forces him to relinquish his advocacy for a synchronic, close reading of literary utterances when he comes to discuss Afro-American dialect poetry. Social institutions, and far more than "literary" criteria, are implied when he asserts:

> When using a word we wake into resonance, as it were, its entire previous history. A text is embedded in specific historical time; it has what linguists call a diachronic structure. To read fully is to restore all that one can of the immediacies of value and intent in which speech actually occurs. (114)

Here, contextualization, rethinking the "intent" of the speaker, and "institutional" considerations are all advocated in a way that hardly seems opposed to the critical strategies of the Black Aesthetic.

To concentrate exclusively on the shortcomings and contradictions of Stepto and Gates, however, is to minimize their achievements. For both writers have suggested, in stimulating ways, that Afro-American literature can be incorporated into a contemporary universe of literary-theoretical discourse. True, the terms on which they propose incorporation amount in one instance to a theology of literacy and, in another, to a mysterious semiotics of literary consciousness. Nonetheless, the very act of proposing that a sound, theoretical orientation toward an Afro-American literary tradition is necessary constitutes a logical second step after the paradigmatic establishment of that tradition by the Black Aesthetic.

Furthermore, Stepto and Gates are both better critics than theoreticians. Hence, they provide interpretations of texts that are, at times, quite striking. (Gates's reflections on structuralism and his structuralist reading of the *Narrative of the Life of Frederick Douglass* are quite provocative.) In addition, neither is so imprisoned by his theoretical claims that he refuses to acknowledge the claims of radically competing theories. For example, the essay by Sherley Anne Williams entitled "The Blues Roots of Contemporary Afro-American Poetry" (72–87) that appears in *Afro-American Literature* is based on the work of Henderson and stands in direct contrast in its methodology to the stipulations on written, non-institutional, literary art adduced by Stepto and Gates. And although Robert Hemenway, in his fine essay on Zora Neale Hurston's relationship to Afro-American folk processes (122–52), makes a gallant attempt to join the camp of Stepto and Gates, his work finally suggests the type of linguistic, expressive continuum implied by Henderson rather than the segmented model of Gates. Finally, Robert O'Meally's brilliant essay on Frederick Douglass's *Narrative* (192–211) is antithetical at every turn to Stepto's notion that critical "literacy" is a function of the reader's understanding of written "metaphor," or inscribed instances of "poetic rhetoric *in isolatio*" (9). For it is O'Meally's agile contextualizing of Douglass's work within the continuum of Afro-American verbal behavior that enables him to provide a reading of the work that suggests "intertextual" possibilities that are far more engaging than those suggested by Stepto's own reading of the *Narrative* (178–91).

In his editorial capacity, therefore, Stepto has rendered a service to the scholarly community by refusing to allow his theory of the "literary" to foreclose the inclusion of essays that contradict, or sharply qualify, his own explicit claims. Unfortunately, he and his coeditor did not work as effectively in their choice of course designs—the models of "reconstructed" instruction toward which the whole of *Afro-American Literature* is directed (if we are to believe the volume's title). Briefly, the section entitled "Afro-American Literature Course Designs" reflects all of the theoretical confusions that have been surveyed heretofore. There are models for courses based on weak distinctions between "literary" and "socio-historical" principles (237); the assumption that literature is an "act of language" (234); the notion that the "oral tradition is . . . a language with a grammar, a syntax, and standards of eloquence of its own" (237); the idea that folk forms are "literary" genres (246); and, finally, the assumption that "interdisciplinary" status can be achieved merely by bringing together different forms of art rather than by summoning methods and models from an array of intellectual disciplines (250–55). The concluding course designs, thus, capture the novelty and promise, as well as the shortcomings, of the new theoretical prospect. The types of distinctions, concerns, and endeavors they suggest are, indeed, significant for the future study of Afro-American literature and verbal art. What they lack—i.e., sound theories of ordinary and literary discourse, an adequate theory of semantics, and a comprehensive theory of reading—will, one hopes, be provided in time by scholars of Afro-American literature who are as persuaded as the reconstructionists that the Afro-American literary tradition can, indeed, withstand sharp critical scrutiny and can survive (as a subject of study) the limitations of early attempts at its literary-theoretical comprehension.

VIII

In *Ideology and Utopia,* Karl Mannheim writes:

To-day we have arrived at the point where we can see clearly that there are differences in modes of thought, not only in different historical periods but also in different cultures. Slowly it dawns upon us that not only does the content of thought change but also its categorical structure. Only very recently has it become possible to investigate the hypothesis that, in the past as well as the present, the dominant modes of thought are supplanted by new categories when the social basis of the group of which these thought-forms are characteristic disintegrates or is transformed under the impact of social change.[46]

The generational shifts discussed in the preceding pages attest the accuracy of Mannheim's observation. The notion of "generational shift," as I have defined it, begins with the assumption that changes in the "categorical structure" of thought are coextensive with social change. The literary-theoretical goal of an analysis deriving from the concept of generational shifts is a "systematic and total formulation" of problems of Afro-American literary study. For only by investigating the guiding assumptions (the "categories" of thought, as it were) of recent Afro-American literary criticism can one gain a sense of the virtues and limitations of what have stood during the past four decades as opposing generational paradigms. What emerges from such an investigation is, first, a realization of the socially- and generationally-conditioned selectivity, or partiality, of such paradigms. They can be as meetly defined by their exclusions as by their manifest content. The quasi-political rhetoric of the Black Aesthetic seems to compete (at its weakest points) with the quasi-religious and semiotic jargon of the reconstructionists for a kind of flawed critical ascendancy.

Yet what also emerges from an investigation of generational shifts in re-cent Afro-American literary criticism is the sense that this criticism has progressed during the past forty years to a point where some "systematic" formulation of theoretical problems is possible. The extremism and short-sightedness of recent generations have been counterbalanced, that is to say, by their serious dedication to the analysis of an object that did not even exist in the world prior to the mid-sixties. The perceptual reorientations of recent generations have served as enabling conditions for a "mode of thought" that takes the theoretical investigation of a unique tradition of *Afro-American literature* as a normative enterprise.

Given the foregoing discussion, it is perhaps clear that my own preference where such theoretical investigation is concerned is the kind of holistic, cultural-anthropological approach that is implicit in the work of Henderson and other spokesmen for the Black Aesthetic. This does not mean, however, that I seek to minimize the importance of the necessary and forceful call that the reconstructionists have issued for serious literary-theoretical endeavors on the part of Afro-Americanists. Still, I am persuaded that at this juncture in the progress of critical generations the theoretical prospect that I call the "an-thropology of art" is the most realistic and fruitful approach to the future study of Afro-American literature and culture.[47] The guiding assumption of the anthropology of art is coextensive with basic tenets of the Black Aesthetic insofar as both prospects assert that works of Afro-American literature and verbal art can not be adequately understood unless they are contextualized within the interdependent systems of Afro-American culture. But the anthro-pology of art *departs from both the Black Aesthetic and the reconstructionist prospects in its assumption that art can not be studied without serious attention to the methods and models of many disciplines.* The contextualization of a work of literary or verbal art, from the perspective of the anthropology of art, is an "interdisciplinary" enterprise in the most contemporary sense of that word. Rather than ignoring (or denigrating) the research and insights of scholars in the nature, social, and behavioral sciences, the anthropology of art views such efforts as positive, rational attempts to comprehend the full dimensions of human behavior. And such efforts serve the literary-theoretical investigator as guides and contributions to an understanding of the symbolic dimensions of human behavior that comprise Afro-American literature and verbal art.

In his essay "Ideology as a Cultural System," Clifford Geertz writes: "The sociology of knowledge ought to be called the sociology of meaning, for what is socially determined is not the nature of conception but the vehicles of conception."[48] I think the anthropology of art stands today not only as a "vehicle of conception" rich in theoretical possibilities, but also as a "categorical structure" that may signal a next generational shift in the criticism of Afro-American literature.

Notes

1 Lewis S. Feuer, *Ideology and Ideologists* (Oxford, 1975), 70. Professor Chester Fontenot was kind enough to remind me that T. S. Eliot's "Tradition and the Individual Talent" and Harold Bloom's *The Anxiety of Influence* also offer approaches to questions of the relationships between old and new generations of intellectuals or writers.

2 Thomas S. Kuhn, *The Structure of Scientific Revolutions* (Chicago, 1970).

3 Richard Wright, "The Literature of the Negro in the United States," in *White Man, Listen!* (Garden City, NY, 1964), 69–105. All citations from Wright's essay refer to this edition and are hereafter marked by page numbers in parentheses.

4 Brown, Davis, and Lee, eds., *The Negro Caravan* (New York, 1941; Arno repr. 1969), 7. All citations from the work refer to this edition and are hereafter marked by page numbers in parentheses.

5 In *The American Negro Writer And His Roots, Selected Papers From The First Conference of Negro Writers, March, 1959* (New York, 1960), 39–40.

6 For historical details on the events of this period, the reader may wish to consult John Hope Franklin, "A Brief History," in *The Black American Reference Book*, ed. Mabel M. Smythe (Englewood Cliffs, NJ, 1976), 1–89.

7 The phrase was originally uttered as part of a call-and-response chant between Carmichael and his audience during the course of a several-day protest march in Mississippi.

8 From Stokely Carmichael and Charles V. Hamilton, *Black Power: The Politics of Liberation in America* (New York, 1967) 43–44.

9 In this volume, 165–71. All citations are hereafter marked by page numbers in parentheses.

10 For an account of this enterprise, the reader may consult Theodore R. Hudson, *From LeRoi Jones to Amiri Baraka: The Literary Works* (Durham, N.C., 1973), 20–25.

11 In this volume, 184–98.

12 *Understanding the New Black Poetry: Black Speech and Black Music as Poetic References* (New York, 1973), 1–69. All citations refer to this edition and are hereafter marked by page numbers in parentheses.

13 Kuhn, *Structure* (Chicago, 1970), 175. All citations refer to this edition and are hereafter marked by page numbers in parentheses.

14   In "The Artworld," in *Philosophy Looks at the Arts,* ed. Joseph Margolis (Philadelphia, 1978), 132–45, Arthur Danto writes, "terrain is constituted artistic in virtue of artistic theories, so that one use of theories, in addition to helping us discriminate art from the rest, consists in making art possible." The *theoretical* constraints of the integrationist paradigm excluded "Negro" expressive works from the American, literary artworld.

15   Albert Hofstadter, "On the Grounds of Aesthetic Judgment," in *Contemporary Aesthetics,* ed. Matthew Lipman (Boston, 1973), 473–74. In both the concept "artworld" and "reference public," I have interpreted the Black Aesthetic as an institutional theory of art. For a recent critique of such theories, the reader may consult Marx W. Wartofsky, "Art, Artworlds, and Ideology," *Journal of Aesthetics and Art Criticism,* 38 (1980), 239–47. In contrast to the "institutional" dimensions of the Black Aesthetic are its idealistic assumptions.

16   For reflections of field theory and on the work of Trier, see John Lyons, *Semantics,* I (Cambridge, 1977), 250–61.

17   I have discussed the romantic idealism of the Black Aesthetic in "The Black Spokesman as Critic: Reflections on the Black Aesthetic," the fifth chapter of my book entitled *The Journey Back: Issues in Black Literature and Criticism* (Chicago, 1980), 132–43.

18   Stephen Henderson, "Saturation: Progress Report on a Theory of Black Poetry," *Black World,* 24 (1975), 14.

19   The words on the creation of system are, of course, those of William Blake's Los, drawn from *Jerusalem.* Los, like the Black Aestheticians, also refused at points to "reason" or "compare," feeling that the imperative "business" was "to create."

20   Henderson, "Saturation," p. 9.

21   Henderson, "The Question of Form," in *A Dark and Sudden Beauty: Two Essays in Black American Poetry by George Kent and Stephen Henderson,* ed. Houston A. Baker, Jr. (Philadelphia, 1977), 24.

22   Henderson, "Question of Form," 32.

23   I have in mind Robert E. Hemenway, author of the superb scholarly effort *Zora Neale Hurston: A Literary Biography* (Urbana, 1977) and Lawrence W. Levine, author of the important book *Black Culture and Black Consciousness: Afro-American Folk Thought From Slavery to Freedom* (New York, 1977).

24   "Black Cultural Nationalism," in *The Black Aesthetic,* 33.

25   Neal, "The Black Contribution to American Letters: Part II, The Writer as Activist—1960 and After," in *The Black American Reference Book,* ed. Mable M. Smythe, (Englewood Cliffs, N.J., 1976), 781–82. All citations refer to this edition and are hereafter marked by page numbers in parentheses.

26   I have in mind the conferences of black writers sponsored by the Howard University Institute for the Arts and the Humanities. Also important, I think, were the symposia held at the University of Pennsylvania in 1975 and 1977. Proceedings of these national gatherings can be found in *The Image of Black Folk in American Literature* (Washington, D.C., 1976) and in *Reading Black: Essays in the Criticism of African, Caribbean, and Afro-American Literature* (Ithaca, N.Y., 1976).

27   The symposium was entitled "The Function of Black American Poetry, 1760–1977," and it was sponsored by the Afro-American Studies Program at the University of Pennsylvania, March 24–26, 1977. Selected proceedings of this symposium appeared in George Kent and Stephen Henderson, *A Dark and Sudden Beauty: Two Essays in Black American Poetry* (Philadelphia, 1977).

28 Feuer, *Ideology and Ideologists*, 57.

29 I have discussed this phenomenon at length in *The Journey Back*, 126–31.

30 It is difficult to date the first, contemporary usage of this term. Ben J. Wattenberg and Richard Scammon's article entitled "Black Progress and Liberal Rhetoric" (*Commentary*, April 1973, 35–44), which proclaimed that 52 percent of Black Americans could be defined as "middle class," certainly gave life to ongoing attempts to define what E. Franklin Frazier designated the "Black Bourgeoisie" in his seminal study *Black Bourgeoisie* (Glencoe, Ill., 1957). The special issue of *Ebony* magazine entitled "The Black Middle Class" (August 1973) seems to have been prompted as much by the necessity to answer Wattenberg and Scammon as by a desire to "update" Frazier at a time when (between 1960 and 1970) the number of blacks employed in professional and technical operations had increased by 131 percent and the number of blacks in the clerical force had grown by 121 percent. Some of the major investigative issues that are signalled by the employment of the term "new black middle class" are addressed by William Julius Wilson in his study *The Declining Significance of Race: Blacks and Changing American Institutions* (Chicago, 1978). In 1979 and 1980, the Afro-American Studies Program of the University of Pennsylvania took up the issues raised by Wilson and by the concept of a "new black middle class" in its annual spring symposia. The proceedings of those symposia can be found in: *The Declining Significance of Race?: A Dialogue Among Black and White Social Scientists*, ed. Joseph R. Washington, Jr. (Philadelphia, 1979) and *Dilemmas of the New Black Middle Class*, ed. Joseph R. Washington, Jr., in manuscript. Essentially, the term "new black middle class" seems to denote a stratum of Afro-American professionals whose education, occupations, and income place them on a level near that of their similarly-employed white counterparts.

31 Quoted from William Julius Wilson, "The Declining Significance of Race: Myth or Reality," in *The Declining Significance of Race?* ed. Joseph R. Washington, Jr., 15.

32 Dexter Fisher and Robert B. Stepto, eds., *Afro-American Literature: The Reconstruction of Instruction* (New York, 1979). All citations refer to this edition and are hereafter marked by page numbers in parentheses.

33 Sir David Ross, *Aristotle* (London, 1923), 73–74. "Prime" matter is unlike "secondary matter" since the latter can not only "exist apart" (e.g., "tissues" may or may not be combined into organs) but can also be severed in reality (i.e., organs may be broken up into their component tissues). It is the inseparability of "form" and "matter" where Stepto is concerned (his "myth" is both structured and structuring) that gives his pregeneric myth the character of "prime" or "informed" matter (See Ross, 71).

34 *Metaphysics*, in *Aristotle's Metaphysics*, ed. John Warrington (London, 1956), 346. When Aristotle discusses "The Prime Mover" in one of the books of the *Metaphysics*, he sets forth what according to Sir David Ross is his only "systemic essay in theology" (Warrington, 331). Stepto, in adducing the agentless operation of his pregeneric myth, is on similar theological ground, attempting to find some thing that is "eternal, substance, and actuality" (Warrington, 345) to move the great sphere of Afro-American literary lights.

35 Quoted from *Afro-American Literature*, 20–21.

36 T. S. Eliot, "Tradition and the Individual Talent," in *Selected Essays* (New York, 1950), 3–11. According to Eliot, the poet can not know what valuable poetic "work" is to be done "unless he lives in what is not merely the present, but the present moment of the past, unless he is conscious, not of what is dead, but of what is already living" (11).

37 Matthew Arnold, "The Study of Poetry," in *The Works of Matthew Arnold*, IV (New York,

1970), 2. All citations refer to this edition and are hereafter marked by page numbers in parentheses.

38 These "factors" are treated in detail by Samuel R. Levin in *The Semantics of Metaphor* (Baltimore, 1977) and by Robert Rogers in *Metaphor: A Psychoanalytic View* (Berkeley, 1978). Additional theoretical discussion of metaphor can be found in the stimulating issue of *Critical Inquiry*, 5 (Autumn 1978) devoted to the subject.

39 I refer to Neal's "The Black Contribution to American Letters," which I discussed in an earlier section of this essay.

40 Gerard Genette defines the text as "subject" in *Figures* (Paris, 1966). Georges Poulet and Paul Ricoeur have also entered reflections on the process whereby "critical thought *becomes* the thought criticized." The quotation here is from Maria Corti's *An Introduction to Literary Semiotics* (Bloomington, 1978), 43.

41 I have discussed the concept of "the destruction of the text" in *The Journey Back*, 127–28. In his essay "And Shine Swam On," which serves as the "Afterword" for the anthology *Black Fire*, eds. Larry Neal and LeRoi Jones (New York, 1968), Neal says that true Afro-American poetry lies in verbal and musical performance, not in *written* texts: "The text could be destroyed and no one would be hurt in the least by it" (653).

42 By "Whorfianism" I mean the scholarly position assumed by Benjamin Lee Whorf. Whorf, in his studies of the Hopi Indians, emphasized the interpenetration of language and reality; the worldview of the Hopi, according to Whorf, is coded into their language. Hence, language and worldview are coextensive (mild Whorfianism) or coterminous (strong Whorfianism), and this makes for a kind of linguistic determinism in human affairs. For a more detailed view of Whorf's thought, consult *Language, Thought and Reality,* ed. John B. Carroll, a collection of Whorf's essays published by the MIT Press in 1956.

43 Instead of language determining worldview, the individual worldview (under the aspect of "privacy") determines, or fashions, its own peculiar language.

44 Umberto Eco, *A Theory of Semiotics* (Bloomington, Ind., 1976), 6–7.

45 This is not, however, an injunction to regard Henderson as an expert on Black English Vernacular as a subject of study *in itself*. For such expert testimony one must turn to the work of Geneva Smitherman, William Labov, and others. A good beginning, of course, is Lorenzo Turner's pioneering study *Africanisms in the Gullah Dialect.*

46 *Ideology and Utopia: An Introduction to the Sociology of Knowledge* (New York, 1936), 82–83. My reading in "ideology" and the "sociology of knowledge" prompted this essay on generational shifts. It seemed appropriate to situate the discussion within its proper ambit as a means of concluding.

47 In *The Journey Back: Issues in Black Literature and Criticism,* I discuss the assumptions and methodoloyg of this approach to literary study.

48 In *The Interpretation of Cultures: Selected Essays by Clifford Geertz* (New York, 1973), 212.

W. Lawrence Hogue

Literary Production: A Silence in Afro-American Critical Practice

(1986)

Recent advances in modern linguistics, along with developments in semiotics and Michel Foucault's concept of discursive formations, have eroded many of the assumptions and presuppositions traditionally associated with literature and criticism. This erosion has proven fundamental. Literary modes and categories inherited from the past no longer accommodate the concerns and questions posed by a new generation of literary scholars and intellectuals. The traditional concept of realism has been proven inadequate. The proposition that the writer is the "creator" of something "original" has come under serious attack. The unquestioned assumption of the text's literariness—that is, that the text possesses certain qualities that place it above the matrices of historical conditions—has been undermined profoundly. Definitions of artistic beauty, greatness in literary texts, and literary worth and value have been deemed subjective and ideological. The conjecture that the writer writes to tell the "truth" has been denounced vehemently. Last, the once acceptable assumptions that critical practice is an innocent activity and that the literary text is inextricably owned by and exclusively associated with the discipline of "literature" have been quelled almost completely.

Developments in semiotics and Foucault's concept of discursive formations produce the theoretical space that allows the literary critic to shift criticism's concerns and focus from a juridical to a theoretical status. In traditional or normative critical practices, the text is subordinated to what Pierre Macherey calls an "external principle of legality," an "aesthetic legality [that] has a juridical rather than a theoretical status; . . . its rules merely re-

This essay first appeared in W. Lawrence Hogue, *Discourse and the Other: The Production of the Afro-American Text* (Durham, N.C., 1986).

strain the writer's activity. Because it is powerless to examine the work on its own terms . . . , [normative] criticism resorts to a corroding resentment."[1] In its theoretical status, critical practice is a certain "form of knowledge" which has a particular condition for its existence.

Further, these developments allow the formation of critical practices that shift criticism's focus from the world of creation, the scene of charismatic authorship, to a specific productive process, a set of operations that transform a given language into something new. The literary text becomes not a tangible object that can be held in hand, but a textual system that transposes one or more systems of sign into another. This textual system is composed of a dispersion of its statements and its gaps and silences. The fact that the text permits and excludes certain statements exposes its exclusionary judgments and shows how it functions as a cultural object with social impact that can be calculated politically.

These advancements and developments have produced the critical and theoretical options for Afro-American and other minority texts, and for self-conscious and avant-garde texts—texts whose formations are different from or exist outside established definitions of the literary experience—to be assessed and explained. They give this new generation of literary critics and scholars the theoretical option to ask new questions of the literary text, to examine its mode of production. They also give the critical option to reexamine and reassess those American texts that have been deemed "great" by institutions such as review journals and magazines, English departments, editors, and granting and awarding agencies within the ruling cultural apparatus.

In any literate society there exist a number of distinct modes of literary production that Terry Eagleton defines as "a unity of certain forces and social relations of literary production."[2] Most literary productions belong to the dominant formation's cultural apparatus, which includes the specific institutions of literary production and distribution—editors, publishing houses, bookstores, and libraries. The cultural apparatus also encompasses a range of secondary supporting institutions—among them literary academies, English departments, literary criticism, the concept of literature, granting and awarding agencies—whose function is more directly ideological. These secondary supportive institutions are concerned with the definition and dissemination of certain codified literary standards, conventions, stereotypes, and assumptions.

The concept of literature, produced historically and ideologically, generates these established literary conventions, stereotypes, and assumptions. The current definition of literature began taking shape during the latter half of the eighteenth century. With a Latin root, *littera,* literature was, in effect, a condition of reading: of being able to read and of having read. It was close to the modern sense of literacy.

In its modern form, however, literature has come to mean, as Raymond Williams notes, "taste," "sensibility," and "discrimination."³ These terms become the unifying concepts of modern literature. They comprise a practice that produces the organization into which forms of imaginative writing are compressed. These forms reflect a historically and ideologically produced way of viewing literary texts. In short, literature becomes a construction "fashioned by particular people for particular reasons."⁴

Editors, publishers, critics, and reviewers function as a kind of conduit for many of the established cultural ideological, and intellectual preferences. They are instrumental in keeping certain ideas, social habits, myths, moral conventions, and stereotypes alive in the public's mind—usually under the pretext of not wanting to upset the status quo or offend the public. These editors and critics seek their own definitions of the literary experience in all texts that come to their attention. They evaluate texts by pointing out their contribution to "knowledge" and by explaining how they reproduce certain values, conventions, stereotypes, and perspectives. They certify those literary texts that speak the discourse better, that conform to the established literary standards and criteria. They exclude those texts that do not conform in subject or perspective, on the grounds that they are inferior aesthetically—thereby effecting certain silences in the discourse of literature.

My intention is not to put forth the simplistic argument that the only literary texts published are those that reproduce mainstream literary conventions, values, and stereotypes. English departments, literary journals and magazines, editors, and publishers often espouse values and meanings that are antithetical to those of mainstream society. But these antithetical values and meanings are compatible with specific forms of discourse that allow them to be appropriated. They either speak a particular language or accept a particular form that will not permit certain meanings and positions to be articulated.⁵

Publishers, in particular, play a crucial role in reproducing established literary conventions and stereotypes by catering to the normative, hypothesized reader. In *The Sociology of Literature,* Robert Escarpit contends that with the rise of the middle class in eighteenth-century England, literature ceased to be the privilege of men of letters.⁶ It shifted its focus and concerns from the aristocracy to the bourgeoisie who demanded a literature that suited their own concerns, that reproduced their values.

With this large middle-class audience the publisher found himself, and still does, caught between the writer's desire and the public's demands. To accommodate, the publisher influences his writer in the interest of the public by giving advances for the production of particular kinds of books. He influences the public through censoring and advertising in the interest of the writer. In short, the publisher induces a compatible writer-public relationship. But, as Maria Corti explains, the publisher fails to make a distinction between the "effective, virtual reader" and the "hypothesized reader."[7]

A consequence of the publisher's appeal to the mass "hypothesized reader" is that marginal and "other" groups are not seen as constituting a real audience. This oversight contributes to the weeding out or exclusion of certain literary texts. This induced writer-public relationship also coerces some writers with nonconformist perspectives and values into writing for the "hypothesized reader." When a writer is forced to write for an alien reader, Robert Escarpit points out, a "sort of detachment results which may allow the author to have an ideology different from that of his readers and to have to decide on the meaning not only of his own work, but of literature itself."[8]

Criticism as practiced by editors, publishers, reviewers, and critics, then, is not scientific; it is a preeminently political exercise that works upon and mediates the reception of literary texts. It is an active and ongoing part of literature and the cultural apparatus as they produce objects whose "effects" function to reproduce a particular literary experience, or particular literary conventions and stereotypes. As a series of interventions within the uses to which so-called literary texts are to be put, critical practice sends out signals as to the worth and value of literary texts. Those literary texts that reproduce particular literary "experiences" are promoted and certified. Those that do not reproduce certain "experiences" or ideological effects are repressed or subordinated.

Perhaps a discussion of Michel Foucault's concepts of discourse and discursive formations can facilitate an understanding of how critical practice and the concept of literature exclude certain forms of literature, and how critical practice's assumptions, represented as value judgments or as "natural" criteria, actually operate within a network of discursive regulations that finally include the broadest ideological constraints and practices.

For Michel Foucault, a discourse is *any* group of statements that exists under the positive condition of a complex group of relations. He calls this group of relations *discursive*. The regularity that binds the object's relations he calls *discursive formation*.[9] A discursive formation does not connect concepts or words with one another. Instead, it offers concepts the objects of which they can speak. It determines the group of relations that a discourse must establish before it can speak of a particular object. These relations characterize not the language used by discourse but discourse itself as a practice. The conditions to which the group of relations are subjected Foucault calls the *rules of formation*.[10]

Within a discourse exist relations of mutual delimitation. The whole group of relations forms a principle of determination that permits and excludes a certain number of statements. This means that a discourse does not occupy all the possible space that is open to it by the mere nature of its system of formation. It is essentially incomplete. The incompleteness is manifested in gaps, silences, discontinuities, and limitations.

But discourse conceals its incompleteness, its mode of formation. It naturalizes itself by inscribing its discursive practice in its method of category selection. For Foucault, the archaeologist's function is to demask this process of naturalization, to expose the various ways in which discourse, or any form of representation, deludes. In inserting this signifying process into the social process, we can see not just how literary texts, canons, standards, myths, and conventions are produced, but also how culture, as well, is produced or invented, rather than being "natural," absolute, or eternal.

Without demasking this process of naturalization, a "natural" or mainstream definition of the literary "experience" will continue to universalize the ideological and historical forces that produced it. Its agents will continue to assume that literature reflects or mirrors the social reality rather than being a production of it. They will continue to assume that "universal" standards exist to measure the literary text's value and worth, rather than seeing its worth as determined within a cultural or ideological context.

For almost a century, Afro-American critics and writers have been aware of the ways in which ideological pressures have dictated the canon of American literature. They also have been aware of the exclusion of certain Afro-American literary texts, images, and conventions from that canon. If we read the letters and fiction of the nineteenth-century writer Charles Chesnutt, which will be discussed in detail in the next chapter, we can discern clearly his awareness that certain literary images, stereotypes, and conventions are sanctioned and promoted by editors, publishers, and critics, and that other Afro-American images and stereotypes are repressed or subordinated. If we read the essays of Zora Neale Hurston almost fifty years later, we again can discern that she too was quite aware of the pressures by ruling literary institutions to prohibit certain Afro-American images and texts. Recently, Mary Helen Washington in *Black-Eyed Susans*, Barbara Smith in *Home Girls:*

A Black Feminist Anthology and in *Some of Us Are Brave,* and others have continued to document the exclusion of blacks and women from the established literary practices in America.

But Chesnutt, Hurston, Washington, Smith, and Afro-American critics of the twentieth century have not examined conceptually the discursive nature of exclusion either in American literature, or in Afro-American and women's literatures. Most Afro-American critical practices, which are my concern here, do not engage their own productive process. They universalize the ideological and historical forces that produce them. They are also silent on the production of Afro-American texts. These critical practices ignore the various literary and ideological forces that actually cause certain Afro-American texts to be published, promoted, and certified and others to be subordinated and/or excluded. They ignore the historically and ideologically established way of viewing literary texts and how this established way affects the production of Afro-American literary texts.

In an article entitled "Generational Shifts and the Recent Criticism of Afro-American Literature," Houston A. Baker, Jr., delineates three dominant critical practices that have defined Afro-American literature in the past forty years. Baker argues that "poetics of integration" defined Afro-American literature during the 1940s and 1950s. The assumptions and criteria for this practice, for defining Afro-American literature, were established by Arthur P. Davis and reached their maturity with Richard Wright. In the introduction to *The Negro Caravan* (1941), Davis writes:

> The editors . . . do not believe that the expression "Negro Literature" is an accurate one, and in spite of its convenient brevity, they have avoided using it. "Negro Literature" has no application if it means *structural peculiarity,* or a Negro school of writing. The Negro writes in the forms evolved in English and American literature. . . . The editors consider Negro writers to be American writers, and literature by American Negroes to be a segment of American literature.[11]

Davis reiterates this integrationist critical practice in his essay, "Integration and Race Literature," which, as Baker informs us, he presented to the first conference on Afro-American writers sponsored by the American society of African Culture in 1959. Here Davis explains, "The integration controversy is another crisis, and from it we hope that the Negro will move permanently into full participation of American life—social, economic, political, and literary."[12]

In his essay "The Literature of the Negro in the United States," published in 1957, Richard Wright viewed the Supreme Court case of *Brown v. Board of Education* as the beginning of the end of racial discrimination in the United States. Wright believed that Afro-American literature would become indistinguishable from the literature of the dominant American society: "At the present moment there is no one dominant note in Negro literary expression. As the Negro merges into the mainstream of American life, there might result actually a disappearance of Negro as such."[13] In the 1950s this "poetics of integration" operated within a network of discursive regulations that included the broadest ideological constraints and practices. It was a part of a dominant assimilationist ideological base—in many instances sanctioned by the dominant American cultural apparatus—whose practices were reproduced in Afro-American cultural, political, and literary arenas.

As major Afro-American writers and critics in the 1940s and 1950s, Wright and Davis were able, through their anthologies, reviews, criticisms, and status within the literary world, to establish a tradition and promote a body of Afro-American literature that reflected the values, conventions, and stereotypes of their integrationist perspective on literary texts. For example, during the 1940s and 1950s when Gwendolyn Brooks was writing "mainstream" poetry, Wright was instrumental in getting her work published by Harper and Row.[14]

Arthur P. Davis in his many anthologies also promoted a particular kind of integrationist Afro-American literature. For example, in *From the Dark Tower: Afro-American Writers 1900–1960*, Davis states that a "major Negro writer is one whose work deals largely with the black experience, measures up to appropriate aesthetic standards, and influences to some extent his contemporaries and/or those who come after."[15] For Davis, "appropriate aesthetic standards" are those standards sanctioned by the dominant American literary establishment. Discussing Paul Laurence Dunbar and Charles Chesnutt, Davis implies that they are "major" Negro writers because both "appeared in America's best periodicals of the age, and both had their works produced by the finest publishing houses."[16]

Davis includes Richard Wright, Chester Himes, Ann Petry, and Julian Mayfield in his section on "Toward the Mainstream" as "major" Negro writers because their naturalist works had the "message of protest against America's treatment of its black minority."[17] Their works have the "spiritual commitment and climate out of which full integration could develop."[18] Owen Dodson's *Boy at the Window* and Gwendolyn Brooks's *Maud Martha* are considered minor works and therefore are excluded because they give "intimate and subtle vignettes of middle class living."

But this integrationist way of viewing Afro-American literary texts, by the mere nature of its concerns, excluded other perspectives (in the next chapter, see Wright's treatment of Hurston's *Their Eyes Were Watching God*). With strong-willed determination to "merge into the mainstream of American life," to write "in the forms evolved in English and American literature," both Wright and Davis accept as "natural" the mainstream literary assumptions about literature. They assume that English and American literature has standards and criteria which Afro-American writers must reproduce if they are to write "good" literature. In not interpreting these fundamental assumptions as a function of some broader ideological practice, or as belonging to a literary discourse that permits and excludes certain literary texts, both Davis and Wright ignore the literary and ideological forces that produce Afro-American literature. In addition, they ignore how their own critical practice is the product of exclusionary judgments and how it therefore defines an Afro-American tradition that appropriates certain Afro-American texts and excludes others.

In his essay "Generational Shifts and the Recent Criticism of Afro-American Literature," Baker further contends that a group of Afro-American writers, intellectuals, and critics—who had a different ideological disposition toward American egalitarianism than those who espoused poetics of integration—emerged in the 1960s: "The emerging generation sets itself the task of analyzing the nature, aims, ends, and arts of those hundreds of thousands of their own people who were assaulting America's manifest structures of exclusion."[19] The critical practice that accompanied this new ideological shift within the Afro-American political arena was one of cultural nationalism, which has its own "structures of exclusion." This nationalist critical practice has its origins in Langston Hughes's writing in the 1920s and its culmination in Amiri Baraka's cultural nationalism of the 1960s and Addison Gayle's black aesthetic of the 1970s. In discussing who will become the "great Negro artist" and what his subject will be, Hughes writes:

> But then there are the low-down folks, the so-called common element, and they are the majority—may the Lord be praised! The people who have their nip of gin on Saturday nights are not too important to themselves . . . to watch the lazy world go round. They . . . do not particularly care whether they are like white folks or anybody else. Their joy funs, bang! into ecstasy. Their religion soars to a shout. Work maybe a little today, rest a little tomorrow. Play a while. Sing a while. O, let's dance. These common people are not afraid of spirituals. . . . They furnish a wealth of colorful, distinctive material for any artist because

they still hold their own individuality in the face of American standard-izations. And perhaps these common people will give to the world its truly great Negro artist, the one who is not afraid to be himself.[20]

Hughes's advocacy of an Afro-American literature emphasizing "the common people" who "do not care whether they are like white folks," who still "hold their own individuality in the face of American standardizations," is echoed in the cultural nationalism of Amiri Baraka in the 1960s:

> Where is the Negro-ness of a literature written in imitation of the meanest of social intelligences to be found in American culture, i.e., the white middle class? How can it even begin to express the emotional predicament of black western man? Such a literature, even if its "characters *are* black, takes on the emotional barrenness of its model, and the blackness of the characters is like the blackness of Al Jolson, an unconvincing device. It is like using black checkers instead of white. They [are] still checkers.[21]

Hughes's and Baraka's advocacy of a nationalist Afro-American literature culminated in the black arts movement of the 1960s and in the black aesthetic critical practice of the late sixties and early seventies whose leading exponents included Ron Karenga, Holt Fuller, and Addison Gayle. These black aestheticians—through their critical texts and major Afro-American review journals and magazines like *Black World, First World, Black Books Bulletin, The Black Scholar*—define Afro-American literature along cultural nationalist criteria. They define the worth of Afro-American literary texts according to how accurately these texts reproduce the cultural nationalist's ideologically defined Afro-American historical experience. These black aestheticians seek their meaning of the Afro-American experience in all Afro-American texts that come to their attention—praising those that reproduce their values, conventions, and stereotypes and condemning those that do not. In *The Way of the New World: The Black Novel in America*, Addison Gayle, using the black aesthetic criteria, determines the worth and value of Afro-American texts from William Wells Brown's *Clotel, or The President's Daughter* (1853) to Ernest J. Gaines's *The Autobiography of Miss Jane Pittman* (1971). Gayle praises those texts—like Delany's *Blake*, Chesnutt's *The Marrow of Tradition*, McKay's *Banana Bottom* and *Home to Harlem*, Killens's *And Then We Heard the Thunder*, and Gaines's *Miss Jane Pittman*—that reproduce stereotypes, conventions, and values from the Afro-American experience of the cultural nationalist world view.

These black aestheticians also exclude those Afro-American texts that do not reproduce the values and conventions of their world view. In *The Way of the New World,* Gayle criticizes texts such as Johnson's *The Autobiography of an Ex-Coloured Man,* Wright's *Native Son,* and Ellison's *Invisible Man,* that use mainstream conventions and stereotypes such as alienation, existentialism, and naturalism to define the Afro-American. In using literature to further their political ends, Gayle and other black aestheticians understand the political function of literature. They know that it implies a particular form of politics, that all literary theories presuppose a certain use of literature. They understand that literature is a social institution that functions to keep certain cultural forms, values, and myths before the reading public. Their strategy is to promote those Afro-American texts that present their preferred myths and cultural forms. But this black aesthetic theory of literature is silent completely on how established literary institutions and apparatuses, throughout American literary history, have affected the production of Afro-American literature. Missing is a discussion of the various literary and ideological forces and institutions that promote those Afro-American texts that reproduce the literary values, conventions, and stereotypes of the dominant literary establishment and exclude and subordinate others. In being silent on literary production, Gayle and other black aestheticians cannot explain why certain Afro-American images and paradigms are promoted and others excluded. They cannot explain how literature is a social institution which reproduces certain codified values, conventions, or world views—be they mainstream American or black cultural nationalist. Of course, such a discussion would cause these black aestheticians to confront openly the ideological nature and function, and therefore the constraints and exclusions, of their own cultural nationalist critical practice.

In the late 1970s two Afro-American critical texts—Robert Stepto's *From Behind the Veil: A Study of Afro-American Narrative* and Houston A. Baker's *The Journey Back: Issues in Black Literature and Criticism*—established new critical perspectives for defining Afro-American literary traditions and canons. They are also silent on literary production. Stepto's *From Behind the Veil* is a "history or fiction of the historical consciousness of an Afro-American art form—namely, the Afro-American written narrative."[22] It works from three fundamental assumptions. First, Stepto assumes that Afro-American culture has its own store of "pregeneric myths" which are "shared stories or myths that not only exist prior to literary form, but eventually shape the forms that comprise a given culture's literary canon."[23] For Stepto, the primary Afro-American pregeneric myth is the "quest for freedom and literacy." Second, he assumes that once the pregeneric myth is in search of its literary forms, the Afro-American critic must "attempt to define and discuss how the myth both assumes and does not assume the properties of genre."[24] Third, Stepto assumes that if an Afro-American literary tradition does exist, it exists not because there is a "sizeable chronology of [Afro-American] authors and texts," but because these Afro-American authors and texts "collectively seek their own literary forms . . . bound historically and linguistically to a shared pregeneric myth."[25]

In *From Behind the Veil's* first section, Stepto delineates four types of slave narratives—the eclectic, the integrated, the generic, and the authenticating. This section ends by describing how Booker T. Washington's *Up From Slavery* and W. E. B. DuBois's *The Souls of Black Folk* reproduce the generic and authenticating slave narratives. In the book's second section, Stepto demonstrates how certain "major" contemporary Afro-American narratives reproduce the types of narrative discussed in the first sections. Johnson's *The Autobiography of an Ex-Coloured Man,* Stepto argues, reproduces the generic and authenticating narratives of Washington and DuBois. Richard Wright's *Black Boy* reproduces Frederic Douglass's *Narrative,* and Ellison's *Invisible Man* reproduces both Washington's and Douglass's. Stepto isolates an Afro-American cultural myth, the pregeneric myth, and uses it to define an Afro-American literary tradition.

From Behind the Veil is valuable for a number of reasons. First, as Stepto points out in the preface, it is different or innovative because it avoids "writing yet another survey of Afro-American literature that systematically moves from texts to nonliterary structures and passively allows those structures to become the literature's collective history."[26] Second, *From Behind the Veil* is valuable because it frees Afro-American texts from the matrix of dominant American critical practices, from the dominant Western historical and ideological way of defining literary texts. The book places certain Afro-American texts in an Afro-American matrix which supports their ideological assumptions. Like the black aestheticians, Stepto understands that a literary text's value and worth are determined within a particular cultural context.

Unlike these black aestheticians, however, Stepto does not understand that all literary theories imply a particular form of politics or presuppose a certain use of literature. The mere fact that Stepto selects the "search for freedom and literacy" rather than another Afro-American myth, such as communal struggle, indicates that the choice is ideological, that his Afro-American tradition in *From Behind the Veil* is a discourse that permits and excludes. In not exposing his motives for selecting the pregeneric myth and in not informing the reader that the pregeneric myth is one of many Afro-American myths, Stepto deludes the reader into believing that the "search for freedom and literacy" is *the* pregeneric myth, is a "collective history," and that all Afro-American writers share it.

Making salient *From Behind the Veil*'s attempt to conceal its mode of production prompts the reader to ask other questions about the book. What is its cultural and ideological function? What is the relationship between Stepto's pregeneric myth and certain dominant American literary myths? What is the relationship between the dominant literary way of viewing literary texts and Stepto's way of viewing Afro-American written narratives? If we examine the "major" Afro-American written narratives that Stepto uses to establish the Afro-American pregeneric canon, we see that these narratives reproduce established American literary conventions and values. Booker T. Washington's *Up from Slavery* reproduces the dominant myth of the Protestant work ethic, for example, while Wright's *Black Boy,* Johnson's *The Autobiography of an Ex-Coloured Man,* and Ellison's *Invisible Man* chronicle the American myth of the rugged individual's quest for freedom.

This means that *From Behind the Veil* promotes those Afro-American texts that reproduce mainstream American literary myths and values. It also means that it excludes, represses, or subordinates those Afro-American texts—such as Delany's *Blake,* Bontemps's *Black Thunder,* Zora Neale Hurston's *Their Eyes Were Watching God,* or Reed's *Mumbo Jumbo*—that do not reproduce mainstream American literary myths and conventions. In its silence on literary production, *From Behind the Veil* deludes the reader into believing that the Afro-American pregeneric literary canon it produces, and the Afro-American images and representations the canon's selected texts present, reflect the Afro-American social reality. Of course, a discussion of literary production would force Stepto to become aware of his own ideological and cultural function as he produces a "natural" myth about Afro-American literary texts.

Houston A. Baker, in *The Journey Back,* like Stepto identifies myths and linguistic structures from the Afro-American historical past and uses them to construct a theory of the Afro-American literary tradition. But like Stepto he also ignores the fact that Afro-American myths, stereotypes, and cultural forms are not innocent, that they are bound culturally and historically—even within the Afro-American social reality—and therefore have political and ideological functions.

In *The Journey Back,* Baker examines how black narrative texts written in English "preserve and communicate culturally unique meanings."[27] First, he describes the place occupied by works of black literature in black American culture, and second, he delineates how writers such as Hammon, Wheatley, Vassa, the slave autobiographer, Wright, Ellison, Baldwin, Baraka, and Brooks "journey through difficult straits" and in the process preserve in language details of their "voyages": "Through his [the black writer's] work we are allowed to witness, if not the trip itself, at least a representation of the voyage that provides some view of our emergence."[28] As with Stepto's work, the value of Baker's *The Journey Back* lies in the fact that it understands that a literary text's value and worth are determined within a particular cultural context. *The Journey Back* turns to an Afro-American cultural context to establish criteria for interpreting and determining the worth and value of Afro-American texts.

But in failing to deal with language as being culturally biased, with the production of these cultural forms, and with each black writer's "representation of the voyage" as production, Baker neglects to reveal the force of meaning of a culture and its literature. First, in arguing that Afro-American writers can preserve in language the Afro-American historical past, Baker assumes that language reflects the social reality. But language is socially and historically produced; it is saturated with cultural and historical codes. In *Selected Writings in Language, Culture, and Personality,* Edward Sapir points out:

> Human beings do not live in the objective world alone, nor alone in the world of social activity as ordinarily understood, but are very much at the mercy of the particular language which has become the medium of expression for their society. It is quite an illusion to imagine that one adjusts to reality essentially without the use of language. . . . The fact of the matter is that the "real world" is to a large extent unconsciously built upon the language habits of the group.[29]

To assume that language is transparent is to ignore the role language plays in understanding people, social history, culture, and the laws of how a society functions.

Second, in assuming that the black writer's "journey back" and his "representation of the voyage" are a reflection of the Afro-American historical past, Baker falls into an antiquated and heavily critiqued realism. According to realism, reading assumes a crossing from expression to the self, from representation to the world, from words to things, and from language to reality. But in light of the fact that modern linguistics has informed us that language is not transparent and that Foucault has informed us that all discourses, including literary texts, permit and exclude, it becomes difficult to accept Baker's supposition that the writer's "journey back" mirrors the Afro-

342 W. Lawrence Hogue

American social reality. Instead, the "journey back" is a production of the Afro-American social reality.

Furthermore, Baker's "anthropology of art" ignores not only the writer himself or herself, but also his or her awarenesses—be they political, racial, or sexual—and how these awarenesses affect the writer's production of the "trips" and "voyages" into the past. But, more important, Baker's "anthropology of art" is silent on literary production. It ignores the role of the institutions within the dominant cultural apparatus, as well that of Afro-American critical practices, in producing Afro-American texts and determining the shape of Afro-American literature. Therefore it is not surprising that he chooses Hammon, Wheatley, and Vassa—who reproduce many of the accepted social and literary conventions, stereotypes, and myths about the Afro-American—to represent Afro-American literature in the eighteenth century. Baker explains "On a first view, 'acculturation' seems to explain everything: Hammon's progress toward Christian orthodoxy, Wheatley's engagement with the God and muses of her white overlords, Vassa's detailing . . . of his education as a gentleman."[30] If Baker's "anthropology of art" included a discussion of literary production, it would allow him to raise questions about those aborted and repressed Afro-American texts that do not give acculturationist representations of the Afro-American in the eighteenth century.

This critique of Stepto and Baker, who identify and naturalize certain Afro-American myths and linguistic structures, can serve as a model for understanding the silences, limitations, and possibilities of other Afro-American critical studies in canonical formation. In the past ten years, black women scholars and writers have worked intensely for canon formation of black women's literature. Through interviews with black women writers and through scholarly endeavors they have identified cultural patterns and forms, perspectives, subjects, and values that are unique or peculiar to black women writers. Barbara Christian's *Black Women Novelists: The Development of a Tradtion, 1892–1976* is a seminal work in black women writers' canon formation. In delineating "recurrent" themes and images in the fiction of black women novelists from Francis Harper's *Iola LeRoy* (1892) to Alice Walker's *Meridian* (1976), Christian establishes a tradition in novels by black women. In the first three historical chapters Christian traces the development of dominant recurring Afro-American stereotypes and images—the mammy, the mulatto, the wench, violent relationships between mother and father, continuity between generations, and insularity—and the impact they had on the production of American and black women's fiction. The next three chapters in *Black Women Novelists* are devoted to the novels of Paule Marshall, Toni Morrison, and Alice Walker who each have "written two novels" and are "in the process of developing" their own critical visions.[31] The three novelists, Christian argues, are "very much a part of the tradition" that preceded them, but are also "developing it in some critical way."[32] In the final chapter Christian looks at the "whole tradition" and tries to "draw some conclusions about its major characteristics and about what directions it may be moving."[33]

In *Black Women Novelists,* Christian executes her intention profoundly. Like Baker and Stepto, she establishes a tradition to interpret black women writers. It is a tradition that comes from black women writers. In establishing this tradition, Christian gives us an Afro-American historical framework to use in understanding certain issues pertinent to black women, and in seeing how black women writers have textualized these issues.

But certain developments in literary theory have forced us to ask additional, or different, questions about the literary text. These new questions give us the critical practice. As I stated earlier, many of the traditional literary assumptions that supported literature and criticism in their traditional forms have eroded. Since the text does not reflect the social reality, what is its need or function? What are the ideological and literary forces that produce the literary text? Why is a particular text published and promoted, another published and excluded, and still another never published?

In *Black Women Novelists* Barbara Christian is quite conscious of some of these questions. She reminds her reader constantly that the literary text does not reflect the social reality. When she is discussing the Afro-American social reality produced in Harper's *Iola LeRoy,* she acknowledges that there is a "discrepancy between the substance of her novel and Harper's detailed observations of the life most black women were leading in the period of Reconstruction, a discrepancy that has something to do with the form of the novel at that time and the image of black women in American society."[34] This means that Christian is aware of certain ideological and literary forces that produce the "image of black women in American society." When Christian writes about the communities described in the works of Marshall, Morrison, and Walker, she points out that she is "not equating the communities these authors present with the Black community. . . . The communities these authors present are more particular."[35] In addition, without revealing a clearly defined discursive formation that produces the book, Christian makes it clear that *Black Women Novelists* is "not intended to be a definitive work. I am not commenting on every black woman who has ever written a novel."[36]

Yet despite this awareness Christian's critical practice tends to lapse into normative criticism, which assumes that there is some "universal" model in social reality that can be used to measure the accuracy of the literary text. Though Christian makes it clear that there is a discrepancy between the social reality described in Harper's novel and the social reality within which she lived and wrote, she gives no insights into *Iola LeRoy* as a production, and does not explain how it "comes to be what it is because of the specific determinations of its mode of production."[37] Without discussing the issue of literary production, Christian's critical practice cannot explain fully how images of black women are tied inextricably to the production of literary texts, or why certain black women novelists are published and promoted, others published and excluded, and still others aborted at editors' and publishers' desks.

Second, despite her awareness that images of black women in fiction are incongruent with those in the social reality, Christian's critical practice lapses at times into antiquated realism. In her opinion, a "problem with Fauset's novels is that [Fauset] gives us this particular Negro [a light-complexioned, upper-middle-class black heroine] exclusively and as the representative of what the race is capable of doing."[38] But for Fauset's heroine to be "representative" of the race is to assume that literature mirrors the social reality. Fauset's novels are not representations of the social real but productions of it. The crucial question should be what are the literary and ideological forces, the "specific determinations" of their modes of production, that cause Fauset's novels to reproduce this image of the "Negro exclusively"? Whom does this produced image serve?

Third, because she does not discuss literary production, Christian cannot discuss the political and cultural significance of certain dominant American and Afro-American literary conventions and stereotypes. Although Christian informs us that the communities produced by Marshall, Morrison, and Walker do not reflect the "Black community," she never gives us insight into these writers' "communities" as produced myths or cultural objects.

Last, in chapters four through six, Christian discusses the works of Marshall, Morrison, and Walker to show how they reproduce already delineated themes and issues. Christian's argument for choosing these three novelists is that "each has written two novels and is in the process of developing her own critical vision." But one other contemporary black woman novelist, Kristin Hunter, has written three novels. Why is she excluded from Christian's tradition? Here, as with Baker and Stepto, we see how canon formation is informed by an external ideological discourse. Moreover, unless critics inform their readers of the political ramifications of their ideological discourse—as Christian attempts to do in *Black Women Novelists*—they will delude readers into believing that the tradition they espouse and the texts they select to generate that tradition really constitute the black women tradition or the Afro-American tradition.

Other anthologies and critical texts—*Sturdy Black Bridges: Visions of Black Women in Literature* (edited by Roseann P. Bell et al.), Mary Helen Washington's *Black-eyed Susans* and *Midnight Birds*, Amiri Baraka's *Confirmation*, Barbara Smith's *Some Are Brave*, Claudia Tate's *Black Women Writers at Work*, and Mari Evans's *Black Women Writers: A Critical Evaluation*—continue the examination of black women writers ferreting out traditions. But as in the cases of Stepto and Baker, these interviews and critical studies of black women writers first assume that all black women writers share the same ideological concerns about black women experience or culture. In this assumption, certain black women writers like Kristin Hunter and Pauline Hopkins who do not reproduce the prevailing women's "themes" and "issues" are subordinated or excluded. Hunter and Hopkins do not deal in their fiction with feminist categories such as black women's historical oppression, the brutal and violent relationships between black men and black women, and black women's sexual awareness. Consequently, they do not fit comfortably into feminist canon formation that organizes black women's texts around these issues.

Second, these interviews and critical studies exclude a discussion of the literary and ideological forces that have given shape, and continue to give shape, to a body of literature called black women's literature. Without a discussion of literary production, these critical studies are not able to explain why certain black women writers are published and promoted and others published and ignored. Are certain black women writers published and promoted because they reproduce established American literary myths and conventions? Are other black women writers published and promoted because they reproduce certain sanctioned Afro-American stereotypes and conventions? Are others published and ignored because they fail to reproduce sanctioned literary myths and conventions?

As I have stated earlier, the value of these Afro-American critical studies lies in the fact that they identify Afro-American cultural patterns and forms, or choose certain Afro-American world views, to produce Afro-American literary traditions, canons, and myths. They establish a critical matrix that receives Afro-American texts more favorably, that defines the worth of Afro-American literature within an Afro-American cultural context. But what these Afro-American critical studies fail to take into consideration is that Afro-American myths, definitions, and linguistic structures are not "natural" in their use by Afro-American writers or by the dominant American literary establishment. They are produced. Further, any use of them in ignorance of the nature of their production or function can lead to an entrapment. Afro-American myths and conventions are inextricably tied to the production of Afro-American texts that in turn determines which images or representations of the Afro-American will appear before the American public. To fail to examine this process is to be entrapped into believing that these images and representations are reflections of the Afro-American social reality rather than productions of it—productions that have political and social functions, be they Afro-American or American.

With an awareness of the role literary production plays in the definition of Afro-American literature, we can begin to see how literature is one of the social institutions within the cultural apparatus, or even within oppressed, marginal social groups within society. We can see how literature provides indices and coherent myths for social subjects (individuals) as they seek equilibrium. But when a racial or cultural group is not in control of its literary productions and when a racial or cultural group fails to discern clearly the different world views within the race or culture that inform the production of the literature, as in the case of Afro-America, it must become aware of the ideological and literary forces that produce literature. It must also be concerned with whose interest literary productions serve. Thus far, most Afro-American critical practices are silent on literary production.

Notes

1 Pierre Macherey, *A Theory of Literary Production* (London, 1978), 16.
2 Terry Eagleton, *Criticism and Ideology* (London, 1976), 45.
3 Raymond Williams, *Marxism and Literature* (Oxford, 1977), 48.
4 Terry Eagleton, *Literary Theory: An Introduction* (Minneapolis, 1983), 11.
5 Eagleton, *Literary Theory*, 200.
6 Robert Escarpit, *The Sociology of Literature* (London, 1971), 49.
7 Maria Corti, *An Introduction to Literary Semiotics* (Bloomington, Ind., 1978), 34.
8 Escarpit, *The Sociology of Literature*, 59.
9 Michel Foucault, *The Archaeology of Knowledge* (New York, 1972), 10.
10 Ibid., 38.
11 Houston A. Baker, Jr., "Generational Shifts and the Recent Criticism of Afro-American Literature," in this volume, 284.
12 Ibid.

13 Richard Wright, "The Literature of the Negro in the United States," in Addison Gayle, ed., *Black Expression* (New York, 1969), 228.
14 Claudia Tate, ed., *Black Women Writers at Work* (New York, 1983), 193.
15 Arthur P. Davis, *From the Dark Tower: Afro-American Writers 1900–1960* (Washington, D.C., 1974), xiv.
16 Ibid., 6.
17 Ibid., 139.
18 Ibid., 138.
19 Baker, "Generational Shifts," 286.
20 Langston Hughes, "The Negro Artist and the Racial Mountain," in this volume 55–59.
21 LeRoi Jones, "The Myth of a 'Negro Literature,'" in this volume, 168.
22 Robert Stepto, *From Behind the Veil: A Study of Afro-American Narrative* (Urbana, Ill., 1979), x.
23 Ibid., ix.
24 Ibid.
25 Ibid., ix–x.
26 Ibid., x.
27 Houston A. Baker, Jr., *The Journey Back: Issues in Black Literature and Criticism* (Chicago, 1980), xii.
28 Ibid., 1.
29 Edward Sapir, *Selected Writings in Language, Culture, and Personality* (Berkeley, 1949), 162.
30 Baker, *The Journey Back*, 19.
31 Barbara Christian, *Black Women Novelists: The Development of a Tradition, 1892–1976* (Westport, Conn., 1980), x.
32 Ibid., x.
33 Ibid.
34 Ibid., 5.
35 Ibid., 239, 240.
36 Ibid., xi.
37 Eagleton, *Criticism and Ideology*, 48.
38 Christian, *Black Women Novelists*, 41.

Barbara Christian

The Race for Theory

(1987)

I have seized this occasion to break the silence among those of us, critics, as we are now called, who have been intimidated, devalued by what I call the race for theory. I have become convinced that there has been a takeover in the literary world by Western philosophers from the old literary elite, the neutral humanists. Philosophers have been able to effect such a takeover because so much of the literature of the West has become pallid, laden with despair, self-indulgent, and disconnected. The New Philosophers, eager to understand a world that is today fast escaping their political control, have redefined literature so that the distinctions implied by that term, that is, the distinctions between everything written and those things written to evoke feeling as well as to express thought, have been blurred. They have changed literary critical language to suit their own purposes as philosophers, and they have reinvented the meaning of theory.

My first response to this realization was to ignore it. Perhaps, in spite of the egocentrism of this trend, some good might come of it. I had, I felt, more pressing and interesting things to do, such as reading and studying the history and literature of black women, a history that had been totally ignored, a contemporary literature bursting with originality, passion, insight, and beauty. But unfortunately it is difficult to ignore this new takeover, theory has become a commodity because that helps determine whether we are hired or promoted in academic institutions—worse, whether we are heard at all. Due to this new orientation, works (a word which evokes labor) have become texts. Critics are no longer concerned with literature, but with other critics' texts, for the critic yearning for attention has displaced the writer and has conceived of himself as the center. Interestingly in the first part of this

This essay first appeared in *Cultural Critique*, 6 (1987).

century, at least in England and America, the critic was usually also a writer of poetry, plays, or novels. But today, as a new generation of professionals develops, he or she is increasingly an academic. Activities such as teaching or writing one's response to specific works of literature have, among this group, become subordinated to one primary thrust, that moment when one creates a theory, thus fixing a constellation of ideas for a time at least, a fixing which no doubt will be replaced in another month or so by somebody else's competing theory as the race accelerates. Perhaps because those who have effected the takeover have the power (although they deny it) first of all to be published, and thereby to determine the ideas which are deemed valuable, some of our most daring and potentially radical critics (and by *our* I mean black, women, Third World) have been influenced, even co-opted, into speaking a language and defining their discussion in terms alien to and opposed to our needs and orientation. At least so far, the creative writers I study have resisted this language.[1]

For people of color have always theorized—but in forms quite different from the Western form of abstract logic. And I am inclined to say that our theorizing (and I intentionally use the verb rather than the noun) is often in narrative forms, in the stories we create, in riddles and proverbs, in the play with language, since dynamic rather than fixed ideas seem more to our liking. How else have we managed to survive with such spiritedness the assault on our bodies, social institutions, countries, our very humanity? And women, at least the women I grew up around, continuously speculated about the nature of life through pithy language that unmasked the power relations of their world. It is this language, and the grace and pleasure with which they played with it, that I find celebrated, refined, critiqued in the works of writers like Toni Morrison and Alice Walker. My folk, in other words, have always been a race of theory—though more in the form of the hieroglyph, a written figure which is both sensual and abstract, both beautiful and communicative. In my own work I try to illuminate and explain these hieroglyphs, which is, I think, an activity quite different from the creating of the hieroglyphs themselves. As the Buddhists would say, the finger pointing at the moon is not the moon.

In this discussion, however, I am more concerned with the issue raised by my first use of the term, *the race of theory*, in relation to its academic hegemony, and possibly of its inappropriateness to the energetic emerging literatures in the world today. The pervasiveness of this academic hegemony is an issue continually spoken about—but usually in hidden groups, lest we, who are disturbed by it, appear ignorant to the reigning academic elite. Among the folk who speak in muted tones are people of color, feminists, radical critics, creative writers, who have struggled for much longer than a decade to make their voices, their various voices, heard, and for whom literature is not an occasion for discourse among critics but is necessary nourishment for their people and one way by which they come to understand their lives better. Clichéd though this may be, it bears, I think, repeating here.

The race for theory, with its linguistic jargon, its emphasis on quoting its prophets, its tendency towards 'Biblical' exegesis, its refusal even to mention specific works of creative writers, far less contemporary ones, its preoccupations with mechanical analyses of language, graphs, algebraic equations, its gross generalizations about culture, has silenced many of us to the extent that some of us feel we can no longer discuss our own literature, while others have developed intense writing blocks and are puzzled by the incomprehensibility of the language set adrift in literary circles. There have been, in the last year, any number of occasions on which I had to convince literary critics who have pioneered entire new areas of critical inquiry that they did have something to say. Some of us are continually harassed to invent wholesale theories regardless of the complexity of the literature we study. I, for one, am tired of being asked to produce a black feminist literary theory as if I were a mechanical man. For I believe such theory is prescriptive—it ought to have some relationship to practice. Since I can count on one hand the number of people attempting to be black feminist literary critics in the world today, I consider it presumptuous of me to invent a theory of how we *ought* to read. Instead, I think we need to read the works of our writers in our various ways and remain open to the intricacies of the intersection of language, class, race, and gender in the literature. And it would help if we share our process, that is, our practice, as much as possible since, finally, our work is a collective endeavor.

The insidious quality of this race for theory is symbolized for me by a term like 'Minority Discourse'[2]—a label that is borrowed from the reigning theory of the day but which is untrue to the literatures being produced by our writers, for many of our literatures (certainly Afro-American literature) are central, not minor. I have used the passive voice in my last sentence construction, contrary to the rules of Black English, which like all languages has a particular value system, since I have not placed responsibility on any particular person or group. But that is precisely because this new ideology has become so prevalent among us that it behaves like so many of the other ideologies with which we have had to contend. It appears to have neither head nor center. At the least, though, we can say that the terms 'minority' and 'discourse' are located firmly in a Western dualistic or 'binary' frame which sees the rest of the world as minor, and tries to convince the rest of the world that it is major, usually through force and then through language, even as it claims many of the ideas that we, its 'historical' other, have known and spoken about for so long. For many of us have never conceived of ourselves only as somebody's *other.*

Let me not give the impression that by objecting to the race for theory I ally myself with or agree with the neutral humanists who see literature as pure expression and will not admit to the obvious control of its production, value, and distribution by those who have power, who deny, in other words, that literature is, of necessity, political. I am studying an entire body of literature that has been denigrated for centuries by such terms as *political.* For an entire century Afro-American writers, from Charles Chestnutt [*sic*] in the nineteenth century through Richard Wright in the 1930s, Imamu Baraka in the 1960s, Alice Walker in the 1970s, have protested the literary hierarchy of dominance which declares when literature is literature, when literature is great, depending on what it thinks is to its advantage. The Black Arts Movement of the 1960s, out of which Black Studies, the Feminist Literary Movement of the 1970s, and Women's Studies grew, articulated precisely those issues, which came *not* from the declarations of the New Western Philosophers but from these groups' reflections on their own lives. That Western scholars have long believed their ideas to be universal has been strongly opposed by many such groups. Some of my colleagues do not see black critical writers of previous decades as eloquent enough. Clearly they have not read Wright's 'A Blueprint for Negro Writing,' Ellison's *Shadow and Act,* Chesnutt's resignation from being a writer, or Alice Walker's 'In search of Zora Neale Hurston.'³ There are two reasons for this general ignorance of what our writer-critics have said. One is that black writing has been generally ignored in the USA. Since we, as Toni Morrison has put it, are seen as a discredited people, it is no surprise, then, that our creations are also discredited. But this is also due to the fact that until recently, dominant critics in the Western world have also been creative writers who have had access to the upper-middle-class institutions of education and, until recently, our writers have decidedly been excluded from these institutions and in fact have often been opposed to them. Because of the academic world's general ignorance about the literature of black people, and of women, whose work too has been discredited, it is not surprising that so many of our critics think that the position arguing that literature is political begins with these New Philosophers. Unfortunately, many of our young critics do not investigate the reasons *why* that statement—literature is political—is now acceptable when before it was not; nor do we look to our own antecedents for the sophisticated arguments upon which we can build in order to change the tendency of any established Western idea to become hegemonic.

For I feel that the new emphasis on literary critical theory is as hegemonic as the world which it attacks. I see the language it creates as one which mystifies rather than clarifies our condition, making it possible for a few people who know that particular language to control the critical scene—that language surfaced, interestingly enough, just when the literature of peoples of color, of black women, of Latin Americans, of Africans, began to move to 'the center.' Such words as *center* and *periphery* are themselves instructive. *Discourse, canon, texts,* words, as Latinate as the tradition from which they come, are quite familiar to me. Because I went to a Catholic Mission school in the West Indies I must confess that I cannot hear the word 'canon' without smelling incense, that the word 'text' immediately brings back agonizing memories of Biblical exegesis, that 'discourse' reeks for me of metaphysics forced down my throat in those courses that traced *world* philosophy from Aristotle through Thomas Aquinas to Heidegger. 'Periphery' too is a word I heard throughout my childhood, for if anything was seen as being at the periphery, it was those small Caribbean islands which had neither land mass nor military power. Still I noted how intensely important this periphery was, for US troups were continually invading one island or another if any change in political control even seemed to be occurring. As I lived among folk for whom language was an absolutely necessary way of validating our existence, I was told that the minds of the world lived only in the small continent of Europe. The metaphysical language of the New Philosophy, then, I must admit, is repulsive to me and is one reason why I raced from philosophy to literature, since the latter seemed to me to have the possibilities of rendering the world as large and as complicated as I experienced it, as sensual as I knew it was. In literature I sensed the possibility of the integration of feeling/knowledge, rather than the split between the abstract and the emotional in which Western philosophy inevitably indulged.

Now I am being told that philosophers are the ones who write literature, that authors are dead, irrelevant, mere vessels through which their narratives ooze, that they do not work nor have they the faintest idea what they are doing; rather, they produce texts as disembodied as the angels. I am frankly astonished that scholars who call themselves marxists or postmarxists could seriously use such metaphysical language even as they attempt to deconstruct the philosophical tradition from which their language comes. And as a student of literature, I am appalled by the sheer ugliness of the language, its lack of clarity, its unnecessarily complicated sentence constructions, its lack of pleasurableness, its alienating quality. It is the kind of writing for which composition teachers would give a freshman a resounding F.

Because I am a curious person, however, I postponed readings of black women writers I was working on and read some of the prophets of this new literary orientation. These writers did announce their dissatisfaction with some of the cornerstone ideas of their own tradition, a dissatisfaction with which I was born. But in their attempt to change the orientation of Western scholarship, they, as usual, concentrated on themselves and were not in the slightest interested in the worlds they had ignored or controlled. Again I was supposed to know *them*, while they were not at all interested in knowing *me*. Instead they sought to 'deconstruct' the tradition to which they belonged even as they used the same forms, style, language of that tradition, forms that necessarily embody its values. And increasingly as I read them and saw their substitution of their philosophical writings for literary ones, I began to have the uneasy feeling that their folk were not producing any literature worth mentioning. For they always harkened back to the masterpieces of the past, again reifying the very texts they said they were deconstructing. Increasingly, as *their* way, *their* terms, *their* approaches remained central and became the means by which one defined literary critics, many of my own peers who had previously been concentrating on dealing with the other side of the equation, the reclamation and discussion of past and *present* Third World literatures, were diverted into continually discussing the new literary theory.

From my point of view as a critic of contemporary Afro-American women's writing, this orientation is extremely problematic. In attempting to find the deep structures in the literary tradition, a major preoccupation of the new New Criticism, many of us have become obsessed with the nature of reading itself to the extent that we have stopped writing about literature being written today. Since I am slightly paranoid, it has begun to occur to me that the literature being produced *is* precisely one of the reasons why this new philosophical-literary-critical theory of relativity is so prominent. In other words, the literature of blacks, women of South America and Africa, etc., as overtly 'political' literature, was being preempted by a new Western concept which proclaimed that reality does not exist, that everything is relative, and that every text is silent about something—which indeed it must necessarily be.

There is, of course, much to be learned from exploring how we know what we know, how we read what we read, an exploration which, of necessity, can have no end. But there also has to be a 'what,' and that 'what,' when it is even mentioned by the New Philosophers, are texts of the past, primarily Western male texts, whose norms are again being transferred onto Third World, female texts as theories of reading proliferate. Inevitably a hierarchy has now developed between what is called theoretical criticism and practical criticism, as mind is deemed superior to matter. I have no quarrel with those who wish to philosophize about how we know what we know. But I do resent the fact that this particular orientation is so privileged and has diverted so many of us from doing the first readings of the literature being written today as well as of past works about which nothing has been written. I note, for example, that there is little work done on Gloria Naylor, that most of Alice Walker's works have not been commented on—despite the rage around *The Color Purple*[4]—that there has yet to be an in-depth study of Frances Harper, the nineteenth-century abolitionist poet and novelist. If our emphasis on theoretical criticism continues, critics of the future may have to reclaim the writers we are now ignoring, that is, if they are even aware these artists exist.

I am particularly perturbed by the movement to exalt theory, as well, because of my own adult history. I was an active member of the Black Arts Movement of the 1960s and know how dangerous theory can become. Many today may not be aware of this, but the Black Arts Movement tried to create Black Literary Theory and in doing so became prescriptive. My fear is that when Theory is not rooted in practice, it becomes prescriptive, exclusive, elitist.

An example of this prescriptiveness is the approach the Black Arts Movement took towards language. For it, blackness resided in the use of black talk which they defined as hip urban language. So that when Nikki Giovanni reviewed Paule Marshall's *Chosen Place, Timeless People,* she criticized the novel on the grounds that it was not black, for the language was too elegant, too white.[5] Blacks, she said, did not speak that way. Having come from the West Indies where we do, some of the time, speak that way, I was amazed by the narrowness of her vision. The emphasis on *one way* to be black resulted in the works of Southern writers being seen as non-black since the black talk of Georgia does not sound like the black talk of Philadelphia. Because the ideologues, like Baraka, came from the urban centers, they tended to privilege their way of speaking, thinking, writing, and to condemn other kinds of writing as not being black enough. Whole areas of the canon were assessed according to the dictum of the Black Arts Nationalist point of view, as in Addison Gayle's *The Way of the New World,* while other works were ignored because they did not fit the scheme of cultural nationalism.[6] Older writers like Ralph Ellison and James Baldwin were condemned because they saw that the intersection of Western and African influences resulted in a new Afro-American culture, a position with which many of the Black Nationalist ideologues disagreed. Writers were told that writing love poems was not being black. Further examples abound.

It is true that the Black Arts Movement resulted in a necessary and important critique both of previous Afro-American literature and of the white-established literary world. But in attempting to take over power, it, as Ishmael Reed satirizes so well in *Mumbo Jumbo,* became much like its opponent, monolithic and downright repressive.[7]

It is this tendency towards the monolithic, monotheistic, and so on, that worries me about the race for theory. Constructs like the *center* and the *periphery* reveal that tendency to want to make the world less complex by organizing it according to one principle, to fix it through an idea which is really an ideal. Many of us are particularly sensitive to monolithism because one major element of ideologies of dominance, such as sexism and racism, is to dehumanize people by stereotyping them, by denying them their variousness and complexity. Inevitably, monolithism becomes a meta-system, in which there is a controlling ideal, especially in relation to pleasure. Language as one form of pleasure is immediately restricted, and becomes heavy, abstract, prescriptive, monotonous.

Variety, multiplicity, eroticism are difficult to control. And it may very well be that these are the reasons why writers are often seen as *persona non grata* by political states, whatever form they take, since writers/artists have a tendency to refuse to give up their way of seeing the world and of playing with possibilities; in fact, their very expression relies on that insistence. Perhaps that is why creative literature, even when written by politically reactionary people, can be so freeing, for in having to embody ideas and recreate the world, writers cannot merely produce 'one way.'

The characteristics of the Black Arts Movement are, I am afraid, being repeated again today, certainly in the other area to which I am especially tuned. In the race for theory, feminists, eager to enter the halls of power, have attempted their own prescriptions. So often I have read books on feminist literary theory that restrict the definition of what *feminist* means and over-generalize about so much of the world that most women as well as men are excluded. Seldom do feminist theorists take into account the complexity of life—that women are of many races and ethnic backgrounds with different histories and cultures and that as a rule women belong to different classes that have different concerns. Seldom do they note these distinctions, because if they did they could not articulate a theory. Often as a way of clearing themselves they do acknowledge that women of color, for example, do exist, then go on to do what they were going to do anyway, which is to invent a theory that has little relevance for us.

That tendency towards monolithism is precisely how I see the French feminist theorists. They concentrate on the female body as the means to creating a female language, since language, they say, is male and necessarily conceives of woman as other.[8] Clearly many of them have been irritated by the theories of Lacan for whom language is phallic. But suppose there are peoples in the world whose language was invented primarily in relation to women, who after all are the ones who relate to children and teach language. Some Native American languages, for example, use female pronouns when speaking about non-gender-specific activity. Who knows who, according to gender, created languages. Further, by positing the body as the source of everything French feminists return to the old myth that biology determines everything and ignore the fact that gender is a social rather than a biological construct.

I could go on critiquing the positions of French feminists who are themselves more various in their points of view than the label which is used to describe them, but that is not my point. What I am concerned about is the authority this school now has in feminist scholarship—the way it has become *authoritative discourse,* monologic, which occurs precisely because it does have access to the means of promulgating its ideas. The Black Arts Movement was able to do this for a time because of the political movements of the 1960s—so too with the French feminists who could not be inventing 'theory' if a space had not been created by the women's movement. In both cases, both groups posited a theory that excluded many of the people who made that space possible. Hence one of the reasons for the surge of Afro-American women's writing during the 1970s and its emphasis on sexism in the black community is precisely that when the ideologues of the 1960s said *black,* they meant *black male.*[9]

I and many of my sisters do not see the world as being so simple. And perhaps that is why we have not rushed to create abstract theories. For we know there are countless women of color, both in America and in the rest of the world, to whom our singular ideas would be applied. There is, therefore, a caution we feel about pronouncing black feminist theory that might be seen as a decisive statement about Third World women. This is not to say we are not theorizing. Certainly our literature is an indication of the ways in which our theorizing, of necessity, is based on our multiplicity of experiences.

There is at least one other lesson I learned from the Black Arts Movement. One reason for its monolithic approach had to do with its desire to destroy the power which controlled black people, but it was a power which many of its ideologues wished to achieve. The nature of our context today is such that an approach which desires power singlemindedly must of necessity become like that which it wishes to destroy. Rather than wanting to change the whole model, many of us want to be at the center. It is this point of view that writers like June Jordan and Audre Lorde continually critique even as they call for empowerment, as they emphasize the fear of difference among us and our need for leaders rather than a reliance on ourselves.

For one must distinguish the desire for power from the need to become empowered—that is, seeing oneself as capable of and having the right to determine one's life. Such empowerment is partially derived from a knowledge of history. The Black Arts Movement did result in the creation of Afro-American Studies as a concept, thus giving it a place in the university where one might engage in the reclamation of Afro-American history and culture and pass it on to others. I am particularly concerned that institutions such as black studies and women's studies, fought for with such vigor and at some sacrifice, are not often seen as important by many of our black or women scholars precisely because the old hierarchy of traditional departments is seen as superior to these "marginal" groups. Yet, it is in this context that many others of us are discovering the extent of our complexity, the interrelationships of different areas of knowledge in relation to a distinctly Afro-American or female experience. Rather than having to view our world as subordinate to others, or rather than having to work as if we were hybrids, we can pursue ourselves as subjects.

My major objection to the race for theory, as some readers have probably guessed by now, really hinges on the question, 'For whom are we doing what we are doing when we do literary criticism?' It is, I think, the central question today, especially for the few of us who have infiltrated academia enough to be wooed by it. The answer to that question determines what orientation we take in our work, the language we use, the purposes for which it is intended.

I can only speak for myself. But what I write and how I write is done in order to save my own life.[10] And I mean that literally. For me literature is a way of knowing that I am not hallucinating, that whatever I feel/know *is*. It is an affirmation that sensuality is intelligence, that sensual language is language that makes sense. My response, then, is directed to those who write what I read and to those who read what I read—put conconcretely—to Toni

Morrison and to people who read Toni Morrison (among whom I would count few academics). That number is increasing, as is the readership of Walker and Marshall. But in no way is the literature Morrison, Marshall, or Walker create supported by the academic world. Nor given the political context of our society, do I expect that to change soon. For there is no reason, given who controls these institutions, for them to be anything other than threatened by these writers.

My readings do presuppose a need, a desire among folk who like me also want to save their own lives. My concern, then, is a passionate one, for the literature of people who are not in power has always been in danger of extinction or of co-optation, not because we do not theorize, but because what we can even imagine, far less who we can reach, is constantly limited by societal structures. For me, literary criticism is promotion as well as understanding, a response to the writer to whom there is often no response, to folk who need the writing as much as they need anything. I know, from literary history, that writing disappears unless there is a response to it. Because I write about writers who are now writing, I hope to help ensure that their tradition has continuity and survives.

So my 'method,' to use a new 'lit. crit.' word, is not fixed but relates to what I read and to the historical context of the writers I read *and* to the many critical activities in which I am engaged, which may or may not involve writing. It is a learning from the language of creative writers, which is one of surprise, so that I might discover what language I might use. For my language is very much based on what I read and how it affects me, that is, on the surprise that comes from reading something that compels you to read differently, as I believe literature does. I, therefore, have no set method, another prerequisite of the new theory, since for me every work suggests a new approach. As risky as that might seem, it is, I believe, what intelligence means—a tuned sensitivity to that which is alive and therefore cannot be known until it is known. Audre Lorde puts it in a far more succinct and sensual way in her essay 'Poetry is not a luxury':

> As they become known to and accepted by us, our feelings and the honest exploration of them become sanctuaries and spawning grounds for the most radical and daring of ideas. They become a safe-house for that difference so necessary to change and the conceptualization of any meaningful action. Right now, I could name at least ten ideas I would have found intolerable or incomprehensible and frightening, except as they came after dreams and poems. This is not idle fantasy, but a disci-

plined attention to the true meaning of 'it feels right to me.' We can train ourselves to respect our feelings and to transpose them into a language so they can be shared. And where that language does not yet exist, it is our poetry which helps to fashion it. Poetry is not only dream and vision; it is the skeleton architecture of our lives. It lays the foundations for a future of change, a bridge across our fears of what has never been before.[11]

Notes

1 For another view of the debate this 'privileged' approach to Afro-American texts has engendered, see Joyce A. Joyce, " 'Who the Cap Fit:' Unconsciousness and Unconscionableness in the Criticism of Houston A. Baker, Jr. and Henry Louis Gates, Jr.," *New Literary History*, 18 (1987), 371–84. I had not read Joyce's essay before I wrote my own. Clearly there are differences between Joyce's view and my own.

2 This paper was originally written for a conference at the University of California at Berkeley entitled "Minority Discourse" and held on 29–31 May 1986.

3 See Ralph Ellison, *Shadow and Act* (New York, 1964); Robert M. Farnsworth, Introduction to Charles Chestnutt, *The Marrow of Tradition* (Ann Arbor, 1969); Addison Gayle, Jr., ed., *The Black Aesthetic* (Garden City, N.Y., 1971); LeRoi Jones, *Home: Social Essays* (New York, 1966); Larry Neal, "The Black Arts Movement," in this volume, 184–98; Alice Walker, "In Search of Zora Neale Hurston," *MS*, 3.9 (March 1975); and Richard Wright, "A Blueprint for Negro Writing," in this volume, 97–106.

4 Alice Walker, *The Color Purple* (New York, 1982). The controversy surrounding the novel and the subsequent film are discussed in Calvin Hernton, *The Sexual Mountain and Black Women Writers* (New York, 1987), chapters 1 and 2.

5 Nikki Giovanni, Review of Paul Marshall, *Chosen Place, Timeless People*, *Negro Digest* 19:3 (January 1970), 51–52, 84.

6 Addison Gayle, Jr., *The Way of the New World: The Black Novel in America* (Garden City, N.Y., 1975).

7 Ishmael Reed, *Mumbo Jumbo* (Garden City, N.Y., 1972).

8 See Ann Rosalind Jones, "Writing the Body: Toward an Understanding of *L'écriture Féminine*," *Feminist Studies*, 7:2 (Summer 1981), 247–63.

9 See June Jordan, *Civil Wars* (New York, 1966); Audre Lorde, "The Master's Tools Will Never Dismantle the Master's House," in Audre Lorde, *Sister Outsider* (Trumansburg, N.Y., 1984), 110–14.

10 This phrase is taken from the title of one of Alice Walker's essays, "Saving the Life That is Your Own: The Importance of Models in the Artist's Life," in Alice Walker, *In Search of Our Mothers' Gardens: Womanist Prose* (New York, 1983).

11 Audre Lorde, "Poetry is not a Luxury," in *Sister Outsider*.

Michael Awkward

Appropriative Gestures:

Theory and

Afro-American Literary Criticism

(1988)

Barbara Christian's "The Race for Theory" leaves no doubt in the mind of its readers that the esteemed black feminist critic is—in the words of the controversial Stephen Knapp and Walter Benn Michaels essay—against theory. Christian's reaction to theory, however, differs from that of Knapp and Michaels, who seek to discredit theory by discussing what they argue are its fallacious oppositions—meaning/intent, knowledge/belief. She also differs from Afro-American critic Joyce Joyce, who discusses what she views as the ideologically deficient theoretical practice of several black critics in order to demonstrate an incompatibility between practical Afrocentric criticism and contemporary literary theory.[1] For Christian neither systematically attacks what she believes are the inadequacies of its most basic tenets nor attempts to address in specific ways what she holds are the flawed critical practices of Afro-Americanist uses of theory. Instead, Christian asserts that theory is a putatively radical enterprise which has done little to change the *status quo* or advance our comprehension of the processes of literary production, and that its ideologically radical practitioners have been 'co-opted into speaking a language and defining their discussion in terms alien to and opposed to our needs and orientation' (349).

The particulars of Christian's attacks on theory certainly are not original, nor are they, I believe, particularly persuasive. By condemning the discourse of literary theory, calling those who employ theoretical paradigms "critic[s] yearning for attention," and implying that literary theory has gained a significant hold on our attention primarily because "so much of the literature of the West has become pallid, laden with despair, self-indulgent and discon-

This essay first appeared in Linda Kauffman, ed., *Gender and Theory: Dialogues in Feminist Criticism* (New York, 1988).

nected," Christian rehearses old arguments which, frankly, I am not interested in addressing. I am aware of no evidence which convincingly suggests
that today's literary critics are, as a group, any more egotistical than their
predecessors, or that figurations of despair historically have proven any less
analytically provocative than those of any other psychological/emotional
state. What I am interested in exploring—and arguing against—are Christian's specific reasons for viewing as counterproductive the theoretical practice of black feminist criticism and other non-hegemonic—nonwhite male—
schools of literary analysis. For I believe that the strategies of reading which
she deplores offer the Afrocentric critic a means of more fully and adequately
decoding the black literary text and canon than what the critic Daniel O'Hara
might call the "fly-by-the-seat-of-one's-pants"[2] approach Christian advances
at the end of her essay as a corrective to "the race for theory."
   Christian characterizes her own critical practice as an effort to save the
emerging, under-appreciated Afro-American woman's text from the types of
critical marginality and canonical oblivion that had previously been the fate
of early- and mid-twentieth century products of black female imaginations.
Clearly, Christian's preservatory impulses are commendable and historically
well founded. Despite the inroads some Afro-American women's texts have
made in small areas in the canon, black women's literature still does not
assume the prominent place in courses and criticism that those who devote a
great deal of scholarly attention to it feel it merits. I do not, then, object to
the tenets which inform Christian's critical practice, nor do I feel that it is
correct to dismiss out of hand the works of those scholars in the field which
are not obviously informed by post-structuralist theories. The types of rereadings of neglected black women's texts and "first readings" of new works
to which Christian has devoted herself can be, when performed in the energetic manner with which she approaches her work, quite helpful to our
understanding of what she has called "the development of the tradition" of
black women's literature. What I do object to where Christian's discussion of
Afro-American critical engagement of literary theory is concerned is her consistent refusal to acknowledge that its employment by several clearly Afrocentric critics has indeed deepened our received knowledge of the textual
production of black writers.
   Christian sees literary theory as a coercive hegemonic force which has
begun to poison the discourse of "some of our most daring and potentially
radical critics (and by *our* I mean black, women, Third World)" (349) whose
adoption of post-structuralist modes of reading suggests that they "have
been influenced, even co-opted" by a hegemonic critical discourse. While

here, as at most points in her essay, she is unwilling to name victims or villains, Christian suggests that, as an enterprise, literary theory has corrupted a previously methodologically sound black feminist criticism, forcing its practitioners either into silence or into the defensive postures of black female natives invaded by an alien, white, phallocentric critical discourse that they employ against their will and better judgment. While the imagery she uses resonates with historically significant indignation—the black female critic as pure Afrocentric maiden corrupted by an institutionally all-powerful white male post-structuralist theory—Christian's representation of theoretically informed black female (and other noncaucasian and/or male) critics as "co-opted" can only be read as an attack on their personal integrity and recent work. She apparently cannot even conceive of the possibility that these critics *choose* to employ theory because they believe it offers provocative means of discussing the texts of nonhegemonic groups, that theory indeed is viewed by them as useful in the critical analysis of the literary products of "the other."

Further, Christian's "resistance to theory" leads her to overstate her claims about a purely descriptive, nontheoretical stage of black feminist criticism. One of its earlier and most eloquent statements, Barbara Smith's groundbreaking essay "Toward a Black Feminist Criticism," is essentially a theoretical—if not post-structuralist—discussion of critical practice and textual production. In this much-anthologized essay, Smith—like all theorists—prescriptively asserts what she believes ought to be the informing principles of the critics she wants to persuade. She defines the limits of the black feminist interpretive project, telling aspiring black feminist critics how Afro-American women's texts ought to be read and suggesting what sorts of findings such readings ought to uncover. Smith says: "Beginning with a primary commitment to exploring how both sexual and racial politics and Black and female identity are inextricable elements in Black women's writings, she would also work from the assumption that Black women writers constitute an identifiable literary tradition. . . . [S]he would think and write out of her own identity and not try to graft the ideas or methodology of white/male literary thought upon the precise materials of Black women's art" (416–17).

While post-structuralist theorists might intervene here and censure Smith's overdetermined collision of biology and ideology—Smith assumes that the black feminist critic will necessarily be a black woman, that whites and black men are incapable of offering the types of analyses she advocates because they "are of course ill-equipped to deal [simultaneously] with the subtleties of racial [and sexual] politics" (412)[3]—it is in her move from theory to practice that contemporary critical theory could be most helpful to her project. For Smith problematically believes that her (now generally accepted) theoretical suggestions—that one analyze in black women's texts figurations of the relationships between race, gender and class, as well as demonstrate the contours of the black woman's literary tradition—will lead necessarily to critical acts such as her still-controversial reading of Toni Morrison's *Sula* as a lesbian novel. Unlike Deborah McDowell, who in "New Directions for Black Feminist Criticism" argues that the problems with Smith's analysis result from a lack of a precise definition of the term "lesbian" and from the fact that Smith's " 'innovative' analysis is pressed to the service of an individual political persuasion" (432), I feel that the problems with Smith's critical maneuvers lie in her lack of awareness of the contemporary literary theories that Christian devalues. Combined with her own convincingly articulated black feminist approach, an engagement of reader-response theory and theories about the textual construction of gendered/ideological readers might have led Smith to be even more innovative. Rather than arguing that Morrison's is a black lesbian text (a reading to which Morrison herself forcefully objected in a recent interview⁴), she might instead have offered a theory of a *black lesbian reader.* Rather than involving herself needlessly and unprofitably in discussions of authorial intent,⁵ Smith might have focused on the *effects on the reader* of *Sula*'s clear and consistent critique of heterosexual institutions, on the text's progressive "lesbianization" of the reader. Whether Morrison *intends* this is, to a certain extent, beside the point; the point of Smith's theorizing is that such a process does—or at least *can*—indeed occur as a necessary function of careful, ideologically informed reading of Morrison's novel. The problem with the move from practical theory to theoretical practice in "Toward a Black Feminist Criticism" is not, as Christian's perspectives suggest, Smith's attempt to "overgeneralize," to *theorize,* about the process of reading, but her insufficient awareness of advances in reader-response theory that would have allowed her to discuss in a more convincing manner her perceptions of the effects of reading Morrison's novel.

My own intent here is not to discredit Smith's essay, which I believe remains the most influential work in the area of black feminist criticism. Rather, it is to suggest the misconceptions that mar Christian's three most forcefully articulated arguments against a black feminist engagement of literary theory: (1) that black feminist criticism and literary theory are essentially incompatible enterprises; (2) that post-structuralism is the cause of (premature) attempts at black feminist literary theory; and (3) that black feminist literary theory has not—and should not have—emerged before the practice of reading black women's texts is more firmly established. Clearly, Smith's essay—and its careful analysis—serves to challenge the general applicability to black feminist criticism of Christian's suppositions. For Smith's 1977 essay (however problematically) *theorizes* despite its lack of a clearly informed awareness of deconstruction, reader-response theory, semiotics, or any of what Smith terms "the ideas or methodology of white/male literary thought," and does so *while* bemoaning the paucity of black feminist critical acts. Despite an obviously antagonistic relationship to white/male hegemony, Smith believes, like the villainous post-structuralist theorists of Christian's essay, that she can offer a prescription, a theory, of how most profitably to read literary texts.

Unlike Smith, Christian is concerned primarily not with theorizing about profitable means by which to approach Afro-American women's literature, but with "help[ing to] ensure that [the black woman's literary] tradition has continuity and survives" by offering "first readings" of new works by Afro-American women. As a consequence, she perceives as quite problematic the insistence that black feminist critics devise theoretical ways of approaching the Afro-American woman's literary tradition. She says:

> Some of us are continually harassed to invent wholesale theories regardless of the complexity of the literature we study. I, for one, am tired of being asked to produce a black feminist literary theory as if I were a mechanical man. For I believe such theory is prescriptive—it ought to have some relationship to practice. Since I can count on one hand the number of people attempting to be black feminist literay critics in the world today, I consider it presumptuous of me to invent a theory of how we *ought* to read. (350)

Certainly Christian's anger is justified if, as she suggests, the requests she has received to offer theoretical models adequate to a discussion of black women's literature have indeed taken the form of intellectual harassment. But she can argue that critical practice in the last fifteen years has not adequately prepared the way for new theories of black women's textual production only by being as restrictive in her definition of "black feminist literary critics" as she accuses feminist literary theorists of being when they define the term "feminist." (Are black feminist critics only black women? If so, they number much more than a handful. Can a gendered and/or racial other learn the ideology, speak the discourse, of "black feminist literary critics"? If not, how should we label such essential works on black women writers as Robert

Hemenway's biography of Zora Neale Hurston, Barbara Johnson's essays on Hurston, Calvin Hernton's *The Sexual Mountain* and *Black Women Writers?*) A multitude of readings—by black and white women and men—have appeared in journals, collections of essays, and books that analyze black women's texts in terms of "the intricacies of the intersection of language, class, race, and gender," enough at least to suggest to Christian, as it has to other black female critics, that black feminist criticism has reached an appropriate time in its history to begin theorizing about its practice and the literary production of Afro-American woman writers.

In *The Resistance to Theory,* Paul de Man suggests:

Literary theory can be said to come into being when the approach to literary texts is no longer based on non-linguistic, that is to say historical and aesthetic, considerations or, to put it somewhat less crudely, when the object of discussion is no longer the meaning or the value but the modalities of production and of reception of meaning and of value prior to their establishment. (7)

I believe that the time has indeed arrived for the black feminist critical move beyond simply "non-linguistic" analyses of the texts of black women writers. As illuminating as a Barbara Christian "first reading" of Toni Morrison's *Beloved* or of new works by Gloria Naylor, Paule Marshall, Alice Walker, Ntozake Shange and Toni Cade Bambara would undoubtedly prove, such readings will do little to insure the survival of the black women's literary tradition. I firmly believe that the tradition's critical establishment has in the past required, and still requires, such self-consciously preservatory acts. But if the literature of black women is to continue to make inroads in the canon, if it is to gain the respect it doubtlessly deserves as an ideologically and aesthetically complex, analytically rich literary tradition within an increasingly theoretical academy, it will require that its critics continue to move beyond description and master the discourse of contemporary literary theory.

I do not mean that Christian must herself undergo a miraculous change in perspective and become a Derridean, Foucauldian or Barthesian poststructuralist critic. I do believe, however, that literary theory provides Afro-Americans and other nonhegemonic groups with a means by which to begin to offer other, currently even more essential, types of responses: text-specific theories of the modalities of black textual production. Whatever the strictly personal or specifically "tribal" uses to which members of oppressed groups put their writers' texts, I believe it is the literary critic's responsibility—whenever he or she acts in the role of critic—to discuss such works in as full, complex, and sophisticated ways as possible. Henry Louis Gates, Jr. states his view of this responsibility in the following way:

> This is the challenge of the critic of black literature in the 1980s: not to shy away from literary theory; rather, to translate it into the black idiom, *renaming* principles of criticism where appropriate, but especially *naming* indigenous black principles of criticism and applying these to explicate our own texts. It is incumbent upon us to protect the integrity of our tradition by bringing to bear upon its criticism any tool of sensitivity to language that is appropriate . . . *any* tool that enables the critic to explain the complex workings of the language of a text.[6] (xxi)

Zora Neale Hurston has argued that the Afro-American is an "appropriative" creature, that "while he lives and moves in the midst of a white civilization, everything he touches is re-interpreted for his own use" (86). Certainly one of the means by which Afro-Americans have, in Christian's words, "managed to survive with such spiritedness the assault on our bodies, social institutions, countries, our very humanity" has been by successfully appropriating putatively superior Western cultural and expressive systems—Christianity, the English language, Western literary genres—and transferring them into forms through which we expressed our culturally distinct black souls. It is this history that suggests that we need not stand before even the most apparently obscure literary theories as silenced, confused, and discursively "blocked" victims of recent developments in the study of literary texts. Literary theory is, despite its origins and white androcentric uses to which it has generally been put, a tool that Afro-American critics can—and have begun to—successfully employ in explications of our own traditions' texts and intertexts. To continue to assert, despite its wonderfully provocative and *useful* employment by figures such as Gates, Hortense Spillers, Houston Baker, and Mary Helen Washington, that literary theory cannot serve the best, *blackest* interests of our literary tradition is to devalue in significant ways these critics' recent contributions to our understanding of black textual production. Such critics have demonstrated irrefutably that theory can be appropriated in ways that will allow us to continue to further our comprehension of Afro-American texts, and to insure both their survival and their impact.

Notes

1   See Steven Knapp and Walter Benn Michaels, "Against Theory," in W. J. T. Mitchell, ed., *Against Theory: Literary Studies and the New Pragmatism* (Chicago, 1985); and Joyce A. Joyce, "The Black Canon: Reconstructing Black American Literary Criticism," *New Literary History* 18:2, 335–44.

2   In *Against Theory.*

3   For a fuller discussion of this collision of biology and ideology in black feminist criticism, see my 1988 essay "Race, Gender, and the Politics of Reading," *Black American Literature Forum* 22:1 (1988), 5–27.

4   In her interview collected in Claudia Tate, ed., *Black Women Writers at Work* (New York, 1983), Morrison asserts—obviously with Smith's comments in mind: "Nobody ever talked about friendship between women unless it was homosexual, and there is no homosexuality in *Sula,*" 118.

5   The problems with Smith's discussion of *Sula* are most glaringly manifested in her attempts to distinguish between textual meaning and authorial intent. She argues that despite the novel's "consistently critical stance toward the heterosexual institutions of male-female relationships, marriage, and the family," 175, Morrison's failure to "approach . . . her subject with the consciousness that a lesbian relationship was at least a possibility for her characters' results from the novelist's overdetermined heterosexual assumptions [that] can veil what may logically be expected to occur in a work," 181.

6   Henry Louis Gates, Jr., *Figures in Black* (New York, 1987).

Toni Morrison

Unspeakable Things Unspoken: The Afro-American

Presence in American Literature

(1989)

planned to call this paper "Canon Fodder," because the terms put me in
mind of a kind of trained muscular response that appears to be on display
in some areas of the recent canon debate. But I changed my mind (so many
have used the phrase) and hope to make clear the appropriateness of the title
I settled on.

My purpose here is to observe the panoply of this most recent and most
anxious series of questions concerning what should or does constitute a
literary canon in order to suggest ways of addressing the Afro-American
presence in American literature that require neither slaughter nor reification—views that may spring the whole literature of an entire nation from the
solitude into which it has been locked. There is something called American
literature that, according to conventional wisdom, is certainly not Chicano
literature, or Afro-American literature, or Asian-American, or Native American, or . . . It is somehow separate from them and they from it, and in spite
of the efforts of recent literary histories, restructured curricula and anthologies, this separate confinement, be it breached or endorsed, is the subject of a
large part of these debates. Although the terms used, like the vocabulary of
earlier canon debates, refer to literary and/or humanistic value, aesthetic
criteria, value-free or socially anchored readings, the contemporary battle
plain is most often understood to be the claims of others against the whitemale origins and definitions of those values; whether those definitions reflect
an eternal, universal and transcending paradigm or whether they constitute
a disguise for a temporal, political and culturally specific program.

Part of the history of this particular debate is located in the successful

This essay first appeared in *Michigan Quarterly Review* (Winter 1989): 1–34.

assault that the feminist scholarship of men and women (black and white) made and continues to make on traditional literary discourse. The male part of the whitemale equation is already deeply engaged, and no one believes the body of literature and its criticism will ever again be what it was in 1965: the protected preserve of the thoughts and works and analytical strategies of whitemen.

It is, however, the "white" part of the question that this paper focuses on, and it is to my great relief that such terms as "white" and "race" can enter serious discussion of literature. Although still a swift and swiftly obeyed call to arms, their use is no longer forbidden.[1] It may appear churlish to doubt the sincerity, or question the proclaimed well-intentioned self-lessness of a nine-hundred-year-old academy struggling through decades of chaos to "maintain standards." Yet of what use is it to go on about "quality" being the only criterion for greatness knowing that the definition of quality is itself the subject of much rage and is seldom universally agreed upon by everyone at all times? Is it to appropriate the term for reasons of state; to be in the position to distribute greatness or withhold it? Or to actively pursue the ways and places in which quality surfaces and stuns us into silence or into language worthy enough to describe it? What is possible is to try to recognize, identify and applaud the fight for and triumph of quality when it is revealed to us and to let go the notion that only the dominant culture or gender can make those judgments, identify that quality or produce it.

Those who claim the superiority of Western culture are entitled to that claim only when Western civilization is measured thoroughly against other civilizations and not found wanting, and when Western civilization owns up to its own sources in the cultures that preceded it.

A large part of the satisfaction I have always received from reading Greek tragedy, for example, is in its similarity to Afro-American communal structures (the function of song and chorus, the heroic struggle between the claims of community and individual hubris) and African religion and philosophy. In other words, that is part of the reason it has quality for me—I feel intellectually at home there. But that could hardly be so for those unfamiliar with my "home," and hardly a requisite for the pleasure they take. The point is, the form (Greek tragedy) makes available these varieties of provocative love because it is masterly—not because the civilization that is its referent was flawless or superior to all others.

One has the feeling that nights are becoming sleepless in some quarters, and it seems to me obvious that the recoil of traditional "humanists" and some postmodern theorists to this particular aspect of the debate, the "race" aspect, is as severe as it is because the claims for attention come from that segment of scholarly and artistic labor in which the mention of "race" is either inevitable or elaborately, painstakingly masked; and if all of the ramifications that the term demands are taken seriously, the bases of Western civilization will require re-thinking. Thus, in spite of its implicit and explicit acknowledgement, "race" is still a virtually unspeakable thing, as can be seen in the apologies, notes of "special use" and circumscribed definitions that accompany it[2]—not least of which is my own deference in surrounding it with quotation marks. Suddenly (for our purposes, suddenly) "race" does not exist. For three hundred years black Americans insisted that "race" was no usefully distinguishing factor in human relationships. During those same three centuries every academic discipline, including theology, history, and natural science, insisted "race" was *the* determining factor in human development. When blacks discovered they had shaped or become a culturally formed race, and that it had specific and revered difference, suddenly they were told there is no such thing as "race," biological or cultural, that matters and that genuinely intellectual exchange cannot accommodate it.[3] In trying to come to some terms about "race" and writing, I am tempted to throw my hands up. It always seemed to me that the people who invented the hierarchy of "race" when it was convenient for them ought not to be the ones to explain it away, now that it does not suit their purposes for it to exist. But there *is* culture and both gender and "race" inform and are informed by it. Afro-American culture exists and though it is clear (and becoming clearer) how it has responded to Western culture, the instances where and means by which it has shaped Western culture are poorly recognized or understood.

I want to address ways in which the presence of Afro-American literature and the awareness of its culture both resuscitate the study of literature in the United States and raise that study's standards. In pursuit of that goal, it will suit my purposes to contextualize the route canon debates have taken in Western literary criticism.

I do not believe this current anxiety can be attributed solely to the routine, even cyclical arguments within literary communities reflecting unpredictable yet inevitable shifts in taste, relevance or perception. Shifts in which an enthusiasm for and official endorsement of William Dean Howells, for example, withered; or in which the legalization of Mark Twain in critical court rose and fell like the fathoming of a sounding line (for which he may or may not have named himself); or even the slow, delayed but steady swell of attention and devotion on which Emily Dickinson soared to what is now, surely, a permanent crest of respect. No. Those were discoveries, reappraisals of individual artists. Serious but not destabilizing. Such accommodations were simple because the questions they posed were simple: Are there one hundred sterling examples of high literary art in American literature and no more? One hundred and six? If one or two fall into disrepute, is there space, then, for one or two others in the vestibule, waiting like girls for bells chimed by future husbands who alone can promise them security, legitimacy—and in whose hands alone rests the gift of critical longevity? Interesting questions, but, as I say, not endangering.

Nor is this detectable academic sleeplessness the consequence of a much more radical shift, such as the mid-nineteenth century one heralding the authenticity of American literature itself. Or an even earlier upheaval—receding now into the distant past—in which theology and thereby Latin, was displaced for the equally rigorous study of the classics and Greek to be followed by what was considered a strangely arrogant and upstart proposal: that English literature was a suitable course of study for an aristocratic education, and not simply morally instructive fodder designed for the working classes. (The Chaucer Society was founded in 1848, four hundred years after Chaucer died.) No. This exchange seems unusual somehow, keener. It has a more strenuously argued (and felt) defense and a more vigorously insistent attack. And both defenses and attacks have spilled out of the academy into the popular press. Why? Resistance to displacement within or expansion of a canon is not, after all, surprising or unwarranted. That's what canonization is for. (And the question of whether there should be a canon or not seems disingenuous to me—there always is one whether there should be or not—for it is in the interests of the professional critical community to have one.) Certainly a sharp alertness as to *why* a work is or is not worthy of study is the legitimate occupation of the critic, the pedagogue and the artist. What is astonishing in the contemporary debate is not the resistance to displacement of works or to the expansion of genre within it, but the virulent passion that accompanies this resistance and, more importantly, the quality of its defense weaponry. The guns are very big; the trigger-fingers quick. But I am convinced the mechanism of the defenders of the flame is faulty. Not only may the hands of the gun-slinging cowboy-scholars be blown off, not only may the target be missed, but the subject of the conflagration (the sacred texts) is sacrificed, disfigured in the battle. This canon fodder may kill the canon. And I, at least, do not intend to live without Aeschylus or William Shakespeare, or James or Twain or Hawthorne, or Melville, etc., etc., etc.

There must be some way to enhance canon readings without enshrining them.

When Milan Kundera, in *The Art of the Novel*, identified the historical territory of the novel by saying "The novel is Europe's creation" and that "The only context for grasping a novel's worth is the history of the European novel," the *New Yorker* reviewer stiffened. Kundera's "personal 'idea of the novel,'" he wrote,

> is so profoundly Eurocentric that it's likely to seem exotic, even perverse, to American readers. . . . *The Art of the Novel* gives off the occasional (but pungent) whiff of cultural arrogance, and we may feel that Kundera's discourse . . . reveals an aspect of his character that we'd rather not have known about. . . . In order to become the artist he now is, the Czech novelist had to discover himself a second time, as a European. But what if that second, grander possibility hadn't been there to be discovered? What if Broch, Kafka, Musil—all that reading—had never been a part of his education, or had entered it only as exotic, alien presence? Kundera's polemical fervor in *The Art of the Novel* annoys us, as American readers, because we feel defensive, excluded from the transcendent 'idea of the novel' that for him seems simply to have been there for the taking. (If only he had cited, in his redeeming version of the novel's history, a few more heroes from the New World's culture.) Our novelists don't discover cultural values within themselves; they invent them.[4]

Kundera's views, obliterating American writers (with the exception of William Faulkner) from his own canon, are relegated to a "smugness" that Terrence Rafferty disassociates from Kundera's imaginative work and applies to the "sublime confidence" of his critical prose. The confidence of an exile who has the sentimental education of, and the choice to become, a European.

I was refreshed by Rafferty's comments. With the substitution of certain phrases, his observations and the justifiable umbrage he takes can be appropriated entirely by Afro-American writers regarding their own exclusion from the "transcendent 'idea of the novel.'"

For the present turbulence seems not to be about the flexibility of a canon, its range among and between Western countries, but about its miscegenation. The word is informative here and I do mean its use. A powerful ingredient in this debate concerns the incursion of third-world or so-called minority literature into a Eurocentric stronghold. When the topic of third world culture is raised, unlike the topic of Scandinavian culture, for example, a possible threat to and implicit criticism of the reigning equilibrium is seen to be raised as well. From the seventeenth century to the twentieth, the arguments resisting that incursion have marched in predictable sequence: (1) there is no Afro-American (or third world) art. (2) it exists but is inferior. (3) it exists and is superior when it measures up to the "universal" criteria of Western art. (4) it is not so much "art" as ore—rich ore—that requires a Western or Eurocentric smith to refine it from its "natural" state into an aesthetically complex form.

A few comments on a larger, older, but no less telling academic struggle—an extremely successful one—may be helpful here. It is telling because it sheds light on certain aspects of this current debate and may locate its sources. I made reference above to the radical upheaval in canon-building that took place at the inauguration of classical studies and Greek. This canonical rerouting from scholasticism to humanism, was not merely radical, it must have been (may I say it?) savage. And it took some seventy years to accomplish. Seventy years to eliminate Egypt as the cradle of civilization *and* its model and replace it with Greece. The triumph of that process was that Greece lost its own origins and became itself original. A number of scholars in various disciplines (history, anthropology, ethnobotany, etc.) have put forward their research into cross-cultural and intercultural transmissions with varying degrees of success in the reception of their work. I am reminded of the curious publishing history of Ivan van Sertima's work, *They Came Before Columbus,* which researches the African presence in Ancient America. I am reminded of Edward Said's *Orientalism,* and especially the work of Martin Bernal, a linguist, trained in Chinese history, who has defined himself as an interloper in the field of classical civilization but who has offered, in *Black Athena,* a stunning investigation of the field. According to Bernal, there are two "models" of Greek history: one views Greece as Aryan or European (the Aryan Model); the other sees it as Levantine—absorbed by Egyptian and Semitic culture (the Ancient Model). "If I am right," writes Professor Bernal, "in urging the overthrow of the Aryan Model and its replacement by the Revised Ancient one, it will be necessary not only to rethink the fundamental bases of 'Western Civilization' but also to recognize the penetration of racism and 'continental chauvinism' into all our historiography, or philosophy of writing history. The Ancient Model had no major 'internal' deficiencies or weaknesses in explanatory power. It was overthrown for external reasons.

For eighteenth and nineteenth century Romantics and racists it was simply intolerable for Greece, which was seen not merely as the epitome of Europe but also as its pure childhood, to have been the result of the mixture of native Europeans and *colonizing* Africans and Semites. Therefore the Ancient Model had to be overthrown and replaced by something more acceptable."[5]

It is difficult not to be persuaded by the weight of documentation Martin Bernal brings to his task and his rather dazzling analytical insights. What struck me in his analysis were the *process* of the fabrication of Ancient Greece and the *motives* for the fabrication. The latter (motive) involved the concept of purity, of progress. The former (process) required misreading, predetermined selectivity of authentic sources, and—silence. From the Christian theological appropriation of Israel (the Levant), to the early nineteenth-century work of the prodigious Karl Müller, work that effectively dismissed the Greeks' own record of their influences and origins as their "Egypto-mania," their tendency to be "wonderstruck" by Egyptian culture, a tendency "manifested in the 'delusion' that Egyptians and other non-European 'barbarians' had possessed superior cultures, from which the Greeks had borrowed massively,"[6] on through the Romantic response to the Enlightenment, and the decline into disfavor of the Phoenicians, "the essential force behind the rejection of the tradition of massive Phoenician influence on early Greece was the rise of racial—as opposed to religious—anti-semitism. This was because the Phoenicians were correctly perceived to have been culturally very close to the Jews."[7]

I have quoted at perhaps too great a length from Bernal's text because *motive,* so seldom an element brought to bear on the history of history, is located, delineated and confronted in Bernal's research, and has helped my own thinking about the process and motives of scholarly attention to and an appraisal of Afro-American presence in the literature of the United States.

Canon building is Empire building. Canon defense is national defense. Canon debate, whatever the terrain, nature and range (of criticism, of history, of the history of knowledge, of the definition of language, the universality of aesthetic principles, the sociology of art, the humanistic imagination), is the clash of cultures. And *all* of the interests are vested.

In such a melee as this one—a provocative, healthy, explosive melee—extraordinarily profound work is being done. Some of the controversy, however, has degenerated into *ad hominem* and unwarranted speculation on the personal habits of artists, specious and silly arguments about politics (the destabilizing forces are dismissed as merely political; the status quo sees itself as not—as though the term "*a*political" were only its prefix and not the most obviously political stance imaginable since one of the functions of political ideology is to pass itself off as immutable, natural and "innocent"), and covert expressions of critical inquiry designed to neutralize and disguise the political interests of the discourse. Yet much of the research and analysis has rendered speakable what was formerly unspoken and has made humanistic studies, once again, the place where one has to go to find out what's going on. Cultures, whether silenced or monologistic, whether repressed or repressing, seek meaning in the language and images available to them.

Silences are being broken, lost things have been found and at least two generations of scholars are disentangling received knowledge from the apparatus of control, most notably those who are engaged in investigations of French and British Colonialist Literature, American slave narratives, and the delineation of the Afro-American literary tradition.

Now that Afro-American artistic presence has been "discovered" actually to exist, now that serious scholarship has moved from silencing the witnesses and erasing their meaningful place in and contribution to American culture, it is no longer acceptable merely to imagine us and imagine for us. We have always been imagining ourselves. We are not Isak Dinesen's "aspects of nature," nor Conrad's unspeaking. We are the subjects of our own narrative, witnesses to and participants in our own experience, and, in no way coincidentally, in the experience of those with whom we have come in contact. We are not, in fact, "other." We are choices. And to read imaginative literature by and about us is to choose to examine centers of the self and to have the opportunity to compare these centers with the "raceless" one with which we are, all of us, most familiar.

II

Recent approaches to the reading of Afro-American literature have come some distance; have addressed those arguments, mentioned earlier, (which are not arguments, but attitudes) that have, since the seventeenth century, effectively silenced the autonomy of that literature. As for the charge that "there is no Afro-American art," contemporary critical analysis of the literature and the recent surge of reprints and rediscoveries have buried it, and are pressing on to expand the traditional canon to include classic Afro-American works where generically and chronologically appropriate, and to devise strategies for reading and thinking about these texts.

As to the second silencing charge, "Afro-American art exists, but is inferior," again, close readings and careful research into the culture out of which the art is born have addressed and still address the labels that once passed for stringent analysis but can no more: that it is imitative, excessive, sensational, mimetic (merely), and unintellectual, though very often "moving," "passionate," "naturalistic," "realistic" or sociologically "revealing." These labels may be construed as compliments or pejoratives and if valid, and shown as such, so much the better. More often than not, however, they are the lazy, easy brand-name applications when the hard work of analysis is deemed too hard, or when the critic does not have access to the scope the work demands. Strategies designed to counter this lazy labeling include the application of recent literary theories to Afro-American literature so that noncanonical texts can be incorporated into existing and forming critical discourse.

The third charge, that "Afro-American art exists, but is superior only when it measures up to the 'universal' criteria of Western art," produces the most seductive form of analysis, for both writer and critic, because comparisons are a major form of knowledge and flattery. The risks, nevertheless, are twofold: (1) the gathering of a culture's difference into the skirts of the Queen is a neutralization designed and constituted to elevate and maintain hegemony. (2) circumscribing and limiting the literature to a mere reaction to or denial of the Queen, judging the work solely in terms of its referents to Eurocentric criteria, or its sociological accuracy, political correctness or its pretense of having no politics at all, cripple the literature and infantilize the serious work of imaginative writing. This response-oriented concept of Afro-American literature contains the seeds of the next (fourth) charge: that when Afro-American art is worthy, it is because it is "raw" and "rich," like ore, and like ore needs refining by Western intelligences. Finding or imposing Western influences in/on Afro-American literature has value, but when its sole purpose is to *place* value only where that influence is located it is pernicious.

My unease stems from the possible, probable, consequences these approaches may have upon the work itself. They can lead to an incipient orphanization of the work in order to issue its adoption papers. They can confine the discourse to the advocacy of diversification within the canon and/or a kind of benign coexistence near or within reach of the already sacred texts. Either of these two positions can quickly become another kind of silencing if permitted to ignore the indigenous created qualities of the writing. So many questions surface and irritate. What have these critiques made of the work's own canvas? Its paint, its frame, its framelessness, its spaces? Another list of approved subjects? Of approved treatments? More self-censoring, more exclusion of the specificity of the culture, the gender, the language? Is there perhaps an alternative utility in these studies? To advance power or locate its fissures? To oppose elitist interests in order to enthrone egalitarian effacement? Or is it merely to rank and grade the readable product as distinct from the writeable production? Can this criticism reveal ways in which the author combats and confronts received prejudices and even creates *other terms* in which to rethink one's attachment to or intolerance of the material of these works? What is important in all of this is that the critic not be engaged in laying claim on behalf of the text to his or her own dominance and power. Nor to exchange his or her professional anxieties for the imagined turbulence of the text. "The text should become a problem of passion, not a pretext for it."

There are at least three focuses that seem to me to be neither reactionary nor simple pluralism, nor the even simpler methods by which the study of Afro-American literature remains the helpful doorman into the halls of sociology. Each of them, however, requires wakefulness.

One is the development of a theory of literature that truly accommodates Afro-American literature: one that is based on its culture, its history, and the artistic strategies the works employ to negotiate the world it inhabits.

Another is the examination and reinterpretation of the American canon, the founding nineteenth-century works, for the "unspeakable things unspoken"; for the ways in which the presence of Afro-Americans has shaped the choices, the language, the structure—the meaning of so much American literature. A search, in other words, for the ghost in the machine.

A third is the examination of contemporary and/or noncanonical literature for this presence, regardless of its category as mainstream, minority, or what you will. I am always amazed by the resonances, the structural gearshifts, and the *uses* to which Afro-American narrative, persona and idiom are put in contemporary "white" literature. And in Afro-American literature itself the question of difference, of essence, is critical. What makes a work "Black"? The most valuable point of entry into the question of cultural (or racial) distinction, the one most fraught, is its language—its unpoliced, seditious, confrontational, manipulative, inventive, disruptive, masked and unmasking language. Such a penetration will entail the most careful study, one in which the impact of Afro-American presence on modernity becomes clear and is no longer a well-kept secret.

I would like to touch, for just a moment, on focuses two and three.

We can agree, I think, that invisible things are not necessarily "not-there"; that a void may be empty, but is not a vacuum. In addition, certain absences are so stressed, so ornate, so planned, they call attention to themselves; arrest us with intentionality and purpose, like neighborhoods that are defined by the population held away from them. Looking at the scope of American literature, I can't help thinking that the question should never have been "Why am I, an Afro-American, absent from it?" It is not a particularly interesting query anyway. The spectacularly interesting question is "What intellectual feats had to be performed by the author or his critic to erase me from a society seething with my presence, and what effect has that performance had on the work?" What are the strategies of escape from knowledge? Of willful oblivion? I am not recommending an inquiry into the obvious impulse that overtakes a soldier sitting in a World War I trench to think of salmon fishing. That kind of pointed "turning from," deliberate escapism or transcendence may be life-saving in a circumstance of immediate duress. The exploration I am suggesting is, how does one sit in the audience observing, watching the performance of Young America, say, in the nineteenth century, say, and reconstruct the play, its director, its plot and its cast in such a manner that its very point never surfaces? Not why. How? Ten years after Tocqueville's prediction in 1840 that "'Finding no stuff for the ideal in what is real and true, poets would flee to imaginary regions . . .' in 1850 at the height of slavery and burgeoning abolitionism, American writers chose romance."[8] Where, I wonder, in these romances is the shadow of the presence from which the text has fled? Where does it heighten, where does it dislocate, where does it necessitate novelistic invention; what does it release; what does it hobble?

The device (or arsenal) that serves the purpose of flight can be Romanticism versus verisimilitude; new criticism versus shabbily disguised and questionably sanctioned "moral uplift"; the "complex series of evasions," that is sometimes believed to be the essence of modernism; the perception of the evolution of art; the cultivation of irony, parody; the nostalgia for "literary language"; the rhetorically unconstrained textuality versus socially anchored textuality, and the undoing of textuality altogether. These critical strategies can (but need not) be put into service to reconstruct the historical world to suit specific cultural and political purposes. Many of these strategies have produced powerfully creative work. Whatever *uses* to which Romanticism is put, however suspicious its origins, it has produced an incontestably wonderful body of work. In other instances these strategies have succeeded in paralyzing both the work and its criticism. In still others they have led to a virtual infantilization of the writer's intellect, his sensibility, his craft. They have reduced the meditations on theory into a "power struggle among sects" reading unauthored and unauthorable material, rather than an outcome of reading *with* the author the text both construct.

In other words, the critical process has made wonderful work of some wonderful work, and recently the means of access to the old debates have altered. The problem now is putting the question. Is the nineteenth century flight from blackness, for example, successful in mainstream American literature? Beautiful? Artistically problematic? Is the text sabotaged by its own proclamations of "universality"? Are there ghosts in the machine? Active but unsummoned presences that can distort the workings of the machine and can also *make* it work? These kinds of questions have been consistently put by critics of Colonial Literature vis-à-vis Africa and India and other third world countries. American literature would benefit from similar critiques. I am made melancholy when I consider that the act of defending the Eurocentric Western posture in literature as not only "universal" but also "race-free" may have resulted in lobotomizing that literature and in diminishing both the art and the artist. Like the surgical removal of legs so that the body can remain enthroned, immobile, static—under house arrest, so to speak. It may be, of course, that contemporary writers deliberately exclude from their conscious writerly world the subjective appraisal of groups perceived as "other," and whitemale writers frequently abjure and deny the excitement of framing or locating their literature in the political world. Nineteenth-century writers, however, would never have given it a thought. Mainstream writers in Young America understood their competition to be national, cultural, but only in relationship to the Old World, certainly not vis-à-vis an ancient race (whether Native American or African) that was stripped of articulateness and intellectual thought, rendered, in D. H. Lawrence's term, "uncreate." For these early American writers, how could there be competition with nations or peoples who were presumed unable to handle or uninterested in handling the written word? One could write about them, but there was never the danger of their "writing back." Just as one could speak to them without fear of their "talking back." One could even observe them, hold them in prolonged gaze, without encountering the risk of being observed, viewed, or judged in return. And if, on occasion, they were themselves viewed and judged, it was out of a political necessity and, for the purposes of art, could not matter. Or so thought Young America. It could never have occurred to Edgar Allan Poe in 1848 that I, for example, might read *The Gold Bug* and watch his efforts to render my grandfather's speech to something as close to braying as possible, an effort so intense you can see the perspiration—and the stupidity—when Jupiter says "I knows," and Mr. Poe spells the verb "nose."*

Yet in spite or because of this monologism there is a great, ornamental, prescribed absence in early American literature and, I submit, it is instructive. It only seems that the canon of American literature is "naturally" or "inevitably" "white." In fact it is studiously so. In fact these absences of vital presences in Young American literature may be the insistent fruit of the scholarship rather than the text. Perhaps some of these writers, although under current house arrest, have much more to say than has been realized. Perhaps some were not so much transcending politics, or escaping blackness, as they were transforming it into intelligible, accessible, yet artistic modes of discourse. To ignore this possibility by never questioning the strategies of transformation is to disenfranchise the writer, diminish the text and render the bulk of the literature aesthetically and historically incoherent—an exorbitant price for cultural (whitemale) purity, and, I believe, a spendthrift one. The reexamination of founding literature of the United States for the unspeakable unspoken may reveal those texts to have deeper and other meanings, deeper and the power, deeper and other significances.

One such writer, in particular, it has been almost impossible to keep under lock and key is Herman Melville.

Among several astute scholars, Michael Rogin has done one of the most exhaustive studies of how deeply Melville's social thought is woven into his writing. He calls our attention to the connection Melville made between American slavery and American freedom, how heightened the one rendered the other. And he has provided evidence of the impact on the work of Melville's family, milieu, and, most importantly, the raging, all-encompassing conflict of the time: slavery. He has reminded us that it was Melville's father-in-law who had, as judge, decided the case that made the Fugitive Slave Law law, and that "other evidence in *Moby Dick* also suggests the impact of Shaw's ruling on the climax of Melville's tale. Melville conceived the final confrontation between Ahab and the white whale some time in the first half of 1851. He may well have written his last chapters only after returning from a trip to New York in June. [Judge Shaw's decision was handed down in April, 1851]. When New York antislavery leaders William Seward and John van Buren

---

*Author's Note: Older America is not always distinguishable from its infancy. We may pardon Edgar Allan Poe in 1848 but it should have occurred to Kenneth Lynn in 1986 that some young Native American might read his Hemingway biography and see herself described as "squaw" by this respected scholar, and that some young men might shudder reading the words "buck" and "half-breed" so casually included in his scholarly speculations.

wrote public letters protesting the *Sims* ruling, the New York *Herald* responded. Its attack on "The Anti-Slavery Agitators' began: "Did you ever see a whale? Did you ever see a mighty whale struggling?"[9]

Rogin also traces the chronology of the whale from its "birth in a state of nature" to its final end as commodity.[10] Central to his argument is that Melville in *Moby Dick* was being allegorically and insistently political in his choice of the whale. But within his chronology, one singular whale transcends all others, goes beyond nature, adventure, politics and commodity to an abstraction. What is this abstraction? This "wicked idea"? Interpretation has been varied. It has been viewed as an allegory of the state in which Ahab is Calhoun, or Daniel Webster; an allegory of capitalism and corruption, God and man, the individual and fate, and most commonly, the single allegorical meaning of the white whale is understood to be brute, indifferent Nature, and Ahab the madman who challenges that Nature.

But let us consider, again, the principal actor, Ahab, created by an author who calls himself Typee, signed himself Tawney, identified himself as Ishmael, and who had written several books before *Moby Dick* criticizing missionary forays into various paradises.

Ahab loses sight of the commercial value of his ship's voyage, its point, and pursues an idea in order to destroy it. His intention, revenge, "an audacious, immitigable and supernatural revenge," develops stature—maturity—when we realize that he is not a man mourning his lost leg or a scar on his face. However intense and dislocating his fever and recovery had been after his encounter with the white whale, however satisfactorily "male" this vengeance is read, the vanity of it is almost adolescent. But if the whale is more than blind, indifferent Nature unsubduable by masculine aggression, if it is as much its adjective as it is its noun, we can consider the possibility that Melville's "truth" was his recognition of the moment in America when whiteness became ideology. And if the white whale is the ideology of race, what Ahab has lost to it is personal dismemberment and family and society and his own place as a human in the world. The trauma of racism is, for the racist and the victim, the severe fragmentation of the self, and has always seemed to me a cause (not a symptom) of psychosis—strangely of no interest to psychiatry. Ahab, then, is navigating between an idea of civilization that he renounces and an idea of savagery he must annihilate, because the two cannot coexist. The former is based on the latter. What is terrible in its complexity is that the idea of savagery is not the missionary one: it is white racial ideology that is savage and if, indeed, a white, nineteenth-century, American male took on not abolition, not the amelioration of racist institutions or their laws, but the very concept of whiteness as an inhuman idea, he would be very alone, very desperate, and very doomed. Madness would be the only appropriate description of such audacity, and "he heaves me," the most succinct and appropriate description of that obsession.

I would not like to be understood to argue that Melville was engaged in some simple and simple-minded black/white didacticism, or that he was satanizing white people. Nothing like that. What I am suggesting is that he was overwhelmed by the philosophical and metaphysical inconsistencies of an extraordinary and unprecedented idea that had its fullest manifestation in his own time in his own country, and that that idea was the successful assertion of whiteness as ideology.

On the *Pequod* the multiracial, mainly foreign, proletariat is at work to produce a commodity, but it is diverted and converted from that labor to Ahab's more significant intellectual quest. We leave whale as commerce and confront whale as metaphor. With that interpretation in place, two of the most famous chapters of the book become luminous in a completely new way. One is Chapter 9, The Sermon. In Father Mapple's thrilling rendition of Jonah's trials, emphasis is given to the purpose of Jonah's salvation. He is saved from the fish's belly for one single purpose, "To preach the Truth to the face of Falsehood! That was it!" Only then the reward "Delight"—which strongly calls to mind Ahab's lonely necessity. "Delight is to him . . . who against the proud gods and commodores of this earth, ever stand forth his own inexorable self. . . . Delight is to him whose strong arms yet support him, when the ship of this base treacherous world has gone down beneath him. Delight is to him who gives no quarter in the truth and kills, burns, and destroys all *sin* though he pluck it out from under the robes of Senators and Judges. Delight—top-gallant delight is to him who acknowledges no law or lord, but the Lord his God, and is only a *patriot to heaven*" [italics mine]. No one, I think, has denied that the sermon is designed to be prophetic, but it seems unremarked what the nature of the sin is—the sin that must be destroyed, regardless. Nature? A sin? The terms do not apply. Capitalism? Perhaps. Capitalism fed greed, lent itself inexorably to corruption, but probably was not in and of itself sinful to Melville. Sin suggests a moral outrage within the bounds of man to repair. The concept of racial superiority would fit seamlessly. It is difficult to read those words ("destruction of sin," "patriot to heaven") and not hear in them the description of a different Ahab. Not an adolescent male in adult clothing, a maniacal egocentric, or the "exotic plant" that V. S. Parrington thought Melville was. Not even a morally fine liberal voice adjusting, balancing, compromising with racial institutions. But another Ahab: the only white male American heroic enough to try to slay the monster that was devouring the world as he knew it.

Another chapter that seems freshly lit by this reading is Chapter 42, The Whiteness of the Whale. Melville points to the do-or-die significance of his effort to say something unsayable in this chapter. "I almost despair," he writes, "of putting it in a comprehensive form. It was the whiteness of the whale that above all things appalled me. But how can I hope to explain myself here; and yet in some dim, random way, explain myself I must, *else all these chapters might be naught*" [italics mine]. The language of this chapter ranges between benevolent, beautiful images of whiteness and whiteness as sinister and shocking. After dissecting the ineffable, he concludes: "Therefore . . . symbolize whatever grand or gracious he will by whiteness, no man can deny that in its profoundest *idealized significance* it calls up a peculiar apparition to the soul." I stress "idealized significance" to emphasize and make clear (if such clarity needs stating) that Melville is not exploring white *people*, but whiteness idealized. Then, after informing the reader of his "hope to light upon some chance clue to conduct us to the hidden course we seek," he tries to nail it. To provide the key to the "hidden course." His struggle to do so is gigantic. He cannot. Nor can we. But in nonfigurative language, he identifies the imaginative tools needed to solve the problem: "subtlety appeals to subtlety, and without imagination no man can follow another into these halls." And his final observation reverberates with personal trauma. "This visible [colored] world seems formed in love, the invisible [white] spheres were formed in fright." The necessity for whiteness as privileged "natural" state, the invention of it, was indeed formed in fright.

"Slavery," writes Rogin, "confirmed Melville's isolation, decisively established in *Moby Dick*, from the dominant consciousness of his time." I differ on this point and submit that Melville's hostility and repugnance for slavery would have found company. There were many white Americans of his acquaintance who felt repelled by slavery, wrote journalism about it, spoke about it, legislated on it and were active in abolishing it. His attitude to slavery alone would not have condemned him to the almost autistic separation visited upon him. And if he felt convinced that blacks were worthy of being treated like whites, or that capitalism was dangerous—he had company or could have found it. But to question the very notion of white progress, the very idea of racial superiority, of whiteness as privileged place in the evolutionary ladder of humankind, and to meditate on the fraudulent, self-destroying philosophy of that superiority, to "pluck it out from under the robes of Senators and Judges," to drag the "judge himself to the bar,"—that was dangerous, solitary, radical work. Especially then. Especially now. To be "only a patriot to heaven" is no mean aspiration in Young America for a writer—or the captain of a whaling ship.

A complex, heaving, disorderly, profound text is *Moby Dick*, and among its several meanings it seems to me this "unspeakable" one has remained the "hidden course," the "truth in the Face of Falsehood." To this day no novelist has so wrestled with its subject. To this day literary analyses of canonical texts have shied away from that perspective: the informing and determining Afro-American presence in traditional American literature. The chapters I have made reference to are only a fraction of the instances where the text surrenders such insights, and points a helpful finger toward the ways in which the ghost drives the machine.

Melville is not the only author whose works double their fascination and their power when scoured for this presence and the writerly strategies taken to address or deny it. Edgar Allan Poe will sustain such a reading. So will Nathaniel Hawthorne and Mark Twain; and in the twentieth century, Willa Cather, Ernest Hemingway, F. Scott Fitzgerald, and William Faulkner, to name a few. Canonical American literature is begging for such attention.

It seems to me a more than fruitful project to produce some cogent analysis showing instances where early American literature identifies itself, risks itself, to assert its antithesis to blackness. How its linguistic gestures prove the intimate relationship to what is being nulled by implying a full descriptive apparatus (identity) to a presence-that-is-assumed-not-to-exist. Afro-American critical inquiry can do this work.

I mentioned earlier that finding or imposing Western influences in/on Afro-American literature had value provided the valued process does not become self-anointing. There is an adjacent project to be undertaken—the third focus in my list: the examination of contemporary literature (both the sacred and the profane) for the impact Afro-American presence has had on the structure of the work, the linguistic practice, and fictional enterprise in which it is engaged. Like focus two, this critical process must also eschew the pernicious goal of equating the fact of that presence with the achievement of the work. A work does not get better because it is responsive to another culture; nor does it become automatically flawed because of that responsiveness. The point is to clarify, not to enlist. And it does not "go without saying" that a work written by an Afro-American is automatically subsumed by an enforcing Afro-American presence. There is a clear flight from blackness in a great deal of Afro-American literature. In others there is the duel with blackness, and in some cases, as they say, "You'd never know."

III

It is on this area, the impact of Afro-American culture on contemporary American literature, that I now wish to comment. I have already said that works by Afro-Americans can respond to this presence (just as non-black works do) in a number of ways. The question of what constitutes the art of a black writer, for whom that modifier is more search than fact, has some urgency. In other words, other than melanin and subject matter, what, in fact, may make me a black writer? Other than my own ethnicity—what is going on in my work that makes me believe it is demonstrably inseparable from a cultural specificity that is Afro-American?

Please forgive the use of my own work in these observations. I use it not because it provides the best example, but because I know it best, know what I did and why, and know how central these queries are to me. Writing is, *after* all, an act of language, its practice. But *first* of all it is an effort of the will to discover.

Let me suggest some of the ways in which I activate language and ways in which that language activates me. I will limit this perusal by calling attention only to the first sentences of the books I've written, and hope that in exploring the choices I made, prior points are illuminated.

The Bluest Eye begins "Quiet as it's kept, there were no marigolds in the fall of 1941." That sentence, like the ones that open each succeeding book, is simple, uncomplicated. Of all the sentences that begin all the books, only two of them have dependent clauses: the other three are simple sentences and two are stripped down to virtually subject, verb, modifier. Nothing fancy here. No words need looking up; they are ordinary, everyday words. Yet I hoped the simplicity was not simple-minded, but devious, even loaded. And that the process of selecting each word, for itself and its relationship to the others in the sentence, along with the rejection of others for their echoes, for what is determined and what is not determined, what is almost there and what must be gleaned, would not theatricalize itself, would not erect a proscenium—at least not a noticeable one. So important to me was this unstaging, that in this first novel I summarized the whole of the book on the first page. (In the first edition, it was printed in its entirety on the jacket.)

The opening phrase of this sentence, "Quiet as it's kept," had several attractions for me. First, it was a familiar phrase familiar to me as a child listening to adults; to black women conversing with one another; telling a story, an anecdote, gossip about some one or event within the circle, the family, the neighborhood. The words are conspiratorial. "Shh, don't tell any-one else," and "No one is allowed to know this." It is a secret between us and a secret that is being kept from us. The conspiracy is both held and withheld, exposed and sustained. In some sense it was precisely what the act of writing the book was: the public exposure of a private confidence. In order fully to comprehend the duality of that position, one needs to think of the immediate political climate in which the writing took place, 1965–1969, during great social upheaval in the life of black people. The publication (as opposed to the writing) involved the exposure; the writing was the disclosure of secrets, secrets "we" shared and those withheld from us by ourselves and by the world outside the community.

"Quiet as it's kept," is also a figure of speech that is written, in this instance, but clearly chosen for how speakerly it is, how it speaks and bespeaks a particular world and its ambience. Further, in addition to its "back fence" connotation, its suggestion of illicit gossip, of thrilling revelation, there is also, in the "whisper," the assumption (on the part of the reader) that the teller is on the inside, knows something others do not, and is going to be generous with this privileged information. The intimacy I was aiming for, the intimacy between the reader and the page, could start up immediately be-cause the secret is being shared, at best, and eavesdropped upon, at the least. Sudden familiarity or instant intimacy seemed crucial to me then, writing my first novel. I did not want the reader to have time to wonder "What do I have to do, to give up, in order to read this? What defense do I need, what distance maintain?" Because I know (and the reader does not—he or she has to wait for the second sentence) that this is a terrible story about things one would rather not know anything about.

What, then, is the Big Secret about to be shared? The thing we (reader and I) are "in" on? A botanical aberration. Pollution, perhaps. A skip, perhaps, in the natural order of things: a September, an autumn, a fall without mari-golds. Bright common, strong and sturdy marigolds. When? In 1941, and since that is a momentous year (the beginning of World War II for the United States), the "fall" of 1941, just before the declaration of war, has a "closet" innuendo. In the temperate zone where there is a season known as "fall" during which one expects marigolds to be at their peak, in the months before the beginning of U.S. participation in World War II, something grim is about to be divulged. The next sentence will make it clear that the sayer, the one who knows, is a child speaking, mimicking the adult black women on the porch or in the back yard. The opening phrase is an effort to be grown-up about this shocking information. The point of view of a child alters the priority an adult would assign the information. "We thought it was because Pecola was having her father's baby that the marigolds did not grow" foregrounds the flowers, backgrounds illicit, traumatic, incomprehensible sex coming to its dreaded fruition. This foregrounding of "trivial" information and backgrounding of shocking knowledge secures the point of view but gives the reader pause about whether the voice of children can be trusted at all or is more trustworthy than an adult's. The reader is thereby protected from a confrontation too soon with the painful details, while simultaneously provoked into a desire to know them. The novelty, I thought, would be in having this story of female violation revealed from the vantage point of the victims or could-be victims of rape—the persons no one inquired of (certainly not in 1965)—the girls themselves. And since the victim does not have the vocabulary to understand the violence or its context, gullible, vulnerable girl friends, looking back as the knowing adults they pretended to be in the beginning, would have to do that for her, and would have to fill those silences with their own reflective lives. Thus, the opening provides the stroke that announces something more than a secret shared, but a silence broken, a void filled, an unspeakable thing spoken at last. And they draw the connection between a minor destabilization in seasonal flora with the insignificant destruction of a black girl. Of course "minor" and "insignificant" represent the outside world's view—for the girls both phenomena are earthshaking depositories of information they spend that whole year of childhood (and afterwards) trying to fathom, and cannot. If they have any success, it will be in transferring the problem of fathoming to the presumably adult reader, to the inner circle of listeners. At the least they have distributed the weight of these problematical questions to a larger constituency, and justified the public exposure of a privacy. If the conspiracy that the opening words announce is entered into by the reader, then the book can be seen to open with its close: a speculation on the disruption of "nature," as being a social disruption with tragic individual consequences in which the reader, as part of the population of the text, is implicated.

However a problem, unsolved, lies in the central chamber of the novel. The shattered world I built (to complement what is happening to Pecola), its pieces held together by seasons in childtime and commenting at every turn on the incompatible and barren white-family primer, does not in its present form handle effectively the silence at its center. The void that is Pecola's "unbeing." It should have had a shape—like the emptiness left by a boom or a cry. It required a sophistication unavailable to me, and some deft manipulation of the voices around her. She is not *seen* by herself until she hallucinates a self. And the fact of her hallucination becomes a point of outside-the-book conversation, but does not work in the reading process.

Also, although I was pressing for a female expressiveness (a challenge that resurfaced in *Sula*), it eluded me for the most part, and I had to content myself with female personae because I was not able to secure throughout the work the feminine subtext that is present in the opening sentence (the women gossiping, eager and aghast in "Quiet as it's kept"). The shambles this struggle became is most evident in the section on Pauline Breedlove where I resorted to two voices, hers and the urging narrator's, both of which are extremely unsatisfactory to me. It is interesting to me now that where I thought I would have the most difficulty subverting the language to a feminine mode, I had the least: connecting Cholly's "rape" by the whitemen to his own of his daughter. This most masculine act of aggression becomes feminized in my language, "passive," and, I think, more accurately repellent when deprived of the male "glamor of shame" rape is (or once was) routinely given.

The points I have tried to illustrate are that my choices of language (speakerly, aural, colloquial), my reliance for full comprehension on codes embedded in black culture, my effort to effect immediate co-conspiracy and intimacy (without any distancing, explanatory fabric), as well as my (failed) attempt to shape a silence while breaking it are attempts (many unsatisfactory) to transfigure the complexity and wealth of Afro-American culture into a language worthy of the culture.

In *Sula*, it's necessary to concentrate on *two* first sentences because what survives in print is not the one I had intended to be the first. Originally the book opened with "Except for World War II nothing ever interfered with National Suicide Day." With some encouragement, I recognized that it was a false beginning. "*In medias res*" with a vengeance, because there was no *res* to be in the middle of—no implied world in which to locate the specificity and the resonances in the sentence. More to the point, I knew I was writing a second novel, and that it too would be about people in a black community not just foregrounded but totally dominant; and that it was about black women—also foregrounded and dominant. In 1988, certainly, I would not need (or feel the need for) the sentence—the short section—that now opens *Sula*. The threshold between the reader and the black-topic text need not be the safe, welcoming lobby I persuaded myself it needed at that time. My preference was the demolition of the lobby altogether. As can be seen from *The Bluest Eye,* and in every other book I have written, only *Sula* has this "entrance." The others refuse the "presentation"; refuse the seductive safe harbor; the line of demarcation between the sacred and the obscene, public and private, them and us. Refuse, in effect, to cater to the diminished expectations of the reader, or his or her alarm heightened by the emotional luggage one carries into the black-topic text. (I should remind you that *Sula* was begun in 1969, while my first book was in proof, in a period of extraordinary political activity.)

Since I had become convinced that the effectiveness of the original beginning was only in my head, the job at hand became how to construct an alternate beginning that would not force the work to genuflect and would complement the outlaw quality in it. The problem presented itself this way: to fashion a door. Instead of having the text open wide the moment the cover is opened (or, as in *The Bluest Eye,* to have the book stand exposed before the cover is even touched, much less opened, by placing the complete "plot" on the first page—and finally on the cover of the first edition), here I was to posit a door, turn its knob and beckon for some four or five pages. I had determined not to mention any characters in those pages, there would be no people in the lobby—but I did, rather heavy-handedly in my view, end the welcome aboard with the mention of Shadrack and Sula. It was a craven (to me, still) surrender to a worn-out technique of novel writing: the overt announcement to the reader whom to pay attention to. Yet the bulk of the opening I finally wrote is about the community, a view of it, and the view is not from within (this is a door, after all) but from the point of view of a stranger—the "valley man" who might happen to be there on some errand, but who obviously does not live there and to and for whom all this is mightily strange, even exotic. You can see why I despise much of this beginning. Yet I tried to place in the opening sentence the signature terms of loss: "There used to be a neighborhood here; not any more." That may not be the world's worst sentence, but it doesn't "play," as they say in the theater.

My new first sentence became "In that place, where they tore the nightshade and blackberry patches from their roots to make room for the Medallion City Golf Course, there was once a neighborhood." Instead of my original plan, here I am introducing an outside-the-circle reader into the circle. I am translating the anonymous into the specific, a "place" into a "neighborhood," and letting a stranger in through whose eyes it can be viewed. In between "place" and "neighborhood" I now have to squeeze the specificity and the *difference;* the nostalgia, the history, and the nostalgia for the history; the violence done to it and the consequences of that violence. (It took three months, those four pages, a whole summer of nights.) The nostalgia is sounded by "once"; the history and a longing for it is implied in the connotation of "neighborhood." The violence lurks in having something torn out by its roots—it will not, cannot grow again. Its consequences are that what has been destroyed is considered weeds, refuse necessarily removed in urban "development" by the unspecified but no less known "they" who do not, cannot, afford to differentiate what is displaced, and would not care that this is "refuse" of a certain kind. Both plants have darkness in them: "black" and "night." One is unusual (nightshade) and has two darkness words: "night" and "shade." The other (blackberry) is common. A familiar plant and an exotic one. A harmless one and a dangerous one. One produces a nourishing berry; one delivers toxic ones. But they both thrived here together, *in that place when it was a neighborhood.* Both are gone now, and the description that follows is of the other specific things, in this black community, destroyed in the wake of the golf course. Golf course conveys what it is not, in this context: not houses, or factories, or even a public park, and certainly not residents. It is a manicured place where the likelihood of the former residents showing up is almost nil.

I want to get back to those berries for a moment (to explain, perhaps, the length of time it took for the language of that section to arrive). I always thought of Sula as quintessentially black, metaphysically black, if you will, which is not melanin and certainly not unquestioning fidelity to the tribe. She is new world black and new world woman extracting choice from choicelessness, responding inventively to found things. Improvisational. Daring, disruptive, imaginative, modern, out-of-the-house, outlawed, un-policing, uncontained and uncontainable. And dangerously female. In her final conversation with Nel she refers to herself as a special kind of black person woman, one with choices. Like a redwood, she says. (With all due respect to the dream landscape of Freud, trees have always seemed feminine to me.) In any case, my perception of Sula's double-dose of *chosen* blackness and *biological* blackness is in the presence of those two words of darkness in "nightshade" as well as in the uncommon quality of the vine itself. One variety is called "enchanter," and the other "bittersweet" because the berries taste bitter at first and then sweet. Also nightshade was thought to counter-act witchcraft. All of this seemed a wonderful constellation of signs for Sula. And "blackberry patch" seemed equally appropriate for Nel: nourishing, never needing to be tended or cultivated, once rooted and bearing. Reliably sweet but thorn-bound. Her process of becoming, heralded by the explosive dissolving of her fragilely-held-together ball of string and fur (when the thorns of her self-protection are removed by Eva), puts her back in touch with the complex, contradictory, evasive, independent, liquid modernity Sula insisted upon. A modernity which overturns pre-war definitions, ushers in the Jazz Age (an age *defined* by Afro-American art and culture), and requires new kinds of intelligences to define oneself.

The stage-setting of the first four pages is embarrassing to me now, but the pains I have taken to explain it may be helpful in identifying the strategies one can be forced to resort to in trying to accommodate the mere fact of writing about, for and out of black culture while accommodating and re-sponding to mainstream "white" culture. The "valley man's" guidance into the territory was my compromise. Perhaps it "worked," but it was not the work I wanted to do.

Had I begun with Shadrack, I would have ignored the smiling welcome and put the reader into immediate confrontation with his wound and his scar. The difference my preferred (original) beginning would have made would be calling greater attention to the traumatic displacement this most wasteful capitalist war had on black people in particular, and throwing into relief the creative, if outlawed, determination to survive it whole. Sula as (feminine) solubility and Shadrack's (male) fixative are two extreme ways of dealing with displacement—a prevalent theme in the narrative of black peo-ple. In the final opening I replicated the demiurge of discriminatory, pros-ecutorial racial oppression in the loss to commercial "progress" of the village, but the references to the community's stability and creativeness (music, dancing, craft, religion, irony, wit all referred to in the "valley man's" pres-ence) refract and subsume their pain while they are in the thick of it. It is a softer embrace than Shadrack's organized, public madness—his disruptive remembering presence which helps (for a while) to cement the community, until Sula challenges them.

"The North Carolina Mutual Life Insurance agent promised to fly from Mercy to the other side of Lake Superior at 3:00."

This declarative sentence is designed to mock a journalistic style; with a minor alteration it could be the opening of an item in a smalltown news-paper. It has the tone of an everyday event of minimal local interest. Yet I wanted it to contain (as does the scene that takes place when the agent fulfills his promise) the information that *Song of Solomon* both centers on and radiates from.

The name of the insurance company is real, a well known black-owned company dependent on black clients, and in its corporate name are "life" and "mutual"; *agent* being the necessary ingredient of what enables the relationship between them. The sentence also moves from North Carolina to Lake Superior—geographical locations, but with a sly implication that the move from North Carolina (the south) to Lake Superior (the north) might not actually involve progress to some "superior state"—which, of course it does not. The two other significant words are "fly," upon which the novel centers and "Mercy," the name of the place from which he is to fly. Both constitute the heartbeat of the narrative. Where is the insurance man flying to? The other side of Lake Superior is Canada, of course, the historic terminus of the escape route for black people looking for asylum. "Mercy," the other significant term, is the grace note; the earnest though, with one exception, unspoken wish of the narrative's population. Some grant it; some never find it; one, at least, makes it the text and cry of her extemporaneous sermon upon the death of her granddaughter. It touches, turns and returns to Guitar at the end of the book—he who is least deserving of it—and moves him to make it his own final gift. It is what one wishes for Hagar; what is unavailable to and unsought by Macon Dead, senior; what his wife learns to demand from him, and what can never come from the white world as is signified by the inversion of the name of the hospital from Mercy to "no-Mercy." It is only available from within. The center of the narrative is flight; the springboard is mercy.

But the sentence turns, as all sentences do, on the verb: promised. The insurance agent does not declare, announce, or threaten his act. He promises, as though a contract is being executed—faithfully—between himself and others. Promises broken, or kept; the difficulty of ferreting out loyalties and ties that bind or bruise wend their way throughout the action and the shifting relationships. So the agent's flight, like that of the Solomon in the title, although toward asylum (Canada, or freedom, or home, or the company of the welcoming dead), and although it carries the possibility of failure and the certainty of danger, is toward change, an alternative way, a cessation of things-as-they-are. It should not be understood as a simple desperate act, the end of a fruitless life, a life without gesture, without examination, but as obedience to a deeper contract with his people. It is his commitment to them, regardless of whether, in all its details, they understand it. There is, however, in their response to his action, a tenderness, some contrition, and mounting respect ("They didn't know he had it in him.") and an awareness that the gesture enclosed rather than repudiated themselves. The note he leaves asks for forgiveness. It is tacked on his door as a mild invitation to whomever might pass by, but it is not an advertisement. It is an almost Christian declaration of love as well as humility of one who was not able to do more.

There are several other flights in the work and they are motivationally different. Solomon's the most magical, the most theatrical and, for Milkman, the most satisfying. It is also the most problematic—to those he left behind. Milkman's flight binds these two elements of loyalty (Mr. Smith's) and abandon and self-interest (Solomon's) into a third thing: a merging of fealty and risk that suggests the "agency" for "mutual" "life," which he offers at the end and which is echoed in the hills behind him, and is the marriage of surrender and domination, acceptance and rule, commitment to a group *through* ultimate isolation. Guitar recognizes this marriage and recalls enough of how lost he himself is to put his weapon down.

The journalistic style at the beginning, its rhythm of a familiar, hand-me-down dignity is pulled along by an accretion of detail displayed in a meandering unremarkableness. Simple words, uncomplex sentence structures, persistent understatement, highly aural syntax—but the ordinariness of the language, its colloquial, vernacular, humorous and, upon occasion, parabolic quality sabotage expectations and mask judgments when it can no longer defer them. The composition of red, white and blue in the opening scene provides the national canvas/flag upon which the narrative works and against which the lives of these black people must be seen, but which must not overwhelm the enterprise the novel is engaged in. It is a composition of color that heralds Milkman's birth, protects his youth, hides its purpose and through which he must burst (through blue Buicks, red tulips in his waking dream, and his sisters' white stockings, ribbons and gloves) before discovering that the gold of his search is really Pilate's yellow orange and the glittering metal of the box in her ear.

These spaces, which I am filling in, and can fill in because they were planned, can conceivably be filled in with other significances. That is planned as well. The point is that into these spaces should fall the ruminations of the reader and his or her invented or recollected or misunderstood knowingness. The reader as narrator asks the questions the community asks, and both reader and "voice" stand among the crowd, within it, with privileged intimacy and contact, but without any more privileged information than the crowd has. That egalitarianism which places us all (reader, the novel's population, the narrator's voice) on the same footing reflected for me the force of flight and mercy, and the precious, imaginative yet realistic gaze of black people who (at one time, anyway) did not mythologize what or whom it mythologized. The "song" itself contains this unblinking evaluation of the miraculous and heroic flight of the legendary Solomon, an unblinking gaze which is lurking in the tender but amused choral-community response to the agent's flight. Sotto (but not completely) is my own giggle (in Afro-American terms) of the proto-myth of the journey to manhood. Whenever characters are cloaked in Western fable, they are in deep trouble; but the African myth is also contaminated. Unprogressive, unreconstructed, self-born Pilate is unimpressed by Solomon's flight and knocks Milkman down when, made new by his appropriation of his own family's fable, he returns to educate her with it. Upon hearing all he has to say, her only interest is filial. "Papa? . . . I've been carryin' Papa?" And her longing to hear the song, finally, is a longing for balm to die by, not a submissive obedience to history—anybody's.

The opening sentence of *Tar Baby,* "He believed he was safe," is the second version of itself. The first, "He thought he was safe," was discarded because "thought" did not contain the doubt I wanted to plant in the reader's mind about whether or not he really was—safe. "Thought" came to me at once because it was the verb my parents and grandparents used when describing what they had dreamed the night before. Not "I dreamt," or "It seemed" or even "I saw or did" this or that—but "I thought." It gave the dream narrative distance (a dream is not "real") and power (the control implied in *thinking* rather than *dreaming*). But to use "thought" seemed to undercut the faith of the character and the distrust I wanted to suggest to the reader. "Believe" was chosen to do the work properly. And the person who does the believing is, in a way, about to enter a dream world, and convinces himself, eventually, that he is in control of it. He believed; was convinced. And although the word suggests his conviction, it does not reassure the reader. If I had wanted the reader to trust this person's point of view I would have written "He was safe." Or, "Finally, he was safe." The unease about this view of safety is important because safety itself is the desire of each person in the novel. Locating it, creating it, losing it.

   You may recall that I was interested in working out the mystery of a piece of lore, a folk tale, which is also about safety and danger and the skills needed to secure the one and recognize and avoid the other. I was not, of course, interested in retelling the tale; I suppose that is an idea to pursue, but it is certainly not interesting enough to engage me for four years. I have said, elsewhere, that the exploration of the Tar Baby tale was like stroking a pet to see what the anatomy was like but not to disturb or distort its mystery. Folklore may have begun as allegory for natural or social phenomena; it may have been employed as a retreat from contemporary issues in art, but folklore can also contain myths that reactivate themselves endlessly through providers—the people who repeat, reshape, reconstitute and reinterpret them. The Tar Baby tale seemed to me to be about masks. Not masks as covering what is to be hidden, but how masks come to life, take life over, exercise the tensions between itself and what it covers. For Son, the most effective and mask is none. For the others the construction is careful and delicately borne, but the masks they make have a life of their own and collide with those they come in contact with. The texture of the novel seemed to want leanness, architecture that was worn and ancient like a piece of mask sculpture: exaggerated, breathing, just athwart the representational life it displaced. Thus, the first and last sentences had to match, as the exterior planes match the interior, concave ones inside the mask. Therefore "He believed he was safe" would be the twin of "Lickety split, lickety split, lickety lickety split." This close is (1) the last sentence of the folk tale. (2) the action of the character. (3) the indeterminate ending that follows from the untrustworthy beginning. (4) the complimentary meter of its twin sister [u u / u u / with u u u / u u u /], and (5) the wide and marvelous space between the contradiction of those two images: from a dream of safety to the sound of running feet. The whole mediated world in between. This masked and unmasked; enchanted, disenchanted; wounded and wounding world is played out on and by the varieties of interpretation (Western and Afro-American) the Tar Baby myth has been (and continues to be) subjected to. Winging's one's way through the vise and expulsion of history becomes possible in creative encounters with that history. Nothing, in those encounters, is safe, or should be. Safety is the foetus of power as well as protection from it, as the uses to which masks and myths are put in Afro-American culture remind us.

"124 was spiteful. Full of a baby's venom."

Beginning *Beloved* with numerals rather than spelled out numbers, it was my intention to give the house an identity separate from the street or even the city; to name it the way "Sweet Home" was named; the way plantations were named, but not with nouns or "proper" names—with numbers instead because numbers have no adjectives, no posture of coziness or grandeur or the haughty yearning of arrivistes and estate builders for the parallel beautifications of the nation they left behind, laying claim to instant history and legend. Numbers here constitute an address, a thrilling enough prospect for slaves who had owned nothing, least of all an address. And although the numbers, unlike words, can have no modifiers, I give these an adjective—spiteful (There are three others). The address is therefore personalized, but personalized by its own activity, not the pasted on desire for personality.

Also there is something about numerals that makes them spoken, heard, in this context, because one expects words to read in a book, not numbers to say, or hear. And the sound of the novel, sometimes cacaphonous, sometimes harmonious, must be an inner ear sound or a sound just beyond hearing, infusing the text with a musical emphasis that words can do sometimes even better than music can. Thus the second sentence is not one: it is a phrase that properly, grammatically, belongs as a dependent clause with the first. Had I done that, however, (124 was spiteful, comma, full of a baby's venom, or 124 was full of a baby's venom) I could not have had the accent on *full* [/ u u / u / u pause / u u u u / u].

Whatever the risks of confronting the reader with what must be immediately incomprehensible in that simple, declarative authoritative sentence, the risk of unsettling him or her, I determined to take. Because the *in medias res* opening that I am so committed to is here excessively demanding. It is abrupt, and should appear so. No native informant here. The reader is snatched, yanked, thrown into an environment completely foreign, and I want it as the first stroke of the shared experience that might be possible between the reader and the novel's population. Snatched just as the slaves were from one place to another, from any place to another, without preparation and without defense. No lobby, no door, no entrance—a gangplank, perhaps (but a very short one). And the house into which this snatching— this kidnapping—propels one, changes from spiteful to loud to quiet, as the sounds in the body of the ship itself may have changed. A few words have to be read before it is clear that 124 refers to a house (in most of the early drafts "The women *in the house* knew it" was simply "The women knew it." "House" was not mentioned for seventeen lines), and a few more have to be read to discover why it is spiteful, or rather the source of the spite. By then it is clear, if not at once, that something is beyond control, but is not beyond understanding since it is not beyond accommodation by both the "women" and the "children." The fully realized presence of the haunting is both a major incumbent of the narrative and sleight of hand. One of its purposes is to keep the reader preoccupied with the nature of the incredible spirit world while being supplied a controlled diet of the incredible political world.

The subliminal, the underground life of a novel is the area most likely to link arms with the reader and facilitate making it one's own. Because one must, to get from the first sentence to the next, and the next and the next.The friendly observation post I was content to build and man in *Sula* (with the stranger in the midst), or the down-home journalism of *Song of Solomon* or the calculated mistrust of the point of view in *Tar Baby* would not serve here. Here I wanted the compelling confusion of being there as they (the characters) are; suddenly, without comfort or succor from the "author," with only imagination, intelligence, and necessity available for the journey. The painterly language of *Song of Solomon* was not useful to me in *Beloved*. There is practically no color whatsoever in its pages, and when there is, it is so stark and remarked upon, it is virtually raw. Color seen for the first time, without its history. No built architecture as in *Tar Baby,* no play with Western chronology as in *Sula;* no exchange between book life and "real" life discourse—with printed text units rubbing up against seasonal black childtime units as in *The Bluest Eye.* No compound of houses, no neighborhood, no sculpture, no paint, no time, especially no time because memory, pre-historic memory, has no time. There is just a little music, each other and the urgency of what is at stake. Which is all they had. For that work, the work of language is to get out of the way.

I hope you understand that in this explication of how I practice language is a search for and deliberate posture of vulnerability to those aspects of Afro-American culture that can inform and position my work. I sometimes know when the work works, when *nommo* has effectively summoned, by reading and listening to those who have entered the text. I learn nothing from those who resist it, except, of course, the sometimes fascinating display of their struggle. My expectations of and my gratitude to the critics who enter, are great. To those who talk about how as well as what; who identify the workings as well as the work; for whom the study of Afro-American literature is neither a crash course in neighborliness and tolerance, nor an infant to be carried, instructed or chastised or even whipped like a child, but the serious study of art forms that have much work to do, but are already legitimatized by their own cultural sources and predecessors—in or out of the canon—I owe much.

For an author, regarding canons, it is very simple: in fifty, a hundred or more years his or her work may be relished for its beauty or its insight or its power; or it may be condemned for its vacuousness and pretension—and junked. Or in fifty or a hundred years the critic (as canon builder) may be applauded for his or her intelligent scholarship and powers of critical inquiry. Or laughed at for ignorance and shabbily disguised assertions of power—and junked. It's possible that the reputations of both will thrive, or that both will decay. In any case, as far as the future is concerned, when one writes, as critic or as author, all necks are on the line.

Notes

1   See *"Race," Writing, and Difference,* ed. Henry Louis Gates (Chicago, 1986).
2   Among many examples, Ivan van Sertima, *They Came Before Columbus, The African Presence in Ancient America* (New York, 1976), xvi–xvii.
3   Tzvetan Todorov, " 'Race,' Writing, and Culture," translated by Loulou Mack, in Gates, *"Race," Writing, and Difference,* 370–80.
4   Terrence Rafferty, "Articles of Faith," *The New Yorker,* 16 May 1988, 110–18.
5   Martin Bernal, *Black Athena: The Afroasiatic Roots of Classical Civilization,* volume 1: *The Fabrication of Ancient Greece 1785–1985* (Rutgers, N.J., 1987), 2.
6   Ibid., 310.
7   Ibid., 337.
8   See Michael Paul Rogin, *Subversive Genealogy: The Politics and Art of Herman Melville* (Berkeley, 1985), 15.
9   Ibid., 107 and 142.
10 Ibid., 112.

Gender, Theory, and
African American Feminist Criticism

Alice Walker

In Search of Our Mothers' Gardens

(1972)

I described her own nature and temperament. Told how they needed a larger life for their expression. . . . I pointed out that in lieu of proper channels, her emotions had overflowed into paths that dissipated them. I talked, beautifully I thought, about an art that would be born, an art that would open the way for women the likes of her. I asked her to hope, and build up an inner life against the coming of that day. . . . I sang, with a strange quiver in my voice, a promise song.—Jean Toomer, "Avey," Cane

The poet speaking to a prostitute who falls asleep while he's talking—

When the poet Jean Toomer walked through the South in the early twenties, he discovered a curious thing: black women whose spirituality was so intense, so deep, so *unconscious,* that they were themselves unaware of the richness they held. They stumbled blindly through their lives: creatures so abused and mutilated in body, so dimmed and confused by pain, that they considered themselves unworthy even of hope. In the selfless abstractions their bodies became to the men who used them, they became more than "sexual objects," more even than mere women: they became "Saints." Instead of being perceived as whole persons, their bodies became shrines: what was thought to be their minds became temples suitable for worship. These crazy Saints stared out at the world, wildly, like lunatics—or quietly, like suicides; and the "God" that was in their gaze was as mute as a great stone.

Who were these Saints? These crazy, loony, pitiful women?

Some of them, without a doubt, were our mothers and grandmothers.

In the still heat of the post-Reconstruction South, this is how they seemed to Jean Toomer: exquisite butterflies trapped in an evil honey, toiling away

This essay first appeared in Alice Walker, *In Search of Our Mothers' Gardens* (New York, 1972).

their lives in an era, a century, that did not acknowledge them, except as "the *mule* of the world." They dreamed dreams that no one knew—not even themselves, in any coherent fashion—and saw visions no one could understand. They wandered or sat about the countryside crooning lullabies to ghosts, and drawing the mother of Christ in charcoal on courthouse walls.

They forced their minds to desert their bodies and their striving spirits sought to rise, like frail whirlwinds from the hard red clay. And when those frail whirlwinds fell, in scattered particles, upon the ground, no one mourned. Instead, men lit candles to celebrate the emptiness that remained, as people do who enter a beautiful but vacant space to resurrect a God.

Our mothers and grandmothers, some of them: moving to music not yet written. And they waited.

They waited for a day when the unknown thing that was in them would be made known; but guessed, somehow in their darkness, that on the day of their revelation they would be long dead. Therefore to Toomer they walked, and even ran, in slow motion. For they were going nowhere immediate, and the future was not yet within their grasp. And men took our mothers and grandmothers, "but got no pleasure from it." So complex was their passion and their calm.

To Toomer, they lay vacant and fallow as autumn fields, with harvest time never in sight: and he saw them enter loveless marriages, without joy; and become prostitutes, without resistance; and become mothers of children, without fulfillment.

For these grandmothers and mothers of ours were not Saints, but Artists; driven to a numb and bleeding madness by the springs of creativity in them for which there was no release. They were Creators, who lived lives of spiritual waste, because they were so rich in spirituality—which is the basis of Art—that the strain of enduring their unused and unwanted talent drove them insane. Throwing away this spirituality was their pathetic attempt to lighten the soul to a weight their work-worn, sexually abused bodies could bear.

What did it mean for a black woman to be an artist in our grandmothers' time? In our great-grandmothers' day? It is a question with an answer cruel enough to stop the blood.

Did you have a genius of a great-great-grandmother who died under some ignorant and depraved white overseer's lash? Or was she required to bake biscuits for a lazy backwater tramp, when she cried out in her soul to paint watercolors of sunsets, or the rain falling on the green and peaceful pasturelands? Or was her body broken and forced to bear children (who were more often than not sold away from her)—eight, ten, fifteen, twenty children—when her one joy was the thought of modeling heroic figures of rebellion, in stone or clay?

How was the creativity of the black woman kept alive, year after year and century after century, when for most of the years black people have been in America, it was a punishable crime for a black person to read or write? And the freedom to paint, to sculpt, to expand the mind with action did not exist. Consider, if you can bear to imagine it, what might have been the result if singing, too, had been forbidden by law. Listen to the voices of Bessie Smith, Billie Holiday, Nina Simone, Roberta Flack, and Aretha Franklin, among others, and imagine those voices muzzled for life. Then you may begin to comprehend the lives of our "crazy," "Sainted" mothers and grandmothers. The agony of the lives of women who might have been Poets, Novelists, Essayists, and Short-Story Writers (over a period of centuries), who died with their real gifts stifled within them.

And, if this were the end of the story, we would have cause to cry out in my paraphrase of Okot p'Bitek's great poem:

> O, my clanswomen
> Let us all cry together!
> Come,
> Let us mourn the death of our mother,
> The death of a Queen
> The ash that was produced
> By a great fire!
> O, this homestead is utterly dead
> Close the gates
> With *lacari* thorns,
> For our mother
> The creator of the Stool is lost!
> And all the young women
> Have perished in the wilderness!

But this is not the end of the story, for all the young women—our mothers and grandmothers, *ourselves*—have not perished in the wilderness. And if we ask ourselves why, and search for and find the answer, we will know beyond all efforts to erase it from our minds, just exactly who, and of what, we black American women are.

One example, perhaps the most pathetic, most misunderstood one, can provide a backdrop for our mothers' work: Phillis Wheatley, a slave in the 1700s.

Virginia Woolf, in her book *A Room of One's Own*, wrote that in order for a woman to write fiction she must have two things, certainly: a room of her own (with key and lock) and enough money to support herself.

What then are we to make of Phillis Wheatley, a slave, who owned not even herself? This sickly, frail black girl who required a servant of her own at times—her health was so precarious—and who, had she been white, would have been easily considered the intellectual superior of all the women and most of the men in the society of her day.

Virginia Woolf wrote further, speaking of course not of our Phillis, that "any woman born with a great gift in the sixteenth century [insert "eighteenth century," insert "black woman," insert "born or made a slave"] would certainly have gone crazed, shot herself, or ended her days in some lonely cottage outside the village, half witch, half wizard [insert "Saint"], feared and mocked at. For it needs little skill and psychology to be sure that a highly gifted girl who had tried to use her gift for poetry would have been so thwarted and hindered by contrary instincts [add "chains, guns, the lash, the ownership of one's body by someone else, submission to an alien religion"], that she must have lost her health and sanity to a certainty."

The key words, as they relate to Phillis, are "contrary instincts." For when we read the poetry of Phillis Wheatley—as when we read the novels of Nella Larsen or the oddly false-sounding autobiography of that freest of all black women writers, Zora Hurston—evidence of "contrary instincts" is everywhere. Her loyalties were completely divided, as was, without question, her mind.

But how could this be otherwise? Captured at seven, a slave of wealthy, doting whites who instilled in her the "savagery" of the Africa they "rescued" her from, one wonders if she was even able to remember her homeland as she had known it, or as it really was.

Yet, because she did try to use her gift for poetry in a world that made her a slave, she was "so thwarted and hindered by . . . contrary instincts, that she . . . lost her health. . . ." In the last years of her brief life, burdened not only with the need to express her gift but also with a penniless, friendless "freedom" and several small children for whom she was forced to do strenuous work to feed, she lost her health, certainly. Suffering from malnutrition and neglect and who knows what mental agonies, Phillis Wheatley died.

So torn by "contrary instincts" was black, kidnapped, enslaved Phillis that her description of "the Goddess"—as she poetically called the Liberty she did not have—is ironically, cruelly humorous. And, in fact, has held Phillis up to ridicule for more than a century. It is usually read prior to hanging Phillis's memory as that of a fool. She wrote:

> The Goddess comes, she moves divinely fair,
> Olive and laurel binds her *golden* hair.
> Wherever shines this native of the skies,
> Unnumber'd charms and recent graces rise. [My italics]

It is obvious that Phillis, the slave, combed the "Goddess's" hair every morning; prior, perhaps, to bringing in the milk, or fixing her mistress's lunch. She took her imagery from the one thing she saw elevated above all others.

With the benefit of hindsight we ask, "How could she?"

But at last, Phillis, we understand. No more snickering when your stiff, struggling, ambivalent lines are forced on us. We know now that you were not an idiot or a traitor; only a sickly little black girl, snatched from your home and country and made a slave; a woman who still struggled to sing the song that was your gift, although in a land of barbarians who praised you for your bewildered tongue. It is not so much what you sang, as that you kept alive, in so many of our ancestors, *the notion of song.*

Black women are called, in the folklore that so aptly identifies one's status in society, "the *mule* of the world," because we have been handed the burdens that everyone else—*everyone* else—refused to carry. We have also been called "Matriarchs," "Superwomen," and "Mean and Evil Bitches." Not to mention "Castraters" and "Sapphire's Mama." When we have pleaded for understanding, our character has been distorted; when we have asked for simple caring, we have been handed empty inspirational appellations, then stuck in the farthest corner. When we have asked for love, we have been given children. In short, even our plainer gifts, our labors of fidelity and love, have been knocked down our throats. To be an artist and a black woman, even today, lowers our status in many respects, rather than raises it: and yet, artists we will be.

Therefore we must fearlessly pull out of ourselves and look at and identify with our lives the living creativity some of our great-grandmothers were not allowed to know. I stress *some* of them because it is well known that the majority of our great-grandmothers knew, even without "knowing" it, the reality of their spirituality, even if they didn't recognize it beyond what happened in the singing at church—and they never had any intention of giving it up.

How they did it—those millions of black women who were not Phillis Wheatley, or Lucy Terry or Frances Harper or Zora Hurston or Nella Larsen or Bessie Smith; or Elizabeth Catlett, or Katherine Dunham, either—brings me to the title of this essay, "In Search of Our Mothers' Gardens," which is a personal account that is yet shared, in its theme and its meaning, by all of us. I found, while thinking about the far-reaching world of the creative black woman, that often the truest answer to a question that really matters can be found very close.

In the late 1920s my mother ran away from home to marry my father. Marriage, if not running away, was expected of seventeen-year-old girls. By the time she was twenty, she had two children and was pregnant with a third. Five children later, I was born. And this is how I came to know my mother: she seemed a large, soft, loving-eyed woman who was rarely impatient in our home. Her quick, violent temper was on view only a few times a year, when she battled with the white landlord who had the misfortune to suggest to her that her children did not need to go to school.

She made all the clothes we wore, even my brothers' overalls. She made all the towels and sheets we used. She spent the summers canning vegetables and fruits. She spent the winter evenings making quilts enough to cover all our beds.

During the "working" day, she labored beside—not behind—my father in the fields. Her day began before sunup, and did not end until late at night. There was never a moment for her to sit down, undisturbed, to unravel her own private thoughts; never a time free from interruption—by work or the noisy inquiries of her many children. And yet, it is to my mother—and all our mothers who were not famous—that I went in search of the secret of what has fed that muzzled and often mutilated, but vibrant, creative spirit that the black woman has inherited, and that pops out in wild and unlikely places to this day.

But when, you will ask, did my overworked mother have time to know or care about feeding the creative spirit?

The answer is so simple that many of us have spent years discovering it. We have constantly looked high, when we should have looked high—and low.

For example: in the Smithsonian Institution in Washington, D.C., there hangs a quilt unlike any other in the world. In fanciful, inspired, and yet simple and identifiable figures, it portrays the story of the Crucifixion. It is considered rare, beyond price. Though it follows no known pattern of quilt-making, and though it is made of bits and pieces of worthless rags, it is obviously the work of a person of powerful imagination and deep spiritual feeling. Below this quilt I saw a note that says it was made by "an anonymous Black woman in Alabama, a hundred years ago."

If we could locate this "anonymous" black woman from Alabama, she would turn out to be one of our grandmothers—an artist who left her mark in the only materials she could afford, and in the only medium her position in society allowed her to use.

As Virginia Woolf wrote further, in *A Room of One's Own:*

Yet genius of a sort must have existed among women as it must have existed among the working class. [Change this to "slaves" and "the wives and daughters of sharecroppers."] Now and again an Emily Brontë or a Robert Burns [change this to "a Zora Hurston or a Richard Wright"] blazes out and proves its presence. But certainly it never got itself on to paper. When, however, one reads of a witch being ducked, of a woman possessed by devils [or "Sainthood"], of a wise woman selling herbs [our root workers], or even a very remarkable man who had a mother, then I think we are on the track of a lost novelist, a suppressed poet, of some mute and inglorious Jane Austen. . . . Indeed, I would venture to guess that Anon, who wrote so many poems without signing them, was often a woman. . . .

And so our mothers and grandmothers have, more often than not anonymously, handed on the creative spark, the seed of the flower they themselves never hoped to see: or like a sealed letter they could not plainly read.

And so it is, certainly, with my own mother. Unlike "Ma" Rainey's songs, which retained their creator's name even while blasting forth from Bessie Smith's mouth, no song or poem will bear my mother's name. Yet so many of the stories that I write, that we all write, are my mother's stories. Only recently did I fully realize this: that through years of listening to my mother's stories of her life, I have absorbed not only the stories themselves, but something of the manner in which she spoke, something of the urgency that involves the knowledge that her stories—like her life—must be recorded. It is probably for this reason that so much of what I have written is about characters whose counterparts in real life are so much older than I am.

But the telling of these stories, which came from my mother's lips as naturally as breathing, was not the only way my mother showed herself as an artist. For stories, too, were subject to being distracted, to dying without conclusion. Dinners must be started, and cotton must be gathered before the big rains. The artist that was and is my mother showed itself to me only after many years. This is what I finally noticed:

Like Mem, a character in *The Third Life of Grange Copeland,* my mother adorned with flowers whatever shabby house we were forced to live in. And not just your typical straggly country stand of zinnias, either. She planted ambitious gardens—and still does—with over fifty different varieties of plants that bloom profusely from early March until late November. Before she left home for the fields, she watered her flowers, chopped up the grass, and laid out new beds. When she returned from the fields she might divide clumps of bulbs, dig a cold pit, uproot and replant roses, or prune branches from her taller bushes or trees—until night came and it was too dark to see.

Whatever she planted grew as if by magic, and her fame as a grower of flowers spread over three counties. Because of her creativity with her flowers, even my memories of poverty are seen through a screen of blooms—sunflowers, petunias, roses, dahlias, forsythia, spirea, delphiniums, verbena . . . and on and on.

And I remember people coming to my mother's yard to be given cuttings from her flowers; I hear again the praise showered on her because whatever rocky soil she landed on, she turned into a garden. A garden so brilliant with colors, so original in its design, so magnificent with life and creativity, that to this day people drive by our house in Georgia—perfect strangers and imperfect strangers—and ask to stand or walk among my mother's art.

I notice that it is only when my mother is working in her flowers that she is radiant, almost to the point of being invisible—except as Creator: hand and eye. She is involved in work her soul must have. Ordering the universe in the image of her personal conception of Beauty.

Her face, as she prepares the Art that is her gift, is a legacy of respect she leaves to me, for all that illuminates and cherishes life. She has handed down respect for the possibilities—and the will to grasp them.

For her, so hindered and intruded upon in so many ways, being an artist has still been a daily part of her life. This ability to hold on, even in very simple ways, is work black women have done for a very long time.

This poem is not enough, but it is something, for the woman who literally covered the holes in our walls with sunflowers:

They were women then
My mama's generation
Husky of voice—Stout of
Step
With fists as well as
Hands
How they battered down
Doors
And ironed
Starched white
Shirts
How they led
Armies
Headragged Generals
Across mined
Fields
Bobby-trapped
Kitchens
To discover books
Desks
A place for us
How they knew what we
Must know
Without knowing a page
Of it
Themselves.

Guided by my heritage of a love of beauty and a respect for strength—in search of my mother's garden, I found my own.

And perhaps in Africa over two hundred years ago, there was just such a mother; perhaps she painted vivid and daring decorations in oranges and yellows and greens on the walls of her hut; perhaps she sang—in a voice like Roberta Flack's—*sweetly* over the compounds of her village; perhaps she wove the most stunning mats or told the most ingenious stories of all the village storytellers. Perhaps she was herself a poet—though only her daughter's name is signed to the poems that we know.

Perhaps Phillis Wheatley's mother was also an artist.

Perhaps in more than Phillis Wheatley's biological life is her mother's signature made clear.

Barbara Smith

Toward a Black Feminist Criticism

(1977)

For all my sisters, especially Beverly and Demita

I do not know where to begin. Long before I tried to write this I realized that I was attempting something unprecedented, something dangerous merely by writing about black women writers from a feminist perspective and about black lesbian writers from any perspective at all. These things have not been done. Not by white male critics, expectedly. Not by black male critics. Not by white women critics who think of themselves as feminists. And most crucially not by black women critics who, although they pay the most attention to black women writers as a group, seldom use a consistent feminist analysis or write about black lesbian literature. All segments of the literary world—whether establishment, progressive, black, female, or lesbian—do not know, or at least act as if they do not know, that black women writers and black lesbian writers exist.

For whites, this specialized lack of knowledge is inextricably connected to their not knowing in any concrete or politically transforming way that black women of any description dwell in this place. Black women's existence, experience and culture, and the brutally complex systems of oppression which shape these, are in the 'real world' of white and/or male consciousness beneath consideration, invisible, unknown.

This invisibility, which goes beyond anything that either black men or white women experience and tell about in their writing, is one reason it is so difficult for me to know where to start. It seems overwhelming to break such

This essay earlier appeared in Gloria Hull, Patricia Bell Scott, and Barbara Smith, eds., *But Some of Us Are Brave* (New York, 1982).

a massive silence. Even more numbing, however, is the realization that so many of the women who will read this have not yet noticed us missing either from their reading matter, their politics or their lives. It is galling that ostensible feminists and acknowledged lesbians have been so blinded to the implications of any womanhood that is not white womanhood and that they have yet to struggle with the deep racism in themselves that is at the source of this blindness.

I think of the thousands and thousands of books, magazines and articles which have been devoted, by this time, to the subject of women's writing and I am filled with rage at the fraction of those pages that mention black and other Third World women. I finally do not know how to begin because in 1977 I want to be writing this for a black feminist publication, for black women who know and love these writers as I do and who, if they do not yet know their names, have at least profoundly felt the pain of their absence.

The conditions that coalesce into the impossibilities of this essay have as much to do with politics as with the practice of literature. Any discussion of Afro-American writers can rightfully begin with the fact that for most of the time we have been in this country we have been categorically denied not only literacy, but the most minimal possibility of a decent human life. In her landmark essay "In Search of Our Mothers' Gardens," Alice Walker discloses how the political, economic and social restrictions of slavery and racism have historically stunted the creative lives of black women.[1]

At the present time I feel that the politics of feminism have a direct relationship to the state of black women's literature. A viable, autonomous black feminist movement in this country would open up the space needed for the exploration of black women's lives and the creation of consciously black woman-identified art. At the same time a redefinition of the goals and strategies of the white feminist movement would lead to much needed change in the focus and content of what is now generally accepted as women's culture.

I want to make in this essay some connections between the politics of black women's lives, what we write about and our situation as artists. In order to do this I will look at how black women have been viewed critically by outsiders, demonstrate the necessity for black feminist criticism, and try to understand what the existence or nonexistence of black lesbian writing reveals about the state of black women's culture and the intensity of *all* black women's oppression.

The role that criticism plays in making a body of literature recognizable and real hardly needs to be explained here. The necessity for nonhostile and perceptive analysis of works written by persons outside the mainstream of white/male cultural rule has been proven by the black cultural resurgence of the 1960s and 1970s and by the even more recent growth of feminist literary scholarship. For books to be real and remembered they have to be talked about. For books to be understood they must be examined in such a way that the basic intentions of the writers are at least considered. Because of racism, black literature has usually been viewed as a discrete subcategory of American literature and there have been black critics of black literature who did much to keep it alive long before it caught the attention of whites. Before the advent of specifically feminist criticism in this decade, books by white women, on the other hand, were not clearly perceived as the cultural manifestation of an oppressed people. It took the surfacing of the second wave of the North American feminist movement to expose the fact that these works contain a stunningly accurate record of the impact of patriarchal values and practice upon the lives of women and more significantly that literature by women provides essential insights into female experience.

In speaking about the current situation of black women writers, it is important to remember that the existence of a feminist movement was an essential precondition to the growth of feminist literature, criticism and women's studies, which focused at the beginning almost entirely upon investigations of literature. The fact that a parallel black feminist movement has been much slower in evolving cannot help but have impact upon the situation of black women writers and artists and explains in part why during this very same period we have been so ignored.

There is no political movement to give power or support to those who want to examine black women's experience through studying our history, literature and culture. There is no political presence that demands a minimal level of consciousness and respect from those who write or talk about our lives. Finally, there is not a developed body of black feminist political theory whose assumptions could be used in the study of black women's art. When black women's books are dealt with at all, it is usually in the context of black literature which largely ignores the implications of sexual politics. When white women look at black women's works they are of course ill-equipped to deal with the subtleties of racial politics. A black feminist approach to literature that embodies the realization that the politics of sex as well as the politics of race and class are crucially interlocking factors in the works of black women writers is an absolute necessity. Until a black feminist criticism exists we will not even know what these writers mean. The citations from a variety of critics which follow prove that without a black feminist critical perspective not only are books by black women misunderstood, they are destroyed in the process.

Jerry H. Bryant, the *Nation's* white male reviewer of Alice Walker's *In Love and Trouble: Stories of Black Women,* wrote in 1973: "The subtitle of the collection, "Stories of Black Women," is probably an attempt by the publisher to exploit not only black subjects but feminine ones. There is nothing feminist about these stories, however."[2] Blackness and feminism are to his mind mutually exclusive and peripheral to the act of writing fiction. Bryant of course does not consider that Walker might have titled the work herself, nor did he apparently read the book which unequivocally reveals the author's feminist consciousness.

In *The Negro Novel in America,* a book that black critics recognize as one of the worst examples of white racist pseudoscholarship, Robert Bone cavalierly dismisses Ann Petry's classic, *The Street.* He perceives it to be "a superficial social analysis" of how slums victimize their black inhabitants.[3] He further objects that:

> It is an attempt to interpret slum life in terms of *Negro* experience, when a larger frame of reference is required. As Alain Locke has observed, "*Knock on Any Door* is superior to *The Street* because it designates class and environment, rather than mere race and environment, as its antagonist."[4]

Neither Robert Bone nor Alain Locke, the black male critic he cites, can recognize that *The Street* is one of the best delineations in literature of how sex, race *and* class interact to oppress black women.

In her review of Toni Morrison's *Sula* for *The New York Times Book Review* in 1973, putative feminist Sara Blackburn makes similarly racist comments. She writes:

> Toni Morrison is far too talented to remain only a marvelous recorder of the black side of provincial American life. If she is to maintain the large and serious audience she deserves, she is going to have to address a riskier contemporary reality than this beautiful but nevertheless distanced novel. *And if she does this, it seems to me that she might easily transcend that early and unintentionally limiting classification 'black woman writer' and take her place among the most serious, important and talented American novelists now working.*[5] [Italics mine]

Recognizing Morrison's exquisite gift, Blackburn unashamedly asserts that Morrison is "too talented" to deal with mere black folk, particularly those double nonentities, black women. In order to be accepted as "serious," "important," "talented" and "American," she must obviously focus her efforts upon chronicling the doings of white men.

The mishandling of black women writers by whites is paralleled more often by their not being handled at all, particularly in feminist criticism. Although Elaine Showalter in her review essay on literary criticism for *Signs* states that: "The best work being produced today [in feminist criticism] is exacting and cosmopolitan," her essay is neither.[6] If it were, she would not have failed to mention a single black or Third World woman writer, whether "major" or "minor," to cite her questionable categories. That she also does not even hint that lesbian writers of any color exist renders her purported overview virtually meaningless. Showalter obviously thinks that the identities of being black and female are mutually exclusive, as this statement illustrates: "Furthermore, there are other literary subcultures (black American novelists, for example) whose history offers a precedent for feminist scholarship to use."[7] The idea of critics like Showalter *using* black literature is chilling, a case of barely disguised cultural imperialism. The final insult is that she footnotes the preceding remark by pointing readers to works on black literature by white males Robert Bone and Roger Rosenblatt.

Two recent works by white women, Ellen Moers's *Literary Women: The great writers* and Patricia Meyer Spacks's *The Female Imagination*, evidence the same racist flaw.[8] Moers includes the names of four black and one Puertorriqueña writer in her seventy pages of bibliographical notes and does not deal at all with Third World women in the body of her book. Spacks refers to a comparison between Negroes (sic) and women in Mary Ellmann's *Thinking About Women* under the index entry, "blacks, women and." "Black Boy (Wright)" is the preceding entry. Nothing follows. Again there is absolutely no recognition that black and female identity ever coexist, specifically in a group of black women writers. Perhaps one can assume that these women do not know who black women writers are, that they have little opportunity like most Americans to learn about them. Perhaps. Their ignorance seems suspiciously selective, however, particularly in the light of the dozens of truly obscure white women writers they are able to unearth. Spacks was herself employed at Wellesley College at the same time that Alice Walker was there teaching one of the first courses on black women writers in the country.

I am not trying to encourage racist criticism of black women writers like that of Sara Blackburn, to cite only one example. As a beginning I would at least like to see in print white women's acknowledgment of the contradictions of who and what are being left out of their research and writing.[9]

Black male critics can also act as if they do not know that black women writers exist and are, of course, hampered by an inability to comprehend black women's experience in sexual as well as racial terms. Unfortunately there are also those who are as virulently sexist in their treatment of black women writers as their white male counterparts. Darwin Turner's discussion of Zora Neale Hurston in his *In a Minor Chord: Three Afro-American Writers and Their Search for Identity* is a frightening example of the near assassination of a great black woman writer.[10] His descriptions of her and her work as "artful," "coy," "irrational," "superficial" and "shallow" bear no relationship to the actual quality of her achievements. Turner is completely insensitive to the sexual political dynamics of Hurston's life and writing.

In a recent interview, the notoriously misogynist writer, Ishmael Reed, comments in this way upon the low sales of his newest novel:

> but the book only sold 8000 copies. I don't mind giving out the figure: 8000. Maybe if I was one of those young *female* Afro-American writers that are so hot now, I'd sell more. You know, fill my books with ghetto women who can *do no wrong*. . . . But come on, I think I could have sold 8000 copies by myself.[11]

The politics of the situation of black women are glaringly illuminated by this statement. Neither Reed nor his white male interviewer has the slightest compunction about attacking black women in print. They need not fear widespread public denunciation since Reed's statement is in perfect agreement with the values of a society that hates black people, women and black women. Finally the two of them feel free to base their actions on the premise that black women are powerless to alter either their political or their cultural oppression.

In her introduction to "A Bibliography of Works Written by American Black Women" Ora Williams quotes some of the reactions of her colleagues toward her efforts to do research on black women. She writes:

> Others have reacted negatively with such statements as, "I really don't think you are going to find very much written." "Have 'they' written anything that is any good?" and "I wouldn't go overboard with this woman's lib thing." When discussions touched on the possibility of teaching a course in which emphasis would be on the literature by black

women, one response was, "Ha, ha. That will certainly be the most
nothing course ever offered!"[12]

A remark by Alice Walker capsulizes what all the preceding examples
indicate about the position of black women writers and the reasons for the
damaging criticism about them. In response to her interviewer's question
"Why do you think that the black woman writer has been so ignored in
America? Does she have even more difficulty than the black male writer, who
perhaps has just begun to gain recognition?" Walker replies:

> There are two reasons why the black woman writer is not taken as seri-
> ously as the black male writer. One is that she's a woman. Critics seem
> unusually ill-equipped to intelligently discuss and analyze the works of
> black women. Generally, they do not even make the attempt; they pre-
> fer, rather, to talk about the lives of black women writers, not about
> what they write. And, since black women writers are not—it would
> seem—very likable—until recently they were the least willing worship-
> pers of male supremacy—comments about them tend to be cruel.[13]

A convincing case for black feminist criticism can obviously be built solely
upon the basis of the negativity of what already exists. It is far more gratify-
ing, however, to demonstrate its necessity by showing how it can serve to
reveal for the first time the profound subtleties of this particular body of
literature.

Before suggesting how a black feminist approach might be used to examine a specific work I will outline some of the principles that I think a black
feminist critic could use. Beginning with a primary commitment to exploring how both sexual and racial politics and black and female identity are
inextricable elements in black women's writings, she would also work from
the assumption that black women writers constitute an identifiable literary tradition. The breadth of her familiarity with these writers would have
shown her that not only is theirs a verifiable historical tradition that parallels in time the tradition of black men and white women writing in this country, but that thematically, stylistically, aesthetically and conceptually black
women writers manifest common approaches to the act of creating literature
as a direct result of the specific political, social and economic experience
they have been obliged to share. The way, for example, that Zora Neale
Hurston, Margaret Walker, Toni Morrison and Alice Walker incorporate the
traditional black female activities of rootworking, herbal medicine, conjure
and midwifery into the fabric of their stories is not mere coincidence, nor is

their use of specifically black female language to express their own and their characters' thoughts accidental. The use of black women's language and cultural experience in books *by* black women *about* black women results in a miraculously rich coalescing of form and content and also takes their writing far beyond the confines of white/male literary structures. The black feminist critic would find innumerable commonalities in works by black women.

Another principle which grows out of the concept of a tradition and which would also help to strengthen this tradition would be for the critic to look first for precedents and insights in interpretation within the works of other black women. In other words she would think and write out of her own identity and not try to graft the ideas or methodology of white/male literary thought upon the precious materials of black women's art. Black feminist criticism would by definition be highly innovative, embodying the daring spirit of the works themselves. The black feminist critic would be constantly aware of the political implications of her work and would assert the connections between it and the political situation of all black women. Logically developed, black feminist criticism would owe its existence to a black feminist movement while at the same time contributing ideas that women in the movement could use.

Black feminist criticism applied to a particular work can overturn previous assumptions about it and expose for the first time its actual dimensions. At the "Lesbians and Literature" discussion at the 1976 Modern Language Association convention Bertha Harris suggested that if in a woman writer's work a sentence refuses to do what it is supposed to do, if there are strong images of women and if there is a refusal to be linear, the result is innately lesbian literature. As usual, I wanted to see if these ideas might be applied to the black women writers that I know and quickly realized that many of their works were, in Harris's sense, lesbian. Not because women are lovers, but because they are the central figures, are positively portrayed and have pivotal relationships with one another. The form and language of these works are also nothing like what white patriarchal culture requires or expects.

I was particularly struck by the way in which Toni Morrison's novels *The Bluest Eye* and *Sula* could be explored from this new perspective.[14] In both works the relationships between girls and women are essential, yet at the same time physical sexuality is overtly expressed only between men and women. Despite the apparent heterosexuality of the female characters, I discovered in re-reading *Sula* that it works as a lesbian novel not only because of the passionate friendship between Sula and Nel, but because of Morrison's consistently critical stance toward the heterosexual institutions of male/female relationships, marriage and the family. Consciously or not, Morrison's work poses both lesbian and feminist questions about black women's autonomy and their impact upon each other's lives.

Sula and Nel find each other in 1922 when each of them is 12, on the brink of puberty and the discovery of boys. Even as awakening sexuality "clotted their dreams," each girl desires "a someone" obviously female with whom to share her feelings. Morrison writes:

> for it was in dreams that the two girls had met. Long before Edna Finch's Mellow House opened, even before they marched through the chocolate halls of Garfield Primary School . . . they had already made each other's acquaintance in the delirium of their noon dreams. They were solitary little girls whose loneliness was so profound it intoxicated them and sent them stumbling into Technicolored visions that always included a presence, a someone who, quite like the dreamer, shared the delight of the dream. When Nel, an only child, sat on the steps of her back porch surrounded by the high silence of her mother's incredibly orderly house, feeling the neatness pointing at her back, she studied the poplars and fell easily into a picture of herself lying on a flower bed, tangled in her own hair, waiting for some fiery prince. He approached but never quite arrived. But always, watching the dream along with her, were some smiling sympathetic eyes. Someone as interested as she herself in the flow of her imagined hair, the thickness of the mattress of flowers, the voile sleeves that closed below her elbows in gold-threaded cuffs.
>
> Similarly, Sula, also an only child, but wedged into a household of throbbing disorder constantly awry with things, people, voices and the slamming of doors, spent hours in the attic behind a roll of linoleum galloping through her own mind on a gray-and-white horse tasting sugar and smelling roses in full view of someone who shared both the taste and the speed.
>
> So when they met, first in those chocolate halls and next through the ropes of the swing, they felt the ease and comfort of old friends. Because each had discovered years before that they were neither white nor male, and that all freedom and triumph was forbidden to them, they had set about creating something else to be. Their meeting was fortunate, for it let them use each other to grow on. Daughters of distant mothers and incomprehensible fathers (Sula's because he was dead; Nel's because he wasn't), they found in each other's eyes the intimacy they were looking for. (*Sula*, 51–52)

As this beautiful passage shows, their relationship, from the very beginning, is suffused with an erotic romanticism. The dreams in which they are initially drawn to each other are actually complementary aspects of the same sensuous fairytale. Nel imagines a "fiery prince" who never quite arrives while Sula gallops like a prince "on a gray-and-white horse."[15] The "real world" of patriarchy requires, however, that they channel this energy away from each other to the opposite sex. Lorraine Bethel explains this dynamic in her essay "Conversations with Ourselves: Black Female Relationships in Toni Cade Bambara's *Gorilla, My Love* and Toni Morrison's *Sula*." She writes:

> I am not suggesting that Sula and Nel are being consciously sexual, or that their relationship has an overt lesbian nature. I am suggesting, however, that there is a certain sensuality in their interactions that is reinforced by the mirror-like nature of their relationship. Sexual exploration and coming of age is a natural part of adolescence. Sula and Nel discover men together, and though their flirtations with males are an important part of their sexual exploration, the sensuality that they experience in each other's company is equally important.[16]

Sula and Nel must also struggle with the constrictions of racism upon their lives. The knowledge that "they were neither white nor male" is the inherent explanation of their need for each other. Morrison depicts in literature the necessary bonding that has always taken place between black women for the sake of barest survival. Together the two girls can find the courage to create themselves.

Their relationship is severed only when Nel marries Jude, an unexceptional young man who thinks of her as "the hem—the tuck and fold that hid his raveling edges" (83). Sula's inventive wildness cannot overcome social pressure or the influence of Nel's parents who "had succeeded in rubbing down to a dull glow any sparkle or splutter she had" (83). Nel falls prey to convention while Sula escapes it. Yet at the wedding which ends the first phase of their relationship, Nel's final action is to look past her husband toward Sula:

> a slim figure in blue, gliding, with just a hint of a strut, down the path towards the road. . . . Even from the rear Nel could tell that it was Sula and that she was smiling; that something deep down in that litheness was amused. (85)

When Sula returns ten years later, her rebelliousness full-blown, a major source of the town's suspicions stems from the fact that although she is almost thirty, she is still unmarried. Sula's grandmother, Eva, does not hesitate to bring up the matter as soon as she arrives. She asks "When you gone to get married? You need to have some babies. It'll settle you. . . . Ain't no woman got no business floatin' around without no man" (92). Sula replies: "I don't want to make somebody else. I want to make myself" (92). Self-definition is a dangerous activity for any women to engage in, especially a black one, and it expectedly earns Sula pariah status in Medallion.

Morrison clearly points out that it is the fact that Sula has not been tamed or broken by the exigencies of heterosexual family life which most galls the others. She writes:

> Among the weighty evidence piling up was the fact that Sula did not look her age. She was near thirty and, unlike them, had lost no teeth, suffered no bruises, developed no ring of fat at the waist or pocket at the back of her neck. (115)

In other words she is not a domestic serf, a woman run down by obligatory childbearing or a victim of battering. Sula also sleeps with the husbands of the town once and then discards them, needing them even less than her own mother did, for sexual gratification and affection. The town reacts to her disavowal of patriarchal values by becoming fanatically serious about their own family obligations, as if in this way they might counteract Sula's radical criticism of their lives.

Sula's presence in her community functions much like the presence of lesbians everywhere to expose the contradictions of supposedly normal life. The opening paragraph of the essay "Woman Identified Woman" has amazing relevance as an explanation of Sula's position and character in the novel. It asks:

> What is a lesbian? A lesbian is the rage of all women condensed to the point of explosion. She is the woman who, often beginning at an extremely early age, acts in accordance with her inner compulsion to be a more complete and freer human being than her society—perhaps then, but certainly later—cares to allow her. These needs and actions, over a period of years, bring her into painful conflict with people, situations, the accepted ways of thinking, feeling and behaving, until she is in a state of continual war with everything around her, and usually with herself. She may not be fully conscious of the political implications of what for her began as personal necessity, but on some level she has not been able to accept the limitations and oppression laid on her by the most basic role of her society—the female role.[17]

The limitations of the *black* female role are even greater in a racist and sexist society as is the amount of courage it takes to challenge them. It is no wonder that the townspeople see Sula's independence as imminently dangerous.

Morrison is also careful to show the reader that despite their years of separation and their opposing paths, Nel and Sula's relationship retains its primacy for each of them. Nel feels transformed when Sula returns and thinks:

> It was like getting the use of an eye back, having a cataract removed. Her old friend had come home. Sula. Who made her laugh, who made her see old things with new eyes, in whose presence she felt clever, gentle and a littly raunchy. (95)

Laughing together in the familiar "rib-scraping" way. Nel feels "new, soft and new" (98). Morrison uses here the visual imagery which symbolizes the women's closeness throughout the novel.

Sula fractures this closeness, however, by sleeping with Nel's husband, an act of little import according to her system of values. Nel, of course, cannot understand. Sula thinks ruefully:

> Nel was the one person who had wanted nothing from her, who had accepted all aspects of her. Now she wanted everything, and all because of *that*. Nel was the first person who had been real to her, whose name she knew, who had seen as she had the slant of life that made it possible to stretch it to its limits. Now Nel was one of *them*. (119–20)

Sula also thinks at the realization of losing Nel about how unsatisfactory her relationships with men have been and admits: "She had been looking all along for a friend, and it took her a while to discover that a lover was not a comrade and could never be—for a woman" (121). The nearest that Sula comes to actually loving a man is in a brief affair with Ajax and what she values most about him is the intellectual companionship he provides, the brilliance he "allows" her to show.

Sula's feelings about sex with men are also consistent with a lesbian interpretation of the novel. Morrison writes:

> She went to bed with men as frequently as she could. It was the only place where she could find what she was looking for: *misery and the ability to feel deep sorrow.* . . . During the lovemaking she found and needed to find the cutting edge. When she left off cooperating with her body and began to assert herself in the act, particles of strength gathered

in her like steel shavings drawn to a spacious magnetic center, forming a tight cluster that nothing, it seemed, could break. *And there was utmost irony and outrage in lying under someone, in a position of surrender, feeling her own abiding strength and limitless power.* . . . When her partner disengaged himself, she looked up at him in wonder trying to recall his name . . . waiting impatiently for him to turn away . . . *leaving her to the postcoital privateness in which she met herself, welcomed herself and joined herself in matchless harmony.* (122–23) [Italics mine]

Sula uses men for sex which results not in communion with them, but in her further delving into self.

Ultimately the deepest communion and communication in the novel occurs between two women who love each other. After their last painful meeting, which does not bring reconciliation, Sula thinks as Nel leaves her:

"So she will walk on down that road, her back so straight in that old green coat . . . thinking how much I have cost her and never remember the days when we were two throats and one eye and we had no price." (147)

It is difficult to imagine a more evocative metaphor for what women can be to each other, the "pricelessness" they achieve in refusing to sell themselves for male approval, the total worth that they can only find in each other's eyes.

Decades later the novel concludes with Nel's final comprehension of the source of the grief that has plagued her from the time her husband walked out. Morrison writes:

"All that time, all that time, I thought I was missing Jude." And the loss pressed down on her chest and came up into her throat. "We was girls together," she said as though explaining something. "O Lord, Sula," she cried, "girl, girl, girlgirlgirl."

It was a fine cry—loud and long—but it had no bottom and it had no top, just circles and circles of sorrow. (174)

Again Morrison exquisitely conveys what women, black women, mean to each other. This final passage verifies the depth of Sula and Nel's relationship and its centrality to an accurate interpretation of the work.

Sula is an exceedingly lesbian novel in the emotions expressed, in the definition of female character, and in the way that the politics of heterosexuality are portrayed. The very meaning of lesbianism is being expanded in literature, just as it is being redefined through politics. The confusion that many readers have felt about *Sula* may well have a lesbian explanation. If one sees Sula's inexplicable "evil" and nonconformity as the evil of not being male-identified, many elements in the novel become clear. The work might be clearer still if Morrison had approached her subject with the consciousness that a lesbian relationship was at least a possibility for her characters. Obviously Morrison did not *intend* the reader to perceive Sula and Nel's relationship as inherently lesbian. However, this lack of intention only shows the way in which heterosexist assumptions can veil what may logically be expected to occur in a work. What I have tried to do here is not to prove that Morrison wrote something that she did not, but to point out how a black feminist critical perspective at least allows consideration of this level of the novel's meaning.

In her interview in *Conditions: One* Adrienne Rich talks about unconsummated relationships and the need to reevaluate the meaning of intense yet supposedly nonerotic connections between women. She asserts: "We need a lot more documentation about what actually happened: I think we can also imagine it, because we know it happened—we know it out of our own lives."[18] Black women are still in the position of having to "imagine," discover and verify black lesbian literature because so little has been written from an avowedly lesbian perspective. The near nonexistence of black lesbian literature which other black lesbians and I so deeply feel has everything to do with the politics of our lives, the total suppression of identity that all black women, lesbian or not, must face. This literary silence is again intensified by the unavailability of an autonomous black feminist movement through which we could fight our oppression and also begin to name ourselves.

In a speech, "The Autonomy of Black Lesbian Women," Wilmette Brown comments upon the connection between our political reality and the literature we must invent:

> Because the isolation of Black lesbian women, given that we are superfreaks, given that our lesbianism defies both the sexual identity that capital gives us and the racial identity that capital gives us, the isolation of Black lesbian women from heterosexual Black women is very profound. Very profound. I have searched throughout Black history, Black literature, whatever, looking for some women that I could see were somehow lesbian. Now I know that in a certain sense they were all lesbian. But that was a very painful search.[19]

Heterosexual privilege is usually the only privilege that black women have. None of us have racial or sexual privilege, almost none of us have class privilege, maintaining "straightness" is our last resort. Being out, particularly out in print, is the final renunciation of any claim to the crumbs of tolerance that nonthreatening ladylike black women are sometimes fed. I am convinced that it is our lack of privilege and power in every other sphere that allows so few black women to make the leap that many white women, particularly writers, have been able to make in this decade, not merely because they are white or have economic leverage, but because they have had the strength and support of a movement behind them.

As black lesbians we must be out not only in white society, but in the black community as well, which is at least as homophobic. That the sanctions against black lesbians are extremely high is well illustrated in this comment by black male writer Ishmael Reed. Speaking about the inroads that whites make into black culture, he asserts:

> In Manhattan you find people actively trying to impede intellectual debate among Afro-Americans. The powerful "liberal/radical/existentialist" influences of the Manhattan literary and drama establishment speak through tokens, like for example that ancient notion of the *one* black ideologue (who's usually a Communist), the *one* black poetess (who's usually a feminist lesbian).[20]

To Reed, "feminist" and "lesbian" are the most pejorative terms he can hurl at a black woman and totally invalidate anything she might say, regardless of her actual politics or sexual identity. Such accusations are quite effective for keeping black women writers who are writing with integrity and strength from any conceivable perspective in line, but especially ones who are actually feminist and lesbian. Unfortunately Reed's reactionary attitude is all too typical. A community which has not confronted sexism, because a widespread black feminist movement has not required it to, has likewise not been challenged to examine its heterosexism. Even at this moment I am not convinced that one can write explicitly as a black lesbian and live to tell about it.

Yet there are a handful of black women who have risked everything for truth. Audre Lorde, Pat Parker and Ann Allen Shockley have at least broken ground in the vast wilderness of works that do not exist.[21] Black feminist criticism will again have an essential role not only in creating a climate in which black lesbian writers can survive, but in undertaking the total reassessment of black literature and literary history needed to reveal the black woman-identified women that Wilmette Brown and so many of us are looking for.

Although I have concentrated here upon what does not exist and what needs to be done, a few black feminist critics have already begun this work. Gloria T. Hull at the University of Delaware has discovered in her research on black women poets of the Harlem Renaissance that many of the women who are considered minor writers of the period were in constant contact with each other and provided both intellectual stimulation and psychological support for each other's work. At least one of these writers, Angelina Weld Grimké, wrote many unpublished love poems to women. Lorraine Bethel, a recent graduate of Yale College, has done substantial work on black women writers, particularly in her senior essay, "This Infinity of Conscious Pain: Blues Lyricism and Hurston's Black Female Folk Aesthetic and Cultural Sensibility in *Their Eyes Were Watching God,*" in which she brilliantly defines and uses the principles of black feminist criticism. Elaine Scott at the State University of New York at Old Westbury is also involved in highly creative and politically resonant research on Hurston and other writers.

The fact that these critics are young and, except for Hull, unpublished merely indicates the impediments we face. Undoubtedly there are other women working and writing whom I do not even know, simply because there is no place to read them. As Michele Wallace states in her article "A Black feminist's search for sisterhood":

> We exist as women who are Black who are feminists, each stranded for the moment, working independently because there is not yet an environment in this society remotely congenial to our struggle—[or our thoughts].[22]

I only hope that this essay is one way of breaking our silence and our isolation, of helping us to know each other.

Just as I did not know where to start I am not sure how to end. I feel that I have tried to say too much and at the same time have left too much unsaid. What I want this essay to do is lead everyone who reads it to examine *everything* that they have ever thought and believed about feminist culture and to ask themselves how their thoughts connect to the reality of black women's writing and lives. I want to encourage in white women, as a first step, a sane accountability to all the women who write and live on this soil. I want most of all for black women and black lesbians somehow not to be so alone. This last will require the most expansive of revolutions as well as many new words to tell us how to make this revolution real. I finally want to express how much easier both my waking and my sleeping hours would be if there were one book in existence that would tell me something specific about my life. One book based in black feminist and black lesbian experience, fiction or nonfiction. Just one work to reflect the reality that I and the black women whom I love are trying to create. When such a book exists then each of us will not only know better how to live, but how to dream.

Notes

1   Alice Walker, "In Search of Our Mothers' Gardens," *Ms.*, May 1974, and *Southern Exposure*, 4.4, *Generations: Women in the South,* Winter 1977, 60–64.
2   Jerry H. Bryant, "The Outskirts of a New City," *Nation*, 12 (November 1973), 502.
3   Robert Bone, *The Negro Novel in America* (New Haven, Conn., 1958), 180.
4   Ibid. (*Knock on Any Door* [New York, 1947] is a novel by black writer Willard Motley.)
5   Sara Blackburn, "You Still Can't Go Home Again," *The New York Times Book Review,* 30 December 1973, 3.
6   Elaine Showalter, "Review Essay: Literary Criticism," *Signs* 2 (Winter 1975), 460.
7   Ibid., 445.
8   Ellen Moers, *Literary Women: The Great Writers* (Garden City, N.Y., 1977); Patricia Meyer Spacks, *The Female Imagination* (New York, 1976).
9   An article by Nancy Hoffman, "White Women, Black Women: Inventing an Adequate Pedagogy," *Women's Studies Newsletter,* 5.1 and 2 (Spring 1977), 21–24, gives valuable insights into how white women can approach the writing of black women.
10   Darwin T. Turner, *In a Minor Chord: Three Afro-American Writers and Their Search for Identity* (Carbondale and Edwardsville, Ill., 1971).
11   John Domini, "Roots and Racism: An Interview with Ishmael Reed," *Boston Phoenix*, 5 April 1977, 20.
12   Ora Williams, "A Bibliography of Works Written by American Black Women," *College Language Association Journal*, 15.3 (March 1972), 355. There is an expanded book-length version of this bibliography: *American Black Women in the Arts and Social Sciences: A Bibliographic Survey*, rev. ed. (Metuchen, N.J., 1978).
13   John O'Brien, ed., *Interviews with Black Writers* (New York, 1973), 201.
14   Toni Morrison, *The Bluest Eye* (New York, 1970) and *Sula* (New York, 1974). All subsequent references to this work will be designated in the text.
15   My sister, Beverly Smith, pointed out this connection to me.
16   Lorraine Bethel, "Conversations with Ourselves: Black Female Relationships in Toni Cade Bambara's *Gorilla, My Love* and Toni Morrison's *Sula*," unpublished paper written at Yale, 1976. (Bethel has worked from a premise similar to mine in a much more developed treatment of the novel.)
17   New York Radicalesbians, "Woman Identified Woman," in *Lesbians Speak Out* (Oakland, 1974), 87.
18   Elly Bulkin, "An interview with Adrienne Rich: Part I," *Conditions: One* (April 1977), 62.
19   Wilmette Brown, "The autonomy of Black lesbian women," MS of speech delivered 24 July 1976, Toronto, Canada, 7.
20   Domini, "Roots and racism," 18.
21   Audre Lorde, *New York Head Shop and Museum* (Detroit, 1974); *Coal* (New York, 1976); *Between Our Selves* (Point Reyes, Calif., 1976); *The Black Unicorn* (New York, 1978).

Pat Parker, *Child of Myself* (Oakland, 1972 and 1974); *Pit Stop* (Oakland, 1973); *Woman-slaughter* (Oakland, 1978); *Movement in Black* (Oakland, 1978).

Ann Allen Shockley, *Loving Her* (Indianapolis, 1974).

There is at least one Black lesbian writers' collective, Jemima, in New York. They do public readings and have available a collection of their poems. They can be contacted c/o Boyce, 41-11 Parsons Blvd., Flushing, N.Y. 11355.

22   Michele Wallace, "A Black Feminist's Search for Sisterhood," *Village Voice*, 28 July 1975, 7.

Deborah E. McDowell

New Directions for Black

Feminist Criticism

(1980)

What is commonly called literary history," writes Louise Bernikow, "is actually a record of choices. Which writers have survived their times and which have not depends upon who noticed them and chose to record their notice."[1] Women writers have fallen victim to arbitrary selection. Their writings have been "patronized, slighted, and misunderstood by a cultural establishment operating according to male norms out of male perceptions."[2] Both literary history's "sins of omission" and literary criticism's inaccurate and partisan judgments of women writers have come under attack since the early 1970s by feminist critics.[3] To date, no one has formulated a precise or complete definition of feminist criticism, but since its inception, its theorists and practitioners have agreed that it is a "corrective, unmasking the omissions and distortions of the past—the errors of a literary critical tradition that arise from and reflect a culture created, perpetuated, and dominated by men."[4]

These early theorists and practitioners of feminist literary criticism were largely white females who, wittingly or not, perpetrated against the Black woman writer the same exclusive practices they so vehemently decried in white male scholars. Seeing the experiences of white women, particularly white middle-class women, as normative, white female scholars proceeded blindly to exclude the work of Black women writers from literary anthologies and critical studies. Among the most flagrant examples of this chauvinism is Patricia Meyer Spacks's *The Female Imagination*. In a weak defense of her book's exclusive focus on women in the Anglo-American literary tradition, Spacks quotes Phyllis Chesler (a white female psychologist): "I have no theory to offer of Third World female psychology in America. . . . As a

This essay first appeared in *Black American Literature Forum*, 14 (1980).

white woman, I'm reluctant and unable to construct theories about experiences I haven't had."[5] But, as Alice Walker observes, "Spacks never lived in nineteenth-century Yorkshire, so why theorize about the Brontës?"[6]

Not only have Black women writers been "disenfranchised" from critical works by white women scholars on the "female tradition," but they have also been frequently excised from those on the Afro-American literary tradition by Black scholars, most of whom are males. For example, Robert Stepto's *From Behind the Veil: A Study of Afro-American Narrative* purports to be "a history . . . of the historical consciousness of an Afro-American art form—namely, the Afro-American written narrative."[7] Yet, Black women writers are conspicuously absent from the table of contents. Though Stepto does have a token two-page discussion of Zora Neale Hurston's *Their Eyes Were Watching God* in which he refers to it as a "seminal narrative in Afro-American letters,"[8] he did not feel that the novel merited its own chapter or the thorough analysis accorded the other works he discusses.

When Black women writers are neither ignored altogether nor merely given honorable mention, they are critically misunderstood and summarily dismissed. In *The Negro Novel in America*, for example, Robert Bone's reading of Jessie Fauset's novels is both partisan and superficial and might explain the reasons Fauset remains obscure. Bone argues that Fauset is the foremost member of the "Rear Guard" of writers "who lagged behind," clinging to established literary traditions. The "Rear Guard" drew their source material from the Negro middle class in their efforts "to orient Negro art toward white opinion," and "to apprise educated whites of the existence of respectable Negroes." Bone adds that Fauset's emphasis on the Black middle class results in novels that are "uniformly sophomoric, trivial and dull."[9]

While David Littlejohn praises Black fiction since 1940, he denigrates the work of Fauset and Nella Larsen. He maintains that "the newer writers are obviously writing as men, for men," and are avoiding the "very close and steamy" writing that is the result of "any subculture's taking itself too seriously, defining the world and its values exclusively in the terms of its own restrictive norms and concerns."[10] This "phallic criticism,"[11] to use Mary Ellman's term, is based on masculine-centered values and definitions. It has dominated the criticism of Black women writers and has done much to guarantee that most would be, in Alice Walker's words, "casually pilloried and consigned to a sneering oblivion."[12]

Suffice it to say that the critical community has not favored Black women writers. The recognition among Black female critics and writers that white women, white men, and Black men consider their experiences as normative and Black women's experiences as deviant has given rise to Black feminist criticism. Much as in white feminist criticism, the critical postulates of Black women's literature are only skeletally defined. Although there is no concrete definition of Black feminist criticism, a handful of Black female scholars have begun the necessary enterprise of resurrecting forgotten Black women writers and revising misinformed critical opinions of them. Justifiably enraged by the critical establishment's neglect and mishandling of Black women writers, these critics are calling for, in the words of Barbara Smith, "nonhostile and perceptive analysis of works written by persons outside the 'mainstream' of white/male cultural rule."[13]

Despite the urgency and timeliness of the enterprise, however, no substantial body of Black feminist criticism—either in theory or practice—exists, a fact which might be explained partially by our limited access to and control of the media.[14] Another explanation for the paucity of Black feminist criticism, notes Barbara Smith, is the lack of a "developed body of Black feminist political theory whose assumptions could be used in the study of Black women's art."

Despite the strained circumstances under which Black feminist critics labor, a few committed Black female scholars have broken necessary ground. For the remainder of this essay I would like to focus on selected writings of Black feminist critics, discussing their strengths and weaknesses and suggesting new directions toward which the criticism might move and pitfalls that it might avoid.

Unfortunately, Black feminist scholarship has been decidedly more practical than theoretical, and the theories developed thus far have often lacked sophistication and have been marred by slogans, rhetoric, and idealism. The articles that attempt to apply these theoretical tenets often lack precision and detail. These limitations are not without reason. As Dorin Schumacher observes, "the feminist critic has few philosophical shelters, pillars, or guideposts," and thus "feminist criticism is fraught with intellectual and professional risks, offering more opportunity for creativity, yet greater possibility of errors."[15]

The earliest theoretical statement on Black feminist criticism is Barbara Smith's "Toward a Black Feminist Criticism." Though its importance as a groundbreaking piece of scholarship cannot be denied, it suffers from lack of precision and detail. In justifying the need for a Black feminist aesthetic, Smith argues that "a Black feminist approach to literature that embodies the realization that the politics of sex as well as the politics of race and class are crucially interlocking factors in the works of Black women writers is an absolute necessity." Until such an approach exists, she continues, "we will not even know what these writers mean."

Smith points out that "thematically, stylistically, aesthetically, and conceptually Black women writers manifest common approaches to the act of creating literature as a direct result of the specific political, social, and economic experience they have been obliged to share." She offers, as an example, the incorporation of rootworking, herbal medicine, conjure, and midwifery in the stories of Zora Neale Hurston, Margaret Walker, Toni Morrison, and Alice Walker. While these folk elements certainly do appear in the work of the writers, they also appear in the works of certain Black male writers, a fact that Smith omits. If Black women writers use these elements differently from Black male writers, such a distinction must be made before one can effectively articulate the basis of a Black feminist aesthetic.

Smith maintains further that Zora Neale Hurston, Margaret Walker, Toni Morrison, and Alice Walker use a "specifically black female language to express their own and their characters' thoughts," but she fails to describe or to provide examples of this unique language. Of course, we have come recently to acknowledge that "many of our habits of language usage are sex-derived, sex-associated, and/or sex-distinctive," that "the ways in which men and women internalize and manipulate language" are undeniably sex-related.[16] But this realization in itself simply paves the way for further investigation that can begin by exploring some critical questions. For example, is there a monolithic Black female language? Do Black female high school dropouts, welfare mothers, college graduates, and Ph.D.s share a common language? Are there regional variations in this common language? Further, some Black male critics have tried to describe the uniquely "Black linguistic elegance"[17] that characterizes Black poetry. Are there noticeable differences between the languages of Black females and Black males? These and other questions must be addressed with precision if current feminist terminology is to function beyond mere critical jargon.

Smith turns from her discussion of the commonalities among Black women writers to describe the nature of her critical enterprise. "Black feminist criticism would by definition be highly innovative," she maintains. "Applied to a particular work [it] can overturn previous assumptions about [the work] and expose for the first time its actual dimensions." Smith then proceeds to demonstrate this critical postulate by interpreting Toni Morrison's *Sula* as a lesbian novel, an interpretation she believes is maintained in "the emotions expressed, in the definition of female character and in the way that the politics of heterosexuality are portrayed." Smith vacillates between argu-

ing forthrightly for the validity of her interpretation and recanting or over-
qualifying it in a way that undercuts her own credibility.

According to Smith, "if in a woman writer's work a sentence refuses to do
what it is supposed to do, if there are strong images of women and if there is a
refusal to be linear, the result is innately lesbian literature." She adds, "because of Morrison's consistently critical stance toward the heterosexual institutions of male-female relationships, marriage, and the family," *Sula* works
as a lesbian novel. This definition of lesbianism is vague and imprecise; it
subsumes far more Black women writers, particularly contemporary ones,
than not into the canon of Lesbian writers. For example, Jessie Fauset, Nella
Larsen, and Zora Neale Hurston all criticize major socializing institutions, as
do Gwendolyn Brooks, Alice Walker, and Toni Cade Bambara. Further, if we
apply Smith's definition of lesbianism, there are probably a few Black male
writers who qualify as well. All of this is to say that Smith has simultaneously
oversimplified and obscured the issue of lesbianism. Obviously aware of the
delicacy of her position, she interjects that "the very meaning of lesbianism
is being expanded in literature." Unfortunately, her qualification does not
strengthen her argument. One of the major tasks ahead of Black feminist
critics who write from a lesbian perspective, then, is to define lesbianism and
lesbian literature precisely. Until they can offer a definition which is not
vacuous, their attempts to distinguish Black lesbian writers from those who
are not will be hindered.[18]

Even as I call for firmer definitions of lesbianism and lesbian literature, I
question whether a lesbian aesthetic is not finally a reductive approach to the
study of Black women's literature which possibly ignores other equally important aspects of the literature. For example, reading *Sula* solely from a
lesbian perspective overlooks the novel's density and complexity, its skillful
blend of folklore, omens, and dreams, its metaphorical and symbolic richness. Although I do not quarrel with Smith's appeal for fresher, more innovative approaches to Black women's literature, I suspect that "innovative" analysis is pressed to the service of an individual political persuasion. One's
personal and political presuppositions enter into one's critical judgments.
Nevertheless, we should heed Annette Kolodny's warning for feminist critics to

> be wary of reading literature as though it were polemic. . . . If when
> using literary materials to make what is essentially a political point, we
> find ourselves virtually rewriting a text, ignoring certain aspects of plot
> or characterization, or over-simplifying the action to fit our "political"

thesis, then we are neither practicing an honest criticism nor saying anything useful about the nature of art (or about the art of political persuasion, for that matter).[19]

Alerting feminist critics to the dangers of political ideology yoked with aesthetic judgment is not synonymous with denying that feminist criticism is a valid and necessary cultural and political enterprise. Indeed, it is both possible and useful to translate ideological positions into aesthetic ones, but if the criticism is to be responsible, the two must be balanced.

Because it is a cultural and political enterprise, feminist critics, in the main, believe that their criticism can effect social change. Smith certainly argues for socially relevant criticism in her conclusion that "Black feminist criticism would owe its existence to a Black feminist movement while at the same time contributing ideas that women in the movement could use." This is an exciting idea in itself, but we should ask: What ideas, specifically, would Black feminist criticism contribute to the movement? Further, even though the proposition of a fruitful relationship between political activism and the academy is an interesting (and necessary) one, I doubt its feasibility. I am not sure that either in theory or in practice Black feminist criticism will be able to alter significantly circumstances that have led to the oppression of Black women. Moreover, as Lillian Robinson pointedly remarks, there is no assurance that feminist aesthetics "will be productive of a vision of art or of social relations that is of the slightest use to the masses of women, or even one that acknowledges the existence and struggle of such women."[20] I agree with Robinson that "ideological criticism must take place in the context of a political movement that can put it to work. The revolution is simply not going to be made by literary journals."[21] I should say that I am not arguing a defeatist position with respect to the social and political uses to which feminist criticism can be put. Just as it is both possible and useful to translate ideological positions into aesthetic ones, it must likewise be possible and useful to translate aesthetic positions into the machinery for social change.

Despite the shortcomings of Smith's article, she raises critical issues on which Black feminist critics can build. There are many tasks ahead of these critics, not the least of which is to attempt to formulate some clear definitions of what Black feminist criticism is. I use the term here simply to refer to Black female critics who analyze the works of Black female writers from a feminist or political perspective. But the term can also apply to any criticism written by a Black woman regardless of her subject or perspective—a book written by a male from a feminist or political perspective, a book written by a

Black woman or about Black women authors in general, or any writings by women.[22]

In addition to defining the methodology, Black feminist critics need to determine the extent to which their criticism intersects with that of white feminist critics. Barbara Smith and others have rightfully challenged white women scholars to become more accountable to Black and Third World women writers, but will that require white women to use a different set of critical tools when studying Black women writers? Are white women's theories predicated upon culturally specific values and assumptions? Andrea Benton Rushing has attempted to answer these questions in her series of articles on images of Black women in literature. She maintains, for example, that critical categories of women, based on analyses of white women characters, are Euro-American in derivation and hence inappropriate to a consideration of Black women characters.[23] Such distinctions are necessary and, if held uniformly, can materially alter the shape of Black feminist scholarship.

Regardless of which theoretical framework Black feminist critics choose, they must have an informed handle on Black literature and Black culture in general. Such a grounding can give this scholarship more texture and completeness and perhaps prevent some of the problems that have had a vitiating effect on the criticism.

This footing in Black history and culture serves as a basis for the study of the literature. Termed "contextual" by theoreticians, this approach is often frowned upon if not dismissed entirely by critics who insist exclusively upon textual and linguistic analysis. Its limitations notwithstanding, I firmly believe that the contextual approach to Black women's literature exposes the conditions under which literature is produced, published, and reviewed. This approach is not only useful but necessary to Black feminist critics.

To those working with Black women writers prior to 1940, the contextual approach is especially useful. In researching Jessie Fauset, Nella Larsen, and Zora Neale Hurston, for example, it is useful to determine what the prevalent attitudes about Black women were during the time that they wrote. There is much information in the Black "little" magazines published during the Harlem Renaissance. An examination of *The Messenger*, for instance, reveals that the dominant social attitudes about Black women were strikingly consistent with traditional middle-class expectations of women. *The Messenger* ran a monthly symposium for some time entitled "Negro Womanhood's Greatest Needs." While a few female contributors stressed the importance of women being equal to men socially, professionally, and economically, the majority emphasized that a woman's place was in the home. It was her duty "to cling to the home [since] great men and women evolve from the environment of the hearthstone."[24]

One of the most startling entries came from a woman who wrote:

The New Negro Woman, with her head erect and spirit undaunted, is resolutely marching forward, ever conscious of her historic and noble mission of doing her bit toward the liberation of her people in particular and the human race in general. Upon her shoulders rests the big task to create and keep alive, in the breast of black men, a holy and consuming passion to break with the slave traditions of the past; to spurn and over-come the fatal, insidious inferiority complex of the present, which . . . bobs up ever and anon, to arrest the progress of the New Negro Man-hood Movement; and to fight with increasing vigor, with dauntless courage, unrelenting zeal and intelligent vision for the attainment of the stature of a full man, a free race and a new world.[25]

Not only does the contributor charge the Black woman with a formidable task, but she also sees her solely in relation to Black men.

This information enhances our understanding of what Fauset, Larsen, and Hurston confronted in attempting to offer alternative images of Black women. Moreover, it helps to clarify certain textual problems and ambigu-ities of their work. Though Fauset and Hurston, for example, explored femi-nist concerns, they leaned toward ambivalence. Fauset especially is alter-nately forthright and cagey, radical and traditional, on issues that confront women. Her first novel, *There Is Confusion* (1924), is flawed by an unantici-pated and abrupt reversal in characterization that brings the central female character more in line with a feminine norm. Similarly, in her last novel, *Seraph on the Swanee* (1948), Zora Neale Hurston depicts a female character who shows promise for growth and change, for a departure from the conven-tional expectations of womanhood, but who in the end apotheosizes mar-riage, motherhood, and domestic servitude.

These two examples alone clearly capture the tension between social pres-sure and artistic integrity which is felt, to some extent, by all women writers. As Tillie Olsen points out, the fear of reprisal from the publishing and critical arenas is a looming obstacle to the woman writer's coming into her own authentic voice. "Fear—the need to please, to be safe—in the literary realm too. Founded fear. Power is still in the hands of men. Power of validation, publication, approval, reputation. . . ."[26]

While insisting on the validity, usefulness, and necessity of contextual ap-proaches to Black women's literature, the Black feminist critic must not ignore the importance of rigorous textual analysis. I am aware of many feminist critics' stubborn resistance to the critical methodology handed down by white men. Although the resistance is certainly politically consistent and logical, I agree with Annette Kolodny that feminist criticism would be "shortsighted if it summarily rejected all the inherited tools of critical analysis simply because they are male and western." We should, rather, salvage what we find useful in past methodologies, reject what we do not, and, where necessary, move toward "inventing new methods of analysis."[27] Particularly useful is Lillian Robinson's suggestion that "a radical kind of textual criticism . . . could usefully study the way the texture of sentences, choice of metaphors, patterns of exposition and narrative relate to [feminist] ideology."[28]

This rigorous textual analysis involves, as Barbara Smith recommends, isolating as many thematic, stylistic, and linguistic commonalities among Black women writers as possible. Among contemporary Black female novelists, the thematic parallels are legion. In Alice Walker and Toni Morrison, for example, the theme of the thwarted female artist figures prominently.[29] Pauline Breedlove in Morrison's The Bluest Eye, for example, is obsessed with ordering things:

> Jars on shelves at canning, peach pits on the step, sticks, stones, leaves. . . . Whatever portable plurality she found, she organized into neat lines, according to their size, shape or gradations of color. . . . She missed without knowing what she missed—paints and crayons.[30]

Similarly, Eva Peace in Sula is forever ordering the pleats in her dress. And Sula's strange and destructive behavior is explained as "the consequence of an idle imagination."

> Had she paints, clay, or knew the discipline of the dance, or strings; had she anything to engage her tremendous curiosity and her gift for metaphor, she might have exchanged the restlessness and preoccupation with whim for an activity that provided her with all she yearned for. And like any artist with no form, she became dangerous.[31]

Likewise, Meridian's mother in Alice Walker's novel Meridian makes artificial flowers and prayer pillows too small for kneeling.

The use of "clothing as iconography"[32] is central to writings by Black women. For example, in one of Jessie Fauset's early short stories, "The Sleeper Wakes" (1920), Amy, the protagonist, is associated with pink clothing (suggesting innocence and immaturity) while she is blinded by fairy-tale notions of love and marriage. However, after she declares her independence from her racist and sexist husband, Amy no longer wears pink. The imagery of clothing is abundant in Zora Neale Hurston's *Their Eyes Were Watching God* (1937). Janie's apron, her silks and satins, her head scarves, and finally her overalls all symbolize various stages of her journey from captivity to liberation. Finally, in Alice Walker's *Meridian*, Meridian's railroad cap and dungarees are emblems of her rejection of conventional images and expectations of womanhood.

A final theme that recurs in the novels of Black women writers is the motif of the journey. Though one can also find this same motif in the works of Black male writers, they do not use it in the same way as do Black female writers.[33] For example, the journey of the Black male character in works by Black men takes him underground. It is a "descent into the underworld,"[34] and is primarily political and social in its implications. Ralph Ellison's *Invisible Man*, Imamu Amiri Baraka's *The System of Dante's Hell*, and Richard Wright's "The Man Who Lived Underground" exemplify this quest. The Black female's journey, on the other hand, though at times touching the political and social, is basically a personal and psychological journey. The female character in the works of Black women is in a state of becoming "part of an evolutionary spiral, moving from victimization to consciousness."[35] The heroines in Zora Neale Hurston's *Their Eyes Were Watching God*, in Alice Walker's *Meridian*, and in Toni Cade Bambara's *The Salt Eaters* are emblematic of this distinction.

Even though isolating such thematic and imagistic commonalities should continue to be one of the Black feminist critic's most urgent tasks, she should beware of generalizing on the basis of too few examples. If one argues authoritatively for the existence of a Black female "consciousness" or "vision" or "literary tradition," one must be sure that the parallels found recur with enough consistency to support these generalizations. Further, Black feminist critics should not become obsessed in searching for common themes and images in Black women's works. As I pointed out earlier, investigating the question of "female" language is critical and may well be among the most challenging jobs awaiting the Black feminist critic. The growing body of research on gender-specific uses of language might aid these critics. In fact, wherever possible, feminist critics should draw on the scholarship of feminists in other disciplines.

An equally challenging and necessary task ahead of the Black feminist critic is a thoroughgoing examination of the works of Black male writers. In her introduction to *Midnight Birds*, Mary Helen Washington argues for the importance of giving Black women writers their due first:

> Black women are searching for a specific language, specific symbols, specific images with which to record their lives, and, even though they can claim a rightful place in the Afro-American tradition and the feminist tradition of women writers, it is also clear that, for purposes of liberation, black women writers will first insist on their own name, their own space.[36]

I likewise believe that the immediate concern of Black feminist critics must be to develop a fuller understanding of Black women writers who have not received the critical attention Black male writers have. Yet, I cannot advocate indefinitely such a separatist position, for the countless thematic, stylistic, and imagistic parallels between Black male and female writers must be examined. Black feminist critics should explore these parallels in an effort to determine the ways in which these commonalities are manifested differently in Black women's writing and the ways in which they coincide with writings by Black men.

Of course, there are feminist critics who are already examining Black male writers, but much of the scholarship has been limited to discussions of the negative images of Black women found in the works of these authors.[37] Although this scholarship served an important function in pioneering Black feminist critics, it has virtually run its course. Feminist critics run the risk of plunging their work into cliché and triviality if they continue merely to focus on how Black men treat Black women in literature. Hortense Spillers offers a more sophisticated approach to this issue in her discussion of the power of language and myth in female relations in James Baldwin's *If Beale Street Could Talk*. One of Spillers's most cogent points is that "woman-freedom, or its negation, is tied to the assertions of myth, or ways of saying things."[38]

Black feminist criticism is a knotty issue, and while I have attempted to describe it, to call for clearer definitions of its methodology, to offer warnings of its limitations, I await the day when Black feminist criticism will expand to embrace other modes of critical inquiry. In other words, I am philosophically opposed to what Annis Pratt calls "methodolatry." Wole Soyinka has offered one of the most cogent defenses against critical absolutism. He explains:

> The danger which a literary ideology poses is the act of consecration—and of course excommunication. Thanks to the tendency of the modern consumer-mind to facilitate digestion by putting in strict categories what are essentially fluid operations of the creative mind upon social and natural phenomena, the formulation of a literary ideology tends to

congeal sooner or later into instant capsules which, administered also to the writer, may end by asphyxiating the creative process.[39]

Whether Black feminist criticism will or should remain a separatist enterprise is a debatable point. Black feminist critics ought to move from this issue to consider the specific language of Black women's literature, to describe the ways Black women writers employ literary devices in a distinct way, and to compare the way Black women writers create their own mythic structures. If they focus on these and other pertinent issues, Black feminist critics will have laid the cornerstone for a sound, thorough articulation of the Black feminist aesthetic.

Notes

1 Louise Bernikow, *The World Split Open: Four Centuries of Women Poets in England and America, 1552–1950* (New York, 1974), 3.

2 William Morgan, "Feminism and Literary Study: A Reply to Annette Kolodny," *Critical Inquiry,* 2 (Summer 1976), B11.

3 The year 1970 was the beginning of the Modern Language Association's Commission on the Status of Women, which offered panels and workshops that were feminist in approach.

4 Statement by Barbara Desmarais quoted in Annis Pratt, "The New Feminist Criticisms: Exploring the History of the New Space," in *Beyond Intellectual Sexism: A New Woman, A New Reality,* ed. Joan I. Roberts (New York, 1976), 176.

5 Patricia Meyer Spacks, *The Female Imagination* (New York, 1976), 5. Ellen Moers, *Literary Women: The Great Writers* (Garden City, N.Y., 1977) is another example of what Alice Walker terms "white female chauvinism."

6 Alice Walker, "One Child of One's Own—An Essay on Creativity," *Ms.,* August 1979, 50.

7 Robert Stepto, *From Behind the Veil: A Study of Afro-American Narrative* (Urbana, Ill., 1979), x. Other sexist critical works include Donald B. Gibson, ed., *Five Black Writers* (New York, 1970), a collection of essays on Wright, Ellison, Baldwin, Hughes, and Leroi Jones, and Jean Wagner, *Black Poets of the United States: From Paul Lawrence Dunbar to Langston Hughes,* trans. Kenneth Douglas (Urbana, Ill., 1973).

8 Stepto, *From Behind the Veil,* 166.

9 Robert Bone, *The Negro Novel in America* (1958; reprint, New Haven, Conn., 1972), 97, 101.

10 David Littlejohn, *Black on White: A Critical Survey of Writing by American Negroes* (New York, 1966), 48–49.

11 Ellman's concept of "phallic criticism" is discussed in a chapter of the same name in her *Thinking About Women* (New York, 1968), 28–54.

12 Introduction to *Zora Neale Hurston: A Literary Biography* by Robert Hemenway (Urbana, Ill., 1976), xiv. Although Walker makes this observation specifically about Hurston, it is one that can apply to a number of Black women writers.

13 Barbara Smith, "Toward a Black Feminist Criticism," in this volume, 411–12.

14 See Evelyn Hammonds, "Toward a Black Feminist Aesthetic," *Sojourner,* October 1980, 7, for a discussion of the limitations on Black feminist critics. She correctly points out that Black

feminist critics "have no newspapers, no mass-marketed magazines or journals that are explicitly oriented toward the involvement of women of color in the feminist movement."

15 Dorin Schumacher, "Subjectives: A Theory of the Critical Process," in *Feminist Literary Criticism: Explorations in Theory*, ed. Josephine Donovan (Lexington, Kent., 1975), 34.

16 Annette Kolodny, "The Feminist as Literary Critic," Critical Response, *Critical Inquiry*, 2 (Summer 1976), 824–25. See also Cheris Kramer, Barrie Thorne, and Nancy Henley, "Perspectives on Language and Communication," *Signs*, 3 (Spring 1978), 638–51, and Nelly Furman, "The Study of Women and Language: Comment on Vol. 3, no. 3," *Signs*, 4 (Fall 1978), 152–85.

17 Stephen Henderson, *Understanding the New Black Poetry: Black Speech and Black Music as Poetic References* (New York, 1973), 31–46.

18 Some attempts have been made to define or at least discuss lesbianism. See Adrienne Rich's two essays, "It Is the Lesbian in Us . . ." and "The Meaning of Our Love for Woman Is What We Have," in *On Lies, Secrets and Silence* (New York, 1979), 199–202 and 223–30, respectively. See also Bertha Harris's "*What We Mean to Say*: Notes Toward Defining the Nature of Lesbian Literature," *Heresies*, 1 (Fall 1977), 5–8, and Blanche Cook's " 'Women Alone Stir My Imagination': Lesbianism and the Cultural Tradition," *Signs*, 4 (Summer 1979): 718–39. Also, at least one bibliography of Black lesbian writers has been compiled. See Ann Allen Shockley's "The Black Lesbian in American Literature: An Overview," *Conditions: Five*, 2 (Fall 1979): 133–42.

19 Annette Kolodny, "Some Notes on Defining a 'Feminist Literary Criticism,' " *Critical Inquiry*, 2 (Fall 1975), 90.

20 Lillian S. Robinson, "Working Women Writing," *Sex, Class, and Culture* (Bloomington, Ind., 1978), 226.

21 Robinson, "The Critical Task," *Sex, Class, and Culture*, 52.

22 I am borrowing here from Kolodny, who makes similar statements in "Some Notes on Defining a 'Feminist Literary Criticism,' " 75.

23 Andrea Benton Rushing, "Images of Black Women in Afro-American Poetry," in *The Afro-American Woman: Struggles and Images*, ed. Sharon Harley and Rosalyn Terborg-Penn (Port Washington, N.Y., 1978), 74–84. She argues that few of the stereotypic traits which Mary Ellman describes in *Thinking About Women* "seem appropriate to Afro-American images of black women." See also her "Images of Black Women in Modern African Poetry: An Overview," in *Sturdy Black Bridges: Visions of Black Women in Literature*, ed. Roseann P. Bell et al. (New York, 1979), 18–24. Rushing argues similarly that Mary Ann Ferguson's categories of women (the submissive wife, the mother angel or "mom," the woman on a pedestal, for example) cannot be applied to Black women characters, whose cultural imperatives are different from white women's.

24 *The Messenger,* 9 (April 1927), 109.

25 *The Messenger,* 5 (July 1923), 757.

26 Tillie Olsen, *Silences* (New York, 1978), 257.

27 Kolodny, "Some Notes on Defining a 'Feminist Literary Criticism,' " 89.

28 Lillian S. Robinson, "Dwelling in Decencies: Radical Criticism and Feminist Perspectives," in *Feminist Criticism*, ed. Cheryl Brown and Karen Olsen (Metuchen, N.J., 1978), 34.

29 For a discussion of Toni Morrison's frustrated female artists see Renita Weems, "Artists Without Art Form: A Look at One Black Woman's World of Unrevered Black Women," *Conditions: Five*, 2 (Fall 1979), 48–58. See also Alice Walker's classic essay, "In Search of Our

Mothers' Gardens," in this volume, 401–9, for a discussion of Black women's creativity in general.

30   Toni Morrison, *The Bluest Eye* (New York, 1970), 88–89.

31   Toni Morrison, *Sula* (New York, 1980), 105.

32   Kolodny, "Some Notes on Defining a 'Feminist Literary Criticism,'" 86.

33   In an NEH Summer Seminar at Yale University in the summer of 1980, Carolyn Naylor of Santa Clara University suggested this to me.

34   For a discussion of this idea see Michael G. Cooke, "The Descent into the Underworld and Modern Black Fiction," *Iowa Review,* 5 (Fall 1974), 72–90.

35   Mary Helen Washington, *Midnight Birds: Stories of Contemporary Black Women Writers* (Garden City, N.Y., 1980), 43.

36   Ibid., xvii.

37   See Saundra Towns, "The Black Woman as Whore: Genesis of the Myth," *The Black Position* 3 (1974), 39–59, and Sylvia Keady, "Richard Wright's Women Characters and Inequality," *Black American Literature Forum* 10 (1976), 124–28, for example.

38   Hortense Spillers, "The Politics of Intimacy: A Discussion," in Bell et al., eds., *Sturdy Black Bridges,* 88.

39   Wole Soyinka, *Myth, Literature and the African World* (London, 1976), 61.

Mary Helen Washington

"The Darkened Eye Restored:" Notes Toward

a Literary History of Black Women

(1987)

When Gwendolyn Brooks won the Pulitzer prize for her second book of poems, *Annie Allen,* in 1950, *Negro Digest* sent a male reporter who covered the story and wrote a brief "homey" article about the life of a Pulitzer-prize-winning poet. The article begins with a list of people who didn't believe Brooks had won the prize—her son, her mother, her husband, friends—even the poet herself. It then catalogs all the negative experiences Brooks had after winning the prize—phones ringing, people dropping in, work interrupted, the family overwhelmed. It mentions her husband, Henry Blakely, as a poet who devotes only occasional time to poetry because "he feels no one family can support two poets." We also learn that the poet was "shy and self conscious" (her terms) until she married Blakely who helped her to lose some of her "social backwardness" (the reporter's terms). The last paragraph of the article, devoted to the poet's nine-year-old son, includes one of the boy's poems (But not a line from the poet who has just won the Pulitzer!) and ends with the son's rejection of his mother's fame because it has upset his life: "All the attention is wearing off now and I sure am glad. I don't like to be so famous. You have too many people talking to you. You never have any peace."[1] The entire article was an act of sabotage, situating Brooks in a domestic milieu where her "proper" role as wife and mother could be asserted and her role as serious artist—a role this reporter obviously found too threatening to even consider—could be undercut.

Three years later when Brooks published her first—and still her only novel—*Maud Martha* (1953), a novel about a woman's anger, repressions, and silences, the critical reviews were equally condescending and dismissive.

This essay first appeared in Mary Helen Washington, ed., *Invented Lives: Narratives of Black Women 1860–1960* (New York, 1987).

Despite Brooks's stature as a Pulitzer-prize-winning poet, the reviews were short, ranging in length from one hundred and sixty to six hundred words, and many were unsigned. Here is a novel that deals with the most compelling themes in contemporary literature: the struggle to sustain one's identity against a racist and sexist society, the silences that result from repressed anger, the need to assert a creative life. Had *Maud Martha* been written by a man about a man's experience, it would have been considered a brilliant modernist text. But these reviewers, unable to place *Maud Martha* in any literary context, chose instead to concentrate on female cheerfulness, calling Maud Martha "a spunky and sophisticated Negro girl" who, they said, had a marvelous "ability to turn unhappiness and anger into a joke."[2]

Consider the way Ralph Ellison's first novel, *Invisible Man,* was received the year before *Maud Martha* when Ellison was still relatively unknown. *The New Republic, Crisis, The Nation, The New Yorker,* and *The Atlantic* published lengthy and signed reviews, ranging in length from six hundred to twenty-one hundred words. Wright Morris and Irving Howe were called in to write serious critical assessments for the *Times* and *The Nation.* Although Brooks's protagonist was never compared to any other literary character, Ellison's nameless hero was considered not only "the embodiment of the Negro race but the "conscience of all races." The titles of Ellison's reviews—"Black & Blue," "Underground Notes," "Brother Betrayed," "Black Man's Burdens"— suggest the universality of the invisible man's struggle. The title of Brooks's reviews—"Young Girl Growing Up" and "Daydreams of Flight," beside being misleading, deny any relationship between the protagonist's personal experiences and the historical experiences of her people. Ellison himself was compared to Richard Wright, Dostoyevski, and Faulkner; Brooks, only to the unspecified "imagists." Most critically, Ellison's work was placed in a tradition; it was described as an example of the "picaresque" tradition and the pilgrim/journey tradition by all reviews. (Later it would be considered a descendant of the slave narrative tradition.) *Maud Martha,* the reviewers said, "stood alone."[3]

Reading these reviews I was struck not only by their resistance to the deeper meaning in *Maud Martha* but by their absolute refusal to see Brooks's novel as part of any tradition in Afro-American or mainstream American literature. Is this because few critics could picture the questing figure, the powerful articulate voice in the tradition as a plain, dark-skinned housewife living in a kitchenette apartment on the south side of Chicago? As I have written earlier, I realize that the supreme confidence of the Ellison text—its epic sweep, its eloquent flow of words, its conscious manipulation of historical situations—invites its greater critical acceptance. By comparison, the *Maud Martha* test is hesitant, self-doubting, retentive, mute. Maud is restricted, for a good part of the novel, to a domestic life that seems narrow and limited—even to her. And, yet, if the terms *invisibility, double-consciousness, the black mask* have any meaning at all for the Afro-American literary tradition, then *Maud Martha*, whose protagonist is more intimately acquainted with the meanings of those words than any male character, belongs unquestionably to that tradition.

Tradition. Now there's a word that nags the feminist critic. A word that has so often been used to exclude or misrepresent women. It is always something of a shock to see black women, sharing equally (and sometimes more than equally) in the labor and strife of black people, expunged from the text when that history becomes shaped into what we call tradition. Why is the fugitive slave, the fiery orator, the political activist, the abolitionist always represented as a black *man?*[4] How does the heroic voice and heroic image of the black woman get suppressed in a culture that depended on her heroism for its survival? What we have to recognize is that the creation of the fiction of tradition is a matter of power, not justice, and that that power has always been in the hands of men—mostly white but some black. Women are the disinherited. Our "ritual journeys," our "articulate voices," our "symbolic spaces" are rarely the same as men's. Those differences and the assumption that those differences make women inherently inferior plus the appropriation by men of the power to define tradition account for women's absence from our written records.

In the early 1890s when a number of leading black intellectuals decided to form "an organization of Colored authors, scholars, and artists," with the expressed intent of raising "the standard of intellectual endeavor among American Negroes," one of the invited members wrote to declare himself "decidedly opposed to the admission of women to membership" because "literary matters and social matters do not mix." He need not have concerned himself since the distinguished luminaries, among them Alexander Crummell, Francis Grimké, and W. E. B. DuBois, proposed from the beginning that the American Negro Academy—a kind of think tank for that intellectual black elite called the Talented Tenth—be open only to "*men* of African descent."[5] Imagine, if you can, black women intellectuals and activists, who in the 1890s had taken on such issues as the moral integrity of black women, lynching, and the education of black youth, being considered social decorations. I mention this egregious example of sexism in the black intellectual community—which by and large was and still is far more egalitarian than their white counterparts—because it underscores an attitude toward black women that has helped to maintain and perpetuate a male-dominated literary and critical tradition. Women have worked assiduously in this tradition as writers, as editors, sometimes, though rarely, as critics, and yet every study of Afro-American narrative, every anthology of *the* Afro-American literary tradition has set forth a model of literary paternity in which each male author vies with his predecessor for greater authenticity, greater control over *his* voice, thus fulfilling the mission his *forefathers* left unfinished.

Women in this model are sometimes granted a place as a stepdaughter who prefigures and directs us to the real heirs (like Ellison and Wright) but they do not influence and determine the direction and shape of the literary canon.[6] Women's writing is considered singular and anomalous, not universal and representative, and for some mysterious reason, writing about black women is not considered as racially significant as writing about black men. Zora Neale Hurston was chastised by critic Benjamin Brawley because "Her interest . . . is not in solving problems, the chief concern being with individuals."[7] And, in his now-famous contemptuous review of Hurston's *Their Eyes Were Watching God,* Richard Wright objects to her novel because her characters (unlike his) live in a "safe and narrow orbit . . . between laughter and tears."[8] Male critics go to great lengths to explain the political naïveté or racial ambivalence of male writers while they harshly criticize women writers for the same kinds of shortcomings. In Wright's essay, "Literature of the Negro of the United States," he forgives George Moses Horton, an early black poet, for being "a split man," trapped in a culture of which he was not really a part; but Phillis Wheatley, he says, is fully culpable. She was, Wright claims, so fully at one with white colonial culture that she developed "innocently," free "to give utterance to what she felt without the humiliating pressure of the color line."[9]

Banished to the "nigger pews" in the Christian churches of Colonial Boston, deprived of the companionship of other blacks, totally under the control of whites, "torn by contrary instincts," Phillis Wheatley was never "at one with her culture." As a new generation of critics, led by William Robinson, Alice Walker, and Merle A. Richmond, has shown us, Phillis Wheatley was a young slave woman whose choice to be an artist in the repressive, racist era of Colonial America represents "the triumph of the artist amid catastrophe."[10]

With the exception of a handful of autobiographical narratives from the nineteenth century, the black woman's realities are virtually suppressed until the period of the Harlem Renaissance and later. Essentially the black woman as artist, as intellectual spokesperson for her own cultural apprenticeship, has not existed before, for anyone. At the source of her own symbol-making task, this community of writers confronts, therefore, a tradition of work that is quite recent, its continuities, broken and sporadic.[11]

Without exception the writings of black women had been dismissed by Afro-American literary critics until they were rediscovered and reevaluated by feminist critics. Examples: Linda Brent's (Harriet Jacobs) slave narrative, *Incidents in the Life of a Slave Girl* (1860), was judged by male historians to be inauthentic because her story was "too melodramatic" and not "representative."[12] Contemporary feminist critics have documented Brent's life as not only entirely authentic but "representative" of the experience of many slave women. Except for Barbara Christian's *Black Women Novelists* and other texts that specifically deal with women writers, critical texts have never considered Frances Harper and Pauline Hopkins makers of early black literary traditions. Like many white women writers of the nineteenth century, they were dismissed as "sentimentalists," even though their male counterparts wrote similarly sentimental novels. Zora Hurston's *Their Eyes Were Watching God* was declared by Richard Wright to be a novel that carried "no theme, no message, no thought," and during the thirty years that Wright dominated the black literary scene, Hurston's novel was out of print.[13] Nella Larsen was also out of print for many years and was not until recently considered a major Harlem Renaissance writer. Ann Petry is usually analyzed as a disciple of Wright's school of social protest fiction, and Dorothy West has not been written about seriously since Robert Bone's *The Negro Novel in America* in 1965. Brooks's novel, *Maud Martha,* though it perfectly expresses the race alienation of the 1950s, was totally eclipsed by Ellison's *Invisible Man* and never considered a vital part of the Afro-American canon.

If there is a single distinguishing feature of the literature of black women— and this accounts for their lack of recognition—it is this: their literature is about black women; it takes the trouble to record the thoughts, words, feelings, and deeds of black women, experiences that make the realities of being black in America look very different from what men have written. There are no women in this tradition hibernating in dark holes contemplating their invisibility; there are no women dismembering the bodies or crushing the skulls of either women or men; and few, if any, women in the literature of black women succeed in heroic quests without the support of other women or men in their communities. Women talk to other women in this tradition, and their friendships with other women—mothers, sisters, grand-mothers, friends, lovers—are vital to their growth and well-being. A common scene recurring in the fiction of black women writers is one in which women (usually two) gather together in a small room to share intimacies that can be trusted only to a kindred female spirit. That intimacy is a tool, allowing women writers to represent women more fully. The friendship between Sappho and Dora in *Contending Forces,* Janie and Pheoby in *Their Eyes Were Watching God,* Linda and her grandmother in *Incidents in the Life of a Slave Girl,* Helga and Mrs. Hayes-Rore in *Quicksand,* Cleo and her sisters in *The Living Is Easy* emphasize this concern with female bonding and suggest that female relationships are an essential aspect of self-definition for women.

I do not want black women writers to be misrepresented as apolitical because of their deep concern for the personal lives of their characters. Their texts are clearly involved with issues of social justice: the rape of black women, the lynching of black men, slavery and Reconstruction, class distinctions among blacks, and all forms of discrimination against black people. No romantic heroines, these women work, and experience discrimination against them in the workplace, a subject that almost never surfaces in the writings of men. At the beginning of *Contending Forces,* Sappho Clark brings her stenography work home with her because blacks are not allowed in the office. Iola Leroy is twice dismissed from jobs when her co-workers discover her race. The educated Helga Crane seeks work as a domestic in Chicago because black women are barred from the professions and from clerical work. Maud Martha also finds work as a domestic where she encounters the brutal condescension of her white employers. These examples have a special meaning for me because in the 1920s my mother and my five aunts migrated to Cleveland, Ohio, from Indianapolis and, in spite of their many talents, they found every door except the kitchen door closed to them. My youngest aunt was trained as a bookkeeper and was so good at her work that her white employer at Guardian Savings of Indianapolis allowed her to work at the branch in a black area. The Cleveland Trust Company was not so liberal, however, so in Cleveland (as Toni Morrison asks, "What could go wrong in Ohio?") she went to work in what is known in the black community as "private family." Her thwarted career is not simply a narrow personal tragedy. As these texts make clear to us—and they are the only texts that tell this story—several generations of competent and talented black women, all of whom *had* to work, were denied access to the most ordinary kind of jobs and therefore to any kind of economic freedom.

Women's sexuality is another subject treated very differently by women and men writers. In the male slave narrative, for example, sexuality is nearly always avoided, and when it does surface it is to report the sexual abuse of female slaves. The male slave narrator was under no compulsion to discuss his own sexuality nor that of other men. As far as we know, the only slave narrator forced to admit a sexual life was Linda Brent who bore two children as a single woman rather than submit to forced concubinage. Her reluctance to publish *Incidents* because it was not the life of "a Heroine with no degradation associated with it" shows that sexuality literally made a woman an unfit subject for literature. In Harlem Renaissance literature, as Barbara Christian reminds us, only male writers felt free to celebrate exoticized sexuality: "The garb of uninhibited passion wears better on a male, who after all, does not have to carry the burden of the race's morality or lack of it."[14] In Renaissance literature, Nella Larsen does represent Helga as a sexual being but that treatment of sex is never celebratory. Helga's sexuality is constantly thwarted, ending as Hazel Carby notes, not in exotic passion but in biological entrapment. In *The Living Is Easy*, Cleo connects sexuality to women's repression and refuses any kind of sexual life, preferring instead emotional intimacy with her sisters and their children. The only women in these excerpts who revels in her sexuality is Janie Crawford in *Their Eyes Were Watching God*, and, significantly, even in this seemingly idyllic treatment of erotic love, female sexuality is always associated with violence. Janie's mother and grandmother are sexually exploited and Janie is beaten by her glorious lover, Tea Cake, so that he can prove his superiority to other men. What do these stories say about female sexuality? It seems to me that all of them point to the fundamental issue of whether or not women can exert control over their sexuality. Helga Crane, for example, fights against the sexual attraction she feels for Dr. Anderson because that attraction makes her feel out of control. Cleo, who is controlled by her husband in all other aspects of her life, controls him by refusing sex. In *Contending Forces*, Sappho forces her lover to undergo a series of tests in order to determine the constancy of his love. And surely the clearest statement of women's anxiety about sexuality and the need for control over one's female body is made by Linda Brent when she tries to explain to her white female audience why she deliberately chose to bear two children outside of marriage to a white man who was not her owner: "It seems less degrading to give one's self, than to submit to compulsion. There is something akin to freedom in having a lover *who has no control over you*, [emphasis mine] except that which he gains by kindness and attachment."[15] Given this deep alienation from and anxiety about heterosexual relationships, we might wonder if any of these women considered taking

women as lovers. If they did, they wrote about such affairs in private places—
letters, journals, diaries, poetry—if they wrote about them at all. In a diary,
which she kept in the 1920s and 1930s, Alice Dunbar-Nelson is more explicit
about sexual intimacy among black women than any writer of that period
that I know, but even her revelations are quite guarded: "And Fay, lovely little
Fay. One day we saw each other, *one day,* and a year has passed. And still we
cannot meet again . . ."[16]

The anxiety of black women writers over the representation of sexuality
goes back to the nineteenth century and the prescription for womanly "virtues" which made slave women automatically immoral and less "feminine
than white women," but that anxiety is evident even in contemporary texts
many of which avoid any kind of sexual vulnerability or project the most
extreme forms of sexual vulnerability onto children and poor women. Once
again the issue is control, and control is bought by cordoning off those
aspects of sexuality that threaten to make women feel powerless. If pleasure
and danger are concomitant aspects of sexuality, it seems clear to me that
black women writers have, out of historical necessity, registered far more of
the latter than the former.

> For a woman to write, she must experiment with "altering and adapting
> the current shape of her thought without crushing or distorting it."[17]

Although many black women writers in some way challenge conventional
notions of what is possible for women characters, "dissenting" from traditions that demand female subordination, I want to single out Zora Neale
Hurston and Gwendolyn Brooks for creating narrative strategies whose major concern is the empowerment of women. Both Hurston and Brooks enter
fiction through a side door: Hurston was a folklorist and anthropolgist;
Brooks is primarily a poet. As outsiders both were freer to experiment with
fictional forms, the result being that they were able to choose forms that resist female entrapment. Janie Crawford's quest in *Their Eyes Were Watching
God* is to recover her own voice and her own sense of autonomy. By framing
the story with Janie telling her tale to her friend Pheoby, Hurston makes
Janie's self-conscious reflections on her life the central narrative concern.
Though Hurston often denies this quest story in favor of the romantic plot,
her interest in Janie's heroic potential is unmistakable. In *Maud Martha*
Brooks also dislodges the romance plot, first by inventing a woman who does
not fit the profile of a romantic heroine and then by making the death of
romance essential to Maud's growth. Being a wife, "in every way considering
and replenishing him," is in conflict with Maud's own desire for what she

vaguely terms "more life." And finally the narrative form itself, as it enacts Maud's rage, her muteness, her indirection, places narrative emphasis on the unsparing, meticulous, courageous consciousness of Maud Martha, making that female consciousness the heroic center of the text. The text that was so arrogantly dismissed in 1953 returns, subversively, in the 1980s, with its rejection of male power, as a critique of the very patriarchal authority that sought its dismissal.

Obviously we will have to learn to read the Afro-American literary tradition in new ways, for continuing on in the old way is impossible. In the past ten or fifteen years the crucial task of reconstruction has been carried on by a number of scholars whose work has made it possible to document black women as artists, as intellectuals, as symbol makers. The continuities of this tradition, as Hortense Spillers tells us, are broken and sporadic, but the knitting together of these fragments has begun. As I look around at my own library shelves I see the texts that have helped to make my work possible. First those pioneering studies undertaken to pave the way for the rest of us: Barbara Christian's, *Black Women Novelists, The Development of a Tradition, 1892–1976*; the invaluable sourcebook, *All the Women Are White, All the Blacks Are Men, But Some of Us Are Brave*, edited by Gloria L. Hull, Patricia Bell Scott, and Barbara Smith; Marilyn Richardson's bibliography, *Black Women and Religion*; Ora Williams's bibliography, *American Black Women*; those early anthologies of black women's literature, *The Black Woman*, edited by Toni Cade Bambara; Pat Crutchfield Exum's *Keeping the Faith*; and *Sturdy Black Bridges: Visions of Black Women in Literature*, edited by Beverly Guy-Sheftall, Roseann P. Bell and Bettye J. Parker.

Robert Hemenway's biography, *Zora Neale Hurston: A Literary Biography*, and Alice Walker's *I Love Myself When I Am Laughing . . . And Then Again When I Am Looking Mean and Impressive: A Zora Neale Hurston Reader* are the major scholarly works that allowed us to reclaim Hurston. Two books on black women's spiritual autobiography, Jean McMahon Humez's *Gifts of Power*, an edition of the writings of Rebecca Jackson Cox, as well as William Andrews's *Sisters of the Spirit* have reclaimed a unique part of black women's early literary tradition. Gloria Hull's edition of Alice Dunbar-Nelson's diary, *Give Us Each Day*, and Dorothy Sterling's *We Are Your Sisters*, a documentary portrayal of nineteenth-century black women, provide evidence of the rich cultural history of black women that is to be found in nontraditional sources. Paula Giddings's history of black women, *When and Where I Enter: The Impact of Black Women on Race and Sex in America* documents the political, social, and literary work of black women.

Deborah E. McDowell's Beacon Press series on black women's fiction has already reissued a number of out-of-print novels, for example, *The Street, Like One of the Family,* and *Iola Leroy.* Rutgers University Press has reissued *Quicksand* and *Passing.* In 1987 a number of important works on black women will be published: Jean Fagan Yellin's definitive edition of Harriet Jacobs's *Incidents in the Life of a Slave Girl* and Hazel Carby's ground-breaking work on black women's narrative tradition: *Reconstructing Womanhood: The Emergence of the Afro-American Woman Novelist.*

As we continue the work of reconstructing a literary history that insists on black women as central to that history, as we reject the old male-dominated accounts of history, refusing to be cramped into the little spaces men have allotted women, we should be aware that this is an act of enlightenment, not simply repudiation. In her 1892 text on black women, *A Voice from the South,* Anna Julia Cooper says that a world in which the female is made subordinate is like a body with one eye bandaged. When the bandage is removed, the body is filled with light: "It sees a circle where before it saw a segment. The darkened eye restored, every member rejoices with it."[18] The making of a literary history in which black women are fully represented is a search for full vision, to create a circle where now we have but a segment.

Notes

1 Frank Harriott, "The Life of a Pulitzer Poet," *Negro Digest,* August 1950, 14–16.

2 1953 reviews of *Maud Martha: The New Yorker,* 10 October, unsigned, 160 words; Hubert Creekmore, "Daydreams in Flight," *New York Times Book Review,* 4 October, 400 words; Nicolas Monjo, "Young Girl Growing Up," *Saturday Review,* 31 October, 140 words; and Coleman Rosenberger, *New York Herald Times,* 18 October, 600 words.

3 1952 reviews of *Invisible Man:* George Mayberry, "Underground Notes," *The New Republic,* 21 April, 600 words; Irving Howe, "A Negro in America," *The Nation,* 10 May, 950 words; Anthony West, "Black Man's Burden," *The New Yorker,* 31 May, 2,100 words; C. J. Rolo, "Candide in Harlem," *The Atlantic,* July, 450 words; Wright Morris, "The World Below," *New York Times Book Review* 13 April, 900 words; "Black & Blue," *Time,* 14 April, 850 words; and J. E. Cassidy "A Brother Betrayed," *Commonweal,* 2 May, 850 words.
1953 reviews of *Maud Martha: The New Yorker,* 10 October, 160 words; Hubert Creekmore, "Daydreams in Flight," *New York Times Book Review* 4 October, 400 words; Nicolas Monjo "Young Girl Growing Up," *Saturday Review* 31 October, 140 words; and Coleman Rosenberger, *New York Herald Tribune* 18 October, 600 words.
The diction of the reviews, too, is revealing. The tone of *Invisible Man* was defined as "vigorous, imaginative, violently humorous and quietly tragic" (*New Republic*), "searing and exalted" (*The Nation*), while *Maud Martha* drew "freshness, warm cheerfulness . . . [and] vitality" (*New York Times*), "ingratiating" (*Saturday Review*). Several reviews of Ellison used "gusto," for Brooks, "liveliness." Brooks's "Negro heroine" (*New York Times*), was

characterized as a "young colored woman" (*Saturday Review*) and a "spunky and sophisti-cated Negro girl" (*New York Times*); Ellison's character as a "hero" and "pilgrim" (*New Republic*).

Matters of style received mixed response in both novels. *Maud Martha's* "impressionistic style" was deemed "not quite sharp or firm enough" and her "remarkable gift" was seen (in the same review) as "mimicry" and an "ability to turn unhappiness and anger into a joke"—a gift that her style did not engender (*New York Times*). The *Saturday Review* said: "Its form is no more than a random narration of loosely assembled incidents" and called its "frame-work . . . somewhat ramshackle." Only the *New York Times* noticed a significance in her style, and likened the "flashes . . . of sensitive lightness" to Imagist poetics, as well as commenting on the "finer qualities of insight and rhythm."

Both authors are criticized along the same lines concerning form and style, but in the reviews of Brooks, her style is the topic that draws the most attention, and the review is favorable or unfavorable depending upon whether or not the reviewer is personally at-tracted to "impressionism." Ellison's novel is treated more seriously than Brooks's because his novel is seen as addressing a broader range of issues, despite his sometimes "hysterical" style.

This position is most apparent in Howe's review in *The Nation*. Howe asks serious questions about traditional literary devices, such as narrative stance and voice, and method of charac-terization, despite the book's lack of "finish." (Ellison's first-person narration is discussed by all reviewers, while Brooks's narrative style is hardly mentioned in any review.) Implicit in Howe's stance toward *Invisible Man* is an assumption that this is a serious novel to be investigated rigorously in accordance with the (high) standards of the academy. Despite those qualities of tone and style that Howe criticizes it for, *Invisible Man* is important, finally, because it fits into the literary tradition of the epic journey of discovery. Howe calls it a "searing and exalted record of a Negro's journey toward contemporary American in search of success, companionship, and finally himself."

4   The extent to which black men are considered representative of the race was suggested to me most emphatically in *Black Women in Nineteenth-Century American Life: Their Words, Their Thoughts, Their Feelings,* ed. Bert James Loewenberg and Ruth Bogin (University Park, Penn., 1976). In their introduction, "Women, Blacks, History," the editors make this comment: "Not only do black women seldom appear in treatments of black history, but historians have been content to permit the male to represent the female in almost every significant category. Thus it is the male who is the representative abolitionist, fugitive slave, or political activist. The black male is the leader, the entrepreneur, the politician, the man of thought. When historians discuss black abolitionist writers and lecturers, they are men. David Walker, Charles Leriox Remond, and a procession of male stalwarts preempt the list in conventional accounts. Particularly later when black history was consciously written, it was the male, not the female, who recorded it. Women are conspicuous by their silence." (4)

5   Alfred A. Moss, Jr., *The American Negro Academy: Voice of the Talented Tenth* (Baton Rouge, 1981). According to Moss, The American Negro Academy, the first major black American learned society was founded March 5, 1897 in Washington, D.C. The constitution of the ANA defined it as "an organization of authors, scholars, artists, and those distinguished in other walks of life, men of African descent, for the promotion of Letters, Science, and Art." While Dubois argued for a more democratic membership "because we find men who are not

distinguished in science or literature or art are just the men we want," he did not, apparently argue for women. Theophilus G. Steward, one of the invited members, was the only one who specifically declared himself opposed to the admission of women. (38, 42)

6 Nearly every Afro-American literary history reads the tradition as primarily a male tradition, beginning with the male slave narrative as the source which generates the essential texts in the canon. With absolute predictability the Frederick Douglass 1845 *Narrative* is the text that issues the call, and the response comes back loud and clear from W. E. B. DuBois, James Weldon Johnson, Richard Wright, James Baldwin, and Ralph Ellison. So firmly established is this male hegemony that even men's arguments with one another (Wright, Baldwin, Ellison) get written into the tradition as a way of interpreting its development. As most feminist critics have noted, women writers cannot simply be inserted into the gaps, or be used to prefigure male writers, the tradition has to be conceptualized from a feminist viewpoint.

7 Benjamin Brawley, *The Negro Genius: A New Appraisal of the Achievement of the American Negro in Literature and the Fine Arts* (New York, 1969), 258. Of the thirteen portraits of writers and artists in this book, only two are of women.

8 Richard Wright, " 'Between Laughter and Tears,' " *New Masses,* 5 (October 1937), 25–26.

9 Richard Wright, "The Literature of the Negro of the United States," in *White Man Listen!* (Garden City, N.Y., 1964), 76.

10 William Robinson, *Phillis Wheatley in the Black American Beginnings* (Detroit, 1976); Alice Walker, "In Search of Our Mothers' Gardens," in this volume, 401–9; and M. A. Richmond, *Bid the Vassal Soar: Interpretive Essays on the Life and Poetry of Phillis Wheatley and George Moses Horton* (Washington, D.C., 1974).

11 Hortense J. Spillers, "A Hateful Passion, A Lost Love," *Feminist Studies,* 9.2 (Summer 1983), 297.

12 In *Reconstructing Womanhood: The Emergence of the Afro-American Woman Novelist* (New York, 1987), Hazel Carby discusses this dismissal of the Brent narrative by John Blassingame in *The Slave Community: Plantation Life in the Antebellum South* (New York, 1979).

13 Wright " 'Beyond Laughter and Tears.' "

14 Barbara Christian, *Black Women Novelists: The Development of a Tradition 1892–1976* (Westport, Conn., 1980), 40.

15 Linda Brent, *Incidents in the Life of a Slave Girl,* ed. L. Maria Child (New York, 1973), 55.

16 Gloria T. Hull, ed., *Give Us Each Day: The Diary of Alice Dunbar-Nelson* (New York, 1984), 421–22.

17 In *Writing Beyond the Ending: Narrative Strategies of Twentieth-Century Women Writers* (Bloomington, Ind., 1985), 32, Rachel Blau DuPlessis quotes Virginia Woolf's prescription for women's writing, "Women and Fiction," in *Granite and Rainbow* (New York, 1958), 80.

18 Anna J. Cooper, *A Voice from the South by a Black Woman of the South* (Xenia, Oh., 1892), 123.

THEMATIC Q'S OF CORREGIDORA

Hortense J. Spillers

Mama's Baby, Papa's Maybe:

An American Grammar Book

(1987)

COLLECTIVE PRONOUN.

HOW CAN IS MARKED BUT NAMELESSNESS.

↳ NAMELESS = DEFINING.

Let's face it. I am a marked woman, but not everybody knows my name. "Peaches" and "Brown Sugar," "Sapphire" and "Earth Mother," "Aunty," "Granny," God's "Holy Fool," a "Miss Ebony First," or "Black Woman at the Podium"; I describe a locus of confounded identities, a meeting ground of investments and privations in the national treasury of rhetorical wealth. My country needs me, and if I were not here, I would have to be invented.

STEREOTYPES.

THE "I" IS THE LOCUS OF CONFOUNDING IDENTITIES.

W. E. B. DuBois predicted as early as 1903 that the twentieth century would be the century of the "color line." We could add to this spatiotemporal configuration another thematic of analogously terrible weight: if the "black woman" can be seen as a particular figuration of the split subject that psycho-analytic theory posits, then this century marks the site of "its" profoundest revelation. The problem before us is deceptively simple: the terms enclosed in quotation marks in the preceding paragraph isolate overdetermined nominative properties. Embedded in bizarre axiological ground, they demon-strate a sort of telegraphic coding; they are markers so loaded with mythical prepossession that there is no easy way for the agents buried beneath them to come clean. In that regard, the names by which I am called in the public place render an example of signifying property *plus*. In order for me to speak a truer word concerning myself, I must strip down through layers of attenu-ated meanings, made an excess in time, over time, assigned by a particular historical order, and there await whatever marvels of my own inventiveness. The personal pronouns are offered in the service of a collective function.

In certain human societies, a child's identity is determined through the line of the Mother, but the United States, from at least one author's point of view, is not one of them: "In essence, the Negro community has been forced

This essay first appeared in *Diacritics*, 17.2 (1987).

into a matriarchal structure which, because it is so far out of line with the *rest of American society*, seriously retards the progress of the group as a whole, and imposes a crushing burden on the Negro male and, in consequence, on a great many Negro women as well."[1]

The notorious bastard, from Vico's banished Roman mothers of such sons, to Caliban, to Heathcliff, and Joe Christmas, has no official female equivalent. Because the traditional rites and laws of inheritance rarely pertain to the female child, bastard status signals to those who need to know which son of the Father's is the legitimate heir and which one the impostor. For that reason, property seems wholly the business of the male. A "she" cannot, therefore, qualify for bastard, or "natural son" status, and that she cannot provides further insight into the coils and recoils of patriarchal wealth and fortune. According to Daniel Patrick Moynihan's celebrated "Report" of the late sixties, the "Negro Family" has no Father to speak of—his Name, his Law, his Symbolic function mark the impressive missing agencies in the essential life of the black community, the "Report" maintains, and it is, surprisingly, the fault of the Daughter, or the female line. This stunning reversal of the castration thematic, displacing the Name and the Law of the Father to the territory of the Mother and Daughter, becomes an aspect of the African-American female's misnaming. We attempt to undo this misnaming in order to reclaim the relationship between Fathers and Daughters within this social matrix for a quite different structure of cultural fictions. For Daughters and Fathers are here made to manifest the very same *rhetorical* symptoms of absence and denial, to embody the double and contrastive agencies of a *prescribed* internecine degradation. "Sapphire" enacts her "Old Man" in drag, just as her "Old Man" becomes "Sapphire" in outrageous caricature.

In other words, in the historic outline of dominance, the respective subject-positions of "female" and "male" adhere to no symbolic integrity. At a time when current critical discourses appear to compel us more and more decidedly toward gender "undecidability," it would appear reactionary, if not dumb, to insist on the integrity of female/male gender. But undressing these conflations of meaning, as they appear under the rule of dominance, would restore, as figurative possibility, not only Power to the Female (for Maternity), but also Power to the Male (for Paternity). We would gain, in short, the *potential* for gender differentiation as it might express itself along a range of stress points, including human biology in its intersection with the project of culture.

Though among the most readily available "whipping boys" of fairly recent public discourse concerning African-Americans and national policy, "The

Moynihan Report" is by no means unprecedented in its conclusions; it belongs, rather, to a class of symbolic paradigms that (1) inscribe "ethnicity" as a scene of negation and (2) confirm the human body as a metonymic figure for an entire repertoire of human and social arrangements. In that regard, the "Report" pursues a behavioral rule of public documentary. Under the Moynihan rule, "ethnicity" itself identifies a total objectification of human and cultural motives—the "white" family, by implication, and the "Negro Family," by outright assertion, in a constant opposition of binary meanings. Apparently spontaneous, these "actants" are *wholly* generated, with neither past nor future, as tribal currents moving out of time. Moynihan's "Families" are pure present and always tense. "Ethnicity" in this case freezes in meaning, takes on constancy, assumes the look and the affects of the Eternal. We could say, then, that in its powerful stillness, "ethnicity," from the point of view of the "Report," embodies nothing more than a mode of memorial time, as Roland Barthes outlines the dynamics of myth.[2] As a signifier that has no movement in the field of signification, the use of "ethnicity" for the living becomes purely appreciative, although one would be unwise not to concede its dangerous and fatal effects.

"Ethnicity" perceived as mythical time enables a writer to perform a variety of conceptual moves all at once. Under its hegemony, the human body becomes a defenseless target for rape and veneration, and the body, in its material and abstract phase, a resource for metaphor. For example, Moynihan's "tangle of pathology" provides the descriptive strategy for the work's fourth chapter, which suggests that "underachievement" in black males of the lower classes is primarily the fault of black females, who achieve out of all proportion, both to their numbers in the community and to the paradigmatic example before the nation: "Ours is a society which presumes male leadership in private and public affairs. . . . A subculture, such as that of the Negro American, in which this is not the pattern, is placed at a distinct disadvantage" (75). Between charts and diagrams, we are asked to consider the impact of qualitative measure on the black male's performance on standardized examinations, matriculation in schools of higher and professional training, etc. Even though Moynihan sounds a critique on his own argument here, he quickly withdraws from its possibilities, suggesting that black males should reign because that is the way the majority culture carries things out: "It is clearly a disadvantage for a minority group to be operating under one principle, while the great majority of the population . . . is operating on another" (75). Those persons living according to the perceived "matriarchal" pattern are, therefore, caught in a state of social "pathology."

Even though Daughters have their own agenda with reference to this order
of Fathers (imagining for the moment that Moynihan's fiction—and others
like it—does not represent an adequate one and that there *is*, once we discover him, a Father here), my contention that these social and cultural
subjects make doubles, unstable in their respective identities, in effect trans-
ports us to a common historical ground, the sociopolitical order of the New
World. That order, with its human sequence written in blood, *represents* for
its African and indigenous peoples a scene of *actual* mutilation, dismemberment, and exile. First of all, their New-World, diasporic plight marked a *theft
of the body*—a willful and violent (and unimaginable from this distance)
severing of the captive body from its motive will, its active desire. Under
these conditions, we lose at least *gender* difference *in the outcome,* and the
female body and the male body become a territory of cultural and political
maneuver, not at all gender-related, gender-specific. But this body, at least
from the point of view of the captive community, focuses a private and
particular space, at which point of convergence biological, sexual, social,
cultural, linguistic, ritualistic, and psychological fortunes join. This profound intimacy of interlocking detail is disrupted, however, by externally
imposed meanings and uses: (1) the captive body becomes the source of an
irresistible, destructive sensuality; (2) at the same time—in stunning contradiction—the captive body reduces to a thing, becoming *being for* the captor;
(3) in this absence *from* a subject position, the captured sexualities provide
a physical and biological expression of "otherness"; (4) as a category of
"otherness," the captive body translates into a potential for pornotroping
and embodies sheer physical powerlessness that slides into a more general
"powerlessness," resonating through various centers of human and social
meaning.

But I would make a distinction in this case between "body" and "flesh" and
impose that distinction as the central one between captive and liberated
subject-positions. In that sense, before the "body" there is the "flesh," that
zero degree of social conceptualization that does not escape concealment
under the brush of discourse, or the reflexes of iconography. Even though
the European hegemonies stole bodies—some of them female—out of West
African communities in concert with the African "middleman," we regard
this human and social irreparability as high crimes against the *flesh,* as the
person of African females and African males registered the wounding. If we
think of the "flesh" as a primary narrative, then we mean its seared, divided,
ripped-apartness, riveted to the ship's hold, fallen, or "escaped" overboard.

One of the most poignant aspects of William Goodell's contemporaneous study of the North American slave codes gives precise expression to the tortures and instruments of captivity.[3] Reporting an instance of Jonathan Edwards's observations on the tortures of enslavement, Goodell narrates: "The smack of the whip is all day long in the ears of those who are on the plantation, or in the vicinity; and it is used with such dexterity and severity as not only to lacerate the skin, but to tear out small portions of the flesh at almost every stake" (221). The anatomical specifications of rupture, of altered human tissue, take on the objective description of laboratory prose—eyes beaten out, arms, backs, skulls branded, a left jaw, a right ankle, punctured; teeth missing, as the calculated work of iron, whips, chains, knives, the canine patrol, the bullet.

These undecipherable markings on the captive body render a kind of hieroglyphics of the flesh whose severe disjunctures come to be hidden to the cultural seeing by skin color. We might well ask if this phenomenon of marking and branding actually "transfers" from one generation to another, finding its various *symbolic substitutions* in an efficacy of meanings that repeat the initiating moments? As Elaine Scarry describes the mechanisms of torture these lacerations, woundings, fissures, tears, scars, openings, ruptures, lesions, rendings, punctures of the flesh create the distance between what I would designate a cultural *vestibularity* and the *culture*, whose state apparatus, including judges, attorneys, "owners," "soul drivers," "overseers," and "men of God," apparently colludes with a protocol of "search and destroy."[4] This body whose flesh carries the female and the male to the frontiers of survival bears in person the marks of a cultural text whose inside has been turned outside.

The flesh is the concentration of "ethnicity" that contemporary critical discourses neither acknowledge nor discourse away. It is this "flesh and blood" entity, in the vestibule (or "pre-view") of a colonized North America, that is essentially ejected from "The Female Body in Western Culture,"[5] but it makes good theory, or commemorative "herstory" to want to "forget," or to have failed to realize, that the African female subject, under these historic conditions, is not only the target of rape—in one sense, an interiorized violation of body and mind—but also the topic of specifically *externalized* acts of torture and prostration that we imagine as the peculiar province of *male* brutality and torture inflicted by other males. A female body strung from a tree limb, or bleeding from the breast on any given day of field work because the "overseer," standing the length of a whip, has popped her flesh open, adds a lexical and living dimension to the narratives of women in culture and society.[6] This materialized scene of unprotected female flesh—of

female flesh "ungendered"—offers a praxis and a theory, a text for living and
for dying, and a method for reading both through their diverse mediations.
Among the myriad uses to which the enslaved community was put, Goodell identifies its value for medical research: "Assortments of diseased, *damaged,* and disabled Negroes, deemed incurable and otherwise worthless are
bought up, it seems . . . by medical institutions, to be experimented and
operated upon, for purposes of 'medical education' and the interest of medical science" (86–87; Goodell's emphasis). From the *Charleston Mercury* for
October 12, 1838, Goodell notes this advertisement:

> 'To planters and others.—Wanted, fifty Negroes, any person, having sick
> Negroes, considered incurable by their respective physicians, and wish-
> ing to dispose of them, Dr. S. will pay cash for Negroes affected with
> scrofula, or king's evil, confirmed hypochondriasm, apoplexy, diseases
> of the liver, kidneys, spleen, stomach and intestines, bladder and its
> appendages, diarrhea, dysentery, etc. The highest cash price will be
> paid, on application as above.' at No. 110 Church Street, Charleston. (87;
> Goodell's emphasis)

This profitable "atomizing" of the captive body provides another angle on
the divided flesh: we lose any hint or suggestion of a dimension of ethics, of
relatedness between human personality and its anatomical features, between
one human personality and another, between human personality and cultural institutions. To that extent, the procedures adopted for the captive flesh
demarcate a total objectification, as the entire captive community becomes a
living laboratory.

The captive body, then, brings into focus a gathering of social realities as
well as a metaphor for value so thoroughly interwoven in their literal and
figurative emphases that distinctions between them are virtually useless.
Even though the captive flesh/body has been "liberated," and no one need
pretend that even the quotation marks do not *matter,* dominant symbolic
activity, the ruling episteme that releases the dynamics of naming and valuation, remains grounded in the originating metaphors of captivity and mutilation so that it is as if neither time nor history, nor historiography and its
topics, shows movement, as the human subject is "murdered" over and over
again by the passions of a bloodless and anonymous archaism, showing itself
in endless disguise. Faulkner's young Chick Mallison in *The Mansion* calls
"it" by other names—"the ancient subterrene atavistic fear . . ."[7] And I would
call it the Great Long National Shame. But people do not talk like that anymore—it is "embarrassing," just as the retrieval of mutilated female bodies

will likely be "backward" for some people. Neither the shameface of the embarrassed, nor the not-looking-back of the self-assured is of much interest to us, and will not help at all if rigor is our dream. We might concede, at the very least, that sticks and bricks *might* break our bones, but words will most certainly *kill* us.

The symbolic order that I wish to trace in this writing, calling it an "American grammar," begins at the "beginning," which is really a rupture and a radically different kind of cultural continuation. The massive demographic shifts, the violent formation of a modern African consciousness, that take place on the subsaharan Continent during the initiative strikes which open the Atlantic Slave Trade in the fifteenth century of our Christ, interrupted hundreds of years of black African culture. We write and think, then, about an outcome of aspects of African-American life in the United States under the pressure of those events. I might as well add that the familiarity of this narrative does nothing to appease the hunger of recorded memory, nor does the persistence of the repeated rob these well-known, oft-told events of their power, even now, to startle. In a very real sense, every writing as revision makes the "discovery" all over again.

2

The narratives by African peoples and their descendants, though not as numeorus from those early centuries of the "execrable trade" as the researcher would wish, suggest, in their rare occurrence, that the visual shock waves touched off when African and European "met" reverberated on both sides of the encounter. The narrative of the "Life of Olaudah Equiano, or Gustavus Vassa, the African. Written by Himself," first published in London in 1789, makes it quite clear that the first Europeans Equiano observed on what is now Nigerian soil were as unreal for him as he and others must have been for the European captors.[8] The cruelty of "these white men with horrible looks, red faces, and long hair," of these "spirits," as the narrator would have it, occupies several pages of Equiano's attention, alongside a first-hand account of Nigerian interior life (27 ff.). We are justified in regarding the outcome of Equiano's experience in the same light as he himself might have—as a "fall," as a veritable descent into the loss of communicative force.

If, as Todorov points out, the Mayan and Aztec peoples "lost control of communication"[9] in light of Spanish intervention, we could observe, similarly, that Vassa falls among men whose language is not only strange to him, but whose habits and practices strike him as "astonishing":

[The sea, the slave ship] filled me with astonishment, which was soon converted into terror, when I was carried on board. I was immediately handled, and tossed up to see if I were sound, by some of the crew; and I was now persuaded that I had gotten into a world of bad spirits, and that they were going to kill me. Their complexions, too, differing so much from ours, their long hair, and the language they spoke (which was different from any I had ever heard), united to confirm me in this belief.

The captivating party does not only "earn" the right to dispose of the captive body as it sees fit, but gains, consequently, the right to name and "name" it: Equiano, for instance, identifies at least three different names that he is given in numerous passages between his Benin homeland and the Virginia colony, the latter and England—"Michael," "Jacob," "Gustavus Vassa" (35; 36).

The nicknames by which African-American women have been called, or regarded, or imagined on the New World scene—the opening lines of this essay provide examples—demonstrate the powers of distortion that the dominant community seizes as its unlawful prerogative. Moynihan's "Negro Family," then, borrows its narrative energies from the grid of associations, from the semantic and iconic folds buried deep in the collective past, that come to surround and signify the captive person. Though there is no absolute point of chronological initiation, we might repeat certain familiar impression points that lend shape to the business of dehumanized naming. Expecting to find direct and amplified reference to African women during the opening years of the Trade, the observer is disappointed time and again that this cultural subject is concealed beneath the mighty debris of the itemized account, between the lines of the massive logs of commercial enterprise that overrun the sense of clarity we believed we had gained concerning this collective humiliation. Elizabeth Donnan's enormous, four-volume documentation becomes a case in point.[10]

Turning directly to this source, we discover what we had not expected to find—that this aspect of the search is rendered problematic and that observations of a field of manners and its related sociometries are an outgrowth of the industry of the "exterior other,"[11] called "anthropology" later on. The European males who laded and captained these galleys and who policed and corralled these human beings, in hundreds of vessels from Liverpool to Elmina, to Jamaica; from the Cayenne Islands, to the ports at Charleston and Salem, and for three centuries of human life, were not curious about this "cargo" that bled, packed like so many live sardines among the immovable objects. Such inveterate obscene blindness might be denied, point blank, as a possibility for *anyone,* except that we know it happened.

Donnan's first volume covers three centuries of European "discovery" and "conquest," beginning 50 years before pious Cristobal, Christum Ferens, the bearer of Christ, laid claim to what he thought was the "Indies." From Gomes Eannes de Azurara's "Chronicle of the Discovery and Conquest of Guinea, 1441–1448"[12], we learn that the Portuguese probably gain the dubious distinction of having introduced black Africans to the European market of servitude. We are also reminded that "Geography" is not a divine gift. Quite to the contrary, its boundaries were shifted during the European "Age of Conquest" in giddy desperation, according to the dictates of conquering armies, the edicts of prelates, the peculiar myopia of the medieval Christian mind. Looking for the "Nile River," for example, according to the fifteenth-century Portuguese notion, is someone's joke. For all that the pre-Columbian "explorers" knew about the sciences of navigation and geography, we are surprised that more parties of them did not end up "discovering" Europe. Perhaps, from a certain angle, that is precisely all that they found— an alternative reading of ego. The Portuguese, having little idea where the Nile ran, at least understood right away that there were men and women darker-skinned than themselves, but they were not specifically knowledgeable, or ingenious, about the various families and groupings represented by them. De Azurara records encounters with "Moors," "Mooresses," "Mulattoes," and people "black as Ethiops" (1:28), but it seems that the "Land of Guinea," or of "Black Men," or of "The Negroes" (1:35) was located anywhere southeast of Cape Verde, the Canaries, and the River Senegal, looking at an eighteenth-century European version of the subsaharan Continent along the West African coast (1:frontispiece).

Three genetic distinctions are available to the Portuguese eye, all along the riffs of melanin in the skin: in a field of captives, some of the observed are "white enough, fair to look upon, and well-proportioned." Others are less "white like mulattoes," and still others "black as Ethiops, and so ugly, both in features and in body, as almost to appear (to those who saw them) the images of a lower hemisphere" (1:28). By implication, this "third man," standing for the most aberrant phenotype to the observing eye, embodies the linguistic community most unknown to the European. Arabic translators among the Europeans could at least "talk" to the "Moors" and instruct them to ransom themselves, or else. . . .

Typically, there is in this grammar of description the perspective of "declension," not of simultaneity, and its point of initiation is solipsistic—it begins with a narrative self, in an apparent unity of feeling, and unlike Equiano, who also saw "ugly" when he looked out, this collective self uncovers the means by which to subjugate the "foreign code of conscience," whose most easily remarkable and irremediable difference is perceived in skin color. By the time of De Azurara's mid-fifteenth century narrative and a century and a half before Shakespeare's "old black ram" of an Othello "tups" that "white ewe" of a Desdemona, the magic of skin color is already installed as a decisive factor in human dealings.

In De Azurara's narrative, we observe males looking at other males, as "female" is subsumed here under the general category of estrangement. Few places in these excerpts carve out a distinct female space, though there are moments of portrayal that perceive female captives in the implications of sociocultural function. When the field of captives (referred to above) is divided among the spoilers, no heed is paid to relations, as fathers are separated from sons, husbands from wives, brothers from sisters and brothers, mothers from children—male and female. It seems clear that the political program of European Christianity promotes this hierarchical view among *males*, although it remains puzzling to us exactly how this version of Christianity transforms the "pagan" also into the "ugly." It appears that human beings came up with degrees of "fair" and then the "hideous," in its overtones of bestiality, as the opposite of "fair," all by themselves, without stage direction, even though there is the curious and blazing exception of Nietzsche's Socrates, who was Athens's ugliest and wisest and best citizen. The intimate choreography that the Portuguese narrator sets going between the "faithless" and the "ugly" transforms a partnership of dancers into a single figure. Once the "faithless," indiscriminate of the three stops of Portuguese skin color, are transported to Europe, they become an *altered* human factor:

And so their lot was now quite contrary to what it had been, since before they had lived in perdition of soul and body; of their souls, in that they were yet pagans, without the clearness and the light of the Holy Faith; and of their bodies, in that they lived like beasts, without any custom of reasonable beings—for they had no knowledge of bread and wine, and they were without covering of clothes, or the lodgment of houses; and worse than all, through the great ignorance that was in them, in that they had no understanding of good, but only knew how to live in bestial sloth. (1:30)

The altered human factor renders an alterity of European ego, an invention, or "discovery" as decisive in the full range of its social implications as the birth of a newborn. According to the semantic alignments of the excerpted passage, personhood, for this European observer, locates an immediately outward and superficial determination, gauged by quite arbitrarily opposed and *specular* categories: that these "pagans" did not have "bread" and "wine" did not mean that they were feastless, as Equiano observes about the Benin diet, c. 1745, in the province of Essaka:

> Our manner of living is entirely plain; for as yet the natives are unacquainted with those refinements in cookery which debauch the taste; bullocks, goats, and poultry supply the greatest part of their food. (These constitute likewise the principal wealth of the country, and the chief articles of its commerce.) The flesh is usually stewed in a pan; to make it savory we sometimes use pepper, and other spices, and we have salt made of wood ashes. Our vegetables are mostly plaintains, eadas, yams, beans and Indian corn. The head of the family usually eats alone; his wives and slaves have also their separate tables. . . . (1:8)

Just as fufu serves the Ghanaian diet today as a starch-and-bread-substitute, palm wine (an item by the same name in the eighteenth-century palate of the Benin community) need not be Heitz Cellars Martha's Vineyard and vice-versa in order for a guest, say, to imagine that she has enjoyed. That African housing arrangements of the fifteenth century did not resemble those familiar to De Azurara's narrator need not have meant that the African communities he encountered were without dwellings. Again, Equiano's narrative suggests that by the middle of the eighteenth century, at least, African living patterns were not only quite distinct in their sociometrical implications, but that also their architectonics accurately reflected the climate and availability of resources in the local circumstance: "These houses never exceed one story in height; they are always built of wood, or stakes driven into the ground, crossed with wattles, and neatly plastered within and without" (1:9). Hierarchical impulse in *both* De Azurara's and Equiano's narratives translates all *perceived* difference as a fundamental degradation *or* transcendence, but at least in Equiano's case, cultural practices are not observed in any intimate connection with skin color. For all intents and purposes, the politics of melanin, not isolated in its strange powers from the imperatives of a mercantile and competitive economics of European nation-states, will make of "transcendence" and "degradation" the basis of a historic violence that will rewrite the histories of modern Europe and black Africa. These mutually exclusive nominative elements come to rest on the same governing semantics—the ahistorical, or symptoms of the "sacred."

By August 1518, the Spanish king, Francisco de Los Covos, under the aegis of a powerful negation, could order "4000 negro slaves both male and female, provided they be Christians" to be taken to the Caribbean, "the islands and the mainland of the ocean sea already discovered or to be discovered" (1:42). Though the notorious "Middle Passage" appears to the investigator as a vast background without boundaries in time and space, we see it related in Donnan's accounts to the opening up of the entire Western hemisphere for the specific purposes of enslavement and colonization. De Azurara's narrative belongs, then, to a discourse of appropriation whose strategies will prove fatal to communities along the coastline of West Africa, stretching, according to Olaudah Equiano, "3400 miles, from Senegal to Angola, and [will include] a variety of kingdoms" (1:5).

The conditions of "Middle Passage" are among the most incredible narratives available to the student, as it remains not easily imaginable. Late in the chronicles of the Atlantic Slave Trade, Britain's Parliament entertained discussions concerning possible "regulations" for slave vessels. A Captain Perry visited the Liverpool port, and among the ships that he inspected was "The Brookes," probably the most well-known image of the slave galley with its representative *personae* etched into the drawing like so many cartoon figures. Elizabeth Donnan's second volume carries the "Brookes Plan," along with an elaborate delineation of its dimensions from the investigative reporting of Perry himself: "Let it now be supposed . . . further, that every man slave is to be allowed six feet by one foot four inches for room, every woman five feet ten by one foot four, every boy five feet by one foot two, and every girl four feet six by one foot . . ." (2:592, n). The owner of "The Brookes," James Jones, had recommended that "five females be reckoned as four males, and three boys or girls as equal to two grown persons" (2:592).

These scaled inequalities complement the commanding terms of the dehumanizing, ungendering, and defacing project of African persons that De Azurara's narrator might have recognized. It has been pointed out to me that these measurements do reveal the application of the gender rule to the material conditions of passage, but I would suggest that "gendering" takes place within the confines of the domestic, an essential metaphor that then spreads its tentacles for male and female subject over a wider ground of human and social purposes. Domesticity appears to gain its power by way of a common origin of cultural fictions that are grounded in the specificity of proper names, more exactly, a patronymic, which, in turn, situates those persons it "covers" in a particular place. Contrarily, the cargo of a ship might not be regarded as elements of the domestic, even though the vessel that carries it is sometimes romantically (ironically?) personified as "she." The human cargo of a slave vessel—in the fundamental effacement and remission of African family and proper names—offers a *counter*-narrative to notions of the domestic.

Those African persons in "Middle Passage" were literally suspended in the "oceanic," if we think of the latter in its Freudian orientation as an analogy for undifferentiated identity: removed from the indigenous land and culture, and not-yet "American" either, these captive persons, without names that their captors would recognize, were in movement across the Atlantic, but they were also *nowhere* at all. Inasmuch as, on any given day, we might imagine, the captive personality did not know where s/he was, we could say that they were the culturally "unmade," thrown in the midst of a figurative darkness that "exposed" their destinies to an unknown course. Often enough for the captains of these galleys, navigational science of the day was not sufficient to guarantee the intended destination. We might say that the slave ship, its crew, and its human-as-cargo stand for a wild and unclaimed richness of *possibility* that is not interrupted, not "counted"/"accounted," or differentiated, until its movement gains the land thousands of miles away from the point of departure. Under these conditions, one is neither female, nor male, as both subjects are taken into "account" as *quantities*. The female in "Middle Passage," as the apparently smaller physical mass, occupies "less room" in a directly translatable money economy. But she is, nevertheless, quantifiable by the same rules of accounting as her male counterpart.

It is not only difficult for the student to find "female" in "Middle Passage," but also, as Herbert S. Klein observes, "African women did not enter the Atlantic slave trade in anything like the numbers of African men.[13] At all ages, men outnumbered women on the slave ships bound for America from Africa" (29). Though this observation does not change the reality of African women's captivity and servitude in New World communities, it does provide a perspective from which to contemplate the *internal* African slave trade, which, according to Africanists, remained a predominantly *female* market. Klein nevertheless affirms that those females forced into the trade were segregated "from men for policing purposes" (35). He claims that both "were allotted the same space between decks . . . and both were fed the same food" (35). It is not altogether clear from Klein's observations *for whom* the "police" kept vigil. It is certainly known from evidence presented in Donnan's third volume ("New England and the Middle Colonies") that insurrection was both frequent and feared in passage, and we have not yet found a great deal of evidence to support a thesis that female captives participated in insurrection-ary activity.[14] Because it was the rule, however—not the exception—that the African female, in both indigenous African cultures and in what becomes her "home," performed tasks of hard physical labor—so much so that the quintessential "slave" is *not* a male, but a female—we wonder at the seeming docility of the subject, granting her a "feminization" that enslavement kept at bay. Indeed, across the spate of discourse that I examined for this writing, the acts of enslavement and responses to it comprise a more or less agonistic engagement of confrontational hostilities among males. The visual and historical evidence betrays the dominant discourse on the matter as incomplete, but *counter*-evidence is inadequate as well: the sexual violation of captive females and their own express rage against their oppressors did not constitute events that captains and their crews rushed to record in letters to their sponsoring companies, or sons on board in letters home to their New England mamas.

One suspects that there are several ways to snare a mockingbird, so that insurrection might have involved, from time to time, rather more subtle means than mutiny on the "Felicity," for instance. At any rate, we get very little notion in the written record of the life of women, children, and infants in "Middle Passage," and no idea of the fate of the pregnant female captive and the unborn, which startling thematic bell hooks addresses in the opening chapter of her pathfinding work.[15] From hooks's lead, however, we might guess that the "reproduction of mothering" in this historic instance carries few of the benefits of a *patriarchilized* female gender, which, from one point of view, is the *only* female gender there is.

The relative silence of the record on this point constitutes a portion of the disquieting lacunae that feminist investigation seeks to fill. Such silence is the nickname of distortion, of the unknown human factor that a revised public discourse would both undo *and* reveal. This cultural subject is inscribed historically as anonymity/anomie in various public documents of European-American mal(e)venture, from Portuguese De Azurara in the middle of the fifteenth century, to South Carolina's Henry Laurens in the eighteenth.

What confuses and enriches the picture is precisely the sameness of anonymous portrayal that adheres tenaciously across the division of gender. In the vertical columns of accounts and ledgers that comprise Donnan's work, the terms "Negroes" and "Slaves" denote a common status. For instance, entries in one account, from September 1700 through September 1702, are specifically descriptive of the names of ships and the private traders in Barbados who will receive the stipulated goods, but "No. Negroes" and "Sum sold for per head" are so exactly arithmetical that it is as if these additions and multiplications belong to the other side of an equation.[16] One is struck by the detail and precision that characterize these accounts, as a narrative, or story, is always implied by a man or woman's *name*: "Wm. Webster," "John Dunn," "Thos. Brownbill," "Robt. Knowles." But the "other" side of the page, as it were, equally precise, throws no *face* in view. It seems that nothing breaks the uniformity in this guise. If in no other way, the destruction of the African name, of kin, of linguistic, and ritual connections is so obvious in the vital stats sheet that we tend to overlook it. Quite naturally, the trader is not interested, in any *semantic* sense, in this "baggage" that he must deliver, but that he is not is all the more reason to search out the metaphorical implications of *naming* as one of the key sources of a bitter Americanizing for African persons.

The loss of the indigenous name/land provides a metaphor of displacement for other human and cultural features and relations, including the displacement of the genitalia, the female's and the male's desire that engenders future. The fact that the enslaved person's access to the issue of his/her own body is not entirely clear in this historic period throws in crisis all aspects of the blood relations, as captors apparently felt no obligation to acknowledge them. Actually trying to understand how the confusions of consanguinity worked becomes the project, because the outcome goes far to explain the rule of gender and its application to the African female in captivity.

3

Even though the essays in Claire C. Robertson's and Martin A. Klein's *Women and Slavery in Africa* have specifically to do with aspects of the internal African slave trade, some of their observations shed light on the captivities of the Diaspora. At least these observations have the benefit of altering the kind of questions we might ask of these silent chapters. For example, Robertson's essay, which opens the volume, discusses the term "slavery" in a wide variety of relationships. The enslaved person as *property* identifies the most familiar element of a most startling proposition. But to overlap *kinlessness* on the requirements of property might enlarge our view of the conditions of enslavement. Looking specifically at documents from the West African societies of Songhay and Dahomey, Claude Meillassoux elaborates several features of the property/kinless constellation that are highly suggestive for our own quite different purposes.[17]

Meillassoux argues that "slavery creates an economic and social agent whose virtue lies in being outside the kinship system."[18] Because the Atlantic trade involved heterogeneous social and ethnic formations in an explicit power relationship, we certainly cannot mean "kinship system" in precisely the same way that Meillassoux observes at work within the intricate calculus of descent among West African societies. However, the idea becomes useful as a point of contemplation when we try to sharpen our own sense of the African female's reproductive uses within the disaporic enterprise of enslavement and the genetic reproduction of the enslaved. In effect, under conditions of captivity, the offspring of the female does not "belong" to the Mother, nor is s/he "related" to the "owner," though the latter "possesses" it, and in the African-American instance, often fathered it, *and*, as often, without whatever benefit of patrimony. In the social outline that Meillassoux is pursuing, the offspring of the enslaved, "being unrelated both to their begetters and to their owners . . . , find themselves in the situation of being orphans" (50).

In the context of the United States, we could not say that the enslaved offspring was "orphaned," but the child does become, under the press of a patronymic, patrifocal, patrilineal, and patriarchal order, the man/woman on the boundary, whose human and familial status, by the very nature of the case, had yet to be defined. I would call this enforced state of breach another instance of vestibular cultural formation where "kinship" loses meaning, *since it can be invaded at any given and arbitrary moment by the property relations.* I certainly do not mean to say that African peoples in the New World did not maintain the powerful ties of sympathy that bind blood-relations in a network of feeling, of continuity. It is precisely *that* relationship—not customarily recognized by the code of slavery—that historians have long identified as the inviolable "Black Family" and further suggest that this structure remains one of the supreme social achievements of African-Americans under conditions of enslavement.[19]

Indeed, the *revised* "Black Family" of enslavement has engendered an older tradition of historiographical and sociological writings than we usually think. Ironically enough, E. Franklin Frazier's *Negro Family in the United States* likely provides the closest *contemporary* narrative of conceptualization for the "Moynihan Report."[20] Originally published in 1939, Frazier's work underwent two redactions in 1948 and 1966. Even though Frazier's outlook on this familial configuration remains basically sanguine, I would support Angela Davis's skeptical reading of Frazier's "Black Matriarchate."[21] *"Except where the master's will was concerned,"* Frazier contends, this matriarchal figure "developed a spirit of independence and a keen sense of her personal rights."²² The "exception" in this instance tends to be overwhelming, as the African-American female's "dominance" and "strength" come to be interpreted by later generations—both black and white, oddly enough—as a "pathology," as an instrument of castration. Frazier's larger point, we might suppose, is that African-Americans developed such resourcefulness under conditions of captivity that "family" must be conceded as one of their redoubtable social attainments. This line of interpretation is pursued by Blassingame and Eugene Genovese²³, among other U.S. historians, and indeed assumes a centrality of focus in our own thinking about the impact and outcome of captivity.   **ABSTRACT.**

It seems clear, however, that "Family," as we practice and understand it "in the West"—the *vertical* transfer of a bloodline, of a patronymic, of titles and entitlements, of real estate and the prerogatives of "cold cash," from *fathers* to *sons* and in the supposedly free exchange of affectional ties between a male and a female of *his* choice—becomes the mythically revered privilege of a free and freed community. In that sense, African peoples in the historic Diaspora had nothing to prove, *if* the point had been that they were not capable of "family" (read "civilization"), since it is stunningly evident, in Equiano's narrative, for instance, that Africans were not only capable of the concept and the practice of "family," including "slaves," but in modes of elaboration and naming that were at least as complex as those of the "nuclear family" "in the West."

Whether or not we decide that the support systems that African-Americans derived under conditions of captivity should be called "family," or something else, strikes me as supremely impertinent. The point remains that the captive persons were *forced* into patterns of *dispersal*, beginning with the Trade itself, into the *horizontal* relatedness of language groups, discourse formations, bloodlines, names, and properties by the legal arrangements of enslavement. It is true that the most "well-meaning" of "masters" (and there must have been *some*) *could not, did not* alter the *ideological* and hegemonic mandates of dominance. It must be conceded that African-Americans, under the press of a hostile and compulsory patriarchal order, bound and determined to destroy them, or to preserve them only in the service and at the behest of the "master" class, exercised a degree of courage and will to survive that startles the imagination even now. Although it makes good revisionist history to read this tale *liberally,* it is probably truer than we know at this distance (and truer than contemporary social practice in the community would suggest on occasion) that the captive person developed, time and again, certain ethical and sentimental features that tied her and him, *across* the landscape to others, often sold from hand to hand, of the same and different blood in a common fabric of memory and inspiration.

We might choose to call this connectedness "family," or "support structure," but that is a rather different case from the moves of a dominant symbolic order, pledged to maintain the supremacy of race. It is that order that forces "family" to modify itself when it does not mean family of the "master," or dominant enclave. It is this rhetorical and symbolic move that declares primacy over any other human and social claim, and in that political order of things, "kin," just as gender formation, has no decisive legal or social efficacy.

We return frequently to Frederick Douglass's careful elaborations of the arrangements of captivity, and we are astonished each reading by two dispersed, yet poignantly related, familial enactments that suggest a connection between "kinship" and "property."[24] Douglass tells us early in the opening chapter of the 1845 *Narrative* that he was separated in infancy from his mother: "For what this separation is [sic] done, I do not know, unless it be to hinder the development of the child's affection toward its mother, and to blunt and destroy the natural affection of the mother for the child. This is the inevitable result" (22).

Perhaps one of the assertions that Meillassoux advances concerning indigenous African formations of enslavement might be turned as a question, against the perspective of Douglass's witness: is the genetic reproduction of the slave and the recognition of the rights of the slave to his or her offspring a check on the *profitability* of slavery? And how so, if so? We see vaguely the route to framing a response, especially to the question's second half and perhaps to the first: the enslaved must not be permitted to perceive that he or she has any human rights that matter. Certainly if "kinship" were possible, the property relations would be undermined, since the offspring would then "belong" to a mother and a father. In the system that Douglass articulates, genetic reproduction becomes, then, not an elaboration of the life-principle in its cultural overlap, but an extension of the boundaries of proliferating properties. Meillassoux goes so far as to argue that "slavery exists where the slave class is reproduced through institutional apparatus: war and market" (50). Since, in the United States, the market of slavery identified the chief institutional means for maintaining a class of enforced servile labor, it seems that the biological reproduction of the enslaved was not alone sufficient to reenforce the *estate* of slavery. If, as Meillassoux contends, "femininity loses its sacredness in slavery" (64), then so does "motherhood" as female blood-rite/right. To that extent, the captive female body locates precisely a moment of converging political and social vectors that mark the flesh as a prime

commodity of exchange. While this proposition is open to further exploration, suffice it to say now that this open exchange of female bodies in the raw
offers a kind of Ur-text to the dynamics of signification and representation
that the gendered female would unravel.

For Douglass, the loss of his mother eventuates in alienation from his
brother and sisters, who live in the same house with him: "The early separation of us from our mother had well nigh blotted the fact of our relationship
from our memories" (45). What could this mean? The *physical* proximity of
the siblings survives the mother's death. They grasp their connection in the
physical sense, but Douglass appears to mean a *psychological* bonding whose
success mandates the *mother's* presence. Could we say, then, that the *feeling*
of kinship is *not* inevitable? That it describes a relationship that appears
"natural," but must be "cultivated" under actual material conditions? If the
child's humanity is mirrored initially in the eyes of its mother, or the mater-
nal function, then we might be able to guess that the social subject grasps the
whole dynamic of resemblance and kinship by way of the same source.

There is an amazing thematic synonymity on this point between aspects of
Douglass's *Narrative* and Malcolm El-Hajj Malik El Shabazz's *Autobiography
of Malcolm X*.[25] Through the loss of the mother, in the latter contemporary
instance, to the institution of "insanity" and the state—a full century after
Douglass's writing and under social conditions that might be designated a
postemancipation neoenslavement—Malcolm and his siblings, robbed of
their activist father in a kkk-like ambush, are not only widely dispersed
across a makeshift social terrain, but also show symptoms of estrangement
and "disremembering" that require many years to heal, and even then, only
by way of Malcolm's prison ordeal turned, eventually, into a redemptive
occurrence.

The destructive loss of the natural mother, whose biological/genetic relationship to the child remains unique and unambiguous, opens the enslaved
young to social ambiguity and chaos: the ambiguity of his/her fatherhood
and to a structure of other relational elements, now threatened, that would
declare the young's connection to a genetic and historic future by way of
their own siblings. That the father in Douglass's case was most likely the
"master," not by any means special to Douglass, involves a hideous paradox.
Fatherhood, at best a supreme cultural courtesy, attenuates here on the one
hand into a monstrous accumulation of power on the other. One has been
"made" and "bought" by disparate currencies, linking back to a common
origin of exchange and domination. The denied genetic link becomes the
chief strategy of an undenied ownership, as if the interrogation into the

father's identity—the blank space where his proper name will fit—were answered by the fact, *de jure* of a material possession. "And this is done," Douglass asserts, "too obviously to administer to the [masters'] own lusts, and make a gratification of their wicked desires profitable as well as pleasurable" (23).

Whether or not the captive female and/or her sexual oppressor derived "pleasure" from their seductions and couplings is not a question we can politely ask. Whether or not "pleasure" is possible at all under conditions that I would aver as nonfreedom for both or either of the parties has not been settled. Indeed, we could go so far as to entertain the very real possibility that "sexuality," as a term of implied relationship and desire, is dubiously appropriate, manageable, or accurate to *any* of the familial arrangements under a system of enslavement, from the master's family to the captive enclave. Under these arrangements, the customary lexis of sexuality, including "reproduction," "motherhood," "pleasure," and "desire" are thrown into unrelieved crisis.

If the testimony of Linda Brent/Harriet Jacobs is to be believed, the official mistresses of slavery's "masters" constitute a privileged class of the tormented, if such contradiction can be entertained.[26] Linda Brent/Harriet Jacobs recounts in the course of her narrative scenes from a "psychodrama," opposing herself and "Mrs. Flint," in what we have come to consider the classic alignment between captive woman and free. Suspecting that her husband, Dr. Flint, has sexual designs on the young Linda (and the doctor is nearly humorously incompetent at it, according to the story line), Mrs. Flint assumes the role of a perambulatory nightmare who visits the captive woman in the spirit of a veiled seduction. Mrs. Flint imitates the incubus who "rides" its victim in order to exact confession, expiation, and anything else that the immaterial power might want. (Gayle Jones's *Corregidora* [New York, 1975] weaves a contemporary fictional situation around the historic motif of entangled female sexualities.) This narrative scene from Brent's work, dictated to Lydia Maria Child, provides an instance of a repeated sequence, purportedly based on "real" life. But the scene in question appears to so commingle its signals with the fictive, with casebook narratives from psychoanalysis, that we are certain that the narrator has her hands on an explosive moment of New-World/U.S. history that feminist investigation is beginning to unravel. The narrator recalls:

Sometimes I woke up, and found her bending over me. At other times she whispered in my ear, as though it were her husband who was speaking to me, and listened to hear what I would answer. If she startled me, on such occasion, she would glide stealthily away; and the next morning she would tell me I had been talking in my sleep, and ask who I was talking to. At last, I began to be fearful for my life. . . . (33)

The "jealous mistress" here (but "jealous" for whom?) forms an analogy with the "master" to the extent that male dominative modes give the male the material means to fully act out what the female might only *wish*. The mistress in the case of Brent's narrative becomes a metaphor for *his* madness that arises in the ecstasy of unchecked power. Mrs. Flint enacts a male alibi and prosthetic motion that is mobilized *at night,* at the material place of the dream work. In both male and female instances, the subject attempts to *inculcate* his or her will into the vulnerable, supine body. Though this is barely hinted on the surface of the text, we might say that Brent, between the lines of her narrative, demarcates a sexuality that is neuterbound, inasmuch as it represents an open vulnerability to a gigantic sexualized repertoire that may be alternately expressed as male/female. Since the gendered female *exists* for the male, we might suggest that the ungendered female—in an amazing stroke of pansexual potential—might be invaded/raided by another *woman* or man.

If *Incidents in the Life of a Slave Girl* were a novel, and not the memoirs of an escaped female captive, then we might say that "Mrs. Flint" is also the narrator's projection, her creation, so that for all her pious and correct umbrage toward the outrage of her captivity, some aspect of Linda Brent is released in a manifold repetition crisis that the doctor's wife comes to stand in for. In the case of both an imagined fiction and the narrative we have from Brent/Jacobs/Child, published only four years before the official proclamations of Freedom, we could say that African-American women's community and Anglo-American women's community, under certain shared cultural conditions, were the twin actants on a common psychic landscape, were subject to the same fabric of dread and humiliation. Neither could claim her body and its various productions—for quite different reasons, albeit—as her own, and in the case of the doctor's wife, *she* appears not to have wanted *her* body at all, but to desire to enter someone else's, specifically, Linda Brent's, in an apparently classic instance of sexual "jealousy" and appropriation. In fact, from one point of view, we cannot unravel one female's narrative from the other's, cannot decipher one without tripping over the other. In that sense, these "threads cable-strong" of an incestuous, interracial genealogy uncover slavery in the United States as one of the richest displays of the psychoanalytic dimensions of culture before the science of European psychoanalysis takes hold.

4

But just as we duly regard similarities between life conditions of American women—captive and free—we must observe those undeniable contrasts and differences so decisive that the African-American female's historic claim to the territory of womanhood and "femininity" still tends to rest too solidly on the subtle and shifting calibrations of a liberal ideology. Valerie Smith's reading of the tale of Linda Brent as a tale of "garreting" enables our notion that female gender for captive women's community is the tale writ between the lines and in the not-quite spaces of an American domesticity.[27] It is this tale that we try to make clearer, or, keeping with the metaphor, "bring on line."

If the point is that the historic conditions of African-American women might be read as an unprecedented occasion in the national context, then gender and the arrangements of gender are both crucial and evasive. Holding, however, to a specialized reading of female gender as an *outcome* of a certain political, sociocultural empowerment within the context of the United States, we would regard dispossession as the *loss* of gender, or one of the chief elements in an altered reading of gender: "Women are considered of no value, *unless* they continually increase their owner's stock. They were put on par with animals."[28] Linda Brent's witness appears to contradict the point I would make, but I am suggesting that even though the enslaved female reproduced other enslaved persons, we do not read "birth" in this instance as a reproduction of mothering precisely because the female, like the male, has been robbed of the parental right, the parental function. One treads dangerous ground in suggesting an equation between female gender and mothering; in fact, feminist inquiry/praxis and the actual day-to-day living of numberless American women—black and white—have gone far to break the enthrallment of a female subject-position to the theoretical and actual situation of maternity. Our task here would be lightened considerably if we could simply slide over the powerful "No," the significant *exception*. In the historic formation to which I point, however, motherhood and female gendering/ ungendering appear so intimately aligned that they *seem* to speak the same language. At least it is plausible to say that motherhood, while it does not exhaust the problematics of female gender, offers one prominent line of approach to it. I would go farther: Because African-American women experienced uncertainty regarding their infants' lives in the historic situation, gendering, in its coeval reference to African-American women, *insinuates* an implicit and unresolved puzzle both within current feminist discourse *and* within those discursive communities that investigate the entire problematics of culture. Are we mistaken to suspect that history—at least in this instance—repeats itself yet again?

Every feature of social and human differentiation disappears in public discourses regarding the African-American person, as we encounter, in the juridical codes of slavery, personality reified. William Goodell's study not only demonstrates the rhetorical and moral passions of the abolitionist project, but also lends insight into the corpus of law that underwrites enslavement. If "slave" is perceived as the essence of stillness (an early version of "ethnicity"), or of an undynamic human state, fixed in time and space, then the law articulates this impossibility as its inherent feature: "Slaves shall be deemed, sold, taken, reputed and adjudged in law to be *chattels personal,* in the hands of their owners and possessors, and their executors, administrators, and assigns, to all intents, constructions, and purposes whatsoever" (23; Goodell emphasis).

Even though we tend to parody and simplify matters to behave as if the various civil codes of the slave-holding United States were monolithically informed, unified, and executed in their application, or that the "code" itself is spontaneously generated in an undivided historic moment, we read it nevertheless as exactly this—the *peak points,* the salient and characteristic features of a human and social procedure that evolves over a natural historical sequence and represents, consequently, the narrative *shorthand* of a transaction that is riddled, *in practice,* with contradictions, accident, and surprise. We could suppose that the legal encodations of enslavement stand for the statistically average case, that the legal code provides the *topics* of a project increasingly threatened and self-conscious. It is, perhaps, not by chance that the laws regarding slavery appear to crystallize in the precise moment when agitation against the arrangement becomes articulate in certain European and New-World communities. In that regard, the slave codes that Goodell describes are themselves an instance of the counter and isolated text that seeks to silence the contradictions and antitheses engendered by it. For example, aspects of Article 461 of the South Carolina Civil Code call attention to just the sort of uneasy oxymoronic character that the "peculiar institution" attempts to sustain in transforming *personality* into *property.*

(1) The "slave" is movable by nature, but "immovable by the operation of law."[29] As I read this, law itself is compelled to a point of saturation, or a reverse zero degree, beyond which it cannot move in the behalf of the en-

slaved *or* the free. We recall, too, that the "master," under these perversions of judicial power, is impelled to *treat* the enslaved as property, and not as person. These laws stand for the kind of social formulation that armed forces will help excise from a living context in the campaigns of civil war. They also embody the untenable human relationship that Henry David Thoreau believed occasioned acts of "civil disobedience," the moral philosophy to which Martin Luther King, Jr. would subscribe in the latter half of the twentieth century.

(2) Slaves shall be *reputed* and *considered* real estate, "subject to be mortgaged, according to the rules prescribed by law."[30] I emphasize "reputed" and "considered" as predicate adjectives that invite attention because they denote a *contrivance,* not an intransitive "is," or the transfer of nominative property from one syntactic point to another by way of a weakened copulative. The status of the "reputed" can change, as it will significantly before the nineteenth century closes. The mood here—the "shall be"—is pointedly subjunctive, or the situation devoutly to be wished. The slave-holding class is forced, in time, to think and do something else is the narrative of violence that enslavement itself has been preparing for a couple of centuries.

Louisiana's and South Carolina's written codes offer a paradigm for praxis in those instances where a *written* text is missing. In that case, the "chattel principle has . . . been affirmed and maintained by the courts, and involved in legislative acts."[31] In Maryland, a legislative enactment of 1798 shows so forceful a synonymity of motives between branches of comparable governance that a line between "judicial" and "legislative" functions is useless to draw: "In case the personal property of a ward shall consist of specific articles, such as slaves, working beasts, animals of any kind, stock, furniture, plates, books, and so forth, the Court if it shall deem it advantageous to the ward, may at any time, pass an order for the sale thereof" (56). This inanimate and corporate ownership—the voting district of a ward—is here spoken for, or might be, as a single slave-holding male in determinations concerning property.

The eye pauses, however, not so much at the provisions of this enactment as at the details of its delineation. Everywhere in the descriptive document, we are stunned by the simultaneity of disparate items in a grammatical series: "Slave" appears in the same context with beasts of burden, *all* and *any* animal(s), various livestock, and a virtually endless profusion of domestic content from the culinary item to the book. Unlike the taxonomy of Borges's "Certain Chinese encyclopedia," whose contemplation opens Foucault's *Order of Things,*[32] these items from a certain American encyclopedia do not sustain discrete and localized "powers of contagion," nor has the ground of their concatenation been desiccated beneath them. That imposed uniformity comprises the shock, that somehow this mix of named things, live and inanimate, collapsed by contiguity to the same text of "realism," carries a disturbingly prominent item of misplacement. To that extent, the project of liberation for African-Americans has found urgency in two passionate motivations that are twinned—(1) to break apart, to rupture violently the laws of American behavior that make such *syntax* possible; (2) to introduce a new *semantic* field/fold more appropriate to his/her own historic movement. I regard this twin compulsion as distinct, though related, moments of the very same narrative process that might appear as a concentration or a dispersal. The narratives of Linda Brent, Frederick Douglass, and Malcolm El-Hajj Malik El-Shabazz (aspects of which are examined in this essay) each represent both narrative ambitions as they occur under the auspices of "author."

Relatedly, we might interpret the whole career of African-Americans, a decisive factor in national political life since the mid-seventeenth century, in light of the *intervening, intruding* tale, or the tale—like Brent's "garret" space— "between the lines," which are already inscribed, as a *metaphor* of social and cultural management. According to this reading, gender, or sex-role assignation, or the clear differentiation of sexual stuff, sustained elsewhere in the culture, does not emerge for the African-American female in this historic instance, except indirectly, except as a way to reenforce through the process of birthing, "the reproduction of the relations of production" that involves "the reproduction of the values and behavior patterns necessary to maintain the system of hierarchy in its various aspects of gender, class, and race or ethnicity."[33] Following Strobel's lead, I would suggest that the foregoing identifies one of the three categories of reproductive labor that African-American females carry out under the regime of captivity. But this replication of ideology is never simple in the case of female subject-positions, and it appears to acquire a thickened layer of motives in the case of African-American females.

If we can account for an originary narrative and judicial principle that might have engendered a "Moynihan Report," many years into the twentieth century, we cannot do much better than look at Goodell's reading of the *partus sequitur ventrem:* the condition of the slave mother is "forever entailed on all her remotest posterity." This maxim of civil law, in Goodell's view, the "genuine and degrading principle of slavery, inasmuch as it places the slave upon a level with brute animals, prevails universally in the slave-holding states" (27). But what is the "condition" of the mother? Is it the "condition" of enslavement the writer means, or does he mean the "mark" and the "knowledge" of the *mother* upon the child that here translates into the culturally forbidden and impure? In an elision of terms, "mother" and "enslavement" are indistinct categories of the illegitimate inasmuch as each of these synonymous elements defines, in effect, a cultural situation that is *father-lacking*. Goodell, who does not only report this maxim of law as an aspect of his own factuality, but also regards it, as does Douglass, as a fundamental degradation, supposes descent and identity through the female line as comparable to a brute animality. Knowing already that there are human communities that align social reproductive procedure according to the line of the mother, and Goodell himself might have known it some years later, we can only conclude that the provisions of patriarchy, here exacerbated by the preponderant powers of an enslaving class, declare Mother Right, by definition, a negating feature of human community.

Even though we are not even talking about *any* of the matriarchal features of social production/reproduction—matrifocality, matrilinearity, matriarchy—when we speak of the enslaved person, we perceive that the dominant culture, in a fatal misunderstanding, assigns a matriarchist value where it does not belong; actually *misnames* the power of the female regarding the enslaved community. Such naming is false because the female could not, in fact, claim her child, and false, once again, because "motherhood" is not perceived in the prevailing social climate as a legitimate procedure of cultural inheritance.

The African-American male has been touched, therefore, by the *mother,* *handed* by her in ways that he cannot escape, and in ways that the white American male is allowed to temporize by a fatherly reprieve. This human and historic development—the text that has been inscribed on the benighted heart of the continent—takes us to the center of an inexorable difference in the depths of American women's community: the African-American woman, the mother, the daughter, becomes historically the powerful and shadowy evocation of a cultural synthesis long evaporated—the law of the Mother—only and precisely because legal enslavement removed the African-American male not so much from sight as from *mimetic* view as a partner in the prevailing social fiction of the Father's name, the Father's law.

Therefore, the female, in this order of things, breaks in upon the imagination with a forcefulness that marks both a denial and an "illegitimacy." Because of this peculiar American denial, the black American male embodies the *only* American community of males which has had the specific occasion to learn *who* the female is within itself, the infant child who bears the life against the could-be fateful gamble, against the odds of pulverization and murder, including her own. It is the heritage of the *mother* that the African-American male must regain as an aspect of his own personhood—the power of "yes" to the "female" within.

This different cultural text actually reconfigures, in historically ordained discourse, certain *representational* potentialities for African-Americans: (1) motherhood as female blood-rite is outraged, is denied, at the *very same time* that it becomes the founding term of a human and social enactment; (2) a dual fatherhood is set in motion, comprised of the African father's *banished* name and body and the captor father's mocking presence. In this play of paradox, only the female stands *in the flesh,* both mother and mother-dispossessed. This problematizing of gender places her, in my view, *out* of the traditional symbolics of female gender, and it is our task to make a place for this different social subject. In doing so, we are less interested in joining the ranks of gendered femaleness than gaining the *insurgent* ground as female social subject. Actually *claiming* the monstrosity (of a female with the potential to "name"), which her culture imposes in blindness, "Sapphire" might rewrite after all a radically different text for a female empowerment.

Notes

1 Daniel P. Moynihan, *The Negro Family: The Case for National Action* (Washington, D.C., 1965), 75.
2 Roland Barthes, translated by Annette Lavers, *Mythologies* (New York, 1972), 109–59, esp. 122–23.
3 William Goodell, *The American Slave Code in Theory and Practice Shown by Its Statutes, Judicial Decisions, and Illustrative Facts* (New York, 1853).
4 Elaine Scarry, *The Body in Pain: The Making and Unmaking of the World* (New York, 1985), 27–59.
5 Susan Rubin Suleiman, ed., *The Female Body in Western Culture* (Cambridge, Mass., 1986).
6 Angela Y. Davis, *Women, Race, and Class* (New York, 1981), 9.
7 William Faulkner, *The Mansion* (New York, 1965), 227.
8 Olaudah Equiano, "The Life of Olaudah Equiano, or Gustavus Vass, The African, Written by Himself," in Arna Bontemps, ed., *Great Slave Narratives* (Boston, 1969), 1–192.
9 Tzvetan Todorov, translated by Richard Howard, *The Conquest of America: The Question of the Other* (New York, 1984), 61.
10 Elizabeth Donnan, ed., *Documents Illustrative of the History of the Slave Trade to America,* 4 vols. (Washington, D.C., 1932).
11 Todorov, *Conquest of America,* 3.
12 Gomes Eannes de Azurara, translated by C. Raymond Beazley and Edgar Prestage, *The Chronicle of the Discovery and Conquest of Guinea,* in Donnan, ed., *History of the Slave Trade,* 1:18–41.

13 Herbert S. Klein, "African Women in the Atlantic Slave Trade," in Claire C. Robertson and Martin A. Klien, eds., *Women and Slavery in Africa* (Madison, Wisc., 1983).

14 See Deborah Gray White, *Ar'n't I A Woman? Female Slaves in the Plantation South* (New York, 1985), 63–64.

15 See hooks, bell, *Ain't I A Woman: Black Women and Feminism* (Boston, 1981), 15–49.

16 See Donnan, ed., *History of the Slave Trade,* 2:25.

17 Claude Meillassoux, "Female Slavery," in Robertson and Klein, eds., *Women and Slavery in Africa,* 49–67.

18 Meillassoux, "Female Slavery," 50.

19 See John Blassingame, *The Slave Community: Plantation Life in the Antebellum South* (New York, 1972), 79 ff.

20 E. Franklin Frazier, *The Negro Family in the United States* (Chicago, 1966).

21 Davis, *Women, Race, and Class,* 14.

22 Frazier, *Negro Family in the United States,* 47; emphasis mine.

23 Eugene Genovese, *Roll, Jordan, Roll: The World the Slaves Made* (New York, 1974), 70–75.

24 Frederick Douglass, *Narrative of the Life of Frederick Douglass An American Slave, Written by Himself* (1845; reprint, New York, 1968).

25 Malcolm El-Hajj Malik El-Shabazz (with Alex Haley), *Autobiography of Malcolm X* (New York, 1966), 21ff.

26 Linda Brent/Harriet Jacobs, *Incidents in the Life of a Slave Girl,* edited by Lydia Maria Child (New York, 1973), 29–35.

27 Valerie Smith, "Loopholes of Retreat: Architecture and Ideology in Harriet Jacobs's *Incidents in the Life of a Slave Girl,*" Paper presented at the American Studies Association Meeting (San Diego, 1985).

28 Brent, *Incidents in the Life of a Slave Girl,* 49; emphasis mine.

29 Goodell, *American Slave Code,* 24.

30 Ibid.

31 Ibid., 25.

32 Michel Foucault, *The Order of Things: An Archaeology of Human Sciences* (New York, 1973).

33 Margaret Strobel, "Slavery and Reproductive Labor in Mombasa," in Robertson and Klein, eds., *Women and Slavery in Africa,* 121.

Valerie Smith

Gender and Afro-Americanist Literary

Theory and Criticism

(1988)

This essay attempts to contribute to the ongoing process of writing black literary feminism by mapping the changing status of gender in Afro-Americanist discourse and suggesting future directions in which the study of representations of race and gender might move.[1] Such an effort to position issues of gender in relation to questions of race seems particularly necessary now that increasing numbers of "others"—black men, white women, and white men—are studying and theorizing about black women's literary and cultural productions.

If, as Hazel V. Carby has argued, the black feminist enterprise cannot be defined solely in terms of a shared experience between "black women as critics and black women as writers who represent black women's reality,"[2] then the time is right to ask ourselves what we mean when we talk about black feminism; to engage discrete instances of black feminist criticism in discussion with each other; and to consider black feminism in relation to the professional and institutional circumstances out of which it is produced and within which it is disseminated. Moreover, given that white men and women and black men have different investments in black feminism than black women do, those of us who consider questions of race and gender must develop a way of talking about the varying kinds of political and professional returns we receive from working on these sorts of issues.

The project of this essay is complicated by the fact that the narrative of the place of gender in Afro-Americanist theoretical and critical discourse is highly charged.[3] Indeed, at one level, rehearsing the history of omissions and misreadings seems almost beside the point, since recent black feminist work is more concerned with developing ways of reading and talking about figura-

This essay first appeared in Elaine Showalter, ed., *Speaking of Gender* (New York, 1988).

tions of race and gender than with focusing on absences in the work of others. Moreover, to criticize the work of black men within the context of a volume edited by a white feminist would suggest that I had chosen, at least for the time being, one set of allies at the expense of another. And yet, at another level it seems to me that if oppositional discourses—black feminist, Afro-Americanist, feminist, Marxist, and so on—are to keep their edge even as they move into the academic mainstream—then practitioners must develop a mode of self-evaluation, and sustain a dialogue with those involved in related enterprises. To fail to confront the contingencies that both enable and impede our theoretical work, is to risk replicating the exclusionary self-mystification, the pretense to objectivity, that characterizes phallocentric humanism.

Therefore in order to suggest how questions of gender might, in the future, expand the possibilities of Afro-Americanist discourse, I have identified ways in which the issue of gender has entered in the past. My hope is that if those of us working on the connections between race, class, and gender in cultural productions acknowledge the relation of our theoretical work to our personal circumstances, then we will be able to expand the radical possibilities of our scholarship. When we consider our relation to the institutions within which we work and by means of which our ideas are circulated, we will be able to resist the conditions that commodify and threaten to divide us.[4]

I

The conditions of oppression provide the subtext of all Afro-Americanist literary criticism and theory. Whether a critic/theorist explores representations of the experience of oppression or strategies by which that experience is transformed, he/she assumes the existence of an "other" against whom/which blacks struggle. In the classic tradition of Afro-Americanist criticism and theory, one dominated by male-authored and -edited texts, the oppressive "other" is a figure of white power, whether individual or institutional. Texts as diverse as Arthur P. Davis's thematic, integrationist, historical "Integration and Race Literature" and Robert B. Stepto's self-consciously dehistoricized study, *From Behind the Veil: A Study of Afro-American Narrative,* thus assume the experience of racism, the economic, social, and political articulations of racial oppression.

The discourse of Afro-Americanist literary study is therefore, like Anglo-American feminist discourse, clearly oppositional in origin and impulse, arising out of a specific kind of exclusion from both mainstream culture and criticism and literary history. Yet despite the challenge they offer to the canon and its custodians, both disciplines in their early stages have replicated the totalizing impulses of the tradition they seek to undermine. Among white feminists, this impulse has taken the form of presuming that one may generalize and theorize about women's experience on the basis of the lives and works of white women from the middle class. Similarly, Afro-Americanists, mostly male, have assumed that one may theorize about the experience of blacks in a racist culture on the basis of the lives of black men alone. As the increasingly visible presence of black feminists in the academy has introduced the issue of race into feminist theory, so has it raised the subject of gender in Afro-Americanist discourse. Black feminists have interrogated and explored the ways in which the experience of race affects the experience of gender, even as they examine ways in which the culturally constructed experience of gender, specifically of womanhood, affects the experience of race.

My consideration of the changing status of gender in Afro-Americanist discourse proceeds from the assumption that gender has generally been treated as a woman's issue, something women worry about but that is beside the point for men: one that gets raised "when and where [black women] enter."[5] Although it is generally not an explicit subject in male-authored discourse, I argue that the non-sex-specific voice of the male critic may be read as male. I consider some of the ways in which contemporary black literary feminism has gendered Afro-Americanist discourse during the past decade. Finally, I suggest directions in which gender study might productively move this field of literary explorations. My argument concentrates on contributions that the issue of gender can make to Afro-Americanist discourse; however, it has implications for ways in which oppositional fields of literary study might conceive of and represent those whom it marginalizes.

II

Historically, Afro-Americanist criticism before the advent of feminism dealt with issues of gender in one of three ways: in a biographical framework permeated by sexual stereotypes of women; in assertions of male authority within the Black Arts movement; and in an ostensibly gender-blind literary history that did not give equal weight to women's texts.

Darwin Turner's *In a Minor Chord: Three Afro-American Writers and Their Search for Identity* (1971) represents a moment before feminist and other modes of literary theory had influenced Afro-Americanist criticism. In his book Turner seeks to explain the inconsistency in quality and output of three skilled writers of the Harlem Renaissance—Jean Toomer, Countee Cullen, and Zora Neale Hurston—by reading their work in relation to their lives. The difficulties of such a method have been foregrounded by developments of the past two decades, but those difficulties are complicated by the difference between the way in which he uses biography to explain Toomer's and Cullen's work on the one hand and Hurston's on the other.

A key to the differential status he accords Hurston may be found as early as his "Introduction," where he describes his writers in the following manner: "Jean Toomer, generally acknowledged to be the most artistic craftsman of those who wrote before 1950; Countee Cullen, the precocious poet laureate of the Renaissance; and Zora Neale Hurston, the most competent black female novelist before 1950."[6] By describing Hurston in terms of her gender identity, her male counterparts in terms of their craft, Turner reveals his assumption that womanhood, but not manhood, has an impact on literary and artistic production.

Turner's Toomer and Cullen chapters are structured differently from his Hurston chapter. In the first two, he begins by establishing their literary power. He then reads the unevenness of their careers against the backdrop of changes in their biographical circumstances, but does not suggest ways in which either Cullen's or Toomer's relation to constructions of masculinity figure in their writing. One might ask today how Toomer's assumptions of male privilege could have prompted him to eschew his racial identity and constitute himself as a raceless American.

The Hurston chapter is set up quite differently from these first two. Instead of establishing her literary power, Turner opens the chapter with an extended examination of her personal eccentricities. Drawing from her autobiography and recollections of her foes and associates alike, he devotes the first third of this chapter to creating an image of Hurston as one who was indifferent to her own and other blacks' dignity, obsequious to whites, opportunistic, and politically retrograde. The bridge from the assessment of her character to the evaluation of her work is the following paragraph:

> The Zora Neale Hurston who takes shape from her autobiography and from the accounts of those who knew her is an imaginative, somewhat shallow, quick-tempered woman, desperate for recognition and reassurance to assuage her feelings of inferiority; a blind follower of that social code which approves arrogance toward one's assumed peers and inferiors but requires total psychological commitment to a subservient

posture before one's supposed superiors. It is in reference to this image that one must examine her novels, her folklore, and her view of the Southern scene.(98)

The references in this passage to Hurston's intellectual insubstantiality and erratic temperament characterize her in terms of cliches about women's character and gifts. What is even more problematic about this analysis, however, is Turner's assertion that this information is necessary if one is to understand Hurston's work. His *caveat* thus confirms one's sense that in 1971, gender was an issue for women but not for men.

Turner's view of gender in terms of feminine identity affects his reading of the text for which Hurston is best known, *Their Eyes Were Watching God*. In a pivotal scene in the novel, the protagonist, Janie, speaks of her own sense of loss to her husband on his deathbed, a man who throughout their marriage has silenced her. Janie says:

> "Listen, Jody, you ain't de Jody ah run off down de road wid. You's whut's left after he died. Ah run off tuh keep house wid you in uh wonderful way. But you wasn't satisfied wid me de way Ah was. Naw! Mah own mind had tuh be squeezed and crowded out tuh make room for yours in me."
>
> "Shut up! Ah wish thunder and lightnin' would kill yuh!"
>
> "Ah know it. And now you got tuh die tuh find out dat you got tuh pacify somebody besides yo'self if you wants any love and sympathy in dis world. You ain't tried tuh pacify *nobody* but yo'self. Too busy listening tuh yo' own big voice."[7]

This exchange is read today within a feminist framework as a victory for a woman denied her right to speak for herself and in her own voice. In 1971, however, this scene of Janie's speaking out against the man who has verbally and physically abused her was read as a sign of the author's racial self-hatred. Thus Turner writes,

> Either personal insensitivity or an inability to recognize aesthetic inappropriateness caused Miss Hurston to besmirch *Their Eyes Were Watching God* with one of the crudest scenes which she ever wrote . . . Never was [Jody's] conduct so cruel as to deserve the vindictive attack which Janie unleashes while he is dying. For Janie, the behavior seems grotesquely out of character. It is characteristic, however, of Miss Hurston's continual emphasis upon intraracial and intrafamilial hatred.[8]

The next phase of Afro-Americanist critical theory that emerged during the Black Arts Movement of the late sixties and early seventies was much more overtly masculinist. Generally understood to represent the aesthetic counterpart of the Black Nationalist Movement, the discourse of this movement similarly enshrines the possibilities of black male power, relegating black women to the position to which Stokely Carmichael assigned them, "prone."

Black Aestheticians concur that black art ought to transform the lives and consciousness of black people. Yet the supreme confidence their essays display testifies more to male fantasies of authority than women's; hence, writing in one of the first anthologies of the movement in 1972, Addison Gayle dismisses the subtle achievements, the nuanced inscriptions of resistance found in the work of a poet like Phillis Wheatley. He writes: "Oblivious of the lot of her fellow blacks, she sang not of a separate nation, but of a Christian Eden."[9]

The sexual politics of the movement become clearer in those essays when the black aesthetic enterprise gets articulated in terms of the recovery of black male sexual power. As Julian Mayfield in the same anthology hints in his essay tellingly entitled "You Touch My Black Aesthetic and I'll Touch Yours," Gayle elsewhere links black male sexuality explicitly to the construction of an Afro-American literary tradition, arguing that "The inability of [white liberals] to see the black man as other than an impotent sexual force accounts for much of the negative criticism by white writers about black literature."[10] While the celebration of black manhood came from the political need to reclaim racial pride, like other radical movements of the 1970s, the Black Arts movement marginalized feminist politics, as we see in Don L. Lee's (Haki Madhubuti's) appraisal of the protagonist of one of Mari Evans's poems:

> The woman herein recreated is not fragmented, hysterical, doesn't have sexual problems with her mate, doesn't feel caught up in a "liberated womanhood" complex/bag—which is to say she is not out to define herself (that is, from the position of weakness, as "the others" do) and thus will not be looked upon as an aberration of the twentieth-century white woman.[11]

In the pioneering work on Afro-American narrative carried out in the late 1970s, critics did not denigrate women's texts, but often ignored them altogether, generalizing about black writing on the basis of strategies and themes found in writing by black men. Mary Helen Washington has argued perceptively that this ostensibly gender-blind discourse actually inscribes the masculine experience of oppression and liberation.[12] When, for instance, Robert Stepto describes a "pregeneric myth," "the quest for freedom and literacy," that informs all black writing, he outlines a pattern more prevalent in male-authored than woman-authored texts.[13] Thus, Frederick Douglass may privilege the moment at which he acquired literacy in his *Narrative of the Life of an American Slave,* but Harriet Jacobs makes virtually no mention of how she came to learn to read and to write. Maya Angelou in *I Know Why The Caged Bird Sings* emphasizes the liberating power of her love of reading, but that gift tends to be celebrated more throughout the body of black men's narratives than in those by women.

A gender-specific analysis of black narrative might now consider the source of the male narrator/protagonist's investment in literacy, the relationship between literacy and the assertion of male power, or the specifically masculine legacy that Douglass and other male slave narrators bequeath to future Afro-American writers. Considerations of gender might also foreground the alternative legacy of a woman slave narrator such as Jacobs. A tradition set in motion by her *Incidents in the Life of a Slave Girl* would necessarily focus on more indirect, surreptitious assertions of power and suggest differences in the ways in which Afro-American men and women represent their relation to language.

III

Marginalized within Afro-Americanist literary discourse, and ignored in similar ways in Anglo-American feminist writing, the black feminist voice emerged in the late seventies with increasing insistence. In recent years, black feminists have introduced the issue of gender into the ostensibly gender-blind discourse of Afro-Americanist literary theory by responding to their own omission from the category "black."[14] Pivotal works such as Frederick Douglass's *Narrative of the Life of Frederick Douglass, an American Slave, Written by Himself,* Richard Wright's *Native Son,* and Ralph Ellison's *Invisible Man,* to name but a few, have traditionally been understood as representations of the struggles of black people under the conditions of race and class oppression. From their earliest essays, however—Barbara Smith's "Toward a Black Feminist Criticism," Deborah E. McDowell's "New Directions for Black Feminist Criticism," and Mary Helen Washington's "New Lives and New Letters: Black Women Writers at the End of the Seventies,"—black feminists have argued that classic critical and imaginative texts such as these that construct themselves and are constructed by readers as "black" might more precisely and productively be read as "black male": representations of the struggles of a black male subject against (a) white male other(s) within the context of a gender-specific ritual ground and symbolic landscape. As Washington has recently written,

> Women have worked assiduously in [the Afro-American literary] tradition as writers, as editors, sometimes, though rarely as critics, and yet every study of Afro-American narrative, every anthology of *the* Afro-American literary tradition has set forth a model of literary paternity in which each male author vies with his predecessor for greater authenticity, greater control over *his* voice, thus fulfilling the mission his *forefathers* left unfinished.
>
> Women in this model are sometimes granted a place as a stepdaughter who prefigures and directs us to the real heirs (like Ellison and Wright) but they do not influence and determine the direction and shape of the literary canon.[15]

The black feminist gendering of Afro-American literary discourse has taken several forms. As I have suggested, their sense of having been omitted from or marginalized within the tradition has prompted them to call attention to the masculinist assumptions of the canon and its custodians. Their bibliographical and editorial projects have expanded and diversified the body of texts taught by and written about by members of the scholarly community.[16] In critical books and essays they complicate received ideas about the contours of the Afro-American tradition by exploring suppressed rituals, conventions, and narrative strategies in the writings of black women.[17] In their most recent work they theorize the interconnections among cultural constructions of race, class, *and* gender in both the language and the ideological assumptions of black texts.

Black feminists have also gendered the discourse of Afro-Americanist theory by writing specifically as women. This self-inscription may take the form of articulating a tradition of black women writing. However self-critical, this process of tradition-building provides intellectual and political antecedents for contemporary black feminists. I have in mind here Hazel V. Carby's brilliant and subtly nuanced *Reconstructing Womanhood: The Emergence of the Black Woman Novelist,* which examines the ways in which early black women's writing shaped and was in turn shaped by contemporary ideological debates about race, womanhood, and imperialism. Her Neo-Marxist study helps to locate historically her own and her contemporaries' enterprise.

The strategies of attribution in Mary Helen Washington's critical writing (for instance, the "Introduction" to *Invented Lives*) inscribe Washington within a community of historical as well as contemporary black feminist voices. Moreover, she writes herself as a black woman by challenging the boundaries that traditionally have separated personal, political, and theoretical writing, boundaries that support a hierarchy that has always excluded black women's cultural productions. Thus she locates her project not only within the context of black women's critical and imaginative writing, but also within that of the experiences of her women relatives.

Although it currently enjoys an unprecedented florescence, black literary feminism is not only a contemporary phenomenon. In the introduction to *A Voice from the South by a Black Woman from the South* (1892), an early instance of black feminist theoretical writing, a chapter entitled "Un [sic] Raison d'Etre," Anna Julia Cooper locates the space from which she as a black woman writes. If the race problem is the central issue facing the United States after the Civil War, then as the nation seeks to work out "the colored man's inheritance and apportionment," all pertinent constituencies must speak for themselves. Yet by Cooper's estimation, the American South is, Sphinxlike, more spoken about than speaking in this debate. The black male voice is, in particular, a "muffled strain," a "jarring chord," a "vague and uncomprehended cadenza." And black women are most silent of all, "the one mute and voiceless note." She argues that whites may not speak for blacks, nor can black men, preoccupied with their own concerns, "reproduce the exact voice of the Black Woman." The essays that comprise the rest of the volume are concerned largely with defining the character—gendering—the voice of black women, to determine what they specifically may add to the ongoing analysis of American culture.

As Carby shows, Cooper, like other early black women intellectuals (including Harriet Jacobs, Frances Ellen Watkins Harper, Ida B. Wells, and others), participates in and transforms the contemporaneous debates about the status of women. Cooper begins from the prevailing assumption that men and women inhabit and dominate separate spheres. She identifies men, predictably, with the workplace outside the home, the political arena, and commerce, women with home, hearth, and the attendant responsibilities. However, that separation is for her the source of women's power. Precisely because women are the care-givers, childrearers, and teachers of manners, they occupy a more influential role in culture than do men. Black men of achievement may represent the possibility of individual accomplishment, Cooper writes, but they cannot stand for the race. Only black women, as the conduit through which the race renews itself, can say: "when and where I enter, in the quiet, undisputed dignity of my womanhood, without violence and without suing or special patronage, then and there the whole *Negro race enters with me.*" Precisely because black women are for her the generative source, or "root" of the race (29), they must be nurtured and treated respectfully, for "the position of woman in society determines the vital elements of its regeneration and progress."

Cooper's analysis might at first seem retrograde, for she appears to appropriate for her own uses a cultural conception of womanhood that minimizes women's influence by relegating them to the domestic sphere. However, when read in the context of her remarks about the higher education of women, Cooper's enterprise seems rather more radical than conciliatory. If the contemporary discourse declared higher education incompatible with femininity, Cooper argues to the contrary that higher education is essential to women's fulfillment of their role. To her mind, given the centrality of black women to the future of the race, they must be educated "for the duties and responsibilities that await the intelligent wife, the Christian mother, the earnest, virtuous, helpful woman, at once the lever and the fulcrum for uplifting the race" (45).

Cooper clearly does not advocate a course specifically tailored for ladies. Rather, she believes that the standard curriculum itself might enable women to project their own talents into the world while itself undergoing a necessary transformation. She writes,

Now I claim that it is the prevalence of the Higher Education among women, the making it a common everyday affair for women to reason and think and express their thought, the training and stimulus which enable and encourage women to administer to the world the bread it needs as well as the sugar it cries for; in short it is the transmitting the potential forces of her soul into dynamic factors that has given symmetry and completeness to the world's agencies. . . .

Religion, science, art, economics, have all needed the feminine flavor; and literature, the expression of what is permanent and best in all of these may be gauged at any time to measure the strength of the feminine ingredient. You will not find theology consigning infants to lakes of unquenchable fire long after women have had a chance to grasp, master, and wield its dogmas. You will not find science annihilating personality from the government of the Universe . . . you will not find jurisprudence formulating as an axiom the absurdity that man and wife are one, and that one the man . . . in fine, you will not find the law of love shut out from the affairs of men after the feminine half of the world's truth is completed. (57–58)

As higher education is critical to the training of black women, so must the teaching of women transform black men. When women become more powerful and influential nurturers, then not only will girls become strong and self-reliant, but boys will "supplement their virility by tenderness and sensibility" as well (61). Men and women so trained will likewise have a salutary effect on culture; when black men and women alike participate in the process of analyzing and reconstructing society, true progress is possible. Only then, in an accumulative period (as Cooper designates the turn of the century) will ideologies of wealth, conquest, and leisure be counterbalanced by "the conservation of those deeper moral forces which make for the happiness of homes and the righteousness of the country" (133).

Cooper's reflections on black women's cultural position might be read as background to her chapter on literature, "The Negro as Presented in American Literature," arguably the earliest sample of black feminist literary criticism. Cooper does not here take black women writers, or even black male writers as her subject. Rather, she analyzes issues of representation as they suggest themselves in writing by white men (Albion Tourgée, George Washington Cable, and William Dean Howells, for instance) about black people. As she had earlier argued that no one group may represent another in the political sphere, in this essay she questions the ability of whites to represent blacks in literature.

The issue of gender does not figure explicitly in Cooper's analysis here the way it does in her other essays, nor does it figure as centrally as the issue of race does. However, her rhetoric and concern with representation derive from the perspective of black women as she had earlier constructed it. One might therefore say that her discourse here is gendered, that Cooper is writing as a black woman.

For contemporary readers, *A Voice from the South* is of particular importance because it anticipates many of the issues black feminists continue to engage: the elitism and racism of white feminists, the sexism of black men, the specificity of the black woman's cultural position. Its significance as a prototype is especially clear given that here Cooper defines in her own terms the status and meaning of womanhood and lays claim to that inheritance for black women.

The heightened visibility of black feminist scholarly and imaginative writers has made gender issues increasingly important to male Afro-Americanists as well. Controversial responses by Stanley Crouch, Mel Watkins, Darryl Pinckney, and others to the fiction of black women demonstrate that works which foreground women's experience of their culturally constructed gender roles in turn prompt men to write out of their own. That is to say that these woman-centered texts, installments in a largely male-centered tradition, have prompted increasing numbers of male reviewers to identify themselves with and respond from the perspective of men who consider themselves to be marginalized.

Stanley Crouch's October 1987 *New Republic* review of Toni Morrison's *Beloved* exhibits the assumptions of such writing. Crouch ostensibly takes issue with Morrison for adhering to a post-Baldwinian position which assumes the literary value of stories of martyrdom and for casting her fictions in a melodramatic prose style. To his mind, it was bad enough when black male writers based narratives on the experience of the atrocities of racism; black women only compound the problem by introducing sexism to the litany of abuses. The rhetoric of Crouch's review suggests, however, that he submerges an *ad feminam* argument beneath an apparently philosophical disagreement.

First, in his actual denunciation of the feminist content of Morrison's work, he focuses on its political incorrectness, not on the limits of transforming suffering into art. He argues that the concern with gender oppression derives from a white feminist agenda, and constitutes nothing more than a recapitulation of ideologically repressive, time-worn stereotypes of black male behavior. The problem with this position, one that recurs throughout similar pieces, is the way that it seeks to marginalize the gendered content of the work in question. He suggests all-too-eagerly that any response to sexism is derivative and diversionary, beside the point of some larger political (or in this case aesthetic) project. Because gender oppression is not his issue, it is therefore not a "real" issue. As if to substantiate this claim, he indicts Morrison for the ways in which a white feminist like Diane Johnson writes about (fetishizes?) her.

A second way in which his response here seems gendered is the fact that he uses this review as the occasion to take pot shots not only at Morrison, but also at any number of other black women writers, including Alice Walker. Of Walker he writes:

Writers like Alice Walker revealed little more than their own inclination to melodrama, militant self-pity, guilt-mongering, and pretensions to

mystic wisdom. What the Walkers really achieved was a position parallel to the one held by Uncle Remus in *Song of the South:* the ex-slave
supplies the white children and the white adults with insights into
human nature and the complexity of the world through the tales of Brer
Rabbit. Better, these black women writers took over the role played by
the black maids in so many old films: when poor little white missy is at a
loss, she is given guidance by an Aunt Jemima lookalike.[18]

Finally, the rhetoric of his conclusion reveals the place of gender in his
literary hierarchy, for he writes that Morrison lacks the "passion" and the
"courage" to render slavery in a way that confronts "the ambiguities of the
human soul, which transcend race." Had she this "courage," this "passion,"
he writes, her work "might stand next to, or outdistance, Ernest Gaines's *The
Autobiography of Miss Jane Pittman* and Charles Johnson's *Oxherding Tale.*"
This formulation clearly constructs the literary marketplace in the terms of a
competition between the sexes for turf.[19]

IV

Thankfully, the scholarly discourse authored by male Afro-Americanists has
begun to address the relationship between issues of race and gender more
productively. Recent work by critic/theorists such as Melvin Dixon, Houston A. Baker, Henry Louis Gates, Jr., and Richard Yarborough exempli-
fies new directions that gender study in Afro-Americanist discourse might
take.[20] For instance, in a *New York Times* review of Washington's *Invented
Lives,* Gates posits compellingly the contours of a black feminist tradition.
Governed by neither Bloom's anxiety of influence nor Gilbert and Gubar's
feminist response to it, an anxiety of authorship, this tradition, Gates argues,
reveals its own specific characteristics. First, he notes, it is unique in generating virulent attacks by other blacks. Second, it is not especially self-
promoting. Third and most importantly, he writes:

> [Black] female authors claim other black women as their ancestors
> (such as Zora Neale Hurston and Ann Petry) whereas most older black
> male writers denied any black influence at all—or worse, eagerly
> claimed a white paternity. No, the writers in this movement have been
> intent upon bonding with other women. And the "patricide" that char-
> acterized Mr. Baldwin's and Mr. Ellison's declarations of independence
> from Richard Wright has no counterpart in matricide. Indeed, Toni
> Morrison's generous stewardship has served as the model for bonding

and the creation of a literary sisterhood that seems to take for granted that good writing will find a publisher. Gone forever is the notion that only one black writer can emerge from the group, in splendid commercial isolation, as "the" black writer of the decade.[21]

As Gates so trenchantly describes the status of women's gender in the construction of literary tradition, Baker analyzes the place of male gender in the construction of Afro-American critical tradition. In his essay, "Discovering America: Generational Shifts, Afro-American Literary Criticism, and the Study of Expressive Culture,"[22] Baker analyzes changes in the assumptions of Afro-American literary critical and theoretical writing during the past four decades. The movement he charts, from Integrationist Poetics through Black Aesthetics to Reconstructionism, productively suggests ways in which each stage in the development of the theory refutes its predecessor and "[establishes] a new framework for intellectual inquiry" (67). What is of particular value, however, is the implicit narrative that links each stage to the next, and suggests that the dynamics of the male acquisition of power actually inform the critical position of each generation.

In the highly allusive extended epigraph to this essay, Baker casts the connection of black expressive culture to literary criticism and theory in terms of the perennial battle between fathers and sons. Anxiety about paternity, he writes, occasions integrationist attempts to assert themselves into a legitimating relation with the white male structure of power: "the players are always founding (white) fathers, or black men who believe there are only a few more chords to be unknot(ted) before Afro-American paternity is secure" (65).

Baker illustrates this premise first by showing that Integrationists such as Arthur P. Davis and Richard Wright believe in a notion of American pluralism and thus anticipate a time when Afro-American literature will lose its specificity and be subsumed into a larger, "classless, raceless" Western literature. He then argues that the Black Aestheticians of the late sixties and early seventies "[invert] the literary-critical optimism and axiology" of the previous generation (73). Amiri Baraka (LeRoi Jones), Larry Neal, Stephen Henderson, and others argue in contrast to the Integrationists that by imitating the strategies and techniques of mainstream white literature, Afro-American writers have diverted the genuine emotional referents and authentic experiential categories of Afro-American life. They therefore support the notion of a "sui generis tradition of Afro-American art and a unique 'standard of criticism' suitable for analyzing it" (74).

The late seventies and early eighties saw the rise of the Reconstructionists, scholars who sought to employ insights and analytical methods acquired from contemporary literary-theoretical discourse in the pedagogy and study of Afro-American literature. Baker argues that as the Aestheticians rewrote the Integrationists, the Reconstructionists refuted the Aestheticians, valorizing the idea of America—which he calls AMERICA—in a manner unlike the Integrationists' position. As he demonstrates, "[the Reconstructionists'] goal was not to help actualize AMERICA by conceding cultural identity. Instead, they assumed that cultural identity was not at issue, suggesting that an advanced, theoretical vocabulary for the study of human expression was both transcultural and constitutive" (89).

Baker's reading of Afro-American literary history is of particular value precisely because it problematizes that history in fresh ways. Black feminists have demythologized the tradition by calling attention to the kinds of assumptions that have excluded black women's writing; they argue by implication that the failure to comprehend women's experience has prevented male Afro-Americanists from recognizing the forms of women's oppression and expression. Baker demythologizes that tradition from a different, albeit gender-based direction; he suggests that the critics' experience of masculinity, as much as their response to social and political change, has affected the way they read the work of earlier critics. What is needed now, I would argue, is some discussion of how the male Afro-Americanists' experiences of their relation to power, and to the rise of feminism, has affected their responses, respectively, to each other and to black women in the profession.

V

As Afro-Americanist discourse has exposed the absences in the work of mainstream critics, questions of gender have forced the Afro-Americanist tradition to be increasingly self-evaluative and self-critical. Not at all diversionary, these explorations rather complicate the field, for they enable considerations of the various ways in which people of color, male and female alike, experience the conditions of oppression. Indeed, further elaborations upon the relationship between gender, race, and class, hold great promise for enriching the discipline. Textually grounded future work needs to be done, for instance, on the way constructions of masculinity affect the experience of race, and the way that connection is represented in literature. Afro-Americanists might also expand upon Baker's work and consider the relationship of gender to the dynamic among critics from which black literary history derives and out of which black intellectual history develops. Insofar as considerations of gender, like those of race and class, are grounded simultaneously in personal and intellectual experience, further explorations of gender issues might prompt Afro-Americanists to reflect upon the politics of our position as black men and black women in the academy. At a time when being black and/or working on questions of race and gender have a certain marketability, it would be useful to consider the effect of our commodification on our work and on our relations to each other. Black male critics and theorists might explore the nature of the contradictions that arise when they undertake black feminist projects. And perhaps most importantly, black feminists ourselves must name openly the conflicts that inhere in our position as critics and theorists in an area of literary study traditionally dominated by males and whites.

Notes

1   The critics and theorists currently engaged in this project include Abena Busia, Hazel V. Carby, Barbara Christian, Frances Smith Foster, Mae Henderson, Gloria Hull, Deborah McDowell, Nellie Y. McKay, Hortense Spillers, Claudia Tate, Cheryl Wall, Mary Helen Washington, and Gloria Watkins (bell hooks).

2   Hazel V. Carby, *Reconstructing Womanhood: The Emergence of the Afro-American Woman Novelist* (New York, 1987), 9.

3   I wish to thank Marianne Hirsch, Victoria Kahn, Sally Shuttleworth, Elaine Showalter, and Robert Stepto for their suggestions and advice.

4   My thoughts about the relation between what we write and our place within institutions have been influenced by the following texts: Elly Bulkin, Minnie Bruce Pratt, and Barbara Smith, *Yours in Struggle: Three Feminist Perspectives on Anti-Semitism and Racism* (Brooklyn, N.Y., 1984); Teresa de Lauretis, *Technologies of Gender: Essays on Theory, Film, and Fiction* (Bloomington, Ind., 1987); Biddy Martin and Chandra Talpade Mohanty, "Feminist Politics: What's Home Got to Do With It?" and Nancy K. Miller, "Changing the Subject: Authorship, Writing, and the Reader," in Teresa de Lauretis, ed., *Feminist Studies/Critical Studies* (Bloomington, Ind., 1986), 191–212 and 102–120 respectively; and Adrienne Rich, *Blood, Bread, and Poetry: Selected Prose 1979–1985.*

5   Anna Julia Cooper, *A Voice from the South by a Black Woman of the South* (Xenia, Ohio, 1892), 31.

6   Darwin T. Turner, *In A Minor Chord: Three Afro-American Writers and Their Search for Identity* (Carbondale and Edwardsville, Ill., 1971), xix.

7   Zora Neale Hurston, *Their Eyes Were Watching God* (1937) (Urbana, Ill., 1978), 133.

8   Turner, *In A Minor Chord*, 108.

9   Addison Gayle, Jr., "The Function of Black Literature at the Present Time," in Gayle, ed., *The Black Aesthetic* (Garden City, N.Y., 1972), 384.

10   See Gayle, "Introduction" to *The Black Aesthetic*, xx, and Julian Mayfield, "You Touch My Black Aesthetic and I'll Touch Yours," in *The Black Aesthetic*, 25.

11   Don L. Lee (Haki Madhubuti), "Toward a Definition: Black Poetry of the Sixties (After Leroi Jones)," in this volume, 217–18.

12   See her essay, " 'The Darkened Eye Restored': Notes Toward a Literary History of Black Women," in this volume, 442–53.

13   See Robert B. Stepto, *From Behind the Veil: A Study of Afro-American Narrative* (Urbana, Ill., 1979).

14   Of course, black feminists have called attention to the racist and classist assumptions of white feminist discourse as well, but for my purposes here I wish to focus on their impact on Afro-Americanist theory.

15   Mary Helen Washington, " 'The Darkened Eye Restored,' " in this volume, 445.

16   See, for instance, the reprints series that McDowell edits for Beacon Press and her Rutgers University Press reprint of Nella Larsen's *Quicksand* (1928) and *Passing* (1929); Washington's three anthologies, *Black-Eyed Susans* (New York, 1975), *Midnight Birds* (New York, 1980), and *Invented Lives* (New York, 1987) and her Feminist Press edition of Paule Marshall's *Brown Girl, Brownstones* (1981); Nellie McKay's edition of Louise Meriwether's *Daddy Was a Number Runner* (New York, 1970); and Gloria T. Hull's edition of Alice Dunbar-Nelson's letters, *Give Us Each Day* (New York, 1984), to name but a few. Black women are not exclusively responsible for these kinds of editorial projects. See also, William Andrews, *Sisters of the Spirit: Three Black Women's Autobiographies of the Nineteenth Century* (Bloomington, 1986); Henry Louis Gates's edition of Harriet E. Wilson's *Our Nig* (New York, 1983) and his Oxford University Press reprints series; and Jean Fagan Yellin's edition of Harriet Jacobs's *Incidents in the Life of a Slave Girl* (Cambridge, 1987).

17   See, for instance, Barbara Christian, *Black Women Novelists: The Development of a Tradition, 1892–1976* (Westport, Conn., 1980); Gloria T. Hull, *Color, Sex, and Poetry: Three Women Writers of The Harlem Renaissance* (Bloomington, Ind., 1987); Deborah E. McDowell, " 'The Changing Same': Generational Connections and Black Women Novelists," *New Literary History*, 18 (Winter 1987), 281–30; and Hortense Spillers, "A Hateful Passion, a Lost Love," *Feminist Studies*, 9 (1983), 293–323.

18   Stanley Crouch, "Aunt Medea," a review of *Beloved* by Toni Morrison, *The New Republic*, 19 October 1987, 39.

19   Deborah McDowell discusses the implications of this brand of black feminist-baiting thoroughly and subtly in her essay "Reading Family Matters" in the collection *Changing Our Own Words: Essays on Criticism, Theory, and Writing by Black Women*, ed. Cheryl Wall (New Brunswick, N.J., 1989).

20   In addition to the Baker and Gates cited below, I refer as well to Melvin Dixon, *Ride Out the Wilderness: Geography and Identity in Afro-American Literature* (Urbana, Ill., 1987) and Richard Yarborough, "Ideology and Black Characterization in the Early Afro-American Novel" (n.p.).

21   Henry Louis Gates, Jr., "Reclaiming Their Tradition," review of *Invented Lives*, ed. Mary Helen Washington, *The New York Times Book Review*, 3, 34–35.

22   Houston A. Baker, Jr., "Discovering America: Generational Shifts, Afro-American Literary Criticism, and the Study of Expressive Culture," in *Blues, Ideology, and Afro-American Literature: A Vernacular Theory* (Chicago, 1984).

Barbara Christian

But What Do We Think We're Doing Anyway: The State of Black Feminist Criticism(s) or My Version of a Little Bit of History

(1989)

In August 1974, a rather unique event occurred. *Black World*, probably the most widely read publication of Afro-American literature, culture, and political thought at that time, used on its cover a picture of the then practically unknown writer Zora Neale Hurston.[1] Under Zora's then unfamiliar photograph was a caption in bold letters, "Black Women Image Makers," which was the title of the essay by Mary Helen Washington featured in the issue. Alongside the Washington essay were three other pieces: an essay now considered a classic, June Jordan's "On Richard Wright and Zora Neale Hurston: Notes Towards a Balancing of Love and Hate," an essay on major works of Zora Neale Hurston, "The Novelist/Anthropologist/Life Work," by poet Ellease Southerland, and a short piece criticizing the television version of Ernest Gaines's *The Autobiography of Miss Jane Pittman,* by black psychologist Alvin Ramsey. It was not particularly striking that the image of a black woman writer graced the cover of *Black World;* Gwendolyn Brooks's picture, for example, had appeared on a previous *Black World* cover. Nor was it especially noteworthy that literary analyses of an Afro-American woman writer appeared in that journal. That certainly had occurred before. What was so striking about this issue of *Black World* was the tone of the individual pieces and the effect of their juxtaposition.

Mary Helen Washington's essay sounded a strong chord—that there was indeed a growing number of contemporary Afro-American women writers whose perspective underlined the centrality of women's lives to their creative vision. June Jordan's essay placed Hurston, a relatively unknown Afro-American woman writer, alongside Richard Wright, who is probably the best

This essay first appeared in Cheryl A. Wall, ed., *Changing Our Own Words* (New Brunswick, N.J., 1989).

known of Afro-American writers, and illuminated how their apparently antithetical worldviews were *both* necessary ways of viewing the complexity of
Afro-American life, which Jordan made clear was not monolithic. Ellease
Southerland reviewed many of Hurston's works, pointing out their significance to Afro-American literature and therefore indicating the existence of
major Afro-American women writers in the past. And in criticizing the television version of *The Autobiography of Miss Jane Pittman*, Ramsey objected
that that commercial white medium had omitted the message of struggle in
Ernest Gaines's novel and turned it into an individual woman's story—a
foreshadowing of criticism that would be repeated when, periodically, images of black women from literature were translated into visual media.

What the configuration of the August 1974 *Black World* suggested to me,
as I am sure it did to others, was the growing visibility of Afro-American
women and the significant impact they were having on contemporary black
culture. The articulation of that impact had been the basis for Toni Cade's
edition of *The Black Woman* in 1970.[2] But that collection had not dealt specifically with literature/creativity. Coupled with the publication of Alice
Walker's "In Search of Our Mothers' Gardens," only a few months before in
the May issue of *Ms.*,[3] the August 1794 *Black World* signaled a shift in position
among those interested in Afro-American literature about women's creativity. Perhaps because I had experienced a decade of the intense literary activity of the 1960s, but also much antifemale black cultural nationalist rhetoric, these two publications had a lightning effect on me. Afro-American
women were making public, were able to make public, their search for
themselves in literary culture.

I begin my reflections on the state (history) of black feminist criticism(s)
with this memory because it seems to me we so quickly forget the recent
past. Perhaps some of us have never known it. Like many of us who lived
through the literary activism of the sixties, we of the eighties may forget that
which just recently preceded us and may therefore misconstrue the period in
which we are acting.

Less than twenty years ago, without using the self-consciously academic
word *theory*, Mary Helen Washington articulated a concept that was original,
startling even, to many of us immersed in the study of Afro-American literature, among whom were few academics, who knew little or cared less about
this literature. In "Black Women Image Makers" Washington stated what for
me is still a basic tenet of black feminist criticism: "We should be about the
business of *reading, absorbing,* and giving *critical* attention to those writers
whose understanding of the black woman can take us *further*" (emphasis

mine).[4] The names of the writers Washington listed, with the exception of Gwendolyn Brooks, were then all virtually unknown; interestingly, after a period when poetry and drama were the preeminent genre of Afro-American literature, practically all of these writers—Maya Angelou, Toni Cader Bambara, Paule Marshall, Toni Morrison, Alice Walker—were practicing fiction writers. While all of the writers were contemporary, Washington implied through her analysis that their vision and craft suggested that previous Afro-American women writers existed. Hence Zora Neale Hurston's picture on the cover of this issue connoted a specific meaning—that of a literary foremother who had been neglected by Afro-Americanists of the past but who was finally being recognized by her daughters and reinstated as a major figure in the Afro-American literary tradition.

It is important for us to remember that in 1974, even before the publication of Robert Henenway's biography of Hurston in 1977 or the reissuing of *Their Eyes Were Watching God,* the articulation of the possibility of a tradition of Afro-American women writers occurred not in a fancy academic journal but in two magazines: *Ms.,* a new popular magazine that came out of the women's movement, and *Black World,* a long-standing black journal unknown to most academics and possibly scorned by some.

Walker's essay and *Black World's* August 1974 issue gave me a focus and are the recognizable points that I can recall as to when I consciously began to work on black women writers. I had, of course, unconsciously begun my own search before reading those pieces. I had spent some portion of the late sixties and early seventies asking my "elders" in the black arts movement whether there were black women who had written before Gwendolyn Brooks or Lorraine Hansberry. Younger poets such as Sonia Sanchez, Nikki Giovanni, Carolyn Rodgers, June Jordan, and Audre Lorde were, of course, quite visible by that time. And by 1974, Morrison and Walker had each published a novel. But only through accident or sheer stint of effort did I discover Paule Marshall's *Brown Girl, Brownstones* (1959) or Hurston's *Their Eyes Were Watching God* (1937)—an indication that the contemporary writers I was then reading might too fade into oblivion. Although in the sixties the works of neglected Afro-American male writers of the Harlem Renaissance were beginning to resurface, for example, Jean Toomer's *Cane,* I was told the women writers of that period were terrible—not worth my trouble. However, because of the conjuncture of the black arts movement and the women's movement, I asked questions I probably would not have otherwise thought of.

If movements have any effect, it is to give us a context within which to imagine questions we would not have imagined before, to ask questions we might not have asked before. The publication of the *Black World* August 1974 issue as well as Walker's essay was rooted in the conjuncture of those two movements, rather than in the theoretizing of any individual scholar, and most emphatically in the literature of contemporary Afro-American women who were able to be published as they had not been before, precisely because that conjuncture was occurring.

That the development of black feminist criticism(s) is firmly rooted in this conjuncture is crystal clear from a pivotal essay of the 1970s: Barbara Smith's "Toward a Black Feminist Criticism," which was originally published in *Conditions II* in 1977. By that time Smith was not only calling on critics to read, absorb, and pay attention to black women writers, as Washington had, but also to write about that body of literature from a feminist perspective. What *feminist* meant for Smith went beyond Washington's emphasis on image making. Critics, she believed, needed to demonstrate how the literature exposed "the brutally complex systems of oppression"[5]—that of sexism, racism, and economic exploitation which affected so gravely the experience and culture of black women. As important, Smith was among the first to point out that black lesbian literature was thoroughly ignored in critical journals, an indication of the homophobia existent in the literary world.

Because the U.S. women's movement had begun to extend itself into academic arenas and because women's voices had been so thoroughly suppressed, by the middle seventies there was a visible increase of interest among academics in women's literature. Yet despite the existence of powerful contemporary Afro-American women writers who continued to be major explorers of Afro-American women's lives—writers, such as Bambara, Jordan, Lorde, Morrison, Shange, Walker, Sherley Anne Williams (the list could be much longer)—little commentary on their works could be found in feminist journals. In many ways, they continued to be characterized by such journals as black, not women, writers. Nor, generally speaking, were critics who studied these writers considered either in the Afro-American or feminist literary worlds—far less the mainstream literary establishment—to be working on an important body of literature central to American letters. By 1977, Smith knew that the sexism of Afro-American literary/intellectual circles and the racism of white feminist literary journals resulted in a kind of homelessness for critical works on black women or other third world women writers. She underlined this fact in her landmark essay: "I think of the thousands and thousands of books which have been devoted by this time to the subject of Women's Writing and I am filled with rage at the fraction of these pages that mention black and other Third World women. I finally do not know how to begin, because in 1977 I want to be writing this for a black feminist publication."[6]

At that time, most feminist journals were practically all white publications; their content dealt almost exclusively with white women as if they were the only women in the United States. The extent to which the mid twentieth-century women's movement was becoming, like its nineteenth-century predecessor, infected by racism seemed all too clear, and the split between a black and a white women's movement that occurred in the nineteenth century seemed to be repeating itself.

Smith seemed to believe that the lack of inclusion of women-of-color writers and critics in the burgeoning literature on women's voices was due, in part, to "the fact that a parallel black feminist movement had been slower in evolving," and that that fact "could not help but have impact upon the situation of black women writers and artists and explains in part why during that very same period we have been so ignored."[7] My experience, however, suggests that other factors were more prominently at work, factors Smith also mentioned. In calling for a "body of black feminist political theory," she pointed out that such a theory was necessary since those who had access to critical publications—white male and, increasingly, black male and white female critics—apparently did not *know how* to respond to the works of black women. More accurately, I think these critics might have been resistant to this body of writing which unavoidably demonstrated the intersections of sexism and racism so central to Afro-American women's lives and therefore threatened not only white men's view of themselves, but black men and white women's view of themselves as well. Smith concludes that "undoubtedly there are other [black] women working and writing whom I do not know, simply because there is no place to read them."[8]

I can personally attest to that fact. By 1977 I was well into the writing of the book that would become *Black Women Novelists: The Development of a Tradition* (1980) and had independently stumbled on two pivotal concepts that Smith articulated in her essay: "the need to demonstrate that black women's writing constituted an identifiable literary tradition" and the importance of looking "for precedents and insights in interpretation within the works of other black women."[9] I found, however, that it was virtually impossible to locate either the works of many nineteenth-century writers or those of contemporary writers, whose books went in and out of print like ping-pong balls. For example, I xeroxed *Brown Girl, Brownstones* (please forgive me, Paule) any number of times because it simply was not available and I wanted to use it in the classes I had begun to teach on Afro-American women's literature. At times I felt more like a detective than a literary critic as I chased clues to find a book I knew existed but which I had begun to think I had hallucinated.

Particularly difficult, I felt, was the dearth of historical material on Afro-American women, that is, on the contexts within which the literature had evolved—contexts I increasingly saw as a necessary foundation for the development of a contemporary black feminist perspective. Other than Gerda Lerner's *Black Women in White America* (1973), I could not find a single full-length analysis of Afro-American women's history. And despite the proliferation of Afro-American and women's history books in the 1970s, I found in most of them only a few paragraphs devoted to black women, the favorites being Harriet Tubman in the black studies ones and Sojourner Truth in the women's studies ones. As a result, in preparation for my book, I, untrained in history, had created a patchwork quilt of historical facts gathered here and there. I remember being positively elated when Sharon Harley and Rosalyn Terborg Penn's collection of historical essays—*The Afro-American Woman* (1978)—was published. But by then, I had almost completed my manuscript. If Afro-American women critics were to turn to black women of the past for insights, their words and works needed to be accessible and had to be located in a cogent historical analysis.

As well, what was stunning to me as I worked on *Black Women Novelists* was the resistance I experienced among scholars to my subject matter. Colleagues of mine, some of whom had my best interest at heart, warned me that I was going to ruin my academic career by studying an insignificant, some said nonexistent, body of literature. Yet I knew it was fortunate for me that I was situated in an Afro-American studies rather than in an English department, where not even the intercession of the Virgin would have allowed me to do research on black women writers. I also found that lit crit journals were not interested in the essays I had begun to write on black women writers. The sustenance I received during those years of writing *Black Women Novelists* came not from the academic/literary world but from small groups of women in bookstores, Y's, in my classes and writers groups for whom this literature was not so much an object of study but was, as it is for me, lifesaving.

Many contemporary Afro-American critics imply in their analyses that only those Afro-Americans in the academy—college faculty and students—read Afro-American literature. I have found quite the opposite to be true. For it was "ordinary" black women, women in the churches, private reading groups, women like my hairdresser and her clients, secondary school teachers, typists, my women friends, many of whom were single mothers, who discussed *The Bluest Eye* (1970) or *In Love and Trouble* (1973) with an intensity unheard of in the academic world. In fact most of my colleagues did not even know these books existed when women I knew were calling these writers by their first name—Alice, Paule, Toni, June—indicating their sense of an intimacy with them. They did not necessarily buy the books but often begged, "borrowed," or "liberated" them—so that book sales were not always indicative of their interest. I had had similar experiences during the 1960s. Postal clerks, winos, as well as the folk who hung out in Micheaux's, the black bookstore in Harlem, knew Baldwin's, Wright's, Ellison's works and talked vociferously about them when many of the folk at CCNY and Columbia had never read one of these writers. Ralph Ellison wrote an extremely provocative blurb for *Our Nig* when he pointed out that Harriet Wilson's novel demonstrated that there is more "free-floating" literacy among blacks than we acknowledge.

No doubt we are influenced by what publishers say people should read or do read. When I began sending out sections of *Black Women Novelists,* practically all academic presses as well as trade presses commented that my subject was not important—that people were not interested in black women writers. Couldn't I write a book on the social problems of black women? Affected by the rhetoric à la Moynihan, most of these presses could hardly believe black women were artists—a point we might remember as some of us today minimize the craft and artistry of these writers in favor of intellectual or social analysis. In response to these comments I could not point to any precedents, for in 1978 there had not been published a full-length study of black women writers. I believe if it were not for the incredible publicity that Toni Morrison's *Song of Solomon* received in 1978, and the fact that one of my chapters was devoted to her work, I would not have been able to publish *Black Women Novelists* when I did. Smith was right on target when she suggested that there might be other black women critics writing and working about whom she did not know because there was no place to read them.

That situation began to change by 1980, however. And I think it is important for us to recall some of the major signs of that change. One such sign was the black sexism issue of the *Black Scholar* published in May/June of 1979 which grew out of black sociologist Robert Staples's extremely critical response to Ntozake Shange's play *for colored girls who have considered suicide when the rainbow is enuf* and Michele Wallace's critique of the sexism in the civil rights movement—*Black Macho and the Myth of the Superwoman* (1979).[10] In his critique of Shange and Wallace, Staples insinuated that black feminists were being promoted by the white media—a stance that would be reiterated years later by some critics in the *Color Purple* debate. Although the debate among the Afro-American women and men on the issue was not a specifically "literary" debate, its very existence indicated the effect Afro-American women's literature was having on Afro-American intellectual circles. What was also interesting about the debate was the intense involvement of Afro-American women writers themselves who unabashedly responded to Staples. Audre Lorde put it succinctly: "Black feminists speak as women and do not need others to speak for us."[11]

Such speaking had certainly ignited the literary world. In the 1970s black women published more novels than they had in any other decade. Some, like Morrison and Walker, were beginning to be acknowledged as great American novelists. Poets such as Lorde, Jordan, Sherley Williams, and Lucille Clifton, to mention a few, were clearly literary/political activists as well as writers in the Afro-American and women's communities. And many of these writers, most of whom were not academicians (e.g., Walker in "One Child of One's Own," Lorde in "The Uses of the Erotic"), were themselves doing black feminist criticism. Increasingly even academicians could not deny the effect this body of literature was having on various communities in American life. Simultaneously, critical essays and analysis began to appear in literary academic as well as in more generalized intellectual journals.

That a black feminist criticism was beginning to receive attention from the academic world was one basis for Deborah McDowell's essay "New Directions for Black Feminist Criticism," which originally appeared in an academic journal, *Black American Literature Forum*, in 1980.[12] In responding to Smith's call for a black feminist criticism, McDowell emphasized the need for clear definitions and methodologies, a sign as well of the increasing emphasis on theory surfacing in the academic world. She asked whether black feminist criticism was relegated only to black women who wrote about black women writers. Did they have to write from a feminist/political perspective to be black feminist critics? Could white women/black men/white men do black feminist criticism? a question which indicated that this literature was beginning to attract a wider group of critics.

McDowell's questions continue to have much relevance as more and more critics of different persuasions, genders, and races write critical essays on Afro-American women writers. Just recently, in April 1988, Michele Wallace published a piece in the *Village Voice* which seemed almost a parody of the August 1974 *Black World* issue.[13] The piece was advertised in the content listing with the titillating title "Who Owns Zora Neale Hurston: Critics Carve up the Legend," and featured on the first page of its text was a big photograph of Zora, who had become the darling of the literary world. Wallace counter-pointed the perspectives of black women, black men, white women, even one prominent white male critic who had written about Hurston. Every-one apparently was getting into the act, though with clearly different pur-poses, as Wallace insinuated that Hurston had become a commodity. Wal-lace's own title for her piece, "Who Dat Say Who Dat When I Say Who Dat?" spoken as if by Hurston herself, underlined the ironic implications of the proliferation of Hurston criticism, much of which, Wallace implied, was severed from Hurston's roots and most of which ignored Hurston's god-desslike mischievousness.

"Who Dat Say Who Dat When I Say Who Dat?" took me back to McDow-ell's essay and her suggestions of parameters for a black feminist criticism. In addition to the ones articulated by Washington in 1974 and Smith in 1977, McDowell emphasized the need for both contextual and textual analysis—contextual, in that the critic needed to have a knowledge of Afro-American history and culture, and women's situation within it, and textual, that is, paying careful attention to the individual text. If one were to combine Wash-ington's, Smith's, and McDowell's suggestions, few of the critical works cited by Wallace would even come close to doing black feminist criticism. Wallace acceded that "Black literature needs a rainbow coalition," but she wondered if some critical approaches did not silence Hurston. While Hurston's and other Afro-American women's writing are deep enough, full enough to be approached from any number of perspectives, their work demands rigorous attention as does any other serious writing.

The question as to who the critic is and how that affects her/his interpreta-tion was very much on my mind when I put together *Black Feminist Criticism* in 1983–1984.[14] In thinking about my own attempts to do such criticism, I in-creasingly felt that critics needed to let go of their distanced and false stance of objectivity and to expose their own point of view—the tangle of back-ground, influences, political perspectives, training, situations that helped form and inform their interpretations. Inspired by feminist discussions about objectivity and subjectivity, I constructed an introduction to my vol-ume that, rather than the usual formal introduction found in most lit crit books, was intended to introduce me in my specific context. It was a person-alized way of indicating some of my biases, not the least of which was the fact that the literature I chose to study was central to an understanding of my own life, and not *only* an intellectual pursuit. Such exposure would, I thought, help the reader evaluate more effectively the choices I had made about the language I used, the specific issues I approached, the particular writers I emphasized. By then I realized I did not want to write about every contemporary Afro-American woman writer—some did not speak to me—and that the extent of my own personal involvement with the writer's work was one aspect of my doing black feminist criticism.

But even more to the point, I thought that black feminist criticism needed to break some of the restricted forms, personalize the staid language associated with the critic—forms that seemed opposed to the works of the writers as well as the culture from which they came—and forms that many readers found intimidating and boring. In the introduction dialogue I used call and response, jazz riffs, techniques found in writers like Hughes and Hurston, as well as the anecdote, a device I had found so effective in the essays of Jordan and Walker, as ways of reflecting on my own process.

In fact the form of the book was based on the idea of process as a critical aspect of an evolving feminist approach—that is, a resistance to art as artifact, to ideas as fixed, and a commitment to open-endedness, possibility, fluidity—to change. These qualities were significant characteristics of the writers I studied. Inspired by Jordan's adroit use of headnotes in *Civil Wars*, I compiled a collection not of every essay I had written between 1975 and 1985 but examples of writing events I considered necessary to doing black feminist criticism—most of which were not essays written originally for academic outlets. For me, doing black feminist criticism involved a literary activism that went beyond the halls of academe, not because I had so legislated but because in practice that is what it often, happily, had to be.

I also intended the book to be a tracing of that journey some of us had been making since 1974, a journey guided by what I considered to be another important element of doing this type of criticism, that is, on being a participant in an ongoing dialogue between the writer and those who were reading the writer, most of whom were not academics and for whom that writing was life-sustaining, lifesaving. As the race for theory began to accelerate in 1984, I became concerned that that dialogue was drying up as critics rushed to construct theories in languages that many writers abhorred and which few readers understood or enjoyed or could use. In particular I was struck by a talk I had had with one major writer who told me she had gone to a lit crit panel on her work but could not comprehend one word, nor could she recognize her work in anything that was said. To whom, she asked, were we critics speaking?

Finally, I used the phrase *Black Feminist Criticism* as the title of my book because it seemed to me, in 1984, as it still does that few black women critics were willing to claim the term *feminist* in their titles. *Women* was an acceptable term, but the political implications of the term *feminist* meant that it was fast giving way to the more neutral term *gender.* I believed it was important to place the term on the black literary map, so to speak, even if it were only a reminder of an orientation no longer in vogue.

My introduction was an appeal to practice as one decisive factor in defining a black feminist criticism. In 1985 Hortense Spillers contributed another point of view. Along with Marjorie Pryse, she edited a volume entitled *Conjuring: Black Women, Fiction and Literary Tradition,*[15] which included essays by black and white women as well as black men. The subtitle was particularly striking to me since the volume privileged fiction, as had the majority of such collections, including my own. And I began to wonder why, in this rich period of Afro-American women's poetry, that genre was being so summarily ignored.

Spillers's afterword, entitled "Cross-Currents, Discontinuities: Black Women's Fiction," made it clear that "the community of black women writing in the U.S. can be regarded as a vivid new fact of national life." She defines this community as "those composed of fiction writers, as well as writers of criticism who are also teachers of literature."[16] In emphasizing the overlapping of these categories, she saw that the academy was fast becoming the site of this community and pointed to one reason why perhaps criticism had taken the direction it had. She might have added as well that new development might be one reason criticism had become so focused on fiction. Perhaps intellectual analysis is more suited to fiction and the essay than it is to poetry and drama—genres that insist on the emotions, the passions, the senses as well as the intellect as equally effective ways of knowing.

In characterizing Afro-American women's fiction as a series of discontinuities and relating these discontinuities to other American writing—to Faulkner, Dreiser, Wright—Spillers constructed a picture of American literature unthinkable in the academic world of 1974. And by using language associated with "new" critical approaches, she demonstrated how an overview of Afro-American women's fiction converged with the more conventional American literary tradition. Her essay extended the perimeters of black feminist criticism(s) in that they could now be situated in the study of American letters as an entirety. Spillers was clearly responding to the impetus for revised canons by showing how Afro-American women's fiction intersected with the currents of other literatures in the United States.

Canon formation has become one of the thorny dilemmas for the black feminist critic. Even as white women, blacks, people of color attempt to reconstruct that body of American literature considered to the *the* literature, we find ourselves confronted with the realization that we may be imitating the very structure that shut our literatures out in the first place. And that judgments we make about, for example, the BBBS (Big Black Books) are determined not only by "quality," that elusive term, but by what we academicians value, what points of view, what genre and forms we privilege.

We finally must wonder about whether this activity, which cannot be value free, will stifle the literatures we have been promoting. For while few white male American critics feel compelled to insinuate "white" literary works into *our* characterizations of American history and culture, we are almost always in a position of having to insinuate our works into their schema.[17] Spillers concludes her afterword with a provocative statement: "The day will come, I would dare to predict, when the black American women's writing community will reflect the currents of both the New new critical procedures and the various literatures concurrent with them."[18] One might also turn that statement around. We might wonder, given that Afro-American women's writing is so clearly at the vortex of sex, race, and class factors that mitigate the notion of democracy at the core of "traditional" American literatures, whether one might want to predict the day when other literatures will reflect the currents of the black American women's writing community.

While Spillers was still concerned with Afro-American women's literature as a recognizable literary tradition, Hazel Carby, in the introduction to her *Reconstructing Womanhood* (1987), was positively negative about the use of the term *tradition*. In "Rethinking Black Feminist Theory," Carby insisted that black feminist criticism has "too frequently been reduced to an experiential relationship that is assumed to exist between black women as readers and black women as writers who represent black women's reality" and that "this reliance on a common or shared experience is essentialist and ahistorical." Her book, she stated, "does not assume the existence of a tradition or traditions of Afro-American intellectual thought that have been constructed as paradigmatic of Afro-American history."[19]

In what frame is her book situated? Carby tells us that her inquiry "works within the theoretical premises of societies—'structured in dominance' by class, by race, and by gender and is a materialist account of the cultural production of black women intellectuals within the social relations that inscribed them."[20] As Valerie Smith pointed out in her review of Carby's book in *Women's Review of Books*, *Reconstructing Womanhood* signals a new direction in black feminist criticism in that Carby is not as much interested in Afro-American women writers as she is in constructing a black female intellectual history.[21]

Ironically, in reconstructing that history, Carby turns to creative writers/ novelists. Perhaps that is because Afro-American writers, female and male, are central, pivotal, predominant figures in Afro-American intellectual history. Why that is so would take volumes to investigate, but one explanation might be that the usual modes of European/American intellectual production were not accessible to or particularly effective for Afro-Americans. That is, the thoroughly rationalist approach of European intellectual discourse might have seemed to them to be too one-dimensional, too narrow, more easily co-opted than narratives, poetry, nonlinear forms where the ambiguities and contradictions of their reality could be more freely expressed and that in these forms they could address themselves to various audiences— their own folk as well as those readers of the dominant culture. In any case, a large number if not the majority of those considered intellectuals in the Afro-American world, female or male, were or attempted to be creative writers— which might account for some of the focus Afro-American intellectual critics have had on creative literature.

No doubt Carby's emphasis on the reconstruction of a black female intellectual history is needed. And that history can now be imagined and speculated about by her and others, as it could not have been even a decade ago, because the words and works of Afro-American women of the past are more accessible. Yet Carby's approach, as she articulates it, does not seem to allow for other emphases within the arena of black feminist criticism, and the work she can now do is possible because others pursued different orientations from her own. Twenty years ago, scholars who used the language and approach she uses (and it is indeed a primarily academic language) were completely opposed to the inclusion of gender as central to their analyses and in fact called that term "essentialist." Nor could Carby be doing the work she is doing unless a space for it was created by a powerful contemporary Afro-American women's literature which in part comes out of the very paradigm she denies. What, I wonder, would Frances Harper or Pauline Hopkins think of her denial of the possibility of Afro-American literary history?

In addition, as my and other overviews of the development of Afro-American literature suggest, there is more of an inclination in the academic and publishing worlds (and we might ask why) to accept sociological/political analyses of black writers—female, male—whether they be from a materialist or bourgeois point of view, than to conceive of them as artists with their own ideas, imagination, forms. This seems to be a privilege reserved for only a few selected white men. Finally one must ask whether the study of an intellectual tradition necessitates the denial of an imaginative, creative

512 Barbara Christian

one? Who is to say that the European emphasis on rational intellectual discourse as the measure of a people's history is superior to those traditions that value creativity, expression, paradox in the constructing of their historical process?

Carby's introduction brings the debate as to what black feminist criticism is full circle, back to Mary Helen Washington's essay in the August 1974 *Black World* in that Washington's assumptions about the relationship between black women's writings and the reality of a shared experience among black women are held suspect—a question worth pursuing. What is so riveting to me is that the term *black feminist criticism* continues to be undefineable—not fixed. For many that might seem catastrophic; for me it is an indication that so much still needs to be done—for example, reading the works of the writers, in order to understand their ramifications. Even as I cannot believe all that has been accomplished in the last fifteen years—a complete revision of, conceptualization of nineteenth-century Afro-American literature, and a redirecting of definitions in contemporary life about women's sexuality, motherhood, relationships, history, race/class, gender intersections, political structures, spirituality as perceived through the lens of contemporary Afro-American women—there is so much yet to do.

So—what do we think we're doing anyway? More precisely, what might we have to do at this juncture, in 1990?

For one—we might have to confront the positives and negatives of what it means to become institutionalized in universities.

Does this mean we will no longer respond to the communal/erotic art that poetry and drama can be because it is so difficult to reduce these forms to ideological wrangling? As Audre Lorde has so profoundly expressed, it is often in poetry that we imagine that which we have been afraid to imagine— that poetry is an important source of imagining new ideas for change.

Does our emphasis on definitions and theories mean that we will close ourselves to those, the many, who know or care little about the intense debates that take so much of our time in universities? Can we conceive of our literary critical activities as related to the activism necessary to substantively change black women's lives?

Does our scholarly advancement mean that more and more of us will turn to the study of past writers as a safer pursuit in the university which apparently has difficulty engaging in the study of present-day literatures? As necessary as the study of the past is, it is just as important to be engaged in the history that we are now making—one that has been so powerfully ignited by the contemporary writers.

In spite of the critical clamor, how many of us have actually produced sustained readings, critiques?

Can we ignore the fact that fewer and fewer blacks are receiving Ph.D.s? In fact, only 820 in 1986. Although black women are not the only ones who can do feminist criticism, it would be a significant loss if they were absent from this enterprise.

Do we assume that this orientation will be here even at the turn of the century?

To whom are *we* accountable? And what social relations are in/scribing us?

Does history teach us anything about the relationship between ideas, language, and practice? By 2000 will our voices sound like women's voices, black women's voices to anyone?

What do we want to do anyway and for whom do we think we're doing it?

Notes

The title of this chapter is a riff on Gloria T. Hull's title, "What It Is I Think She's Doing Anyhow," in Barbara Smith, ed., *Home Girls: A Black Feminist Anthology* (New York, 1983), 124–42.

1   *Black World* 23, 10 (August 1974).
2   Toni Cade, *The Black Woman* (New York, 1970).
3   Alice Walker, "In Search of Our Mothers' Gardens," in this volume, 401–9.
4   Mary Helen Washington, "Black Women Image Makers," *Black World* 23, 10 (August 1974), 10–19; quote, 11.
5   Barbara Smith, "Toward a Black Feminist Criticism," in this volume, 410.
6   Ibid., 411.
7   Ibid., 412.
8   Ibid., 425.
9   Ibid., 416–17.
10 "The Black Sexism Debate," *Black Scholar* 10, 8–9 (May/June 1979), 14–67.
11 Audre Lorde, "The Great American Disease," *Black Scholar* 10, 8–9 (May/June 1979), 17.
12 Deborah E. McDowell, "New Directions for Black Feminist Criticism," in this volume, 428–41.
13 Michele Wallace, "Who Dat Say Who Dat When I Say Who Dat?" *Village Voice Literary Supplement,* April 12, 1988, 18–21.
14 Barbara Christian, *Black Feminist Criticism: Perspectives on Black Women Writers* (New York, 1985).

15   Marjorie Pryse and Hortense Spillers, eds., *Conjuring; Black Women Fiction and Literary Tradition* (Bloomington, Ind., 1985).

16   Hortense Spillers, "Afterword: Crosscurrents, Discontinuities: Black Women's Fiction," in Pryse and Spillers, *Conjuring,* 249–61.

17   For a current overview of canonical issues in American literature see Frederick Crews, "Whose American Renaissance," *New York Review of Books,* October 27, 1988, 68–81. For an alternate view on the dangers of canonical formation in Afro-American literature, see Theodore D. Mason, Jr., "Between the Populist and the Scientist; Ideology and Power in Recent Afro-American Literary Criticism, or The Dozens as Scholarship," *Callaloo* II, 3 (Summer, 1988): 606–15.

18   Spillers, "Afterword," 259.

19   Hazel Carby, "Woman's Era: Rethinking Black Feminist Theory," *Reconstructing Womanhood: The Emergence of the Afro-American Woman Novelist* (New York, 1987), 16.

20   Ibid., 17.

21   Valerie Smith, "A Self-Critical Tradition," *Women's Review of Books,* 5. 5 (February 1988), 15.

Sherley Anne Williams

Some Implications of Womanist Theory

(1990)

I am an Afro-Americanist and enough of an Africanist to know something of the enormous differences between African literatures and Afro-
American literature, and something, too, of the remarkable parallels and
similarities between them. We do in English, after all, trace our literary roots
back to the same foreparents, the Senegalese-American, Phillis Wheatley and
the Nigerian-American, Gustavas Vassa or Olaudah Equiano, the African. So
you must make your own analogies with what follows here; I am assuming
that feminist criticism receives much the same reception it has met with
among Afro-American critics, male and female. Often, feminist concerns are
seen as a divisive, white importation that further fragments an already divided and embattled race, as trivial mind games unworthy of response while
black people everywhere confront massive economic and social problems. I
don't deny feminism's potential for divisiveness, but the concerns of women
are neither trivial nor petty. The relation between male and female is the very
foundation of human society. If black men refuse to engage the unease at the
race's heart, they cannot speak or even see truthfully anywhere else.

Feminist readings can lead to misapprehensions of particular texts or even
of a whole tradition, but certain of its formulations offer us a vocabulary that
can be made meaningful in terms of our own experience. Feminist theory,
like black aesthetics, offers us not only the possibility of changing one's
reading of the world, but of changing the world itself. And like black aesthetics, it is far more egalitarian than the prevailing mode. What follows,
then, is both a critique of feminist theory and an application of that branch of
it Alice Walker has called "womanist."[1] It is as much *bolekaja* criticism as

This essay first appeared in Henry Louis Gates, Jr., ed., *Reading Black, Reading Feminist* (New
York, 1990).

"feminist" theory, for black women writers have been urging black men not so much to "come down [and] fight," as to come down and talk, even before Chinweizu, Jemie, and Madubuike coined a critical term to describe our challenge.[2]

Feminist criticism, to paraphrase Elaine Showalter's words in the "Introduction" to The New Feminist Criticism,[3] challenges the fundamental theoretical assumptions of literary history and criticism by demanding a radical rethinking and revisioning of the conceptual grounds of literary study that have been based almost entirely on male literary experiences. Some of the implications of this radical revisioning have already been realized in Afro-American literature. The works of forgotten black women writers are being resurrected and critics are at work revising the slighting, often misinformed critical opinions of their works. We have a fuller understanding of these writers because feminist criticism has begun to eliminate much of the phallocentrism from our readings of their work and to recover the female aesthetics said to distinguish female creativity from male. We can see the results of this inquiry in the numerous monographs and articles that have appeared in the nine years since the publication of Barbara Smith's groundbreaking essay, "Towards a Black Feminist Criticism" and in the fact that some black male critics are now numbered among the ranks of feminist critics.

Much of the present interest in black feminist criticism is rooted in the fact that black women writers are among the most exciting writers on the contemporary American literary scene, but the interest began in the confrontation of black women readers in the early seventies with black female portraiture (or its lack) in fiction by black male writers. Deborah E. McDowell, in "New Directions for Black Feminist Theory,"[4] values these pioneering studies of negative and derogatory female portraiture as an impetus to early black feminist inquiry and acknowledges that a black feminist criticism must do more than "merely focus on how black men have treated black women in literature." McDowell's major concern is with encouraging the development of theories that will help us to properly see and understand the themes, motifs, and idioms used by black women writers, but she raises other important issues as well. She touches upon one of the most disturbing aspects of current black feminist criticism, its separatism—its tendency to see not only a distinct black female culture but to see that culture as a separate cultural form having more in common with white female experience than with the facticity of Afro-American life. This proposition is problematic, even as a theoretical conjecture, especially since even its adherents have conceded that, until quite recently, black women's literary experiences were excluded from consideration in the literature of white feminists. For this reason, I prefer Alice Walker's term, *womanist*, as the referent for what I attempt here. Womanist theory is, by definition, "committed to the survival and wholeness of entire people," female *and* male, as well as to a valorization of women's works in all their varieties and multitudes. That commitment places it squarely within the challenge of engagement implicit in *bolekaja* criticism.

McDowell also calls for black feminist critics to turn their attention to the "challenging and necessary task" of a thoroughgoing examination of the works of black male writers, and suggests a line of inquiry that implicitly affirms kinship among Afro-American writers, "the countless thematic, stylistic, and imagistic parallels between black male and black female writing." Her call, however, does not go far enough. By limiting the studies of writings by black males to efforts "to determine the ways in which these commonalities are manifested differently in black women's writings and the ways in which they coincide with writings by black men," she seems to imply that feminist inquiry can only illuminate works by women and works that include female portraiture, that our rereadings of female image will not also change our readings of men. Womanist inquiry, on the other hand, assumes that it can talk both effectively and productively about men. This is a necessary assumption because the negative, stereotyped images of black women are only a part of the problem of phallocentric writings by black males. In order to understand that problem more fully, we must turn to what black men have written about themselves.

Much literature, classic and popular, by white American males valorizes the white patriarchal ideals of physical aggression, heroic conquest, and intellectual domination. A conventional feminist reading of black male literature, recognizing that a difference in actual circumstances forced distinguishing and different characteristics on would-be black patriarchs, would see these ideals only partially "encoded" in writings by black American males. Even so, such ideals would be the desired ones and deviation from them taken as signs of diminished masculine self-esteem. That is, explicit social protest about racial prohibitions that restrict black men from exercising patriarchal authority is part of their "heroic quest" because they don't possess all the privileges of white men. Such a reading, of course, tends to reduce the black struggle for justice and equal opportunity to the right to beat one's wife and daughter. Many black men refused to exercise such "rights" and many black women resisted those who tried.[5] Nor was physical aggression really a value in the literature of black males before 1940. Physical force, even when used by nonheroic black men, was almost always defensive, especially

against white people, and, when used against other blacks, generally symbolized the corruption wrought by slavery. The initial *formulation,* however,
does serve to illuminate some instances of black male self-portraiture, particularly in nineteenth-century narrative and fiction.

Nineteenth-century black men, confronted with the impossibility of being
the (white) patriarch, began to subvert certain of patriarchy's ideals and
values to conform to their own images. Thus, the degree to which, and the
basis on which, the hero avoids physical aggression was one means of establishing the hero's noble stature and contributed to the hero's intellectual
equality with—not dominance over—the collective white man. Frederick
Douglass's 1845 autobiography, *Narrative of the Life of Frederick Douglass, An
American Slave,*[6] offers several instances of this subversion and redefinition
of white patriarchal ideals. I focus on what he will later call "The Fight."[7]
Douglass, an "uppity" slave, is hired out to Covey, a "nigger-breaker," to have
his spirit curbed. Douglass's "fight" with Covey marks the turning point in
his development from slave to free man. In the instant he refuses to be
whipped, Douglass ceases "to be a slave in fact." Yet Douglass is not the
aggressor. Douglass seizes Covey by the throat when the latter tries to tie him
up and holds him "uneasy"; though Douglass does draw Covey's blood, he
actually touches him only with the ends of his fingers. Douglass brings the
white man to the ground but never lays violent hands on him; rather, he
"seizes him by the collar." Douglass is thus able to dominate Covey by his
own self-restraint and self-control rather than by *force major.* Douglass takes
a great delight in having bested Covey while conforming to a semblance of
the master-slave relationship. In the later retelling of the episode he returns
"a polite, 'Yes, sir,'" to Covey's outraged, "Are you going to continue to
resist?" and concludes, "I was victorious because my aim had not been to
injure him but to prevent his injuring me."

Robert B. Stepto, in *From Behind the Veil*[8] (itself a brilliant example of the
use to which genre studies can be put), details the brilliant strokes by which
"Douglass reinforces his posture as an articulate hero"—that is, the intellectual equal of the white men who introduce and thus vouch for the authenticity of Douglass and his narrative before the white world. In "supplant[ing
the white men] as the definitive historian[s] of his past," Douglass self-
consciously reverses the usual patterns of authentication in black texts; this
manifestation of his intellectual independence is characterized by the same
restraint and subtlety as his description of his successful psychological rite of
passage.

The pattern of self-restraint, of physical self-control as an avenue to moral superiority and intellectual equality vis-à-vis white society, dominates male self-portraiture in the nineteenth century, where achieving heroic stature is most often the means by which the black male hero also assumes the mantle of the "patriarch." But the black patriarch in the nineteenth century has more to do with providing for and protecting his "dependents" than with wielding authority or exploiting their dependency so as to achieve his own privilege. Once free, Douglass marries, takes a job, becomes a leader in the struggle for the abolition of slavery; Josiah Henson, the model for Harriet Beecher Stowe's *Uncle Tom*,[9] escapes from slavery with his wife beside him and two children on his back, works on the Underground Railroad, and founds a black township in Canada. Dr. Miller, the hero of Charles Chesnutt's turn-of-the-century novel, *The Marrow of Tradition*,[10] is a husband, father, son, and founder of a hospital and school for blacks. Black male heroic stature was most often achieved within the context of marriage, family, and black community—all of which depend on a relationship with, if not a black woman, at least other black people.

The nature of the black male character's heroic quest and the means by which the hero achieves intellectual parity begin to change in the twentieth century. The heroic quest through the early thirties was a largely introspective one whose goal was the reintegration of the educated hero with the unlettered black masses who symbolized his negro-ness.[11] But the valuation of black community and black family (often an extended family) continues until 1940. Richard Wright's *Native Son* began a period in which the black heroic quest was increasingly externalized. A perceptive, though not necessarily articulate or educated, protagonist seeks recognition from the white power structure and in the process comes to recognize—and realize—himself. By the mid 1960s, white society was typically characterized by physically frail and cowardly, morally weak, sexually impotent, effeminate white men and superfeminine white women who personified the official standard of feminine beauty—delicate, dainty, sexually inhibited until liberated by a hyperpotent black man.[12] The goal of the black hero's quest was to dominate the one and marry the other. Black community, once the object of heroic quest, was, in these works, an impediment to its success; black female portraiture, when present, was often no more than demeaning stereotypes used to justify what even the hero sometimes recognized as a pathological obsession with the white woman. This kind of heroic quest is a dominant feature in some important contemporary texts; however, black male self-portraiture, by the late 1970s, was presented within a broader spectrum of themes— patriarchal responsibility, sibling relations, and male bonding—that were self-questioning rather than self-satisfied or self-righteous.[13] These few texts can be construed as a positive response to the black feminist criticism of the early seventies. Yet they are largely neglected by the Afro-American critical establishment which, by and large, leaves to *The New York Times* the task of canonizing our literature. The present interest in black women's writing arose outside that hegemony, as had the interest in black poetry in the late sixties. And, like the black aesthetics that arose as a response to black arts poetry, black feminist criticism runs the risk of being narrowly proscriptive rather than broadly analytic.

Michele Wallace, using a combination of fiction and nonfiction prose—the novels of Richard Wright, Ralph Ellison, and James Baldwin, the essays of Baldwin, Norman Mailer, and Eldridge Cleaver—suggests, in *Black Macho and the Myth of the Superwoman*,[14] a black feminist reading of the development of modern black male self-image that is similar to what I have said here. Wallace was roundly damned and told by sister feminists "to read it again," as though we ourselves had not suspected, even suggested, these things before. And no one has quite dared since then to hold up the record black men have written of themselves. Rather, since black men gave little evidence of talking to us, we talked to each other.

Having confronted what black men have said about us, it is now time for black feminist critics to confront black male writers with what they have said about themselves. What is needed is a thoroughgoing examination of male images in the works of black male writers. This is a necessary step in ending the separatist tendency in Afro-American criticism and in achieving in Afro-American literature feminist's theory's avowed aim of "challenging the fundamental theoretical assumptions of traditional literary history and criticism." Black women as readers and writers have been kept out of literary endeavor, so we had, and have, a lot to say. But to focus solely on ourselves is to fall into the same hole The Brother has dug for himself—narcissism, isolation, inarticulation, obscurity. Of course we must keep talking to and about ourselves, but literature, as Chinweizu and Walker remind us, is about community and dialogue; theories or ways of reading ought actively to promote the enlargement of both.

Notes

1   Alice Walker, *In Search of Our Mothers' Gardens* (San Diego, 1984), xi.
2   Onwuchekwa Jemie, Chinweizu, Ihechukwu Madbuike, *Toward the Decolonization of African Literature* (Washington, D.C., 1983), xii.

3   Elaine Showalter, ed. *The New Feminist Criticism: Essays on Women, Literature and Theory* (New York, 1985), 8.

4   Deborah McDowell, "New Directions for Black Feminist Criticism," in this volume, 428–41.

5   Further research in both traditional and contemporary Afro-American orature just might document that the community valued going "upside" anyone's head as a *last,* rather than the first, resort at least as much as they admired the ability or will to do so.

6   Frederick Douglass, *Narrative of the Life of an American Slave Written by Himself,* ed. Benjamin Quarles (1845; reprint, Cambridge, Mass., 1960), 103–104.

7   Frederick Douglass, *My Bondage and My Freedom* (1855; reprint, New York, 1969), 243.

8   Robert B. Stepto, *From Behind the Veil* (Urbana, Ill.: 1979), 16–26.

9   Josiah Henson, *Father Henson's Own Story* (1849; reprint, Literature House, 1970).

10   Charles Chesnutt, *The Marrow of Tradition* (1901; reprint, Ann Arbor, Mich., 1969).

11   The key texts include James Weldon Johnson's *The Autobiography of an Ex-Colored Man* (1912; New York, 1927), Jeam Toomer's *Cane* (New York, 1923), and Langston Hughes's *Not Without Laughter* (1930; New York, 1969).

12   The terminology is drawn from Eldridge Cleaver's *Soul on Ice* (New York, 1968), but the portrayal can be found in the works of black male writers from Richard Wright and Ralph Ellison to Ishmael Reed.

13   Ernest J. Gaines's *In My Father's House* (New York, 1978) and Wesley Brown's *Tragic Magic* (New York, 1978) come most readily to mind; however, the works of William Melvin Kelley, John McCluskey, and John A. Williams present a range of black male characters that still awaits close discussion.

14   Michelle Wallace, *Black Macho and the Myth of the Superwoman* (New York, 1978).

Useful Sources for Related Reading

The Harlem Renaissance

Anderson, Jervis. *This Was Harlem: A Cultural Portrait, 1900–1950.* New York: Farrar, Straus, and Giroux, 1982.

Baker, Houston A., Jr. *Modernism and the Harlem Renaissance.* Chicago: U of Chicago P, 1987.

Bontemps, Arna, ed. *The Harlem Renaissance Remembered.* New York: Dodd, Mead and Co., 1972.

Davis, Arthur P. *From the Dark Tower: Afro-American Writers 1900–1960.* Washington, D.C., Howard UP, 1974.

Ford, Nick Aaron. *The Contemporary Negro Novel: A Study in Race Relations.* Boston: Meador Publishing Co., 1936.

Huggins, Nathan. *Harlem Renaissance.* New York: Oxford UP, 1971.

Hull, Gloria T. *Color, Sex, and Poetry: Three Women Writers of the Harlem Renaissance.* Bloomington: Indiana UP, 1987.

Johnson, James Weldon. Introduction. *The Book of American Negro Poetry.* Ed. James Weldon Johnson. 1922. Reprint, Harcourt: San Diego, 1969.

Lewis, David L. *When Harlem Was in Vogue.* New York: Oxford UP, 1981.

Locke, Alain, ed. *The New Negro.* 1925. Reprint, New York: Atheneum, 1968.

Singh, Amritjit, William Shiver, and Stanley Brodwin, eds. *The Harlem Renaissance: Reevaluations.* New York: Garland Publishing, 1989.

Wintz, Cary. *Black Culture and the Harlem Renaissance.* Houston: Rice UP, 1988.

Humanistic/Ethical Criticism and the Protest Tradition

Baldwin, James. *Nobody Knows My Name: More Notes of a Native Son.* New York: Dell, 1961.

———. *Notes of a Native Son.* Boston: Beacon P, 1955.

Brown, Sterling. *The Negro in American Fiction* and *Negro Poetry and Drama.* 1937. Reprint, New York: Atheneum, 1969.

Ellison, Ralph. *Going to the Territory.* New York: Random, 1986.

———. *Shadow and Act.* New York: Random House, 1964.

Ford, Nick Aaron. "A Blueprint for Negro Authors." *Phylon* 11 (1950): 374–77.

Jackson, Blyden. *The Waiting Years: Essays on American Negro Literature.* Baton Rouge: Louisiana State UP, 1976.

Walker, Margaret. *How I Wrote Jubilee and Other Essays on Life and Literature.* Ed. Maryemma Graham. New York: The Feminist P, 1990.

Wright, Richard. "How 'Bigger' Was Born." *Native Son.* New York: Harper and Row, 1940.

The Black Arts Movement

Gayle, Addison. *The Way of the New World: The Black Novel in America.* New York: Doubleday, 1975.

Gayle, Addison, ed. *The Black Aesthetic.* New York: Doubleday, 1971.

Gerald, Carolyn F. "The Black Writer and His Role." *Negro Digest* 18 (1969): 42–48.

Jones, LeRoi. *Home: Social Essays.* New York: William Morrow, 1966.

Jones, LeRoi and Larry Neal, eds. *Black Fire: An Anthology of Afro-American Writing.* New York: William Morrow, 1968.

Kent, George. *Blackness and the Adventure of Western Culture.* Chicago: Third World P, 1972.

Mason, Ernest D. "Black Art and the Configurations of Experience: The Philosophy of the Black Aesthetic." *CLA Journal* 27 (1983): 1–17.

Neal, Larry. *Visions of a Liberated Future: Black Arts Movement Writings.* New York: Thunder's Mouth P, 1989.

Structuralism, Post-Structuralism, and the African American Critic

Baker, Houston A., Jr. *Blues, Ideology, and Afro-American Literature: A Vernacular Theory.* Chicago: U of Chicago P, 1984.

———. "In Dubious Battle." *New Literary History: A Journal of Theory and Interpretation* 18.2 (1987): 363–69.

———. *The Journey Back: Issues in Black Literature and Criticism.* Chicago: U of Chicago P, 1980.

Baker, Houston A., Jr., and Patricia Redmond, eds. *Afro-American Literary Studies in the 1990s.* Chicago: U of Chicago P, 1989.

Cooke, Michael G. *Afro-American Literature in the Twentieth-Century: The Achievement of Intimacy.* New Haven: Yale UP, 1984.

Fisher, Dexter, and Robert Stepto, eds. *Afro-American Literature: The Reconstruction of Instruction.* New York: Modern Language Association, 1979.

Gates, Henry Louis, Jr. *The Signifying Monkey: A Theory of African-American Literary Criticism.* New York: Oxford, 1988.

———. "'What's Love Got To Do with It?' Critical Theory, Integrity, and the Black Idiom." *New Literary History: A Journal of Theory and Interpretation* 18.2 (1987): 345–62.

Gates, Henry Louis, Jr., ed. *Black Literature and Literary Theory.* New York: Methuen, 1984.

Joyce, Joyce. "The Black Canon: Reconstructing Black American Literary Criticism." *New Literary History: A Journal of Theory and Interpretation* 18.2 (1987): 335–44.

———. "'Who the Cap Fit': Unconsciousness and Unconscionableness in the Criticism of Houston A. Baker, Jr., and Henry Louis Gates, Jr." *New Literary History: A Journal of Theory and Interpretation* 18.2 (1987): 371–84.

Gender, Theory, and African American Feminist Criticism

Awkward, Michael. "Race, Gender, and the Politics of Reading." *Black American Literature Forum* 22.1 (1988): 5–27.

Braxton, Joanne M. and Andree Nicola McLaughlin, eds. *Wild Women in the Whirlwind: Afra-American Culture and The Contemporary Literary Renaissance.* New Brunswick: Rutgers UP, 1990.

Cade, Toni, ed. *The Black Woman.* New York: New American Library, 1970.

Evans, Mari, ed. *Black Women Writers (1950–1980) A Critical Evaluation.* New York: Anchor, 1984.

hooks, bell. *Ain't I A Woman: Black Women and Feminism.* Boston: South End P, 1981.

——. *Feminist Theory: From Margin to Center.* Boston: South End P, 1984.

Hull, Gloria T., Patricia Bell-Scott, and Barbara Smith, eds. *All the Women Are White, All the Men Are Black, but Some of Us Are Brave.* New York: The Feminist P, 1982.

McKay, Nellie. "Reflections on Black Women Writers: Revising the Literary Canon." *The Impact of Feminist Research in the Academy.* Ed. Christie Farnham. Bloomington: Indiana UP, 1987. 174–89.

Pryse, Marjorie and Hortense J. Spillers, eds. *Conjuring: Black Women, Fiction, and Literary Tradition.* Bloomington: Indiana UP, 1985.

Wall, Cheryl, ed. *Changing Our Own Words: Essays on Criticism, Theory, and Writing by Black Women.* New Brunswick: Rutgers UP, 1989.

Acknowledgment of Copyrights

The editor gratefully acknowledges the following contributors, their works, and their publishers with the following copyright notices. This critical anthology would not have been possible without the cooperation of numerous literary agents, literary estates, and permission editors.

Awkward, Michael, "Appropriative Gestures: Theory and Afro-American Literary Criticism," from *Gender and Theory: Dialogues in Feminist Criticism*, edited by Linda Kauffman. © 1988. Reprinted by permission of Basil Blackwell, London and the author.

Baker, Houston A., Jr. "Generational Shifts and the Recent Criticism of Afro-American Literature," from *Black American Literature Forum*, Vol. 15. © 1981. Reprinted by permission of the publisher and the author.

Baldwin, James, "Everybody's Protest Novel," from *Notes of a Native Son*. © 1955. Reprinted by permission of Beacon Press, Boston. 1955.

Christian, Barbara, "The Race for Theory," from *Cultural Critique*, Vol. 6, 1987. © Oxford University Press. Reprinted by permission.

Christian, Barbara, "But What Do We Think We're Doing Anyhow: The State of Black Feminist Criticism(s) or My Version of a Little Bit of History," from *Changing Our Own Words*, edited by Cheryl Wall, Rutgers University Press. © 1989. Reprinted by permission.

Davis, Arthur P., "Integration and Negro Literature," from *Phylon*, Vol. 17, No. 2. © 1956. Reprinted by permission of *Phylon*.

Ellison, Ralph, "Twentieth-Century Fiction and the Black Mask of Humanity," from *Shadow and Act*. © 1964. Reprinted by permission of Random House.

Fabio, Sarah Webster, "Tripping with Black Writing," from *The Black Aesthetic*, edited by Addison Gayle, Jr. © 1971 by Sarah Webster Fabio. Reprinted by permission of Cheryl Fabio-Bradford.

Fuller, Hoyt, "Towards a Black Aesthetic," from *The Critic*, Vol. 26, No. 5, 1968. © 1968 by Hoyt Fuller. Reprinted by permission of Mary Stevens.

Gates, Henry Louis, Jr., "Preface to Blackness: Text and Pretext," from *Afro-American Literature: The Reconstruction of Instruction*, edited by Dexter Fisher and Robert Stepto. © Modern Language Association, 1979. Reprinted by permission.

Gayle, Addison, Jr., "Cultural Strangulation: Black Literature and the White Aesthetic," from

About the Critics

Angelyn Mitchell is an assistant professor of English at Georgetown University, where she teaches African American literature.

Michael Awkward is an associate professor of English at the University of Michigan, Ann Arbor. He is the author of *Inspiriting Influences: Tradition, Revision, and Afro-American Women's Novels* (1989) as well as several articles focusing on issues of race and gender.

Houston A. Baker, Jr., is the Albert M. Greenfield Professor of Human Relations at the University of Pennsylvania where he also serves as director of the Center for the Study of Black Literature and Culture. He is also the author of numerous books and articles on African American literature and culture, including *Workings of the Spirit: The Poetics of Afro-American Women's Writing* (1991).

James Baldwin (1924–1987) was a preeminent novelist and essayist whose works include *Go Tell It on the Mountain* (1953), *Giovanni's Room* (1956), and *The Fire Next Time* (1963).

William Stanley Braithwaite (1878–1962) was a noted poet, critic, editor, and anthologist.

Sterling A. Brown (1901–1989) was a professor of English at Howard University and a noted poet. His major publications include *Southern Road* (1932), a volume of poetry, and *The Negro in American Literature* and *Negro Poetry and Drama* (1938).

Barbara Christian is a professor in the Afro-American Studies Department at University of California, Berkeley. A leading black feminist critic, she is the author of *Black Women Novelists: The Development of a Tradition* (1980).

Arthur P. Davis is professor emeritus of English at Howard University. His major works include *Cavalcade: Negro American Writing from 1760 to the Present* (1971, edited with J. Saunders Redding) and *From the Dark Tower: Afro-American Writers, 1900–1960* (1974).

W. E. B. DuBois (1868–1963) was a pioneering figure in twentieth-century African American culture and thought. Editor of the *Crisis* for many years, DuBois also taught at Atlanta University. His major works include *The Souls of Black Folk* (1903).

Ralph Ellison (1914–1994) was the author of *Invisible Man* (1952) as well as two collections of essays, *Shadow and Act* (1964) and *Going to the Territory* (1986).

Sarah Webster Fabio (1928–1979) was a key participant in the Black Arts Movement, particularly in the Oakland and San Francisco areas. Her major works include *A Mirror: A Soul* (1969) and *Black Talk: Soul, Shield, and Sword* (1973).

Jessie Fauset (1882–1961) was an educator, an editor for the *Crisis,* and a novelist. Her novels include *There Is Confusion* (1924) and *Plum Bun: A Novel without a Moral* (1928).

Hoyt Fuller (1925–1981) was one of the most influential figures in the Black Arts Movement. A writer and an editor, Fuller edited Johnson Publishing Company's *Negro Digest/Black World* and later founded his own publication *First World.*

Henry Louis Gates, Jr., is the W. E. B. DuBois Professor of African-American Studies at Harvard University. A prolific literary and cultural critic, Gates has written numerous essays on race, gender, and literary theory. His works include *The Signifying Monkey: A Theory of African-American Literary Criticism* (1988).

Addison Gayle, Jr., (1932–1991) was the editor of the landmark anthology *The Black Aesthetic* (1971). A major theoretician of the Black Arts Movement, Gayle taught at Bernard M. Baruch College.

W. Lawrence Hogue is an associate professor of English at the University of Houston and is the author of *Discourse and the Other: The Production of the Afro-American Text* (1986).

Langston Hughes (1902–1967) was an acclaimed poet as well as a dramatist, novelist, anthologist, and short story writer; he was perhaps the best known of the Harlem Renaissance writers.

Zora Neale Hurston (1891–1960) was a novelist, short story writer, dramatist, and folklorist. Her works include *Their Eyes Were Watching God* (1937) and *Tell My Horse* (1938).

LeRoi Jones (Amiri Baraka) is another of the primary architects of the Black Arts Movements. An essayist, anthologist, poet and playwright, he is best known for his plays *Dutchman* (1964) and *The Slave* (1964).

George Kent (1920–1982) was a professor of English at several institutions, including the University of Chicago. His major publications include *Blackness and the Adventure of Western Culture* (1972).

Don L. Lee (Haki Madhubuti) is founder and editor of *Black Books Bulletin* and Third World Press as well as cofounder and director of the Institute of Positive Education. A Black Arts Movement member, he has published several collections of poetry.

Alain Locke (1886–1954) was considered by some to be the "godfather" of the Harlem Renaissance. Editor of the landmark anthology *The New Negro* (1925), Locke was professor of English and philosophy at Howard University.

Deborah McDowell is an associate professor of English at the University of Virginia. A leading feminist critic, McDowell is the general editor of the Beacon Press Black Women Writers series.

Toni Morrison is the 1993 Nobel Prize in literature recipient. The author of six novels, she is currently the Robert Goheen Professor in the Humanities Council at Princeton University.

Larry Neal (1937–1981) was one of the central figure of the Black Arts Movement. An essayist, lecturer, and social activist, Neal was also an accomplished poet.

J. Saunders Redding (1906–1988) was the Newman I. White Professor of American Studies and Human Letters at Cornell University. His books include *To Make a Poet Black* (1939) and *On Being Black in America* (1951).

George S. Schuyler (1895–1977) was a journalist and novelist. His major works include *Black No More* (1931) and *Black and Conservative* (1966).

Barbara Smith is cofounder of Kitchen Table Press and the author of several essays on black feminist thought.

Valerie Smith is an associate professor of English at the University of California, Los Angeles.

Author of several essays on black feminist criticism, she is the author of *Self-Discovery and Authority in Afro-American Narrative* (1987).

Hortense J. Spillers is professor of English at Cornell University. Author of numerous essays on black feminist criticism, she co-edited *Conjuring: Black Women, Fiction, and Literary Tradition* (1985).

Robert B. Stepto is professor of English, Afro-American Studies, and American Studies at Yale University. His works include *From Behind the Veil: A Study of Afro-American Narrative* (1979).

Alice Walker is an acclaimed novelist, poet, and essayist. In addition to her numerous collections of poetry, her novels include *Possessing the Secret of Joy* (1992) and *The Temple of My Familiar* (1989).

Margaret Walker is professor emeritus of English at Jackson State University. She is the author of *Jubilee* (1966) and *Richard Wright: Daemonic Genius* (1988).

Mary Helen Washington is a professor of English at the University of Maryland, College Park. A noted anthologist and literary critic, she is the editor of *Invented Lives: Narratives of Black Women 1860–1960* (1987) and *Black-Eyed Susans/Midnight Birds* (1990).

Sherley Anne Williams is professor of English at the University of California, San Diego and is the author of *Dessa Rose* (1986).

Richard Wright (1908–1960) was a prolific novelist. His works include *Native Son* (1940), *Black Boy* (1945), and the sociodocumentary *Twelve Million Black Voices* (1941).

Index of Selected Names